POPULAR CONTENTION
IN GREAT BRITAIN
1758–1834

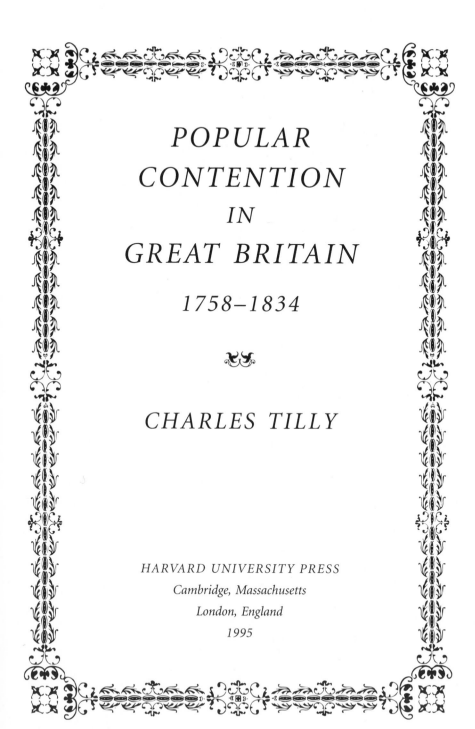

POPULAR CONTENTION IN GREAT BRITAIN

1758–1834

CHARLES TILLY

HARVARD UNIVERSITY PRESS

Cambridge, Massachusetts

London, England

1995

Library of Congress Cataloging-in-Publication Data

Tilly, Charles.
Popular contention in Great Britain, 1758–1834 / Charles Tilly.
p.   cm.
Includes bibliographical references (p.   ) and index.
ISBN 0-674-68980-1
1. Working class—Great Britain—Political activity—History—18th century.
2. Working class—Great Britain—Political activity—History—19th century.
3. Popular culture—Great Britain—History—18th century.
4. Popular culture—Great Britain—History—19th century.
5. Dissenters—Great Britain—History—18th century.
6. Dissenters—Great Britain—History—19th century.
I. Title.
HD8395.T55   1995
322′ .2′0941—dc20

94-48325

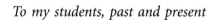

To my students, past and present

❧ *PREFACE* ❧

LIFE IS A GREAT DAWDLE, a putting off until tomorrow of tasks that look painful today. In his author credits for an article published in 1990, Eliot Wirshbo says he has "published articles on Homer, Hesiod and Virgil, and continues to amass data for a major work on dawdling." (I wish I had said it first, but I procrastinated!) In his Ely Lecture to the American Economic Association, George Akerlof cast a pleasant light on procrastination when he contrasted it with blind obedience: "Procrastination occurs when present costs are unduly salient in comparison with future costs, leading individuals to postpone tasks until tomorrow without foreseeing that when tomorrow comes, the required action will be delayed yet again. Irrational obedience to authority or escalation of commitment occurs when the salience of an action today depends upon its deviation from previous actions." Although Akerlof portrays both procrastination and this sort of unthinking obedience as irrational deviations from enlightened self-interest, I take comfort from the implication that when I dawdle I am rebelling, in my small way, against tyranny.

The trouble with dawdling, however, is that in the conscientious heart it stirs up guilt. This book provides a case in point. It reports work I began more than twenty years ago, and have not yet finished. Two or three years, to be sure, went into designing the research and experimenting with the available evidence, ten years into collecting and refining the evidence. But that still leaves the seven years or so since I began writing the book's first chapter—years of excitement, procrastination, and guilt. (The other books I've written during those years simply provide more evidence of procrastination on this one.) Writing the book, furthermore, has raised so many new questions that my agenda remains at least as long as it ever was. In the course of writing it, indeed, I amputated two chapters from the original design, one on variation from place to place, group to group, and issue to issue, the other on causes—two substantial omissions, you will agree. I decided the book already had enough limbs without those phantoms. But that leaves more work for the future.

Research groups at the University of Michigan, then at the New School for Social Research, gave me essential assistance. For help with gathering and preparing the evidence I am grateful to Cathy Adams, Margarita Alario, Amy Alpert, Tim Beckett, John Boyd, Brian Brown, Tom Buoye, Laurie Burns, Keith Clarke, Sam Cohn, Carol Conell, Paul Cooney, Maria Emilia Correa, Carmen Espaillat, Phylis Floyd, Malou Furnas, Bill Golson, Harry Grzelewski, Martha Guest, Dawn Hendricks, Nancy Horn, David Jordan, Laura Kalmanowiecki, Hyun Kim, Radhika Lal, Chris Lord, Ann Matheson, Madeleine McCarney, Chris McKesson, Debbie McKesson, Frank Munger, Fred Murphy, Barbara Nadon, Raúl Onoro, Mary Parks, Michael Pearlman, Shirley Peeples, Diane Poland, Michael Polen, Marline Reiss, Maria Ríos, Debbie Ripley, Mark Ryan, Emilie Schmeidler, Bobbi Schweitzer, Anuradha Seth, Steve Simmons, Rebecca Skinner, Lael Sorensen, Erica Stanley, Marc Steinberg, Carlos de la Torre, Nick Trippel, Sheila Wilder, Hong Xu, Raúl Zambrano, and the host of more temporary workers they supervised; at the risk of injustice to others, let me single out Nancy Horn, David Jordan, and Bobbi Schweitzer for the strenuous years they devoted to the research project. In recent years, Kim Geiger has kept computers (including mine) running at the Center for Studies of Social Change, while Eloise Linger and Kenyalyn Makone have kept the center as a whole operating.

For criticism of the manuscript at many different stages I thank Guy Baldwin, Perry Chang, Sam Clark, Carmenza Gallo, Michael Hanagan, Behrooz Moazami, Charles Sabel, Anton Schuurman, Wayne Te Brake, Harrison White, Viviana Zelizer, and two wise, anonymous readers for Harvard University Press. Although I have neglected to produce the total recasting of the book he demanded, I have benefited from the page-by-page criticism Sidney Tarrow gave earlier versions of the manuscript. Audiences at Brown University, Columbia University, the University of Michigan, the New School for Social Research, the Russell Sage Foundation, the American Historical Association, and the Social Science History

Association raised critical questions concerning earlier versions of the argument and evidence. Members of my New School proseminars on political processes (including co-chairs Richard Bensel, Jeff Goodwin, and Tony Pereira) suffered through repeated presentations of chapter drafts, issuing many helpful calls for clarification and improvement. With a light but sure hand, Camille Smith prepared the manuscript for publication.

Financial support came from the Horace Rackham School of Graduate Studies, University of Michigan; the Russell Sage Foundation; the New School; the National Endowment for the Humanities; and, preeminently, the National Science Foundation. After eighteen years of generous funding, NSF told me I'd better stop dawdling and finish my book. Maybe Akerlof is right.

ⓘ CONTENTS ⓘ

❦ ABBREVIATIONS ❧

ADD   Additional Manuscripts (British Library, London)

AR   Annual Register

BL   British Library

BN Fr   Bibliothèque Nationale, Paris, Fonds Français

GM   Gentleman's Magazine

HO   Home Office (papers, Public Record Office, London)

HPD   Hansard's Parliamentary Debates

LC   London Chronicle

LT   Times of London

MC   Morning Chronicle

MEPO   Metropolitan Police (papers, Public Record Office)

MOP   Mirror of Parliament

MP   Member of Parliament

PRO   Public Record Office

SP   State Papers (Public Record Office)

FROM MUTINY TO
MASS MOBILIZATION

IN RETROSPECT, many North Americans called those years of battle the French and Indian War. Within German territories, people remembered the Third Silesian War. Eventually, however, most Europeans came to think of the far-flung struggles from 1756 to 1763 as the Seven Years War. No matter what its name, Great Britain lay at the conflict's center. By the end of the 1750s British armies and navies had been making war almost continuously for half a century. On the oceans as well as in Germany, France, Scotland, Canada, Ireland, and India they had broadcast British claims to primacy among the world's nations. Victoriously violent and always alert for another fight on land or sea, British armed forces terrified their neighbors into a broad European coalition to contain them.

In 1756 the major armed conflict with France had sprung from colonial competition between the two great powers. Yet another time Great Britain—that is, England, Wales, and Scotland—had mobilized for war. The government and its agents borrowed money, raised taxes, outfitted privateers, authorized press gangs, and hired mercenaries. In 1757 Parliament reorganized the conscripted militia as a national defense force. Crowds attacked agents of conscription throughout much of eastern England that year. By then, Britons had been fighting taxes, resisting impressment, and grumbling audibly about corruption in high places for fifty years, but their state had continued to grow, to centralize, and to make war.

After initial blows such as losing Minorca, by 1758 British forces were dislodging the French from their North American colonies and flexing British muscle elsewhere. Anyone browsing the columns of the *London Chronicle* for 10–12 January 1758 therefore encountered plenty of military news. "According to the last Accounts from Hamburgh," reported a middle page of that issue, "the slowness of the Siege of Harbourg arose from the Unwillingness of the Hanoverian General to destroy the Castle, and more especially, the new Works, but finding the French persisted obstinately in defending the Place, he at length unmasked two Batteries of fifteen Pieces of Cannon, which in a few Days rendered the Place utterly indefensible, and compelled M. de Perouse to accept the Terms proposed." Other items on the same page ran:

> We hear that in Consequence of the Message sent by the king of Prussia concerning the Multitude of Austrian Prisoners in his Hand, the Empress Queen agreed to allow them Three Halfpence per Day, which the Prisoners refused, and offered to fight under his Prussian Majesty against any Power, except the House of Austria . . .

> Yesterday the sum of 161. 15s. 6d. was paid into the Hands of John Fielding, Esq. by the Rev. Mr. Gilbert Bennet of Lincoln, for the Use of the Marine Society, it being a Collection made by that Clergyman at a Card Assembly in that City . . .

> Monday sennight [that is, seven nights = a week ago Monday; compare fortnight] three Men and two Women took a Boat at Limehouse to go on board a Privateer in the River, to take Leave of their Friends on board; but when the Boat was going alongside the Vessel, two of the Officers declared they should not come on board, and immediately threw two nine Pound Balls into the Boat, which staved it. The two Women and one Man were drowned; The Waterman saved himself by getting hold of the Cable. The officers have absconded.

> Yesterday fifteen Men belonging to the Namur Man of War, who had forced their way out of the Ship at Portsmouth, by which some of them were wounded, came to petition the Lords of the Admiralty, but they were all ordered to be taken up, and tried for Mutiny.

Great Britain had obviously gone to war, and civilian life felt war's repercussions.

With the militia draft, impressment for the navy, and aggressive, often unscrupulous recruitment for the army all in action, resistance to military service once again became an everyday event. Take that intriguing item about sailors who jumped ship, petitioned, and were held for mutiny. On

Saturday 7 January 1758, according to the *London Chronicle*'s report from Portsmouth, "several Prest Men, on board of the Namur Man of War, lying along-side of the Jetty Head, who had been refused Liberty to come on Shore to see their Friends, forced their Way onto the Dock; the Lieutenant of the Ship ordered some of the Marines to fire at them, which they accordingly did, and wounded one or two; however they all got out of Dock, and gave three Cheers. Several of the Workmen had very nigh been shot; one of the Balls went into a Plank, where there was a Number at Work" (LC 7–10 Jan. 1758). "It is reported," said the *Annual Register* of the same affair, "that the badness of their provisions was the cause of their complaint" (AR 1758: 78). That did not end the adventure. The pressed sailors went to London, where fifteen of them sought an audience with the Lords of the Admiralty to complain about bad provisions and rough treatment. The Lords ordered them put in irons and returned to Portsmouth for mutiny trials.

On 21 January a court martial on board the *Newark,* near Gosport, sentenced all fifteen sailors to death and sent them to await hanging on the *Royal Anne.* On the 30th:

> This day being appointed for the execution of the 15 seamen, belonging to the Namur, the boats from every ship in commission, manned and armed, attended, and rowed guard round the Royal Anne. A little before 12 o'clock the prisoners were brought up, in order to be executed, and the halters were fixing, when they were informed his majesty had shown mercy to 14, but they were to draw lots who should be the man that was to suffer death. Matthew McCan, the second man that drew, had the unfortunate chance; and accordingly, at a gun fired as a signal, he was run up the yard-arm, where he hung for near an hour. The reprieved were turned over to the Grafton and Sunderland, bound to the East Indies. (AR 1758: 81)

The Admiralty needed sailors for its European war, for its conquests in India, and for the protection of its seafaring merchants. It was getting them through force, fraud, and purchase. It did not like losing them either to desertion or to a larger number of executions than the minimum that would guarantee a healthy dose of fear.

Some Britons—generally not in military service—showed more enthusiasm for the war than pressed sailors could muster. In a great reversal,

Britain had recently allied herself with Prussia against France and Austria. Prussia's king, Frederick the Great, had accordingly gained a popular following in England. On 24 January "some Persons assembled in a riotous Manner on Tower-Hill, and broke several Windows, Candles not being soon enough lighted in Honour of the King of Prussia's Birth Day. The same night the Mob committed great Violences in Surry-Street in the Strand, particularly at the Coach-Office, not a Window was left with a whole Pane of Glass" (LC 24–26 Jan. 1758). Thus eighteenth-century Englishmen enforced their demands for public displays of proper sentiments.

Only a minor share of 1758's contention, however, grew so directly from war. Around the end of January a gang of smugglers encountered troops in Sussex, and killed dragoon Thomas Cole (LC 28–30 Sept. 1758). On 6 February about ten sailors broke up a sporting event in Cold Bath Fields, where men and boys were stoning cocks, and carried off the cocks (LC 7–9 Feb. 1758). On 9 March a full two hundred sailors in Portsmouth entered a public house, smashed everything, poured out all the beer, then went off to wreck other pubs (AR 1758). The same day,

> a man, who has a wife and five small children, stood on the pillory at the end of Dyot-street, Broad St. Giles's, for assaulting a girl about ten years of age, with an intent to ravish her. Several hundred of the female sex, of the Amazonian kind, assembled near the pillory, and, notwithstanding all the Peace officers could do to prevent it, treated the poor wretch so inhumanly, that it is said he is since dead of the wounds; but some of them will likely pay dear for their sport, several having been since taken into custody. (LC 10–13 March 1758)

In June "A large mob of weavers, labourers, and other disorderly persons" near Shawhill, Wiltshire, tore down fences and leveled embankments of gardens and orchards "under pretence that they were purloin'd from the common" (GM June 1758: 287). A few days later fishermen on the Thames threatened to kill any member of the Under Water Bailiff's party who stepped ashore to enforce his ban on catching "spawn and fry" with fine-meshed nets; the bailiff's party retreated prudently (LC 9–12 June 1758). On the 22d of the same month the crew of the privateer Prince of Wales took arms and defended themselves from what the *Annual Register* called "the hottest press for seamen on the Thames that has been known since the war began" (AR 1758: 99).

July 1758 arrived no duller than June. On 12 July several hundred people tore down a Bloomsbury house adjacent to one whose collapse had recently killed seven people; they threatened to tear down three or four more (LC 14 July 1758). The same day a "great concourse of people" who had gathered to watch the execution of convicted French spy Dr. Florence Hensey "committed some disorders" when he received a two-week stay of execution (AR 1758: 101, erroneously dating the event 4 July). On 13 July the *London Chronicle* reported that "great quarrels" had arisen because persons who had paid 2s. and 2s. 6d. to sit on the scaffolding during the execution had demanded their money back. They never did see their entertainment: Hensey escaped execution and disappeared.

On through the year the *Chronicle* chronicled local conflicts in the same columns with reactions to the war, and with struggles engendered directly by the crown's efforts to mobilize for war. The paper also reported multiple prosecutions of women and men who, the previous year, had joined in public resistance to the militia draft or in the "pillaging" of food supplies. Local conflicts occurred more frequently than events concerning nationally articulated issues. Although wartime pressures on food supplies, labor, and political liberties formed the context of all sorts of conflicts, local or otherwise, conflicts varied in the directness and explicitness of their connection to military mobilization. Battles between smugglers and troops, vengeance against pub owners and child molesters, destruction of enclosures, and pulling down of dangerous houses sometimes referred to war or involved military personnel, but they did the work of everyday popular politics.

In these snapshots of popular contention—of occasions on which people gathered and made claims on other people, including holders of power—we glimpse the issues that brought eighteenth-century Britons into open confrontation with one another , as well as the kinds of actors who joined the fray. Clearly military men often participated in conflicts with the state, on both sides of the line. Patently vengeance against moral and political offenders occupied a prominent place in the contention of ordinary people. Evidently local people and local issues, rather than nationally organized programs and parties, entered repeatedly into the day's collective confrontations. As compared with our own time, these British conflicts of 1758 breathe the musty air of antiquity. In popular contention, a great deal has changed since then.

Contention in 1833

Instead of being spread out evenly over the succeeding two centuries, however, many of the critical changes in popular contention from 1758 to the present crowded into a few decades around the end of the eighteenth century. More like a volcano than a glacier, the forms of conflict changed in bursts. By the 1820s and 1830s, as a result, many features of today's contention were already visible. A comparison of 1833's conflicts with those of 1758 will help us see them.

Three quarters of a century after 1758, Great Britain had been at peace in Europe and America for eighteen years. The vast effort of the Napoleonic Wars had outstripped any previous mobilization, and had made Britain into the world's most powerful state. In the midst of war (1801), Great Britain had become part of the (forcibly and uneasily) United Kingdom of Great Britain and Ireland. The wars with Napoleon ended, Britain had shifted its warmaking power to Asian conquests and—with the critical exception of Ireland—deployed its troops less and less at home.

Not that domestic conflict had ended, or contentious claims ceased. Consider a series of events that occurred in Great Britain during the first few days of January 1833. Factory weavers of Paisley, near Glasgow, capped a long struggle by holding a public meeting with the town's cloth manufacturers, and by bargaining through a minimum wage. In Nairn (Inverness), a "rabble" attacked the coach of newly elected MP (Member of Parliament) Colonel Baillie, as he changed horses on his way south. ("The better classes," tut-tutted a report the *Morning Chronicle* of 10 January reprinted from the *Inverness Journal,* "were scandalised by so lawless an outrage.") In Edinburgh another MP, George Sinclair, chaired a meeting of the Society for the Abolition of Church Patronage; unsurprisingly, the participants sent a petition to Parliament urging the abolition of church patronage in Scotland. A wardmote (that is, a general assembly of the Ward) in Cripplegate Without, London, resolved to petition the Court of Common Council for the regular election of aldermen and open meetings of the Court. In Chelsea a group of men who were playing dominoes in a pub left their game and beat a man they accused of being a common informer.

Nor was that all. A dinner of 150–200 Midlothian Whig electors cheered their MP, Sir John Dalrymple, in Dalkeith as he proclaimed the need for further reforms in government. In Withyam (Sussex) a group of un-authorized hunters—poachers, in authorities' eyes—fought a "desperate affray" with Lord De La Warr's gamekeepers, breaking a warden's arm in two places. At a meeting in Liverpool the reelected MP Lord Sandon described himself as satisfied with the recent Reform Bill, prepared to press for church reforms, but hostile to such proposed innovations as voting by ballot.

Amid all the news from England, Scotland, and Wales filtered reports of a Tithe War in Ireland: resistance by Catholic cottagers to Anglican divines' collections of the obligatory ecclesiastical tithe. These abundant reports take us through only the first four days of January 1833 (LT 3, 7, 9, 11, 19 Jan., 2 Feb. 1833; MC 3, 7, 10, 11, 18 Jan. 1833; MOP 11 Feb. 1834); the remainder of the year saw well over six hundred similar events—events in which people gathered publicly and made visible claims on others, including powerholders—occur somewhere in Great Britain.

Claim-making events of 1833 shared some features with those of 1758. Poachers continued to ply their trade and to battle gamekeepers. Un-masked informers were no more likely to escape a beating in 1833 than seventy-five years before. Disgruntled citizens still stoned the coaches of unpopular public figures, and failure to illuminate on an occasion of general celebration still sometimes attracted window-smashers, although those particular forms of direct action were fading from prominence.

Other forms of contention, however, had altered greatly. Pubs and coffeehouses figured much more often as the sites or starting points of contention in 1833 than they had in 1758. By 1833 the proportion of claim-making events that included physical violence had greatly declined. Attacks on prisoners pilloried for sexual offenses, common in the 1750s, had disappeared with the pillory itself, as had the public tribute to a popular figure who was placed in the stocks or otherwise subjected to judicial humiliation; indeed, public punishments were on their way out, in favor of various forms of transportation and incarceration (Beattie 1986).

Still more had changed by 1833. Turnouts—occasions on which work-ers in a trade of a given town gathered, deliberated, decided to quit work, went from shop to shop inducing those who were still working to join them, deliberated again, then presented common demands to all the local masters—had become more frequent by 1833. As an alternative to the turnout, the firm-by-firm strike was, however, gaining ground in regions of large-scale manufacturing such as Lancashire. Public assemblies such as wardmotes and vestry meetings had gained importance. Named associations—the Society for the Abolition of Church Patronage, the National Political Union, the Society for Improving the Condition of Factory Children, and so on—had taken on new prominence. MPs and Parliament figured prominently as objects or initiators of claims. Above all, in 1833 the apparatus of public meetings recurred constantly: advertised assemblies open to all who shared an interest, elections of chairmen, presentations of speakers, resolutions, votes, acclamations, petitions.

Some meetings featured open debates and a few conducted organizational business, but many consisted essentially of public displays of united will. At the Edinburgh meeting, for example, MP Sinclair opened the session by declaring:

> . . . we come before you a society already established and some years in operation, and none can be expected to take a part in our proceedings who is not himself a member of the institution, and consequently an approver of its objects. I know there are many men of great piety, intelligence, and respectability, who consider that to be the bulwark of our church which we consider to be its bane. If those individuals choose to hold any meeting for the purpose of expressing their opinions, they shall not experience from any member of this association the least interruption, and, on the other hand, I may venture to hope we shall experience no interruption to our proceedings. The object this society has in view is the entire and unqualified abolition of patronage. (LT 19 Jan. 1833, from the *Edinburgh Observer*)

Not all meetings, however, proceeded so decorously. In the spring of 1833, radical and (chiefly) reformist organizers in the National Union of the Working Classes began planning a National Convention bringing together delegates from towns throughout Britain. From the French Revolution of 1789 onward, the demand for a grassroots Convention had stated a claim to popular sovereignty (Belchem 1978, 1981; Epstein 1990; Parssinen 1973). Since the parliamentary reform of 1832 had essentially extended the suffrage of capitalists and petty bourgeois but excluded the great mass of workers, the program had taken on a more specifically working-class air than in the days of worker-bourgeois alliance. "The plan," noted Francis Place, "was such that they might evade the law at their first set out, for they could call it an universal suffrage association; even honest Lord Althorpe could not find fault with it, since he had his own Agricultural Association, which was similar as a body, to the proposed delegates" (BL ADD 27797).

On 4 May the *Poor Mans Guardian* announced a general meeting in Cold Bath Fields for 13 May. The meeting's organizers, speaking for the National Political Union and the National Union of the Working Classes, issued a manifesto entitled "A National Convention, the Only Proper Remedy." It began:

FELLOW CITIZENS, The majority of the hereditary legislators obstinately and impudently oppose our just claims to representation. Treat their opposition with contempt; set the privileged villains and usurpers at defiance. This political club of hereditary self-elected law-makers has no proper authority either to concede or to withhold our just and irrefragable right to representation. Their privilege of nullifying the expressed will of the majority of the nation is an unjustifiable usurpation, repugnant to reason and justice, which ought not to be tolerated for an instant longer. (Black 1969: 85)

By excluding workers, in short, a Parliament elected under the terms of 1832's Reform Act remained unjustly unrepresentative. The manifesto went on to propose a popularly elected National Convention. The petition the organizers had prepared for the meeting protested against individual land ownership, primogeniture, the funding system, and legislation protecting large landowners (Chase 1988).

The government smelled trouble. Justifying his force's preparations for the meeting in a letter of 20 May to Home Secretary Melbourne, Police Commissioner Richard Mayne remarked that most of those likely to assemble "were men of desperate characters holding principles subversive of all existing Institutions, and destructive of property; that language of the most inflammatory sort was used by them; that the Unions were taught by their leaders that an opportunity was now afforded them for carrying into effect such principles, and that in this way only, could they hope to improve their condition" (PRO MEPO 1/44). Despite the government's prohibition of the meeting in a proclamation dated 11 May, three hundred people assembled; after the Metropolitan Police arrived, the crowd swelled to three or four thousand. Altogether, about 1,800 policemen gathered to contain them.

As the meeting's elected chairman (veteran radical James Mee, who described himself as a "poor, industrious mechanic") spoke, four hundred policemen left the nearby stables in which they had hidden themselves and marched into the crowd swinging truncheons; one policeman was killed and many civilians were wounded. (A jury ruled the policeman's death justifiable homicide, and Richard Carlile's radical *Gauntlet* published the jurymen's names in gold letters: Wiener 1983: 193; Thurston 1967: 129–135.) Police captured four flags: an American flag; a tricolor with a beehive and the inscription "Equal rights and equal laws"; a small flag with a beehive, a bundle of sticks and united hands; and a black flag featuring a death's head, crossbones, and the motto Liberty or Death (BL ADD 27797; MEPO 1/44, MC 13 May 1833–13 May 1834 LT 13 May 1833–25 Aug. 1834 ; GM 13 May 1833, 1 Jan. 1834; AR 31 May, 31 Dec. 1833; HPD 16 May–12 July 1833 ; MOP 16 May–23 Aug. 1833). The Cold Bath Fields meeting turned into something very like a violent demonstration. The open meeting in general had become a kind of demonstration—indoor or outdoor—a coordinated way of publicizing support for a particular claim on holders of power. Frequently a special-purpose association, society, or club called the meeting. What is more, meetings recurrently concerned national issues, emphatically including issues that the government and Parliament were on their way to deciding.

Although British people had assembled and made demands in other ways for many centuries, as of 1833 they had not long used the special-purpose association and its meetings for that purpose. Members of the eighteenth-century ruling classes, it is true, frequently formed associations for discussion, celebration, commemoration, or diversion; they had sometimes turned their associations to the ends of national politics. The early years of the French Revolution, furthermore, saw a proliferation of politically oriented associations until the government, at war with France, closed them down in 1794 and thereafter. Except for the more conventional religious congregations, however, any sort of mass-membership organization remained suspect, and subject to tight control by public authorities, into the 1820s. The lobby—literally, an organized effort to buttonhole MPs in the Parliament building's lobby—on behalf of recognized interests only came into its own during the eighteenth century.

Whether local interests and ordinary people had a right to exert the same sort of pressure kept controversy boiling into the nineteenth century. *A fortiori*, general public meetings and street demonstrations on behalf of self-defined interests took a long time to gain acceptance.

At the very start of 1780, for example, the Sheriff of Surrey had called a meeting of "noblemen, gentlemen, clergy, and freeholders" to discuss ways of trimming war-swollen governmental expenditures, and to form Committees of Correspondence on the American model to coordinate discussion with like-minded people in other parts of Great Britain (LC 7 Jan. 1780: 26). Promoted by the Reverend Christopher Wyvill and members of the parliamentary opposition, similar meetings were taking place through much of Britain. But on 7 February another meeting of Surrey freeholders, convened by Lord Onslow, adopted a resolution declaring:

> Lest the proceedings of the Meeting called by the late High Sheriff of the County, on the 21st day of January last, should be considered the general sense of the County, we whose names are hereunto subscribed, the Sheriff, Lieutenant, Noblemen, Gentlemen, Clergy, and Freeholders of the County of Surrey, having taken into our serious consideration the said proceedings, do not object to the general prayer of the petition then agreed to, but we do, as good and loyal subjects, strongly protest against the Resolution for an Association and Committee of Correspondence, for the purposes therein mentioned, because we think such Associations and Committees of the most dangerous tendency, and coupled with Petitions, can, as we conceive, have no other meaning, than to overawe and control the free discussion and determination of the several matters contained therein by Parliament, the only power intrusted by the constitution to judge and decide upon the same, thereby assuming a self-constituted power to overturn the legislature, the establishment of which was the great object of the glorious Revolution. (LC 8 Feb. 1780: 135)

Responding exactly one month later to a series of petitions against wastefulness in public expenditure from the newly formed Yorkshire Association, William Burrell said in Parliament: "He for one approved of petitions; he was himself a petitioner, but he totally disapproved of committees and associations . . . He knew of no way to collect the voice of the majority of the people, but by the majority of the freeholders; and . . . not above an eighth of that description had signed the petitions . . .

They plainly aimed at the destruction of the independency of Parliament, by tying down the members to certain measures" (Butterfield 1968: 253). Formidable coalitions, organized on a national scale, crystallized on both sides of the issue. The right to form associations and make demands in their names—which indirectly asserted popular sovereignty—remained essentially contested in 1780. So did any other public and collective effort to influence Parliament's decisions. By 1833, despite a stringently restricted suffrage, these practices had become routine and uncontested.

Even then, foreigners found British routines surprising. Alexis de Tocqueville, who in August 1833 attended a London gathering on behalf of aid to exiled Poles, found British public meetings an impressive instrument of democracy, where ordinary workers had the chance to speak up and be heard. Although such meetings usually elected as chair a senior or prestigious participant who would enforce a rough parliamentary decorum and often endorsed resolutions or petitions prepared in advance, in principle all participants had the right to speak, and many did. "An extraordinary feature of the meeting," Tocqueville mused, "was the way the aristocrats who were present had to give way without saying a word; indeed, they were obliged to flatter popular passions and prejudices in order to get indulgence and applause" (Tocqueville 1958: 17).

Tocqueville's countryman Baron d'Haussez, who visited England the same year, found the public *méting* (as he called it) ridiculous and offensive, for essentially the same reasons that made Tocqueville admire it. It was in the public meeting, thought d'Haussez, that one saw the English people "deliberating on the law, criticizing the behavior of the Cabinet, deciding everything, and returning home sure that it has done great things, that it has a will, that it thought everything the speakers said, in fact that the speakers said nothing the people had not inspired" (d'Haussez 1833: 189–190). D'Haussez complained of strident, promise-filled oratory, of petitions prepared in advance, of the presence of shopkeepers and badly dressed workers. "A meeting," he continued, "only brings together the lowest social classes, the most inflammable, the least likely to be guided by reason, and to balance the good and bad in a particular program. It will follow the plans of the turbulent, anxious, and dangerous party, and will lend popular support to its leaders" (ibid.: 193). In short, public meetings smacked of direct democracy and popular sovereignty.

From their French perspectives, both Tocqueville and d'Haussez saw that the British had fashioned a new political instrument, and were using it enthusiastically. In 1833 the great themes of public meetings were elections, the behavior of the national government, treatment of the Irish, administration of local affairs, maintenance of trade, the abolition of slavery, and taxes—essentially the same issues Parliament was debating that very year. Although meetings also tended to local affairs and private interests, they had become a major device for exerting pressure in national politics.

What Changed, and Why?

If we extended our detailed inventory of events beyond the first four days of 1833 we would notice the accompaniment of public meetings by marches, rallies, displays of party symbols, and so on through the routines that twentieth-century westerners—British or otherwise—associate with street politics and social movements. We would also witness a proliferation of turnouts and strikes, not to mention formation of new special-interest associations. Between 1758 and 1833 a new variety of claim-making had taken shape in Britain. Today, to a large degree, citizens of Britain and other western countries still make claims by means of similar routines. British contention had moved from the alien world of the eighteenth century into our own era. Mass popular politics had taken hold on a national scale in Great Britain. Further changes separate today's politics from those of 1833, notably the later-nineteenth-century elaboration of national party structures with a greatly expanded electorate, the twentieth-century checking of Parliament by a vast governmental bureaucracy, and the enormous capitalization of publicity via mass media. Still, by 1833 a well-established set of routines, most of them still recognizable today, linked local and popular politics to national affairs.

Two interdependent sets of changes in British life between 1758 and 1833 constituted the development of mass national politics. Both involved ordinary people: persons who individually exercised little power over the state and whose main business consisted of production and/or reproduction. First, relations, routine and otherwise, between ordinary people and power-holders on a national scale (emphatically including persons who staffed or controlled the national state) altered significantly; collectively, ordinary people acquired the capacity to intervene repeatedly in national affairs, as powerholders began regularly to take them into account (although by no means always to serve their interests) when making decisions that had direct consequences for ordinary people's lives. Taxation, military service, political representation, treatment of the poor, religious administration, official corruption, and much more that had long fallen under the nearly exclusive jurisdiction of the ruling classes became regular and accepted objects of popular influence. Officials and notables by no means began to do the people's bidding, but in taking controversial actions they strove increasingly to anticipate popular reactions, to co-opt or repress popular leaders, to prevent demonstrations of opposition, and even to bargain with carriers—authentic or otherwise—of popular demands. In small but significant ways, British politics became more democratic.

Second, the means by which ordinary people made collective claims on other people, including powerholders and the state, underwent a deep transformation; increasingly they involved large-scale, coordinated interaction that established direct contact between ordinary people and agents of the national state. Our initial comparison between 1758 and 1833 provides a rough sense of what changed in these regards, but no more than hints of when, how, and why. My chief aims in this book are to document those deep changes and to search out their causes. We will seek those causes in large mutations of the British economy and the British state, in significant alterations of routine politics, and in the internal history of popular collective action. We will touch on the processes that created mass national politics in Great Britain and elsewhere.

Let us not exaggerate the simplicity, unilinearity, or completeness of changes between 1758 and 1833. The Reform Act of 1832 created a propertied electorate in which few ordinary people, by any plausible definition of "ordinary," could vote; although the legislation preserved the previous electoral rights of particular residents, in some boroughs that had been fairly open before 1832 the Act actually excluded whole categories of ordinary electors—notably nonresident freeholders and residents holding property worth less than £10 per year—from suffrage they had previously enjoyed. Almost immediately (as the 1833 assembly in Cold Bath Fields illustrates) radical and reformist militants joined to mobilize demands for expanded representation, even including manhood suffrage. During the following fifteen years, Chartism stated workers' loud complaint against their near-exclusion from direct participation in national politics. The rich and the landed still wielded disproportionate power over the national fate. Ordinary people still had a greater chance to involve themselves in open-air claim-making, in the politics of the street, than in the crucial arenas of decisionmaking, whether local or national. In the 1758 adventure with which this chapter began, in contrast, pressed sailors proceeded directly to the Lords of the Admiralty instead of appealing to local patrons; during the eighteenth century that was an exceptional proceeding, but it happened. Changes between 1758 and 1833 followed zigzags rather than straight lines. Seen from the perspective of 1758, nevertheless, Britain's condition in 1833 stood dramatically closer to something we can reasonably call mass national politics.

We can even speak of democracy. Democracy, in standard meanings of the term, has three elements: (1) a broad and relatively equal definition of citizenship; (2) obligatory, definitive consultation of citizens on state policy and personnel; (3) protection of citizens, including members of minorities, against arbitrary action by agents of the state. To the degree that these three conditions apply, we can call a state democratic. Neither in 1758 nor in 1833 did Great Britain qualify strongly as a democracy by these standards. In 1833, for example, women, servants, and wage-laborers lacked major rights of citizenship enjoyed by propertied adult males. At some points between those dates—notably during the repressive years of the 1790s—British democracy actually receded, especially with respect to protection of citizens from arbitrary state action. Yet over the period as a whole the breadth and equality of citizenship, the extent of consultation, and even the protection of citizens expanded significantly. To that extent, Great Britain became more democratic.

Among the world's states, Britain was precocious. Other countries were moving in the same general direction, but in most of them public meetings, demonstrations, special-interest associations, and related forms of interaction became standard instruments of popular politics only considerably later in the century. In France and Germany, for example, the crucial changes occurred in the 1840s and 1850s; in Italy, later than that. British North America, it is true, followed roughly the same timetable as the mother country, especially before the United States gained its independence. But on the whole Great Britain led the way. The migration of the English word "meeting" into French (*meeting*), Spanish (*mitin*), and Russian (*miting*) reflects that British priority.

These changes mattered. Alterations in the means by which people collectively made claims significantly affected who was heard and how powerholders behaved: by 1833, royal ministers and Justices of the Peace alike had to pay attention when new associations formed and made demands; they could no longer escape simply by invoking royal privilege or the law of riot. The examination of everyday contention allows us to follow continuous alterations in the means people used to forward or protect their collective interests.

The very routines of conflict and collective action underwent a deep transformation from the eighteenth to the nineteenth century. The transformation occurred, I believe, as the result of a great concentration of capital, a substantial augmentation and alteration in the national state's power, and a series of struggles that arose in response to those changes. More specifically, the growth of mercantile influence and the increasing importance of Parliament and national officials (therefore, to some extent, of national elections) for the fates of ordinary people generated threats and opportunities. Those threats and opportunities in turn stimulated interested parties to attempt new sorts of defense and offense: to match association with association, to gain electoral power, to make direct claims on their national government. Through long, strenuous interaction with authorities, enemies, and allies, those ordinary people fashioned new ways of acting together on their interests and forced their interlocutors to change their own ways of making and responding to claims. Cumulatively, struggles of ordinary people with powerholders wrought great changes in the British structure of power.

In this book I investigate how and why the forms of collective interaction involving ordinary people changed in Britain between 1750 and 1840. I inquire as well into the correlates and consequences of those deep changes. More precisely, the book concerns collective *contention*: the discontinuous making of claims that bear on other people's interests. *Continuous* claim-making includes parliamentary representation, routine activities of trade unions, day-to-day operation of friendship networks, and similar unceasing exertions of influence; I discuss them where relevant and possible, but focus on claim-making in which people gather, act together, and then disperse—that is, *discontinuous* claim-making.

Collective action as a whole includes all joint effort on behalf of shared interests. Not all of it is contentious; religious groups, for example, often act together to express a common devotion, sporting groups for the joy of action and of the sociability it brings, kinship groups to reinforce their internal solidarity and mutual aid. Even overtly political groups often gather for banquets, festivals, and testimonials. These are important activities, but they do not come into this book except when they become the occasions of public claim-making. The discussions that follow chiefly concern the world of conflict, of contradictory interests, of claims, threats, and promises, of coercion, coalition, and co-optation, of negotiation, of politics. The chapters to come present masses of evidence about mutinies, meetings, marches, petition drives, demonstrations, turnouts, window-breaking, street battles, attacks on informers, and other forms of contention, and bring the evidence to bear on the description and explanation of critical changes in the claim-making of Britain's ordinary people.

The denser evidence about political processes in this book extends from the 1750s to the 1830s. More precisely, I examine events in the years from 1758 to 1834—arbitrary dates selected because of the availability of evidence, but designed to span a great deal of political change and to provide a first glimpse of the changes following the Reform Act of 1832. Those dates correspond roughly to the lifetime of the rough-hewn radical William Cobbett, who lived from 1762 to 1835. After a period as an outspoken Loyalist in the 1790s, Cobbett veered sharply toward radicalism early in the new century, and remained a vociferous critic of regimes and corrupt practices for the rest of his life. As an important political figure of the 1820s and 1830s, Cobbett constantly testified to how much had changed in his lifetime—generally, he thought, for the worse. He reacted strongly to the deployment of 1,800 Metropolitan Police to break up and contain the 1833 meeting at Cold Bath Fields.

During parliamentary debate on the affair, the former army serjeant-major attacked the use of police, saying:

it was something new in England to see peace-officers in uniform, embodied in companies and battalions, marching in rank and file, commanded by serjeants and colonels—under the mock name of superintendents. It was once the boast of Englishmen that we had no *gens d'armes* and no *mouchards*. Get rid of the *gendarmerie*, and let us have peace-officers of our own choosing, as formerly; if not, the people must arm themselves. They might say, that that would be destroying part of the institutions of the country, but were these policemen any part of the Constitution of England? Why, he was a grown up and married man before ever the word "Police" was applied to a body of men in England; even the Attorney General might well recollect the time when there were a few—a very few police Magistrates with the 300 l. a year, and their few Bow-street Runners, as they were called in those days; but now there was a host of Magistrates, with salaries of 800 l. and whole regiments at their beck. (HPD 14 June 1833: 804–805)

Later Cobbett complained that a police spy, William Popay, not only helped instigate the Cold Bath Fields meeting but also identified the man tried (and acquitted) for murdering a policeman during the police effort to disperse the crowd (MOP 27 June 1833: 2584). Popay's exposure as an *agent provocateur* reinforced the radical cause in a time of its deep disarray.

Cobbett was often wrong. To the end of his life, for example, he challenged the claim that England's population had expanded, often capping his argument by observing that village churches had been built to hold many more people than now appeared on a Sunday; even the decennial censuses that began in 1801 did not convince him. Nevertheless, he had a keen sense of changes in political practice. Cobbett's reminiscences remind us that not only the forms of popular contention but also governmental responses to it altered greatly over the three-quarters of a century at hand. Our problem is to examine changes in contention, changes in power, and their mutual influence.

What's at Issue?

Politicians, philosophers, historians, and political scientists have written many incompatible tales about the creation of mass national politics. The best-known stories speak of Progress, of Struggle, and of Disorder. The fable of Progress portrays a wise crafting of new institutions in the face of inexorable social changes by agents as various as statesmen, the Middle Class, the Working Class, or British Common Sense (for example, Bendix 1964; Binder et al. 1971; Deutsch 1966; Di Palma 1990; Karl 1990; Marshall 1950; Nelson 1987; North and Thomas 1973; O'Donnell and Schmitter 1986; Weiner and Huntington 1987). The tale of Struggle gives us opposing forces—most often, social classes—battling out the future, and forming new political arrangements as peace treaties along the way (for example, Bright and Harding 1984; Corrigan 1980; Genet and Le Mené 1987; Jessop 1972; Moore 1966; Peattie and Rein 1983; Roy 1984; Tarrow 1989a). In its optimistic version, of course, Struggle produces Progress. The story of Disorder differs sharply. It portrays a coherent society overrun by the flood of industrialization, population growth, secularization, or modernization, suffering the political consequences, and coping as best it can (for example, Goldstone 1991; Grew 1978; Halebsky 1976; Huntington 1968; Kornhauser 1959; Lerner 1956; Smelser 1959).

The tales compete, but they also connect. Progress becomes Disorder, as Albert Hirschman has said, to the extent that the observer considers it illusory because of the futility of tinkering with social relations, the likelihood that reforms will generate perverse effects, and the jeopardy in which new advantages put old achievements (Hirschman 1991, 1993). The happiest versions of the Struggle story, furthermore, present a rising class as the agent of Progress. Nevertheless, at their cores the three sorts of tales contradict one another; they cannot all be true at once. This book stands resolutely in the middle ground, the category of struggle. I present the creation of mass national politics in Britain as a by-product of great struggles and provisional settlements in the course of which all parties had programs and interests but no one intended to create the political arrangements that actually emerged. Instead of staging a public contest among competing theories, however, the book plunges into the concrete history of British political change.

Why should we care? After all, Jonathan Clark has dismissed the importance of popular politics during the very period I address in this book. In general, Clark claims, popular agitation provided ruling politicians with arguments and pretexts but otherwise had no significant impact on the actual course of national political life. Ordinary people, furthermore, played little part in defining even the options of their own politics:

> The apparent unavailability of vast areas of meliorist social reform later at the centre of populist radical attention meant that the common man was still presented with relatively simple options of obedience and revolt, and it would be wrong to underestimate the revolutionary possibilities of early-nineteenth-century Britain and Ireland. Proletarian mass meet-

ings, violence and threats were therefore still widely perceived as merely the first steps toward insurrection, as indeed they were in Ireland in 1798. Since economic fluctuations and postwar disruptions were largely beyond the power of the State to remedy, the natural solution to such dangers seemed a reassertion of traditional ideals of social order, and the presence or absence of revolution would be treated as an index of the effectiveness of those ideals. What finally made them untenable was not the scale of popular disorder, which declined sharply with economic recovery in the 1820s, but the intellectual challenge offered to those ideals by the alternative ideals and practice of sectarianism and atheism, and the political articulation which they received. (Clark 1985: 374–375)

Ordinary people, in short, *might* have influenced national politics directly by making a revolution (which would presumably have consisted of an angry, destructive outburst), but having failed to do so provided no more than arguments for the men who ran the great national show.

Elsewhere (notably in Clark 1985: 393–420), Clark echoes Robert Southey and other conservatives of the 1830s in contending that the repeal of the Test and Corporation Acts (1828) and Catholic Emancipation (1829), by shaking the support hitherto accorded the regime by loyal Tories, mined the foundations of the old political system, which then washed away in the flood caused by parliamentary reform. Thus high politics alone really matters, and popular politics is at best an epiphenomenon. Clark concedes that from 1832 onward the "old regime" broke up: voters aligned themselves much more strongly by party than they had since 1688. But before 1832, he claims, high politics—the politics that really counted on a national scale—neither bent significantly in response to the economic and demographic changes then sweeping England nor connected in important ways with the politics of the masses.

In the course of a brilliant polemic, Clark has hit a number of exposed targets in recent social and political history (see Innes 1987, 1991). But his scattershot arrows have also gone very wide of the mark. The same recent historiography on which Clark draws has established the wide popular mobilization that accompanied national political crises such as those posed by John Wilkes in the 1760s or by sympathizers with the French Revolution in the 1790s (for example, Belchem 1978, 1981, 1985b; Bohstedt 1983; Brewer 1976; Colley 1992; Drescher 1986; Foster 1974;

Harrison 1988; Kumar 1983; Lottes 1979; O'Gorman 1982; Palmer 1988; Parssinen 1973; Steinberg 1989; Thompson 1963; Vester 1970). It has not, to be sure, established that popular mobilization made a great difference to the courses or outcomes of these crises. The question remains contested in the present state of knowledge; this book sharpens the question without resolving it definitively.

Recent work has shown that popular politics fused local and national concerns. It has made a convincing case, furthermore, that out-of-doors action played a significant part in popular politics, just as it did in industrial conflict. It has demonstrated substantial popular involvement in local and national election campaigns (Money 1990; O'Gorman 1989; Phillips 1982, 1990). It has traced the intersection between popular festivities and major political issues (Colley 1980, 1986, 1992; Epstein 1988; Golby and Purdue 1984; Hole 1989; Money 1977). It indicates, although less clearly, that the agenda, form, and language of popular collective action changed significantly between the 1760s and the 1840s. It thereby makes more pressing this book's questions: how, when, and why did the character of popular contention change? What difference did those changes make?

John Brewer's study of the period from 1688 to 1780 in Great Britain brings out strong connections among changes in war, state organization, fiscal structure, elite politics, and popular collective action (Brewer 1989). So far, students of popular politics have not drawn appropriate conclusions from Brewer's analysis (for a beginning, however, see Stone 1994). The state appears in studies of the subject as an agent of repression and an object of claims, but not as a growing organization whose war-driven alterations shaped and interacted with the changing character of popular collective action. Especially for the period after 1780, this investigation clarifies those relations.

Such an inquiry into British experience should therefore contribute to our general understanding of collective action. Great Britain has long stood as a model of democratization and of muddling through without revolution (for example, Bendix 1964; Clark 1986; Katznelson and Zolberg 1986; Moore 1966; Powell 1973; Royle and Walvin 1982; Rueschemeyer; Stephens and Stephens 1992; Thomas 1978; Thomis and Holt 1977). Clarifying how British popular politics changed between the 1750s and the 1830s will therefore help test general models of democratization, revolution, and political change. Students of collective action now divide sharply over the relationships among shared identities and beliefs, durable social relations, material interests, class formation, and collective action (see Aya 1990; Cohen and Arato 1992; Johnson 1990; Klandermans; Kriesi and Tarrow 1988; McAdam, McCarthy, and Zald 1988; McPhail 1991; Melucci 1989; Scott 1985, 1990; Sewell 1990a, 1990b; Somers 1992; Tarrow 1988, 1989a, 1993). Close examination of British contention will inevitably bear on those controversies.

Finally, specialists in collective action are still having great trouble specifying the connections between very large structural transformations such as industrialization or urbanization and alterations in the character of popular struggles (in addition to the items just cited, see Alapuro 1988; Aminzade 1981; Birnbaum 1988; Blickle 1988; Bright and Harding 1984; Cameron 1974; Cronin and Schneer 1982; Eisenberg 1989; Hanagan and Tilly 1989; Kerbo 1982; Mommsen and Hirschfeld 1982; Moore 1979; Price 1991; Roy 1984; Rule 1988; Steinberg 1989; Tarrow 1989b; Zimmerman 1983). Again, a proper understanding of Britain's experience will help us pin down those crucial relations. Although this book is aimed chiefly at popular politics in Great Britain, its findings ramify across the terrain of collective action in other times and places.

In particular, British popular contention bears on the relationship between shared perceptions and identities, on one side, and response to political opportunities, on the other. An understandable but fruitless debate has long pitted one against the other, with advocates of perceptions and identities insisting on cultural shaping of collective action while analysts of political opportunities stressed calculating rationality—often individual rationality at that. In this book I exit from the debate. I argue, first, that previous controversies have gotten nowhere because of the shared fixation on individual and collective states of mind, asking in essence, "What do those actors *really* want?" on the presumption that intentions are unitary and clear, exist prior to action, and cause social action. A shift from the consciousness of actors to relations among actors and the shared understandings they entail not only dissolves that unanswerable question but also leads directly to a program of empirical inquiry into interaction and an investigation of the constraints under which interaction occurs. It passes from a world of individuals, of self-propelled billiard balls, to a world of social connectedness, of arteries and living cells.

I argue further that routine social activities—notably production, reproduction, exchange, and consumption—form durable and multiple networks of social relations, which in their turn serve as the bases of collective interaction. Which clusters of social relations, therefore which shared identities, memories, and beliefs, come into play in collective action varies dramatically and rapidly as a function of political opportunity. Hence two rhythms in the alteration of collective action: a jagged short-term rhythm depending heavily on shifts in the relative strategic positions, shared understandings, and resources of connected actors; a smoother long-term rhythm depending more heavily on the incremental transformation of social relations in the course of such processes as proletarianization and state formation. While rarely entering the discussion explicitly, such a view informs the analyses in this book from start to finish.

To the extent that the political interaction of the bulk of Britain's population matters, the study of popular contention can also contribute substantially to European political history. It forms a significant part of the effort to explain the emergence of mass popular politics on a national scale in Great Britain and elsewhere after 1750. In their struggles with powerholders between the 1750s and the 1840s, British citizens hammered out new ways of pursuing popular politics, ways that were strongly affected by the contemporaneous reorganization of capital and of the state, that reshaped the state's repressive apparatus, that created new relationships between constituents and their national representatives, and that laid the basis for most people's participation in national politics for some time after 1832.

Popular collective action, furthermore, influenced national politics in at least four ways: (1) by forcing rulers to bargain, at least indirectly, over such issues as the political rights of religious minorities and the treatment of the poor; (2) by inciting repressive efforts such as the organization of the Metropolitan Police, which had their own durable effects on the state's organization as well as reshaping local collective action; (3) by transforming the connections among groups of participants in collective interaction, notably when alliances formed between fragments of the ruling classes and activists from the ranks of ordinary people; and (4) (more rarely) by stimulating struggles and realignments among powerholders such as those which occurred around John Wilkes, Catholic Emancipation, and parliamentary reform. Even more rarely, popular collective interaction contributed to a fifth outcome: a direct, genuine alteration in the national structure of power; the expanded suffrage for merchants and manufacturers afforded by the Reform Act of 1832 (which resulted from the government's frightened but astutely minimal concessions to popular mobilization) gave them a presence in British politics they had not previously enjoyed. If those things are true—and this book provides some evidence for each of them—then the study of popular contention takes us well into the mainstream of political change. The challenge is to explain the forms, evolution, and impact of popular contention.

We therefore have several major reasons for paying close attention to the evolution of popular collective interaction in Great Britain. Within Britain, popular collective interaction both reflected and shaped national politics. Within Britain, the changing forms of public claim-making also affected how people pursued private ends: fed themselves, found work, expressed approval or disapproval for their neighbors' behavior. Within the West as a whole, British models of political participation influenced the formation of political institutions elsewhere, both through the direct impact of British control as in India or North America and through Britain's standing as an exemplar at crucial moments like the revolutions of 1848. Variants of the nationalization of polity and economy that occurred in Britain, finally, occurred in many other parts of the West; a proper understanding of British experience should therefore help us understand the transformations of popular politics in other parts of the world. We can gain from grasping both the overall changes that occurred in Great Britain during the seventy-five years following 1758 and the complex social processes through which alterations in contention actually occurred.

Contending Ideas

Rather than rush to transhistorical models, however, we will do well to get the British experience right. What have historians to teach us? British historians have written their own versions of the three classic tales: Progress, Struggle, and Disorder. Until the 1960s they usually conflated Progress and Struggle in different sorts of Whig history while distinguishing them sharply from Disorder. *Disorderly* analyses treated popular action as a relatively direct response to hardship, stress, or social dissolution. In his authoritative general history of George III's reign, J. Steven Watson epitomized the disorderly interpretation: "Violence there was in plenty in the settled England of 1760. Riots and disorders were part of the way of life, a regular distraction from the drabness of the life of the poor, a release of emotion and energy; and as such they were taken for granted by the upper classes and did little to weaken the system" (Watson 1960: 38).

Struggle and Progress analyses, in contrast, mapped popular contention into the overall development of effective, informed mass politics, a long pilgrimage from scattered, short-run protests to united, long-run programs for change (for example, Cole and Postgate 1961). Friedrich Engels set the tone for progressive analyses by postulating the passage of English workers through stages: from (1) crime to (2) revolts against machinery to (3) trade unions, strikes, and attacks against knobsticks to (4) a future revolution. "People who endure so much to bend one single bourgeois," wrote Engels, "will be able to break the power of the whole bourgeoisie" (Engels 1969: 252). For Engels, Chartism (still vigorous when he wrote in 1844) was the harbinger of decisive working-class collective action against capitalists.

Writing a few years later, after Chartism had collapsed, Karl Marx still saw English history as heading toward revolution. Reviewing François Guizot's *Pourquoi la révolution d'Angleterre a-t-elle réussi?* Marx saw the "constitutional monarchy" of 1689 as having produced a favorable climate for eighteenth-century capitalist expansion, with a consequent growth of an industrial bourgeoisie to complement England's already powerful mercantile bourgeoisie. The bourgeoisie "became so omnipotent that, even before it gained direct political power as a result of the Reform Bill, it forced its opponents to legislate in *its* interests and in accordance with *its* requirements. It captured direct representation in Parliament and used this to destroy the last remnants of real power left to the landed proprietors." "And while M. Guizot compliments the English," continued Marx, "on the failure of republicanism and socialism—those base, tumorous growths of French society—to shake the foundations of an infinitely beneficent monarchy, class conflicts in English society have reached a pitch unequalled in any other country: a bourgeoisie with unprecedented wealth and productive forces is confronted here by a proletariat which equally has no precedent in power and concentration" (Marx 1973: 255). Thus, for Marx, an ultimately progressive class struggle informed English history from the Glorious Revolution to the revolution that was now in preparation.

In the 1960s historians abandoned the simpler versions of both disorderly and progressive-struggle models. The 1960s seem, at least in retrospect, a golden age of Marxist historiography. In 1959 E. J. Hobsbawm had published his *Primitive Rebels,* which dealt with Britain only in passing but dramatized the idea of a "pre-political" form of popular collective action, lacking organized leadership and a well-developed analysis on a national scale, expressing strongly felt dissatisfaction with exploitation and injustice on a local or regional scale. Soon after arrived George Rudé's *Wilkes and Liberty* (1962), his *Crowd in History* (1964), and the Hobsbawm-Rudé *Captain Swing* (1968). Meanwhile, E. P. Thompson published what was to become the most influential and controversial book of all, his *Making of the English Working Class* (1963).

Thompson's work transformed the historiography of class formation. No one who reads the book will have trouble understanding why. *The Making* combines scintillating history with slashing polemic. Thompson stalks two different preys: the capitalist interpretation of economic history, and economistic Marxism. "In this tradition," Thompson has said of the latter,

> the very simplified notion of the creation of the working class was that of a determined process: steam power plus the factory system equals the working class. Some kind of raw material, like peasants "flocking to factories," was then processed into so many yards of class-conscious proletarians. I was polemicizing against this notion in order to show the existing plebeian consciousness refracted by new experiences in social being, which experiences were handled in cultural ways by the people, thus giving rise to a transformed consciousness. (quoted in Abelove et al. 1983: 7)

Assuming, rather than demonstrating, a common experience throughout England, Thompson traces transformations in class action and consciousness between the 1780s and the reform mobilization of 1832. "This book," he wrote, "can be seen as a biography of the English working class from its adolescence until its early manhood. In the years between 1780 and 1832 most English working people came to feel an identity of interests as between themselves, and as against their rulers and employers" (Thompson 1963: 11). Thompson insisted on this sense of class not as a thing or a position but as a dynamic relationship to antagonists. The *making* of the English working class, in his account, consisted of bringing to full consciousness that dynamic relationship of workers to employers and rulers, with the accompanying recognition that workers had the power to act against their exploiters.

Weaving together diverse texts ranging from pamphlets to speeches to poetry to popular slogans to threatening letters, Thompson arrived at an interpretation of changes in working-class consciousness over the course of successive struggles from the 1780s to the 1830s. The basic transformation in that period, he declared,

> is the formation of "the working class." This is revealed, first, in the growth of class consciousness: the consciousness of an identity of interests as between all these diverse groups of working people and as against the interests of other classes. And, second, in the growth of corresponding forms of political and industrial organisation. By 1832 there were strongly-based and self-conscious working-class institutions—trade unions, friendly societies, educational and religious movements, political organisations, periodicals—working-class intellectual traditions, working-class community patterns, and a working-class structure of feeling. (ibid.: 194)

The same transformation, in Thompson's account, took English workers from John Bunyan to Bronterre O'Brien, from defense of the old moral economy to demands for power in the industrial economy, from scattered attacks against local enemies to mass movements, from Methodism to Chartism. On the way, according to Thompson, workers passed through great revolutionary conspiracies such as those which underlay Luddism and the repeated workers' insurrections of 1817–1820.

With enormous verve, then, Thompson fought against both the condescending reluctance of conservative and liberal historians to take working-class visions seriously and the readiness of Marxist historians to attribute working-class action directly to workers' material situations without passing through the processes by which workers struggled toward shared conceptions of themselves and their fate. Having read Thompson, a generation of historians adopted the metaphor of "making," the idea of class as process and relationship rather than position, the methodological injunction to consider utterances, slogans, threatening letters, speeches, pamphlets, and songs as texts, the search for shared consciousness as the culmination of class formation. Thompson's writings had such great power that they reinforced a tendency already present in the progressive analyses of earlier decades: to organize the entire analysis of changes in popular politics around the rise of the working class. Even those who have disagreed sharply with Thompson have accepted that theoretical frame.

In the 1970s and 1980s Thompson's position, indeed the whole body of Marxist work, nevertheless came under bitter attack (Donnelly 1976). Craig Calhoun (1982) devoted an entire monograph to the assertion that what Thompson saw as class formation actually consisted largely of parochial and unconnected workers' defense of their beleaguered communities against the inroads of industrial capitalism. J. C. D. Clark scored the whole of what he called the Old Guard ("that cohort of scholars whose minds were formed in the matrix of inter-war Marxism, and their later heirs"), singling out Thompson's "exceedingly reductionist analysis" of eighteenth-century class relations for particular scorn (Clark 1986: 2, 50).

Clark identified what he saw as a quasi-conspiracy of Old Guard historians to maintain the myth of radicalism in the face of powerful evidence that British politics, popular and otherwise, remained attached to old institutions until well into the nineteenth century:

> The Old Guard solution was a familiar one: radicalism was really there all the time, only one can't see it. It goes underground; but its causes and essence remain the same. The Levellers and Diggers of the 1640s came to the surface again, reincarnated as the English Jacobins of the 1790s (with, perhaps, a brief anticipation in the Wilkesite disturbances). Meanwhile, justified resentment must have simmered below the surface. A further problem then became easy to resolve: subversive agitation is clearly present in the 1790s and after c. 1817, but the intervening period offered an awkward gap. Of course, the revolutionary tradition must have gone underground once more. (ibid.: 98)

"Such an argument," continued Clark, "was exceedingly useful for historians: it was wholly untestable" (ibid.). By 1990, to be sure, he was conceding "revolutionary stresses" in 1790s England due chiefly to material suffering (Clark 1990: 69). He then argued that from 1530 to 1820 "the most consistent theme both of popular sentiment and of ideological exegesis was anti-Catholicism" (ibid.: 40), which allowed for some coherent popular mobilization but still rejected any imputation of radicalism to the English masses. By 1994 he was acknowledging the "turbulence and fierce passions of the populace" and concluding: "If eighteenth-century England was relatively free from profound political upheaval, this must be attributed to the increasing hegemonic efficiency of the regime of peer and bishop, squire and parson, rather than to the presence of a Lockeian consensus about the justice of the settlement of 1689 or a passively deferential submission to the rule of the elite" (Clark 1994: 41). Ironically, as Joanna Innes noted, the argument brought Clark close to the classic radical claim that a small, tight oligarchy ran eighteenth-century England (Innes 1991).

From Old Hat Whig-Liberal historians and Old Guard Marxist historians, Clark also distinguishes the Class of '68, who are, according to one of Clark's reviewers, "the soggy romantics nostalgic for the 'radical' euphoria of the late 1960s, who are fond of something called 'popular politics,' and moral crowds" (Goldie 1987: 88). Prominent among them is John Brewer, whose work has, indeed, confirmed the active participation of eighteenth-century people in politics despite their lack of a vote in parliamentary elections (Brewer 1976, 1979–80). In the 1760s Brewer sees "considerable overlap between an incipient political radicalism and the manifestations of social discontent" (1976: 18). Brewer has shown us the widespread use of mockery, symbolic objects, ritual retaliation, and dramatization in the street theater of popular politics. With the American resistance and Wilkes movement of the 1760s, he has identified the growth of demands for popular representation, for something approaching popular sovereignty.

Dealing with a period before Thompson's starting date of 1790, Brewer properly takes no position on the major question Thompson addresses and Clark attacks: whether a solidary and effective working class was forming in the era of the French Wars and beyond. Gareth Stedman Jones, who focuses on the period after Thompson's terminus of 1832, takes a strong position thereon. He complains that Thompson's conception of class consciousness "still assumes a relatively direct relationship between 'social being' and 'social consciousness' which leaves little independent space to the ideological context within which the coherence of a particular language of class can be reconstituted" (Stedman Jones 1983: 101). He claims, in contrast, that class consciousness "formed part of a language whose systematic linkages were supplied by the assumptions of radicalism: a vision and analysis of social and political evils which certainly long predated the advent of class consciousness, however defined" (ibid.: 102). "It was not consciousness . . . that produced politics," he declares, "but politics that produced consciousness" (ibid.: 19). Stedman Jones, like

Thompson, treats popular collective action—in this case the action of Chartists—as a product of shared consciousness. But Stedman Jones sees the consciousness as deriving from a largely autonomous body of political thought with strong roots in eighteenth-century radicalism. That is actually what he means by "politics" (see Mayfield and Thorne 1992).

Stedman Jones's trajectory continues. With Patrick Joyce and James Vernon the linguistic turn comes full circle on Marxism. Hesitantly in Joyce's case, triumphantly in Vernon's, these revisionists reject any evidence of class action in which the actors' own language does not indicate that they are self-consciously striving on behalf of shared membership in a class. "Although social constituencies we might choose to call classes express certain values," writes Joyce (1991: 15), "this does not make the values *themselves* ones of class. Meanings are an altogether different matter. To assume that they can be gratuitously given a class label merely by dint of their social constituency is to open the door to almost any cultural manifestation as the expression of class" (emphasis in original). Joyce explicitly criticizes Eric Hobsbawm's presentation of evidence concerning distinctive working-class styles of life on these grounds.

Vernon plunges even deeper into subjectivism by centering his account of popular political life on "the creation of political subjectivities" (1993: 7). "Central to such an account," he declares, "is the recognition that politics is about far more than orthodox political institutions and their representative systems. Instead it turns upon the idea of English political culture as an arena of struggle in which competing groups contested one another's definitions of the public political sphere according to their interpretation of the constitution" (ibid.). This bold reduction of popular politics to discourse and subjectivity enables Vernon to interpret nineteenth-century British political change as the snuffing out of democracy, since it incorporated once-radical popular subjectivities into the limited gray instrumentalities of liberal constitutionalism: "The invention of democracy in England was then a sham" (ibid.: 336).

Common Action and Shared Understanding

Schematically, these competing accounts of popular collective interaction vary along two dimensions: the alleged social bases of common action and the alleged extent and character of shared understanding. The most commonly proposed bases of action range from social stress to political mobilization to group struggle. *Social stress* ideas, in their broadest and purest form, presume that social life consists of a confrontation between sharply defined individuals and an overarching society, that social change causes disorder, that conflict stems from the malfunctioning of ordinary regulatory mechanisms, and that the chief effect of contention is to disrupt normal social processes. Except in the event of a general breakdown, in this view, contention has little or nothing to do with the true structure of power.

Social stress arguments lead to the expectation of a close correspondence between the pace of social change and the frequency of contention, of disproportionate participation in contention by individuals and groups that rapid social change is displacing, of a tendency for contention to arise from accumulated frustrations, of a large distance between everyday contention and the real wielding of power, of trivial impact by the contention of ordinary people on the actual direction of political change. We have already witnessed J. C. D. Clark applying just such reasoning to the evolution of British social protest after 1820. For the eighteenth century, Ian Christie similarly declares that popular turbulence "was a fact of life which the ruling classes in Britain had learned to put up with as a matter of course. Dearth was not the only spark to the tinder. There were formidable riots against the reorganization of the militia in the 1750s and the early 1760s. Unemployment and wage disputes caused others in London in 1765 and in 1768–9. Political excitement could give rise to intimidating disturbances" (Christie 1984: 33). Christie writes of fire and explosion, of excitement, of propensity to riot. Despite several decades of battering by social historians, social stress interpretations have somehow survived. Applied to British contention between 1750 and 1840, such reasoning suggests, for example, that the rapid growth of London created a displaced, drifting population which easily joined street disturbances and destructive mass movements, much as Charles Dickens's dull-witted Barnaby Rudge, having strayed from the protective ties of his home at London's edge, joined the thugs of Lord George Gordon.

Political mobilization ideas indicate that whatever stress ordinary people may have endured, the critical difference between action and inaction was the extent to which they had become involved in organized movements: associations, churches, Friendly Societies, unions, parties, and others.

Malcolm Thomis and Peter Holt, surveying the prospects for revolution in Britain between 1789 and 1848, argue that:

> Apart from providing an outstanding example of accomplished revolution which others might wish to copy, the French Revolution gave rise to an enormous political debate, in which working men featured for almost the first time. Though excluded from Parliament as well as from government, the working classes could not henceforward be excluded from the arguments and discussions that surrounded these subjects, however desperately successive governments might endeavour to enforce their exclusion. (Thomis and Holt 1977: 123)

Thomis and Holt go on to emphasize the significance of the London Corresponding Society, the Hampden Clubs, the National Union of Working Classes, and the National Charter Association in focusing the omnipresent rays of working-class discontent on the tinder of organized action. The organizational vehicle and the doctrine, in short, create their own public. Neither sheer stress nor articulated interests underlie popular political interaction.

Group struggle ideas go beyond the notion of political mobilization to contradict the social-stress line of analysis in almost every particular; they assert that individuals and social relations among them are the fundamental social realities, that individuals and groups have shared interests and create shared meanings, that social life consists of interactions among interest-oriented groups, that contention constitutes a consequential element of those interactions. Group struggle arguments promote the expectation of disproportionate involvement in contention by members of coherent groups having well-defined interests at risk, and of strong connections between everyday contention and large changes in the structure of power. Applied to eighteenth- and nineteenth-century Britain, such a perspective predicts substantial interdependence between the actions of Parliament and struggles in the streets.

The second dimension of variation among accounts of popular collective action concerns intentions and consciousness: direct impulse, imposed consciousness, or shared understanding. At the extreme of *direct impulse* we find the idea that hunger or poverty drives people directly into inchoate collective action, or into the ranks of organized protesters—whether or not the leaders' doctrines correspond to their own interests

or intentions. In the case of *imposed consciousness,* people have accepted—
or have been unable to escape—ideologies constructed by others, and act
together on the premises of those ideologies. *Shared understanding* implies
that people know what they are doing together, either because they have
a traditional analysis to draw on, because someone else has proposed an
appealing analysis, or because they have formed their own conception in
the course of previous struggles.

All concrete historical analyses of conflict lie somewhere between the
extremes. Analyzing urban crowds during the first half of the eighteenth
century, Nicholas Rogers approves Henry Fielding's observation that "the
interventions of the crowd were essentially reactive, defining the limits of
the possible" (Rogers 1989: 388). While allowing for complexity and
variation, Rogers ultimately places popular collective action in the zone
defined by imposed consciousness and political mobilization, with strong
emphasis on influence from "above." Norman Gash assigns even less
autonomy to popular interaction. In discussing the conflicts that beset
Britain after the end of the Napoleonic Wars, for example, he declares:
"What faced the government in 1816 and 1817 was prolonged and
widespread economic distress and social discontent, which produced
innumerable incidents of differing degrees of illegality and violence, from
simple industrial disputes to the opportunistic tactics of a few theoretical
revolutionaries. Riot and disorder were the immemorial reaction of the
common people to distress and grievance" (Gash 1979: 79). With that
analysis, Gash places himself near, but not quite in, the social-stress/di-
rect-impulse corner of our range.

Speaking of the mid-nineteenth century, John Stevenson argues that
by then "there were forms of organisation, methods of expressing grievances, and sufficient effective influence for the major interest groups to
contain conflicts within the existing political framework" (Stevenson
1979: 319). His argument stands much closer to the group-struggle pole,
and allows considerable room for shared understanding. But Stevenson
keeps his distance from a pure group-struggle analysis by arguing as well
that "England did not experience revolutionary upheaval or counter-revo-
lutionary violence to the degree experienced by many other societies in
this period, in spite of the stresses imposed by urbanisation, industrialisation, and the transition from oligarchic government to the beginnings
of mass democracy" (ibid.: 323). To the extent that we take the "in spite

of" seriously, these observations pull Stevenson's analysis back in the direction of social stress.

Mark Harrison, in his survey of 528 crowds that gathered for various purposes in Manchester, Norwich, Liverpool, and (especially) Bristol between 1790 and 1835, rebels against the idea that contention changed form significantly over the period, but presents the events as coherent products of their settings (Harrison 1988). He also rejects group-struggle analyses, even when his evidence seems to support them. On the whole, his *ad hoc* interpretations give considerable weight to shared understanding, deny the predominance of social stress, and consider political mobilization of high importance. Thus his work, too, occupies a position within our two dimensions somewhere between John Brewer and John Stevenson.

In general, then, competing accounts of popular collective interaction in eighteenth- and nineteenth-century Britain fall into the sort of array depicted in the two panels of Figure 1.1: above the diagonal, authors emphasizing shared understanding and group struggle; below, authors insisting on direct impulse and social stress. The correlation between positions on the two dimensions is strong but imperfect. No one who insists on direct impulse, for example, also considers group struggle to provide the basis for common action; analysts of group struggle tend to argue shared understanding; yet those who emphasize shared understanding divide with respect to political mobilization and group struggle; hence we can usefully distinguish the two dimensions.

It need not be true, of course, that all popular collective interaction took place at a single location with respect to the two dimensions: very likely barroom brawls partake more of social stress and direct impulse than do clashes between the supporters of rival candidates for Parliament. Authors differ both in their placement of such events and in their estimates of relative prevalence among different categories of events. Any particular author therefore actually occupies not a point, but a preferred space within the diagram. Three different ideas intersect in that space: a set of implicit theories concerning the causes of different varieties of popular collective interaction; a notion of the relative frequency of those different varieties; an estimate of which varieties come closest to expressing the deep interests, aspirations, impulses, or desires of ordinary people. Together, these ideas define a center of gravity for the author's analysis.

My explanations in this book cluster toward the group-struggle end of the range, as well as insisting that shared understanding plays a major part in popular collective interaction. Their genealogy runs variously to Hobsbawm, to Rudé, to Thompson, to Brewer, to non-British analyses of social movements, revolutions, and collective action. They recognize that political entrepreneurs promulgate and even occasionally impose ideolo-

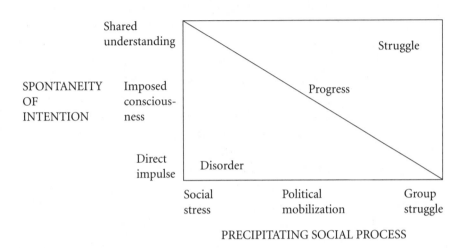

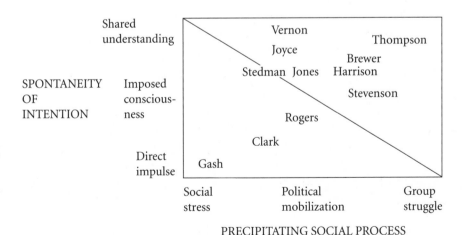

Figure 1.1. Alternative accounts of popular collective action

gies and programs, but emphasize the negotiation with ordinary people that enters into political entrepreneurs' efforts. My arguments accent the salience of interests, of opportunities for the realization of interests, of coherent groups, of shared beliefs, of social classes, of coalitions, of mobilization and organized collective interaction, of repression and facilitation. They identify a close correspondence between open contention and the routine exercise of power. They attribute to the struggles of ordinary people a significant impact on national affairs. They challenge ideas below the diagram's diagonal, ideas resembling those of Norman Gash, J. C. D. Clark and (to a lesser extent) Gareth Stedman Jones.

As will soon be obvious, nevertheless, my analysis breaks with almost all of these earlier ways of explaining popular collective interaction. It does so by shifting the emphasis from what roared in the hearts, minds, and bellies of ordinary people to how all sorts of people made claims on one another, from individual or group orientations to patterns of interaction, from personal perceptions to shared understandings, from psyches to social ties, from actions to transactions. It stresses, furthermore, claim-making that bore on political power, on power with respect to the means of government. While paying repeated attention to class formation and class conflict, I take up struggles that bore on political power whether or not they sprang from or affected class antagonisms, class consciousness, or class structure.

Those choices mark out a distinctive position with respect to contemporary thinking about political mobilization and collective action in general. Even when recognizing the importance of strategic interaction, most scholars of the subject have sought to provide accounts of the action of actors—individuals, communities, classes, organizations, and others—taken singly. The sharpest disputes have concerned the extent to which the actors pursued some sort of narrow, rational, and conscious self-interest, as opposed to solidarity, identity, or diffuse emotion. My analyses of British contention move the emphasis to the history and logic of interaction, of struggle itself. More than anything else, in the pages to come, I ask how and why the forms of involvement of ordinary British people in politically relevant struggles changed between the 1750s and the 1830s.

In so doing, I return to the questions, but not the answers and causal accounts, of a properly discredited subject: political modernization. Theories of political modernization that proliferated in the 1950s and 1960s were an intellectual disaster: teleological, unilinear, arrogant, unhistorical, and vague (Bendix 1967; Berting and Blockmans 1987; Chilcote and Johnson 1983; Roy 1984; Taylor 1979; Tilly 1975; 1985b, 1989; for a contrary view, see Weiner and Huntington 1987). No one should try to resurrect them. Yet they raised two questions for which we still lack satisfactory answers: (1) When a capitalist economy first expands rapidly, why does so much else—demography, education, household structure, urban organization, political struggle—change at the same time? (2) Under what conditions and through what processes do citizens become durably involved in national politics by means of elections, parties, associations, mass communications, and organized interests (see Nelson 1987)?

Together, this pair of questions pose the problem of relations between the appearance of mass national politics and other momentous social changes. My arguments and evidence feature the impact of an expanding, warmaking state and a growing, capitalizing economy on a wide variety of other changes, including alterations in the forms of popular struggle. But they also establish that struggle has its own partly autonomous history, a history that does not reduce simply to a reflection of the changing organization of production or of the changing structure of state power, a history that in itself influences the organization of production and the structure of state power.

Here we arrive at my own most contentious claim: that the prior path of collective claim-making constrains its subsequent forms, influencing the very issues, actors, settings, and outcomes of popular struggle. The particular path of contention has an important impact, I argue, because each shared effort to press claims lays down a settlement among parties to the transaction, a memory of the interaction, new information about the likely outcomes of different sorts of interactions, and a changed web of relations within and among the participating sets of people. Between 1823 and 1829, for example, the British government's reluctant negotiation with Daniel O'Connell and his Catholic Association over Catholic Emancipation—despite issuing in the Association's dissolution and restriction of the Irish franchise—established a compelling model and precedent for the action of mass-subscription associations in national politics. Advocates of parliamentary reform soon profited by the model and the precedent. At the same time, mass mobilization over Catholic

Emancipation facilitated Robert Peel's institution of the Metropolitan Police (a form of organization itself based strongly on British experiments with repression in Ireland). As Cobbett's complaint of 1833 suggests, the New Police, in their turn, significantly constrained subsequent popular collective interaction in London.

I will present the argument and evidence for such connections later on. For now, we merely have to recognize the importance of following the actual path of contention and of avoiding obvious traps: the resort to simple dichotomies such as traditional/modern or pre-political/political, the fabrication of unilinear models of change, the reduction of contention to a straightforward expression of changes in production, political power, or popular mentality, the imposition of teleologies in which the later forms of claim-making somehow determine the earlier ones.

At a time when many historians and social scientists have begun to think that all social action dissolves into discourse, a dissolution that makes it inaccessible to the conventional procedures of social science, in this book I make a large wager on the coherence and external knowability of the political processes I examine. Gareth Stedman Jones and Joan Wallach Scott, for example, reject E. P. Thompson's claim to have shown how struggle between capitalists and authorities, on the one hand, and workers, on the other, created strong, coherent, unified class consciousness, which in turn informed workers' interaction with capitalists and authorities (Stedman Jones 1983; Scott 1987, 1988) . Although their epistemological positions remain unclear, the Stedman Jones and Scott critiques of Thompson assign such large autonomy to discourse as to deny the possibility of ever establishing cause-effect relations among the material conditions in which workers and capitalists lived, the languages they spoke, the collective interaction they carried on, and the impact of that collective interaction on the subsequent structure of power.

While reserving the right to criticize and modify Thompson's own account of class formation, I side strongly with Thompson in this dispute. I regard culture—shared understandings and their objectifications—as the frame within which social action takes place, and discourse as a major means of action, but I deny that culture and discourse exhaust social reality. My analyses make plenty of allowance for social construction—as the discussion of contentious repertoires will soon make clear—but they assert connections of cause and effect among material conditions, common identities, social relations, shared beliefs, memories, and experiences, collective interaction, and the reordering of power. They assume a world in which:

social relations (rather than individual mentalities or societies) are
    the fundamental realities;
relative to a particular set of social relations, individuals and groups
    have articulated interests that are ascertainable prior to the
    interaction we are seeking to explain;
routine social interaction affects the distribution of resources and
    social ties among different segments of the population and
    thereby influences their relative capacity to act collectively;
although they always negotiate, often innovate, and sometimes rebel,
    people interact within limits set by the beliefs and conventions
    they have established in the course of previous interactions;
individual action and collective interaction lay down residues in the
    form of information, beliefs, conventions, commitments, social
    ties, geographical distributions, and artifacts that strongly
    constrain subsequent rounds of interaction and interaction; and
these residues not only restrict but also enable interaction through
    the accumulation of shared knowledge and social relations.

In short, my arguments deny that all social experience reduces to agentless text, and affirm that the development of mass national politics concerns the ascertainable actions of real people.

Where does that leave culture, political or otherwise? If we mean by culture shared understandings and their representations in actions or objects—a defensible approximation of what most analysts mean by it—the entire book concerns culture (see Morawska and Spohn 1994 for a survey of recent work on the subject). The attempt of pressed sailors to reach the Lords of the Admiralty, women's attack on a pilloried rapist, the routines of public meetings, the Cold Bath Fields call for a National Convention, and the other contentious events we have already examined would be inexplicable without reference to communication within frames of shared understandings. What is more, culture constrained holders of power: British conservatives read the advocacy of political rights for Catholics as a threat to a Protestant constitution, courts accepted arguments that made the killing of a policeman "justifiable homicide," masters recognized obligations to their unemployed workers, householders knew the meaning of lighted candles in a window, mayors saw some justice in poor people's demands for bread at a price they could afford to pay. More generally, claim-makers implicitly (and sometimes explictly) calculated and compared the likely outcomes of various contentious strategies on the basis of collectively accumulated experience with the objects of their claims, on the basis of causal reasoning derived from collective memory, on the basis of shared standards of justice and worth.

I break with many treatments of culture, nevertheless, in denying that it acts like a numinous cloud hovering over social life, shifting in its own winds, and producing social action as rain or snow. In my analyses I reject the common conception of culture as a residuum that remains after the factoring out of interest and compulsion, and the notion of culture as occupying the terrains of value and belief, but not of practice. Instead, I assume that culture inheres in concrete social relations and the often fragmentary, inconsistent, and episodic interpretations people make of them. People create, adapt, apply, and deploy shared understandings— culture—in social interaction, just as the shared understandings they have at their disposal constrain their sense of what is possible and desirable.

The widely shared eighteenth-century belief that a community's poor people had a right to basic foodstuffs at a price they could afford, which often extended into the community's collective right to seize food being hoarded or shipped off to other markets, rested on decades of local practice, but once in place it justified crowd action against millers, bakers, merchants, and local officials. As collective seizures of food lost their feasibility and effectiveness, however, ordinary people abandoned ideas and practices of a moral economy (Bohstedt 1992; Thompson 1971, 1991). Again, in its popular variants the labor theory of value emerged from struggle between masters and workers, but once in existence designated likely enemies and possible allies differently from the conception of a trade as a corporate community. Thus culture and contention intertwine.

Culture becomes most salient, explicit, and crucial to my analysis in three related ideas: (1) that actors anticipate the likely consequences of their actions and interactions on the basis of accumulated, interpreted, social experience; (2) that the means of interaction available to any pair of interacting parties incorporate shared understandings derived from the previous course of their interaction; and (3) that each interaction transforms, however slightly, those shared understandings. Indeed, those three arguments provide the chief basis for thinking that collective interaction, far from being a mere reflection of supposedly deeper processes, has a continuous, cumulative, coherent history.

I do not pretend to have entered the minds of eighteenth- and nineteenth-century Britons, to have reconstructed their individual experiences in detail. Instead I have concentrated on interaction, on the public conversation of claims, counterclaims, and associated actions. This concentration will not satisfy anyone who believes that conscious individual experience constitutes the crux and essential content of history, therefore that deep individual motives provide the only genuine causes of historical action. Breaking with that profound individualism, I argue that shared understandings, interactions, and social ties have a cumulative, observable logic in contention as they do elsewhere.

On that premise, my analyses follow three parallel arcs. At a very general level, I describe how the British state and economy changed over the three-quarters of a century from the 1750s to the 1830s. That account relies almost entirely on other people's syntheses of British history; I make no claims for its originality, but put considerable stock in its adequacy, since those large changes supply some of the causes and effects in my proposed explanation of changes in popular collective interaction. At a second level, I hazard descriptions and explanations of alterations in the political positions and activities of Great Britain's ordinary people; although I bring some new evidence to bear on these alterations, I draw heavily on other historians' studies of particular groups, localities, and events. Most of the new evidence in this book falls into the third arc, which follows the ways that the bulk of Britain's population made public and collective claims on others, when they did so. I scrutinize description after description of open contention for evidence concerning how and why popular politics and collective claim-making changed so profoundly.

Repertoires of Contention

Throughout this book we will watch changes in the ways that people act together in pursuit of shared interests—changes in repertoires of collective interaction. The word *repertoire* helps describe what happens by identifying a limited set of routines that are learned, shared, and acted out through a relatively deliberate process of choice. Repertoires are learned cultural creations, but they do not descend from abstract philosophy or take shape as a result of political propaganda; they emerge from struggle. People learn to break windows in protest, attack pilloried prisoners, tear down dishonored houses, stage public marches, petition, hold formal meetings, organize special-interest associations. At any particular point in history, however, they learn only a rather small number of alternative ways to act collectively.

The limits of that learning, plus the fact that potential collaborators and antagonists likewise have learned a relatively limited set of means, constrain the choices available for collective interaction. The means, furthermore, articulate with, and help shape, a number of social arrangements that are not part of the collective interaction itself, but channel it to some degree: police practices, laws of assembly, rules of association, routines for informal gathering, ways of displaying symbols of affiliation, opposition, or protest, means of reporting news, and so on. By analogy with the various improvisations known to a jazz band or a troupe of strolling players (rather than, say, the more confining music read by a string quartet), people in a given place and time know how to carry out a limited number of alternative collective-action routines, adapting each one to the immediate circumstances and to the reactions of antagonists, authorities, allies, observers, objects of their action, and other persons somehow involved in the struggle. In the manner of jazz musicians, the players embed their known routines in shared understandings, including references to well-known themes and previous performances; remember how the workers at Cold Bath Fields in 1833, before being beaten down by the police, not only called for a National Convention and justified themselves as a legally defensible universal suffrage association, but also displayed an American flag plus a black banner emblazoned with a skull, crossbones, and the words Liberty or Death.

Like their theatrical counterparts, repertoires of collective action designate not individual performances but means of *inter*action among pairs or larger sets of actors. A company, not an individual, maintains a repertoire. The simplest set consists of one actor (say a group of workers) making collective claims, and another actor (say the workers' boss) becoming the object of those claims. That simple set compounds into pairs making claims on each other, into trios of claimants, up to the complex arrays of national politics. Not all collective claims involve overt conflict. Participants in collective celebrations often make claims only on each other, demanding little more than shared affirmation of identity; leaders call on followers for support, and followers declare their solidarity, without necessarily arousing conflicts of interest. When the claims in question would, if realized, affect the interests of other actors, we may speak of *contention*. Repertoires of contention: the established ways in which pairs of actors make and receive claims bearing on each other's interests.

Repertoires have several different levels: action, performance, campaign, and array of performances. Individual *actions* include such elements as window-smashing and cheering, which in different circumstances played significant parts in claim-making, but rarely made up the whole of a claim-making occasion. *Performances* such as the pulling down of a house or the holding of a public meeting, in contrast, often constituted self-contained statements of claims, even if outside of the gathering in question they rested on widespread discussion and preparation; performances generally consisted of multiple actions in recurrent sequences. A candidate's organization of multiple performances in preparation for a parliamentary election provides one prominent model for a *campaign*, but as they emerged to prominence in the nineteenth century social movements likewise entailed multiple performances and a great deal of behind-the-scenes organizing. The array of performances—or *repertoire* for short—linking any particular set of political actors might compound into one sort of campaign or another, but it remained enormously limited by comparison with the actions, performances, and campaigns those same actors had the technical capacity to produce, even in comparison with those which other sets of actors were actually employing in the same era. Actions, performances, campaigns, and repertoires have their counterparts in the dialogues, plays, play cycles, and whole arrays of dramas available to the interacting players of a particular dramatic company.

A weak version of the repertoire metaphor asserts simply that participants in action attend to one another's assigned parts in the drama and to shared memories of similar events. As a guide to interpretation, even a weak version helps. But I mean a strong version, which implies (1) that social relations, meanings, and actions cluster together in known, recurrent patterns and (2) that many technically possible contentious transactions never occur because the potential participants lack the requisite knowledge, memory, and social connections. In the strong version, the appearance of new forms results from deliberate innovation and strenuous bargaining, as in the process by which employers, workers, and agents of the British state struggled over the boundary between acceptable and unacceptable forms of strike activity. While contenders are constantly innovating, furthermore, they generally innovate at the perimeter of the existing repertoire rather than by breaking entirely with old ways. Most innovations fail and disappear; only a rare few fashion long-term changes in a form of contention. Only very rarely does one whole repertoire give way to another; the period of British history we are examining features one such massive change in repertoire. For these reasons, repertoires of contention have their own distinct histories.

Any repertoire depends on an existing web of social relations and understandings among parties to the interaction. In today's Britain, for example, most connected sets of aggrieved people have the ability to demonstrate, petition, send a delegation to authorities, and so on through a number of routines for stating complaints and demands. All such routines involve at least two parties: an aggrieved or interested group of citizens and a powerholder who is the object of their claims. Although parties to an interaction often disagree sharply over their respective rights and obligations, such routines articulate with broad shared beliefs: beliefs in the propriety of peaceful public airing of grievances, in the rights of individuals to representation, in limits to governmental intervention, and in other premises of representative government. Many Britons have actually joined in performing some of these routines. The alternative routines constitute their collective-interaction repertoire.

Powerful people have distinctive routines for dealing with one another: the ceremonial dinner, the reception, the foxhunt, and so on. But the routines linking relatively powerless people to one another and to authorities of various kinds more often put established rights and privileges at risk. Here, routines involving the mass of the population concern us more than those which were ruling-class monopolies. For the study of popular collective-interaction repertoires forms part of an attempt to explain the development of mass politics on a national scale in Great Britain and other western countries. In 1758 sustained mass intervention in national politics did not exist anywhere in the world. By 1833 it had become almost routine in Great Britain and was beginning to occur elsewhere in Western Europe.

During the eighteenth century, as we have seen, British repertoires were different. The prevailing forms of open conflict above a very small scale included seizures of grain, tollgate attacks, disruptions of ceremonies or festivals, group hunting on forbidden territory, invasions of land, orderly destruction of property, shaming routines such as Rough Music, and similar events. Most of these forms of contention had existed for several centuries with relatively little change; the largest alterations in Britain's contentious repertoires between the sixteenth and eighteenth centuries seem to have been the decline of depredations by private armies and gangs of retainers rather than the introduction of distinctively new forms of interaction (Charlesworth 1983; Fletcher 1968; Fletcher and Stevenson 1985; Harris 1987; MacCulloch 1979; Manning 1988; Morrill and Walter 1985; Rogers 1989; Sharp 1980; Stone 1947; Stone 1983; Underdown 1985; Walter and Wrightson 1976; Zagorin 1982).

Like political life as a whole, we might characterize the eighteenth-century repertoire as "parochial," "bifurcated," and "particular." It was *parochial* because most often the interests and interaction involved were concentrated in a single community. It was *bifurcated* because when ordinary people addressed local issues and nearby objects they took impressively direct action to achieve their ends, but when it came to national issues and objects they recurrently addressed their demands to a local patron or authority, who might represent their interest, redress their grievance, fulfill his own obligation, or at least authorize them to act. Thus the collective seizure of grain, which authorities called a "food riot," stated both a grievance against local merchants and the claim that local authorities should act to keep food in the community at a price poor people could afford, while the breaking down of enclosures stated the claim that landlords and authorities should maintain the rights of community members to glean, pasture, gather, or otherwise use unplanted lands to their advantage.

The eighteenth-century repertoire was *particular* because the detailed routines of action varied greatly from group to group, issue to issue, locality to locality. Its forms of contention were also particular in two other regards: varying considerably in detail from one locality to another, and transferring only with difficulty among different settings and political circumstances. The parochial, particular, and bifurcated eighteenth-century repertoire likewise included a good deal of ceremonial, street theater, deployment of strong visual symbols, and destruction of symbolically charged objects. For all its eighteenth-century trappings, the escape of pressed sailors with which this chapter began was exceptional in forging an autonomous link between citizens and their national state.

Although some of these "eighteenth-century" routines survived well into the nineteenth century, they rapidly lost their relative prominence among the means of righting wrongs. Instead, demonstrations, strikes, rallies, public meetings, and similar forms of interaction came to prevail during the nineteenth century. As compared with their predecessors, nineteenth-century forms had a cosmopolitan, modular, and autonomous character. They were *cosmopolitan* in often referring to interests and issues that spanned many localities or affected centers of power whose actions touched many localities. They were *modular* in being easily transferable from one setting or circumstance to another instead of being shaped tightly to particular uses. They were *autonomous* in beginning on the claimants' own initiative and establishing direct communication between claimants and nationally significant centers of power. Yet they involved less direct action and immediate redress of grievances than their eighteenth-century predecessors. Their cosmopolitan and autonomous character meant that they transferred with relative ease from setting to setting and circumstance to circumstance; a wide variety of interests, groups, and localities adopted very similar routines for public meetings and related actions.

We should resist the temptation to label one of the two repertoires as more efficient, more political, or more "revolutionary" than the other. Nor does it help to call one repertoire "traditional" and the other "modern," any more than one can say that contemporary English is superior to that of Shakespeare, as if one were clearly more efficient or sophisticated than the other. The division between "pre-political" and "political," between "backward-looking" and "forward-looking" forms of action, it is true, once helped George Rudé, E. J. Hobsbawm, and other pioneers in the historical study of collective action to dramatize the fact that crowds act coherently instead of impulsively, that the character of crowd action altered visibly during the nineteenth century, and that the alteration linked to the changing struggle for power. When many historians were portraying crowds and protesters as irrational, and ultimately insignificant, historical actors, the message of Rudé and Hobsbawm needed underlining. Following Rudé and Hobsbawm, I myself once wrote about the "modernization" of "protest," distinguishing "reactionary" from "primitive" and "modern" forms of collective action. I soon abandoned those labels and the ideas behind them; I realized that they entailed an unjustified— and unverified—teleology (for laudable skepticism on this score, see Archer 1990).

Many a distinction that works well as a first approximation operates badly as a basis of sustained analysis. So it is here: we must recognize that repertoires of contention are sets of tools for the people involved. Backward/forward, pre-political/political, and similar distinctions classify not the tools, but particular circumstances for using them. The tools serve more than one end, and their relative efficacy depends on the match among tools, tasks, and users. A new repertoire emerged in the nineteenth century because new users took up new tasks and found the available tools inadequate to their problems and abilities. In the course of actual struggles, people making claims and counter-claims fashioned new means of claim-making.

Neither the new tasks nor the new forms of interaction were intrinsically revolutionary. After all, the English had managed two revolutions in the seventeenth century with repertoires similar to those which prevailed in the eighteenth century, but never managed to make one in the nineteenth or twentieth century with their new repertoires. A larger share of interactions in the older repertoire (such as Rough Music and the pulling down of poorhouses) involved direct action against adversaries, while a much greater proportion of the interactions in the newer repertoire (such as the public meeting and the mass petition) took for granted the continued existence of the national structure of power; such forms of action could achieve their aims only cumulatively, in the long run, over many coordinated efforts. The new repertoire gave advantages to those who could easily draw on or create associations, alliances with other aggrieved groups, and contacts with Parliament; it tipped the balance away from ordinary workers and poor people toward bourgeois of various stripes. In these regards, the old repertoire was arguably more revolutionary than the new. Both repertoires reflected and interacted with the organization of power in their own historical contexts. The difference between them lay in the relations of repertoires and actors to their political settings.

Warning: like most useful dichotomies, the reduction of many repertoires to just two simplifies radically for the sake of clarity. No actual group employed all the means of interaction within either of the repertoires, no pair of actors shifted abruptly from one repertoire to the other, no sharp break in repertoires occurred in 1800 or at any other date. We are examining a history of continuous innovation and modulation. Yet surges of change in repertoires did occur, alterations in the contentious repertoires of one pair of actors induced alterations in adjacent pairs, broad conflicts produced more extensive repertoire changes than narrow ones, and some innovations caught on much more rapidly and durably than others. For these reasons, the exaggerated division of continuously changing multiple repertoires into eighteenth- and nineteenth-century sets serves as a useful guide to a complex history.

Insistent Questions, Possible Answers

The analyses in this book concern changing repertoires of contention in Great Britain during the three-quarters of a century following 1758. More than anything else, they pursue a single question: How, why, and with what effects did the ways in which ordinary people made collective claims on other people change in Great Britain between the 1750s and the 1830s? Generalized, the question concerns the emergence of mass national politics in Great Britain and, by extension, elsewhere. It entails a series of more detailed questions:

Under what conditions did significant changes occur in the form or intensity of involvement among different pairs of actors, including powerholders, in open contention?

What caused the basic means by which people made collective claims on others—their repertoires of contention—to alter so greatly during those seventy-five years?

How did those changes affect the relative ability of different contenders to advance their own interests?

What part did changes in the organization of production and of state power play in these transformations of contention?

Given that no revolution occurred in Britain between 1750 and 1840, how close to revolution did changes in production, state power, and contention bring Great Britain, when, and how?

The answers to these subsidiary questions take several different forms, each a partial response to more than one of them. First, the concentration of capital and the related proletarianization of the British workforce altered the interests of workers, of employers, and of several third parties to their relationship—parish officers, royal functionaries, and others. Increasingly employers broke through the constraints of local crafts and made decisions based on the logic of national and international markets. Increasingly workers found they could not exert effective pressure on employers without expanding their scale of organization and redefining solidarity in terms that cut across individual crafts. These changes, in turn, pushed collective interaction toward a larger scale and a national arena.

Second, urbanization, migration, and rapid population growth transformed the organizational bases of local collective interaction, adding weight to those actors who could create, adapt, or infiltrate flexible, efficient associations and assemblies. Associations and assemblies provided the means of connecting and maneuvering substantial numbers of people rapidly.

Third, the rising intensity of British military efforts, at least through 1815, impelled an expansion of taxes, national debt, and service bureaucracies, which increased not only the state's size but also its weight within the economy. In the process Parliament—critical to every decision concerning governmental revenue, expenditure, and personnel—occupied ever more space in political decisions. These changes, too, promoted a shift toward collective interaction that was large in scale and national in scope. In addition, they enhanced the strategic advantage and maneuvering room of formally constituted associations, especially those with national constituencies, as bases for collective interaction. They made parliamentary elections more critical to national issues, encouraged contested elections, drew nonvoters more intensely into electoral campaigns, and encouraged the formation of "paraparliamentary" politics in such guises as national social movements, national petition drives, and calls for a mass platform. These activities in turn expanded the utilization of local assemblies such as vestries in national struggles over power and policy. These processes sharpened the conflict between two different conceptions and organizations of national politics: one vesting fundamental power in a compact between regime and Parliament, the other treating both of them as instruments of a sovereign people.

Fourth, short-run shifts in the mobilization and strategic advantage of different parties to conflicts of interest strongly affected the ebb and flow of contention. The shifts often resulted from circumstances external to the conflicts themselves, as when the end of the Napoleonic Wars brought many former soldiers back into the civilian labor force yet simultaneously reduced the demand for industrial labor.

Fifth, struggles laid down their own history, both because participants in a given struggle remembered what had happened before and planned their actions accordingly and because the outcome of any particular struggle altered the positions of the participants, including third parties. Concessions the government made to a specific type of action by a certain actor, for example, made it easier for other actors to press claims by means of that same type of interaction. The success of one petition drive opened the way to new petition drives, as one association's pressing of its claims set a precedent for another association to press its own claims. Contention, however, also generated repression, which in turn shaped the possibilities for collective interaction. A deep change in British policing, for example, occurred between 1750 and the 1830s; that change involved agents of the state in anticipatory control of potentially unruly crowds. In the course of that internal history of struggle, collective-action innovators and entrepreneurs such as John Wilkes, Lord George Gordon, Orator Hunt, Daniel O'Connell, John Doherty, and Feargus O'Connor sometimes had large impacts on prevailing forms of interaction. They helped create the social movement, with its devices of meeting, marching, petitioning, displaying, and attacking, as a standard means of pursuing shared ends.

Sixth, Britain most closely approached a revolutionary situation—the existence of an alternative to the established government commanding substantial support in significant segments of the national population—during the 1830–32 mobilization around parliamentary reform. The dramatic splits of 1768–1769, 1780, the 1790s, 1816–1820, and 1828–1829 lacked the depth and national scope of reform mobilization. Nevertheless, even that later mobilization fell far short of revolution. Most of its organizers remained committed to the acquisition of power within the existing system, the central coalition of workers and small capitalists brought together contradictory interests, and holders of state power took skillful advantage of both facts.

Finally, the particular history of Great Britain set off British contention from struggles in other western countries. British capitalism and the British state both followed distinctive trajectories over the years from 1758 to 1834, and those paths of change strongly affected the ways ordinary British people acted together on their interests. On the side of capitalism, British landlords and entrepreneurs invested early and heavily in large-scale marketing and relatively concentrated means of production. They thus promoted proletarianization of workers in both agriculture and manufacturing. Their reorganizations of production likewise stimulated rapid shifts from agriculture to manufacturing and services as well as from rural to urban population, which in its turn favored a substitution of relatively long-distance, definitive migration for the churning short-distance movement that had characterized the previous centuries.

On the side of the state, war drove a great expansion of the British state apparatus. Yet as compared with other European powers the British state continued to do a great deal of its work through co-opted members of the ruling classes (notably the parsons and landlords who served as Justices of the Peace) and operated increasingly within limits set by a mighty Parliament. Inside Parliament, furthermore, the Commons gained greater and greater weight.

These political arrangements had emerged from earlier struggles, including multiple rebellions and two revolutions. In 1758 the Glorious Revolution lay only seven decades back, the contested settlement of Hanoverians on the British throne was only forty-four years old, major rebellions against royal power had shaken Scotland several times in the memory of living men and women. In the course of those struggles, Britain's people had gained unusually extensive rights to assembly, association, petition, privacy, and criticism of authorities. During the seventy-five years following 1758, however, two monumental changes altered the everyday uses of those rights, and established new ones: the formation of a new class system, more strongly marked by industrial capitalism, and the bargaining out of mass citizenship on a national scale. In both regards, Britain's experience preceded that of most European neighbors. We will see abundant evidence of the impact of Britain's particular economic and political history on its patterns of contention between 1758 and 1834.

This book, then, oscillates from the general to the particular and back. The particulars concern contentious events, and clusters of them; I place concrete instances of claim-making in their historical contexts. At the general level, however, I attempt two different sorts of synthesis. At one end, I aim to formulate and test models of the impact of changes in the organization of production and state power on popular collective inter-action, as well as to identify general processes by which the character and consequences of struggles affect the forms of subsequent struggles. At the other, I seek to fashion a valid account of the emergence in Great Britain of mass popular politics and the means of claim-making that now prevail through much of the European world. The book oscillates between the two sorts of generalization on the assumptions that (1) the principles underlying the deep transformation of British popular politics apply much more widely among the many countries in which the expansion of capitalist property relations and the growth of a national state coincided, and (2) the very correspondence of particularities in British experience— for example, connections between the rising power of Parliament and the explosion of petition-signing meetings—provides crucial clues to the general causes of change.

What's to Come

The study of changing repertoires in Great Britain raises further questions of great importance. We will explore how the objects and strategies of claim-makers change, for example by looking at the increasing salience of Parliament as an object of claims by local groups. We will look closely at the interaction of challengers with authorities, and at the political outcomes of the interaction—examining, for instance, how changing techniques and intensities of repression affect the means people use to contend for their interests. We will study the impact of a given major struggle and its outcome on those which follow, as in the ways that John Wilkes's innovations in collective action of the 1760s opened the way to subsequent innovators. We will ask what light the systematic analysis of contention sheds on series of events that historians already regard as important moments of change, such as the vast mobilization around the issue of parliamentary reform from 1830 to 1832. We will investigate the influence of the changing organization of production, including the concentration of capital, on the issues and forms of contention. We will inquire, finally, how transformations of the state impinged upon, and interacted with, the course of contention.

The analysis of popular contention provides sufficiently rich evidence to support important conclusions about such matters. Most of all, the attentive decoding of contentious gatherings reveals how the concentration of capital and the expansion of the state pushed popular struggles from local arenas and from a significant reliance on patronage toward autonomous claim-making in national arenas. How this happened, and to what degree, varied from one set of actors to another; hunters and gamekeepers continued to battle in a landlord's posted forest while public meetings that laid claims directly on Parliament began to overshadow assemblies concerning parish affairs. The remainder of this book traces changes and variations in British contention in order to work out exactly how the social transformation of Great Britain from 1758 to 1834 affected the collective interaction of ordinary people, and how that collective interaction shaped the general course of politics.

The more successfully the succeeding chapters accomplish that task, alas, the more it will dissatisfy their most demanding readers. Success will tempt those readers to ask for more: either a fully documented general history of contention and its causes, an equally general treatise on the dynamics of popular contention, or both at once. I do not prove all the book's causal assertions—a full analysis of capitalization and proletarianization, for example, would require much more extensive documentation of changing production, ownership, and exchange—but I do establish that they are generally consistent with the ebb and flow of popular contention. Nor do I offer a full theoretical treatment of contention and popular politics, despite drawing heavily on recent work in those fields. I focus on establishing probable connections between large social changes and alterations in the character of Britain's public claim-making between the 1750s and the 1830s.

The following chapters break into three clusters. Chapters 2 and 3 present overviews of change in the character and context of British struggles over the entire period: first a preliminary survey of actual shifts in issues, actors, and actions from 1758 to 1834, then changes in the state, economy, and class structure. The second section—Chapters 4–7—splits that period into four chronological segments and explores the contention of each segment in its own terms. The final chapter sums up the book's implications thrice: once as a refashioned narrative of popular contention in Great Britain from the 1750s to the 1830s, again as a set of reflections on the foundations of British collective action in the eighteenth and nineteenth centuries, finally as insight into processes by which mass national politics take shape in general. Since today, to a large degree, people making collective claims in western countries still use the repertoires struggling Britons created back then, the study of eighteenth- and nineteenth-century contention promises to help us understand the struggles that shape our own lives.

❧ 2 ❧

CONTENTION UNDER A
MAGNIFYING GLASS

On Thursday, 17 April 1834, London's stock market erupted in a turbulent session. The Bank of England's changing policy on debt management contributed to the market's swings that day, but so did popular contention. "The depression was accelerated," reported the *Morning Chronicle* of 18 April,

> by reports of disturbances having broken out in Merthyr Tydvil. This, however, we are assured on the best authority, is not the fact, the latest accounts from that place not alluding to any such circumstance. Fears are, however, entertained in the city that the occurrences at Oldham will lead to manifestations of feeling in other and more populous towns in the kingdom. The public notice which has been given of a General Meeting of the Trades Unions of the Metropolis and its vicinity next Monday, to present a Petition to the King for the remission of the sentence on the Dorchester Unionists, has also caused some apprehensions for the maintenance of tranquillity in the city. (MC 18 April 1834: 4)

Any report of "disturbance" at Merthyr Tydvil (or Tydfil) recalled the first week of June 1831, when striking miners of that Welsh hill town had sacked the houses of local officials and fought pitched battles with Highland troops, leaving sixteen or seventeen colliers and two soldiers dead. This time the report was false, but it worried holders of capital.

In any case, something *had* happened in Oldham: on Monday the 14th, three constables without warrants had entered the Trades Union Room of the King William IV pub, where the Cotton Spinners Union had assembled. Most likely searching for evidence of a revolutionary conspiracy, they seized some oath-taking documents and suffered an attack from the assembled workers; they managed to arrest two of their attackers, the union secretaries, and to get away. The next morning, as officers were taking the two prisoners to the magistrates, a crowd of some 2,000 people formed in Manchester Street, beat the officers, and rescued the prisoners. Plant police fired at the crowd from the windows of a nearby mill, whose workers were on strike and being replaced by knobsticks. The gunfire killed one man. Members of the crowd then broke the mill's windows and sacked its owner's house.

Lancers finally dispersed the crowd, but on Wednesday the 16th 10,000 workers assembled on Oldham Edge to protest and demand justice; vociferous meetings were continuing in Oldham as the *Chronicle* printed its report (MC 17–29 April, 18 August 1834; LT 17–28 April, 6, 7, 12 June, 14, 18 August 1834, 23 January 1835; GM May 1834; AR 1834). The local Regeneration Society (the political wing of John Doherty's National Spinners' Union) called a general strike, which many trades joined; eventually two knobsticks were convicted of manslaughter and two police officers discharged from their jobs for illegal entry into the union's headquarters (Foster 1974; Kirby and Musson 1975).

As for the "Dorchester Unionists," they were the six agricultural laborers of Tolpuddle, Dorset—the Tolpuddle Martyrs—to whom the Dorchester Assizes had recently (19 March) given sentences of transportation to Australia for swearing and administering oaths in the course of forming a parish Friendly Society; they had dared their bold initiative after their masters had cut wages step by step from ten to seven shillings per week, then threatened to take away yet another shilling. Since the repeal of the Combination Acts in 1824, organizing such societies had been legal, but oath-taking still fell under the ban of a 1797 law originally aimed at secret societies that might subvert the war against France. Organized workers all over the country rightly interpreted the conviction and the sentence as threats to their own rights to organize. Early in April, protest meetings multiplied in Lancashire, Yorkshire and, of course, London.

In London, as the *Chronicle* reported, union leaders, coordinated by the Owenite Grand National Consolidated Trades Union, planned a huge march to give the king a petition requesting commutation of the convicted laborers' sentences. The Union's London District Central Committee organized the march (Parssinen and Prothero 1977). They chose 21 April (Monday, a day off for many workers and the favorite day for workers' assemblies) and organized the demonstration of support with meticulous care. Each "brother in union" was, according to a placard printed and posted in advance, to wear "a crimson riband, one inch wide, between the first and second button-hole, on the left side of his coat" (HO 52/24). Drawn by lot, the order of march was to be as follows:

1. Gold beaters
2. United metal trades
3. Goldsmiths, silversmiths, and jewellers
4. Wood sawyers
5. Tailors
6. Garment dyers, calico glaziers, and calenderers
7. Rope makers
8. Tin-Plate workers
9. Wood turners
10. Scale makers
11. Saddlers
12. Cabinet and chair makers
13. Cordwainers
14. Horse-hair curlers
15. Silk skein dyers
16. Silk weavers
17. Builders
18. Smiths
19. Silk hatters.

Each group was to carry a banner designating the trade and its position in the procession.

The government found the unions' plan legal but alarming. On Saturday 19 April Chief Magistrate Frederick Roe had 2,500 copies of this bill posted around London:

Whereas public Notice has been given that great numbers of Persons intend to assemble on Monday the 21st of April with the intention of accompanying, in procession and array, through the Streets of the Metropolis, a Deputation to present to the Secretary of State a Petition addressed to the King, And Whereas such a Meeting and such Proceedings are highly improper and objectionable, calculated to excite terror in the minds of the peaceable and well disposed Inhabitants of the Metropolis, and may prove dangerous to the public peace as well as to the Individuals engaged in them: The Magistrates of the Police Offices hereby warn all classes of His Majesty's Subjects of the danger to which they will expose themselves by attending such a Meeting, or taking any part in such proceedings. The Magistrates also enjoin Masters to prevent their Apprentices, Workers and Servants from being present at such a Meeting. (HO 60/2)

On the same day, Home Secretary Melbourne alerted magistrates, police, and cavalry to the danger of "disturbance" during the trade union procession that would accompany a union member's funeral in Hammersmith on Sunday 20 April (HO 41/26).

The Whiggish *Chronicle* echoed the Whig government; its editors concluded that the march's intent "can only be to intimidate and overawe the legal authorities by an ostentatious display of physical force" (MC 19 April 1834: 4). The very day of the scheduled march, they added:

We have always contended for the right of the working classes to combine for the protection of their interests in questions with their employers, provided they avoided all attempts at coercion or other unfair means of influencing their own classes. Under the exciting circumstances also of the recent unadvised and injurious formation of the organized societies now called "Trades' Unions" we have fearlessly contended for the sufficiency of the existing laws, and decidedly deprecated any new legislation. We deem the statute in force a sufficiently fair and full protection of the relative rights of masters and men—excepting perhaps the illegal influence obtained by the *physical* means denominated "picketing" and "scouting"—and the numerous convictions in all parts of the kingdom, and the notorious failure of the most offensive unions and "strikes," as a demonstration of the practical sufficiency of the existing law. (MC 21 April 1834: 2)

Even their cautious judgment that the Tolpuddle laborers' sentences were too severe did not keep the *Chronicle*'s editors from deploring the "absurd and dangerous" pronouncements of trade unions, or from decrying the "'SPECTACLE SYSTEM' of public funerals of deceased members of Unions, and numerous public processions . . . such as we are to witness this day" (MC 21 April 1834: 2). Workers had every right, that is, to challenge their own employers on their own ground. But they had no right to enter national politics as united workers.

The anti-union *Times* redoubled with the declaration that "the whole scheme is the most flagrant humbug upon those poor people for the benefit of the 'managers' alone, and this day's farce is got up for the double purpose of cheating the poor gulled members of the Unions with the fancy of their own importance, and frightening the Government by a display of their numerical force" (LT 21 April 1834: 2). The Government swore in 5,000 special constables, stationed 2,812 policemen throughout the city, placed a special guard at the Bank of England, brought in several regiments of regular troops, and even added artillery to their armament (HO 41/26; HO 52/24; Radzinowicz 1968).

Notwithstanding severe warnings from newspaper writers, employers, and public authorities, a large share of London's workers assembled on Monday, and the march went smoothly. Behind leaders in regalia and banners marking the nineteen participating trades, 25,000–30,000 members of metropolitan trade unions assembled near Copenhagen House in Islington, many of them wearing their best clothes and sporting one-inch crimson ribbons on their left lapels. Twelve men shouldered the hefty petition with its 260,000 signatures. They made their way deliberately through King's Cross, Russell Square, Waterloo Place, and Charing Cross to the Whitehall office of Home Secretary Viscount Melbourne—a path that took them from the City's plebeian northern reaches into the stylish West End, past royal territory, and onto the terrain of Parliament.

At the Home Office the assembly's delegates, as well as Robert Owen, tried to deliver their petition to Melbourne, while the mass of the demonstrators filed across Westminster Bridge and awaited the parley's results at Kennington Common. Under-Secretary Phillips, speaking for Melbourne in a scenario that Melbourne had planned well in advance, insisted that Owen (who was not an official member of the deputation) leave, and reported that the Home Secretary "could not receive a Petition presented under such circumstances, and in such a manner," but would transmit to the king a petition duly presented on another day by an unaccompanied delegation (MC 22 April 1834: 1). And so it was. On hearing the news, the thousands of marchers went home peacefully. A day later, Melbourne received the disputed petition.

The debate, however, did not end. Despite the nearly perfect decorum of the occasion, the *Chronicle*'s writers continued to believe that "Assemblages of the whole of the working population are not within the limits of the allowable exercises of liberty" (MC 22 April 1834: 4). A "Well-Wisher of Old England" wrote the *Times* that the upper and middle classes should revive volunteer forces to combat the working-class menace (LT 22 April 1834: 6). In the House of Lords, the Marquess of Londonderry complained that the relative success of the great march had only encouraged the unionists: 15,000 new members had recently signed up, said he, workers were using the funerals of their fellow members as pretexts for additional demonstrations in the streets, and "In his neighbourhood, on Sunday last, there were not fewer than 6,000 or 7,000 men congregated, and moving in procession and array, to the great terror of the peaceable and well-disposed inhabitants" (HPD 28 April 1834: 96). As beggars, three-card-monte dealers, unlicensed vendors, and street preachers today take their places on crowded sidewalks, dissident ordinary citizens moved into the ambiguous space provided by public festivals and ceremonies.

The marquess made the same reference to "terror" as had the chief magistrate's declaration two days before the procession; both echoed the phrase *in terrorem populi*, which was sanctified by the 1714 Riot Act: with an hour's warning, magistrates could label as a riot any assembly of twelve or more persons who frightened the public and threatened to break the law; after the requisite hour, magistrates could have such assemblies broken up by force. Yet the Marquess of Londonderry, Chief Magistrate Roe, the Well-Wisher of Old England, and the *Morning Chronicle* all faced a problem: the orderly workers who marched through London's streets were not clearly breaking any law, not even threatening to break any. Public officials had to recognize that this sort of mobile meeting stayed just within legal limits and built on many precedents. By 1834 what we now call a demonstration had legal standing as a way of making claims, of demonstrating that large numbers of determined people stood behind a particular program, demand, or party.

A Change of Repertoires

What set off this class of events from other public gatherings? Not the large numbers, as such; thousands of people also moved through the streets at such public ceremonies as the procession of Lord Mayor's Day. Nor the public presentation of a petition, which had been common practice for seventy years. The thronged petition march and the funeral processions stood out from other gatherings by the fact that ordinary people clearly identified with formal associations—in this case, trade unions—publicly displayed their numbers, determination, uprightness, and internal discipline in support of a well-defined set of claims. They acted autonomously, and they made demands of the national government: in the event at hand, demands to pardon the Dorchester laborers.

In retrospect, we can see as precedents the behavior of partisans during eighteenth-century elections and the many marches of John Wilkes's supporters during the disputes over his elections to Parliament in 1768 and 1769. By 1780 some public leaders had argued that Committees of Correspondence and similar associations had the right to put pressure on Parliament and the government. The idea of a "mass platform" on which ordinary people could state their views concerning matters coming before Parliament, promoted by such militants as Henry Hunt, had gained credibility after the end of the Napoleonic Wars (Belchem 1978, 1981, 1986). But the right of associations involving relatively powerless people to voice their claims by gathering publicly and marching became well established only in the 1820s and 1830s. The *Morning Chronicle's* commentators were observing a relatively new form of contention.

The newspaper's editors also mentioned "strikes," "picketing," and "scouting"—not only concerted withdrawals from work, but also organized exclusion of potential strikebreakers from places of employment—as unacceptable novelties. In 1834 these forms of collective interaction hovered at the brink of legality; they were becoming common but lacked the standing of the street march or the public meeting. In a longer perspective, nevertheless, it is remarkable how many different forms of contention that remained standard into the twentieth century began to dominate popular action during the four decades from 1790 to 1830.

The newcomers included the public meeting, the petition by a special-interest association, the demonstration, the single-establishment strike, and the national social movement. As compared with the forms of contention that prevailed in the eighteenth century, the innovations more often took a national scale and aimed at national holders of power. They relied less frequently on patrons and other intermediaries to transmit their entreaties or demands to authorities. The participants spoke more frequently in the name of a self-identified interest. Such a form as the public meeting transferred with relative ease from group to group, place to place, issue to issue. In comparison with relatively parochial, particular, and bifurcated eighteenth-century forms of action, they were cosmopolitan, modular, and autonomous. A new repertoire of contention was crystallizing, and displacing an older one.

So many historians of popular contention have either misread or assumed *a priori* the long-term trends—supposedly toward class-conscious militancy, toward compromise and pacification, toward rationality, or toward something else—that previous historiography leaves unclear exactly what we must explain. Accordingly, my aim in this chapter is not to explain the great changes, but to clarify what happened. Later chapters will wallow in explanation, but this one will skim lightly over its surface. The chapter will, in compensation, plunge deeply into the available evidence.

Problems, Sources, Methods

The analyses that follow do not recount the full history of British collective action. They concentrate on moments in which people gathered to make visible, public claims, acted on those claims in one way or another, then turned to other business. In stressing open, collective, discontinuous contention, the analyses neglect individual forms of struggle and resistance as well as the routine operation of political parties, labor unions, patron-client networks, and other powerful means of collective interaction, except when they produce visible contention in the public arena. They do so in an effort to make the analysis of collective interaction manageable, in the conviction that contention is an important subject for its own sake, and in the hope that the careful analysis of collective contention will also lend insight into individual action, continuous contention, and non-contentious collective interaction.

The central body of evidence on which I draw comes from an enumeration of more than 8,000 "contentious gatherings" that occurred in Southeastern England during thirteen years scattered from 1758 to 1820 and in Great Britain as a whole during the seven years from 1828 to 1834. I chose the earlier thirteen years as a compromise among several partly contradictory desiderata: (1) spread over the entire period from 1750 to

1827; (2) availability of sources (for example Kent's trade directory for London) permitting an analysis of the geographic and social contexts of different kinds of contention; (3) adjacent years, where possible, in order to increase the continuity of the record; and (4) few enough periods that a small group of readers and transcribers could actually get through the sources in four or five years of part-time effort.

Although one might defend 1758 as a starting point because of its situation in the midst of the Seven Years War, in historical perspective nothing sets that year off from its neighbors; as the inquiry began, 1758 merely seemed the first year for which my group, working chiefly in the United States, could assemble broad evidence that would be roughly comparable to evidence available for later years. Sheer lack of time and resources made it impossible for me to collect systematic evidence for all of Great Britain during the thirteen earlier years. When it came to analyzing Great Britain as a whole, continuity became all the more important, not only because of the desirability of following recurrent conflicts through their courses but also because of the necessity of examining a great deal of evidence on the contexts of contention. After a good deal of experimentation with different sets of years, I chose 1828–1834 because in that period the British state made decisions—notably on parliamentary reform—that significantly affected the politics of the rest of the century. These two decisions yielded an odd array of years, but an interesting one.

In a contentious gathering (CG), a number of people—here, ten or more—outside of the government gathered in a publicly accessible place and made claims on at least one person outside their own number, claims which if realized would affect the interests of their object. My collaborators and I searched publications of the time and cataloged a total of 8,088 CGs; the appendix provides a detailed description of our sources and procedures. This catalog constitutes the core of my evidence on changes and variations in collective-action repertoires.

The "contentious gathering" acts as a spotlight. If we run a spotlight slowly across a dark terrain, how much we see at any instant depends as much on the power and focus of the beam as on the contents of the terrain. At any given look, furthermore, the frequency and mix of objects the spotlight brings into view are unreliable guides to their actual numbers and proportions across the whole terrain. If the beam sweeps from a fixed point, it best identifies objects lying close to that location. Slow movement of the light, however, does provide us with useful information about where there are many objects and where few; the spotlight works better in comparison than in description.

Similarly, the boundaries of the category "contentious gathering" are deliberately arbitrary, but broad enough to catch a wide range of collective interaction. The definition takes in just about every event for which authorities and observers used such terms as riot, disorder, disturbance, or affray, but also includes a great many peaceful meetings, processions, and other assemblies that escaped the wrath of authorities. Since salutes, cheers, and professions of support count as claims, the word "contentious" slightly misstates the character of events in the catalog. (Other possible terms—protest, claim-making, and so on—are either more cumbersome, more misleading, or both.) In any case, even professions of support for one party typically involved opposition to another party. Almost all the gatherings identified by the definition entailed genuine conflicts of interest; they included the public taking of stands that could—and often did—cost the actors and the objects of their action something.

In order to shield myself from an otherwise inevitable barrage of accusations and misunderstandings, let me make a few declarations of unfaith. I do not believe national periodicals of the eighteenth and nineteenth centuries contain complete, unbiased enumerations and descriptions of all sorts of conflict. I do not think that "contentious gatherings" exhaust or represent all the means of collective action and interaction that were available to British people back then. I do not pretend that one can sum seizures of grain, parades, mass meetings, machine-breaking incidents, and demonstrations into a single number somehow indexing the quantity of anger, disturbance, or militancy prevailing in a whole complex country. I do not imagine that platoons of machine-readable data, strenuously disciplined, will line up in neat rows and shout out unexpected but true answers to great historical questions. I do not suppose, finally, that the forms of contention in Britain—or anywhere else—fall into a natural progression from traditional to modern, from simple to sophisticated, from expressive to instrumental, from ineffective to effective. Let me hope that readers and critics of this book will avoid attributing to me any of those views.

Yet I do believe some things. I assert that constraining histories of popular contention by reference to large, uniform catalogs of events reduces the temptation to let a few spectacular and well-documented conflicts dominate interpretations of change. My investigations convince me that contentious gatherings, however trivial taken one by one, had a significant cumulative effect on the conduct of public business in Britain. I am ready to argue that reports in periodicals contain sufficient information to document the larger changes and variations in popular contention over the eighteenth and nineteenth centuries. I think it possible to identify and allow for biases in the sources we consult. I claim that Britain's contentious gatherings provide some evidence for alterations in a wider range of conflict and collective interaction, such as the day-to-day use of interpersonal networks. I suppose that large changes in the numbers and proportions of different kinds of gathering constitute evidence of more general shifts in the character of popular involvement in political struggle. I have some confidence that traces of the major social changes affecting popular contention appear in existing accounts of contentious gatherings, if only one has the patience and ingenuity to search them out. The general sense of the ebb and flow of contention conveyed by our sources deserves some credence.

Not everyone will accept that judgment. Roger Wells, who has dug deep into local records of conflict between 1793 and 1801, warns that "The press, even at the end of the eighteenth century, is an inconclusive source" (Wells 1988: 93). If we are looking for utter completeness, Wells is unquestionably correct. Drawing on multiple archives and periodicals, for example, Wells tabulates thirteen "disturbances" in Kent, Surrey, or Sussex from January through May 1795, during the great subsistence crisis (ibid.: 425). My group found reports on only four of these events in the *Times,* the *London Chronicle, Gentleman's Magazine,* or the *Annual Register.* Two of them our stringent rules disqualified because the reports did not establish clearly that ten or more persons had gathered in the same publicly accessible place and made claims on others. However, we also found a fourteenth open conflict over food at Brighthelmstone on 16 April, where "about 200 women and girls assembled before the Inn where the market is held, with a loaf of bread and a steak of beef hoisted on sticks, which they occasionally let fall to express their meaning that those articles must be lowered in price" (LC 23 April 1795: 388). Wells's catalog misses that event. Thus the score runs Wells Only 9, Tilly Only 1, Both

4. Many comparisons of our sample with detailed monographs come out in similar fashion. Wells has suggested, furthermore, that even his sources underestimate the number of "disturbances" (Wells 1990: 157).

So what should we conclude? Certainly that the enumerations drawn from periodicals miss many relevant events, especially smaller and vaguely reported events; that should warn us against attributing much importance to small differences and to comparisons based on small numbers of CGs. Since even Wells's exhaustive search misses events, however, the real question is whether unknown biases in the periodicals' reporting—we can, after all, usually adjust for known biases—vitiate large comparisons among periods, regions, social groups, or forms of action. With due confirmation wherever possible from other sources, I argue that we can draw reliable conclusions from those comparisons (see Appendix 1 for further discussion of reliability). The rigorous, uniform application of well-defined procedures reflects what happened between 1758 and 1834 at an unusual angle. Yet in that reflection we can still observe relations among reflected objects. Knowing the procedures of selection, furthermore, we can correct for the angle of vision they produce.

That reply, to be sure, leads immediately to another objection: Mark Harrison has complained that my research employs "a method for search for data related to collective behaviour which is designed to satisfy the retrieval needs of the computer, rather than a rich appreciation of context" (Harrison 1988: 17). On the contrary, I have had to push and bend computers ruthlessly in order to make them accept the rich material in the files of contentious gatherings. In fact, Harrison's basic procedure— the inventorying of crowd events from newspapers, supplemented by other sources—strikingly resembles my own. If Harrison's observation contains a legitimate reservation, it is that by including a large number of events in comparable form, the machine-readable record sacrificed some of the available detail on the contexts and internal sequences of the best-documented events; beyond a certain limit, comparability, coverage, and density pointed in somewhat different directions. But over 8,000 events, comparability of documentation and coverage of a considerable block of time and space have considerable advantages. One measure is this: From his compilation of crowd events in four English cities between 1790 and 1835, Harrison detects no significant changes in their character or settings; whatever defects my catalogs have, they provide abundant evidence of alterations in the same sorts of events within the Southeast between 1758 and 1834, and a reasonable case for shifts on the national scale as well.

Much depends, in any case, on what we are trying to measure. Wells assumes that historians should be studying something called "social protest," presumably because it gauges ordinary people's attitudes toward such changes as enclosures, freeing of the grain market, proletarianization, and imposition of the New Poor Law (Wells 1990). He is essentially searching for the "hidden transcripts" carrying shared but concealed resentments and aspirations that James Scott (1990) argues become the property of every durably subordinate group and serve as the bases of their concerted action. For that reason, Wells insists on the importance of going beyond the examination of big public events to the accumulation of evidence on arson, cattle-maiming, machine-breaking, perhaps even petty crime.

Indeed it is important to recognize that depending on the current tactical situation the same people turn from making public demands to burning hayricks and vice versa; coming to the Swing rebellion of 1830, we will observe exactly that sort of alternation. It is likewise important to see how risky it would be to infer a general state of mind and its changes from only one variety of action. But I reject that enterprise on two different grounds: first because it conflates the action with the presumably underlying attitude without allowing for the problematic connection between the two; second because it hinders treatment of this book's central problem, how and why the very means of collective interaction change and vary so dramatically in history. How and why, in particular, did mass national politics take shape? The study of changing attitudes, however profound, will not solve that problem. We must displace the inquiry toward social interaction, toward relations among groups, toward struggle, toward contention.

My doughty band of explorers was not the first to tread the ground of contention. We often encountered events already described by R. B. Rose, George Rudé, Eric Hobsbawm, the Hammonds, the Webbs, E. P. Thompson, John Bohstedt, John Stevenson, Andrew Charlesworth, and other cartographers of British conflicts. Although consulting their analyses seldom identified outright errors in the narratives we had drawn from our own sources, it provided essential context and interpretation while offering reassurance that we were dealing with similar sorts of evidence. The difference was that our catalog also includes thousands of events of which no mention appears in standard historical analyses—not because other historians did not have access to the sources, but most often because other historians found them routine, redundant, or trivial. That is the point: to include both the sensational and the routine in order to see how ways of acting together varied and changed.

A catalog of contentious gatherings will not answer every conceivable question about the evolution of collective interaction in Great Britain. For one thing, the evidence from 1758 to 1820 concentrates in the Southeast plus London: Kent, Middlesex, Surrey, and Sussex. It therefore says little about regional variation before 1828, and vastly underrepresents such important eighteenth-century forms of struggle as combats of hunters and gamekeepers, encounters between smugglers and coast guards, attacks on tollgates, and seizures of grain. Nor does it provide much insight concerning Scottish, Welsh, or Cornish perspectives on the country's great conflicts. Within the Southeastern region, furthermore, the catalog provides less dense coverage of contentious events in the eighteenth century than in the nineteenth. For that reason, in my discussion of CGs from 1758 to 1820 I incessantly compare and augment findings from the CG catalog with evidence from British archives and the work of other historians. Repeatedly in later chapters I call attention to differences in contention between the commercialized, urban Southeast and the diverse remainder of Great Britain.

In addition, a significant share of collective action and, especially, preparation for collective action took place outside of contentious gatherings. Some important struggles took place in the shelter of judicial proceedings; gleaners whose rights to enter harvested fields farmers challenged increasingly in the century after 1750, for example, carried on a major part of their counter-attack by means of appeals to royal courts (King 1989). Others typically occurred so secretly or on such a small scale that they escape the net; after some hesitation, John Archer makes the case for arson, poaching, and sometimes even animal-maiming—actions that rarely generated contentious gatherings as defined here—as forms of "social protest" in nineteenth-century East Anglia (Archer 1990; see also Carter 1980). Behind-the-scenes planning and manipulating, private persuasion, patronage, conversation in pubs and coffeehouses, arguments in shops, and routine actions of associations all form parts of the history of collective interaction. To the extent that they are known, standardized, and subject to choice, they belong to repertoires of contention, but they appear only indirectly in contentious gatherings.

The scattered selection of years—1758, 1759, 1768, 1769, 1780, 1781, 1789, 1795, 1801, 1807, 1811, 1819, 1820, 1828–1834—renders impossible some potentially interesting analyses of variation over time. The conventional list of eighteenth-century financial crises, for example, includes 1761, 1763, 1772, 1778, 1793, and 1797 (Hoppit 1986), none of which appears on our list; no one can use the evidence to examine the impact of financial crises on popular contention. Nor would it be easy to examine the influence of swings in food supply, military success, or George III's sanity, all of which require more continuous sets of years. My analyses have not, furthermore, ruled out definitively the possibility that changes in the selectivity or reporting style of periodicals account for some apparent shifts in contention, including a massive long-term increase in the sheer frequency of CGs. Sustained comparisons with other sources including governmental correspondence and local histories convince me that evidence for trends inferred from the periodicals also appears outside them. In any case, the material I have gathered constitutes the first step in a close analysis of reporting practices.

The evidence does not cover the collective interaction of all segments of the British population equally. Judging from the discrepancy between the vast number of petitions submitted by antislavery forces (especially religious groups of one kind or another) and the relatively small number of CGs concerning slavery reported in our sources, it is reasonable to suppose that the sources underreported religious meetings in which congregants made contentious claims (Drescher 1986). Groups, especially rich and powerful groups, that had easy access to power through patronage or direct representation rarely appeared in contentious gatherings except as objects of claims; they had less risky, more efficient ways to pursue their collective ends than by gathering publicly to state claims. As contenders such as organized Catholics or Protestant Dissenters actually gained power through contention, they generally moved toward routine political negotiation, influence-wielding, and maneuvering within government channels; they abandoned for most purposes the field of public contention. Therefore the study of open contention gathers an uneven sample of all collective interaction, and uncovers only part of contentious repertoires.

Finally, events outside Great Britain—notably in Ireland and, before independence, in America—now and then stimulated collective interaction and shaped its consequences in England, Wales, or Scotland. Those events figure in the catalog only insofar as participants in British contentious gatherings called attention to them directly. As the analysis unfolds, I draw information on these crucial matters from whatever sources I can, but on the whole the evidence concerning them remains thinner than when the discussion turns to moments of open contention.

Despite these limitations, scrutiny of contentious gatherings has large advantages over other possible means of analyzing popular collective interaction. It provides a way to make comparable observations over substantial chunks of space, time, and social situation, and therefore to facilitate identification of differences among places, periods, and settings. Because many individuals and groups appear in multiple gatherings at different times, following them from event to event helps trace changes in the behavior of individuals and groups.

Enough residues of non-contentious collective interaction appear in reports of contention to make possible guarded inferences concerning the variation and evolution of collective interaction as a whole—inferences that we can test, to some degree, by closer examination of particular places, periods, groups, and social settings. The method, furthermore, requires no *a priori* decisions as to which groups, places, issues, and forms of action figure prominently in contention and therefore deserve singling out; thus it offers means of putting detailed case studies into context, and of linking them with one another.

Reliance on periodicals as a major source of information likewise has merits that outweigh its obvious drawbacks. Reporters, editors, and information networks, to be sure, inject their biases into the reports that newspapers and other periodicals print, as well as into their selection of items worthy of printing. Comparisons with other sources suggest, unsurprisingly, that our periodicals overrepresent events from the Southeast and events that involve explicit references to national politics, while underrepresenting local labor disputes and run-of-the-mill brawls. (The over- and under-representation, however, do not disguise significant differences from one region to another or from one sort of event to another.)

These features of our sources will give any British historian pause. But consider the choices before us. On a national scale, the chief alternative sources for catalogs of contention are (1) regional and local periodicals; (2) surviving correspondence of local observers with government officials (which means especially the correspondence of magistrates and other dignitaries with the Secretaries of State or, from March 1782, the Home Secretary); (3) internal records of governmental administrations, particularly the Home Office, the Treasury Office, the War Office and, toward the end of our period, various police forces; and (4) judicial proceedings.

When any of these sources contains information on contention, it is often richer and more attentive to context than are contemporary periodicals. Yet any of them mentions a much smaller proportion of all contentious gatherings, bias and selectivity are often severe, and the volume of material an investigator must examine in order to constitute anything like a national catalog is overwhelming. As compared with the general and county correspondence series of the Secretaries of State, and then of the Home Office—the most obvious rivals to our periodicals as sources for the kind of inventory we have undertaken—our sources report many more events, especially of the more routine and nonviolent varieties. With the equivalent of the already large effort our catalog of contentious gatherings from periodicals entailed, it would most likely have been impossible to examine more than two or three of our twenty years by means of any one of the alternative sources, much less all of them.

Methodological implications: use periodicals as a primary source, identify the biases of the periodicals as clearly and reliably as possible, take the biases into account in any interpretation of the evidence, check the evidence in the periodicals against samples of all the other sources when possible, and undertake some overlapping inquiries that employ the full range of sources to examine particular events, groups, places, and transformations about which the catalogs of contention also provide evidence. My collaborators and I have done all these things; time and again we have compared our own catalogs with other periodicals, standard historical works, and archival materials (see Appendix 1 for a summary). These supplementary studies have convinced me that for an equivalent effort no other array of sources would produce as informative a picture of contention's changing modalities in Great Britain from 1758 to 1834 as does our collection of periodicals.

On 29 October 1831, when ultra-Tory MP Sir Charles Wetherell re-turned to Bristol after the House of Lords had rejected the Reform Bill, four days of mayhem and arson began in Bristol; in one of nineteenth-century Britain's most violent series of contentious gatherings 17 people died (chiefly at the hands of the military), hundreds were injured, esti-mates of property damage ran from £65,000 to £400,000, 81 people were convicted for their participation, 31 of them for capital offenses (Steven-son 1992; Harrison 1988; Phillips 1992; Amey 1979; Caple 1990). When Francis Place wrote an account of Bristol's struggles, his sources were *Hansard's, Mirror of Parliament,* the *United Service Journal,* the *Annual Register, Blackwood's Magazine,* the *Morning Chronicle,* and a few other newspapers (BL ADD 27790). Place had, to be sure, little access to the official correspondence that now stuffs national and regional archives. But his choices confirm the possibility of assembling an intelligible ac-count of those complex events from the array of periodicals that has served my inquiry.

The pages of this book teem with tables, most of them summarizing characteristics of contentious gatherings year by year. The tables bear about the same relationship to the story I am telling as a marked roadmap bears to a journey. Being descriptive and flat, they present neither the idiosyncrasies of particular events nor the motive power that leads from event to event. Like roadmaps, nevertheless, they have three precious uses. First, they greatly limit the number of plausible causal stories we can tell about the complex sequence of events they document; they rule out many stories—for instance, stories of unchanging popular politics driven chiefly by impulse and hardship—historians have sometimes told. Second, they identify phenomena for explanation—for example, the relative decline of direct action and physical violence in public claim-making—that other-wise easily escape attention or specification. Finally, they clarify the roads not taken, where popular contention might have gone, but did not, as in Britain's brushes with revolutionary situations and movements. I offer many descriptions of individual events, many explanations of actions singly or collectively, many efforts to account for patterns of difference and change, all outside the ubiquitous statistical tables. But the summary statistics constrain the descriptions and explanations, serving as maps whose main features no telling can ignore.

I have, in presenting the quantitative evidence, made a decision that will disappoint, or even offend, many social scientists. The evidence lends itself not only to the statistical descriptions every chapter contains but also to the modeling and estimation of causal relationships, for example between the increasing power of Parliament and the nationalization of claim-making. Although I am pursuing such quantitative causal analyses enthusiastically elsewhere, I have excluded them almost entirely from this book. That for three reasons: first because their presentation, with the essential explication of sources and methods, would encumber an already dense narrative; second, because I want the book to retell the story of British popular contention within the plane in which historians of Britain ordinarily work, rather than to displace the analysis onto a different plane; third, because the discipline of laying out causal accounts in words clarifies what quantitative modeling will eventually have to represent, verify, and falsify. The book, furthermore, reports little quantitative tracing of covariation in contention's characteristics from place to place, group to group, or even issue to issue; its numbers concentrate instead on year-to-year changes. Although the pages to come contain many descriptive numbers, they therefore report very few full-fledged quantitative analyses.

A Calendar of Contention

As Britain's new repertoire of contention came into use between the 1750s and the 1830s, the scale and frequency of open contention increased significantly. Evidence from the catalog of contentious gatherings establishes the change clearly. The catalog, you will remember, covers thirteen years scattered unevenly from 1758 to 1820 for the Southeast (Middlesex, Surrey, Sussex, and Kent) and seven adjacent years, 1828–1834, for the whole of Great Britain. Before examining the catalog's detail, let us glance at its headings, the twenty individual years.

1758 (14 CGs): The third year of war with France and the second of the Newcastle-Pitt coalition ministry, 1758 was also a year of high food prices and rising war taxes. The year's contentious gatherings featured not only the mutiny of pressed sailors at Portsmouth but also window-breaking celebrations of the king of Prussia's birthday, struggles over fishing in the Thames, a fight between smugglers and troops, a brawl between sailors and owners of gamecocks, the collective pulling down of unsafe houses, crowd looting of a pastry shop, an assembly of farmers in favor of legalizing broad-wheeled carriages, another meeting to nominate a candidate for Parliament, as well as attacks on plundering soldiers, on a child molester, on a pawnbroker, and on surgeons who tried to carry off for dissection the bodies of criminals hanged at Tyburn. In 1758 direct action—often violent—dominated the events that qualified as contentious gatherings. Physical retaliation against malefactors and moral menaces occurred frequently, competitors often came to blows or worse, and decorous public meetings rarely occurred.

1759 (12 CGs): As the war dragged on, taxes continued their rise, prices abated slightly, while British troops won victories over France in North America and on the seas; after the military failures of previous years, people called 1759 *annus mirabilis,* Year of Miracles. During the year various crowds in the Southeast attacked officers charged with enforcing observation of the Sabbath, tried to rescue men seized by a press gang, pelted a pair of extortionists in the Cheapside pillory, smashed the shop of a Quaker who opened his shop on Sunday, broke the windows of another Quaker who did not illuminate his house for the Prince of Wales's birthday, and harassed ladies of fashion in St. James's Park; meanwhile, a hired gang kidnapped their patron's divorced wife, a General Court of the East India Company thanked Admiral Pocock and Commodore Steevens for their "wise conduct and gallant behaviour" in the East Indies, a meeting in St. James's praised the king for his conduct of the war and opened a subscription for recruitment of soldiers, a delegation went to compliment His Majesty on the taking of Quebec, newly recruited soldiers mutinied, and 15 or 16 men boarded and plundered a merchant vessel at Beachy Head. The CGs of 1759, like those of the previous year, frequently took the form of direct and violent retaliation for wrongdoing. Mutiny and enforced compliance with a public celebration again made the news, while public meetings remained the province of powerful people.

1768 (111 CGs): The stormy sixty-year reign of George III had begun in 1760. In 1768—a year of peace and steady taxes despite serious stirrings in the American colonies, discussions in Parliament of the "Discontents in America," and moderately declining prices after the acute highs of 1766 and 1767—John Wilkes returned from exile, went to prison, was tried and sentenced, won multiple parliamentary elections, but saw Parliament refuse doggedly to seat him. The contentious gatherings of the year reflected the struggles over Wilkes, but also included extensive demands by workers. Among other things, sailors and rivermen repeatedly marched through London and laid their economic demands before public authorities. In addition, orderly crowds gathered in public places and staged symbolic, mocking attacks on such figures as the king's favorite, Lord Bute. Public marches and unauthorized assemblies figured more prominently in London's life than they had in 1758 or 1759.

1769 (67 CGs): A similar year despite a mild decline in the cost of living and a modest rise in taxes, and despite stiffening resistance to both taxation and the quartering of troops in the American colonies. Controversy continued to swirl around Wilkes, as meetings and elections of duly constituted wards and other localities turned into expressions of support for the advocate of popular liberties while he remained in prison and Parliament refused to seat him, but counter-meetings of officials affirmed their devotion to the king as well as their fear of "disorder" and "sedition." Crowds pulled down dangerous buildings, resisted the burial of an executed criminal in consecrated ground, and attacked delegations of merchants and freeholders rumored to oppose clemency for Wilkes.

Elsewhere seamen left their ships and marched to East India House to demand wage increases, and coalheavers assembled to complain of their distress. In Spitalfields major conflicts brewed: throwsters demanded money from silk masters, striking weavers beat up blacklegs or cut cloth from their looms, cutters battled troops, and large numbers of workers coming from the execution of some of the cutters in nearby Bethnal Green (where spectators had stoned the executioners and burned the gallows) sacked the house of a master weaver. In 1769 several contentious currents of the previous years flowed together: avenging actions, militant marches, and workers' battles accompanied an increasing use of public meetings—both authorized and unauthorized—to make statements of opposition and support.

1780 (70 CGs): By 1780 Lord North was chief minister, and Britain was combating revolutionaries in North America. In that year of relatively low prices but rising taxes the agitation of Lord George Gordon's anti-Catholic Protestant Association dominated London's contention; during the early days of June, the destruction of houses, schools, and chapels, smashing of church paraphernalia, burning of Catholic property, extortion of contributions, and freeing of prisoners made London a war zone. Nevertheless, the Southeast also staged meetings on governmental expenditure, tax relief, the American war, governmental reform, and local defense against rioters. (Four years earlier John Wilkes, finally reseated in Parliament as a Member for Middlesex, had filed the first comprehensive parliamentary motion for reform and extension of the franchise; it was not to be the last.) Again, a brawl between soldiers and sailors, fights between smugglers and troops, and attacks on criminals in the pillory all took their place in the year's contention. If the actions of a single association and its followers loomed exceptionally large in 1780, a wide sampling of other characteristic eighteenth-century forms of direct action likewise appeared in London's region.

1781 (29 CGs): Amid major losses in the American war, including the surrender of Cornwallis at Yorktown, 1781 was a year of steady prices and increased taxation. Jailbreaks, rescues of prisoners, battles within prisons, crowds celebrating Lord George Gordon's acquittal, smuggler-officer struggles, attacks on constables, salutes to the king, a landing of privateers, and other violent events gave an unusual range to the year's unplanned gatherings, while meetings against military quartering, for the legalization of interest on tradesmen's bills, opposing committees of correspondence, in support of candidates, in favor of the Middlesex aldermen, and against the American war all added to the variety. In 1780 and 1781 the forms of London's popular collective interaction were proliferating.

1789 (52 CGs): The year began with prices rising slightly, taxes steady, and George III insane. It saw the beginning of the French Revolution, which stimulated a few gatherings in praise of Britain's own revolutions. People at other meetings voiced support for William Pitt or for the government, stated their hostility to abolition of the slave trade, decried a tobacco tax bill, petitioned against parliamentary enclosures, called for repeal of the shop tax, cheered or jeered parliamentary candidates, supported or opposed a regency for the incompetent king, and then celebrated his partial recovery. Outside of regularly convened meetings, operagoers attacked the impresario, circusgoers dealt the same treatment to the circus manager, pub patrons assaulted constables, spectators at a fight beat a constable who tried to stop the bloodshed, a gentleman battled with servants who blocked the opera's entrance, and bystanders avenged themselves on pickpockets. Regularly called public meetings of one sort or another accounted for more than 60 percent of the Southeast's CGs, but the other 40 percent continued the eighteenth-century themes of redress and vengeance.

1795 (108 CGs): Britain was in the heat of war with France, as prices took a characteristic wartime spurt (compounded by a disastrous harvest in 1794) and taxes continued to increase. Parliament debated the suspension of *habeas corpus,* tightened controls over Friendly Societies, and passed a series of other repressive measures. Meetings predominated even more: about two-thirds of all CGs. Participants in 1795's meetings took stands on canal construction and tolls, post road rates, the Seditious Meetings Bill, the Wapping Wet Dock Bill, the Lock and Wharf Bill, and a number of other bills, a combination of journeymen gold beaters, candidates for office, the conduct of the war, prospects for peace, recruitment of seamen, the legitimacy of other meetings, the terms for shipbuilding, new taxes, regulation of the butcher's trade, radical reform, provision prices, bread for the poor, and many another current issue.

Outside of formal meetings, London's other gatherings of 1795 included cheers for members of the royal family at the new Drury Lane Theater and elsewhere, popular opposition to the arrest of a supposed prophet (later declared insane) by the king's messengers, complaints at the market about high provision prices, seizures of meat and flour and attacks on the property of their purveyors, turnouts, and a brawl between soldiers and carriers of sedan chairs. (Elsewhere in England collective seizures of food occurred repeatedly during the spring and summer, while in Ireland the insurrectionary United Irishmen became a mass movement: Wells 1983.) Meanwhile, other people in the Southeast complained against and sometimes mobbed press gangs, broke into coach-houses and inns to loot them, rescued prisoners, jeered the king and stoned his coach while shouting "Bread! Peace!" and assailed William Pitt as he rode home to Downing Street. War and its consequences again became the stimuli for many gatherings, but the range of other national issues engaging public contention was also broadening.

1801 (55 CGs): At the start of 1801, three years after suppression of the United Irishmen, the United Kingdom of Great Britain and Ireland came into being. Only with the harvest of 1801 did an acute subsistence crisis end. During the year Pitt resigned and Britain made a fragile peace with France, as the cost of living reached an all-time high and taxes remained constant. Parliament restricted children's workdays to 12 hours, prohibited children's night work, and forbade the hiring of pauper children less than nine years old to work in cotton mills. As the year went on, Covent Garden operagoers cheered the royal family, smugglers battled troops, workers in East Bourne assembled near the homes of the "principal residents" to complain about high prices, workers at Horsham and elsewhere assembled with similar grievances, a "mob" broke into, sacked, and burned a house in which surgeons had been dissecting a cadaver, another "mob" chased a recruiting officer into hiding, East India sailors fought off a press gang, biscuit-bakers petitioned for increased wages, an "immense concourse of people" tried to hold a forbidden fair, "young bucks" fought with prostitutes, Chinese workers for the East India Company battled one another, Portuguese and American sailors brawled, pupils at Westminster School rebelled against their master, debtors ducked a creditor under a pump at Newgate Prison, two groups of Irish men and women carried on a small war, a lord and a crowd traded brickbats and drubbings over his refusal to illuminate his house for the preliminaries of peace, and so on through a wide variety of issues and actions.

Meetings dipped to only a third of 1801's CGs; they concerned the appointment of officers for the Islington Volunteers, the merits of the Marylebone Volunteers, a churchwarden's services to his vestry, the opening of trade with India, the Calico Prints Duty Bill, aid to the poor, the Lord Mayor's performance, the pope's request that French bishops in English exile resign their sees, the making of peace with France, and thanks to various officers for their public service. While war and peace

continued to attract considerable contention, local issues reasserted themselves quite emphatically.

1807 (108 CGs): The United Kingdom was back at war with France. Prices
had dropped from their record level of 1801, but taxes rose by almost 10
percent over 1806. Amid extensive discussion of military and diplomatic
affairs, Parliament debated and passed the abolition of slave-trading in
all British dominions. During the year people assembled in meetings
(which constituted about three-quarters of all CGs) voiced thanks to the
royal family, supported or opposed Members of Parliament, called for the
repeal of the Tanned Leather Act, resolved to oppose changes in the
charter of the South Sea Company, praised trade with the United States,
supported a candidate for a directorship of the East India Company,
proposed the sending of troops to India, stated their antipathy to political
rights for Catholics, favored revisions in the current Poor Bill, advocated
the admission of naval officers to Parliament, decried ministerial influence
in elections, criticized current tax bills, opposed the malt distillers' monopoly, took positions on the election of directors for the Eagle Insurance
Company, thanked the Lord Mayor for his efforts to prevent robberies,
and encouraged MPs who opposed the slave trade, but, all things considered, said remarkably little about the great parliamentary issue of slavery.

Outside of 1807's meetings, spectators at an execution trampled to
death 30 of their own number, those at another cheered the death of a
murderer, onlookers at the pillory pelted a child molester, would-be
spectators broke into the Royal Circus, a crowd rescued three smugglers
from their captors, other smugglers fought customs officers, a deputation
from Cambridge University presented an anti-Catholic address to the
king, Irishmen smashed a coach that had too few places for them, a group
of "idle persons" who had gathered to gaze at a tobacconist's gorgeous
wife manhandled the beadle who tried to disperse them, supporters met
candidates at campaign dinners, bystanders huzzahed members of the
royal family, people in the street broke into a brothel to rescue a young
girl whom procurers had enticed therein, partisans at an election tore
down the hustings and stoned the hotel of an opposition candidate,
admirers formed a parade for a military hero, butchers and Irishmen
fought to exhaustion, supporters carried the chair of a newly elected MP,

a "mob" treated a brothelkeeper with Rough Music, shoemakers tried to prevent their fellows from working without advances of wages, an informal posse tracked and killed a suspected murderer, participants in the Lord Mayor's Day celebration saluted their mayor, and a number of attacks on dishonored individuals occurred. Although by 1807 public meetings had become the numerically predominant form of contentious gathering, direct action still held its own during that turbulent year.

1811 (a mere 48 CGs): The war with France dragged on in Portugal, in Spain, and on the seas, while the Prince of Wales took office as Regent for a demented king. Prices fell a little from the high levels of the previous two years, as taxes continued to rise. Meetings concerned support for the Regent and other members of the royal family, import restrictions, freedom of the press, the Wet Docks Bill, the Distillery Bill, the Arrest Bill, the Porthaven Harbour Bill, the Kent and Military Canal Bill, the East India Company Bill, the Religious Restriction Bill, parliamentary reform, union of the wards of Cripplegate Without and Cripplegate Within, election of a Lord Mayor, tax assessments, public paving, and nuisance removal. CGs other than meetings included an attack on a Wesleyan meeting house, a mutiny of French prisoners, cheers for the military and members of the royal family, pursuit of a pederast, rescue of arrested pickpockets, commiseration of spectators with the fate of two executed men, assault of a theatergoer who refused to take off his hat during the singing of "God Save the King," bludgeoning of Portuguese sailors by their American colleagues, and other events of the same genre. Outside—but not inside—the Southeast, in the northern industrial districts, machine-breaking reached a new height. Meetings held at about 70 percent of all Southeastern CGs, but surprisingly few of the meetings or other events concerned the great war that was approaching its dénouement.

1819: By this year the frequency of contentious gatherings had leaped far above the usual 50 to 100 of previous years; mentions of 256 Southeast CGs appeared in the periodicals. The year brought high prices for peacetime, although nothing like the heights of 1813 and 1814; taxes had fallen greatly from their 1816 peak. The government continued the round of repression (for example the Coercion Acts of 1817) that followed the postwar mobilization of demands for reform; the Six Acts of 1819 significantly cut back civil liberties. The war with France having finally ended in 1815, an unprecedented wave of demands for parliamentary reform had begun, with Hampden Clubs and Political Unions doing a significant share of the agitation.

The great increase in numbers of CGs from 1819 on makes it impractical to enumerate all their forms and themes. Let us settle for a two-month slice: In August 1819 constables and yeomanry in Manchester fought their battle of Peterloo by shooting down members of a crowd gathered in St. Peter's Fields to hear about parliamentary reform and repeal of the Corn Laws. Londoners were likewise meeting about reform, but were also battling police who stopped a fight, attacking the property of the Regent's Canal Company, and gathering to deplore the Peterloo massacre. During September some 35,000 people marched through London streets demanding radical reform, meetings in Southwark and London likewise called for reform, another meeting in the City called for Livery elections free from outside interference, partisans of a losing candidate for alderman fought supporters of the winner, inhabitants of St. Giles Without, St. Botolph Without, and Farringdon Without met to protest the Magistrates' behavior at Peterloo, people on the street attacked a beggar, and police stopped a bloody brawl. In summary, about three-quarters of 1819's CGs were meetings of one kind or another, chiefly of regularly authorized assemblies such as wardmotes; their great themes were elections, the conduct of local or national government (including responses to Peterloo), bills pending in Parliament, and religious affairs.

1820 (274 CGs): George III died after sixty years as king, and the Regent became George IV. The new king's effort to divorce his long-estranged wife, Caroline, immediately raised a national hue and cry over her right to be queen. Although the Lords (by a mere nine votes) passed a bill depriving Caroline of her rights, the government dropped it in the face of certain defeat by the Commons. As prices dropped rapidly and taxation slackened a little, Parliament, alarmed by the widespread mobilization of workers in favor of reform, added to the repressive Six Acts of 1819 a ban on armed processions; Parliament also enacted summary punishment for trespass and damage of public or private property. Roughly two-thirds of the year's CGs took place as formal meetings, especially of authorized public assemblies, with the chief issues concerning the king and queen, but with local government also coming in for substantial attention. The events of May and June 1820 give a sense of the whole year:

A crowd attacked the executioner at Old Bailey.

At the Freemason's Tavern, the British and Foreign Bible Society honored Lord Teignmouth.

A number of delegations offered condolences and congratulations to the new king.

Meeting in the City of London Tavern, the Benevolent Society of St. Patrick thanked the Duke of Wellington.

Shipowners at the City of London Tavern agreed to petition Parliament against changes in the laws protecting shipping and for repeal of prohibitory duties.

At Freemason's Hall, the Society for the Improvement of Prison Discipline and Reformation of Juvenile Offenders thanked the Duke of Gloucester for his support.

The vestry of St. Mary's, Newington opposed a parliamentary bill for the building of new churches.

A "mob" rescued smugglers from Dover Gaol.

Members of the Pitt Club assembled in Merchant Taylors' Hall and voiced support of the ministry.

A "company of gentlemen" dined at Freemason's Tavern to honor reelected members of Parliament.

A "multitude" in Dover greeted the return of queen Caroline, then others in Canterbury, Sittingbourne, Chatham, Rochester, Stroud, Gravesend, and Dartford cheered her on her way to Westminster.

Crowds in Westminster gathered repeatedly near the queen's house, cheered her, forced passersby to doff their hats in her honor, and broke windows of her presumed opponents.

The British and Foreign School Society joined at Freemason's Tavern to pursue their cause and honor their patrons.

A crowd gathered at Charing Cross in support of troops who were supposedly discontented with their barracks there.

Smugglers on the Kent coast had a "serious affray" with seamen.

Spectators at a military review in Whitehall gave huzzas to the Duke of York.

Irishmen battled each other in Westminster, then fought the police
and troops sent to pacify them.

Southwark electors at a public dinner honored alderman Thorpe.

People gathered in St. Marylebone alternately cheered and jeered
parliamentary leaders and the queen on their way to Parliament.

People elsewhere in London roared and acted out approval of the
queen at her other public appearances.

Householders at the Southwark Town Hall sent a laudatory message
to queen Caroline and opposed the Seditious Meetings Bill.

The deputations of various turnpike trusts assembled at the Crown
and Anchor to state their opposition to the Turnpike
Management Bill.

Participants in an open meeting at Guildhall passed a resolution in
favor of the queen.

The queen's bid for recognition predominated from late in May and all
through June, but other issues continued to attract attention. By 1820
London's CGs were beginning to show recurrent signs of organized
national campaigns to articulate public sentiments about issues before
the government and Parliament.

From 1828 to 1834 we are dealing not only with four counties around
London, but also with all the rest of England, Wales, and Scotland. With
an average of 983 CGs per year—almost three a day, on average—events
come too thick and fast for even a sample enumeration. Let us settle for
a general summary and a few quick examples.

1828 (259 CGs in the Southeast, 336 elsewhere in Great Britain): Prices
were again declining, as they would for most of the following years; taxes
were following a similar trajectory. With the Duke of Wellington prime
minister and with Catholics mobilizing around Daniel O'Connell in
Ireland, repeal of the Test and Corporation Acts (which passed) and
Catholic Emancipation (which failed) became salient national issues. The
drive to open public office for Catholics renewed the energetic but
unsuccessful parliamentary campaigns of 1821 and 1825. To counter the
new drive, the Earl of Winchester and Edward Knatchbull began organizing Protestants in Brunswick Clubs opposing Catholic Emancipation.

Robert Peel (then Home Secretary) and Wellington, however, came to see some concessions to Catholic claims as essential to public order, at least in Ireland. The government's proposal to regulate Friendly Societies likewise excited a good deal of discussion. In 1828 a little over three-quarters of all CGs were public meetings, but in contrast with 1820 most of them were convened by special-interest associations; predictably, Catholic claims, Friendly Societies, government performance, and the Test and Corporation Acts dominated their agendas.

1829 (279 CGs in the Southeast, 362 elsewhere): Contrary to the general trend, prices rose sharply from 1828, and taxes rose modestly, only to fall again in 1830. Wellington and Peel pushed Catholic Emancipation through Parliament in company with dissolution of the Catholic Association and restriction of Irish suffrage, and succeeded in establishing the Metropolitan Police as well. Parliament also passed a bill regulating Friendly Societies; other acts reorganized London Justices of the Peace and the Chester constabulary. About two-thirds of the year's CGs were formal meetings, but the share of them called by associations dropped precipitously as public assemblies and religious congregations became more active. The predominant themes of contention were Catholic Emancipation (38 percent of all CGs) and national government performance, but industrial conflict—for example, turbulent strikes in Spitalfields, Bethnal Green, Manchester, Coventry, and Barnsley—also played a larger part than usual.

1830 (474 CGs in the Southeast, 690 elsewhere): William IV succeeded his deceased brother George IV, a required general election accelerated the campaign for parliamentary reform, and Whigs came to power. Both before and after George's death, Whigs unsuccessfully introduced reform proposals into Parliament. Under the Whig government a cabinet committee drafted a bill containing relatively wide-reaching reforms. While the Tories were still in power Parliament had also passed measures promoting uniform (and uniformed) police forces throughout the country. During the fall, landless laborers in London's hinterland burned hayricks, smashed threshing machines, and marched from farm to farm demanding wage rises, employment guarantees, and remission of the tithe or rents; those events became famous as the "Swing" rebellion, for the mythical avenger Captain Swing.

At the same time, urban political associations (notably the Birmingham Political Union) and national federations of workers (notably John Doherty's National Association for the Protection of Labour) began to form and voice demands on a national scale. Meetings fell to 57 percent of all CGs in our catalog, and various sorts of violent gatherings swelled to 30 percent of the total; what actually happened, however, is that 1830 brought more meetings than ever before, while CGs other than meetings multiplied even faster. Contention in 1830 turned especially on wages, machine-breaking, the abolition of slavery, taxes, elections, and parliamentary reform; participants in 45 meetings, however, inveighed against widow-burning in India.

1831 (656 CGs in the Southeast, 989 elsewhere): The year brought a great mobilization for parliamentary reform, although the Whigs (despite strong endorsement of their position in another election) were still unable to drive their bill through Parliament. In Ireland (outside the catalog of British CGs but certainly not outside the range of British politics), a violent Tithe War broke out over Catholic resistance to supporting the established Episcopal church. Advocates of reform continued to organize and mobilize on the basis of newly formed associations. After the House of Lords rejected the Reform Bill, major street fighting occurred in Derby, Nottingham, and Bristol. With June's turbulent turnout of Merthyr Tydfil and October's bloody struggles in Bristol, 1831 produced more deaths in contention (52) than any other of our nineteenth-century years, although not so many as 1768 or 1780. Violence in the streets notwithstanding, a full 80 percent of all CGs were public meetings, with constituted assemblies such as the inhabitants of Hythe (21 January) or the freeholders of Canterbury (30 April) playing the predominant role. Parliamentary reform and/or national governmental performance were the issues articulated in 63 percent of the year's contentious gatherings.

1832 (502 CGs in the Southeast, 609 elsewhere): A restricted bill for parliamentary reform was finally passed after great ministerial turnover and royal intervention. Scottish and Irish reform bills likewise became law. In the autumn a general election brought in the first reformed House of Commons. Its most notable acts in 1832 reduced the range of offenses to which the death penalty applied. During the critical days of the negotiation over reform (in May), street demonstrations occurred throughout Great Britain. Meetings nevertheless constituted 79 percent of the CGs, as reform, governmental performance, and elections drew the most attention.

1833 (417 CGs in the Southeast, 257 elsewhere): As resistance to British control in Ireland continued to agitate Britain itself, Parliament extended the abolition of slavery to the colonies, passed a major act to regulate women's and children's factory work in Britain, and repealed the East India Company's trading monopoly, but also gave the Lord Lieutenant of Ireland expanded coercive powers. Meetings again ran close to four-fifths of the year's CGs. Policing, elections, local governmental affairs, and taxes all came in for repeated discussion; surprisingly, slavery was the theme in only 6.2 percent of the year's CGs (42 meetings).

1834 (481 CGs in the Southeast, 573 elsewhere): During the year the ministry went from Grey to Melbourne to Peel; under Melbourne Parliament passed the New Poor Law and further narrowed the range of capital punishment. The Grand National Consolidated Trades Union organized and began speaking for workers, but burned out by October. The sentencing of the Tolpuddle laborers for oath-taking stimulated widespread workers' protests, and the debate over the New Poor Law likewise brought thousands into the streets. Meetings increased to just over 80 percent of the year's events, as elections, religious affairs, the Poor Law, governmental performance, and wardmotes drew the most attention.

Even these quick summaries make clear how much the quality of British contention changed between 1758 and 1834. The early years juxtaposed decorous assemblies of the ruling classes with rambunctious direct actions of ordinary people: workers' marches, attacks on symbols, possessions, or persons of reputed malefactors, and rebellions of military recruits. During the following years meetings generalized, direct action inciting or entailing violence became less and less prevalent, and the gap between the forms of elite and mass involvement in contention therefore declined.

In the course of the middle years, the marches and mass meetings of what would eventually become the social movement became much more visible. Across the long years of war with France, we see not only gatherings directly stimulated by press gangs, rising taxes, and other features of the war effort but also a remarkable shift toward meetings that formally called on Parliament to act; by 1819 a substantial majority of all contentious gatherings were formally called public assemblies of one sort or another. In the 1820s and 1830s we see a few of the familiar attacks on miscreants (but practically none of the old collective humiliations) amid large numbers of public meetings, oriented chiefly to current decisions of Parliament.

Numbering the Struggles

To pin down these changes, let us examine the numbers. Table 2.1 and Figures 2.1–2.5 describe the quantitative trends from 1758 to 1834 for the Southeast (Kent, Middlesex, Surrey, and Sussex) and from 1828 to 1834 for the rest of Great Britain. In a typical eighteenth-century year, our sources reported from 50 to 100 events meeting our criteria for contentious gatherings: 10 or more people in the same public place making claims that bore on the interests of others. From 1819 onward our sources for the Southeast reported from 250 to 650 such events each year.

The differences are large: for the Southeast, a qualifying event every fourth or fifth day during the sample years before 1819, one or two per day during most years thereafter. In the peak year of 1831, a full 656 contentious gatherings occurred in Middlesex, Surrey, Kent, or Sussex, and another 989 in the rest of Great Britain. In the years in which we have counts for both the Southeast and the rest of Great Britain, year-to-year fluctuations are similar, even if overall levels are different, for the two geographic areas. This covariation of the two series from 1828 to 1834 provides some reason for thinking that during the earlier years the London series represents changes in Great Britain as a whole.

A *formation,* in the jargon of this analysis, is any person or set of persons whom our sources describe as acting distinctively; for most purposes, it suffices to think of them as individuals and groups involved distinguishably in the action—including involvement by being objects of claims. (Parliament, the king, and other public figures appear among our formations chiefly as absent objects of claims.) We distinguish a new *action* each time any formation changes location or behavior; our files record, among other things, the verb (for example smash, run, salute, request) the sources use to describe that action. Table 2.1 shows that the

Table 2.1. Contentious gatherings, formations, and actions in Great Britain, 1758–1834

	Events			Formations			Actions		
Year	Total	Southeast region	Other Britain	Total	Southeast region	Other Britain	Total	Southeast region	Other Britain
1758	14	14		44	44		78	78	
1759	12	12		53	53		109	109	
1768	111	111		442	442		920	920	
1769	67	67		252	252		506	506	
1780	70	70		312	312		619	619	
1781	29	29		120	120		243	243	
1789	52	52		148	148		290	290	
1795	108	108		397	397		574	574	
1801	55	55		178	178		355	355	
1807	108	108		303	303		574	574	
1811	48	48		163	163		284	284	
1819	256	256		929	929		1,594	1,594	
1820	274	274		1,095	1,095		1,843	1,843	
1828	595	259	336	1,780	862	918	3,331	1,566	1,765
1829	641	279	362	2,249	938	1,311	4,203	1,702	2,501
1830	1,164	474	690	4,291	1,694	2,597	7,972	3,061	4,911
1831	1,645	656	989	5,855	2,379	3,476	11,389	4,280	7,109
1832	1,111	502	609	3,697	1,636	2,061	7,011	2,963	4,048
1833	674	417	257	1,978	1,256	722	3,614	2,224	1,390
1834	1,054	481	573	2,898	1,442	1,456	5,192	2,515	2,677
Total	8,088	4,272	3,816	27,184	14,643	12,541	50,875	26,474	24,401

average event involved three or four formations and seven or eight actions; the number of either gives a crude indication of an event's complexity. By this standard, CGs actually became less complex over time—moved toward more uniform routines having fewer formations and actions per event. The rise of the public meeting epitomizes that change.

How confident can we be of any trends these figures show? What reservations must we keep in mind? First, the base population grew: a correction for population size (Figure 2.2) reduces the gap between the eighteenth and nineteenth centuries from roughly sixfold to fourfold and brings out the vastly higher per capita frequency of contentious gatherings reported in the Southeast, but does not alter the basic chronology of contention.

Second, the gaps in the chronology before 1828 could hide some greater year-to-year swings in contention as well as an earlier start to the post-1811 rise. Although among years of major subsistence crisis the sample includes 1758, 1768, 1795, 1801, and 1811, it entirely misses the crises of 1772–1773 and 1816–1818. During the period of the French Revolution the sample years skip the Church and King riots (1791) and a wave of attacks on recruiters and press gangs (1794). But the selected years do

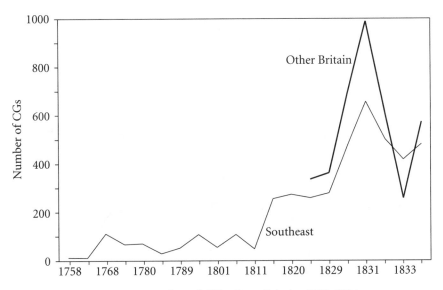

Figure 2.1. Number of CGs, Great Britain, 1758–1834

include major struggles over John Wilkes (1768–1769) and Lord George Gordon (1780), crucial years of the French Revolution and the wars with France (1789, 1795, 1801, 1807, and 1811), the time of Peterloo (1819), and the great outcry over Queen Caroline (1820), as well as the continuous record of contention from 1828 through 1834. All in all, it seems unlikely that missing years are distorting general trends in the data.

Increased reporting accounts for some (but surely not all) of the apparent rise of public contention. It is possible, if rather unlikely, that trends outside the Southeast ran in a quite different direction before 1828. These curves, furthermore, do not establish that nineteenth-century Britons made claims more often than their eighteenth-century counterparts; small-scale and indirect claim-making probably declined significantly after 1800, and could have dropped enough to compensate for the rise in larger-scale, direct claim-making. The evidence in the table and graphs simply indicates that gathering in substantial numbers and making public claims became a much more frequent way of contending in Great Britain after the Napoleonic Wars than it had been earlier. But that was an important change.

Among eighteenth-century years the greatest number of CGs (111) occurred in 1768, a year combining the struggles over John Wilkes's

Figure 2.2. CGs per million population, Great Britain, 1758–1834

imprisonment and electoral campaigns with widespread industrial conflict. The surge between 1811 and 1819 (which apparently began at war's end in 1815) reflects another large round of worker-capitalist confrontations, plus working-class demands for political reforms. The year 1830 brought a new mobilization for parliamentary reform together with the Swing rebellion in southeastern England. Contention of the peak year, 1831, centered on an even more extensive mobilization around the multiple issues of reform.

As the frequency of contentious gatherings rose, their texture changed. Table 2.2 shows the numbers of arrests, woundings, and deaths reported in our accounts of contentious gatherings. These numbers generally run lower than conventional historical figures, for two reasons. First, they include only the casualties incurred in the course of the interaction constituting the contentious gathering or (in the case of arrests) in its intermediate aftermath; small groups and isolated individuals who were arrested, wounded, or killed in related encounters with small numbers of police or troops disappear from these counts. Second, the numbers sum up reports in the periodicals we analyzed, instead of turning to arrest records, hospital reports, or any other supplementary source.

Sometimes the resulting discrepancies are quite large; conventional historical accounts of the Gordon Riots, for example, tally 450 arrests, 285 deaths, and hundreds of persons wounded (Rudé 1971), while the totals in our accounts come to only 161 arrests, 16 persons wounded, and 106 dead. The stories in the *London Chronicle, Gentleman's Magazine*, and the *Annual Register* actually suggest larger totals, but simply do not supply the essential detail. Again, Hobsbawm and Rudé (1968) report 1,976 prisoners brought to trial for participation in the rural rebellions of 1830, while our accounts mention only 1,327 arrests. We must therefore treat the figures on casualties as minima, and hope that the undercounts vary little from year to year. In that fortunate case, casualty statistics will provide reliable indications of year-to-year variation despite being too low.

With these cautions in mind, let us examine the numbers of arrests, woundings, and deaths. In absolute numbers, arrests reached their peak in 1830, when law officers apprehended 1,800 participants in CGs, 1,327 of them in the course of the Swing Rebellion; 1831 came second, with 779 arrests. Among the eighteenth-century years the 174 reported arrests of 1780 led the way. As for wounding, in absolute numbers the bloodiest

Table 2.2. Arrests and casualties in contentious gatherings, Great Britain, 1758–1834

	Arrests			N wounded			N killed		
Year	Total	Southeast region	Other Britain	Total	Southeast region	Other Britain	Total	Southeast region	Other Britain
1758	3	3		1	1		2	2	
1759	24	24		4	4		1	1	
1768	92	92		147	147		75	75	
1769	45	45		19	19		9	9	
1780	174	174		20	20		109	109	
1781	10	10		25	25		11	11	
1789	10	10		10	10		0	0	
1795	33	33		6	6		2	2	
1801	8	8		8	8		2	2	
1807	9	9		32	32		32	32	
1811	29	29		9	9		5	5	
1819	156	156		12	12		5	5	
1820	53	53		25	25		1	1	
1828	312	165	147	40	8	32	11	6	5
1829	398	95	303	64	13	51	11	2	9
1830	1,800	389	1,411	154	83	71	11	4	7
1831	779	244	535	151	38	113	52	4	48
1832	518	154	364	129	31	98	28	7	21
1833	283	114	169	76	24	52	8	3	5
1834	311	193	118	98	41	57	3	0	3
Total	5,047	2,000	3,047	1,030	556	474	378	280	98

year was 1768, with 1780 and the Gordon Riots again surely underreported. In terms of deaths—arguably the most reliable of these statistics—the black medals go to 1768 (75 dead in the Southeast alone) and 1780 (109 deaths).

Figures 2.3, 2.4, and 2.5 follow the numbers of persons arrested, wounded, and killed in CGs from 1758 to 1834. While Table 2.2 presents absolute numbers, the graphs show arrests and casualties per hundred events rather than as an absolute number, since otherwise the sheer increase in frequency of events would hide important shifts. The number wounded is no doubt the least reliable figure, the number killed the most credible; all three curves, however, probably represent general trends from 1758 to 1834 fairly well.

Arrests reached a first peak—two per event, on average—in 1759. The majority of that year's mere dozen events centered on physical attacks of one kind or another: a mutiny, resistance to a press gang, forcible seizure of an estranged wife and, especially, crowd mistreatment of Quakers; 24 arrests came in response to the attacks. In 1780, which saw 2.5 arrests per CG, the street fighting and destruction initiated by Lord George Gordon's Protestant Association invited massive retaliation from the authorities.

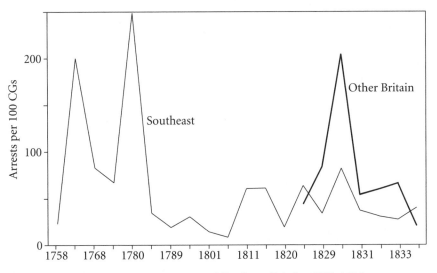

Figure 2.3. Arrests per 100 CGs, Great Britain, 1758–1834

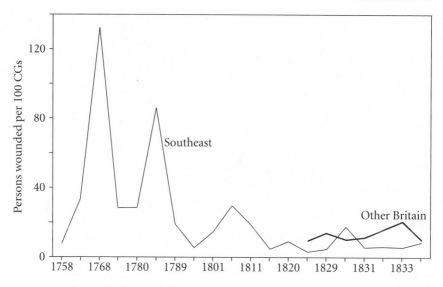

Figure 2.4. Wounded per 100 CGs, Great Britain, 1758–1834

The only nineteenth-century year in our set that rivaled 1759 and 1780 with respect to arrests per CG was 1830, when the massive arrests of landless laborers swelled the totals, more so outside the Southeast than in London's immediate hinterland. In that year the Southeast's arrests concentrated in Kent, where the first great round of "Swing" events occurred.

Wounding and killing followed similar contours, except for the shortage of reported wounds in 1780. No nineteenth-century year except 1807 (a year of frequent crowd attacks on individuals—Catholics, Irishmen, a homosexual, a brothelkeeper, a grasping attorney, and others, not to mention the trampling deaths of 30 spectators at an execution) approached the casualties per event that prevailed before 1789. The general tendency is unmistakable: a massive decline in the prevalence of violence in contention. After 1811, as the number of contentious gatherings multiplied, the likelihood that anyone would be hurt in them, or any significant quantity of property damaged, greatly diminished.

Three complementary changes in contention produced the great pacification. First, within the same general kinds of events participants less frequently used violent means. Parish assemblies, festivals, and street marches became more decorous. Second, the repression of popular collective action changed. As authorities became more reluctant to send troops into ordinary gatherings and as they started creating professional police forces specialized in crowd control, the chances of being wounded or killed in the course of contention diminished radically. Third, and most important, repertoires of contention shifted significantly. The rise of the meeting, the demonstration, the rally, the petition march, and similar forms of action as well as the decline of such routines as Rough Music meant that the sheer opportunity for direct confrontation with enemies or repressive forces dwindled.

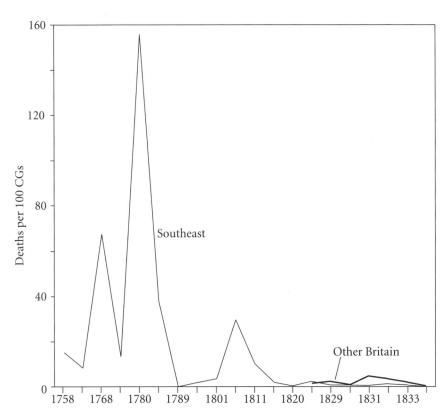

Figure 2.5. Deaths per 100 CGs, Great Britain, 1758–1834

Forms of Contention, Old and New

The following graphs portray some of the relevant changes. Figure 2.6 presents the proportions of meetings and violent gatherings in the South-east over the span from 1758 to 1834. (*Meetings* include gatherings of named associations, official assemblies, and other preplanned public gatherings; *violent gatherings* include hunter-gamekeeper encounters, fights of smugglers with customs officers, attacks on blacklegs, and similar events. The news is obvious: violent sorts of events declined from three-quarters of the total in the 1750s to around one-tenth in the 1830s. Meetings of one kind or another rose from 15 or 20 percent to over 80 percent of all CGs. With the exception of 1801 (when celebrations of the temporary peace, of the king, and of popular heroes swelled the number), the omitted category of nonviolent gatherings other than meetings continued to run from 5 to 10 percent of the total.

In the capital and elsewhere, meetings rose in prominence over the entire period from the 1750s to the 1830s and dominated contention from 1807 onward. The complex, mobile events of the eighteenth century gave way to the standardized meeting, in which an audience assembled in a hall or another enclosed space heard a relatively small number of

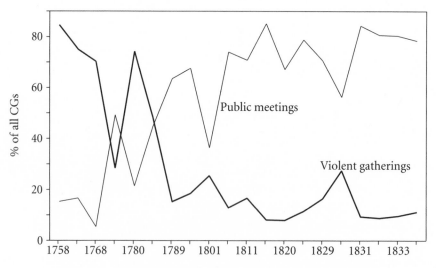

Figure 2.6. Crude event types, Southeastern England, 1758–1834

speakers pass through a familiar routine, often culminating in a resolution or a petition directed to Parliament or other national holders of power.

In the same process, groups taking part in contention altered significantly. The kinds of *individuals* participating probably changed much less than the guises in which they participated. Workers, for example, sometimes joined contention as workers, but they also appeared as parishioners, as members of crowds, as participants in Friendly Societies, as supporters of candidates, and in many other roles. In creating our records of contentious gatherings, we recorded and used the names our sources gave to formations: even if we suspected, for example, that the "mob" reported in the *Times* consisted entirely of workers, we transcribed the label *mob;* if the sources gave more than one name to the same formation, we recorded them all but gave priority to the one that was more precise or, failing that, more prominent in the accounts. Of the possible 10 million people who took part in one or another of the 8,088 CGs in the sample, we know the names of only about 26,000, and of them we rarely know much more than the names and the particular identities they brought to the gathering. The evidence therefore says little about changing patterns of individual participation in contention. It says a great deal, however, about the kinds of constituted groups publicly involved.

Figure 2.7 provides information for greatly aggregated categories of formation. I use these broad, debatable rubrics here in order to avoid burying the major trends in mounds of detail. ("Repressive formations" include military units, constables, police, sheriffs, gamekeepers, and others who have the legal right to coerce members of the public, while the term "inhabitants" refers to freeholders, electors, parishioners, ward members, inhabitants at large, and other sets of people identified by attachment to a common locality.) We might summarize the chief changes—including information from tabulations not shown here—in a series of observations:

1. Crowds, repressive formations, and economically designated groups fell from major to minor importance in British contention, with each one stabilizing at around 5 or 10 percent of the total after 1811.
2. Parliament (which "participated" in CGs chiefly as the absent object of other people's demands) rose from insignificance in the 1750s to a dominant position in the 1830s.
3. The king, ministers, and high officials (who likewise appeared in

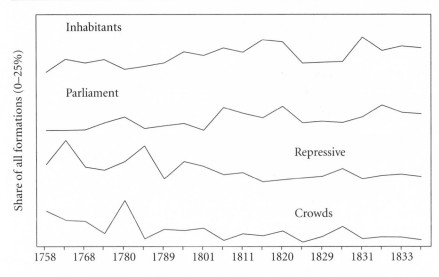

Figure 2.7. Selected formations, Southeastern England, 1758–1834

contentious gatherings primarily as objects of claims) swung considerably in importance, but typically constituted from one-twentieth to
one-tenth of all formations.

4. Fluctuations in the participation of inhabitants and local officials
   generally occurred together, but over the long run inhabitants gained
   in relative importance while officials stayed in the vicinity of 15 percent
   of all formations.

5. Named individuals, religious groups, and organized interests neither
   rose nor fell decisively, but all had a few years of fairly extensive
   involvement in contention.

6. Between 1828 and 1834 changes in the relative involvement of different
   kinds of formation generally occurred simultaneously in the Southeast
   and the rest of Great Britain; named individuals, religious groups, local
   officials, and Parliament offered partial exceptions to the rule.

If we restrict the analysis to formations that participated directly in the
CG, rather than watching or serving as absent objects of claims, the trends
move in the same directions, but obviously the values for such categories
as Parliament, royalty, and national officials run considerably lower; see
Appendix 1, Tables A.3, A.4, and A.6, for details.

All in all, the evidence about broad categories of formations describes the rise to prominence of a pattern in which people united by common residence and/or a shared special interest gathered to call on Parliament to act. In later chapters we will see the pattern forming: freeholders, parishioners, association members, religious congregations, or local residents gathering publicly, even ostentatiously, to announce their preferences on action by the national government, especially by Parliament. In politics local standing and national standing acquired a new connection. If we define citizenship as a set of categorically defined rights and obligations between agents and subjects of a state, then citizenship came into being; it became an accepted basis for making claims on the national state.

Members of my research group transcribed the principal verb our sources used (or that we inferred from the sources) to describe each action, and called it an action-verb. The course of action-verbs within CGs refines the picture of changes in contentious repertoires. In Figure 2.8 we find the verbs from actions having an object, which excludes such actions as "move" and "end." (Roughly half of the 51,000 verbs in the entire set had objects.) The verb dictionary for the entire file covers 2,474 different verbs, from *abate* and *abuse* to *yell at* and *yield*. Here I have grouped the verbs in extremely broad categories in order to bring out

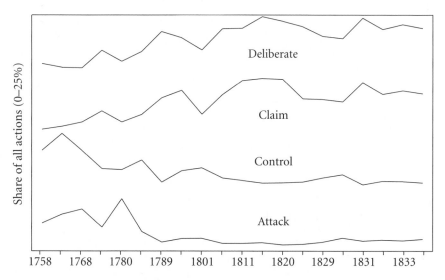

Figure 2.8. Selected actions, Southeastern England, 1758–1834

major trends. Examples of the verbs subsumed under the major headings are as follows:

ATTACK: alarm, annoy, assault, attack, batter, beat, beat off, besiege, beset;

CONTROL: apprehend, arouse, arrange, arrest, calm, capture, carry off, catch, caution;

CLAIM: accede, accept, admit, agitate, agree, allow, assert, claim, dare, defy, egg on;

DELIBERATE: add to, address, adopt, amend, answer, appoint, argue, bring before, call on.

(See Appendix 1, Table A.5, for more details on verb categories.) Altogether, these four portmanteau categories plus the trendless "support" (for example acclaim, acknowledge, admire, aid, applaud, approve, assent, assist, avow) contain 85 percent of the 25,239 actions having objects.

Even with this gross grouping of verbs, the trends between 1758 and 1834 are unmistakable. "Attack" verbs declined irregularly from the 1750s (when they ran about 30 percent of all verbs) to 1811 (when they reached about 10 percent), then remained in the range from 10–20 percent of all actions. The peaks arrived in 1768, 1780, and 1801, years respectively of Wilkes, Gordon, and subsistence struggles. Actions of "control" likewise fell rapidly, but reached their nadir in 1820 and moved back up to almost a quarter of all actions in 1830, the year of Captain Swing. "Claim" verbs had no decisive long-term trend, and appeared more frequently in events outside the Southeast than in London itself; why claims reached their highest level in 1828, during the mobilizations around Catholic Emancipation and repeal of the Test and Corporation Acts, remains to be seen. Consistent with the rise of meetings, "deliberate" verbs rose emphatically over time, although the dramatic drop in deliberation between 1828 and 1830 indicates a temporary return to out-of-doors politics. Again the evidence describes a great shift of repertoires toward planned, controlled assemblies, and a pivot during the second decade of the nineteenth century.

The *major issues* of contentious gatherings, unlike most items in our machine-readable records, do not come directly from the texts; they represent our summaries of the major claims being made in each event, especially those claims which qualified the gathering as contentious in the first place. We recorded just one set of issues per CG. They are therefore not as subtle as the distinctions among individual actions, but they give a sense of themes that connected actions with one another. Altogether, the 8,088 CGs took up about 3,000 different issues, some of them (for example, the many variants on parliamentary reform) barely distinguishable from one another. The alphabetical list begins with these entries:

abolition of slavery pro (that is, in favor of abolition)
additional bishops in India pro
Additional Church Bill anti
Administration Bill anti
Admiralty anti, food demands
admission to infirmary
affray between military
agricultural distress

Figure 2.9 again uses broad categories: attack on a person or object; religious issues of any kind; elections; parliamentary reform. These rubrics plus misery, government, and labor include 77 percent of all principal issues.

Except for the now unsurprising decline of attacks, the graphs of major issues display no long-term trends. They do, however, reveal wide swings

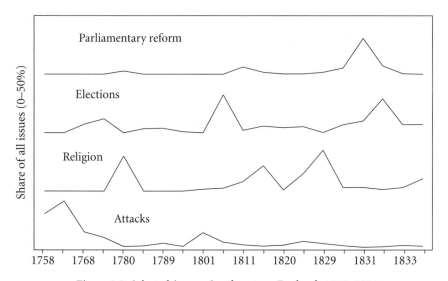

Figure 2.9. Selected issues, Southeastern England, 1758–1834

in the salience of different issues, largely as a function of national politics. Religion, for example, shoots up in 1780 (again, Lord George Gordon), 1819 (a struggle over proposed increases in the tax-supported stipends of London clergy), and 1828–1829 (Test and Corporation plus Catholic Emancipation). The curves for elections emphasize the pivotal polls of 1769, 1807, and 1832.

Most revealing is the chronology of parliamentary reform as a major issue. To be sure, our scattered years miss the grand reform debates of 1782–1785, 1790–1793, 1809–1810, 1816–1817, and 1822. Yet they capture the steps up from 1780 to 1811 to the incomparable heights of 1831, when at least 953 of the 1,645 contentious gatherings in our collection— 58 percent—concerned reform, and another 304 events (18 percent) concerned either elections or the national government. Like reform, many other issues ran in surges, building in a few months from low levels of action to high intensity. That tendency became more pronounced with the nineteenth-century transformation of repertoires, as associations formed, existing groups mobilized, public meetings proliferated, and leaders competed for the attention of Parliament as well as for the allegiance of other activists.

Note, however, the disappearances as well as the new arrivals. Forms of contention that occurred frequently in the Southeast during the eighteenth century's middle decades included:

mutinies of pressed military men breaking windows of householders who failed to illuminate;

collective seizures of food, often coupled with sacking the premises of the merchant;

verbal and physical attacks on malefactors seen in the street or displayed in the pillory;

taking sides at public executions;

workers' marches to public authorities in trade disputes;

ridicule and/or destruction of symbols, effigies, and/or property of public figures or moral offenders;

pulling down and/or sacking of dangerous or offensive houses;

donkeying, or otherwise humiliating, workers who violated collective agreements;

breaking up of theaters at unsatisfactory performances;

liberation of prisoners;
fights between hunters and gamekeepers;
battles between smugglers and royal officers.

Outside of the Southeast, the comparable list includes not only all of these but also destruction of tollgates, invasions of enclosed land, and disruptions of public ceremonies and festivals (see Archer 1990; Bohstedt 1983; Brewer 1976; Brewer and Styles 1980; Carter 1980; Charlesworth 1983; Gilmour 1992; Harrison 1988; Hayter 1978; King 1989; Palmer 1988; Stevenson 1992). None of these ever became a standard feature of a national social movement; they inhabited different political worlds. By the 1820s and 1830s all of these once-common routines had become rare or nonexistent. With them declined direct enforcement of public morality, immediate avenging of shared grievances, claims on actors who were present in person or by proxy, and actions whose claims remained within a local arena.

The pivotal years for decline of these common eighteenth-century forms of contention arrived during the Napoleonic Wars. The changeover to meetings, social movements, and related forms, however, actually occurred in three phases: (1) democratization of the once-elite public meeting that became quite noticeable in the 1780s, as the older routines persisted and elections became frequent occasions for popular voicing of claims; (2) decline of many standard eighteenth-century forms toward the end of the great war; and (3) multiplication of meetings, demonstrations, social movements, and related events after the war's end. Figure 2.10 captures the direction of change by graphing, year by year, Parliament as a proportion of all objects of claims against the proportion of all CGs that were meetings. Clearly the trend ran upward for both meetings and claims on Parliament; the major reversals occurred in 1780, 1801, and 1830—years of Lord George Gordon, economic crisis, and the Swing rebellion respectively. The major point of inflection lies somewhere between 1781 and 1807, depending on what we make of 1801's reversal. The bellicose period from the American Revolution to the Congress of Vienna wrought a great transformation of popular contention in Great Britain. One large set of repertoires displaced another. Although the process of transformation continued beyond the 1830s, the pace of innovation, displacement, and new institutionalization greatly diminished.

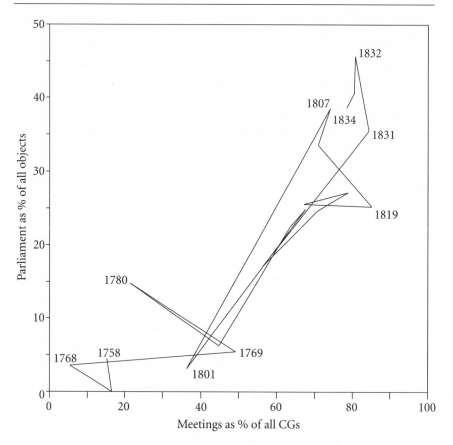

Figure 2.10. Meetings and Parliament, Southeastern England, 1758–1834

If this much of the change seems clear, important questions remain. First, did the transformations affect all groups, issues, and forms of action more or less equally and simultaneously? Or did the interactions comprising repertoires alter at different paces in different places, coming to be favored by various groups with respect to certain issues at distinct times? In particular, did struggles among workers or between workers and employers—which our catalog of contentious gatherings surely underrepresents—follow a different course from those aligning ordinary citizens with or against public authorities which dominate the catalog? When and how, for example, did the firm-by-firm strike emerge as a major form of worker action?

Second, how much of the alteration in repertoires resulted from the rise of new actors and issues rather than from shifts in the strategies of the same actors with regard to similar issues? Is it possible that the large increase in meetings as vehicles for collective claims, for example, stemmed entirely from the arrival of bourgeois and skilled workers on the national political scene?

Third, what part did ruling-class and governmental strategies of control play in the changes? To what extent, for example, did Britain's rulers promote the public meeting, demonstration, or strike as more easily containable alternatives to the eighteenth century's many forms of direct action?

Fourth, what structural changes in Great Britain, if any, favored the transformation of repertoires? Did the growth of a proletariat, the rise of mass consumption, the expanding power of the state, the concentration of capital, or the proliferation of communications have significant impacts on the character of popular struggles?

Fifth, did actors, issues, forms of action, and particular combinations among them differ significantly in revolutionary potential? Did Britain therefore approach revolution more closely at some moments in the change of repertoires than at others? If so, how and why?

Finally, what differences, if any, did changes in repertoire make? Were they nothing but epiphenomena, alternate organizations of ineffectuality? Or did their occurrence significantly affect the likelihoods that different groups of aggrieved persons would achieve their ends—or at least influence the behavior of those who held power?

The previous chapter sketched tentative answers to these questions. But before we can address them seriously, directly, and with evidence in hand, we must know what else was happening in Britain as the prevailing collective-action repertoires changed. Let us turn to a more sustained examination of structural change and potential sources of collective claims in Great Britain between 1750 and 1840.

❧ 3 ❧

CAPITAL, STATE, AND CLASS
IN BRITAIN, 1750–1840

"THE CONDITION OF THE POOR," Alexis de Tocqueville observed in 1833, "is England's greatest evil" (Tocqueville 1958: 41). Three years past a revolution in his home country, the famous observer of mores and politics took advantage of five weeks in England to judge the possibility of revolution across the Channel. "The number of poor people," he declared,

> is growing here at a frightening pace, partly because of defects in the laws. But the chief and permanent cause of the problem is, I think, the concentration of landed property. In England, the number of property-owners is decreasing rather than increasing, and the number of proletarians grows with the population. This state of affairs couples with taxes so high that rich people can't hire poor people as they would if such a large share of their money didn't go to the state; such things can only cause more and more misery . . . In sum, England seems to be in a critical situation, which certain events could quite possibly turn into a violent revolution. Yet if things follow their natural course I don't think the revolution will occur, and I see plenty of chances for the English to change their political and social situation at the cost of great pain but without upheaval and civil war. (Tocqueville 1958: 41–42; see also Spring 1980)

In the swirl of economic growth and political transformation Tocqueville saw an England—and, by extension, a Great Britain—beset by difficulty, divided by class, but somehow able to draw on great reserves of strength. He saw British social structure more clearly than did most contemporary Britons.

Let us examine that Britain closely, trying to discern the major changes separating life in the 1830s from experience eighty or ninety years earlier, in the 1750s. During that time, we shall see, Great Britain underwent massive population growth, greatly expanded its proletariat, urbanized energetically, created major regions of capital-concentrated manufacturing, multiplied its armies and empire, built up the mass and power of its central state, and shifted from relatively parochial, particular, and bifurcated toward relatively cosmopolitan, modular, and autonomous popular participation in politics, while seeing inequality sharpen and a national ruling class of capitalistic landlords retain its hold on the state apparatus but concede new influence to merchants and manufacturers. By Tocqueville's time a new Great Britain had taken shape. Later chapters will return to social changes during their periods in detail, but this chapter will sketch the long-term context of Britain's contention. It will trace few of the specific causal chains connecting various forms of contention to major social changes, likewise reserving that effort for later chapters.

The Britain Tocqueville visited in 1833 had gone through three-quarters of a century, or more, of rapid population growth. At the start of the 1750s Great Britain's 90,000 square miles had housed about 7.4 million people: 6.1 million in England, 0.3 million in Wales, and 1.3 million in Scotland. By the end of the 1830s the number had grown to 18.6 million. During the latter half of the eighteenth century the country's population increased at a respectable 0.7 percent per year. But from 1801 to 1841 the pace doubled to a frenetic 1.4 percent.

Consider the comparison with Tocqueville's France, Britain's principal rival and (after Russia) Europe's second most populous state. Great Britain's population grew much more rapidly than France's. Britain stood at about a third of France's population in 1751. Thereafter, rapid population growth brought Britain up to about two-fifths of France (not counting Napoleon's conquests) in 1801, and to more than half in 1841. Over the entire period from 1751 to 1841, the island's population density rose from 84 persons per square mile (between Sweden and Estonia today) to 208 (on a par with today's Spain, Austria, or Greece). The nearly 150 percent increase in population and density over ninety years signified large changes in Britain's social life.

How did that intense growth occur? Thanks to Wrigley and Schofield's splendid reconstruction of English population history, we know much more about England than about Wales or Scotland. Welsh demographic change remains a mystery. England and Scotland, in any case, went through broadly similar changes. In the last quarter of the seventeenth century, the English population began to grow after a long period of stagnation. It then grew especially because fertility rose; that happened largely because the proportion of the population ever marrying, which had long been low, increased dramatically. While fertility within marriage remained more or less constant, the sheer increase in the number of married couples of childbearing age multiplied the rate at which babies were being born.

As Figure 3.1 (drawn from Wrigley and Schofield 1981) shows, England experienced a rapid increase in its birth rate between the middle of the eighteenth century and the end of the Napoleonic Wars, while the death rate underwent a substantial decline. By twentieth-century standards, however, the levels of fertility and mortality both remained high; crude birth rates of 33 to 42 and crude death rates of 22 to 29 put eighteenth- and nineteenth-century England in the company of 1990s Chad, Nepal, and Laos. England did not actually start a sustained drop of fertility and mortality toward today's low levels until late in the nineteenth century.

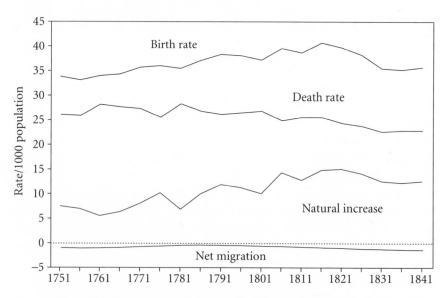

Figure 3.1. Components of change, English population, 1751–1841
Source: Wrigley and Schofield 1981: 528–529.

After the seventeenth century's transatlantic rush, net migration never constituted a major component of England's population change. The modest outmigration from 1750 to 1840, which fluctuated around one per thousand of population per year, resulted from the balance between departure of the English-born and arrival of others, especially Irish, from outside of England. During the wars with Revolutionary and Napoleonic France on the order of 4,000 Irish immigrants arrived each year; the number grew slowly to a peak of 40,000 per year during the 1840s (Floud and McCloskey 1981). But over the entire period from 1750 to 1840 many Irish immigrants moved on to America, and many English emigrants joined them. Net outmigration surged as the Seven Years War ended, dropped somewhat during the American and French wars, then recovered after 1811. Yet natural increase dominated population growth. Through the interplay of migration, fertility, and mortality, the overall growth rate of the English population rose irregularly over most of the period we are examining. It reached its peak around the end of the Napoleonic Wars.

Scotland's rate of population growth described a similar pattern. It reached 1.1 percent per year in the 1790s and ran at 1.2 percent between 1801 and 1841, with the peak decade from 1811 to 1821 (Flinn et al. 1977). Because the Scottish rate of growth always ran a bit slower than that of England and Wales, however, Scotland's share of the British population gradually diminished. Taken together, the populations of England, Wales, and Scotland expanded energetically during the later eighteenth century and with unprecedented vigor during the first half of the nineteenth.

Again, why? When other vital rates remain constant, rising nuptiality of women in their childbearing years elevates fertility. Nuptiality increases played the major part in Britain's rising fertility. But nuptiality may rise through either an increase in the proportion of the population that ever marries or a decrease in the average age at marriage among those who do marry. In England weight shifted from one factor to the other. During the first half of the eighteenth century most of the relatively small rise in fertility resulted from an increase in the proportion of the population ever marrying; fewer people, it appears, spent their lives unmarried as servants, sailors, or soldiers. But after 1750 something different happened: among those who did marry, age at marriage dropped, with a large effect on fertility (Weir 1984a).

As Jack Goldstone has suggested, we might think of the British population as divided into two partly distinct sectors, each with its own somewhat different demographic regime: (1) a Traditional population whose members married at standard ages when niches (farmsteads, places in shops, and the like) were available, and remained unmarried if they reached those standard ages at a time when niches were unavailable, and (2) a Proletarian population, dependent on wage-labor for survival, whose members generally married, but married as a function of the availability of wage-labor: marrying earlier when jobs were plentiful, marrying later or never in times of unemployment (Goldstone 1986; for a different perspective, see Fogel 1994; Komlos 1990).

For several centuries before 1750 the Traditional population predominated. High proportions remained spinsters and bachelors all their lives. More married in good times than bad, because economic expansion opened new niches in agriculture, manufacturing, and services: new farms, new firms, new shops. But even in good times large numbers remained unwed. That was the heyday of the unmarried live-in servant. When a severe squeeze on niches (through enclosures, the expulsion of servants from farms, the elimination of small shops, or population growth itself) occurred, however, it pushed people from the Traditional into the Proletarian sector. Then former Traditionals took wage-work in existing farms, firms, and shops; in the process, they moved toward a Proletarian tuning of marriage age to the availability of jobs.

In such a segmented population, rising income promotes fertility of the Traditional population through declining celibacy, while rising employment promotes fertility of the Proletarian population through declining age at marriage. Over the long run, however, rising income depresses Proletarian fertility (as the minimum standard of expenditure per child and per adult rises from generation to generation) and declining mortality likewise depresses fertility of both Traditional and Proletarian households (as the increasing survival of children burdens household expenditure, space, niches, and jobs). As Goldstone puts it: "it was proletarianization in the context of an industrializing economy that provided increasingly regular employment for wage labour in industry and agriculture that allowed earlier family formation and hence increased fertility among those who did marry, without an offsetting decline in access to marriage among the population as a whole" (Goldstone 1986: 29). Britain's population was proletarianizing rapidly during the eighteenth century. True, the number of male servants shrank and the number of common laborers rose little faster than the whole population. Yet industrial occupations and petty trades grew much more rapidly (Lindert 1980). Within agriculture itself enclosures pushed many cottagers and laborers from control over some land and livestock to nearly complete dependency on wage labor (Snell 1985; Humphries 1990). In Scotland, similarly, sheep farmers displaced thousands of smallholders from the rocky Highlands and drove them into landless labor; from that point on, they ate potatoes instead of oats and milk (Salaman 1985). In the short run, at least, proletarianization meant immiseration.

Proletarians, Landlords, and Others

Let us be clear about the word "proletarian." It often calls up an image of deskilled individuals working at mindless tasks in large factories under strict discipline. Proletarians, however, include many people besides factory hands, miners, and dockworkers. A population is proletarian to the extent that its members produce using productive means owned by others, and receive wages for their labor power. By that criterion, the majority of Britain's eighteenth-century people were proletarians. During the eighteenth century many British proletarians worked in agriculture, many split their time between agriculture and manufacturing, and many manufacturing workers produced at home or in village shops. Although Britain had become an exceptionally industrial country by the mid-eighteenth century, few of its proletarians were working in large shops under strict discipline.

Proletarianization centers on the separation of waged workers from control over means of production. If we follow E. P. Thompson in considering class as a dynamic relationship rather than a personal or categorical attribute, then the growth of a British proletariat consisted of the increasing organization of work around relations between wage-giving owners of productive means and property-poor workers who depended on wages for survival. Parallel but partly separate processes forwarded proletarianization, in this sense, within manufacturing and agriculture. Within manufacturing, merchants in textiles, metalworking, and mining increased their capital, expanded their control over sites of production, relied increasingly on inanimate sources of energy, mechanized to some degree, and imposed greater time-discipline over waged workers who, on the average, were losing their hold on land, craft solidarity, and tools of their trades. Within agriculture, landlords enclosed their properties, adopted improved technologies, mechanized modestly, and let their lands to farmers. The farmers, in their turn, reduced their reliance on long-term live-in servants, preferring seasonal and annual hiring of landless laborers. With hundreds of variations for industries and regions, the two processes enormously increased the number of relations between capitalists and wageworkers in industry and the number of relations between landlords, farmers, and landless laborers in agriculture.

Changes in the agricultural labor force played an important part in Britain's proletarianization. They stemmed from longer-range changes in British agriculture. During the later seventeenth century, the regional differentiation of pastoral, arable, and protoindustrial production in rural areas increased sharply (Kussmaul 1990). London's growing market and the expansion of Britain's industrial exports both played their part in that differentiation. During the eighteenth century, regional specialization stabilized to some degree, although the location of rural industry remained volatile, with East Anglia's and Devon's textiles in decline as those of Lancashire flourished. Merchants gained profits and landlords gained rents, while small landowners lost out. With the rising agricultural prices of the revolutionary and Napoleonic wars, landlords grew wealthier and more powerful, to the detriment of landless laborers and servants but to the advantage of large leaseholders.

Over much of the eighteenth century, smallholders and servants both dwindled. The period of the Napoleonic Wars brought a decisive shift from live-in servants to landless wage-labor; the shift went farther and faster in London's cash-crop hinterland than elsewhere (Kussmaul 1981; Snell 1985). The wartime shift corresponded to a change in poor people's diets: potato-growing spread, and wheat bread became rare (Horn 1980). Class differences in food consumption—and, most likely, in other kinds of consumption as well—sharpened. Increasingly, the farming population divided into three distinct classes: landlords, substantial tenant farmers, and landless laborers. The three classes ate differently, dressed differently, lived in different kinds of housing, and differed hugely in power. At the top of the hierarchy, the owners of great estates continued to consolidate their hold on Britain's land (Allen 1982; Beckett 1984; Stone and Stone 1984).

Most proletarians in agriculture worked, directly or indirectly, for members of the aristocracy or gentry, the English landed elite. The English aristocracy and gentry were still increasing their share of the entire landscape during the eighteenth century; they were both acquiring new land and excluding villagers from customary uses—hunting, fishing, gleaning, and pasturing—of land to which landlords already held title. A huge rise in rents between 1770 and 1815 further increased their hold on the countryside. By the end of the eighteenth century, the aristocracy and gentry held between a quarter and a third of England's entire territory (Stone and Stone 1984).

They did not, in general, work the land themselves. "Slowly," report Lawrence Stone and Jeanne Fawtier Stone,

> . . . they enclosed most of England and leased it out to a relatively small number of large tenant farmers, who in turn hired landless labourers to till the soil. The resultant tripartite social structure of the countryside was quite unlike anything to be seen elsewhere in Europe. Its weakness was the plight of the landless labourers in a bad year, but its strength was the potentiality—and reality—of substantial agricultural improvement and a progressive increase in the total output of food. This both enriched the landlord and fed the poor. (ibid.: 419)

The landlord received the lion's share. In the company of London's finance capitalists, the class of landlords as a whole, furthermore, continued to dominate British national life, including Parliament, well into the nineteenth century: "At the time of the Napoleonic Wars, perhaps seven-eighths of all persons worth £100,000 or more in Britain were landowners" (Rubinstein 1987: 50). They operated a system of patronage that dispensed offices and emoluments to the powerful, favors and mediation to the weak. At the same time, their stewards and agents worked the electoral system on their behalf; between 1730 and 1769 Earl Gower spent an average of £225 per year on the faithful electors of Newcastle-under-Lyme alone, while between 1733 and 1770 the Duke of Bedford averaged 207 pounds per year of political gratuities at Tavistock (Wellenreuther 1979). The county lords lieutenant (who were always peers) named the Justices of the Peace (who ran most of the judicial apparatus) from among the local landed elite. The system perpetuated itself.

When the indefatigable Patrick Colquhoun published his survey of the British Empire at the end of the Napoleonic Wars, he divided the 3,501,781 families and 17,096,803 people of the United Kingdom into the categories of Table 3.1. Roughly speaking, Colquhoun distinguished the aristocracy, the gentry, the great bourgeoisie, the middle bourgeoisie, the petty bourgeoisie, the working class, the Lumpenproletariat, and the armed forces. Within agriculture and other primary industries he counted 384,000 "freeholders of the better sort," 1,050,000 lesser freeholders, 1,540,000 farmers, and 3,154,142 labourers. Landless laborers then came close to half the agricultural population. For another half-century, their share increased at the expense of smallholders and modest farmers.

The 237,000 members of the aristocracy and gentry constituted 1.4 percent of the United Kingdom's families and population, but controlled the bulk of its land. They worked mainly through prosperous farmers, who in turn hired wage-workers. The emergence of that tripartite structure displaced a world holding a similar number of landlords, fewer farmers and landless laborers, but many more smallholders, servants, and semiproletarian workers on the land.

Who else was there? To round out the social-class roster of Great Britain, as Colquhoun's enumeration suggests, we would certainly have to tally a small but crucial set of merchants and industrialists, at first nearly indistinguishable but then, over time, increasingly separate from each other. Among the very wealthy the distinction was sharper; London's traders and bankers constituted a powerful world apart from manufacturing until late in the nineteenth century (Rubinstein 1987). Tradesmen, craftsmen, and laborers in manufacturing, service, and commerce belong on the roll. So do the growing number of professionals, including clergymen, barristers, and full-time officials.

To be sure, we can translate Colquhoun's categories into effective classes only to the extent that their members drew identities from category-to-category relations. During the later eighteenth century, the clearest manifestations of class in this strong sense appeared in the relations between landless laborers and farmers, between craft workers and masters, between petty bourgeois and aristocracy. As the nineteenth century arrived, the division and connection between proletarianizing workers and owners of large shops joined these other intense forms of class relations. Over the period from 1750 to 1840, Britain witnessed the growth of a town-based bourgeoisie, petty bourgeoisie, and proletariat that was unparalleled in previous European experience.

Table 3.1. Patrick Colquhoun's classification of the United Kingdom's population, 1815

Highest Orders: The Royal Family, the Lords Spiritual and Temporal, the Great officers of State, and all above the degree of a Baronet: 576 families, 2,880 people

Second Class: Baronets, Knights, Country Gentlemen, and others having large incomes: 46,861 families, 234,305 people

Third Class: Dignified Clergy, Persons holding considerable employments in the State, elevated positions in the Law, eminent Practitioners in Physic, considerable Merchants, Manufacturers upon a large scale, and Bankers of the first order: 12,200 families, 61,000 people

Fourth Class: Persons holding inferior situations in Church and State, respectable Clergymen of different persuasions, Practitioners in Law and Physic, Teachers of Youth of the superior order, respectable Freeholders, Ship Owners, Merchants and Manufacturers of the second class, Warehousemen and respectable shopkeepers, Artists, respectable Builders, Mechanics, and Persons living on moderate incomes: 233,650 families, 1,168,250 people

Fifth Class: Lesser Freeholders, Shopkeepers of the second order, Innkeepers, Publicans, and Persons engaged in miscellaneous occupations, or living on moderate incomes: 564,799 families, 2,798,475 people

Sixth Class: Working Mechanics, Artisans, Handicrafts, Agricultural Labourers, and others, who subsist by labour in various employments: 2,126,095 families, 8,792,800 people

Menial Servants: 1,279,923 people

Seventh, or Lowest Class: Paupers and their families, Vagrants, Gipsies, Rogues, Vagabonds, and idle and disorderly persons, supported by criminal delinquency: 387,100 families, 1,828,170 people

Officers of the Army, Navy, and Marines, including all Officers on half-pay and superannuated: 10,500 families, 69,000 people

Non-commissioned Officers in the Army, Navy, and Marines, Soldiers, Seamen, and Marines, including Pensioners of the Army, Navy &c.: 120,000 families, 862,000 people

Source: Colquhoun 1815: 106–107.

The Growth of Industry

For the male labor force only, the distribution among large sectors changed roughly as follows (Crafts 1985: 62–63):

	1760	1800	1840
% in agriculture	49.6	39.9	25.0
% in trade, handicraft, mining or manufacturing	23.8	29.5	47.3
% in other industry	26.6	30.6	27.7

Because the labor force was expanding rapidly, the percentages translate into a one-third increase in the size of the male agricultural labor force, a fivefold growth of male workers in trade, handicraft, mining or manufacturing, and nearly a tripling of those in other industry. The sources of the estimates—especially parish records before 1811—make women's employment harder to trace. The best guess, however, is that women's employment in manufacturing grew even more rapidly than men's.

For the period between 1755 and 1811, Peter Lindert's analyses of parish records provide estimates of the percentage change in many categories of the male labor force (Lindert 1980), which appear in Table 3.2. Eighteen-eleven was a war year; the large numbers of soldiers and sailors reflect the wartime mobilization. But the disproportionate increases of the professions, the building trades, the textile trades, mining, laborers, and other services, as well as the declines of farmers, yeomen, and servants, represent longer-term trends. (The falls in commerce and other manufacturing were temporary, apparently effects of war.) Between the 1750s and the 1840s Britain made the shift from a predominantly agricultural (although quite proletarian) labor force to an even more proletarian labor force dominated by nonagricultural employment.

Agriculture's mediocre wages and stagnating employment drove workers into manufacturing and services. During the industrialization of 1750–1850, Britain exploited the secret of coupling cheap labor to new technology in production for export markets. Not that steam power and large workplaces caused most of the expansion. The closer we look, the more the mirage of an eighteenth-century "industrial revolution" wrought by steam-powered machines and factories dissolves (see Cameron 1990; Hartwell 1990; Mokyr 1987, 1993). Lancashire and Yorkshire's West Riding did burgeon with milltowns toward the end of the eighteenth century, but even there handloom weaving in homes and small shops played a major part in the expansion of manufacturing. Coal-fueled steam power began to have a strong effect on textile production only in the 1840s (von Tunzelmann 1978).

As the chronology of changes in production suggests, British economic growth accelerated irregularly from modest in the early eighteenth cen-

Table 3.2. Peter Lindert's estimates of changes in major occupations, 1755–1811

Category	Number in 1755 (thousands)	Number in 1811 (thousands)	Annual % change, 1755–1811
Farmers	110	92	−0.3
Yeomen	65	39	−0.9
Other agricultural*	203	185	−0.2
Professions	9	41	+2.7
Commerce	191	137	−0.6
Building trades*	111	240	+1.4
Textile trades	40	157	+2.5
Other manufacturing*	201	171	−0.3
Mining	14	152	+4.4
Maritime trades	60	136	+1.5
Army	10	266	+6.0
Laborers	191	341	+1.0
Servants	129	78	−0.9
Other services	66	205	+2.0
Other	68	212	+2.1
Total men	1,469	2,328	+0.8

*Excluding laborers.
Source: Lindert 1980.

tury to fairly rapid a century later. N. F. R. Crafts offers the following estimates of average annual percentage rates of growth (Crafts 1985: 45):

Years	National product	National product per capita
700–1760	0.69	0.31
1760–1780	0.70	0.01
1780–1801	1.32	0.35
1801–1831	1.97	0.52

The broad patterns resemble C. Knick Harley's estimates of national income from 1700 to 1841, with economic growth outstripping population growth by a substantial margin only after the Napoleonic Wars (Harley 1982; for refinements, see Harley 1993). Around that time, the English population finally escaped from the Malthusian trap in which for centuries prices had risen in close correlation with aggregate population growth (Wrigley and Schofield 1981; Wrigley 1988).

Over Britain as a whole, agricultural improvements and the construction of roads and canals figured prominently among the contributors to growth. In both cases, new technology mattered less than the expansion of entrepreneurship and the spreading adoption of techniques that had taken shape over the previous centuries. Factories and mills, furthermore, accounted for relatively little of the increase in nonagricultural employment before the later nineteenth century; as late as 1831 only a tenth of England's employed adult males worked in large-scale manufacturing (Wrigley 1986).

The tenth, nevertheless, occupied a disproportionately important place in the British economy. Cotton textiles, in particular, led the way. From 1780 to 1860 total factor productivity in cotton cloth probably rose by more than 2.5 percent per year (Floud and McCloskey 1981). Markets grew even faster, as British cottons undersold domestic textiles across the Channel and elsewhere. Employment grew accordingly. The number of men in textile occupations, especially weaving, greatly increased during the later eighteenth century; it may well have doubled between 1755 and 1801 (Lindert 1980). Exports of goods, especially textiles, produced by relatively unskilled wage-workers established Britain's dominance in the nineteenth-century international market. At home, capitalists, landlords, and prosperous entrepreneurs created a world of fashion and luxury consumption (McKendrick, Brewer, and Plumb 1985).

Urbanization

That world was increasingly urban. The concentration of capital, the acceleration of commerce, and the growth of large firms drew labor to cities. After several centuries of moderate urban growth outside of London, Britain urbanized rapidly in the century after 1750. At the middle of the eighteenth century, London, with around 675,000 inhabitants, was probably Europe's largest city; Constantinople was its chief competitor. After Beijing, indeed, London was quite possibly the second largest city in the world. By 1801 London reached 865,000 people; by 1841, 1.9 million.

Yet the rest of Britain urbanized even more rapidly than London grew between 1750 and 1801, and not much more slowly thereafter. As of 1750 London and its hinterland already belonged to Europe's greatest concentration of urban population, which extended through the Low Countries and northern France. By 1801 the high-density zone extended to northern England, and by 1841 it included central Scotland (de Vries 1984; South Wales, on the other hand, only began its vigorous urbanization after 1880: Dodgshon and Butlin 1978).

The chief centers of urban growth outside the London region were the industrial and commercial regions to the north, where capital concentrated and labor congregated in cities. Glasgow, Liverpool, Birmingham, Hull, Leeds, Manchester, Nottingham, and Sheffield all more than doubled their populations between 1750 and 1800 (de Vries 1984). New turnpikes, with their much-attacked tollgates, concentrated in the regions of expanding industry, which had less of the access to navigable rivers that characterized older centers of manufacturing. Both the number of turnpike trusts and total turnpike mileage increased at an average of 2.2 percent per year between 1750 and 1836 (calculated from Pawson 1977: 114–115). From 1770 onward canals multiplied even faster than turnpikes, moving coal and metal cheaply among the new industrial centers. After 1800 those centers' regions continued to spearhead urban growth. Meanwhile, the old regional capitals—Norwich, Bristol, York, Exeter, and Newcastle—

grew only moderately, or even stagnated. Over the century after 1750, London, manufacturing centers, and the cities that shipped their products dominated Britain's urbanization.

Britain's urban growth resulted from three somewhat different processes. In one case, a region's commercial node absorbed activities that had previously scattered through its hinterland; Manchester grew as an actual site of textile manufacturing, for example, only after long serving as the base for entrepreneurs who controlled household and small-shop production throughout southern Lancashire. In the second case, a capitalist established a major production center in a favorable rural location (often where water power and household manufacturing coincided), so that mills and shops inflated a village into a raw new kind of city; Merthyr Tydfil and Bolton illustrate this second pattern. In the third case, an activity that depended on the expansion of trade, services, and manufacturing drove the growth of an existing center; prospering ports such as Bristol, Hull, and (especially) Liverpool best illustrate this process. In all three cases, substantial migration from elsewhere—most often from the immediate vicinity—played a major part in the city's growth.

The growth of cities and the movement of workers into manufacturing and services rested on dramatic increases in the labor productivity of British agriculture. Although rising imports from Ireland and elsewhere also played their part in the expanding British food supply, within Britain a slow-growing group of agricultural workers fed a fast-growing group of workers outside of agriculture. Crafts estimates that "each agricultural worker's output was capable of feeding 2.7 non-agricultural workers in 1841 compared with 1 in 1760" (Crafts 1985: 138; for a dissenting view, see Gregory Clark 1993). Technical innovations played only a small part in the increase; instead, the spread and refinement of mixed farming on enclosed land stepped up the productivity of land and labor. The rising efficiency of agriculture permitted—or forced—the movement of workers into trade, handicraft and, especially, machinofacture.

Given a relatively unchanging system of suffrage, Britain's urbanization had two strong political effects. First, it increased the underrepresentation of urban areas in a Parliament still elected from counties and long-established boroughs, some of them almost devoid of population. Second, it increased the number of disfranchised men present and actively interested on the occasion of urban elections to Parliament. Urban electoral campaigns became major opportunities for supporters of one national cause or another to voice their shared demands in public.

Income and Inequality

Agricultural workers themselves benefited only modestly from their increasing productivity. Workers as a whole, according to Lindert and Williamson's optimistic estimates, enjoyed real income increases on the order of 150 percent from 1781 to 1851. Agricultural laborers, according to the same estimates, saw their real income rise only about two-thirds. More precisely, the Lindert-Williamson estimates show little change in any large category's real income from 1755 to 1810, then rapid increases among blue-collar and, especially, white-collar workers thereafter, while agricultural laborers gained less than other categories (Lindert and Williamson 1983b). England's cost of living, as Figure 3.2 illustrates, held fairly steady from 1750 to 1790, then rose precipitously during the war years, only to decline almost to prewar levels—although with considerably greater volatility—during the decade after 1811. In the face of very rapid population increases, the leveling of prices itself implies substantial rises

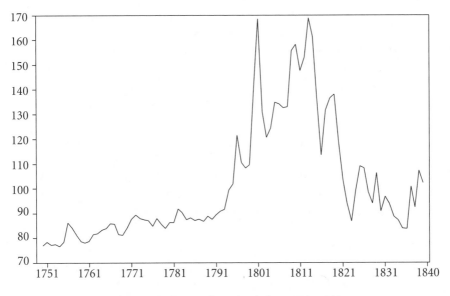

Figure 3.2. Composite price index, 1750–1840

in productivity, which in Great Britain resulted both from agricultural efficiency and from shifts of labor into manufacturing.

Before the decade 1810–1819, however, real income rose little if at all; the rising cost of living canceled out increases in nominal wages. Around 1790, available nutrition limited the average height and weight of British male adults to about 168 cm. (66 in.) and 61 kg. (134 lbs.); at that, an estimated 3 percent of the labor force ate too little for any work at all, while another 17 percent had only the energy for 6 hours of light work, or 1.09 hours of heavy work, per day (Fogel 1994). Conditions worsened, furthermore, during the war. As indicated by the stature of boys recruited to the Marine Society, London's working classes suffered a significant decline in nutrition during the war years (Floud and Wachter 1982: 433; imagine an encounter of William Cobbett, a stout 6'1", with an average London worker!) Meanwhile, the ruling classes grew tall and fat; with exceptions such as willowy William Pitt, Gillray's biting cartoons of the time typically portray gentry and nobility as bloated and gouty, workers as shrunken and gaunt. After Waterloo, however, food supplies expanded and prices declined rapidly. According to Jeffrey Williamson's estimates, cheaper living and higher wages combined to produce a rapid increase of real income for white-collar employees, more modest gains for artisans and other nonagricultural workers, and a slight improvement for farm laborers (Figure 3.3; Williamson 1985a).

Although the figures for artisans and other workers probably portray the trend correctly, C. H. Feinstein has cast great doubt on Williamson's estimates of white-collar income and therefore of overall income inequality (Crafts 1989; Feinstein 1988). The Lindert-Williamson estimates may also exaggerate the benefits to agricultural laborers; K. D. M. Snell's study of rural settlement examinations suggests that in southern England their real income remained roughly constant from 1706 to the 1780s, actually declined significantly with the rapid rise in living costs from the 1780s to the end of the Napoleonic Wars, then failed to regain its eighteenth-century level as the cost of living dropped thereafter. In the Southeast— the grain-growing region that fed London—women suffered serious losses of real income, as the changing organization of production excluded them from agricultural tasks such as grain-cutting (Snell 1985; Humphries 1990). In the same region, cyclical unemployment increased and relief rolls swelled (Boyer 1990; Snell 1985; Wells 1990). Meat all but disappeared from farm laborers' diets (Rule 1986). In agriculture, then, the benefits of rising productivity as well as of enclosures flowed first to farmers (that is, large leaseholders) and then to landlords, whose incomes soared. Landless laborers paid the price.

Over the nine decades from 1750 to 1840, all of Britain's social classes felt the increasing involvement of their country in the world economy. Britain was, remarks Eric Hobsbawm, "in a position to develop its international trade to an abnormal extent, simply because of the monopoly of industrialization, and of relations with the underdeveloped overseas world which she succeeded in establishing between 1780 and 1815" (Hobsbawm 1968: 111). Although as markets European countries mattered more than the rest of the world, Britain's colonies supplied raw materials, finished products, and capital that figured significantly in the homeland's industrialization.

By the mid-eighteenth century those colonies already constituted one of the world's greatest empires, with large territories in India, the West Indies, and North America, not to mention Ireland. During the following ninety years Britain lost many of its American colonies and clamped Ireland into a United Kingdom. In the same period, however, it became the dominant power in India, expanded the West Indian base, gained a

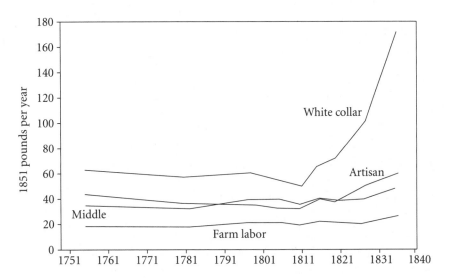

Figure 3.3. Real incomes of occupations, 1755–1835

toehold in the Mediterranean, expanded aggressively into Africa and the Pacific, and picked up bits and pieces elsewhere. After having been the object of competing claims from the 1760s onward, for example, the Islas Malvinas, or Falkland Islands, fell to a British expedition in 1833. Like the Malvinas, much of the new territory came to Britain as prizes of war.

War and the British State

Like all other European states, the British state expanded—both externally and internally—through war and preparation for war. Long before the eighteenth century the British made their presence known in continental wars and the state felt the impact of war. Nevertheless, from the Hundred Years War to the later seventeenth century, British navies and, especially, armies involved themselves in European warmaking less intensively than did rivals such as France, Spain, Sweden, or even the Dutch Republic. After the Restoration of 1660, Charles II and James II began to consolidate control over taxation with an eye to building up both their military capacity and their independence from Parliament. Once the Glorious Revolution defeated the Stuart bid for autonomy, wars against France drove a great expansion of the central fiscal and administrative staff, under tightened parliamentary control. How great that expansion seems depends on whether we look backward or forward: nothing like it had occurred since Henry VIII's reorganization of the state, but the eighteenth-century wars so greatly accelerated the expansion that from the perspective of century's end the beginning looks puny.

In the early eighteenth century Great Britain had plenty of government, but not much state (Braddick 1991). A small but fairly efficient central administration—some 10,000 to 15,000 permanent officers, plus their employees—took care of war, taxes, and national expenditure. The army actually loomed larger than the central administration. Most governmental administration took place at the level of the county or the parish, in the form of decisions and applications undertaken by unpaid committees, councils, or officials. Relief of the poor, for example, preoccupied local officials and burdened parish administration, but occupied almost no space in the national state structure. Justices of the Peace enjoyed an enormous range of powers, approaching those of Eastern Europe's magnates:

They could arrest and punish offenders for drunkenness, vagrancy, profanity, poaching and much else. They supervised ale-houses, decided bastardy cases and exercised jurisdiction over runaway servants or apprentices. They might fix prices and wages, regulate apprenticeships, order highway maintenance, decide poor law policy (as authorities above the parishes), suppress nuisances, oversee markets, license or ban fairs and amusements, appoint constables, assess rates. (Thane 1990: 6)

Looking back at the early 1800s from 1848, Samuel Bamford reported that:

Constables and overseers had, in those days, a very straightforward way of doing business. On receiving an order, or even a direction less tangible, from a magistrate or magistrate's clerk, it was forthwith carried into effect—the magistrate was everything,—the rate-payers and vestry nothing,—and money was expended which was never enquired into afterwards. If the minister, or some one or two of the "gentlemen rate-payers," put a question or so to the overseer when he met him, and the reply was, "Oh, Mr A. or Mr. B the magistrate ordered it," all would be right, and nothing further would be said about the matter. (Bamford 1967: I, 228)

By 1848, as Bamford rightly saw, the magistrates' reign was an era long past; indeed, they were already passing in 1800. The magistrate's eighteenth-century powers stand out the more in comparison with Russian, Prussian, or Ottoman models because the Justices of the Peace neither served in the military nor had significant armed force under their command. That separation from the military helps explain, indeed, the enormous autonomy their rulers were willing to grant them. As the great armed lords of the sixteenth and seventeenth centuries had lost power and autonomy, the unarmed gentry had gained it (Stone 1947, 1983).

Parliament did, it is true, enact the general rules within which local and county officials operated—authorizing such innovations as the Poor Law unions by which sets of adjacent parishes banded together to build poorhouses and common welfare policies. Parliament and the central administration did, now and then, step in to end what they regarded as abuses of local government. Secretaries of State and county Lieutenants General intermittently advised Justices of the Peace and mayors on difficult parish affairs. The system of courts operated under royal sanction and, at a distance, royal supervision. Now and then the national government sent in troops to put down rebellion or enforce royally ratified law. For most of the eighteenth century, nevertheless, Britain's national state did these things by two overlapping means: (1) personal connections built around great lords, and (2) a central administrative structure devoted mainly to military activity, financial support for military activity, and the maintenance of a royal establishment. Joanna Innes (1994) has even spoken of the state's "disengagement" from domestic government during the eighteenth century as a consequence of the central government's preoccupation with wars and international relations.

No need to overstate the case. Having read reams of correspondence between France's eighteenth-century central officials and their provincial interlocutors, and having often recited the Tocquevillian couplet "French centralization: British decentralization," I was amazed to start working in Britain's eighteenth-century State Papers only to find the Secretaries of State's lawyers sending out opinions to local Justices of the Peace on matters that in Old Regime France would rarely have gotten past semi-autonomous municipalities, Estates, or Parlements. With respect to sheer connectedness, by the Seven Years War the British state was more centralized than the French; local officials could choose between passing through patrons, enlisting an MP in their cause, or connecting directly with officers of the central state without contacting the British equivalent of an Intendant, Parlement, provincial Estate, or tax farmer.

In Britain, however, the central apparatus was much less bulky, far more government business passed through unsalaried volunteers drawn from the gentry, fewer people operated royally sanctioned offices essentially as lucrative enterprises, and ordinary people found it harder to make direct connections with full-time officials of the national state. In these regards, the British state resembled the Dutch rather more than the French. And with good reason: in both Britain and the Netherlands burghers and landlords not only had strong incentives to keep the business of government in their own hands but also had the means to resist the crown's demands.

In other regards, however, Britain resembled France more than the Netherlands. Despite being capable of raising large, effective forces in time of war, the eighteenth-century Dutch disbanded their armies and navies in peacetime. As a result of war and imperial expansion, in contrast, the British state already had substantial armed force at its disposal by the early eighteenth century. During the century, the army and navy expanded mightily, while the staff attached to them and the fiscal apparatus grew as well. For the century's first few decades, the state's demand for revenues remained modest—between 15 and 20 percent of per capita income (Mathias and O'Brien 1976). In wartime, from three-fifths to three-quarters of that revenue went to military ends (Brewer 1989). After 1740, however, larger wars meant bigger budgets, more debt service, and an enormous increase in demand for taxes.

During the first half of the eighteenth century British peacetime armies generally amounted to about 35,000 men, a quarter or less of the French forces, and less than half the army Frederick William I was building up in Prussia. (Other armies, paid for by the Irish people, occupied Ireland.) During the War of the Austrian succession (1740–1748), however, Britain tried roughly to triple its forces. As the Seven Years War (1756–1763) began, the army again expanded, eventually (in 1760) to reach 203,000 troops. After the war ended, it settled down at 45,000, including 12,000 charged to Ireland (Barnett 1974; Brewer 1989). Another surge came with the American Revolution. But the mobilization against Napoleon far overshadowed that of previous wars. At their maximum, British armies numbered 237,000 men (Barnett 1974).

As the eighteenth century moved on, the navy's size approached the army's. During the American wars, for example, the navy's authorized strength averaged 82,000 men to the army's 108,000 (Brewer 1989). Since the navy cost substantially more per man to maintain than the army, naval expansion drove a disproportionate increase in military expenditure (French 1990). Successive mobilizations of men for war temporarily depleted Britain's domestic labor force, and reduced unemployment, although the disproportionate recruitment of relatively unskilled laborers for military service meant that the civilian economy lost few skilled hands (O'Brien 1989). But the ends of wars brought demobilization, unemployment and—most likely—increasing property crime (Hay 1982). In addition to their effects on expenditure, debt, and capital accumulation, Britain's many wars therefore had a significant effect on the labor available for agricultural and industrial production.

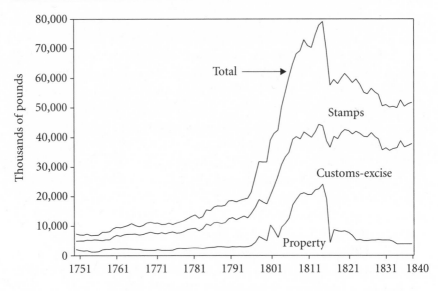

Figure 3.4. Government income, 1750–1840

The defeat of Napoleon did not end the demand for troops, although the shift from continental wars and great alliances changed its character:

> After 1815 therefore the British army's role was very different from in the century after 1715. It was no longer needed, however intermittently, in struggles against great powers, or in deliberate imperial expansion. Nevertheless the existing empire, irrelevant though it now seemed, had to be garrisoned and its frontiers protected against native unrest. The peacetime strength of the British standing army rose to the unprecedented figure of over 100,000 men. However, up to three-quarters of the infantry were overseas, in the empire. The army now became for the first time a largely colonial army, whose units might be exiled for a decade or more at a time. (Barnett 1974: 272–273)

As a result, the army decreased its presence in Britain as its influence in the world at large increased.

Someone had to pay those men. Ultimately, British taxpayers footed much of the bill. By the 1790s national taxes stood at close to 25 percent of commodity output; toward 1810 they reached 35 percent. France, by comparison, was waging its great wars with smaller per capita levies:

under 15 percent of commodity output over almost the entire period from 1720 to 1810 (Mathias and O'Brien 1976; Morineau 1980; O'Brien 1988, 1989). Figures 3.4 and 3.5 reveal the rhythms of expansion. The curves of tax revenues tell us that Britain drew the bulk of its tax revenues from customs and excise rather than assessments on land, income, or property throughout the period from 1750 to 1840. (For the war years, the graph's rubric "property" includes income taxes.) As a matter of principle, Britain's rulers also opposed direct assessment of wealth— which, they reasoned, moved taxation from optional to obligatory (Kennedy 1964). The principle was convenient, since any increase in the land tax directly attacked the fortunes of a landowning ruling class that lacked the fiscal exemptions enjoyed by many of their continental cousins.

During the Napoleonic Wars, it is true, an unprecedented income tax brought in a significant share of state revenue; by the wars' end it supplied roughly a fifth of all government income (Bordo and White 1990). Levied essentially at a flat rate, it lacked the regressive bite of Britain's major eighteenth-century taxes. But with the wars' end, the income tax installed in 1799 disappeared, and Britain (or, by then, the United Kingdom) turned back to heavy reliance on customs and excise, supplementing that

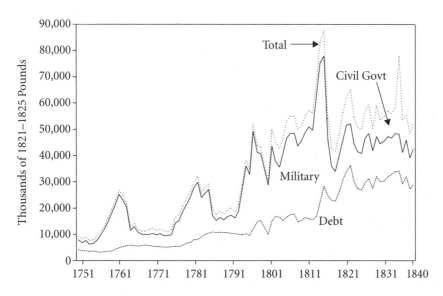

Figure 3.5. Government budgets, 1750–1840

income with stamp duties, proceeds from the Post Office, and a few other minor levies (Levi 1988). With booming foreign trade and a highly commercialized domestic economy, Britain could draw sufficient income to run the state by dipping into commercial flows rather than accumulated stocks of wealth. The postwar British state financed itself with a sharply regressive system of taxation.

Although the curves show increases in tax collections during the Seven Years War and the American War, the great acceleration occurred in the struggle with France that followed the revolution of 1789. Tax collections more than quadrupled from about £17 million in 1790 to almost £80 million in 1815. (During the same interval the Lindert-Williamson cost of living index rose by 45 percent; for the interval 1790–1810, best estimates show an increase of between 70 and 90 percent, still only a quarter of the tax increase: Lindert and Williamson 1983b.) What is more, the well-known ratchet effect occurred: Once the great war ended, taxes did not return to their prewar levels, but settled down at about two-thirds of their wartime peak.

One reason for the ratchet appears clearly in Figure 3.5, which shows where the revenue went. The reason was debt service. Under the impact of borrowing for war, Britain's national debt became permanent, and known to be permanent, toward the end of the seventeenth century; following the Dutch example, Britain moved to a substantial but fully funded public debt (Dickson 1967; 't Hart 1991). Nevertheless, interest on the debt remained a relatively small part of the budget for the following century. Military spending dominated the budget until the end of the Napoleonic Wars; surges of government expenditure faithfully trace the military buildups of 1756–63, 1776–1785, and 1793–1815. But over time the borrowing done to fill the gap between current revenues and military demands added enormously to the national debt, and therefore to interest on loans as a share of the current national budget. After 1770 or so, as a consequence, Britain's financial crises—occasions on which the market for securities suffered severe losses—became more frequent and general (Hoppit 1986). Nevertheless, as compared with the French enemy, the British state borrowed easily in wartime, and was able to suspend the pound's convertibility between 1797 and 1821 without drying up its credit; its previous record of peacetime balanced budgets and of debt retirement served the state well (Bordo and White 1990).

Total debt rose to the cadence of war, as shown in Table 3.3. Clearly, the burden of debt continued long past the peace treaties of 1815. That shift made the state much more beholden to the capitalists who had lent the money than had ever been true before the great wars. The rising level of taxation, furthermore, generated business for bankers, who held the receipts temporarily and issued bank notes or drafts for the transmission of tax payments (Chester 1981).

The graph shows another important side effect of the wars: a significant expansion of civil government as a continuing claim on the national budget. During the later eighteenth century, British government grew chiefly by means of expansion at the level of the parish or the county: Poor Law commissioners took on larger burdens, county magistrates at quarter or petty sessions intervened in parish affairs, and other *ad hoc* administrative arrangements proliferated, while Parliament and the central government generally restricted themselves to authorization and tutelage. Local powerholders drew their incomes from rents (and, in the case of clergy, tithes) rather than taxes; so long as the state taxed them lightly, protected their property, and supported their domination of the

Table 3.3. Total debt of Great Britain/United Kingdom, 1750–1841

Year	Debt	% change per year since previous date
1750	£78 million	
1760	£102 million	+2.7
1770	£131 million	+2.5
1780	£167 million	+2.5
1790	£244 million	+3.9
1801	£456 million	+5.8
1811	£610 million	+2.9
1821	£838 million	+3.2
1831	£786 million	−0.6
1841	£790 million	+0.1

Source: Mitchell and Deane 1971: 401–402.

local population, they could easily afford to volunteer their services. With the French wars of the 1790s and 1800s, however, the central apparatus itself expanded.

The government's nominal staff did not grow very fast, but its activity and expenditure did. In 1797 about 18,000 public officers worked for the national government. Of them, almost 13,000 labored in Customs or Excise; next in order came the Post Office, with 957 employees, and the Stamp Office, with 521. Over 90 percent of all the state's civilian public servants belonged to the fiscal agencies of the crown (Chester 1981: 166–167; the term "civil service" did not come into use until the 1850s; up to then the term "public service" included both military and civilian officers of government).

During the following decades, nonmilitary public service grew more slowly than the population as a whole, rising to a peak of 24,600 in 1815 and then receding to 22,400 in 1829. However, the radical reduction of sinecures (which had been numerous in 1797) meant that the effective workforce increased much more rapidly. The shift from fees to salaries, furthermore, led to a significant increase in the civilian public service budget. Great Britain created a permanent national bureaucracy between 1780 and 1840 (Cohen 1965).

In the process, the weight of government shifted away from the king and his protégés toward Parliament and the administration (Chester 1981). In England, as in other European states, patronage had long cemented the connections between the crown and its ruling class. After the seventeenth-century Civil War annihilated the patronage structure— or at least the access of its beneficiaries to offices of state—the construction of a ruling Whig coalition restored it grandly. By the middle of the eighteenth century, placemen were everywhere; in 1761, 260 royal clients sat in the House of Commons (Brewer 1976). Patronage, John Brewer reminds us, "was the bedrock of politics, and the foundation stone of political stability." During the next decade, the foundation stone began to crack.

American resistance to British efforts at raising revenue after the large expenditures of the Seven Years War helped open the fissure in British politics. The American theme of "no taxation without representation" resonated in Great Britain, where the vast majority of the population paid taxes but had no direct spokesmen (much less spokeswomen) in Parliament. The emergence of coalitions between radicals outside Parliament and reformers within, aided by the development of an active radical press and the rise of such talented polemicists as John Wilkes, fortified the attack on royal clients, and raised the call for parliamentary reform.

The years of war with France played a critical part in the shift. The drive for revenues simultaneously augmented the importance of Parliament as a granter of funds and put pressure on successive ministries to build a more effective fiscal organization; it also forced ministers to report more fully on how they used governmental revenues. William Pitt the Younger did a significant part of the work. He came to power at the end of the American war, confronted the debt accumulated during forty years of intermittent warfare, and oversaw the enormous increase in taxation occasioned by the new war with revolutionary France.

Becoming prime minister in 1783 at the ripe age of twenty-four, Pitt eventually undertook a major reform of the national administration. He not only reorganized government offices but insistently eliminated sinecures held by clients of great magnates. "Lord Liverpool, the next long-serving Prime Minister," notes Eric Evans, "was to remark that Pitt had all but destroyed the patronage network, and in consequence had put government on an entirely different footing. Most important of all, royal patronage was no longer sufficient either to elevate or to sustain a minister not already powerfully supported in Parliament" (Evans 1983: 26–27). Thus Pitt assisted a twofold process that preceded, succeeded, and surpassed him: an enlargement of the state apparatus to meet the expensive demands of war, and a tipping of the balance of governmental power toward Parliament.

Pitt did not work alone. Nor did he eliminate all sinecures or patronage. Through the early decades of the nineteenth century, radicals such as John Wade and William Cobbett pounded away at Old Corruption—the world of placemen and patricians growing rich at the public trough. Not until the Reform Act of 1832 did rich posts and emoluments awarded through personal connections largely disappear from national government (Rubinstein 1983). There, too, Parliament gained the advantage over the king and his connection.

A strong chain connected the expansion of British warmaking, the hurried rise in taxation, the growth of central governmental staff, and the increasing power of Parliament. "The emergence of a peculiarly British version of the fiscal-military state," concludes John Brewer,

> complete with large armies and navies, industrious administrators, high taxes and huge debts, was not the inevitable result of the nation's entry into European war but the unintended consequence of the political crisis which racked the British state after the Glorious Revolution of 1688. Though not inevitable, these changes in government were enduring. The overweening power of the Treasury, a highly centralized financial system, a standing Parliament, heavy taxation, an administrative class of gifted amateurs lacking training in the science of government but with a strong sense of public duty, government deficits and a thriving market in public securities: all these features of modern British politics began under the later Stuarts and Hanoverians. (Brewer 1989: 250)

These profound processes accelerated with the eighteenth century's multiple—and increasingly costly—wars. By the end of the Napoleonic Wars, Britain had a new state, the state dominated a far wider range of social life, and both politicians and ordinary citizens played for decisively new stakes. Their bargaining advanced popular sovereignty, in the sense of deriving the right to rule from the broad consent of the governed. It helped create citizenship, in the sense of rights to demand the state's protection based on simple membership in the large category of recognized natives plus naturalized foreigners. It created a modicum of democracy, in the sense of citizens' rights to check the arbitrary use of state power. It promoted nationalism, in the double sense of collective identification with the state and of ceding priority to the state's requirements over those of families, churches, communities, and other long-established institutions. It even promoted the sovereign's popularity: as George III lost practical power, he became an object of folk devotion (Colley 1984).

As Parliament gained power, however, the demands of those excluded from Parliament became more insistent. Into the 1820s gentry and nobility dominated Parliament. Yet from the 1770s onward they did so in the face of calls for reform of Parliament—which meant, among other things, reallocation of representation so that it corresponded more closely to population and, especially, property. Since a rising share of Britain's property consisted of urban land and capital, reform implied a greater voice for the British bourgeoisie. The voice gained strength from the late eighteenth century onward, and gained a major place on the stage with the Reform Act of 1832. The partial accession of the bourgeoisie to state power once again enlarged the scope of the state. But it left skilled workers both organized and excluded from political power—an invitation to widespread, vigorous collective action.

Repression in Britain

Despite the brawling of pubs and elections, repeated struggles over hunting and smuggling, and the expansion of military forces during the eighteenth century, Britain's landlords, clergy, and officials had for centuries collaborated quite effectively in disarming the common people. At least in England, the state and its close allies could have charmed Max Weber with their near-monopoly of violent means. Even hunting early became a rich man's privilege in Britain: from 1430 onward only freeholders with landed incomes of at least 40s. per annum had the right to hunt, while from 1603 the threshold rose to £10; from the Game Act of 1671 to the Game Reform Act of 1831 landed gentry exercised a legal monopoly of hunting for game; the 1831 law chiefly extended hunting privileges to smaller landlords, while continuing to prohibit game hunting by landless people. Ordinary people's hunting, in short, became criminal during the seventeenth century, and remained that way into the nineteenth.

Although their fifteenth-century forebears had often traveled and fought armed, by the eighteenth century few ordinary Britons owned lethal weapons, and fewer used them. The long disarming of the citizenry helps account for the decline of violent deaths in Britain, the political debates over the creation of militias and yeomanries, the rarity of armed insurrection, the resort of aggrieved laborers to mass begging, machine-breaking, cattle-maiming, or arson rather than direct attacks on farmers, landlords, and vicars, the resistance to new police forces (especially if armed), and the fact that most people killed in collective violence were unarmed civilians, while most killers were armed agents of the state (Archer 1990; Babington 1990; Carter 1980; Cockburn 1991; Emsley 1983a; Hair 1971; Hay et al. 1975; Hayter 1978; Palmer 1988; Philips 1980, 1989; Radzinowicz 1968; Stone 1947, 1983; Storch 1976).

After 1750 an enlarging state acquired even greater repressive powers. (*Repression* includes all efforts by authorities that increase the cost of collective action to the actors; it pairs with *facilitation,* the reduction of collective-action costs.) During the eighteenth century little of the repressive apparatus lay directly in the hands of the national state. Through most of Great Britain the chief professional law-enforcement officers at hand were gamekeepers, who worked for landlords, not governments. Gamekeepers enforced class law; under the game laws in force from 1671 to 1831,

> no one could legally hunt hares, partridges, pheasants or grouse unless he possessed either a freehold worth 100 pounds a year, a leasehold worth 150 pounds a year or was the heir apparent of an esquire or person "of higher degree." Those who did not meet this property qualification were forbidden not only to hunt but also to possess sporting dogs, guns, nets, snares or any other "engine" which could be used to make [*sic*] game. Even the possession of game by "unqualified" persons was prohibited. (Munsche 1981a: 82–83; see also Munsche 1981b; Thompson 1975)

Gamekeepers, sheriffs, aldermen, magistrates, local constables, and volunteer forces policed collective action with little interference from national authorities; only rarely did the army or the militia intervene. (When they did, however, it was often on a large scale: troops killed or fatally wounded 285 people in 1780's Gordon Riots, and 12,000 troops occupied the region between Leicester and York during the Luddite actions of 1811 and 1812: Rudé 1978). Organized public force spread thinly across the land.

That force did not increase greatly from the 1750s to the 1820s. During the wars with revolutionary and Napoleonic France, however, units of yeomanry—mounted volunteer forces recruited especially from small farmers, and frequently led by gentry—began to form and to play an active role in the control of crowds. During the first three decades of the nineteenth century, especially during the Napoleonic Wars, magistrates often called out the yeomanry to back up their constables; when it came to repressing workers and the poor, yeomen had a deserved reputation for greater reliability than the more plebeian militia. When yeomen were not available, nineteenth-century magistrates often resorted to the swearing in of special constables, whose dependability varied greatly with the objects of repression and the class composition of the local community.

Ireland served as a proving ground for Great Britain's police. Three Irish Chief Secretaries introduced major reforms of the Irish police: The Duke of Wellington's Dublin police in 1808, Robert Peel's Peace Preservation Police (soon to be known, not always affectionately, as Bobbies or Peelers) in 1814, and Henry Goulborn's Irish Constabulary in 1822; they set the model for a regular, permanent, centrally disciplined force. By 1828 Irish constables were wearing a standard military-style uniform. Shaped by Irish experience, Home Secretary Peel was plotting a London police force by 1822 (Palmer 1988). The policing of Ireland and Peel's formation of a uniformed London police force in 1829 started a new era in the patrolling of public space. They marked major steps in the creation of regular, professional, bureaucratized police forces coordinated by the state and distinct from its citizenry. From that point on, despite recurrent resistance from its citizenry to police control, Britain's national state vigorously expanded its repressive powers. The expansion went far beyond policing; it included the creation of the first salaried magistrates, the removal of barriers to prosecution, and a shift from capital punishment to various forms of incarceration.

The actual use of repressive force varied as a function of two kinds of threat to state power: pressure of war outside, pressure from domestic challengers inside. Repression also increased when the clients and supporters of the government—especially landlords and capitalists—felt threatened by the multiplication of those proletarians they regarded as the idle poor. In terms of legislation, the repressive landmarks of 1750 to 1840 included the multiple controls enacted against "sedition" during the French revolutionary wars, and the coercive acts against the mobilizations of 1817 to 1820; Appendix 2 provides a chronology of repressive legislation. Not all legislation moved in the direction of greater repression. During the 1820s, for example, Parliament began to dismantle some of the repressive apparatus constructed during the previous wars; the repeal of the Combination Acts in 1824 gave a considerable spur to the formation of working-class associations. Still, the overall effect of these parliamentary actions was to increase the involvement of the national state in the surveillance and control of organization and collective action.

Statute and practice remained far from identical, but they ran in the same general direction. Eighteenth-century English criminal prosecutions depended heavily on the victim's initiative; if the victim could not find the perpetrator of the crime or the goods (if any) that the culprit had taken, he or she had no effective recourse in law. The posting of private rewards for the apprehension of criminals and the recovery of stolen property provided a partial answer for those who had the means of paying rewards. Between the 1690s and the 1830s public authorities frequently offered bounties (including the criminal's "horse, furniture, arms and money") for apprehension of highwaymen and footpads; sometimes the reward included a "Tyburn Ticket" exempting the informer from public duties in the jurisdiction within which the felony occurred (Leslie-Melville 1934). The abolition of statutory rewards in 1818 did not eliminate courts' and public officials' offering of rewards in cases they regarded as heinous.

The indigent, to be sure, had little public recourse for crimes that fell short of felony. During the later eighteenth century, however, private thief-taking associations, increased public offering of rewards, and the frequent enactment of criminal statutes offering fees or shares of fines to those who helped secure a conviction all expanded the scope of search, apprehension, and prosecution. Professional thief-catchers and inform-ers—some of whom specialized in entrapping petty criminals into the commission of felonies—came into their own (Hay and Snyder 1989). Nor, according to the 1817 parliamentary inquiry into the system, did they always escape the temptation of perjury to win a rewarded conviction (Radzinowicz 1968).

At the same time, the pattern of judicial punishment changed sig-nificantly. Up to the early eighteenth century British courts had few choices of punishment other than execution, whipping, or public humili-ation. Courts often sentenced criminals to death, only to see them re-prieved before execution. Conversely, faced with the choice of killing or acquitting for relatively minor offenses, courts often let offenders go, or accepted their claim of benefit of clergy, which by then protected the lives of the literate in general as well as those actually in religious orders. A convicted felon given benefit of clergy escaped with a branded thumb.

Then Parliament and the courts began to shift. As the British popula-tion proletarianized, urbanized, and increased its stock of mobile wealth, and as the wealthy tightened their hold on property, theft, poaching, and other property crimes became more frequent. Parliament, ever mindful of its own stake in property, multiplied the number of property offenses subject to the death sentence. At the same time, Parliament began to reduce the scope of benefit of clergy, and to legitimate long-term incarceration and transportation to the colonies. The law became more sweeping and increasingly punitive.

The courts, for their part, imposed the death penalty less often, but had those condemned executed more often. They shifted from exemplary punishment—singling out one or two victims as dramatic examples, and freeing or failing to pursue the rest—toward prosecution of all offenders. They also began incarcerating as never before. In Surrey, where John Beattie has assembled the finest evidence so far, imprisonment and transportation rose rapidly from 1710, became the primary forms of punishment by the 1740s, and increased to more than 90 percent of all punishments by 1800 (Beattie 1986).

Similar trends affected the repression of collective action. During much of the eighteenth century, and before, British authorities responded to collective action of which they did not approve by means of brutal exemplary punishment: they typically hanged, whipped, or pilloried a few ringleaders, then let the rest go free. As the century wore on, however, they turned increasingly to transportation and imprisonment. Those expedients became even more popular among magistrates during the heightened repression that occurred after the outbreak of wars with Revolutionary France. By the time of the Tolpuddle Martyrs, exile and incarceration had become the standard means of dealing with bumptious claimants.

The histories of repression and of collective action overlapped. In eighteenth-century Britain authorities commonly tolerated or even encouraged the participation of ordinary people in the punishment of offenders. Executions attracted great crowds, sometimes—when the victim had a following or the executioner botched his job—at the expense of public order. In Bradford criminals "were flogged at cart tail . . . A pillory was set up at the bottom of Westgate where the market was held . . . people were allowed to throw eggs or potatoes but not stones." Outside the authorities' sponsorship, "'Riding the stang,' a local variant of rough music, was a common practice in many villages, providing a means of regulating unorthodox behavior and of keeping sexual transgressors at bay" (Koditschek 1990: 55). Workers applied similar sanctions to their fellows who violated collective decisions by continuing to produce during work stoppages, took employment without the trade's sanction, or worked for too low a wage. Thus a continuum ran from solemn official retaliation to the shaming and roughing up of popular justice. The growth of incarceration or transportation and the imposition of constabularies broke the continuum, separated the populace from official punishment, and helped suppress the collective exercise of informal justice.

Repression and collective action not only overlapped but also shaped each other. Claim-makers, objects of their claims, and authorities interacted strategically, seeking to bend the others to their own aims. If magistrates employed special constables and yeomanry to suppress the vast meetings and marches in support of parliamentary reform that proliferated after 1815, for example, radicals and reformers tried to discourage their neighbors from serving in the forces of repression. They also created Hampden Clubs and political unions to establish a modicum of legality for reform-seeking activity. Magistrates in turn looked for ways to declare such associations or their meetings seditious. So the cycle of parry and thrust continued.

Popular Participation in National Politics

Writing in the 1770s, Adam Smith's disciple John Millar thought that the consequence of proletarianization (a term he certainly did not use!) would be to promote democratic politics. As the old style of landlord, with his train of dependents, gave way to the "frugal and industrious merchant," wage-workers would likewise acquire freedom of action:

> It cannot be doubted that these circumstances have a tendency to introduce a democratical government. As persons of inferior rank are placed in a situation which, in point of subsistence, renders them little dependent upon their superiors; as no one order of men continues in the exclusive possession of opulence; and as every man who is industrious may entertain the hope of gaining a fortune; it is to be expected that the prerogatives of the monarch and of the ancient nobility will be gradually undermined, that the privileges of the people will be extended in the same proportion, and that power, the usual attendant, will be in some measure diffused over all the members of the community. (Lehmann 1960: 292)

Millar wrote from Glasgow, where it was no doubt easier in the 1770s to imagine a democratical future than was the case in London. Yet his prognostication contained a kernel of truth for Great Britain as a whole. It took a long time and plenty of struggle, but eventually the spread of wage-labor and the expansion of entrepreneurship reduced the share of the population living directly under the control of aristocrats, gentry, and even their farmers. It promoted a demand for independent political participation.

Indeed, the very means by which the British aristocracy and gentry had consolidated their rule—tightened control over a Parliament whose powers were expanding—generated demands and opportunities for mobilization against oligarchy and for popular power. Eighteenth-century Britain stood out from any other European power in maintaining an electoral system linking every county, and many boroughs within the counties, directly to national centers of decisionmaking. Despite the overwhelmingly aristocratic composition of Parliament itself, parliamentary elections (especially when contested) brought national issues to a local scale and provided opportunities for taking local issues to a national scale. The implication of the Hanoverian ruling classes in an electoral system, as Frank O'Gorman remarks, "involved them in a permanent commitment to Parliament, and thus to parliamentary and representative forms and processes" (1989: 17).

Parliamentary elections took place in two arenas; although they certainly attached successful candidates to national politics, they also sustained, undermined, or established the candidates' positions in local webs of influence and prestige. For that reason, non-electors gained leverage to the extent that competition among candidates occurred. Binding elections to a lawmaking assembly provided opportunities and incentives for non-electors to place pressure on electors, hence for dissident candidates and lawmakers to form alliances with dissident non-electors. To the extent that non-electors acquired power, wealth, and independence outside of the electoral sphere, furthermore, the discrepancy between their political rights and those of the enfranchised became more obvious and galling. The long exclusion from voting and public office of Protestant Dissenters (partial) and Roman Catholics (virtually complete), for example, gave radical MPs grounds for collaboration with a substantial body of non-electors. Great Britain's economic growth and proletarianization therefore increased the stakes of popular politics.

Within the limits set by governmental repression, popular politics expanded in scope. Before the final passage of the Reform Act, public

politics underwent profound changes in Britain. Direct popular participation in national political life broadened and deepened. During the
eighteenth century, broadly speaking, popular politics proceeded on the
basis of the following assumptions:

1. that citizens grouped into legally recognized bodies, such as guilds,
   communities, and religious sects, which exercised collective rights;
2. that the law protected such collective rights;
3. that local authorities had an obligation to enforce and respect the law;
4. that the chosen representatives of such recognized bodies had the right
   and obligation to make public presentations of their demands and
   grievances;
5. that authorities had an obligation to consider those demands and
   grievances, and to act on them when they were just;
6. that outside this framework, no one who had not been convoked by
   established authorities had a clear right to assemble, to state demands
   or grievances, or to act collectively.

As our preliminary examination of contentious repertoires has already
indicated, these implicit principles defined a system of *parochial, particular,* and *bifurcated* popular politics—parochial because ordinary people
had the right to act within localized limits; particular because the forms
of action varied greatly according to issue, group, and locality; bifurcated
because they acted directly at home but ordinarily sought redress or favor
on a national scale through powerful intermediaries. Legal and illegal
claim-making shared these characteristics.

Over the nine decades after 1750 the principles gave way to another
system we might call *cosmopolitan, modular,* and *autonomous.* Groups of
ordinary people came to participate directly in national struggles for
power, and to do so on their own account. On the way, the British people
spread the use of the deliberately organized special-purpose association
as a political instrument. The idea and the fact of mass mobilization
around a national program took shape. As political actors, national
extraparliamentary associations and webs of associations were unknown
in 1750, novel in 1780, commonplace in 1830. Their rise accompanied
proposals for a national convention to legislate on behalf of all the people,
efforts of political entrepreneurs to formulate and popularize national
programs, the use of mass assemblies and marches to demonstrate popu-

lar determination, and doctrines of popular sovereignty (Parssinen 1973). Again, both legal and illegal contention moved in the same direction.

The change occurred in irregular surges: critics of government policy during the American troubles, including John Wilkes, adopted the popular association but used it only intermittently; Lord George Gordon molded his anti-Catholic followers into a temporarily effective Protestant Association in 1780; London's radicals built extensive associations with relatively small followings during the French wars; in 1816 and 1817 Henry Hunt launched a campaign of "cumulative, constitutionally sanctioned protest, open to all, for a programme demanding the constitutionally decreed rights of all" (Belchem 1985: 22); during the following decade, Daniel O'Connell's Catholic Association provided the base for a national—indeed, international—set of demands; by the time Political Unions and similar organizations waged the fight for reform between 1830 and 1832, national and autonomous popular politics had become Britain's regular style.

In this regard, as in so many others, the period of the French Revolution and Empire was pivotal: an increasingly powerful and demanding state called forth a new form of politics. In the same process, contested elections became more common (Phillips 1982). Citizens who lacked the right to vote followed elections, and participated in the campaigning, more and more actively. The rudiments of a two-party system came into being (O'Gorman 1989). Merchants, entrepreneurs, financiers, and members of established trades pressed their claims on the state more and more openly, more and more directly. Voluntary associations, especially among the middle classes, formed to promote self-help, recreation, education, moral reform, and political action alike (Morris 1983, 1990). Pubs and coffeehouses became increasingly important gathering places, and bases for special-interest associations; for example, "box clubs" bringing together members of a particular trade met regularly in pubs, with the innkeepers holding their funds and papers in locked boxes dedicated to them. Labor unions emerged from the informal trade networks that already prevailed during the eighteenth century. Newspapers carried more and more information about the doings of government, Parliament, and powerholders. Within Parliament, private bills on behalf of local constituents first multiplied, then gave way to a proliferation of public bills. Issues of national action—rights of religious minorities, parliamentary reform, slavery, taxes, and so on—came to preoccupy public discussion. In short, associationally based popular politics took shape on a national scale. As all this happened, ordinary Britons came to identify with the national state as never before (Colley 1986, 1992). Bourgeois and skilled workers led the way, but other workers—even agricultural workers, in the long run—followed the same path.

Social Movements and Democracy

Britain's surges of collective activity represented the birth of what we now call the social movement—the sustained, organized challenge to existing authorities in the name of a deprived, excluded, or wronged population. In most cases, the appearance of a social movement incited the formation of counter-movements by those whose interests the movement threatened; thus supporters of the Church of England rallied against Catholic Emancipation, using many of the emancipators' tactics. In the 1820s and 1830s the struggles around Catholic Emancipation, Test and Corporation Acts, the abolition of slavery, the New Poor Law, and, preeminently, parliamentary reform all took shape as social movements and counter-movements.

Most analysts of social movements have confused the historical process in two ways (for critical reviews, see Tarrow 1994; Tilly 1993c). First, they have treated social movements as suprahistorical phenomena appearing in all sorts of social settings, rather than recognizing them as specific historical creations. On a national scale, sustained challenges to authorities in the name of aggrieved categories of citizens have actually been quite rare. Before the late eighteenth century one might identify the Peasants' Revolt, the Pilgrimage of Grace, the seventeenth-century revolutions, and a few other episodes as social movements, but the social movement never became a routine way of doing political business in Great Britain. From the 1790s onward we can see a remarkable expansion and regularization of the national social movement not only in Great Britain but elsewhere in the West.

Second, analysts have imagined that a movement was a *group*—abolitionists, prohibitionists, and so on. In fact, social movements resemble electoral campaigns and wars in being interactions—not between parties or armies but between activists and authorities. As veteran participants in social movements know all too well, coalitions, group memberships, and identities fluctuate, the organization of participants changes rapidly, and tactics alter with the political situation, but the challenge often outlives any particular challenger. Organizers of social movements deliberately compound confusion on this score, for the self-designated leaders of excluded populations have a strong interest in presenting those populations as coherent, unified, and mobilized, as forces to be reckoned with. Notice how much of organizers' efforts go into preparing for a campaign, a demonstration, or a public statement by negotiating agreement among factions and coalition partners whose priorities differ, seeking to get the maximum number of people and groups committed to a common set of complaints or demands, and trying to assure that participants in the joint action will not challenge the illusion of unity in public. Much is at stake: a successful social movement gains some sort of recognition not only for an aggrieved population and its grievances but also for its presumed leadership.

Zald and McCarthy (1979, 1988) usefully distinguish between a social movement as such and a social-movement *organization* (SMO) such as the Birmingham Political Union or the Grand National Consolidated Trades Union. The social movement consists of a series of challenges in the name of an aggrieved population, while the SMO almost never includes the whole of the population in question and sometimes (as in the case of Abolitionism) includes no members of it. SMOs serve, however, as crucial vehicles for social movements just as parties serve as vehicles for electoral campaigns. In the period we are examining, demands for abolition of slavery, for parliamentary reform, for removal of religious disabilities began to take the form of national social movements. In those movements and the counter-movements they inspired, crucial SMOs included the London Abolition Society, the London Corresponding Society, the Catholic Association, and the anti-Catholic Brunswick Clubs.

The tie to electoral campaigns surpasses analogy. Social movements parallel and feed on electoral politics, precisely because they signal the presence of mass support—and even of potential votes—for programs that lack strong voices in existing legislatures. In the West as a whole the national social movement became a significant element of popular politics as participation widened, whether through expansion of the suffrage or through popular pressure on those who had the vote. In Great Britain the flourishing of extraparliamentary (or, better, paraparliamentary) politics followed just such a course; calls for a mass platform, a national convention, or even a people's charter conveyed the idea that the existing representative process excluded people who had a right to be heard (Beer 1957; Belchem 1978, 1981, 1985; Bradley 1986; Brewer 1976, 1979–80, 1980; Dinwiddy 1990; Epstein 1990; Kramnick 1990; Lottes 1979; Morgan 1988; Parssinen 1973). One can make a reasonable case that British political entrepreneurs from John Wilkes to Francis Place *invented* the national social movement as a standard way of making claims; they coordinated marches, meetings, petitions, slogans, publications, and special-purpose associations into nationwide challenges to the existing distribution or use of state power (Tilly 1982a). British popular politics thus provided a new model for the citizens of other western states.

Indeed, Britain made significant steps toward democracy. Democracy remains a much-contested term, torn between ideal conceptions of equality or justice and specific institutional arrangements such as binding popular elections. Nevertheless, prevailing definitions of democracy pivot on the relations between states and citizens: categories of the population sharing publicly defined rights and obligations with regard to the state. In these terms, democracy involves only a few elements: broad, relatively equal standards of citizenship coupled with binding consultation of citizens in regard to state personnel and policy, as well as protection of citizens (especially members of minorities) from arbitrary state action. By these criteria Great Britain of 1750 fell far short of democracy: although by comparison with most other European states Britain offered its citizens substantial protections, national citizenship remained narrow and unequal, while a very small electorate enjoyed the privilege of binding consultation, even that excluding a considerable range of state policy and personnel. The theory of virtual representation, indeed, justified these very restrictions on democracy. Parochial, particular, bifurcated popular claim-making directly reflected the undemocratic state of affairs. In this context, the claims to popular sovereignty that revived during the American Revolution constituted a revolutionary challenge.

The rise of a cosmopolitan, modular, autonomous repertoire of popular claim-making resulted from and promoted a considerable increase in democracy. Between the 1750s and the 1830s Great Britain allowed modest increases in protections of citizens (notably in the realms of assembly and association), broadened and equalized its definition of citizenship somewhat (notably in the 1832 reform but also in the partial incorporation of Ireland into a United Kingdom), and took important steps toward binding consultation through the strengthening of parties, the growth of ministerial responsibility, the rising power of Parliament, and the expansion of popular participation in elections. Such struggles as those of John Wilkes (1760s), county reform associations (1780s), revolutionary radicals (1790s), workers' associations (1810s and 1820s), Catholic Emancipation (1820s), and parliamentary reform (1780s and thereafter) contributed in various, sometimes contradictory, ways to the construction of democracy. Unlike states moving toward democracy from despotism or populist autocracy, Great Britain's earlier investing of a narrowly and unequally defined citizenry with substantial protections and some binding rights of consultation meant that each expansion or equalization of citizenship accelerated democratization in these regards as well. Although Great Britain of 1834 remained undemocratic by twentieth-century standards, it had made significant strides toward democracy in the previous three-quarters of a century.

How did the great changes happen? Britain's military expansion increased the importance of taxation, which in turn enhanced Parliament's power vis-à-vis both local authorities and the crown. That great shift made parliamentary elections more salient not only for legal electors but also for clienteles (actual or potential) of MPs. With MPs collaborating and contesting, the greater salience of elections made them more important and legitimate occasions for the collective display of political preferences by ordinary people, just as they justified the increasing use of associations and public meetings to address popular grievances or demands to individual MPs or to Parliament.

Political entrepreneurs such as John Wilkes, George Gordon, Francis Place, and John Doherty introduced a whole stream of tactical innovations in meeting, petitioning, marching, and publishing that sometimes succeeded, and then tended to survive for others to employ. They took advantage of established rights and institutions such as local deliberative assemblies, parliamentary elections, and petitions to create new political forms. A proliferating press, profiting from rising national income, increasing literacy, intensifying communications by road and water, and eventually the extension of partisan struggles for control of Parliament and governmental policy, facilitated nationalization of politics. State authorities repressed when they could—especially during the intense years of wars with France—but also made tactical concessions that likewise opened up space for new actors or actions, for example in the grudging legal acceptance of John Wilkes's right to criticize royal policy. Powerholders, notably MPs of radical persuasion, sometimes aligned themselves strongly with popular movements, thereby making governmental repression more difficult. The net effect was an unsteady but finally momentous shift toward public meetings, demonstrations, petitions, social movements, and related forms of interaction. It finally amounted to the creation of mass national politics.

To be sure, all these trends varied greatly from place to place. The nationalization of popular politics went farther and faster in Manchester than in Welsh villages, while Kent's agricultural laborers experienced proletarianization more intensely than did those of Devon. London and its hinterland served as the cockpit of Britain's social change, but the growth of large-scale industry marked the London region's landscape less vividly than that of Lancashire. In later chapters I will trace out regional variations in detail and will also take up the implications of social change and variation for popular collective action.

In the meantime, let us recall how profoundly Great Britain changed during the nine decades from 1750 to 1840. During that time, we have seen, Great Britain underwent massive population growth, in the course of which its proletariat greatly expanded. The concentration of land and of capital accelerated the proletariat's growth in agriculture and manufacturing. The country urbanized energetically and created major regions of capital-concentrated manufacturing. Capital accumulated and concentrated as inequality sharpened. A national ruling class of increasingly capitalistic and prosperous landlords retained its hold on the state apparatus while conceding new influence to merchants and manufacturers. All of these changes generated new struggles and new popular claims.

On the side of the state, warfare on the continent, in America, and in distant regions of conquest remained the dominant activity. Even more than its predecessors, the war Great Britain waged intermittently against France from 1793 to 1815 reshaped political and social life. Britain saw its armies and empire multiply, and the mass and power of its central state inflate. War brought prosperity and power to landlords, who took advantage of their situation to accelerate enclosures and proletarianization in agriculture. As this set of changes initiated and interacted with popular struggle, everyday politics shifted from relatively parochial, particular, and bifurcated toward relatively cosmopolitan, modular, and autonomous. Thus a new Britain of associations, social movements, and national class struggles took shape. The form and content of popular contention changed correspondingly.

Is this story coherent and true? Only a close examination of changes in contention and its context between the 1750s and 1830s will tell. That is exactly the business of the chapters to come.

WILKES, GORDON, AND POPULAR VENGEANCE, 1758–1788

STARTING IN 1764, Benjamin Franklin served as Pennsylvania's agent in London. He stood vigorously for the American colonies' rights; in 1765, for example, he lobbied energetically for repeal of the Stamp Act, the fiscal measure that sparked such concerted opposition to British rule in America. For a future revolutionary, he nevertheless took a remarkably disapproving line on popular contention. Writing in April 1768 of what we now regard as a great popular political mobilization, he declared to his son:

> Since my last . . . nothing has been talked or thought of here but elections. There have been amazing contests all over the kingdom, £20 or 30,000 of a side spent in several places, and inconceivable mischief done by debauching the people and making them idle, besides the immediate actual mischief done by drunken mad mobs to houses, windows, &c. The scenes have been horrible. London was illuminated two nights running at the command of the mob for the success of Wilkes in the Middlesex election; the second night exceeded anything of the kind ever seen here on the greatest occasions of rejoicing, as even the small cross streets, lanes, courts, and other out-of-the-way places were all in a blaze with lights, and the principal streets all night long, as the mobs went round again after two o'clock, and obliged people who had extinguished their candles to light them again. Those who refused had all their windows destroyed . . . Tis really an extraordinary event, to see an outlaw and exile, of bad personal character, not worth a farthing, come over from France, set himself up as a candidate for the capital of the kingdom,

miss his election only by being too late in his application, and immediately carrying it for the principal county. The mob (spirited up by
numbers of different ballads sung or roared in every street) requiring
gentlemen and ladies of all ranks as they passed in their carriages to
shout for Wilkes and liberty, marking the same words on all their coaches
and chalk, and No. 45 on every door, which extends a vast way along
the roads into the country. (Franklin 1972: 98–99)

The Wilkes in question was the ungainly gentleman, journalist, rake,
demagogue, and English patriot John Wilkes. Wilkes had entered Parliament for Aylesbury in 1757. In April 1763 issue 45 of Wilkes's paper, *The
North Briton*, printed veiled criticism of the king's speech at the close of
Parliament; the king's speech had praised the Treaty of Paris, settling the
Seven Years War. For that article, Wilkes spent a brief term in the Tower
of London, while the sheriff and the hangman tried to burn No. 45
publicly in Cheapside, only to be pelted by a crowd that rescued the
condemned paper. His judicial appearances during 1763 brought out
cheering throngs and launched the enduring slogan "Wilkes and Liberty."
Contemporaries saw him as a reembodiment of the seventeenth-century
Leveller John Lilburne, so much so that at a public dinner an admirer gave
him the 1710 edition of *The Tryal of Lieutenant Colonel John Lilburne*
(Donnelly 1988). In both Britain and North America the number 45—
embodied in forty-five candles, forty-five toasts, forty-five marching men,
or a coach bearing the number 45—became an instantly recognized
symbol of opposition to arbitrary rule.

George Grenville, George III's chief minister, took Wilkes seriously; in
1763 he planned to make Wilkes's expulsion from the Commons a matter
of parliamentary confidence (Thomas 1975). In 1764, Wilkes was in fact
expelled from the House of Commons, sentenced to jail, then declared
an outlaw. This time he had not only reprinted the infamous No. 45 but
also produced a pornographic parody of Pope's *Essay on Man* (entitled
Essay on Woman), then fled the country. His publisher Williams suffered—or enjoyed—the consequences. Wilkes's lawyer and close collaborator, Serjeant Glynn, argued in court that the jury, not the judge, had
the right to decide whether a publication constituted libel, therefore
whether Williams was guilty of libel. The presiding judge ruled otherwise,

and the jury convicted Williams (Brewer 1980: 156; courts did not concede juries the right to decide whether libel had actually occurred until the 1790s). On Thursday 14 February 1765,

> Mr. Williams, bookseller in *Fleet street,* stood on the pillory in *New Palace Yard, Westminster,* pursuant to his sentence . . . for re-publishing the *North Briton* No. 45 in volumes. The coach that carried him from the *King's Bench* prison to the pillory was No. 45. He was received by the acclamations of a prodigious concourse of people. Opposite to the pillory were erected four ladders, with cords running from each other, on which were hung a Jack Boot, an axe, and a *Scotch* bonnet. The latter, after remaining there some time, was burnt, and the top of the boot chopt off. During his standing also, a purple purse, ornamented with ribbonds of an orange colour, was produced by a gentleman, who began a collection in favor of the culprit, by putting a guinea into it himself, after which, the purse being carried round, many contributed, to the amount . . . of about 200 guineas. Mr. *Williams,* at going into the pillory, and getting out, bowed to the spectators. He held a sprig of laurel in his hand all the time. (GM February 1765: 96; see E. P. Thompson 1991: 276 for a broadside printed on that occasion)

Clearly, Wilkes's cause had popular appeal even in his absence; it inspired a symbol-drenched pageant of opposition to governmental tyranny. Both Scots and establishment Englishmen hated him. After spending four years in leisurely but increasingly debt-ridden exile on the continent, Wilkes slipped back into Britain early in 1768. He appealed unsuccessfully for a pardon, failed in a bid for one parliamentary seat, and then (in March of 1768) won election to a seat in Middlesex. Benjamin Franklin's letter to his son described the riotous Wilkite victory celebration of 29 March.

Wilkes's 1768 parliamentary campaign affronted the British establishment in its direct appeal to the electorate—an appeal by an obscenity-spouting outlaw, no less. (Marchers in an anti-Wilkes procession on 28 March, the first day of the Middlesex election, carried a banner lettered "No Blasphemer.") Thousands of silk weavers from Spitalfields, already famous for their readiness to act collectively, served as Wilkes's private police. Despite the narrowness of the eighteenth-century electorate, the entire campaign smacked of popular sovereignty. It challenged the principle of virtual representation. It threatened the power of authorities to place their allies and clients in Parliament and, by extension, in the government itself. The whiff of popular sovereignty did not please Benjamin Franklin either.

In describing the Wilkite celebrations, Franklin used authorities' language. The word was not "crowd," or "assembly," or "gathering," but *mob*—short for "the mobility" and *mobile vulgus*. Mobs are gatherings of dangerous people performing improper acts. Mobs make riots. Riots, in the language of authorities, are collective actions (whether violent or not) whose impropriety justifies the use of force to terminate them. In the eighteenth-century lexicon they lodged near *outrage* and *sedition*. The words are essentially political labels; they set a distance between observer and actors, mark a line between responsible and irresponsible means of pursuing interests, separate order from disorder. As such, the categories matter. They affect the way authorities behave. In the eighteenth-century setting their use deserves the closest study. But as categories for historical analysis, words such as mob, riot, outrage, and sedition obscure much of what went on.

Whatever we call it, the window-breaking Wilkite celebration had extended from the City over to the fine houses and public buildings of Westminster. Franklin himself lived in Craven Street, off the Strand. That put him by the river, only a stone's throw from Charing Cross, not far from Whitehall—between Parliament and St. James's on one side and the financial centers of the City on the other. It also placed him just off the primary path of frequent processions and marches. They commonly originated at Mansion House or some other symbolically charged location in the City and then proceeded, soberly or tumultuously, down the Strand toward Parliament or St. James's. Charing Cross served, in fact, as the pivot: south toward Parliament or west toward the royal palace. The Wilkites of 1768 broke windows at the Duke of Northumberland's, in Charing Cross, a few steps away from Franklin's house; they may well have rushed down Franklin's street as well.

Writing his friend John Ross in May 1768, Franklin fretted about Britain's public order. "I have urged over and over the Necessity of the Change we desire," he declared,

but this Country itself being at present in a Situation very little better, weakens our Argument that a Royal Government would be better managed and safer to live under than that of a Proprietary. Even this Capital, the Residence of the King, is now a daily Scene of lawless Riot and Confusion. Mobs are patrolling the Streets at Noon Day, some Knocking all down that will not roar for Wilkes and Liberty: Courts of Justice afraid to give Judgment against him: Coalheavers and Porters pulling down the Houses of Coal Merchants that refuse to give them more Wages; Sawyers destroying the new Sawmills; Sailors unrigging all the outward-bound Ships, and suffering none to sail till Merchants agree to raise their Pay; Watermen destroying private Boats and threatning Bridges; Weavers entring Houses by Force, and destroying the Work in the Looms; Soldiers firing among the Mobs and killing Men, Women and Children, which seems only to have produc'd an universal Sullenness, that looks like a great black Cloud coming on, ready to burst in a general Tempest. What the Event will be God only knows: But some Punishment seems preparing for a People who are ungratefully abusing the best Constitution and the best King any Nation was ever blest with, intent on nothing but Luxury, Licentiousness, Power, Places, Pensions and Plunder. (Franklin 1972: 129)

Thus the mobs of London, in Franklin's estimation, posed a serious threat to good government. The authorities agreed: during April they began calling troops into London to check "disorder."

Indeed, all the things Franklin's letter deplored had happened recently in London and vicinity. In April crowds had stopped carriages on behalf of Wilkes, workers had repeatedly attacked blacklegs and masters, and other struggles had burst out every week. If Franklin exaggerated the generality of violence and "universal Sullenness," then, he was not inventing the capital's turbulence. Some of the events, moreover, ended in death. During the boardings of 26 April a large body of coal heavers, according to *Gentleman's Magazine,* "assembled in a riotous manner in Wapping, went on board the colliers, and obliged the men who were at work to leave off; so that the business of delivering ships, in the river, is wholly at a stand . . . This riot was attended with much blood shed, the rioters having met with opposition fought desperately, and several lives were lost" (GM 1768: 197). A week later their leaders met with city officials and made a provisional settlement of the dispute. On the seventh of May "the sailors assembled in a body in St. George's fields, and went to St. James's, with colours flying, drums beating, and fifes playing, and presented a petition to his majesty, setting forth their grievances, and praying relief" (GM 1768: 262). On the ninth,

> a numerous body of watermen assembled before the mansion house, and laid their complaint before the lord mayor, who advised them, to appoint proper persons to draw up a petition to Parliament, which his lordship promised he would present; upon which they gave him three huzzas and went quietly home. The same night a large mob of another kind assembled before the mansion-house, carrying a gallows with a boot hanging to it, and a red cap; but on some of the ringleaders being secured by the peace-officers, the rest dispersed. (GM 1768: 242)

The boot on a gallows offered a punning threat to the king's favorite, Lord Bute; it often appeared in the company of a Scotch bonnet (a symbol of Bute's national origin) or a petticoat (a reference to the popular belief that he was the Princess Dowager's lover).

Political symbols traveled fast and far within the British world. In October 1765 the citizens of Charleston, South Carolina, greeted the arrival of stamped paper in their port:

> In the middle of Broad Street and Church Street, near Mr. Dillon's . . . appeared suspended on a gallows twenty feet high, an effigy, with a figure of the devil on its right hand, and on its left a boot, with a head stuck upon it distinguished by a blue bonnet, to each of which were affixed labels expressive of the sense of the people in their loyalty but tenacious of just liberty. They declared that all internal duties imposed upon them without the consent of their immediate or even virtual, representation, was grievous, oppressive, and unconstitutional, and that an extension of the powers and jurisdiction of admiralty courts in America tended to subvert one of their most darling legal rights, that of trial by juries. (*South Carolina Gazette*, 31 October 1765)

The theme of "no taxation without representation" played counterpoint to the melody of popular sovereignty. Similarly, the Liberty Tree that Bostonians saluted in their opposition to the Stamp Act in August 1765 bore both an effigy of the tax collector and a devil in a boot (Hoerder 1977). The colonial struggles issuing in the American Revolution adopted, to a large degree, the vocabulary, symbols, rituals, and forms of collective action that Benjamin Franklin witnessed in London (Couser et al. 1986; Hoerder 1977; Smith 1965; Walsh 1959; Young 1973).

For British contention of the 1760s, nevertheless, London became the font of innovation. In London the 1760s were, according to George Rudé's expert opinion, "the most remarkable decade of industrial disputes of the whole century," and 1768 was the peak year (Rudé 1971a: 191–192; see also Dobson 1980; Linebaugh 1992). On the day after the crowd at London's Mansion House erected its own gallows,

> A large body of sawyers assembled and pulled down the saw-mill lately erected by Mr. Dingley at Lymehouse, on pretence that it deprived many workmen of employment . . . The coal-heavers assembled again . . . this day and rendezvoused in Stepney-fields, where their numbers considerably increased, and then they repaired with a flag flying, drums beating, and two violins playing before them to Palace-yard, where they were met by Sir John Fielding, who persuaded them to part with their flag, to silence their drums, and to discharge their fidlers; and then talking with their leaders, prevailed upon them to meet some of their masters at his office in the afternoon, and accomodate their differences. (GM 1768: 242–243)

The same day, according to *Gentleman's Magazine,* "the mob which has constantly surrounded the King's Bench prison in St. George's-fields, ever since the imprisonment of Mr. Wilkes, grew outrageous; the riot act was read, and the soldiers ordered to fire. Several persons who were passing along the road at a distance were unfortunately killed; and one youth about 17, son to a stable-keeper in the Borough, was singled out, followed, and shot dead, in an outhouse where he had fled for shelter" (GM 1768: 242). Justice Samuel Gillam had read the Riot Act, whereupon members of the crowd had stoned him. When a "man in a red waistcoat" managed to hit his target, the Justice ordered guards to pursue the red waistcoat. Captain Murray and three grenadiers chased him, lost him, then cornered William Allen—who was neither the waistcoated man nor another stoner of Gillam—and shot him (Rudé 1962). In Wilkite legend, this confrontation and the guards' subsequent killing of five or six more people in the crowd that was stoning them came to be known as the Massacre of St. George's Fields. Wilkes's lawyers, ever alert for opportunities to use the law in publicizing official injustice, managed to have the magistrates in charge at St. George's Fields indicted for murder. Only a few days (and a few bloody altercations) later, Benjamin Franklin wrote his gloomy diagnosis of the capital's condition: infected with Wilkism, enfeebled by sedition.

The Wilkite fever was, indeed, still raging. At the end of April Wilkes had gone to jail, had been released temporarily, only to be sentenced to twenty-two months in prison. During the judicial maneuvering his supporters had thronged the streets, broken windows, and attended his every move. Even pragmatic Americans, Franklin regretted to observe, showed a culpable sympathy for the mob. As he wrote to William Franklin in October 1768, "Wilkes is extinguished. I am sorry to see in the American papers that some People there are so indiscreet as to distinguish themselves in applauding his No. 45, which I suppose they do not know was a Paper in which their King was personally affronted, whom I am sure they love and honour. It hurts you here with sober sensible Men, when they see you so easily infected with the Madness of English Mobs" (Franklin 1972: 224).

Wilkes was not so easily extinguished as that. When Franklin wrote to his son, Wilkes was comfortably ensconced in the King's Bench Prison, keeping congenial company, dining well, and biding his time. In 1769, while still in prison, he won election as a London alderman, found himself expelled from Parliament, then won four more elections to his Middlesex seat, only to face the Commons' refusal to seat him each time. On all these occasions and more, London crowds acted out their disapproval or celebrated their victories in the streets. The year was "one of the great landmarks in the history of extra-parliamentary activity" (Langford 1989: 386).

On 22 March 1769, for example, a large body of City merchants paraded through the streets to present a loyal anti-Radical address to the king; the address begged leave "to express our concern and abhorrence of every attempt to spread sedition, to inflame the minds, and alienate the affection of a free and loyal people from the best of kings, and his government; which we apprehend has of late been encouraged, without the least shadow of foundation, by some ill-designing persons, to answer sinister and selfish purposes" (AR 1769: 195). The unmistakable reference to John Wilkes came not long after Wilkes's third election and third rejection by Parliament. On that occasion, Wilkes's supporters pelted the merchants, attacked their carriages, and deterred three-quarters of them from reaching St. James's; a hearse that followed the merchants bore painted scenes of the shooting of William Allen at St. George's Fields and the attack on a Wilkes follower during the March 1768 Middlesex election (AR 1769; GM 1769).

Wilkes stayed in jail until April 1770; at his release, celebrations occurred throughout Britain and America. Wilkes had yet to become Sheriff in 1771, to be named Lord Mayor in 1774, and finally to reenter Parliament that same year. From those establishment positions, he continued to bombard king and Commons with protests and demands. No man of the people, he nevertheless challenged national authorities with an insolence that resonated at the same frequencies as popular resentments, forwarding the belief that authorities should answer to the populace.

Although Wilkes himself never preached popular sovereignty, indeed resisted diversion of the discussion from his own grievances, he became a symbol of ordinary people's rights to hold their rulers accountable. He went so far as to support, at least for a while, universal manhood suffrage. His outrageous behavior "endeared him to an increasingly politically aware public" (Brewer 1976: 164). His legal maneuvers permanently established the right of British periodicals to report and criticize the actions of Parliament, ministers, and crown (Hill 1985). Wilkes became a major British defender of American rights. Across the Atlantic, Americans treated him as an ally, a hero, and a symbol of liberty. On both sides of the ocean, "Wilkes and Liberty" became the rallying cry of opposition to royal policy.

With Wilkes, furthermore, the voluntary political association became a more prominent base for influence and collective action than it had ever been before. Not that Wilkes's band invented the extraparliamentary political association; at least twenty years earlier Tories, long exiled from political power, had urged their cause among electors by means of deliberately formed clubs; indeed old Tories who knew the technique well joined Wilkes's entourage (Colley 1981). The Wilkes movement, however, generalized the association's use, expanded its membership significantly beyond the electorate, and established it as a standard vehicle for collective action. In February 1769 Wilkes's defenders (notably the clergyman John Horne, later known as Horne Tooke) began meeting at the London Tavern as the Friends of Mr. Wilkes and the Constitution. Soon they organized themselves as the Society of Supporters of the Bill of Rights; the association's members included a number of MPs who had strong ties to the

City of London. It undertook to promote Wilkes's election, to defray his debts and electoral expenses, and to defend constitutional liberties (Goodwin 1979). In a contested innovation, it asked candidates whom it supported to pledge themselves in advance to work for its program.

The new association and its provincial counterparts launched petition after petition to king and Parliament. Both its example and its members influenced the next decade's campaign for parliamentary reform. Members of the Supporters of the Bill of Rights including Horne Tooke also played a significant part in the later London Corresponding Society, which became one of the most visible advocates of parliamentary reform during the French Revolution. An association of extraordinary people pushed for reforms that would advance the interests of ordinary people. They called boldly for annual Parliaments, equal representation, exclusion of placemen from the Commons, reduction of administrative abuses in Ireland, and attention to the grievances of American colonists.

Although Wilkes himself resisted the broadening and radicalization of the programs advocated in his name, his supporters in the Society and in the streets formed an implicit coalition of middle-class dissidents and working-class reformers. With no clear long-run design but great ingenuity and determination in the short run, they opened new paths through the British political system. ("The beginnings of the concerted movement for parliamentary reform," wrote A. S. Turberville (1943: 2) in some perplexity, "are commonly and with good reason traced back to the career of John Wilkes, and it is a singular fact that a man morally so worthless as he should have had so beneficent an influence upon our parliamentary development." The system itself, furthermore, was changing as a result of major transformations in Great Britain's economic organization and social life.

Such an opening cleared the way for more than one sort of claim. In 1780 and 1781 Christopher Wyvill's Yorkshire Association and its counterparts elsewhere in England claimed the right not only to exist but also to petition Parliament for the reduction of wasteful expenditure, and to represent men of property as a whole; in the very act of making demands on Parliament, they constituted a segment of an anti-Parliament (Beer 1957). In expanding his Protestant Association (1779), Lord George Gordon took advantage of the Wilkite precedent for a very different end, the renewed exclusion of Catholics from British public life.

Britain's victories over France in the Seven Years War started the chain of events that led to the so-called Gordon Riots of 1780. In acquiring Quebec Great Britain also absorbed a substantial new Catholic population; the Quebec Act of 1774 acknowledged that fact by according significant political power to the colony's Catholics. The war with American colonists then made the recruitment of Catholic soldiers more urgent than before. The relief act of 1778, among other provisions, allowed English Catholic recruits to take an oath of allegiance to the crown without abjuring Catholicism; the proposal to extend the privilege to Scotland, however, incited vigorous resistance among Scottish Presbyterians in Glasgow and Edinburgh, including Lord George Gordon; the government reversed its decision. While remaining silent during parliamentary debate on the relief act, Edmund Burke, as MP for Bristol, played a major part in drafting the bill, and had presented the petition from Scottish Catholics for relief; he thereby attracted Lord George Gordon's wrath (O'Brien 1992). Gordon's speeches on behalf of the anti-Catholic Scots enhanced his reputation as a bold opponent of arbitrary power, and made him president of the Protestant Association. Radicals, even those who shared Gordon's hatred of the Catholic church, generally kept their distance (Rogers 1990).

Gordon's forces in England took inspiration from the Scottish resistance. Members of the Protestant Association acted against what they saw as an expanding threat to Protestant ascendancy in Great Britain. When Gordon introduced a mass petition against Catholic relief into Parliament on 2 June, the Association's members poured into the streets to await— and influence—results of the parliamentary debate. Fifty thousand of them or more gathered in St. George's Fields, Southwark, previously the assembly point of Wilkes's supporters, then marched to Parliament with the petition; an estimated 14,000 people milled outside Parliament as Gordon presented it (Hibbert 1958). There members of the crowd attacked arriving members of Commons and Lords, smashing some of their coaches in the process. As Parliament discussed whether to receive the petition for an immediate and general debate, Gordon rushed repeatedly from the hall to tell his massed followers about the proceedings.

After the besieged Commons gave a crushing defeat to Gordon's request for consideration, some minor altercations between troops and demonstrators took place outside of Parliament. Guards had to protect members of Parliament as they left the premises, but eventually the vast crowd dispersed. Toward midnight, however, compact groups of activists began to light bonfires in the streets and to sack the Catholic chapels of the Sardinian and Bavarian ambassadors. Over the next five nights groups smashed, looted, and burned more chapels, homes of Catholic dignitaries, and jails that held those arrested in the first rounds of repression.

Although Charles Dickens described Gordon's followers as a blood-thirsty mob, they were remarkably selective in their work: they attacked buildings rather than persons, and selected the buildings with care. The chronicler of Parisian life Louis-Sébastian Mercier, who claimed to have been in London at the time, reported: "One saw them emptying houses in narrow streets, carrying the furniture and goods for burning into a nearby square without causing any other damage or endangering the neighborhood. I saw a three-storey house whose windows they were breaking; next door no window was broken, and the occupants of the neighboring house watched from its windows without danger" (Mercier 1982: 109). In quelling the attackers, in contrast, troops used lethal force; 275 people died in the repression. The military nevertheless took a week to regain control of the streets. Londoners formed a number of local vigilance associations, as much to counter the military presence as to protect themselves from smashers and looters (Rogers 1990). Lord George spent six months in the Tower of London before going on trial for high treason, a charge of which the jury acquitted him.

However much their followers violated the law, both Wilkes and Gordon innovated deliberately at the very edge of the permissible. Both, as E. P. Thompson (1963) suggested, probably benefited from the libertarian Whigs' reluctance to support the use of major force against the populace. Their innovations, when successful, nevertheless changed the structure of power, the prevailing forms of collective action, and the limits of the permissible. Wilkes and his Society of Supporters of the Bill of Rights repeatedly used the law to change the law—forcing, for example, the abandonment of warrants for unnamed offenders. More generally, they and their popular supporters acted out the proposition that the government was responsible to the people as a whole, and succeeded in advancing that principle some distance. Gordon's arrival at Parliament with both a huge petition and thousands of backers likewise took him into the gray zone of intimidation. His ultimate failure, however, reduced the precedent's value; on the whole innovations in collective action stuck much more readily if they gained visible advantages for the actors. Which tactics gained advantages for their users changed systematically over the long run, as a function of alterations in the British economy and polity.

How Britain Was Changing

In the Britain of Wilkes and Gordon, industrialization, war, and consequent governmental expansion were transforming social life. On the whole, the span of years from 1758 to 1788 brought a time of economic and demographic expansion: age at marriage was dropping, natural increase was rising rapidly as a consequence, the manufacturing labor force was growing fast along with total production, while Britain's industrial regions urbanized and entrepreneurs invested in turnpikes and canals. Poverty increased, as usual, along with prosperity. Outside of London, authorities tried to cope with impoverishment by establishing Houses of Industry and expanding Poor Law Unions. Efforts to regulate the poor stimulated widespread conflict outside of the Southeast. Yet these vigorous economic and demographic transformations did not affect popular contention nearly so much in the short run as did alterations in government, especially the prosecution of wars.

During the 1760s and 1770s Britain was not only fighting European wars but also establishing itself as the world's greatest colonial power. By the time of the American Revolution, Holland had clearly lost its once enormous superiority on the seas. British armies were pushing the French and Dutch from India and establishing indirect English rule through much of that subcontinent. With the conclusion of the Seven Years War, Great Britain annexed Senegal, Canada, most of Louisiana, and a number of Caribbean islands. Although Britain battled its American colonists with increasing bitterness for almost two decades, even the independence of the thirteen American colonies did not shake Britain's supremacy on the sea and overseas. The former colonies, indeed, continued to serve as major markets for British goods and major sources of British raw materials.

Britain remained at war from 1756 to 1763 (the Seven Years War), and again from 1776 to 1783 (the American War of Independence). War brought increases in taxes, expansion of state power, and pressure on workers' wages. During the years from 1758 to 1788, as Table 4.1 shows, government revenues increased substantially; the land tax rose a modest

1.1 percent per year, while customs and excise moved up respectively at 2.4 and 2.5 percent annually, and revenue from controversial tax stamps— the Stamp Act that stirred up so much dissent in the American colonies dated from 1765—increased at a rapid 5.3 percent per year. Overall, net governmental income rose at a rate of 2.5 percent per year, while expenditure increased at 0.7 percent. With a lag of three years, the peace of 1783 had brought a rapid reduction in military expenditure, which meant that government books actually ran a nominal surplus from 1787 to 1792. Nevertheless, total debt mounted from £82.1 million pounds in 1758 to £245.1 million in 1788, for a rate of increase of 3.7 percent per year. Debt charges took £2.9 million of the government's £13.2 million total expenditure in 1758, £9.4 million of a £16.3 million total in 1788, a rise from

Table 4.1. Government finance and real income in Britain, 1758–1788

Item	1758	1788	Annual % change
Revenue from customs	1,918	3,996	+2.4%
Revenue from excise	3,477	7,257	+2.5
Revenue from stamps	277	1,322	+5.3
Revenue from land tax	2,139	3,013	+1.1
Debt service expenditure	2,895	9,407	+4.0
Civil government expenditure	1,279	1,522	+0.6
Expenditure on army	4,586	2,099	−2.6
Expenditure on navy	3,893	2,262	−1.8
Total military expenditure	9,026	4,908	−2.1
Farm laborer real income	18.9	19.4	+0.1
Middle worker real income	34.4	25.9	+0.1
Artisan real income	41.6	35.8	−0.4

Note: "Real income" is in 1851 pounds per year. Other figures are in thousands of current pounds sterling.

Sources: Interpolated from Lindert and Williamson 1983b; Williamson 1985; Mitchell and Deane 1971.

a fifth to almost three-fifths of the state's budget at a time when direct military expenditures were declining as shares of a greatly increased total: 68.4 percent of the budget in 1758, 30 percent in 1788. Together, military expenditure and debt charges for military borrowing remained at about 90 percent of the total governmental budget (Mitchell and Deane 1971).

As in other highly commercialized countries, Britain's state revenues depended more heavily on customs and excise than on poll taxes or direct imposition of land and property; the disparity was increasing. While taxes rose, employees of the Excise Office multiplied faster than other branches of government: by 49 percent between 1755 and 1782 (Brewer 1989). War-driven state centralization that spanned the eighteenth century was moving apace during the century's third quarter. As the tax burden increased, real income remained steady or declined for workers, especially for artisans; between 1758 and 1788 artisan income dropped at about 0.4 percent per year, for a total loss of more than 12 percent (computed and interpolated from Lindert and Williamson 1983b and Williamson 1985). Even outside years of failed harvest such as 1766 and 1771, food prices were rising significantly faster than workers' nominal wages. It was not, in short, an easy time.

In this context, national politics had two faces. Seen from one side it consisted of the play of factions among great Whig leaders and their friends: not only Bute, but also Newcastle, Rockingham, the Pitts, Grenville, Townshend, Shelburne, and a dozen more potentates over the twenty-four years in question. Seen from the other side national politics consisted of striving by the king and various allies to pursue grand policies of war, conquest, and diplomacy on a world scale, and to get British subjects to pay for those policies. Great political lords had policy preferences, but they also had interests and allies—both frequently rewarded by the granting of office—to serve. From the political heights, the popular mobilizations that occurred around John Wilkes and Lord George Gordon constituted irritants and obstacles but not politics as such. International merchants and colonial landowners made trade policies, tariffs, and administration of the East India Company critical issues for Parliament and successive ministries. But in the 1760s and 1770s the resistances of East Indians and Irishmen to British rule rarely articulated with popular political struggles inside Britain.

America was different; from the time of Wilkes to the 1780s, as the

American war ground on, it became a touchstone for opposition to royal policy. Far more than a lunatic fringe took up the American cause; in 1770, after all, Edmund Burke himself became British agent for the New York Colonial Assembly. In 1775 a government-encouraged campaign of addresses in favor of the war incited a counter-campaign of antiwar petitions that garnered thousands of signatures (Colley 1992). By 1776, when the king addressed the first session of Parliament after the American Declaration of Independence, the Earl of Shelburne was denouncing the king's defense of British policy as "a string of sophisms, no less wretched in their texture than insolent in their tenor" (Fitzmaurice 1912, II: 1). "English allies of the American cause," observes Paul Langford, "tended to assume that, in the context of 1776, Revolution principles were synonymous with American principles" (Langford 1980: 108). Still, the state's international policies touched ordinary people's politics most directly through efforts to gather the means of war: taxation, press gangs, militia drawings, and the like.

Contention's Flow

With the Wilkite furor, many observers noticed that popular politics was changing rapidly, that ordinary people were mobilizing around national political issues to a degree that no one had seen since the revolutions of the seventeenth century. The conflicts Benjamin Franklin observed often touched national politics in the sense of maneuvering for power in and over the state. As witnessed by the extensive parliamentary debates they incited, Wilkes and his partisans were raising fundamental questions of representation and popular sovereignty both in England and in America. Yet they employed characteristic eighteenth-century idioms: calling for candles in windows and cries of catchwords as signs of support for the cause, carrying out rituals such as the hanging or burning of a boot, marching to the royal palace with flags and violins.

The more usual repertoire of eighteenth-century popular politics, in any case, concentrated on local issues and local figures, whether enemies or friends. Contrary to the ineffectual venting of emotion suggested by such words as "protest" and "mob," its users frequently accomplished their short-run objectives, frequently saw their claims realized. Nor did they merely adopt primitive forms of the actions that nineteenth-century special-interest associations, parties, and movements would employ more efficaciously. Instead, they focused on direct, often violent, disciplining of their objects.

During April 1768, for example, as Benjamin Franklin's fears of popular action mounted, reports of these contentious gatherings appeared in the London press:

2 April: Near Brentford, a crowd stopped a passing carriage and forced its passengers to shout their support for Wilkes and Liberty.

14 April: Journeymen cut cloth from six looms at the home of a Shoreditch master weaver, while in Spitalfields other journeymen likewise cut cloth from looms.

15 April: Participants in a struggle between striking and nonstriking coalheavers in Wapping destroyed houses; on the Brentford road, Wilkes supporters again stopped a carriage and demanded homage to Wilkes and Liberty.

16 April, Shadwell: Coalheavers attacked a dealer whose servant had torn up their handbill.

18 April: Part of the public at an execution on Sutton Common seized the victims' corpses and buried them in defiance of surgeons whom they accused of planning to dissect the bodies—as the surgeons had a legal right to do.

20 April: At the Roundabout Tavern, Wapping, coalheavers attacked an innkeeper–coal dealer.

21 April: After the employees of a bordello in Goodman's Fields attacked a man who was trying to remove his daughter from their premises, a crowd sacked the bawdy house. Meanwhile, in Spitalfields raiding parties of journeymen again cut cloth from looms.

26 April: Coalheavers boarded boats in Wapping and manhandled their masters.

27 April: Wilkes's partisans watched his transportation to prison, then liberated him before he escaped from them and turned himself in.

28 April: Around King's Bench Prison in Southwark, Wilkes's supporters, burning a boot and a bonnet ceremoniously, called for the illumination of houses in honor of their hero.

The prevalence of direct action, often violent, on a local scale marked the events of April. Indeed, it characterized much of eighteenth-century contention.

In the Southeast (Kent, Middlesex, Surrey, and Sussex), we have extensive evidence on popular contention during 1758, 1759, 1768, 1769, 1780, and 1781. Table 4.2 offers a rough breakdown of the occasions of contentious gatherings during those years. (For the record, the initial listing includes a mutiny described in the first chapter. Since it began in Portsmouth and participants only passed through Westminster before returning to the fleet in chains, I have excluded it from the chapter's later tabulations.) Of course the categories overlap; in 1769, for example, almost all of the "other attacks" consisted either of Wilkes's supporters' attempts to force

Table 4.2. Occasions of contentious gatherings in the Southeast, 1758–1781

Type of event	% of annual total						
	1758	1759	1768	1769	1780	1781	Total
Forced illumination of windows	14.3	8.3	9.0	0.0	0.0	0.0	4.3
Other attacks on persons or their property	35.7	33.3	54.1	25.4	62.9	37.9	46.5
Seizure of food or property	14.3	8.3	8.1	3.0	5.7	0.0	5.9
Mutiny	7.1	8.3	0.0	0.0	0.0	0.0	0.7
Resistance to governmental regulation or action	14.3	16.7	0.9	1.5	8.6	13.8	5.3
Meeting to communicate with national government	14.3	25.0	9.0	43.3	21.4	20.7	21.5
Electoral assembly	0.0	0.0	5.4	13.4	0.0	3.4	5.3
Strike, turnout, or gathering for wage demands	0.0	0.0	10.8	3.0	0.0	0.0	4.6
Other gathering	0.0	0.0	2.7	10.4	1.4	24.1	5.9
Total	100.0	99.9	100.0	100.0	100.0	99.9	100.0
Number of CGs	14	12	111	67	70	29	303

acknowledgment of their hero's merits or of strikers' retaliation against masters and nonstrikers. Note the localism and direct action in the majority of these events. Note also the rising importance of assemblies concerning national affairs beginning with 1768. During 1758 and 1759 only five of the twenty-six CGs involved direct statements concerning national politics, and in all five instances the actors came from the ruling classes: the nobility, the East India Company, and so on. The four cases of resistance during those years pitted fishermen, conscripts, smugglers, and ordinary citizens against various government agents.

The dozen gatherings of 1759 included an attack on enforcers of Sabbath closing, another attack on a Quaker who did *not* close on a day of fast, gang kidnapping of an estranged wife, an assault on the house of a Quaker who failed to illuminate for the Prince of Wales's birthday, harassment of fashionable ladies by a crowd in St. James's Park, resistance to a press gang, pelting of two extortionists in the pillory, a mutiny of new recruits, group plundering of a beached ship, meetings to commend naval commanders and to encourage military enlistments, and a noble delegation to the king on the occasion of Quebec's capture. Most of these events began either with an informal group's converging on someone they regarded as their friend or enemy, or with the effort of governmental agents to force the state's will on reluctant citizens. All this despite the fact that during 1759 Parliament was debating war taxes and the Poor Laws, subjects that strongly affected the interests of ordinary people. For the most part, then, popular politics of the 1750s proceeded in a parochial, mediated, reactive mode. The nationalization of struggles in 1768 and 1769 only attenuated those characteristics.

Among relatively powerful people, however, some innovations were appearing. The Wilkite Society of Supporters of the Bill of Rights opened space for other special-purpose associations in British politics, a space invaded in 1780 by Lord George Gordon's anti-Catholic Protestant Association. The formation of large associations in Ireland and America provided another model for English, Welsh, and Scottish political entrepreneurs. During the anticorruption campaigns of 1780, the Yorkshire Association and others like it drew directly on Irish and American models (Butterfield 1968). Reform committees organized great public meetings in London and engineered the submission of huge petitions for shorter Parliaments and the enlargement of county representation; all these tactics proceeded in tight cooperation with opposition members of Parliament, who drew on expressions of extraparliamentary support in the course of parliamentary debate. Elite associations, drawing their membership almost entirely from propertyholders, confirmed the right of British subjects to assemble at their own initiative, deliberate, and petition Parliament or the king. Their activity enlarged the channels of political communication between British localities and national centers of power.

The contention of 1758 to 1788 did not reflect the rise and fall of hardship in any simple manner; where the economic squeeze shaped claim-making, it always did so through the mediation of existing social organization, accumulated beliefs and grievances, prior relations between rich and poor, current political mobilization, and the available repertoires of contention. Tables 4.3 to 4.5 project profiles of contention between 1758 and 1781 from three angles: major issues, participating groups, and types of action. Overall, local rather than national issues predominated:

Table 4.3. Major issues of contentious gatherings in the Southeast, 1758–1781

Issue	% of annual total						Total	N
	1758	1759	1768	1769	1780	1781		
Attacks on objects	15.4	8.3	4.5	1.5	31.4	0.0	10.3	31
Attacks on persons	30.8	41.7	15.3	10.4	2.9	3.4	11.9	36
Turnout/strike	0.0	0.0	12.6	0.0	0.0	0.0	4.6	14
Other labor	15.4	0.0	17.1	4.5	1.4	0.0	8.3	25
Catholic claims	0.0	0.0	0.0	0.0	30.0	0.0	7.0	21
Elections	0.0	0.0	7.2	11.9	0.0	3.4	5.6	17
Wilkes	0.0	0.0	17.1	6.0	0.0	0.0	7.6	23
Royalty	0.0	8.3	1.8	16.4	1.4	3.4	5.3	16
National government	0.0	25.0	5.4	10.4	11.4	24.1	10.3	31
Local government	7.7	0.0	1.8	14.9	2.9	13.8	6.3	19
Other	30.8	16.7	0.0	23.9	18.6	51.7	22.8	69
Total	100.1	100.0	99.9	99.9	100.0	99.8	100.0	302
N	13*	12	111	67	70	29	302	

*Excluding a CG beginning in Portsmouth but touching London, described in Chapter 1.

Table 4.4. Formations participating in contentious gatherings, Southeast, 1758–1781

Type of formation	% of annual total						Total	N
	1758	1759	1768	1769	1780	1781		
Parliament, MP	2.6	0.0	2.3	3.6	9.6	4.2	4.5	55
National officials	0.0	3.8	2.3	2.4	4.2	4.2	3.0	36
Royalty	0.0	5.7	0.9	7.1	1.3	5.8	3.0	36
Gentlemen, nobles	0.0	1.9	2.5	4.8	1.9	1.7	2.6	32
Judges	0.0	1.9	2.9	2.8	9.9	2.5	4.5	55
Mayor	7.7	0.0	1.6	5.2	0.6	0.8	2.1	26
Other local officials	2.6	1.9	0.9	12.7	4.8	13.3	5.7	69
Clergy	2.6	0.0	0.0	0.0	0.6	0.0	0.2	3
Freeholders/electors	2.6	0.0	0.7	0.4	0.3	0.0	0.5	6
Other local assemblies	0.0	5.7	4.1	5.6	1.3	2.5	3.4	42
Members of trade	12.8	1.9	26.7	15.9	2.9	7.5	14.9	182
Other interest	2.6	1.9	3.2	0.8	3.8	3.3	2.8	34
Police	2.6	5.7	3.2	3.2	3.2	5.0	3.4	42
Troops	7.7	15.1	5.9	3.2	8.0	13.3	7.1	86
Unnamed crowd	12.8	13.2	10.6	5.2	19.9	3.3	11.3	138
Named individual	15.4	15.1	9.0	9.1	12.8	3.3	9.9	121
Other	28.2	26.4	23.3	18.3	14.7	29.2	20.9	255
Total	100.2	100.2	100.1	100.3	99.8	99.9	99.8	1,218
N	39	53	442	252	312	120	1,218	

Note: Includes both actors and objects of claims.

Table 4.5. Verbs in all actions of contentious gatherings, Southeast, 1758–1781

Verb	% of annual total						Total	N
	1758	1759	1768	1769	1780	1781		
Assemble	8.3	2.0	4.4	4.9	4.0	3.4	4.3	98
Attack	13.3	17.0	18.2	10.9	24.8	9.6	17.3	396
Cheer	0.0	0.0	0.8	1.9	1.6	1.0	1.2	27
Communicate	0.0	1.0	4.3	5.1	3.4	2.4	3.8	87
Control	20.0	27.0	18.0	10.7	10.5	15.9	14.9	341
Decry	0.0	2.0	1.2	1.7	0.9	1.4	1.3	29
Deliberate	3.3	0.0	0.3	1.7	0.7	2.4	1.0	22
Disperse	3.3	4.0	4.9	4.9	4.2	4.3	4.6	105
End	20.0	10.0	10.9	11.9	10.7	12.0	11.3	259
Fight	1.7	1.0	1.9	1.3	0.2	4.3	1.5	35
Gather	8.3	9.0	7.6	4.9	6.5	7.7	6.9	157
Meet	1.7	2.0	1.6	5.3	2.5	3.8	2.8	64
Move	6.7	11.0	10.0	8.7	11.2	6.7	9.7	221
Negotiate	0.0	1.0	2.2	2.1	0.5	1.0	1.6	36
Petition	0.0	0.0	0.8	1.7	0.9	1.9	1.1	24
Request	0.0	1.0	3.4	4.5	2.9	1.9	3.2	72
Resist	0.0	3.0	1.1	2.1	1.3	1.0	1.4	32
Resolve	1.7	2.0	0.4	3.0	1.1	4.8	1.6	37
Support	3.3	1.0	0.8	1.7	0.7	2.9	1.2	28
Other	8.3	6.0	7.3	10.9	11.4	11.5	9.4	214
Total	99.9	100.0	100.1	99.9	100.0	99.9	100.1	2,284
N	60	100	894	469	553	208	2,284	

attacks on hated persons and objects representing them, local government, labor disputes. National politics (in the form of elections, performance of the national government, appeals to royalty, the Wilkes disputes, and claims for Catholic rights) accounted for about 36 percent of all contentious gatherings over the six years in question. Issues fluctuated in importance from year to year: the Wilkes dispute peaked in 1768, with 17 percent of all events, while Catholic claims (pro and con) became salient only during Lord George Gordon's anti-Catholic mobilization of 1780; twenty-one of that year's seventy CGs pivoted on Catholic rights.

Many events, of course, raised more than a single issue—indeed, resulted from deliberate tactical linking of issues. The Southeast's fifteen meetings of 1780 and 1781 concerning national government, for example, pivoted on the issue of wasteful public expenditure, especially the civil list; but (as their organizers generally intended) they actually involved contests over the power of Parliament to control royal and ministerial spending, over placemen and sinecures, over the legitimacy of extraparliamentary political associations, over the validity of petitions written in the name of associations or of the people as a whole, over the propriety of the American war, ultimately over the same questions of popular sovereignty John Wilkes's campaigns had posed so sharply. They managed to connect patronage, incompetence, waste, and warmaking. They resulted, that is, from the reform-seeking campaign mounted by Christopher Wyvill's Yorkshire Association and then by the London Association.

Following precedents set by the Wilkite Society of Supporters of the Bill of Rights as well as the American Committees of Correspondence, members of the Yorkshire Association's London counterpart and the Protestant Association played major parts in popular mobilization. Organizers of the new associations aimed at enfranchised voters, but they raised issues that engaged the entire population (Black 1963). By 1779 such associations posed a sufficient threat to the existing political order that George III himself was scheming to infiltrate and contain the Yorkshire Association's proceedings (Butterfield 1968).

Note, however, that even the king did not declare such associations *ipso facto* illegal, so long as they confined their official membership to respectable persons. By 1790, indeed, no less a person than Edmund Burke considered it natural to declare that "I certainly have the honour to belong to more clubs than one, in which the constitution of this kingdom, and the principles of the glorious Revolution [of 1688], are held in high reverence, and I reckon myself among the most forward in my zeal for maintaining that constitution and those principles in their utmost purity and vigour" (Burke 1984: 2–3). At that point, associations became suspect only when they began to recruit mass memberships, to speak for the population at large, or to advocate seditious principles. Britain's ruling classes now had their associations, while contesting the rights of other Britons to form or join them.

Ordinary eighteenth-century Britons had few means of speaking out directly on national issues. The humble petition provided the most acceptable way to reach the national government, and especially the king (Fraser 1961). The wars in America stimulated petitions galore: "Between the Stamp Act crisis in 1765 and the constitutional crisis over the Coalition in 1784, petitions with more than a quarter of a million signatures ascended to Parliament or the Crown" (Bradley 1986: ix). Between 1775 and 1778 some 25,000 British subjects petitioned the king in support of peace in America; roughly equal numbers wrote in favor of coercive measures against upstart Americans (Bradley 1986).

Similarly, the first great campaign for abolition of slave trading, in 1787–1788, centered on mass petitioning; Manchester's petition to Parliament bore almost 11,000 signatures, representing 20 percent of the city's entire population (Drescher 1986). The signatories of the time, furthermore, came increasingly from general assemblies of the local population rather than privileged groups; while 89 percent of the petitions on behalf of John Wilkes in 1769–1770 bore the name of the nobility, a corporation, freemen, and so on, only 30 percent of 1788's petitions concerning the slave trade emanated from such elite conclaves (ibid.).

Who took part? Table 4.4 provides evidence. A *formation* is any person or set of persons our sources describe as acting distinctly during a contentious gathering. If tailors or shopkeepers appeared in a formation observers called "parishioners," we called them parishioners; the list of all formations therefore bears little relation to a census of all participants in contentious gatherings. Named individuals—who usually appeared in contention as the objects of praise, support, reprobation, or violence—made up a full fifth of all formations; their proportion, however, was declining irregularly over the period in favor of local and national political officials.

In most years reporters labeled around a tenth of all formations "crowd," "mob," or some similarly vague, derogatory term. Police and troops likewise weighed in at about a tenth of all formations, reaching a peak of 21 percent in the violent events of 1759. Workers swung around 12 percent of the total, reaching their own maximum 21 percent in 1768—a great year for labor conflict, as we have seen. Perhaps the most important fact is negative: together, members of Parliament, national officials, and royalty made up only 4.5 percent of all formations, usually as objects of claims by elite groups. For the most part, CGs involved conflicts among local citizens, or between citizens and local officials.

Verbs describing actions that occurred during CGs—2,284 actions for the entire period—confirm the image of small-scale, often violent local conflict one can draw from the evidence about issues and formations. (Each verb actually represents a set; "negotiate," for example, includes not only negotiate, but also accede, accept, admit, agitate, agree, allow, assert, claim, dare, defy, egg on, encourage, enjoin, excite, exhort, and so on through the alphabet.) "End," with its 11.3 percent of all verbs, is an artifact due to our supplying that verb whenever the available accounts did not say how the gathering dispersed. But attack (17.3 percent) and control (14.9 percent) properly represent the importance of force and counterforce in the CGs of 1758 to 1781. Few of the verbs fall into the categories that typically come from orderly public meetings: cheer, communicate, deliberate, meet, petition, request, resolve, support. Altogether, these verbs make up less than a seventh of the total. Nor do any real trends in the forms of action appear.

Yet the years from 1768 through 1781 stand out from their predecessors in some important regards; during those years the verbs cheer, communicate, disperse, petition, and request—for the most part, verbs closely associated with organized public meetings and nonviolent displays of support—became more common, while control and gather declined in importance. No doubt the most surprising feature of the later period was the coupling of various sorts of attacks to the actions of meetings and associations. The Protestant Association provides the culmination: attacks on Catholics and their buildings in 1780, attacks on prisons holding the Association's activists in 1781. As of 1781 an observer of British contention had every reason to connect associational activity to violence rather than to the restraint it later connoted.

Let us shun teleology. Nothing about the forms of the eighteenth-century repertoire required that they give way to the nineteenth-century forms. Neither set was more advanced, effective, modern, rational, or instrumental than the other. It distorts the explanation of eighteenth-century action to analyze it as a first step toward nineteenth-century action. The point of contrasting the two repertoires is simply to point out that eighteenth-century Britons had distinctive means of claim-making at their disposal, means rooted in the politics and social structure of their time. They were not merely attenuated or immature versions of means that would later arrive at effective maturity.

How the Repertoire Worked

Take the sort of event that authorities and unwary historians called a "food riot"; we might better call it a seizure of food (especially grain or bread), for that action usually lay at its core. Few violent struggles over food occurred in eighteenth-century London and its vicinity, both because London was the hub of a relatively effective national market system and because fearful authorities did what they could to supply London in times of dearth (Walter 1989; Wells 1988). On 24 May 1768, nevertheless, in Hastings (Sussex), "a very tumultuous mob rose there by beat of drum, and insisted upon having wheat at 5s. per bushel. They then went to the house of Mr. White, a farmer in that neighbourhood, dragged him out to the middle of one of his own fields, forced him to stay there while they broke open his granary and destroyed all his wheat; after this they returned and paraded it about the town" (LC 25 May 1768: 498; "destroyed," in this instance, apparently meant seized and carted away). Two days later a group of gentlemen from Westminster met at a house near St. James's to organize a petition to Parliament "for lowering the price of provisions" (LC 28 May 1768: 510). On 1 July of the same year "a great number of Weavers assembled in Bunhill-row and Chiswell-street, where the Country-farmers were selling pease at 10d. a peck, the Weavers got up in seven carts, and sold them at 6d. a peck" (LC 2 July 1768: 6). Thus in a difficult year like 1768, even London witnessed struggles over food.

Elsewhere in Britain conflicts broke out frequently in seasons of grain shortage and high prices. As they had since at least the sixteenth century, they concentrated in regions of rapid and extensive proletarianization, where increasing numbers of people controlled insufficient land to feed themselves and depended on wages for the purchase of food (Charlesworth 1980, 1983, 1994; Manning 1988: 314; Walter 1989; Wells 1979, 1980, 1988). Those people felt immediately the pinch of rising food prices and of unemployment. The August 1766 number of *Gentleman's Magazine* reported, for example:

> The poor near *Honiton* have risen, and seized upon the bags of corn lodged by the farmers in the public houses, brought them into the market, and sold the corn at 5s. 6d. per bushel, paying the money, and returning the bags to the owners; and several hundreds rose and pulled down the bunting mills at *Ottery, Tipton,* and *Sidbury.* They have done damage, as supposed, to the amount of 1900 l.
>
> The poor have also risen at *Crediton.* In short, the case of the poor is become so desperate, that it demands some immediate redress.
>
> Great disturbances amongst the poor have happened lately near *Exeter,* on account of the high price of provisions, having destroyed several flour mills; and burnt down a set of flour mills at *Stoke.* The gentlemen have bought large quantities of flour, which they sell to the poor for three pence half penny per pound, in order to put a stop to those disturbances. (GM August 1766: 386)

The "poor" in this instance, and many other instances, were largely workers in rural manufacturing. Honiton, Ottery, Tipton, Sidbury, Crediton, and Stoke were villages, market towns, and manufacturing centers in Exeter's hinterland, a dense district of serge-weaving. A gazetteer of 1759 indicates that "eighty percent" of Exeter's population was engaged in woolen production (Hoskins 1935: 53). Much of the population therefore depended on marketed food—especially bread—for their survival. In the Southwest the sale of food in controlled public markets had been declining for most of the century in favor of private marketing that directly connected farmers to merchants who supplied major cities; the rise of private marketing reduced the ability of local authorities to intervene in price or supply, and increased the vulnerability of local supplies to the competition of Bristol, London, or other major centers (Chartres 1973).

Devon as a whole sent cattle, sheep, cider, and butter to much of England, particularly to London. But its industrial districts exported serges to Italy, Spain, Portugal, and the rest of Europe. In the 1760s its once flourishing woolen industry had suffered from its loss of markets during the Seven Years War; by 1766 the industry was recovering, although it would never again reach the peak of the 1750s. Proletarian and semiproletarian workers abounded; for them the price of bread governed the comfort of everyday living.

In February 1766, after scattered struggles over food in the previous months, Parliament agreed without a vote to a ban on grain exports and to duty-free imports of American grain. In August the ban expired at a time when much of southern Europe was suffering acute shortages. Farmers and merchants rushed their grain to port, with the result that domestic supplies diminished dramatically and grain prices rose sharply. More provision-related contention occurred in 1766 than in any other eighteenth-century year. The year's struggles over food broke out chiefly in rural manufacturing districts, including those of Devon (Williams 1984; see also Hayter 1978; Shelton 1973; Charlesworth 1983). The risings included the seizure of stored or shipped grain, its sale at below-market prices, attacks on flour mills, and sacking of the premises of local capitalists whom workers blamed for hoarding, high prices, and low wages. Yet they displayed surprising order: note how the workers of Honiton sold seized grain, then returned both money and grainsacks to its owners. Once Parliament reinstated the embargo on grain exports in late September, furthermore, widespread contention over food began to subside.

Struggles over food could reach the scale of insurrection. In February 1773 officials of Penryn (Cornwall) reported that the region's tin miners

broke open the houses of several maltsters, and carried off between 200 and 300 Winchester Bushells of Barly and would have carried off, the whole stock from the Town, had they not been prevented by Lieutenant Hamilton the commander of Pendennis Castle, who upon application immediately came to our assistance, and drove them out of Town, but before our Return, the Town was visited by a fresh Party of about 300 more of those Banditti, with whom we were forced to beat a parly, and come to an agreement to let them have the corn for one third less than the prime cost to the Proprietors. (SP 41/26, 9 February 1773)

Tinners staged similar raids at Padston, Falmouth, Helstone, and Woodbridge, publicly selling grain they seized at below the current market price. They only ceased their action with the dispatch of troops later in February.

To some extent, the poor people who seized grain and attacked profiteers accomplished their aim: they not only took vengeance but also pressed local officials—and, through their mediation, Parliament—to increase the supply of low-priced food. Struggles over food nicely illustrate the parochial, particular, bifurcated, direct-action-oriented character of eighteenth-century contention.

Against Poorhouses and Enclosures

Similarly, resistance to changing control of the poor followed the standard eighteenth-century pattern. Consider Suffolk in the 1760s. When the directors of the newly proposed workhouse for Lees and Wilford Hundreds, to be situated at Melton, met at the White Hart in Wickham Market on 1 August 1765, a crowd of four to five hundred men, plus women and children, surrounded the inn, then forced their way into the room and seized the directors. They destroyed the parish poor records and forced the directors to sign a statement abandoning their plan. Members of the crowd declared they would tear down the existing workhouse at Nacton (Muskett 1980). That did not end Suffolk's action against poorhouses. For a week the group went from workhouse to workhouse tearing the buildings down and demanding that the overseers commit themselves not to rebuild. They demanded "that the poor should be maintained as usual; that they should range at liberty and be their own masters" (Webb and Webb 1963: 141–142). As *Gentleman's Magazine* reported for 5 August 1765:

> Some thousands of rioters assembled in the neighbourhood of *Saxmundham* in *Suffolk*, and destroyed the industry-house, in which the poor were employed. Their pretence was to release the poor to assist in the harvest-work; but the fact was to defeat a late act of Parliament, lately obtained for the relief of the hundreds of *Wilford*, and *Loes*, etc. In this riot, the military were called in, and several lost their lives before the rioters were dispersed. (GM August 1765: 392; note the pejorative use of "riot" and "rioters")

At Saxmundham not only the poor but also many of their less impoverished neighbors considered the new institution improper and intolerable.

In Bulcamp, a few miles north of Saxmundham, a new workhouse was still under construction for Blything Hundred. From Bulcamp we have the testimony of Benjamin Preston, an agricultural laborer in Theberton, Suffolk. At eight o'clock on Monday morning, 5 August 1765, he, Daniel Manning, and fourteen others were hoeing turnips in a farmer's field. Suddenly, as the magistrate's clerk (who may well have supplied the words "riotous" and "rioter") set down his story ten days later,

> several persons whose names he don't know came into the field and took away his and Manning's Hoes, and in a forceable manner compelled them and the other men working in the field to go with them to Bulcamp and assist in pulling down the poor's House which was then erecting there . . . they accordingly joined them and were afterwards joined by several hundreds all armed with sticks, poles, or other instruments . . . some of them (but don't know who, by name) took their Handkerchiefs from their necks and fastened them to poles which they display'd as flags or colours and in this manner proceeded a long huzzaing and making a great noise . . . when they came to Halesworth the people at a publick House (but don't know their names nor can recollect the sign) Invited them to Drink and drew them several Quarts of Beer which they drank and the alehouse people refused to take anything for it . . . as they marched a long a Gentleman who appeared like a Clergyman stop't one of these Riotous persons who was near the Examinant and spoke to those about him and told them the bad consequences of persisting in their design and Desired them to return to their own Homes, which the Examinant and others were inclined to do, but immediately another of the said Rioters (whose name he didn't know) with a Bludgeon in his hand came up to said Gent. and threatened to strike him if he did not go away immediately, and compelled the Examinant and the rest to proceed and they accordingly went on hallowing and making a great noise till they came to Bulcamp where they arrived between 6 and 7 in the Evening . . . when they were at Bulcamp, believes their number might be about 1000 . . . he saw . . . John Saws get one of the Poles, belonging to the Scaffolding of said Building at the South end thereof and . . . Mills with a Pitchfork, Ralph with a peasemake, Canham, Lumkin and Rachan with Staffs, Poles, and other Instruments at various parts of the said Building throwing down and destroying the same . . . there were at the same time many other Persons to the amount of 150 and upwards (whose names he don't know) pulling

down and destroying the aforesaid Building . . . during the whole time
the said Building was pulling down . . . James Stronger was riding upon
a horse, and . . . William Ingledon upon an Ass, Huzzaing and Encouraging the aforesaid Riotous persons to proceed in pulling down the
aforesaid Building and in particular made use of the following Expressions—"My Lads work away, work away. Let's pull Hell down to the
Ground, pull Bulcamp Hell down to the Ground" (these were the names
given to the said Building by the said Rioters) and every time any
material part of the said Building was thrown down there was a general
Shout or Acclamation of Joy among the said Rioters in which the said
Stronger and Ingledon were most remarkably conspicuous . . . at the
time the aforesaid Building was destroyed there was also pulled down
and destroyed a Smith's shop and forge that had been Erected for the
more convenient Executing the Smith's work for the said Building and
a Cottage for the use of the Workmen Employed therein but can't
particularize any of the Persons concerned therein . . . he heard several
of the said Rioters and particularly Canham and Lamkin [sic] say that
it would be a very good and Laudable act to pull down the said Building
for that Rain had been long wanting and that God Almighty would not
suffer it to Rain till that Building was Destroyed and that it happening
to Rain the next Day he heard the said Lumkin and Canham say that
it would not have rained had they not Destroyed the said Building
intended for a Poor's House . . . they Continued at Bulcamp aforesaid
on the 5th Instant till it was Dark when they went to Sir John Rover's
house where they got Victuals and Drink and then to the Revd. Mr.
Burton's and did the same. (SP 37/4; "that" and other indications of
indirect discourse elided)

Other witnesses interrogated that day confirmed Benjamin Preston's account in all essentials but added significant details: that the first three
people to enter the poorhouse under construction were women, that the
crowd had forced the local gentlemen to feed them, that they had threatened to pull down the house of one of the gentlemen, that they had torn
down a fence—no doubt of an enclosed field—at one of the gentlemen's
properties, and so on. Bulcamp's avengers adopted the standard eighteenth-century routine of pulling down a moral offender's house and
wrecking its contents. They even seem to have given their action magical
significance; it brought much-needed rain.

Preston and other laborers testified under threat of prosecution. Yet uncoerced reports gave a similar picture of the struggle at Bulcamp. On 15 August a magistrate's clerk transcribed the testimony of John Garneys, a surgeon of Yexford, Suffolk:

> Says that about one o'clock in the morning of the 6th instant he heard that the mob who had pulled down the House at Bulcamp were at Mr. Buxtons and threatened to go to Mr. Inghams and pull his House down. He went to Mr. Buxton's and there saw said James Stronger, John Lumkin, John Atikins and ___, his wife, Edward Butters, Jacob Spenlove, ___ Taylor and ___ Slade and heard them say they had destroyed the House at Bulcamp which some of them called Little Hell and that they would go to Mr. Ingham and pull his House down unless he delivered them the Books and Papers. Says he thereupon went to Mr. Inghams with as much speed as possible to give him any assistance in his Power and says that between 2 and 3 in the morning of the said 6th instant about 100 of said Rioters were assembled about Mr. Ingham's House among whom were said Stronger, Lumkin, and the others named by him to have been at Mr. Buxton's and said Rioters demanded to see Mr. Ingham and declared if he did not come to them they would pull the House down. That Mr. Ingham's Servant and Examinant did all in their Power to appease said Rioters and assured them Mr. Ingham was not at home (as in truth he was not, he having left his House upon hearing their threats) and to make them quiet gave them Bread and Cheese and Beer but nevertheless they were much Enraged at not finding Mr. Ingham and insisted Examinant had secreted him some where, and threatened that if they discovered he had they would pull his House down, and says that all the Rioters during the time they were there which was about 3 hours behaved very riotously and outrageous and the said Stronger in particular declared he would eat the flesh and Drink the Blood of the Gent. concerned in erecting the said Poors House. Says he heard many of said Rioters declare that as they had such Success in this their first undertaking they would reduce the price of Corn or pull down all the mills about. (SP 37/4; blanks in original text)

Thus questions of prices, employment, and treatment of the poor interlocked tightly. In the case of Bulcamp, the law officer charged to review the proceedings concluded that the poorhouse attack and related events constituted an "enormous riot" but not the treason or the destruction of a dwelling that would justify a felony charge (SP 37/4). Four days after the attack on Bulcamp's poorhouse the people who had threatened Nacton's workhouse directors on 1 August tried to fulfill their threat:

> Several persons riotously assembled to pull down the house of industry, lately erected at Nacton near Ipswich carried their boldness to such length that, neither the expostulations of the magistrates against the illegality of their design, which they openly avowed, the consequences of the riot proclamation act being read, which were explained to them, nor the appearance of a body of regular horse and foot, called in as part of the *posse comitatus,* seemed to make the least impression on them; nay, though the proclamation was read to them with an audible voice, and they seemed to hear it with attention, not a man stirred. (AR 1765: 116–117)

When the magistrates asked members of the assembly why they had come to Nacton, "Several of them answered with firmness, to pull down the House" (Muskett 1980: 29). The commander ordered eleven mounted dragoons to move to the crowd's rear while the remainder of the soldiers faced the rebels. As the troops prepared for attack, the crowd of a hundred or so "fell upon both horses and men with such arms as they had, peasemakes, hedge-stakes, cudgels, etc., but in five minutes the affair was over." Soldiers arrested seven men as examples, and dispersed the rest. "It appears," commented the reporter, "that these unhappy men were deluded by their leaders, who had persuaded them, that the military forces could not fire, or act against them. Many more persons might have been apprehended with ease, but seven were thought enough to make an example of" (AR 1765: 117).

At Bulcamp "Little Hell" was a workhouse under construction. At Nacton the "house of industry" a local crowd proposed to destroy was a recently built workhouse. Poor English villagers had long drawn relief from their own parishes while living at home. The payments were miserable, but they assured survival. The payments, furthermore, were a right. That was "outdoor relief." "Indoor relief"—the workhouse or some other form of incarceration—was now threatening to displace the older system. From the 1730s onward many local authorities of East Anglia responded to the increasing numbers of poor with two important innovations: (1) locking up the poor to work under public supervision and (2) combining the poor-law efforts of a number of adjacent parishes into a single administration. Parliament had legalized both efforts. The building of workhouses for multiple parishes combined the two new enterprises. It also permitted many parishes to reduce their relief payments and ship their local paupers elsewhere. Poor people and their friends or relatives fought indoor relief in the name of established rights.

Poor people struck directly at the provisions their wealthier and more powerful neighbors were making for them. A threatening letter dropped in Raydon discussed the Tattingstone workhouse:

> Gentleman, this to a quaint you all of you cor Serning th Billing of this workhous think to starv the poor theare Stephen Wite Stratford Lews of Barfield Wile of TataSon Loyd hintlesham but let them tak Car of thin Selves for farit that is hap on shall there Brains be Blown out and that as sure as death and fail not and the hous shall not be bilt a toyle for thear shall be 500 planted soon and will di all it and pull Wiles hous down. (Muskett 1980: 28)

That the rich should "think to starve the poor" in workhouses instead of giving them a pittance at home was simply outrageous. The outrage called for direct action against the rich and their hated innovations. It called for pulling down not only workhouses but also the homes of offending officials.

Why should poor people be so ungrateful? Because, they said, parish poor had a right to outdoor relief rather than indoor work. Because, they said, the authorities had no right to lock them up merely for being indigent. They had earned better than Bulcamp Hell. "That a free-born Englishman had the right to be relieved in his own home," remarks Ann Digby, "and should not be relieved by being imprisoned in a workhouse was a recurrent theme in East Anglian popular protest" (Digby 1978: 216). One locked up criminals and madmen, not honest freeborn Englishmen. To be poor and unemployed was—as most authorities admitted—neither criminal nor mad.

Why, then, were officials building poorhouses in East Anglia? They had, of course, an administrative rationale:

> Suffolk's experience of poor law administration had run a somewhat different course from that of most other counties. It had marched ahead

in using the hundred rather than the parish for rationalizing and cheapening the cost of maintaining the poor. In rural areas elsewhere, the grouping of parishes was not generally undertaken until after 1782. In Suffolk, this step was first taken in 1756 when the gentry of the hundreds of Carlford and Colneis, on their own initiative, obtained a local act setting up a governing body of J.P.s, freeholders, leaseholders and clergy to arrange for the building of a workhouse at Nacton and to administer poor relief throughout the two hundreds. This experiment reduced the cost of the poor so effectively that by 1780 all the hundreds of east Suffolk, except Plomesgate, as well as Cosford hundred in west Suffolk, had organized themselves in the same way. (Thirsk and Imray 1958: 23)

Cost-cutting remained the prime concern, for during the nineteenth century, as the costs of indoor relief began to overtake those of outdoor relief, parishes began to shift back to the outdoor variety (ibid.).

But why did relief costs rise so notably in the eighteenth century? One fundamental factor was the significant increase in the number of landless agricultural workers in the region, itself a joint result of property concentration and of natural increase among the landless. Landlords and farmers were buying out smallholders, as they had been for several centuries. They were also squeezing out the common rights to glean, to collect wood, to pasture, to hunt, and to gather wild food which had previously made it possible for poor families to survive on tiny plots of land (Humphries 1990). At the same time, farmers were turning away from the practice of having their laborers live in, and take food at the common board as part of their pay. Employment on farms was becoming more seasonal, with large numbers of workers hired on for peak seasons and let go for the rest of the year (Kussmaul 1981).

These trends meant, of course, seasonal unemployment and dependency for many of East Anglia's laboring families. Finally, decline of the region's rural industry was sharpening the competition for work in the countryside; that competition held laborers' wages to one of the lowest levels in all England. In short, an acute process of rural proletarianization was in action. Once again the farmers and landlords of East Anglia led the way to innovation in the countryside—this time toward the establishment of the "indoor relief" that framers of the 1834 New Poor Law would attempt to generalize. They did so by forming "incorporations" uniting a number of rural parishes in the construction and operation of a single house of industry for the dependent poor.

In the 1750s landlords and parsons of the parishes near Ipswich caught the reform fever. Admiral Vernon donated a site on Nacton Heath for a new workhouse. A blue-ribbon committee supervised its construction. The Nacton House of Industry, a model of its kind, started enrolling paupers from a number of adjacent parishes in 1758. The parish poor went to work weaving sacks, making cordage, and spinning wool for the weavers of Norwich. In 1763 and 1764 Parliament authorized seven more houses of industry in Suffolk: at Bulcamp, Barham, Heckingham, Melton, Oulton, Tattingstone, and Shipmeadow (Webb and Webb 1963). By 1765, however, elite supervision had slackened at Nacton and Saxmundham. Cooperating parishes, furthermore, had dumped into the poorhouse young and old, sick and well, regardless of their ability to work. Poor people of Suffolk resisted the system's extension. They stated their demands in a distinctively eighteenth-century mode.

Enclosures of common lands incited similar direct action to restore the rights of the poor. On 26 July 1765, at West Haddon, Northants, "a number of people assembled . . . under pretence of foot-ball playing; but in an instant formed themselves into a tumultuous mob, and pulled up the fences of a new inclosure there, and laid the whole field open" (GM August 1765: 391). At a dinner meeting in Astrop Wells on 12 September 1765, a report came in

> that a number of rioters from Banbury were assembling at Walkworth, the seat of ___ Eyre Esq., in order to level the fences of his new enclosed estate; and a motion being made, that the gentlemen then present, with their servants, should instantly mount their horses, and give them a meeting, the same was agreed to, and eight gentlemen posted to the place, and found the report true. About forty of the levellers were assembled, who, upon sight of the gentlemen, took to their heels and ran away. In the pursuit eight were taken, but the ringleader, who is known, made his escape. (GM September 1765: 441, blank in original text)

Enclosures also generated contention more indirectly, as they restricted semilegal customary uses of open fields or common land that became more visibly illegal once the land lay between neat markers of private property.

Hunting provides the most important example. Authorities and proprietors called hunting on private land "poaching." Four processes converged to make hunting more contentious during the late eighteenth century: increased raising of game birds for shooting on gentlemen's estates, growth of the landless rural population, growing urban demand for game, and commercialization of poaching to meet that demand (Munsche 1981; see also Archer 1990; Carter 1980; Jones 1979; Thompson 1975). As military forces expanded, furthermore, regulars, yeomen, and volunteers had otherwise unauthorized arms at their disposal, and often used them for illicit hunting. In Dorset:

> In 1780 there was a great battle between keepers and poachers on Chettle Common. One keeper was killed, another had his knee broken by a swindgel. A poacher whose hand was cut off by a keeper's hanger turned out to be a sergeant of dragoons. He was lucky, perhaps because he was popular: his sentence of seven years' transportation was commuted to a short prison sentence; he was allowed to retire on half-pay, and set up as a black-market game dealer in London. His regiment buried his hand, with full honours of war, in Pimperne churchyard. (Chevenix Trench 1967: 117)

Gamekeepers found themselves fighting sportsmen, soldiers, poor householders, and whole bands of commercial hunters.

Seizures of grain, attacks on poorhouses, invasions of enclosed land, and much poaching had in common the choice of local targets, the employment of direct redressing action, the risk or deliberate use of violence, the appeal to patrons for intervention with outside authorities, and the adoption of symbolically charged rituals. They firmly belonged, that is, to the contentious repertoire of their time.

Workers' Contention

Some eighteenth-century contention built on more formal organization than did seizures of food and attacks on workhouses or enclosures. That was especially true of the actions of religious denominations, trade groups, and constituted public assemblies such as wardmotes. During the Wilkes controversy of 1769, ward meetings and similar assemblies repeatedly took stands on the issues. In February 1773 London's publicans met—naturally, at a pub: the Brown Bear and Rummer—to consider raising the price of beer. Government spies reported the proceedings (SP 37/10). And in 1780–81, of course, we have seen Lord George Gordon's Protestant Association alternating between public meetings and street politics.

In the Southeast workers were hyperactive between 1758 and 1788. Bookbinders, bricklayers, carpenters, coalheavers, curriers, hatters, joiners, papermakers, printers, sawyers, seamen, shipyard workers, shoemakers, tailors, and weavers sustained especially high levels of collective action (Dobson 1980). London's tailors, for example, enjoyed a special relationship to Parliament, with fixed hours, wages set at Quarter Sessions, and arbitrated disputes; their journeymen's society had the reputation of being "the most militant and effective trade union in eighteenth-century England" (Dobson 1980: 60). Parliament had enacted its regulations, indeed, when seeking to check the activities of the tailors' underground union in 1720 (Rule 1986). The legislation created powerful levers for collective action. Both masters and journeymen, however, organized to take hold of those levers. The masters tried repeatedly to break their journeymen's union by invoking the law of conspiracy as well as by establishing their own houses of call.

In a petition of 1764, during a major wage dispute, Westminster's master tailors described their journeymen's organization. Those workers, they reported:

> have Exacted much greater Wages from their Masters and have worked less Hours than by Law allowed And not Content with that Imposition they formed themselves into a Kind of Republick and held illegal Meetings at 42 different Public Houses commonly called Houses of Call and appointed from each of those Houses Two Persons to Represent the Body and fform the Grand Committee for the Management of the Town (as they express it) which Grand Committee make Rules and Orders for the Direction of the Masters and the whole Body of Journeymen Taylors And whatever Master or Journeyman refused to comply therewith the Master was not to have any Men to do their Business And the Journey-

man was ffined at the Will of the Body of the Journeymen And until
he paid that fine and cleared his Contempt the other Journeymen would
not suffer him to work for any Master. (SP 37/3)

London's master tailors did not succeed in breaking the union.

Eighteenth-century workers combined extensive organization with readiness to use force. The old rites of retaliation and humiliation definitely
remained part of their arsenal. In 1765 Newcastle-area mineowners tried
to impose a sort of perpetual bond on their workers, who rapidly mobilized to strike (Flinn 1984). On 13 September 1765, in the midst of a
work stoppage of 4,000 pitmen, coal owner J. B. Ridley of Newcastle
reported to the Earl of Northumberland that "some violent proceedings
have this day happened at Sir Ralph Milbanke's Colliery and a Number
of the Wear Water men as they are called, have acquainted one of the
Agents of those Collieries, that the men of six Collieries have resolved to
morrow to destroy all the Engines, Gins etc. belonging to all the Collieries
on that River" (SP 37/4; see also Levine and Wrightson 1991). In December 1775 London magistrates "rescued a journeyman sawyer from a
parade through Wapping (he was tied to a donkey, face to its tail, with a
saw tied to his back and placarded 'WORKING BELOW PRICE')" (Dobson
1980: 90). Among eighteenth-century workers, marching, meeting, and
deliberating were by no means inconsistent with smashing machines or
destroying goods currently in production; these acts of destruction paralleled a local community's pulling down of moral offenders' dwellings.

Weavers of Spitalfields (whom we have already seen protecting Wilkes's
election campaigns, cutting silk from renegade workers' looms, and marching
to petition the king) likewise met repeatedly and formally. In 1765 the
weavers first marched on Parliament after the Lords rejected a bill to raise
the tariff on foreign silks the Commons had passed. Weavers then attacked
the house of the Duke of Bedford, the only peer to speak against the bill
(Leslie-Melville 1934). In the 1770s masters and journeymen met separately, then in general assemblies of the trade, to negotiate wage rates
which the government then ratified and enforced (SP 37/10; Steinberg
1989). In April 1773, for example, weavers assembled in the hope of
marching to petition the king, and left anonymous letters with London's
aldermen asking that the council allow such a march to proceed. On 24
April 1773, indeed, Sir John Fielding laid out an elaborate plan of policing

to make sure that no weavers' assembly would break out of its original location and expand into a riotous march (SP 37/10). In that very year the weavers' action finally precipitated an act of Parliament that regulated the trade to their advantage, with fixed wages and governmental arbitration of disputes between workers and masters. For fifty years thereafter the Spitalfields weavers enjoyed significant protection from the capitalist market's vagaries and the concentration of capital that was occurring rapidly in other branches of British manufacturing. During those secure years they wasted little time marching and petitioning except when Parliament threatened to let protective legislation lapse.

Seamen and coalheavers of London likewise built substantial local organization and took advantage of it for collective action. We have already seen both in action during 1768. In 1769, "The seamen outward-bound, in the East-India company's service, quitted their ships, and went in a body to the East-India house, and demanded an increase of wages; which, however, was not complied with" (AR 1769: 79; legend has it that the use of the word "strike" for an industrial work stoppage originated in the seamen's striking of sails for just such presentations of demands: Dobson 1980). Shoemakers, in contrast, used the standard local techniques of turning out and gathering to coerce their masters; in May 1768 journeymen shoemakers "assembled in a tumultuous manner in Moorfields, and other places, for advancing their wages, and compelling many Masters to sign an agreement to that purpose"; several of them received prison sentences on 1 June (LC 2 June 1768).

Outside of the Southeast, trade disputes more often involved mass strikes, machine-breaking, and attacks on the houses of masters. At the workhouse of Shepton Mallet (Somerset) in July 1776, local clothiers started a trial of the newly invented spinning jenny. Weavers, shearmen, and other industrial workers from nearby towns soon assembled at night, broke into the workhouse, smashed the machines and the building's windows, then invaded a gentleman's house to smash furniture and drink up his beer. Under command of a local magistrate, dragoons arrested five or six people only to be stoned by the remainder. After the reading of the Riot Act, the troops fired, killing one man and wounding six (Randall 1991: 72–73, citing *Gloucester Journal* and *Bath Chronicle*).

Other actions involved appeals to authorities, even to Parliament, as well as direct action. In 1778 and 1779 the stockingers of Nottinghamshire agitated for a bill to regulate wages in framework knitting, a proposal the manufacturers vigorously opposed. When Parliament voted down the bill in June 1779, stockingers smashed the windows of master hosiers in Nottingham, burned the house of one master, attacked cotton mills, and smashed stocking frames (Rose 1963–64). In September of the same year the magistrates of Wigan reported that:

> Ever since Monday last a violent and unruly mob have at different times assembled themselves by Beat of Drum and armed, and have committed violent outrages; their principal Fury has been exerted against some of the Capital Manufacturers in the Cotton and Fustian Manufactories carried on in this Town and in the adjacent villages. They have already extended their outrage and violence to the utter destruction of the engine and works of a Capital Manufacturer residing in this Town, and whose Manufactory was about three miles distant, where they have demolished different kinds of Engines for Carding, Roving and Spinning Cotton Wool, some of which were worked by Water. (ibid.: 78–79, citing W.O. 34/119)

Around Glasgow in 1787 thousands of weavers left work over an imminent wage cut and negotiated fruitlessly with their masters. Then some of them sent threatening letters, harassed masters' families, cut webs from working looms, burned the webs publicly, fought troops sent to disperse them, and suffered three deaths in the affray (Murray 1978).

Relations between stockingers and master hosiers in Nottingham, between workers and manufacturers in Wigan, between weavers and their masters in western Scotland, and between journeymen and master tailors in London obviously differed significantly. Yet their contentious repertoires of the 1760s and 1770s had much in common. Direct action, threats, vengeance against individuals, smashing and breaking, irreverent, shaming, and symbol-charged punishment, borrowing of authorized public celebrations and assemblies joined with an appeal to patrons for mediation beyond the local arena. All these features characterized eighteenth-century repertoires of contention.

Mutations

Yet some things were changing. First of all, we can see a greater density of associations in London than in the rest of the country, even if such entities as the Yorkshire Association and the Protestant Association launched their activity from outside, and even though mass action in Ireland and America provided some of the inspiration and precedent for action in London. Often some group in a provincial center innovated on a small scale, only to see Londoners adopt and perfect their innovation on a large scale. Over the long run, London's associational action led the country. From 1768 onward we can see an acceleration of associational politics with its meeting, marching, petitioning, and campaigning. We can also witness a mild increase in the salience of national issues in popular contention.

How and why did the ways in which ordinary people acted collectively change between the 1750s and the 1830s? The evidence from 1758 to 1788 begins to shed light on the answers. We have some indications of differential change in repertoires, with groups connected on a national scale by elite entrepreneurs, especially those based in London, adopting associational action while groups elsewhere were continuing to deploy the standard means of the eighteenth-century repertoire. The issues of war and peace, on one side, and of capital's expansion, on the other, seem to have stimulated a wide range of resistance and concerted action, including especially the newer associational forms. We have no clear indication so far of ruling-class and governmental strategies of control, except to notice that negotiation with national authorities reshaped meetings, marches, petitions, election campaigns, and other innovations of the period. On the basis of the period's evidence, proletarianization and changes in state power emphatically affected the relatively minor shifts in repertoire. We have suggestions—only suggestions so far—that the emergence of a repertoire based on associational life and strongly oriented to national centers of power could have a large impact on British politics. The Society of Supporters of the Bill of Rights, the Protestant Association, and the Yorkshire Association all helped expand the social bases and political activity of associations outside the elite and in opposition to Parliament. To what extent did they mark a path to the future? An examination of contention between 1789 and 1815 will clarify all these questions.

PLATES

THE PILLORY TRIUMPHANT, 1765 (engraving sold by Sumpter). The bookseller John Williams is pilloried for selling John Wilkes's works.

THE BRENTFORD ELECTION, 1768 (*Oxford Magazine*). A violent encounter between partisans of John Wilkes's ally Serjeant Glynn and of his opponent Sir William Beauchamp Proctor.

FANATICISM REVIVED, 1780 (Carey engraving). Attacks on property of Catholics by supporters of Lord George Gordon's Protestant Association.

THE PROTESTANT ASSOCIATION, 1780 (Wooding engraving). Members of the Protestant Association march to present their anti-Catholic petition to Parliament.

WILLIAM PITT'S PROCESSION, 1784 (Rowlandson engraving). Satire of "Billy" Pitt's procession to dine with the Grocers' Company and receive the freedom of the City; includes John Wilkes, who had recently supported Pitt in Parliament.

THE DELEGATES IN COUNCIL, 1797 (I. Cruikshank engraving). Spokesmen for a naval mutiny meet with Admiral Buckner, while radical and Whig politicians look on from under the table.

HINTS TO FORESTALLERS, 1800 (I. Cruikshank [?] engraving). A market crowd wreaks vengeance on a high-priced merchant-farmer.

Rifle Men!

John the Great supported by corresponding Citizens !!

A Party of the Jazy Club drawing a Cannon loaded with Norfolk Dumplins !!

I. HORNE TOOKE

Whig Club

Feb. 1801

HORNE TOOKE'S ELECTION PROCESSION, 1801 (anonymous engraving). John Horne (Horne Tooke) is borne on a chair by members of the suppressed London Corresponding Society.

WESTMINSTER PARLIAMENTARY ELECTION, 1818 (Scharf aquatint).
Covent Garden with hustings and crowd.

THE PETERLOO MASSACRE, 1819 (Marks aquatint). Manchester Yeomanry ride down spectators at St. Peter's Fields, Manchester.

CROWD PELTS WELLINGTON, 1820 (Lane [?] engraving). During the Queen Caroline affair, people hoot and stone the duke, who supports the king.

THE CATHOLIC ASSOCIATION, 1825 (R. Cruikshank engraving). Prime Minister Canning faces supporters of Daniel O'Connell and his Catholic Association.

METROPOLITAN POLITICAL UNION, 1830 (Heath in *The Looking Glass*).
Daniel O'Connell speaks to a crowd represented as braying asses.

COBBETT AND SWING, 1830 (Seymour woodcut). Cobbett gives copies
of his *Register* to a bill-sticker as hayricks blaze.

THE PITMENS UNION, 1832 (*Northumberland Freeholder*).
Confrontation between coal owners and representatives of the union.

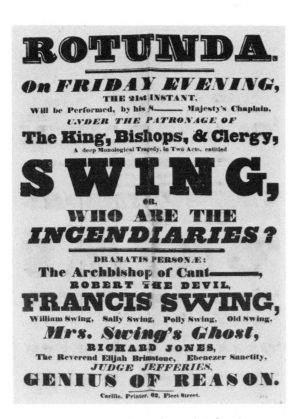

SWING SATIRIZED, 1831 (poster). Advertisement for radical response to the Swing rebellion.

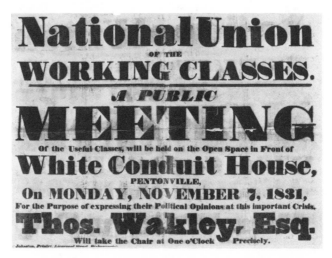

MEETING OF THE NUWC, 1831 (poster). Call to a meeting of the National Union of the Working Classes in the Pentonville district, London.

❧ 5 ❧

REVOLUTION, WAR, AND
OTHER STRUGGLES, 1789–1815

"FROM THE PART Mr. Burke took in the American Revolution," declared Thomas Paine in 1791, "it was natural that I should consider him a friend to mankind" (Paine 1984: 35). Edmund Burke had defended American rights in the 1760s and 1770s; as a new MP, for example, he had played a major part in organizing the repeal of the infamous Stamp Act. Not only that; he had supported relief from political disabilities of Catholics and Protestant Dissenters as well. As an Anglo-Irish outsider from Dublin, Burke had reasons for sympathy with the excluded and oppressed. His *Thoughts on the Cause of the Present Discontents* (1770), with its concessions to popular representation, established the Rocking-ham Whigs as public critics of arbitrary power. Burke and his companions regarded Parliament, not the king, as the nation's voice.

To that limited extent, Burke then stood on the same side as John Wilkes. Indeed, he had worked for Wilkes's admission to Parliament during the controversies of 1769 (O'Brien 1992). But his *Reflections on the Revolution in France,* published in 1790, vehemently rejected broad claims to popular sovereignty as well as revolution. Paine, advocate of popular sovereignty and friend of revolution, flayed Burke as a sort of Cold Warrior: "When the French Revolution broke out," Paine complained, "it certainly afforded to Mr. Burke an opportunity of doing some good, had he been disposed to it; instead of which, no sooner did he see the old prejudices wearing away, than he immediately began sowing the seeds of a new inveteracy, as if he were afraid that England and France would cease to be enemies" (Paine 1984: 36). Paine's *The Rights of Man* countered with stirring advocacy of the French Revolution and the case for establishment of a republican constitution—without revolution if possible, with revolution if necessary—in Great Britain.

Tom Paine knew something about revolution: emigrating to Pennsylvania with Benjamin Franklin's patronage in 1774, he had served the American cause in a variety of capacities thereafter. During his French sojourn of 1789, "From Lafayette Paine received the key to the Bastille to take back to Washington" (Kramnick 1990: 141). Paine drew on a glowing faith in human capacity for ethical self-government. "There is a natural aptness in man, and more so in society," he wrote,

> because it embraces a greater variety of abilities and resource, to accommodate itself to whatever situation it is in. The instant formal government is abolished, society begins to act. A general association takes place, and common interest produces common security . . . When men, as well from natural instinct, as from reciprocal benefits, have habituated themselves to social and civilized life, there is always enough of its principles in practice to carry them through any changes they may find necessary or convenient to make in their government. (Paine 1984: 164)

In the Britain of 1791 these were revolutionary principles. They made popular deliberation and consent prior to parliamentary decisionmaking, not subordinate to it, much less an illegitimate assumption of parliamentary prerogatives. Paine's line of argument struck a resonant chord in Great Britain; volume I sold some 50,000 copies in 1791, volume II perhaps 200,000 copies by 1793. Reprints and excerpts circulated everywhere in pamphlets and the penny press.

Edmund Burke would have none of this innate goodness, with its closely associated ideas of equality and natural rights. Nor would he concede the priority of popular will over Parliament's judgment. Even when supporting American claims during the 1770s, he had argued in terms of defending an excellent English constitution against the abuses of arbitrary authority rather than in terms of making concessions to popular sovereignty, to the idea that government rests, and should rest, on the consent and will of the governed. Although "on at least one occasion he changed his vote to suit the opinion of his electors," during the 1774 campaign for the instruction of MPs he had insisted to his own Bristol electors that, having selected him as a member of the governing assembly for his merits, they had no right to direct his votes (Langford 1988).

There, Burke contradicted the Welsh Dissenter Rev. Dr. Richard Price. Price had been arguing natural rights since defending the American revolt in 1775, but Burke had never accepted that dangerous doctrine. In his first great speech against the French Revolution in March 1790, Burke read from the writings of Price and of Price's friend Joseph Priestley to illustrate the threat their doctrines offered to the established church, hence to the establishment as a whole. Burke rejected Price's advocacy of repeal of the Test and Corporation Acts, which limited the political rights of Protestant Dissenters. Responding to Price's enthusiastic speeches lauding the French Revolution's realization of popular rights, Burke's *Reflections* continued to reject any claim that such rights existed, or would do good if they did exist. Burke attacked populist claims not only on general grounds of political obligation but also on account of their pernicious social consequences. More than once he drew parallels between Parisian mobs and the Gordon rioters of 1780. Nor did those reflections lack popular support; conservatives, including workers who rallied for Church and King, found in the French Revolution something foreign to deplore. The standard loyalist riposte to expressions of favor for revolutionary causes was to parade and burn an effigy of Tom Paine (Booth 1983; Donnelly and Baxter 1975).

Burke did not impugn the right of the Revolution Society, before which Price had spoken, to exist; he challenged its claim to speak for the English people, and to address congratulations directly to the French government. He denied that the English Revolution of 1688 had established royal rule by consent of the governed, going on to insist that popular government would bring disaster. Good government required the preeminence of property and birth: "The power of perpetuating our property in our families is one of the most valuable and interesting circumstances belonging to it, and that which tends the most to the perpetuation of society itself. It makes our weakness subservient to our virtue; it grafts benevolence even upon avarice. The possessors of family wealth, and of the distinction which attends hereditary possession . . . are the natural securities for this transmission" (Burke 1984: 49).

Burke anticipated today's rational-choice theorists by reversing the democratic argument for consent. A form of government was, he wrote, an invention, a necessary invention; once a people had consented to a particular form of government they had an obligation to maintain it rather than to subvert it, for the overthrow of government could only bring vast disorder, the destruction of every interest. Conservatives from Hobbes onward have commonly made precisely that argument. The Old Whig analysis, as Samuel Beer (1957) called it, easily justified such arrangements as rotten boroughs on the ground that they facilitated representation of collective interests. Virtual representation, runs the argument, installed greater wisdom than direct popular representation ever could.

Meanwhile, popular contention increasingly disputed Burke's claim. Organized nonvoters stormed the hustings, workers called for state intervention in their disputes with masters, enemies of policing cited their inborn rights, and working-class leaders called for a mass platform of reforms initiated from below, all in the spirit (and sometimes in the name) of popular sovereignty. In Norwich, after commemorating England's own Glorious Revolution with cannonade, church bells, bonfire, and illuminations on 5 November 1788, citizens followed the French Revolution of 1789 with weekly reports in the local newspaper, visits to Paris, and tableaux on Guild Day; in November 1789 they formed their own Revolution Society (Jewson 1975). The idea of an extraparliamentary national Convention to represent all the people instead of the narrow electorate sprang directly from French example. Mass associations edged closer to acceptability, even when conservatives such as Burke denied their right to speak for the masses. As American resistance had earlier provided a splendid opportunity for British criticism of favoritism and tyranny, the French Revolution's first years placed a concrete example close at hand; it gave British reformers and radicals a wonderfully convenient comparison with the corruption and arbitrary rule they saw at home.

On 17 June 1789, after all, France's deputies to the Third Estate had baptized themselves the National Assembly, merely inviting members of the other Estates to join them. In the name of the Nation, they had declared themselves the supreme political authority. They provided a striking model of popular sovereignty. Although the ensuing war with France dulled the French comparison's luster, the very expansion and centralization of the British state in a time of war—and of taxation—on an unprecedented scale sharpened the debate over popular sovereignty. It raised new questions of consent by those who paid and obeyed, undercut the positions of old elite intermediaries, and made it more urgent for any interest to influence Parliament rather than local patrons or even the king and his entourage. Few ordinary people made explicit arguments from taxation to popular sovereignty, but the expense of war and of a corrupt establishment became prevalent radical complaints and prime arguments for the likely benefits of parliamentary reform.

Despite anti-French nationalism and extensive repression, ordinary people pressed their demands to be heard on the national scene. Between 1789 and 1815 ordinary people gained little or no practical, everyday power in Great Britain; the freedom of radicals among them to assemble, organize, and protest even declined during the years of war. What is more, the extension of associational activity opened space for anti-radicals as well as radicals: the Church and King clubs that attacked militant Dissenters and French sympathizers from 1791 onward benefited from the precedents set by their radical adversaries (Dickinson 1990). In Birmingham local magistrates tolerated, perhaps promoted, the attacks of Church and King activists against the properties of Joseph Priestley, other radicals, and prominent Dissenters on the occasion of their Bastille Day celebrations in 1791. In Manchester local Tories formed a Society to Put Down Levellers in 1793, subjecting radicals and reformers to secret examination and marking some of them for prosecution (Gatrell 1982). Nevertheless the accepted forms of claim-making changed in ways that for the first time since the seventeenth-century revolutions conceded substantial space to the idea and the practice of popular sovereignty.

Edmund Morgan argues that popular sovereignty was a fiction invented by English magnates as a weapon against threats to their position: "Yeomen did not declare their own independence. Their lordly neighbors declared it, in an appeal for support against those other few whom they feared and distrusted as enemies to liberty and to the security of property—against irresponsible kings, against courtiers and bankers, stockjobbers and speculators—and against that unsafe portion of the many whom they also feared and distrusted for the same reason: paupers and laborers who held no land" (Morgan 1988: 169). Perhaps. But whoever first deployed well-articulated arguments for popular sovereignty, from the time of Wilkes onward the arguments had enormous appeal to ordinary Britons. By the late eighteenth century Tom Paine spoke for an increasingly popular view.

The pamphlet debate among Price, Burke, and Paine summed up the political choices open to British people in the age of the French Revolution. Intermediate positions existed, to be sure: Christopher Wyvill, for all the daring of his Yorkshire Association in 1780 and for all his authorship of a pamphlet titled *A Defence of Dr. Price and the Reformers of England,* stuck with the idea that property gave people a stake in the government, while the propertyless whom Paine proposed to empower lacked the essential stability and moderation for self-government (Thompson 1963; Dinwiddy 1971). In 1790, nevertheless, Paine and Burke marked the debate's poles; the fundamental contest concerned the direct representation of the population as a whole. In Sheffield during November 1792, "5,000 'republicans and levellers' in the guise of cutlers, paraded posters showing Edmund Burke riding a pig, the Home Secretary as half-man, half-ass, the Angel of Peace offering Tom Paine's *Rights of Man* to a stricken Britannia; it was Valmy they were celebrating" (Williams 1968: 3). As the previous generation had used the rebellious American colonies, British dissidents seized the French Revolution as a club with which to beat their own rulers.

Associations in France and Britain

Sometimes the weapon was, precisely, a club: a political association. As it happens, many French revolutionaries of 1789 thought that, far from teaching the English, they were finally acquiring the liberties and political means of freeborn Englishmen. When the French Third Estate assembled in May 1789 it soon called itself the Communes in direct imitation of the House of Commons. The emulation extended to popular mobilization. In 1785, for example, the Parisian bookseller Sébastian Hardy had described the English-style *Klubs* around the Palais-Royal recently established under the auspices of the Duke of Chartres as gambling dens set up "to attract foreigners and other rich people of the capital" and started "only to imitate the English" (BN Fr 6685, 16 February 1785). At that point the emulation had little political significance; the Palais Royal simply represented a zone of license partly protected from royal authority. In some regards it paralleled the contained licentiousness of Southwark, where fairs, bars, brothels, assembly-points of workers' marches, and centers of radical gathering neighbored but few police ventured. As with Southwark, the Palais Royal served as an area of exceptionally free political discussion.

Around the beginning of 1787, however, France divided in a great struggle between the tax-seeking monarchy and sovereign courts that defended provincial privileges. Parisian clubs were then "infected with political fever" (Egret 1962: 148). Sensitive to their heat, the government closed down the clubs in August 1787, but in August 1788 relented under the somewhat more liberal ministry of Jacques Necker. Royalists later blamed Necker for having thereby encouraged a revolutionary movement. They had a point.

At that moment French conservatives were right to think of voluntary associations—especially those permitting popular membership and espousing political programs—as a dangerous British innovation. Using criteria similar to those of the British study, but with sources far less systematic and complete, I have assembled a catalog of contentious gatherings in the Paris region as well as four other French regions from 1600 through 1984 (Tilly 1985a, 1986b). In the Parisian catalog for 1780–1788, clandestine workers' guilds surely lay behind some of the workers' strikes and attacks, but not one publicly visible association of any kind made claims or organized collective action. Eighteenth-century France certainly had learned societies, lay religious confraternities, lodges, and underground workers' organizations, but in general French public authorities struck down as a danger to public order any attempt to create political clubs or their equivalent. They also strongly discouraged any associations they did tolerate from making public claims except through the courts and/or the mouths of eminent patrons.

In England's Southeast of 1780, in contrast, not only the Protestant Association and a number of authorized assemblies (such as the Freeholders of Surrey, the Inhabitants of Aldgate Ward, and Publicans) but also a Committee of Correspondence and the City Association made public claims. The Society for Constitutional Information, organized that year, became a major advocate of parliamentary reform. In 1781 several committees (including "friends" of parliamentary candidates) joined the assemblies of inhabitants and freeholders. During the later 1780s an elite "Committee to Conduct the Application to Parliament" managed Protestant Dissenters' unsuccessful campaign for repeal of the mildly restrictive Test and Corporation Acts (Davis 1971: 44). In 1789 the Whig Club, the Humane Society, the London Association, the Club Instituted to Support the Independency of the County (of Middlesex), and the Society for Commemorating the Revolution in Great Britain added their numbers to many local assemblies and *ad hoc* gatherings of merchants, manufacturers, or theater subscribers.

Once the Protestant Association collapsed after its debacle of 1780, mass-membership associations receded from open contention for a time.

But elite associations (the Society for Commemorating the Revolution enlisted, among others, the Lord Mayor, the Lord Mayor Elect, Lord William Russell, and numerous MPs) had an established place among Britain's claim-makers of the 1780s. The Society for the Abolition of the Slave Trade, for example, formed in 1787, became the nucleus of anti-slavery efforts for two decades. "The Anti-Slavery Society," according to R. J. Morris, "created the characteristic forms of the modern pressure group, public meetings, petitions, and reports in the growing newspaper press" (Morris 1990: 409); if that opinion gives too little weight to the other activist organizations of the 1790s, it captures the connection between associations and the emerging apparatus of social movements.

Nor did London monopolize clubs and associations: in later eighteenth-century Birmingham, for example, the Free Debating Society and kindred associations often met in taverns and coffeehouses to air the day's political issues, while poorer people organized clubs for mutual aid and pooled purchases (Money 1977; R. J. Morris 1990; Barry 1993). In coal-producing regions, owners and operators repeatedly used deliberately formed associations to advance their oligopolistic interests from early in the eighteenth century (Flinn 1984). Between 1785 and 1799 masonic lodges were multiplying in industrial areas (Money 1990). On the side of repression, furthermore, associations for the prosecution of felons had proliferated in England over the previous two decades (Philips 1989); as compared with their European neighbors, the eighteenth-century British did an exceptional share of their public business by means of private, special-purpose associations. If we add to secular clubs the work of churches, which frequently served as nurseries for principled collective action, by the end of the eighteenth century Britain's public life teemed with associations; Nonconformist churches had, after all, been conducting much of their collective work through assemblies and associations for a century before 1790 (Nuttall 1971). No doubt a century of tense toleration for congregations outside the state church had opened up an organizational space that generally remained much smaller on the European continent, if not in the religiously polyglot United States.

With its Revolution, France temporarily reversed the cross-channel balance. In 1789 the clubs of Paris and other French cities became major rallying-points for revolutionary demands. In Paris, the Klub National began to meet in the Palais Royal, hitherto a pleasure palace but now the gathering-place of orators, journalists, and political activists. On 29 July, after the attack on the Bastille and the king's recalling of the popular Jacques Necker as minister of finance, people celebrated in the Palais:

> In each arcade of the galleries they had placed a chandelier surrounded with brightly colored lanterns. Everywhere one saw transparencies with these words: *Long live the king; long live the Nation; long live M. Necker.* The eleven arcades of the Klube [*sic*] were illuminated in an even more striking way: in the middle they had placed a transparency with the words *Klub National* and on the sides portraits of the king and of M. Necker, likewise in transparencies. To that brilliant illumination they added a continuous concert, very melodious, played by all the instrumentalists of the Opera and other theaters combined. (BN Fr 6687, 29 July 1789)

By that time, popularly organized clubs, societies, committees, and militias were doing much of the revolutionary work in Paris and all the provinces. For four years—until the Terror, and then Thermidor—special-purpose associations spearheaded popular participation in the French Revolution.

British dissidents returned the French compliment by organizing constitutional societies to demand effective reform. Dr. Price gave the address of 1789 that stimulated Edmund Burke's famous reply before the Revolution Society, which claimed to have met annually since 1688 in commemoration of that year's Glorious Revolution. The London Revolution Society had already committed itself to a populist position at its centennial meeting of 1788, declaring:

1 That all civil and political authority is derived from the people
2 That the abuse of power justifies resistance
3 That the right of private judgment, liberty of conscience, trial by jury, the freedom of the press and the freedom of election ought ever to be held sacred and inviolable. (Goodwin 1979: 87)

They and their allies, furthermore, had recently mobilized in the energetic, if unsuccessful, campaigns of 1787 and 1789 for repeal of those political restrictions on Dissenters imposed by the Test and Corporation Acts. But new associations sprang up immediately. At its 1789 meeting the London Revolution Society itself passed a resolution encouraging the formation of similar societies, linked by correspondence, throughout the kingdom (ibid.: 110). The organization of corresponding societies rather than openly national organizations stayed just within the law, and emulated a tactic used very effectively by rebellious American colonists fifteen years earlier. In Manchester a small group of merchants, manufacturers, and professionals formed their own society in response to the founding of a conservative local Church and King Club in March 1790; it was committed to "government by 'the consent of the governed' and a 'speedy and effective reform' of parliamentary representation" (Bohstedt 1983: 106). Elsewhere, the Manchester society's counterparts recruited many more petty merchants, artisans, and workers. The Sheffield Constitutional Society organized a popular membership in 1791, the first of many, and boasted 2000 members in March 1792 (Royle and Walvin 1982: 50); by the following summer, in Norwich alone, "over 2,000 men were organized in forty small tavern-clubs" (Williams 1968: 64). The London Corresponding Society, formed in the spring of 1792, swelled to more than a thousand members by year's end.

Although it had some roots in the relatively elite Society for Constitutional Information (which in turn maintained close ties to the London Revolution Society), the LCS set a standard for mass-membership associations with its shoemaker-founder Thomas Hardy, its initiation fee of one shilling, and its dues of a penny per week. It soon established collaboration with sister societies in Sheffield, Stockport, Norwich, and Manchester. The corresponding societies became major organizers of the unsuccessful petition drive for parliamentary reform in 1793. By November 1795 the LCS was able to bring out an "immense concourse" around five tribunes in the fields behind Copenhagen House (Islington) to sign petitions against bills increasing security measures for the king and outlawing seditious assemblies; the *Annual Register* estimated the assembly as "not less than an hundred thousand persons" (AR 1795: 43; see also Goodwin 1979).

While the LCS grew cautious as governmental repression checked obvious radicals, the association and the public meeting took on increasing prominence in British repertoires of popular contention. At the edge of the association and the public meeting formed a "radical underworld" of conspirators, confidence men, and zealots who appeared, among other guises, as the United Englishmen or United Britons (McCalman 1988). Even the major repressive legislation of 1794–1799 (banning of the United

Irishmen, partial suspension of *habeas corpus,* the Seditious Meetings Act, the Treasonable Practices Act, the Irish Insurrection Act, the Combination Acts) failed to expunge associational activity.

Public discourse shifted accordingly. Until the 1790s British defenders of political positions commonly invoked religious justifications and argued in terms of general political theory. With the discussion aroused by the French Revolution, it became much more common to offer secular arguments emphasizing the social consequences of one political course or another (Hole 1989; Claeys 1994). At the same time, conceptions of individual rights became much more salient; even apparently backward-looking references to the rights of freeborn Englishmen, which multiplied, emphasized the priority of individual interests over collective order. Popular debating societies, at which shopkeepers and artisans typically paid sixpence to hear a spirited discussion, increasingly slanted their questions to the democratic side (Thale 1989). The struggles of the revolutionary period reshaped the intellectual means with which authors, orators, political leaders, and ordinary people reasoned out the alternatives open to them.

The proliferation of explicitly political associations in the 1790s had its parallels, and perhaps part of its basis, in the organization of labor unions. Tailors, hatters, weavers, and other groups of relatively skilled workers maintained underground unions through most of the eighteenth century. Many trades, furthermore, sustained regional or national networks including "ports of call" at which their tramping members could find sustenance and access to employment. Whenever they struck or otherwise acted collectively on wages and working conditions, such workers ran the risk of prosecution for conspiracy. As illegal bodies, labor unions remained secret; at this remove it is therefore hard to distinguish the action of special-purpose associations from the operation of informal networks within trades. But in general it seems that mutual aid societies and labor unions multiplied from the 1760s to the 1780s only to explode in the associational expansion of the early 1790s and then contract significantly with later repression.

As the previous chapter showed, the years from the 1750s to the 1780s had seen increasing statement of claims for popular sovereignty, a moderate rise in associational activity, some nationalization of demands, as well as a first articulation of programs for parliamentary reform and reduction of religious barriers to political participation. Yet the fundamental repertoire of popular contention had not changed significantly during those years. Most public contention continued to take the form of direct attacks on malefactors or their property, grain seizures, the acting out of shame or commendation, invasions of newly forbidden territories, appeals to patrons, and similar local actions aimed at local targets.

The following period was different. Between 1789 and 1815 Britain's ordinary people took decisive, irreversible steps away from local, particular, and mediated action. Radical entrepreneurs experimented more or less successfully with missionary lecture tours, national conventions, giant petition drives, vast public meetings, and the formation of special-purpose associations. Their opponents, often encouraged by public authorities, adopted some of the same means. The rise of the popular association and of the public meeting was the most visible element in a more general move toward means of contention that voiced a claim to be heard directly on the national scene. Although he employs a very different idiom, Roger Wells sees a similar shift in both rural and urban conflicts on a national scale; for him the 1790s were "a watershed in rural history" (Wells 1990: 157), and another "watershed" for workers' organization (Wells 1988: 168). The weight of contention' shifted decisively toward cosmopolitan, modular, autonomous forms of action.

Why? The answer lies at two levels: external and internal to popular contention. Externally, the rising power of Parliament, the increasing penetration of the national state into local life, the accumulation and concentration of capital, the proletarianization of the working population, and the increasing prominence of merchants and manufacturers in national affairs gave ordinary people and their political entrepreneurs growing capacities and incentives to fight for their rights on a national scale, increasingly by means of efforts to influence Parliament. Internally, the specific histories of collective action and repression formed institutions, knowledge, memories, practices, and legal precedents that set the range of capacities, opportunities, and threats for new collective actors. Authorities' concessions to meetings and marches at one given time facilitated the next round of meetings and marches while making it more difficult for authorities to smash them. But equally ordinary people's acceptance of meetings and marches as proper ways of making claims foreclosed their choices of direct retaliation against enemies and wrongdoers. This set of changes enlarged the places of political brokers, entrepreneurs, and organizations in popular claim-making. More and more, national politics and local contention intertwined.

Economy and Demography

Over the short run, shifts in political opportunity and threat strongly affected the incidence of popular contention; even struggles over food depended heavily on responses of local authorities to shortages and high prices. Similarly, workers acted or failed to act on long-accumulated grievances as a function of short-term changes in their power vis-à-vis capitalists and landlords. Over the longer run, however, transformations of the economy shaped not only the grievances on which ordinary people were prepared to act but also their capacity to act collectively. Between 1789 and 1815 those transformations ran deep. During the titanic struggles with France, Great Britain repeatedly flexed its economic muscle. Manufactures accounted for about nine-tenths of all British exports during the period, and textiles—increasingly cotton textiles—accounted for more than half of all exports (Crafts 1985). Despite a blockade of British trade by France and its allies that severely cramped exports to the Continent, the economy as a whole continued to expand, even accelerated. During the war years, exports of textiles to British colonies, to the United States, to China, and to the rest of the world grew. Correspondingly, imports of raw cotton and of food rose. Ireland and America therefore became increasingly crucial sources of supply.

During the war merchants, manufacturers, and landlords all benefited from the great economic expansion. Merchants gained from Britain's increasingly central position in world trade. Manufacturers gained from labor-saving technologies and managerial innovations in the face of a tight labor market. Landlords and large farmers, pressed at first by war-induced shortages of labor, not only profited from the restriction of food imports, the demand for food to support troops under arms, and the consequent rise in prices, but also used that leverage to organize enclosures and introduce more efficient forms of mixed farming. Rents rose handsomely. Rising food prices and enclosures, in particular, rapidly elevated rents. Rising rents provided an incentive for those who already held some legal title to property to enclose commonly held land; 43 percent of all parliamentary enclosures ever registered took place during the French Wars (Mingay 1989). Meanwhile real incomes, according to optimistic Lindert-Williamson estimates, turned from the slight declines of the previous period to a modest rise of about 0.4 percent per year.

From the bottom, however, things looked different. Rising food prices entailed a substantial increase in the cost of living. Although the overall effects of parliamentary enclosure remain murky and controversial, most likely the loss of common rights struck land-poor laborers hard (ibid.). Class differences in diet, income, and style of life sharpened. Proletarianization accelerated in both agriculture and manufacturing as farm workers lost their claims on land or lodging and artisans gave way to wage-workers; while Alan Armstrong (1988: 57) concludes that "wage-paid labour in agriculture just about succeeded in holding its own during the French wars," K. D. M. Snell's analysis of Southern England indicates a significant decline in real income for agricultural laborers (Snell 1985). As bourgeois property expanded and the population as a whole proletarianized, the proportion of the population falling under the direct control of landlords, or even of their substantial tenant farmers, declined decisively. During the subsistence crisis of 1795 parish elders in southeastern England widely adopted the Speenhamland system, in which poor rates subsidized able-bodied laborers' wages on a sliding scale depending on the current price of food and the composition of the worker's household (Mingay 1989; Boyer 1990).

Nominally independent landless laborers multiplied in city, town, and village, while full-time manufacturing workers and military personnel also increased. Writing in 1816, Robert Southey found the growth of the poor population frightening:

> . . . the great mass of the manufacturing populace, whatever be their wages, live, as the phrase is, from hand to mouth, and make no provision for the morrow . . . being utterly improvident because their moral and religious education has been utterly neglected. The number of paupers, therefore, which elsewhere is stationary, or increases only in proportion to the increase of the other classes of society, is here at all times liable to a sudden and perilous augmentation, from the effects of an unfavorable season, in a climate where the seasons are peculiarly precarious; from the fluctuations of politics affecting a people, to whom foreign commerce has become of too much importance; and even from the

caprice of fashion, in a country where thousands of families are dependent for daily bread upon the taste for silks or stuffs, ribands and buttons, and buckles. Formerly, indeed, these things seldom produced any farther evil than that of a few riots upon market days in times of scarcity. But the same accident, which to a healthy subject would occasion only a slight and temporary inconvenience, scarcely felt at the moment, and drawing no ill consequences after it, will produce gangrene or cancer in a system that is morbidly predisposed, and certain it is, that in these our days a morbid change has been wrought in the great body of the populace. (Southey 1832: I, 76–77)

At bottom, as Southey half-recognized, this vulnerability arose from commercial expansion, from the very vigor of capitalism. In villages as well as cities, merchants, artisans, and wage-workers connected increasingly with one another and with the rest of the world through commercial networks. Not that they formed a happy *ménage à trois;* each pair of them fought frequently.

State, War, and Parliament

Behind the changes in popular contention lay a massive political process. With a two-year interval of uneasy peace, Britain warred with France from 1793 to 1815, at huge expense. The army increased from about 40,000 men in 1789 to 266,000 in 1811, the navy from 16,000 in 1789 to 114,000 in 1797, for a more than sixfold increase of professional military forces, not counting domestic militias. In the Caribbean, British forces (aided by black rebellion in Saint-Domingue) destroyed French commercial predominance, even if they returned most of their conquests at war's end; by 1795 the British had 30,000 troops in the Caribbean. At the same time, Britain stepped up efforts to pacify India and Ireland, whose subordination to Britain the French threatened repeatedly in different ways. In India, Cornwallis and then Wellesley fought Sultan Tipu of Mysore until Tipu's death in 1799 consolidated British power and sealed the expulsion of France from the subcontinent. Meanwhile British forces were seizing the Cape of Good Hope, Ceylon, Malacca, and other territories in adjacent seas. By 1805 Britain wielded major power in a band from Africa to China.

In Ireland, however, challenges to British hegemony continued. Despite the Irish Parliament's passage in 1793, under pressure from Whitehall, of a Catholic relief act that significantly increased popular representation and officeholding, attacks on landlords and insurrectionary plots proliferated. In 1798 a force of 15,000 United Irishmen took Wexford and Enniscorthy before General Lake organized a strong counterforce and dispersed them; a French landing in August 1798 came too late, and succumbed to joint attacks by Lake and Cornwallis. But Ireland continued to resist British rule, and to pay for a large force of British troops; army contingents stationed in Ireland amounted to 10,000 men in 1793, 24,000 in 1798, and 30,000 in 1808 (Palmer 1988). The formation of the United Kingdom brought 100 relatively conservative Irish protestant members into the British Parliament, but did not pacify the colony's ordinary people.

Wars in Europe, Asia, and Ireland greatly increased the crown's military expenditure and its total expenditure. State expenditure grew even faster than revenues, with the obvious consequence that debt increased. After 1789 expenditure on the army and navy grew more than four times as fast as in the previous forty years. Income and expenditure (Table 5.1) give an indication of the change. All major categories of state revenue accelerated dramatically; although Britain was already energetically making war during the decades before 1789, customs, excise, and land tax grew more than twice as fast between 1789 and 1815 as they had between 1758 and 1781. The inclusion of Ireland in the figures for 1815 probably inflates them slightly, but since before 1801 Britain essentially made the Irish occupation pay for itself, the numbers give a reasonable estimate of the changing weight of government in Great Britain.

As a rough measure of taxation's impact, we might express the per capita burden as the approximate number of days' wages it would pay of (1) a farm laborer and (2) a cotton spinner (see Table 5.2). The figures average, of course, across women, men, and children. Yet they serve to show that the household burden of wartime taxes accelerated somewhat after 1795 and momentously after 1801. With respect to workers' ability to pay, taxes more than doubled. If we imagined the average worker's household as having three members and only one wage-earner, the numbers would represent a rise from about a seventh to over a third of household income devoted to taxation of one sort or another.

As happened everywhere in Europe during the eighteenth and nine-

Table 5.1. Government finance and real income in Britain/United Kingdom, 1789–1815

Item	1789	1815	Annual % of change	Rate of change 1758–1788
Revenue from customs	3,647	14,800	+5.5%	+2.4%
Revenue from excise	7,301	29,500	+5.5	+2.5
Revenue from stamps	1,250	6,500	+6.5	+5.3
Revenue from land tax	3,006	8,000	+3.8	+1.1
Debt service expenditure	9,425	30,000	+4.6	+4.0
Civil government expenditure	1,664	5,800	+4.9	+0.6
Expenditure on army	1,899	49,600	+13.4	−2.6
Expenditure on navy	2,073	22,800	+9.7	−1.8
Total expenditure on military	4,447	72,400	+11.3	−2.1
Farm laborer real income	19.69	21.93	+0.4	+0.1
Middle worker real income	35.91	39.98	+0.4	+0.1
Artisan real income	35.71	39.21	+0.4	−0.4

Note: "Real income" is in 1851 pounds per year. Other figures are in thousands of current pounds sterling. 1815 governmental figures refer to the United Kingdom.

Sources: Lindert and Williamson 1983b; Williamson 1985; Mitchell and Deane 1971.

teenth centuries, war swelled the civilian establishment as well. The Alien Act of January 1793, for example, created an Alien Office to control France's émigrés in Britain; it soon became the nerve center of domestic political surveillance and the base of a large network of spies and informers (Hone 1982; Wells 1983; Fryer 1965; Mitchell 1965). In 1794 the government created another new office: the Secretary of War, budgeted at 13,000 pounds (Cohen 1965). Civil government expenditure rose from a modest growth rate of 0.6 percent per year in 1758–1788 to an enormous 4.9 percent per year in 1789–1815.

The result was a massively larger state, and one in which parliamentary consent to taxation and expenditure occupied a much more central position in the political process. In the course of the state's expansion emerged a relatively conservative governing coalition typified (and often led) by William Pitt and a more reformist opposition around Charles James Fox. After 1792 neither cluster provided a comfortable home for the radicals who surged during the French Revolution's early years but eventually fragmented under strong state repression of political association and workers' collective action. While the British state was striking at Englishmen, Welshmen, Scots, and (especially) Irishmen who displayed sympathy for French ideas, indeed, it was also pursuing an extensive if futile effort to organize counter-revolution in France (Fryer 1965; Mitchell 1965). Both Pitt and Fox died in 1806, but their clusters survived into the postwar period. Indeed, the conservative coalition Pitt had soldered together remained connected and politically dominant until 1829.

In matters of state, Pitt the Younger himself marked an age. Pitt's influence helped form a public administration that was much freer of sinecures and patronage than its predecessors. He established cabinet government (rather than a government of ministers individually responsible to the king) as the dominant pattern, and thereby promoted a shift of power toward Parliament that war's rising fiscal burdens already favored. In 1799, after commissioning an unprecedented survey of national income, he even established an income tax that endured, with a brief intermission, until the war's end.

Table 5.2. Days' wages paid per capita in national taxes, 1781–1815

Year	Farm laborer	Cotton spinner
1781	14	7
1789	14	8
1795	12	8
1801	16	10
1807	26	15
1811	28	16
1815	32	18

Sources: Lindert and Williamson 1983b; Williamson 1985; Mitchell and Deane 1971.

Almost all states that go to war accumulate powers they could not exercise in peacetime, and use them to suppress dissent. The British state of the 1790s was no exception. War with a revolutionary foe justified and to some extent caused a marked increase in state repression during the 1790s. The vast mobilization of corresponding societies and other radical organizations immediately activated government informers and spies. By 1792 the government was prosecuting Tom Paine, issuing proclamations against seditious publications, closing down debating societies, and encouraging the formation of antirevolutionary loyalist associations such as John Reeves's Association for the Preservation of Liberty and Property against Republicans and Levellers.

With the start of war against France in February 1793, both organized loyalists and local magistrates attacked radicals. Scottish magistrates soon convicted Thomas Muir and Thomas Fyshe Palmer for their advocacy of an extraparliamentary Convention on the French model. The formation of paramilitary Volunteer Corps in 1794 enlisted patriots against the double threat of French invasion and radical subversion (Western 1956). Parliamentary acts of 1793, 1795, and 1796 first authorized magistrates to send vagrants into military service and then imposed recruitment quotas on local authorities that increased those authorities' incentives to get rid of inconvenient young men by dumping them into the military (Wells 1983).

The militarizing state faced a dilemma. On the one hand, its rulers could not count on unquestioning working-class loyalty. On the other, an expanding need for military manpower both at home and abroad left them no choice but to arm poor men in the nation's defense. "The evidence suggests, then," concludes Linda Colley,

> that in the early years of the war the British government was—rightly or wrongly—as afraid of its own people as it was of the enemy. Labouring men might be the bedrock of the regular forces and fill the ranks of the militia, but they were neither welcome nor very much trusted in the less structured world of the volunteers. Not an armed people, but a propertied and respectable home guard to restrain domestic disorder was what the authorities were most anxious to create at this stage of the conflict. The change came in the winter of 1797, when Napoleon's Army

of England encamped along the French coastline. Desperate, and by now without European allies, the government had no choice but to make the shift from seeking quality support at home to seeking it in quantity. (Colley 1992: 289)

That it did, inventorying the kingdom's military resources in the 1798 Defence of the Realm returns and the census of 1801, canvassing the local availability of men for service, literally and figuratively drumming up patriotic themes, broadcasting the threat of French invasion, and tightening the apparatus of repression.

In 1794 both calls for Conventions and prosecutions of radicals (notably including Hardy of the LCS, whom a jury acquitted) multiplied as Parliament started a stream of repressive legislation: the Seditious Meetings Act, the Treasonable Practices Act, and so on. The controls held until the war's end twenty years later, then provided the model for postwar repressive legislation. They even received substantial political support, as when the December 1795 Yorkshire meeting organized by Christopher Wyvill and his allies to protest the Treasonable Practices and Seditious Meetings bills actually split into his faction and a larger group supporting the government (Dinwiddy 1971). The connection of repression with war sometimes became quite direct, as in Yarmouth during the summer of 1796, when officers of the naval sloop *L'Espiègle* recruited their own men to break up a meeting addressed by radical John Thelwall, seize Thelwall, and return him to the ship for impressment; only a rescue by Thelwall's friends foiled the plot (Thompson 1994; see also Emsley 1983b).

By 1797 repression was working well, fragmenting the organized radical movement throughout Great Britain, if not in Ireland, while driving its more revolutionary segments farther underground. "Several historians have been kind enough to advise us," remarked E. P. Thompson in a characteristic aside, "that Pitt's measures against reformers fell far short of a White Terror. We may thank them for disclosing this hitherto undetected truth: no guillotine was set up at Tyburn. But the Britain of 1796–7, when the 'anarchic cry' went up of 'No Law for Jacobins!', could be an uncomfortable place for reformers" (Thompson 1994: 101). The Acts of 1799 which outlawed the United Englishmen, the United Scotsmen, the United Britons, the United Irish, the London Corresponding

Society, and then any workmen's associations whatsoever merely consolidated repressive practices that were already operating (Goodwin 1979).

In contrast to its dealings with Ireland and India, at home the British state of the wartime period did not endow itself with many new repressive powers and agencies. Instead, it heightened repression by authorizing existing courts and officials to act more forcefully against a wide range of dissidents and by consulting much more extensively with repressive agents. For the most part, Parliament and Whitehall delegated the power to control collective action. Nevertheless, "The regular, Militia, and Volunteer armies, were widely deployed against protesting crowds; the threat of their use, in accordance with *government* policies, was universal" (Wells 1988: 287). During the hundreds of local struggles over food in 1795, for example, magistrates repeatedly called one of the three forces to their aid—not always, we shall see, to good effect. The arm, and arms, of the state, reached farther and farther into local affairs.

Textures of Contention

As the state's involvement (repressive or otherwise) in public contention increased, the forms of claim-making changed significantly. The anecdotal information we have already reviewed strongly suggests a flowering of associational activity, public meetings, popular participation in elections, and direct efforts to influence the national state, especially through Parliament. We can verify these impressions by examining the actual flow of contentious gatherings in the Southeast in 1789, 1795, 1801, 1807, and 1811, and by comparing those years *en bloc* with the years from 1758 to 1781. The crude distribution of occasions for contentious gatherings (Table 5.3) identifies important changes from the 1758–1781 period to the time of the French Revolution and wars. Forced illumination of windows, for example, dwindled to insignificance, while other attacks on persons or their property receded from almost half of all events in 1758–1781 to an average of 12 percent between 1789 and 1811.

Similarly, the Southeast's seizures of food or property declined from almost 6 percent to a little over 1 percent of all CGs, while strikes, turnouts, and wage demands dropped from 4.6 to 1.1 percent of the total. (Elsewhere in Great Britain, we shall see, both subsistence struggles and industrial conflict remained intense; in the Southeast, furthermore, industrial conflict flared again after wartime repression ended.) The great gainers were meetings to communicate with the national government (up from 21.5 to 35.0 percent), electoral assemblies (from 5.3 to 13.5) and the catchall "other gatherings" (5.9 to 33.4). "Other gatherings" include militant marches, crowds that formed in support of popular figures, and similar events that often had implications for national politics. In 1811, for example, the nineteen "other gatherings" consisted of thirteen meetings concerning local affairs such as the improvement of Sandwich harbor and the union of Cripplegate Without and Within in a single ward, plus six public events: three appearances of the Duke of Clarence (then a naval commander, and eventually King William IV), a public promenade of George III, and two other occasions on which a

Table 5.3. Occasions of contentious gatherings in Southeastern England, 1789–1811

Type of event	Total 1758–81	% of annual total					Total
		1789	1795	1801	1807	1811	
Forced illumination of windows	4.3	0.0	0.0	3.6	0.0	0.0	0.5
Other attacks on persons or their property	46.5	15.4	11.1	16.4	9.3	12.5	12.1
Seizure of food or property	5.9	0.0	3.7	0.0	0.0	0.0	1.1
Mutiny	0.7	0.0	0.0	0.0	0.0	0.0	0.0
Resistance to governmental regulation or action	5.3	0.0	4.6	7.3	1.9	2.1	3.2
Meeting to communicate with national government	21.5	61.5	48.1	14.5	17.6	39.6	35.0
Electoral assembly	5.3	3.8	2.8	1.8	38.0	6.2	13.5
Strike, turnout, or gathering for wage demands	4.6	0.0	1.9	1.8	0.9	0.0	1.1
Other gathering	5.9	19.2	27.8	54.5	32.4	39.6	33.4
Total	100.0	99.9	100.0	99.9	100.1	100.0	99.9
Number of CGs	302	52	108	55	108	48	371

crowd watched and commented on the execution of two convicted forgers and spectators at St. James's congratulated a grenadier who had received a medal for action against the French.

Although any dating in this regard is delicate and ultimately arbitrary, we can reasonably say that during these years of war the demonstration took shape in Britain as a standard form of politics. The demonstration consisted, and still consists, of gathering deliberately in a public place, preferably a place combining visibility with symbolic significance, displaying both membership in a politically relevant population and support for some position by means of voice, printed words, or symbolic objects, and communicating collective determination by acting in a disciplined fashion in one space and/or moving through a series of spaces—for example by marching from St. George's Fields to the Houses of Parliament. Demonstrations became favored instruments in the campaigns we now call social movements.

Social movements worked to an implicit scoreboard that accumulated across events the multiples of displayed worthiness, unity, numbers, and commitment to a cause; high commitment could compensate for small numbers, and so on, but in the last accounting cumulated scores mattered. Over decades of campaigning, for example, opponents of the slave trade established a reading of themselves as sober, principled churchgoers whose petitions bespoke a following in the tens of thousands. Cumulative scores mattered because they signaled the presence of a disciplined force that could act unpredictably, even dangerously, outside the bounds of routine politics. We witness negotiation over precisely that accounting during the 1790s in the London Corresponding Society's effort to bring out thousands of ordinary people in visible support of parliamentary reform and the government's counter-effort to disable the LCS by prosecuting its leaders for high treason.

The demonstration accordingly became a major instrument of social movements. During the Bristol by-election of 1812, Henry Hunt lost heavily, since most of his support came from the disfranchised working population "who marched in huge crowds to the cry 'Hunt and Peace' behind a loaf of bread on a pole and a Cap of Liberty, cheered his stentorian harangues, assailed anyone wearing blue with a volley of mud, stones and dead cats, and attacked the White Lion (headquarters of the Loyal and Constitutional Club) and Council House" (Prothero 1979: 82).

The demonstration, stemming in part from the raucous electoral parade, was becoming a major instrument of social movements.

Between 1789 and 1815 demonstrators often used dramatic symbols, as when women demanding cheaper food marched with loaves of bread on sticks, draped with black crepe: a "mourning loaf." To some degree, even the classic forced sale of food at below its current market price gave way to this sort of demonstration, this appeal to authorities local and national for intervention in the market. With many changes of texture, the demonstration has remained a crucial part of Britain's contentious repertoire to this day.

Eighteenth-century forms did not utterly vanish. Many of them reappeared intermittently for years afterward. During the war, for example, outstanding British victories brought renewed demands for the illumination of windows; on 13 October 1797, when the news of Admiral Duncan's naval victory arrived in London, crowds formed outside Thomas Hardy's intentionally unlighted house and battled the guard from the Corresponding Society who had gathered to protect Hardy (Vincent 1977: 90–95). Illumination again became the occasion for violent clashes during the campaign for Queen Caroline in 1820 and at the king's dismissal of Parliament in April 1831, amid the vast mobilization for parliamentary reform. Some workers continued to "donkey" knobsticks—drive them through town (preferably facing backwards) on a real donkey or its figurative double, a stout rail. In Whitechapel (May 1809), a band of Irishmen armed with bludgeons declared "They would kill every bloody Jew" and at a spectator's cry of "England forever" began an indiscriminate attack on bystanders (HO 42/99). Later the same year a theater within a theater opened up in London as for sixty-seven nights people staged dramatic protests against the high prices of the newly opened Covent Garden Theatre, shutting down performance after performance and eventually gaining major concessions from manager-actor John Philip Kemble (Baer 1992).

These are not all: Richard Densham, who preached Evangelical doctrine on the road for the Village Itinerancy Society in 1799, described the reception of his teachings in Rogate, Sussex:

> Soon after I read my text they began to throw rotten eggs and make a noise to disturb the people and many of the more abandoned raised the dust by throwing it with their hands, etc. Soon after I began my sermon

Table 5.4. Verbs in all actions of contentious gatherings, Southeastern England, 1789–1811

Verb	Total 1759–81	% of annual total					Total	N
		1789	1795	1801	1807	1811		
Assemble	4.3	2.7	4.3	4.1	4.6	3.1	4.0	81
Attack	17.3	4.2	5.8	6.0	3.4	3.5	4.7	96
Cheer	1.2	4.6	2.1	5.0	4.9	7.0	4.2	86
Communicate	3.8	0.8	2.2	1.6	1.9	1.2	1.7	35
Control	15.0	4.6	9.9	11.4	6.5	5.5	8.0	163
Decry	1.3	1.9	1.2	1.6	2.3	0.8	1.6	32
Deliberate	1.0	1.2	0.6	0.3	0.4	0.0	0.5	10
Disperse	4.6	3.1	4.3	4.1	2.5	3.9	3.6	73
End	11.3	18.1	13.2	13.9	18.4	14.5	15.5	314
Fight	1.5	0.8	0.9	4.1	0.4	0.8	1.2	25
Gather	6.9	8.5	3.3	7.3	4.2	3.1	4.8	97
Meet	2.8	9.7	8.5	6.3	12.0	11.7	9.6	195
Move	9.7	6.6	7.9	6.9	4.2	4.7	6.2	126
Negotiate	1.6	0.8	0.6	1.3	0.4	0.4	0.6	13
Petition	1.0	1.2	1.9	0.3	0.4	0.4	1.0	20
Request	3.1	2.7	1.3	2.2	1.1	1.2	1.6	32
Resist	1.4	0.4	0.7	2.5	0.2	0.4	0.8	16
Resolve	1.6	9.7	15.6	5.0	15.4	20.3	13.7	279
Support	1.2	2.7	0.9	0.0	1.5	0.8	1.1	23
Other	9.4	15.8	14.8	16.1	15.4	16.8	15.6	316
Total	100.1	100.1	100.0	100.0	100.1	100.1	100.0	2,032
N	2,293	259	674	317	526	256	2,032	

an egg struck me on the back part of my head and run'd down my back which render'd my situation unpleasant from the dreadful stench I endured all the time of preaching . . . When I went to the public house one of the farmers who is the *churchwarden* came to me and wished me to desist from coming again as he thought there would be still greater opposition. (Martin 1978: 180, citing New College MS 41/69)

Elsewhere, Densham complained that his counter-audiences gave him "rough music" (Martin 1978: 180). The direct attack on the outcast, the nonconformist, the moral leper had by no means disappeared from the British repertoire of contention. But such events became rare and peripheral as compared to the repeated public meetings, petition drives, marches, delegations, and other actions by constituted associations or official assemblies. Thus the Southeast's popular contention moved noticeably toward national politics.

The pattern of change in verbs (Table 5.4) reflects the same trends from 1758–81 to 1789–1811:

proportion doubled or more: cheer, meet, resolve;
proportion dropped by half or more: attack, communicate,
    deliberate, negotiate.

The verbs most clearly attached to public meetings and other nonviolent displays of support—cheer, meet, resolve—rose together. Verbs of attack declined, while "control" verbs, which figured prominently in the actions of police and troops, likewise dropped from 15 to 8 percent of the total. Among the verbs that became less common, however, were some that clustered in nonviolent gatherings where people bargained out decisions: communicate, deliberate, negotiate. Within nonviolent public assemblies, that is, people shifted from internal conflict to the display of concerted will. As an example of the forms of action that were declining, here are abstracts of an event in East Bourne (Sussex), not far from Beachy Head, on 6 and 7 February 1801:

Text	*Verb*
On Friday last, a considerable number of labourers, fishermen, and mechanics assembled at East Bourne	ASSEMBLE

and proceeded to the houses of the principal inhabitants	PROCEED
complaining that the excessive price of grain rendered it impossible for them to support their families	COMPLAIN
and requesting that something might be done to enable them to bear the extreme pressure of the times	REQUEST
Mr. Gilbert addressed them on the impropriety of their thus appearing	ADDRESS
but promised that their situations should be taken into consideration	PROMISE
after which they all returned peaceably to their homes	RETURN

The action in East Bourne (which the laborers of nearby Horsham almost duplicated the next day) had a little of the meeting, and a lot of the rebellion; hence Mr. Gilbert's warning about the "impropriety of their thus appearing." Another report tells us that Mr. Gilbert asked whether they had applied for relief, with the implication that a proper protest displayed deference and went through channels. Some events were more ritualized; on 20 November: "a coal-porter exhibited his wife in Smithfield, with a halter round her neck, for sale. He demanded a guinea for her, but she being on hand for some time, until a man of good appearance made the purchase, and packing her, halter and all, into a hackney-coach, drove for Blackfriars bridge amidst the huzzas of the mob" (MC 21 November 1801). That account yielded the string of verbs GATHER, EXHIBIT, DE-MAND, BUY, PACK, DRIVE, HUZZA. (The prefix # means we inferred the verb or transformed a noun into a verb instead of drawing it directly from the text.) The well-known ritual of wife sale (in which the ostensible buyer was often already the wife's lover) yields a very active sequence of verbs. But the verbs of violent events run even more actively. On the 26 and 17 April 1801:

About 8 in the evening a mob assembled before a house in Wych-Street, formerly the Queen of Bohemia tavern (but now supposed to be unoc-cupied), in consequence of some boys who had been at play in the passage, declaring they saw some persons through the key-hole employed in cutting up human bodies. The mob, having increased, at length broke into the house, in which they found several human bodies partly dissected, one body of a man which appeared to have been not long dead, with that of an infant not four months old, untouched, and several tubs with human flesh, andc. The stench was so great, that many were glad to return without viewing the disgusting scene, and many who went in were seized with sickness. Notwithstanding, it was explained to the mob, that the house had been for some time used as an anatomical theatre, they were so enraged as to proceed to destroy the house; but a party of Bow-street officers arriving, at length succeeded in restoring the peace, to the great satisfaction of the neighborhood, who had been much alarmed at an idea that the mob would in their rage set fire to the house. The surgeons, who were in the house, made their escape by a back way, leaving several of their instruments behind them. This is the house in which a committee of the Corresponding Society was seized three years ago. (AR 1801: 14)

Yesterday several of the inhabitants of Wych-street waited upon Mr. Ford, to complain of a mob that had collected about the house late the Queen of Bohemia's Head, where the dead bodies were discovered on Sunday; the mob were proceeding to acts of violence, in consequence of which Mr. Ford immediately directed a party of peace officers to repair to the spot, who dispersed the crowd without any mischief ensuing. (LC 28 April 1801)

Similar accounts appeared in *Gentleman's Magazine* and the *Times.* From all these accounts we extracted the two sequences SEE, CUT UP, DECLARE, ASSEMBLE, INCREASE, BREAK IN, ESCAPE, DESTROY, ALARM // WAIT ON, COMPLAIN, DIRECT, ARRIVE, QUIET. We read the verbs of coercion and violence.

The march of workers in East Bourne, the wife sale in Smithfield, and the gathering at the anatomical theater all represented well-established eighteenth-century forms of action. Increasingly common as of 1801, however, were contentious gatherings in the form of nonviolent assemblies. Here, on 21 March, is a thoroughly routine case:

SOCIETY FOR BETTERING THE CONDITION OF THE POOR. At a MEETING OF THE COMMITTEE, held the 21st Day of March 1801 . . . It appearing to the Committee, by information from different quarters, that the distresses of the poor, occasioned by the high price of bread and of all the necessary articles of life, are greatly increased, and require the exertions of all the other classes of society to alleviate their pressure; and it also appearing that the present funds entrusted to the Committee, at Lloyd's, though managed with a very great degree of judgment and effect, will not be adequate to their object, without further liberal Contributions from the Benevolent, and particularly from the opulent Inhabitants of the West End of the Metropolis; And a Meeting of the Inhabitants of the Metropolis having been fixed for Friday the 27th inst. at the Thatched House Tavern, in St. James's-street, at one o'clock, Resolved unanimously, That it be most earnestly recommended to the Inhabitants of the Metropolis, and more particularly so the Members of this Society, to attend the said Meeting; and to give their support to the measures, now rendered peculiarly necessary to be taken for the relief of their poor and distressed Brethren. Resolved, That this Resolution be signed by the Chairman, and inserted in the Public Papers. (LT 25 March 1801)

The verbs simplify: MEET, RESOLVE, RESOLVE, END. Duller than a workers' march or a wife sale, this gathering hewed to a well-defined aim.

Meetings of this sort had taken place in Britain for half a century, but now this form of action was becoming more and more predominant in the Southeast. Increasingly, furthermore, it drew on substantial participation from ordinary people rather than elites alone. We have seen that popular participation most clearly in the public meetings of the London Corresponding Society and its provincial counterparts. The pattern centers on the assembly planned in advance and aimed at a focused appeal to authorities, especially national authorities. As is still true almost two centuries later, the organizers do their best to display unity of purpose, advertise their cause's worthiness, attract publicity, recruit donors, and draw the attention of public authorities. As of 1801, political entrepreneurs were trying increasingly to influence Parliament.

Through the years from 1789 to 1815, in short, most of the eighteenth century's contentious repertoire survived. Yet it diminished in importance as public meetings, marches, and other elements of the national social movement came into wider and wider use. Although churches continued to play crucial parts in such movements as antislavery, other formally constituted assemblies and special-interest associations began to dominate

Table 5.5. Major issues of contentious gatherings in Southeastern England, 1789–1811

Issue	Total 1758–81	% of annual total					Total	N
		1789	1795	1801	1807	1811		
Attacks on objects	10.2	0.0	0.9	0.0	0.9	0.0	0.5	2
Attacks on persons	11.9	5.8	2.8	14.5	6.5	4.2	6.2	23
Food prices	2.0	0.0	12.0	3.6	0.0	0.0	4.0	15
Taxes	0.3	13.5	1.9	0.0	1.9	2.1	3.2	12
Trade	3.6	0.0	7.4	9.1	4.6	6.3	5.7	21
Catholic claims	6.9	0.0	0.0	1.8	2.8	0.0	1.1	4
Elections	5.6	3.8	0.9	0.0	32.4	2.1	10.5	39
Royalty	10.8	42.3	15.7	10.9	7.4	8.3	15.4	57
National government	10.2	7.7	17.6	20.0	18.5	22.9	17.5	65
Local government	6.3	0.0	3.7	9.1	4.6	6.3	4.6	17
Wardmote	0.7	3.8	3.7	0.0	12.0	2.1	5.4	20
Other	37.1	23.1	33.3	30.9	8.3	45.8	25.9	96
Total	100.0	100.0	99.9	99.9	99.9	100.1	100.0	371
N	302	52	108	55	108	48	371	

contention. Cosmopolitan, autonomous, modular collective action came to prevail over parochial, particular, bifurcated collective action. As a consequence, the frequency of direct attacks on persons and objects greatly declined. If the violence of contention diminished, that does not mean radicalism disappeared. On the contrary, radical mobilization flourished with the model of the French Revolution at hand, then withered in the blast of wartime repression; a few militant networks maintained their coherence by going underground.

Contentious Issues

Major issues of contentious gatherings likewise showed important changes from 1758–1781 to the war years (Table 5.5). Attacks on objects and persons, as we might now expect, dropped from about 22 percent of all CGs to under 7 percent. Catholic claims figured less prominently among the issues of 1789–1811, but a different selection of years for comparison would doubtless have altered that result. A similar observation applies to antislavery. Among the years in question, slavery became the focus of contentious gatherings only in 1789. After their substantial mobilization of 1788, however, antislavery forces were then working chiefly through correspondence and pamphlet-writing rather than petitions and public meetings. Their opponents, however, were mobilizing in 1789: every one of the five meetings around the issue that year brought together planters, West Indies merchants, or both in the name of private property to ask Parliament not to abolish the slave trade.

If the sample years had included the major drives for abolition of the slave trade in 1788, 1792, and 1814, abolitionism and antislavery would look much more like an ascending national social movement (Drescher 1982). After all, "There were more petitions for abolition in the 1780s, the 1790s, the 1810s, and the 1830s than for any other single issue" (Drescher 1986: 59). During the parliamentary elections of 1806 and 1807, furthermore, William Wilberforce and his abolitionist allies made slave trading a significant issue in England's industrial north (Drescher 1994). Around 1789 antislavery organizers were working almost exclusively within Quaker and Evangelical congregations (Davis 1987; Drescher 1982, 1986; Temperley 1981; Walvin 1980, 1981). Most of those petitions surely emanated from meetings that would, if fully described in our sources, qualify as CGs.

While issues of food prices, taxes, the condition of trade, and ward-motes all rose modestly, the great gainers were elections, royalty, and national government. The proportion of all events concerning elections swelled because of the hotly contested polls of 1807, and royalty got a boost from agitation over the king's health in 1789; otherwise, those two categories actually showed little change from the previous period. The most significant increase occurred in national government as an issue: 10.2 percent of all CGs in 1758–1781, over 17 percent of all CGs in each year from 1795 onward. The tabulations of issues, then, indicate a notable nationalization of claims in Britain during the French Revolution and Empire.

During 1811, for example, 34 of the 48 CGs (71 percent) were public meetings; as central issues, they took up calls for parliamentary reform (7 meetings), canals and harbors (4), the Religious Restriction Bill (3), praise and thanks to dignitaries (3), the Distillery Bill (2), city ward government (2), rebuilding the Drury Lane Theater (2), and one each of the Arrest Bill, the Wet Docks Bill, the East India Company Bill, the appointment of the Prince of Wales as Regent, restrictions on imports, freedom of the press, the Lancasterian Educational System, election of a Lord Mayor, tax assessments, agricultural improvements, and street paving; MPs and high government officials, furthermore, frequently presided over the meetings or received their acclamation.

At a meeting of Westminster inhabitants in Palace Yard on 18 March, a Mr. Walker (very likely Thomas Walker, a famous Lancashire radical) declared:

> The obvious cause of all our misfortunes is the want of a due representation of the people. This was the cause of the present enormous amount of taxes, levied for the purpose of carrying on wars, not to protect, but to put down the liberties of the country. It was from this cause that the resources of the country were wasted on contractors and jobbers, while the power of the enemy was daily increasing from the folly and wickedness of our system. The commerce of the country was thrown into a few hands; who, in case of failure, had only to renew their lease of subjection to the Minister of the day. To understand the tactics of the House is now supposed the most important requisites of a Minister; and therefore it was not surprising that the power originally delegated for the protection of the people, is now deployed to shield detected delinquency, and to carry into effect unconstitutional usurpations. It was not to be wondered at, that any attempts at reform should be obstinately resisted by men grown old in selfish pursuits, and degraded by corrupt practices. (LT 19 March 1811)

Note the language of social movements, of indignant concern about national politics in the name of a wronged citizenry. Outside of 1811's decorous meetings, it is true, people of the Southeast rescued prisoners, attacked a Wesleyan meeting house, trampled one another at Carlton House, captured a homosexual rapist, fought in a theater, bludgeoned sailors, and cheered the Prince Regent; these events, many of them violent, dealt chiefly with local issues in rough-and-tumble eighteenth-century style. Elsewhere in England, furthermore, workers of 1811 were smashing machines that threatened their livelihood. Since the day when E. P.

Thompson wrote of Luddism as a well-hidden but formidable national conspiracy, historians have divided sharply as to how much that avenging movement connected with national politics (see, for example, Dinwiddy 1979). By eighteenth-century standards, nevertheless, an impressive share of 1811's contentious gatherings concerned issues that Parliament and the government had currently under consideration.

Although principled public opposition to the war with France never animated a mass movement, the war profoundly affected the issues of British contention. It did so in two ways, indirect and direct. Indirectly, the war limited food supplies and raised prices, stimulated rent rises, accelerated proletarianization, encouraged Irish rebels, and justified repressive measures against radicals; all of these became bases of contention, even when the contenders themselves missed the connection of their claim-making with war.

Directly, some Britons resisted military service or discipline, others cheered those who served, while still others openly stated demands for peace. In 1795, for example, attacks on crimps (civilians who recruited forcibly, and profitably, for the army) occurred widely. On 12 January the *Times* commented:

> However expedient it is to recruit our Land Forces, and strongly as it is requisite to make our Navy respectable, and superior to the enemy, yet in attaining these essential points, the constitutional liberty of the subject should be preserved. It is, therefore, with a degree of regret, we mention that the power of enlisting men for the Land Service, in particular, has been entrusted to persons who have abused the confidence reposed in them and who have used the most unjustifiable means to accomplish their purposes. As an instance, among others, that have previously been brought before the public, we are authorised, from the circumstances of the case, to state that, on Friday last, a very great mob assembled in *London Road*, leading from the Obelisk in St. George's Fields to the Elephant and Castle, at Newington-Butts, and, having intimation that a number of men were there imprisoned by a certain description of *Crimps*, they attacked the house where these persons were confined, demolished the windows, and released eighteen men, who were chained together by hand-cuffs and other iron ligaments. The Borough Magistrates, on hearing of this outrage, immediately sent down their officers;

and the *acting Recruiting Serjeant* being taken into custody, he was, after a short examination, committed to the New Gaol. The circumstances which led to the discovery of this imprisonment, was, that of kidnapping a pot-boy, who, before he was chained down, contrived to break a pane of glass in the drawing-room window (for the house was a private one, and elegantly furnished), from whence he cried out "Murder!" This alarmed the neighbourhood, and, as it had been suspected by them, that persons were illegally confined there, the doors and windows were soon demolished, and the prisoners liberated. The Serjeant and his crew had two women of the town genteely dressed up, for the purpose of inveigling young men into the house, which they stiled their lodgings, where the deluded were instantly hand-cuffed, and, about three or four o'clock in the morning, sent off in coaches, hired for the purpose, to the country. On Saturday, several more youths, who were confined in other parts of the Fields, were released by the Magistrate, amidst the plaudits of a numerous multitude of spectators.

Other attacks on unscrupulous military recruiters occurred throughout the year. Similarly, attacks on authorities charged to draft men for the militia proliferated from 1795 to 1798 (Charlesworth 1983: 127–130).

Attacks on crimps, press gangs, and militia authorities were not the only signs of opposition to the war. On 23 January the London municipality, after hot debate, agreed to send a petition to Parliament complaining about the war's expense and asking for its speedy termination (LT 24 January 1795); in February, July, and November more meetings of dignitaries took the same line. The London Corresponding Society and its provincial counterparts coupled demands for parliamentary reform with calls for an end to the war. The address to the king from the LCS mass meeting of 29 June 1795 concluded:

We conjure you, Sire, in the Name and for the Sake of that Glorious Revolution which seated the House of Brunswick on the Throne, to yield a timely attention to the Cries of a Suffering People, and to exert that Power with which the Constitution has entrusted you; to give them that Free and Equal Representation which can alone enable the British Nation to prevent future and remove the present Calamities; to dismiss from your Councils, those guilty Ministers who have so long with impunity insulted us and betrayed our dearest Interests; to put an immediate

Period to the Ravages of a Cruel and Destructive War; and to restore to us that Peace and Tranquility which are so essentially necessary for your own Personal security and for the Happiness of the People! (HO 42/35)

Ordinary people voiced similar opinions in a different manner. Over and over groups of workers made a triangular connection among economic hardship, the corruption of political institutions, and the pursuit of war, as did the "treasonable paper" found near Bolton in 1807 that read "No King No War The Downfall of the Trade will be the Downfall of the Nation . . . if there was no King and a new set of Ministers . . . the working People might Earn a Living" (Bohstedt 1983: 148).

Londoners made similar connections. On 29 October 1795, as the king went to the House of Lords, crowds hooted royal ministers, including Pitt, then stoned the king's coach. After the king repaired to St. James's and abandoned his state coach for his private carriage to go to Buckingham house, "on his way through the Park, the mob surrounded the carriage, and prevented it from proceeding, crying out, 'Bread! Bread! Peace! Peace!'" (AR 1795: 38). That encounter stimulated Parliament to pass Pitt's Treasonable Practices and Seditious Meetings acts, which in turn called out a series of public meetings against such an assault on the Bill of Rights, as well as another attack in St. James's Park—this one on 17 December, against Pitt himself.

In other years, military mutinies paralleled civilian resistance to the war. The peak came in the spring of 1797, when first the Channel fleet and then crews at the Nore belonging chiefly to the North Sea fleet refused to obey their officers until they received raises in pay and improvements in working conditions. In February and March sailors of the Channel fleet, emulating their civilian counterparts, surreptitiously circulated petitions for redress, then sent them to the baffled Admiralty. When the Admiralty ordered them to sea, every crew refused the order and ran up the red flag as a signal of resistance. Collective bargaining and waiting held the Channel Fleet immobile, under control of its seamen, for a full month. They won their battle: not only improvements in compensation, but also pardons for all mutineers.

The North Sea sailors, however, did less well. After splits among the fleet's mutineers, the rebellion ended in bitter repression, including the hanging of Richard Parker, the mutiny's elected president. United Irishmen, Irish Defenders, and British democrats in the ranks played important parts in sustaining, if not in initiating, the mutinies and in giving them a populist cast (Wells 1983; see also Clark 1990).

Popular action on the war, nevertheless, divided sharply. When Colonel William Tate and his Black legion landed on the Welsh coast in February 1797, hoping for an insurrection to support French plans to invade Ireland, the invaders received no local support; they surrendered within three days. Plenty of Britons joined the government's anti-French and anti-revolutionary causes, from those of Birmingham who attacked Joseph Priestley in the name of Church and King (1791) onward. In 1794 "The celebrations for the [naval victory of the] Glorious First of June were particularly rowdy in London; crowds roamed the streets for several nights in succession demanding that householders illuminate their windows, and smashing the windows of those who refused" (Emsley 1979: 27). From the spring of 1792, furthermore, local authorities repeatedly organized public meetings to express support for the government, sending addresses to the king that voiced loyalty to the crown and opposition to the pernicious doctrines seeping in from France; from November 1992 they were also promoting the formation of loyalist associations such as John Reeves's Association for the Preservation of Liberty and Property against Republicans and Levellers specifically to counter radical associations' mobilization (Dozier 1983).

By no means all expressions of support for the regime, however, resulted so directly from elite promotion. In May 1795, when battered Guards repatriated from the Continent marched into St. James's Park, "an immense crowd was collected to welcome them home with all the sincerity of Englishmen" (LC 12 May 1795). At a time of heightened fear of French invasion, half a million people turned out on both 26 and 28 October 1803 to attend the king's review of 27,000 volunteers (Colley 1984). With the partial exception of loyalist associations, expressions of popular patriotism, unlike those of radicalism, generally borrowed the standard eighteenth-century forms: attacks on offenders, open-air celebrations, and the like.

Any connoisseur of seventeenth- and eighteenth-century French contention who studies these findings has a surprise coming: the unimportance of taxes and public finance. Although British opponents of war in 1795, for example, often made the war's cost one of their talking points, during that year only a single decorous meeting of merchants acted against a specific tax, a new levy on foreign wine. In France, in contrast, the imposition of new taxes and the assessment of old ones repeatedly generated rebellions, sometimes on a national scale. Issues of public finance figured centrally in the fateful French struggles of 1787–1790 and continued to incite resistance throughout the Revolution (Markoff 1986; Tilly 1986). Even if we exclude well-organized social movements such as the winegrowers' widespread demands of 1907 and the shopkeepers' and smallholders' mobilization led by Pierre Poujade in the 1950s, France's last major violent fiscal rebellion, the *révolte des quarante-cinq centimes,* took place as late as 1848–1850 (Gossez 1953).

Between 1789 and 1815 British citizens bore enormous increases in their tax burden and a higher overall rate of payment than their French cousins; yet only twelve of the 371 CGs under consideration focused on taxes. Seven of the twelve occurred in 1789. Not one involved popular resistance to tax collectors: six of them, indeed, were public meetings of merchants, manufacturers, or official bodies protesting the shop tax or the tobacco excise, the seventh a celebration of the shop tax's repeal. This while across the Channel French people were burning tollgates, smashing tax collectors' offices, and assaulting the collectors themselves.

Issues of public finance were not entirely absent from British struggles, as Walker's speech in Palace Yard indicates. The emoluments of high officials provided propaganda for many a radical pamphleteer, taxation raised the question of representation, smugglers fought customs agents, and the installation of tollgates on newly constructed turnpikes invited neighbors to tear them down. Still, the commercialization of the British economy, the preference of Parliament for taxes on transactions and flows of goods rather than property, and the relative insignificance of fiscal exemptions for nobles and dignitaries all made Britain's large fiscal burden more bearable, less incendiary as a political issue. As in many other spheres, a shared sense of injustice was a greater spur to resistance than was the sheer weight of the state's demands. In any case, those tax-related conflicts which did occur almost all took the form of organized pressure on the national government.

The Issue Is Food

Even within the domain of struggle over the food supply we see some evidence of repertoire change. The years from 1789 to 1815, 1794–1795 and 1799–1801 (each counted up to the harvest of the later year) were times of famine in Great Britain; 1811–1812 brought bad times as well. Famine, as Amartya Sen has stated with great lucidity, consists of a killing decline in people's entitlement to food (Sen 1981). Such a decline occurs through many different combinations of food shortage, price rise, and income loss. All three converged in the British crises: bad harvests, already elevated wartime prices shooting upward, both agricultural and industrial workers' loss of wages because of the crisis—the first because of diminished employment in farming, the second because of diversion of demand away from cheap textiles to food. Wheat on the Exeter market rose by 32.3 percent from 1794 to 1795, by 64.6 percent from 1798 to 1799, and another 20.1 percent the following year (Deane and Cole 1971). Although at Exeter wheat prices of 1812 simply maintained their high levels of the three previous years, in Great Britain as a whole the 1811–1812 rise reached 33 percent (ibid.).

High prices, low incomes, and shortages alone do not generate struggles over food. It takes at least these elements: a mobilized and aggrieved population, visible offenders against shared conceptions of justice, and authorities who fail to intervene on the popular side. These mediating factors attenuate the correlation between frequency of contention and fluctuations of food prices. In his analysis of violent events involving fifty people or more in England and Wales from 1790 to 1810, John Bohstedt finds an annual correlation of +.41 between current price levels and frequency of "food riots"; he indicates a somewhat higher (but unspecified) correlation between that frequency and recent rises in prices (Bohstedt 1983).

In London's hinterland the readiness of authorities to intervene surely muted the impact of prices on contention, especially in the later phases of economic crises. During the shortages of 1794–1796, 1799–1801, and 1811–1812, as in 1766, authorities took great care to ensure London's food supply at the expense of other regions, with the consequence that forced sales of food and blockage of shipments concentrated in industrial regions elsewhere. In the Southeast per capita expenditures for poor relief probably reached their all-time high during 1801 (Baugh 1975). This time the newer industrial regions of the North loomed much larger than they had in the 1760s; the geographies of 1794–1796 and 1799–1801 strikingly resembled each other (Booth 1977; Charlesworth 1983; Wells 1988).

Nevertheless, older industrial regions such as Devon continued to resound with struggles over food. Within those regions, likewise, as John Bohstedt argues for Devon, the geography of alimentary contention remained quite constant from 1795 to 1801 (Bohstedt 1983).

It was the forms of action that changed. Although old-fashioned price-fixing seizures of food continued, as compared with the great crisis of 1766, the famines of 1794–1795 and 1799–1801 generated a higher pro-portion of meetings and demonstration-like assemblies. During our sam-ple years for the Southeast, only 13 of the 108 CGs in 1795, 2 of the 55 CGs in 1801, and none of the 48 CGs in 1811 focused on food. In 1795, 9 of the 13 food-related CGs took the form of public meetings either inaugurating subscriptions for the "industrious poor" or pledging to consume wheaten bread in order to spread the supply; the other 4 consisted of an attack on a cheating baker's dwelling in Westminster; a march of "200 women and girls," bread and beef impaled on sticks, in Brighthelmstone; and occasions in which the militia invaded Blatchington and Chichester markets to force the sale of food below current prices; at most 2 of the 13 events resembled the standard grain seizures of 1766. Four more CGs that focused on other issues nevertheless touched on questions of subsistence: two public meetings and the two occasions in October and December in which crowds at St. James's mobbed first nobles and the king, then chief minister Pitt, with calls for bread and peace.

On the whole, British struggles over food seem to have become poli-ticized from the 1790s onward. As Roger Wells sees it, "The 1790s did not witness a simple resort to food rioting on the traditional model; food prices, wages and—crucially—poor relief levels were increasingly juxta-posed" (Wells 1990: 157). On 5 May 1795 the Westminster Forum debated the following question: "Does the present scarcity of Provisions arise from any failure in our natural produce, the monopoly of individuals, or the wickedness of administration in obstinately prosecuting a system of Warfare?" (Thale 1989: 70). Alan Booth speaks of "greater organization and planning by 1800, the increasing use of handbills to advertise riot and co-ordinate rioters, and the use of threat tactics on a much greater scale" (Booth 1977: 100). Direct action and demonstrating combined; in September 1800, for example, crowds surged through the streets of Lon-don calling for bread and attacking the premises of bakers and other food merchants (Wells 1988). At the same time, public meetings calling for parliamentary action or for collective aid by more prosperous citizens became part of the standard repertoire.

Perhaps the most dramatic events, however, were the multiple occasions in which militia units occupied markets and forced sales of food below the going rates. In those days mobilized militias, like other military units, bought their own food on local markets; they therefore suffered from shortages and price rises just as civilians did. On 16 April a regiment of Oxfordshire militia stationed in Sussex had first remonstrated over bad meat supplied by Seaford's butchers and then

> had quitted their barracks at Blatchington, near Seaford, and notwith-standing the endeavours of their officers, had taken their arms and marched with bayonets fixed. That on Thursday evening they, in a very disorderly manner, entered the town of Seaford, and seized all the flour and provisions they could meet with. The next morning (Friday) they marched in the same manner, in number about 500, to Newhaven, and to the Tide Mill near that town where they found a very large quantity of flour. That they seized the horses of the farmers, and of the artillery with which they were carrying it away. They also seized a vessel in the river, laden with flour and corn, on which they placed a guard of twenty men. (LC 21 April 1795: 384)

During their invasions of Seaford and Newhaven, the militiamen had staged below-market public sales of food and drink. Some had returned to barracks with beef on their bayonets, only to encounter royal troops on the way; others went to Newhaven, where they eventually invaded the pubs before spending the night, more or less drunk, in town (Wells 1988). The next day horse artillery from Lewes and Brighthelmstone captured the militiamen and another group from Blatchington who were marching to relieve them. On 14 June militia officers forced a dozen privates convicted of participation in the Seaford-Newhaven affair to form a firing squad and execute two of their own leaders (GM June 1795).

April buzzed with militia interventions in food markets. On 28 April 1795 Archdeacon Turner reported that at Wells (Somerset) "on Saturday last such of the 122 Regt as are now quartered here marched into the Market Place with fixed Bayonets and compelled Persons who had pur-chased large quantities of Butter at ninepence halfpenny pr pound to sell it at eight pence; they afterwards sold Potatoes at a price fixed by themselves. They then went out of the Limits of the City and acted in the same manner" (HO 42/34; see also Wells 1988). In Somerset and elsewhere the militia usually collaborated with the civilian population, which continued its own market interventions. Volunteers were even more inclined than militiamen to aid the locals, or at least to refrain from striking at their neighbors (Bohstedt 1983).

Alien militia units, in contrast, did occasionally serve to repress popular struggles over food. In December, again in Wells, "A great many women supported by a number of other persons had for some days past in the most riotous manner prevented the shipping of Flour for the Capital." The magistrates sent in the Pembroke militia, "whose behaviour was equally active, as prudent, after driving the mob off with Bayonets they secured and protected the Flour and Ship" (HO 42/37). This time the outsider militia served local authorities instead of allying itself with the indignant populace.

The crises of 1799–1801 and 1811–1812 brought fewer struggles over food and concentrated them even more heavily in industrial regions. Still they continued the patterns of 1795. In southern Devon of 1800–1801, for example, the recently organized Volunteers "actually led mobs, often in full uniform" (Charlesworth 1983: 118; see also Bohstedt 1983; Charlesworth 1994). The phrase "food riot" fails to capture the politicized ambience of the period's struggles over subsistence.

Who Contended, and How?

Most of the alterations in the representation of different sorts of formations in contentious gatherings (Table 5.6) follow obviously from other changes we have already noted. As compared with 1758–1781, the categories that more than doubled their share of CGs in 1789–1811 are Parliament/MP, royalty, local assemblies, and other interests than members of a trade. Parliament, which figured exclusively as the object of claims, rose from 4.5 to 15.5 percent of all formations. The major declines appeared among members of trades, unnamed crowds, and unnamed individuals. Aside from the temporary suppression of workers' demands during the war years, the disappearing species were formations such as spectators at executions who attacked the executioner and crowds who took vengeance on unpopular local figures. Formations gaining promi-

Table 5.6. Formations participating in Southeastern contentious gatherings, 1789–1811

Type of formation	Total 1758–81	% of annual total					Total	N
		1789	1795	1801	1807	1811		
Parliament/MP	4.5	12.8	15.1	1.7	22.1	21.5	15.5	184
National officials	3.0	4.1	2.0	3.4	1.0	1.8	2.2	26
Royalty	3.0	14.2	8.3	3.4	3.6	3.7	6.5	77
Gentlemen, nobles	2.6	4.7	2.3	4.5	4.0	10.4	4.5	53
Judges	4.5	0.0	3.0	5.6	1.7	1.8	2.5	30
Mayor	2.1	2.0	1.3	2.2	1.7	2.5	1.8	21
Other local officials	5.7	4.7	11.8	4.5	13.5	10.4	10.1	120
Clergy	0.2	0.0	0.3	3.4	0.3	0.0	0.7	8
Freeholders/electors	0.5	4.7	2.0	3.4	0.7	1.8	2.2	26
Other local assemblies	3.4	4.1	10.1	8.4	10.9	9.8	9.3	110
Members of trade	14.9	11.5	8.8	7.9	4.3	4.3	7.2	86
Other interest	2.8	6.8	5.8	6.2	10.2	6.1	7.1	85
Police	3.4	2.0	2.0	2.2	3.3	3.7	2.6	31
Troops	7.1	0.7	8.1	6.2	1.3	3.1	4.5	53
Unnamed crowd	11.3	3.4	5.0	5.1	2.6	3.7	4.0	48
Named individuals	9.9	4.1	2.8	6.2	2.6	1.2	3.2	38
Other	20.9	20.3	11.3	25.8	16.2	14.1	16.2	193
Total	99.8	100.1	100.0	100.1	100.0	99.9	100.1	1189
N	1,223	148	397	178	303	163	1,189	

Note: Includes both actors and objects of claims.

nence were local people sitting as authorized assemblies (such as ward-motes, official meetings of freeholders) or regularly convened public meetings and the objects of their claims—Parliament as a whole, individual MPs, the Regent, or the king.

The year 1807 featured a national election. During the year's 108 CGs

Parliament or an MP appeared as the object of claims 67 times. Royalty drew claims no more than 11 times. Out of the remaining 225 formations, local assemblies such as meetings of freeholders accounted for 44, interest groups such as the "friends" of candidates for Parliament 42, the once prominent anonymous "mob," "crowd," or "populace" only 20. If the year's contentious gatherings brought out "a little girl," "a young country girl," "a swindler," "idle persons," Irishmen, smugglers, and revenue officers, they also called into action the sons of the clergy, planters and merchants, shareholders, and friends of the deaf and dumb, as well as many local assemblies of electors, freemen, and inhabitants. We see settling into place a routine politics of interest strongly oriented to actors on a national scale. What we do not much see in 1807, as compared with 1789 or even 1795, is popular associations of workers or radicals; repression had driven them underground or out of existence.

The Southeast and the northern industrial regions, however, differed sharply in this regard: in London and the Southeast, gradual and effective repression of public workers' action that lasted until war's end; elsewhere, sporadic revivals of working-class contention reaching a high point in the Luddite years of 1811. In London even the Spitalfields silkweavers, protected as they were by parliamentary statute, made only intermittent, clandestine efforts at organizing during the war years (Steinberg 1989). Craftsmen and tradesmen did, of course, play important parts in London's radical associations throughout the war. As compared with the years before and after, nevertheless, the two decades from 1795 to 1815 marked a low point of London workers' actions as workers rather than as members of local assemblies or mixed crowds. In 1801, for example, the only clearly labeled workers (excluding soldiers and sailors) to appear in Southeastern CGs were as follows:

labourers, fishermen, and mechanics who assembled in East Bourne and Horsham to complain about grain prices;

calico printers who met with merchants at the London Tavern to oppose an additional duty on printed goods;

biscuit-makers who petitioned the Victualling Office for a wage increase;

prostitutes who battled "young bucks" in Southwark;

firemen whom a crowd in Yarmouth kept from hosing a house reputed to hold crimped or impressed sailors;

the executioner who dispatched two convicted murderers before a
jeering crowd of thousands at Newgate;

a coal-porter who successfully exhibited his wife for sale in
Smithfield.

The Southeast's events of 1801 give little evidence of sustained working-
class collective action.

In the industrializing regions of the North things looked quite different.
As magistrate Holland Watson of Stockport wrote to the Secretary of
State on 3 July 1794: "The suspension of the Habeas Corpus Act is very
generally considered as a wise and salutary measure, but you may rely on
it, it by no means prevents the Societies from meeting. They are still very
industrious and unwearied in their exertions and I am fairly convinced it
will require some stronger measures than have yet been adopted to return
them from pursuing their wicked schemes" (HO 42/32)2. In Lancashire
strikes and subsistence struggles continued into the decade after 1789,
while workers joined employers in renewed demands for radical reform. Of
the twenty-nine working-class "protests" Frank Munger cataloged in Lancashire between 1789 and 1799, ten were worker-employer disputes, six
struggles over food, four explicit expressions of national political position
(two of them vigorously anti-reform), one a petition on behalf of handloom weavers, and seven local affrays over various issues; twenty of the
twenty-nine events involved violence (Munger 1977).

Although Lancashire militants, like their London counterparts, felt
increased repression after 1794, organized workers continued to meet and
act between then and the war's end. The United Englishmen persisted in
holding large open-air meetings through 1801, great strikes of weavers
and spinners, respectively, occurred in 1808 and 1810, and attacks on
mills proliferated in 1811–1812; unlike the Luddism of Nottinghamshire
and Yorkshire, however, Lancashire's machine-breaking occurred especially in open marches of workers against major employers and in conjunction with complaints about the food supply (ibid.). Looking back
from 1828, Francis Place saw those attacks as responding directly to the
orders of workers' committees (Ratcliffe and Chaloner 1977). Throughout
the region of machine-breaking, in fact, the old practice of vengeance by
wrecking machines acquired a stronger political rationale and connection;
workers linked action against immoral capitalists with action against a
corrupt state (Dinwiddy 1979).

We should beware, nevertheless, of the temptation to compress the period's working-class actions into an ascending straight line of militancy, radicalism, and right thinking. While documenting widespread working-class collective action outside the London region, John Rule reminds us of events "at Liverpool in 1792 when carpenters, who had a well-established union, threatened to pull down the houses of abolitionists if the slave trade were abolished, at the same time as they were agitating for a wage increase" (Rule 1986: 264). Church and King militants, immolators of Tom Paine's effigy, and those who celebrated military victories in the streets were often workers. Neither the net movement toward national politics, nor the rising opposition of workers to capitalist employers and corrupt state officials, nor the on-balance shift in forms of contention occurred without significant counter-currents. Over Great Britain as a whole, indeed, we witness a surge of worker militancy during the early 1790s, followed in different regions by a leveling or recession that lasted until peace returned in 1815.

Not coincidentally, a similar pattern marked the public presence of organized radicalism. I am not speaking of underlying sentiment; sentiments remained more nearly constant: when ordinary people had a defensible chance to speak out, for example in the protests over food prices of 1801 and 1802, many of them continued to voice hostility to the war, opposition to a governmental power they regarded as corrupt, demands for popular sovereignty, and support for radical leaders such as John Cartwright or Sir Francis Burdett. Suitable occasions simply arrived less frequently after 1794 than before. No doubt the danger of independent radical action helps explain the enormous support Burdett received from nonvoters in his electoral campaigns of 1802, 1804, and 1807, as well as at his commitment to the Tower for defiance of Parliament in 1810 (Dinwiddy 1980). Just as an earlier generation had taken public festivities such as Lord Mayor's Day as authorization to fill the streets and, in the shelter of crowds, shout grievances or forbidden hopes, ordinary people of the late eighteenth century poured out their political preferences during the tolerated street activities of electoral campaigns.

To be sure, "radicalism" in this era ran from the insurrectionary plots of Colonel Despard or the United Irishmen to the petitions and speeches for parliamentary reform of Burdett and his allies. Across this broad range, however, a national network of connections survived wartime repression and reformed in the postwar years (Belchem 1981, 1985b; Dinwiddy 1973, 1990; Donnelly and Baxter 1975; Epstein 1990; Goodwin 1979; Hollis 1980; Hone 1982; Jewson 1975; Koditschek 1990; Lottes 1979; Main 1965–1967; McCalman 1988; Miller 1968; Money 1977; Murray 1978; Parssinen 1972, 1973; Rudé 1978; Thomas 1970; Thomis and Holt 1977; Thompson 1963; Wells 1983; Willis 1976). Radical sentiment and connectedness varied much less than the opportunities for concerted collective action on behalf of radical programs.

It looks, furthermore, as though the same is true of popular loyalism: forming especially as a counter-movement to organized public radicalism, expressions of support for Church and King waxed and waned as a function of the radical presence and of the authorities' tolerance or encouragement (Colley 1992; Dann and Dinwiddy 1988; Dickinson 1990; Dinwiddy 1971; Emsley 1979; Ginter 1966; Innes 1991). It is a pity that British historians have thus far been so obsessed with gauging how radical (or, for that matter, nonradical) workers as a whole became in the 1790s that they have not traced systematically the differential recruitment or interaction of radical and loyalist activists from the working class. The major changes did not occur in sentiments and consciousness but in the forms of collective action that were available to workers and radicals. Between 1789 and 1815, largely through the mobilization and innovation of popular radical associations during the early 1790s, the forms of the social movement on a national scale became much more widely available to ordinary Britons.

Revolution and Popular Sovereignty

Does this mean turn-of-the-century Britain edged close to revolution? Let us be clear about terms: a revolution is a transfer of power over a state in the course of which at least two distinct blocs make incompatible claims to control the state, and some significant portion of the population subject to the state's jurisdiction acquiesces in the claims of each bloc. A full revolutionary sequence thus runs from sundering of sovereignty and hegemony through a period of struggle to reestablishment of sovereignty and hegemony under new management. We can usefully distinguish between revolutionary situations and outcomes. A revolutionary *situation* consists of an open division of sovereignty, while a revolutionary *outcome* entails a definitive transfer of power (see Aya 1990; Kimmel 1990).

By this standard, Great Britain kept its distance from revolution between 1789 and 1815. The only serious revolutionary situation opened up outside of Great Britain, during the great, bloody Irish insurrection; it quickly closed down again. One might consider the substantial shift of power from local authorities and from the king to Parliament a quiet revolution, but not a product of armed struggle—except in the ironic sense that preparation for war fostered the shift of power. Revolutionary programs, sentiments, and organizational networks certainly existed in wartime Britain; the United Englishmen and their allies did maintain a republican vision, extensive communications, and intermittent plans to rally ordinary people against the state. But they lacked both a credible alternative organization that might actually seize power and active support from significant segments of the general population. They lacked the means of revolution. France's example stimulated great enthusiasm and hope for radical political reform in Great Britain during the early 1790s, but even that burst of activism fell far short of a revolutionary situation.

Nevertheless British contention altered greatly through nonrevolutionary changes between 1789 and 1815. Although many eighteenth-century forms of contention—forced illuminations, fights between smugglers and customs officers, electoral brawls, and the like—persisted, they became less frequent. Conflicts over food and wages continued, but took on stronger connections with the state and with national politics than before 1789. Most of all, the burst of radical organizing in the early 1790s greatly increased the use of public meetings, street demonstrations, and related forms of action. Contention became more cosmopolitan, modular, and autonomous.

The change occurred for two related reasons. First, wartime concentration of capital and (especially) of state power combined with the growing weight of Parliament inside the state to increase the salience of national powerholders for all sorts of claimants. We have seen evidence of that connection in the increasing focus on parliamentary reform, the politicization of conflicts over food and wages, struggles over military service, the waxing importance of parliamentary elections, and the general increase in national government (especially Parliament itself) as an issue and object of claims. Second, interaction among authorities, claim-makers, and their opponents or objects reshaped the range of known and permissible collective action. We have seen that recasting in rising demands for a mass platform, expanded use of the mass association, proliferation of corresponding societies, widespread petitioning, multiplying lecture tours, frequent mounting of quasi-demonstrations—the whole apparatus of the social movement.

Sometimes explicitly and often implicitly, these newly dominant forms of action raised claims of popular sovereignty, the principle that the right to rule rests, and ought to rest, on the informed consent of a whole people. As Burke and his conservative confreres sensed, the program of radical reform called for consultation of the population at large and even the instruction of Parliament, just as the public meeting, the petition, and the demonstration claimed the right of people to address their betters directly. Their use did not, of course, guarantee the actual installation of popular sovereignty. As practices, virtual representation and ruling-class entente survived the popular assault. Nevertheless, the expanding repertoire opened up space in public life on a national scale that ordinary people had not previously occupied in Great Britain outside of major revolutions and rebellions. Changes of later years expanded and organized that space, but the stressful time of the French Revolution and war with France indelibly established its existence.

✤ 6 ✤

STATE, CLASS, AND
CONTENTION, 1816–1827

IN 1816 WILLIAM COBBETT, indignant as ever, spat out a comparison between the quelling of rebellion in occupied France and in England's own Cambridgeshire. "It is curious to observe," wrote Cobbett, "the exact pace which is kept by the two Governments, that of the Bourbons and ours, in putting down insurrections in their respective countries. A few days ago, we were told the troops at *Ely* had seized the arms of the people, and, amongst the rest, a great number of *fowling pieces*" (*Cobbett's Weekly Political Register,* 24 September 1816 [American edition, written 29 June]). In Grenoble, Cobbett remarked, once the authorities had succeeded in disarming the turbulent population, they began returning hunting weapons to their owners. British authorities, according to Cobbett, feared to emulate their French counterparts by giving back insurgents' weapons. Thus vigorously victorious Britain had become more timorous, more tyrannical, or both, than decisively defeated France.

Despite Cobbett's parallel, the Grenoble insurrection was not exactly a popular rising. Its chief organizer, Paul Didier, intended a coup on behalf of the Duke of Orleans, who actually was to become king in 1830. Didier had recruited peasants and ex-soldiers, most of whom thought they were acting for Napoleon, now an English captive on St. Helena. On the evening of 4 May 1816 about a thousand villagers began an armed march toward Grenoble. They soon met troops sent by forewarned military authorities. The insurrection fell apart almost immediately, with a loss of eight lives among the insurgents. Executions ordered by military tribunals soon took twenty-five more, including Didier. Under a state of siege, the army did indeed disarm the implicated villages, and did eventually return private arms to their owners. Except for the purpose of lambasting his own government, nevertheless, no Englishman could call the Bourbon government a model of clemency.

Meanwhile, a special commission in Ely was preparing to try eighty-two people accused of "rioting." In East Anglia and adjacent sections of Cambridgeshire, wartime enclosures had completed the proletarianization of agricultural laborers by eliminating squatters and obliterating tenants' rights in the commons; thenceforth the welfare of workers in the region depended almost entirely on the current combination of employment levels, wages, and food prices. By 1816 postwar demobilization had brought massive unemployment and declining wages. As commonly happened at that time of year, furthermore, food prices began rising in the spring; the wage-price scissors closed. During April 1816 agricultural laborers in Cambridgeshire, Essex, Suffolk, and Norfolk had posted bills calling for higher wages, set fire to the properties of landowners or clergy, and smashed agricultural machinery.

From Bildeston (Suffolk), for example, Major Marrie wrote the Home Secretary repeatedly with reports of barn- and stack-burnings, threatening letters, and riotous assemblies; "I fear," he complained on 26 April,

> deep schemes laid, that if something is not done immediately the consequences may be dreadfull, and we may experience by our own hand what Bonaparte long wish [sic] for (our destruction) from some propositions made to some of the farmers by the mob assembled yesterday. I judge there is more intended, than simply the employment of the poor. They (the mob) said if you will join us we will lower the tithe, and then corn will be cheaper, and we shall get work. (HO 42/149; on Major Marrie's incessant alarums and excursions, see also Peacock 1965)

At Downham (Norfolk), a crowd surrounded the house where the magistrates were meeting, broke windows, pelted the officials with stones, glass, and bottles as they escaped, then went off to sack local food stores before the yeomanry rode in to disperse and arrest them. The next day a larger group approached the town until "the Magistrates and the Mob came to terms" for a release of prisoners, two shillings per day wages, and flour at 2s. 6d. per stone (HO 42/150).

In some incidents people assembled to demand (as they said at Brandon on 16 May) "Cheap Bread, a Cheap Loaf and Provisions Cheaper" (Peacock 1965: 78). The peak arrived on 22, 23, and 24 May, when armed crowds tramped through Littleport and Ely demanding work, fair wages, and lower prices, collecting money for drink, sequestering magistrates, sacking houses of declared public enemies, battling troops, and drinking prodigious quantities of commandeered beer. On 25 May Home Secretary Sidmouth dispatched military forces to East Anglia, thereby slowing a series of rebellions that had still been expanding the day before.

Cobbett half-defended attacks on property of the well-to-do: "The destruction of property, in these cases," he commented,

> is an act of vengeance upon the rich, upon the general notion that it is their fault that the poor are not better off. Nor, do these acts of vengeance fail of producing their effect, of which we have proof all over the kingdom. In numerous places the people of property have met, and have agreed to make subscriptions, or to do something or other in order to make employment for the poor, and to raise their wages. Some unfortunate creatures will be hanged at Ely, but, the labourers, all over the kingdom, will obtain an attention to their demands which they could not obtain before. (*Cobbett's Weekly Political Register*, American ed., 24 September 1816)

By June's end the Special Assizes convened in Ely were pronouncing judicial retribution. Although no one had died during the workers' actions, rebellion of this order constituted a capital crime. "They would freely kill," declared Cobbett of the prosecutors and the royal officials behind them, "every man, woman, and child in the district, who was present at the riots; but they want the courage" (ibid.). The Assizes pronounced twenty-four death sentences. Authorities actually had five executions carried out on 28 June, the day before Cobbett wrote his commentary. The other nineteen persons went to prison or transportation. The justices wrought fierce repression to forestall any future rebellion by agricultural workers.

Like his sometime collaborator, rival, and enemy Henry Hunt, Cobbett was a countryman and onetime patriot whom the spectacle of inequality during the long wars with France had radicalized; the difference was that while Hunt was born a country gentleman and began his political pilgrimage in jail for a personal quarrel, Cobbett, son of an innkeeper, had begun as a ploughboy, educated himself, served in the army, entered politics as a loyalist in the United States during the 1790s, returned to England a Tory, and only later acquired both his Hampshire farm and his radical convictions. By the early 1800s, nevertheless, he was spilling his zeal for his own brand of reform into his *Political Register* and a flood of other publications.

At the peace, Cobbett expanded his efforts on behalf of populist radicalism, with special emphasis on the sorry fate of landless laborers. As he saw it, the effects of the late war and of the crushing taxation that had accompanied it constituted the fundamental problem. He claimed that parasitic beneficiaries of a bloated state were defending themselves for their inaction by invoking the treacherous doctrine of "natural decline," of the inevitable collapse of English greatness in favor of such upstarts as the United States. Following Tom Paine's writings on debt and paper money, he singled out the maintenance of a standing army and the acquittal of debts accumulated during the war as the country's great burdens, the dreadful weights that would cause England to founder and perhaps the poor to rebel.

Cobbett had reasons for personal dissatisfaction with British repression. For an article attacking German mercenaries' flogging of English militiamen, he had spent two years (1810–1812) in Newgate Prison. Yet he had maintained his outspoken criticism of arbitrary rule, profitable office-holding, and war-driven taxation. He and Henry Hunt became the most influential British radicals of their time, campaigning vigorously, if quite unsuccessfully, for parliamentary reform. By reform, Hunt and Cobbett meant Parliaments elected annually by a broad male franchise employing the secret ballot; before the end of 1816, indeed, Cobbett joined Hunt in advocating universal manhood suffrage. They argued that such Parliaments, truly representing the national interest, would obliterate the political and financial arrangements that were oppressing ordinary Englishmen. The Cobbett-Hunt program articulated neatly with the widespread popular view that greed among employers and corruption among public officials were sapping age-old citizens' rights. A popularly elected Parliament, people reasoned, would deal severely with greed and corruption.

Hunt and Cobbett publicized those views widely, Hunt chiefly by speaking, Cobbett principally by writing. In 1816 Cobbett began to evade the tax levied on such high-priced papers as his *Political Register* (which then sold for a shilling halfpenny, including fourpence tax, when a common laborer's wage ran about four shillings per day) by printing the lead article as a twopenny broadsheet, the *Weekly Political Pamphlet*. It enjoyed an enormous success; the first issue sold 44,000 copies, to the *Times*'s daily 5,000, within a month. The government-inspired *Courier* called the broadsheet "two penny trash," an epithet Cobbett cheerfully appropriated. The *Political Pamphlet*, alias Two Penny Trash, became Britain's first widely circulated political newspaper for the working classes, the inspiration for such popular tabloids as the *Black Dwarf.*

The conjunction of his new publishing venture with a great campaign for parliamentary reform, however, soon made Britain too hot for Cobbett. A great petition drive for universal suffrage and relief of the poor, a trio of turbulent meetings on behalf of the cause in London's Spa Fields, an attack on the Prince Regent's carriage as he left Parliament, and alarming reports from a large network of anti-radical spies brought parliamentary committees to believe in a revolutionary conspiracy. Early in 1817 Parliament adopted a series of sharply repressive measures: suspension of *habeas corpus*, extensive control over public meetings, arrests of leading radicals, and more. Seeing ministerial handwriting on the wall, Cobbett sailed to America with two of his sons. Although the *Political Register* continued to broadcast his views in England, he himself did not return until 1819. By that time British contention had moved dramatically toward nationwide campaigns for political reform. The age of social movements had begun.

Economy and State, 1816–1827

The great wars of 1792–1815 sharpened divisions within the British economy. Although the continental blockade and the diversion of capital to military activity may have slowed the pace of industrial expansion, the growth of an industrial proletariat continued during the war years, as in the agricultural sector landlords and farmers speeded the growth of landless labor, hence of potential recruits to low-wage jobs in manufacturing. High rates of natural increase, driven especially by younger and more widespread marriage, accelerated Britain's proletarianization. Meanwhile, the disproportionate movement of agricultural laborers into military service produced a wartime labor shortage, which in turn encouraged landlords and farmers to mechanize planting and reaping. While the labor shortage temporarily reduced the impact of proletarianization on wages, military demobilization brought serious unemployment.

The termination of the Napoleonic wars not only poured former agricultural laborers back into civilian life but also threatened landlords' war-driven prosperity. In 1822 Cobbett met a farmer "who said he must be ruined, unless another *good war* should come!" (Cobbett 1967: 59). A combination of abundant harvests and reopened international markets brought agricultural prices crashing down, threatening rents as well. In 1815 the landed interest managed to buffer its losses by Parliament's enactment of a Corn Law limiting grain imports as a function of the domestic price. That measure, however, did nothing to stay the proletarianization of farm workers. The squeeze of landless laborers helped produce East Anglia's agrarian struggles of 1816, about whose repression Cobbett wrote so indignantly.

The glut of labor in postwar agriculture and the rapid growth of the general population spurred the movement into industrial wage-labor as they forwarded the proletarianization of both agricultural and industrial sectors. During the early postwar years the dramatic drop in agricultural prices attacked the incomes of landlords and farmers while contributing to a slight overall increase in other people's real incomes. Despite the relative cheapness of agricultural labor, large farmers therefore continued to substitute machines (notably threshing machines) for workers, to dispense with year-round servants and hired hands, and to impose increased discipline on their laborers. Rising industrial productivity contributed to the wages of well-established industrial workers, but simultaneously promoted proletarianization outside of that select circle.

Capital-concentrated manufacturing drove a modest expansion of the British economy; not until after 1830, however, did technologically innovative capital-intensive increases in productivity really accelerate (Feinstein in Floud and McCloskey 1981). Gains between 1816 and 1827 resulted chiefly from displacement of labor to higher-productivity industries and from intensification of labor discipline. In the bellwether cotton industry, it is true, a momentous shift occurred: continual mechanization of carding and spinning through all the postwar years, rapid introduction of power looms—hence displacement of handloom weavers—in the 1820s. The trade depressions of cotton goods in 1816–1817 and 1826–1827 found textile workers acutely vulnerable. On 29 May 1816, for example, magistrates Ralph Fletcher and James Watkins of Bolton transmitted the complaint from a delegation of local cotton weavers that in consequence of *Failures* which have taken place within a week or two past, notices have been given to upwards of one thousand Weavers, that no more materials will be delivered out to them after those in the Loom shall have been wrought; And also that like notices have been given by *solvent* manufacturers, to upwards of two thousand weavers that they too, must not expect any more materials for weaving to be delivered out to them. From these circumstances their opinion is that before the end of three months One Half of the Weavers of this Town and neighborhood (the whole estimated at twenty thousand five hundred) will be out of Employment. (HO 42/150)

Although the cotton trade recovered somewhat in 1818, handloom weavers would never again see the relative prosperity of the war years. By virtue of its expanding industry, nevertheless, Britain overtook France as the West's preeminent economic power.

After the British state's massive wartime expansion, the postwar years brought a significant administrative contraction. Yet by all standards the state that emerged from the war remained substantially larger than its predecessor of 1789. Corrected for inflation, its expenditure during the postwar decade ran about 2.5 times that of the later eighteenth century. The abolition of the income tax at war's end simply displaced the augmented fiscal burden to customs and excise. Cast as per capita equivalents of daily wages for farm laborers and cotton spinners, the long-term trend of governmental receipts for Great Britain looks as in Table 6.1. The per capita burden of 1815 roughly tripled the wage equivalent of 1758, while

Table 6.1. Days' wages paid per capita in national taxes, 1758–1827

Year	Farm laborer	Cotton spinner
1758	12	6
1781	14	7
1789	14	8
1815	32	18
1827	23	12

Sources: Lindert and Williamson 1983b; Williamson 1985; Mitchell and Dane 1971.

Table 6.2. Government finance and real income in the United Kingdom, 1816–1827

	Annual total		Annual % change	
Item	1816	1827	1816–1827	1789–1815
Revenue from customs	14.3	19.5	+2.9%	+5.5%
Revenue from excise	29.5	20.8	−3.2	+5.5
Revenue from stamps	6.7	7.0	+0.4	+6.5
Revenue from land tax	9.5	5.1	−5.8	+3.8
Debt service expenditure	32.2	29.2	−0.9	+4.6
Civil government expenditure	6.1	6.0	−0.2	+4.9
Expenditure on army and ordnance	39.6	10.2	−13.1	+12.8
Expenditure on navy	16.8	6.5	−9.0	+9.7
Total Expenditure on military	56.4	16.7	−11.7	+11.3
Farm laborer real income	21.8	22.0	+0.1	+0.4
Middle worker real income	30.2	37.2	+1.9	+0.4
Artisan real income	38.9	49.9	+2.3	+0.4

Note: "Real income" is in 1851 pounds per year. Other figures are in millions of current pounds sterling. 1815–1827 governmental figures refer to the United Kingdom.

Sources: Lindert and Williamson 1983b; Williamson 1985; Mitchell and Deane 1971.

that of 1827 still doubled it. Thus the per capita cost of government reached a peak toward the end of the Napoleonic wars but by no means receded to its prewar levels as peace returned.

The army, now engaged largely in overseas conquest, settled at the unprecedented peacetime strength of 100,000 men. Until 1818 substantial British contingents occupied defeated France. The state's full-time administrative staff had not, it is true, expanded enormously: from about 18,000 before the wars to just under 25,000 in 1815, back to 22,000 or 23,000 during the 1820s. But the 18,000 had included many sinecures, which greatly diminished by war's end. Thus the effective governmental staff grew significantly.

As Table 6.2 shows, changes in economy and state structure had visible effects on state finances: continued increase in customs revenues, stagnation or decline in returns from other taxes (especially the land tax), stabilization of payments on the national debt and costs of civil government, great declines in military expenditure—substantial armies in Ireland and overseas drawing major shares of their costs from populations they controlled for the empire. Consistent with imperial conquests, naval budgets contracted less rapidly than those for the army and ordnance.

At home, armed force civilianized. With the partial exception of the yeomanry, the state had seized central control of military means. Especially in Ireland, specialized police forces were growing, and becoming more involved in the control of collective action; although magistrates continued to call for royal troops and yeomanry in times of major conflict, police partially displaced troops from crowd control. In the CGs of Southeast England troops made up 68.5 percent of all repressive formations in 1758–1781, 63.4 percent in 1789–1811, 42.4 percent in 1819–1820.

Judicially, royal courts enjoyed unquestioned priority over the unarmed and unpaid Justices of the Peace, who nevertheless meted out most of the judgments rendered in the land and enjoyed substantial regulatory powers at county and local levels. Within the state, wartime fiscal expansion and the incorporation of Ireland into a United Kingdom had greatly augmented the political weight of Parliament relative both to the monarchy and to regional holders of power. Parliament wielded extensive control over governmental expenditure, wrote regulations prescribing the forms of municipal administration, and met many local demands for assistance, yet left localities on their own to provide for such costs as schools and poor relief. Municipalities continued to exercise highly varied privileges, including many different modes for election of MPs, as a function of their previous tractations with the crown. Ultimately, however, they operated within stringent limits set by Parliament and royal administration. Although radicals such as Cobbett continued to rail against the emoluments and privileges of great royal officers, the patronage politics of Walpole's day had almost entirely dissolved.

By the 1820s the British had created a remarkable state in which the many powers of local and regional officials did not impede substantial central control or the support of an expensive military establishment. This was no Russia, with its combination of regional satraps and crown-dependent officials; no Netherlands, with its French-imposed central structure confronting municipalities that had enjoyed centuries of semi-autonomy; no Prussia, with its great landlords serving simultaneously as army officers, judges, and regional agents of the crown; no Spain, with its web of municipal and noble privilege cramping any possibility of decisive action by the central administration. Despite its appearance of liberty and idiosyncrasy, the British state wielded compact, effective central power. That it used the power disproportionately in the interests of the wealthy and titled does not gainsay that effectiveness. On the contrary, the state's protection of landlords, clergy, and large capitalists reinforced its control over the rest of the population precisely because the state continued to do much of its work through those privileged intermediaries.

From War to Peace to Contention

William Cobbett was therefore right to see the Napoleonic wars as a source of deep changes in British life, their end as an opportunity for mass political activity. The terminations of major wars commonly occasion readjustment among all the actors, international and domestic, who have taken part. Internationally, ends of wars bring the major moments for abolition of old states, creation of new states, changes of rulers, redrawing of boundaries, and reorganization of constitutional forms. In such settlements as the Congress of Vienna, much of the work goes into recasting the state system, especially to the detriment of those who have lost the recent war.

Domestically, the cessation of hostilities undoes some of the arrangements created by military mobilization, but never returns social life to the *status quo ante*. In wartime, the state's expansion of military force, its sustenance of the war effort, and its disciplining of the civilian population in both regards form new state agencies, powers, and varieties of intervention. As war ends, rulers manage not only the demobilization of major military forces and their infrastructure but also the disposition of the apparatus lately erected to draw compliance and the means of war from citizens: inflated taxes, repressive laws, means of surveillance, systems of rationing, and much more. The demobilization of large military forces itself places serious stress on an economy and polity—finding work for veterans in labor markets that are usually contracting after the stimulus of war production, dealing with people who have taken the jobs of absent warriors, caring for the war-disabled, absorbing into civilian routines men who have spent years killing and carousing, disposing safely of military arms, matériel, and real estate.

As they improvise to sustain a war effort, furthermore, rulers usually overcommit the state. They take on more obligations, many of them payable at war's end, than the state's likely future capacity can justify. That is obviously true of financial obligations in the form of government bonds and the like. It is also true of political commitments to military veterans, to collaborating opposition powerholders, and to major social classes that cooperate in support of the war. When debts come due at the peace settlement, some creditors always lose, and often some of them take action to defend their claims. Few rulers, especially among those which have won a war, ever dismantle the whole apparatus, returning fully to the prewar situation. Instead, they typically divert some of the state's expanded capacity to repairing war damage, compensating veterans, paying debts accumulated in wartime borrowing, and taking on new tasks wartime experience has made seem more urgent, attractive, or newly feasible. Hence the famous ratchet effect: the tendency of state budgets and administrative staffs to inflate during a war's prosecution, only to remain far above the prewar level during postwar contraction.

All this takes place, finally, as peace removes the justifications for wartime constriction of civil liberties. Censorship relaxes, surveillance networks disband, spies move to safer pursuits, military jurisdiction over civilian life contracts, laws limiting association and assembly expire, tolerance of influential citizens for arbitrary state action against presumed enemies declines. Almost inevitably, advocates of suppressed causes, grievances, and populations raise their voices in new claims. Their demands activate further claims by parties they now threaten, by those who wish to defend gains they have made in wartime, or by others who learn that in the face of a relaxing state the time is ripe for new claims. As all these processes converge just after a war, the level of contention often rises abruptly. Over European experience as a whole, new bids for power and revolutionary situations—the appearance of challengers who control some part of the state apparatus and command assent from some significant portion of the citizenry—have concentrated disproportionately in postwar years.

Britain's experience from 1789 to 1820 conformed to the model of wartime repression and accumulation of state power, war-end relaxation, and postwar mass mobilization. The Napoleonic wars and their consequences strongly affected the rhythm and themes of popular contention during the postwar years. Wartime activity had greatly expanded the scope, personnel, and resources of the British state, while making Parliament, the authorizer of taxes, ever more salient within the state; something like cabinet government with a responsible prime minister drawn from parliamentary ranks began to take shape.

The flurry of associational activity that arose between 1789 and 1795 subsided rapidly; the repressive apparatus put in place during the later 1790s then restrained the making of popular claims on the state for almost two decades. Yet repression did encourage two rather different sorts of political activity: clandestine organization of revolutionary networks, and adoption by reformers of means—for example, electoral campaigns activating many non-electors—lying barely within the bounds of legality. At least in southeastern England, authorized local assemblies such as electoral meetings, wardmotes, and vestries gained a surprising stimulus from the combination of nationalization and repression. By the peace of 1815, powerholders had to deal with a citizenry much more strongly oriented to national politics than their parents had been in 1789, and better equipped to contend in the national arena.

The double ending of the Napoleonic Wars in 1814 and 1815 likewise illustrated the characteristic turbulence of transitions to peace. No full revolutionary situation formed in Great Britain during 1816 or 1817, but less drastic versions of the characteristic postwar transformations clearly occurred. Britain demobilized 332,000 troops in little more than a year, dumping them into an economy that quickly began to experience agrarian contraction. The postwar government reorganized its repression, intensifying some forms of surveillance and punishment while relaxing others. In 1816, for example, Parliament abolished the pillory and significantly broadened the judicial scope of *habeas corpus.* Yet in the same year Parliament also greatly tightened laws against poaching and passed a Malicious Damage Act for Scotland to punish attacks on mines and factories.

In 1817 Parliament suspended the *habeas corpus* rights it had just broadened, instituted tight controls over meetings of fifty or more persons, stepped up its measures against "seditious and blasphemous" publications, confirmed previous Treason Acts, and passed an Irish Insurrection Act, but also annulled previous penalties against the profession of religious dissent in Ireland. Each year thereafter—notably 1819, with its Six Acts and its friendly societies legislation, and 1824, with its repeal of the Combination Acts—retouched the national pattern of repression in some regards; the net result was to make a wider range of popular associations legal, to subject legally constituted associations to stricter public surveillance, and to increase the penalties for violent direct action and clandestine association.

Contentious Contours

After a five-year cycle of struggle from 1816 through 1820, contention on a national scale declined during the 1820s; the reinforced repression of 1819 and the economic upswing of the early 1820s both contributed to that decline. In the industrial north, however, badly squeezed workers (especially handloom weavers) continued to make claims, especially with the trade depression of 1826. In Great Britain as a whole, the chronology of contention ran this way:

1816: farmworkers' attacks on farmers, landlords, and enclosures; industrial workers' attacks on machinery; struggles over food supply; wage demands; reform meetings.

1817: workers' strikes, assemblies, processions, marches, and insurrections; reform meetings.

1818: reform meetings and demonstrations; major strikes, processions, workers' meetings; attacks on agricultural and industrial machinery.

1819: reform meetings and demonstrations, including responses to Peterloo and Hunt's arrest; electoral gatherings and fights.

1820: electoral gatherings; meetings, processions, delegations, forced illuminations, and street gatherings in support of Queen Caroline; reform meetings, processions, and demonstrations; attempted insurrections; major strikes.

1821: processions and demonstrations (including a vast funeral procession) in support of the queen; reform meetings; coronation celebrations.

1822: workers' gatherings, attacks on agricultural and industrial machinery.

1823: workers' gatherings, strikes, including agitation of Spitalfields weavers against repeal of Protective Act.

1824: workers' meetings, strikes.

1825: strikes, attacks on industrial machinery; organizing meetings of workers.

1826: workers' meetings, strikes, attacks on industrial machinery; meetings against Corn Law; reform meetings; contested electoral assemblies.

1827: workers' meetings.

What was happening? A vast mobilization of popular claims surged in 1815 and 1816, only to be met by renewed repression during the continuing claim-making of 1817–1819. Another large campaign for parliamentary reform rose and fell, joining with the popular outcry against George IV's attempt to exclude his estranged wife, Queen Caroline, from the throne in 1820. The reform agitation of 1821–22, although sufficient to stir Parliament, brought little popular mobilization. With the exception of northern English workers' struggles in 1826, during the later 1820s national attention shifted to Ireland, where Daniel O'Connell and his allies organized the mass-membership Catholic Association and pressed for Catholic emancipation: the granting to Catholics of rights to hold public office, including seats in the UK Parliament.

Within Great Britain but outside of London and its hinterland, workers dominated large-scale contention. In 1816 East Anglia's landless laborers attacked agricultural machinery, burned hayricks, seized food, and (as we have seen) marched into market towns while in Lancashire, Cheshire, and Nottinghamshire their industrial counterparts were smashing frames, demonstrating, and demanding reform. The following year East Anglia's workers remained silent, but those of Yorkshire, Nottinghamshire, and Derbyshire joined in, to the point of participating in an abortive insurrectionary march toward Nottingham, the so-called Pentrich Rebellion. During 1818 weavers and colliers continued to meet, strike, and demonstrate in Lancashire and Cheshire; many workers were enlisting in the cause of parliamentary reform. Preparing for mass action, militant workers formed paramilitary units that began to march and drill in the countryside. In a botched attempt to arrest speaker Henry Hunt, the Lancashire yeomanry and royal hussars broke up a great reform meeting at St. Peter's Fields in Manchester (16 August 1819)—an action soon styled Peterloo in ironic antithesis to Wellington's victory over Napoleon just four years earlier. The massacre, in which 11 people died and 600 suffered injuries, at first stimulated militant responses throughout Great Britain, but actually initiated new repression and a major recession of workers' collective action.

Spring of 1820 saw a series of armed workers' risings in Yorkshire and Lancashire in conjunction with a foiled attempt at insurrection (the Cato Street conspiracy) in London, followed by quiescence. Spies and informers generally kept national authorities well ahead of workers' conspiracies, which the authorities nevertheless often let unfold to the point of incrimination or self-destruction. From 1821 through 1825 among London's workers only the silkweavers (who were losing the legislative protection they had enjoyed for sixty years) acted repeatedly. Then in 1826 workers' attacks on machinery and factories multiplied in Lancashire and Yorkshire, with power-looms coming in for the most serious destruction. Meanwhile, in Ireland a campaign for Catholic emancipation flourished from 1823 onward.

Henry Hunt's career during those years illustrates the changing tempo of contention. During the great flurry of street activity in 1819, Hunt went to jail on his arrest at Peterloo (16 August), made numerous public appearances while out of jail during his indictment and trial, began to stand for election to Parliament from Preston, then finally (May 1820) received a sentence of thirty months' imprisonment in Ilchester gaol on the charge of "unlawful and seditious assembling for the purpose of exciting discontent" (Belchem 1985: 118). Having distanced himself from the sometime allies who plotted the tragicomic, government-infiltrated coup d'état of Cato Street (February 1820), Hunt figured in 1820 as a hero (but not an active presence) during the abortive workers' risings of Huddersfield and Grange Moor. While incarcerated at Ilchester, Hunt kept up a steady stream of legal actions, publications, and communications with allies, then joined a great round of celebrations at his release (October 1822). For the next few years, nevertheless, he concentrated his practical political efforts on electoral campaigns in Somerset (1823 and 1826) and reform within the London municipality. Although reformers continued to meet, write, and fight bitterly among themselves, no significant national mobilization occurred again within Great Britain before 1828's drive for—and against—Catholic emancipation.

Queen Caroline

From Ilchester Gaol, by pen and voice Henry Hunt lavished his advice on the organizers of 1820's great mobilization around the Princess of Wales, the presumptive Queen Caroline. George III's death that year finally put Prince Regent George, long Britain's *de facto* sovereign, in a position to become king. He and his wife Caroline of Brunswick had lived quite separately since shortly after their arranged marriage of 1795. Both had formed other liaisons, he notoriously and multiply, she somewhat more discreetly—but not discreetly enough to avoid being suspected in 1805 of having borne an illegitimate child. Through enemy-of-my-enemy alignments, she attracted support among radical and Whig opponents of the Prince Regent, creating a politically prominent London salon before escaping into continental exile in 1813.

Even in exile, Caroline had maintained a following among the regime's critics. Cobbett himself had written repeatedly in her behalf. As George IV prepared to assume the crown, Caroline (assured of public support by London reformers such as Alderman Matthew Wood) returned to claim her place as queen. George retorted by asking Parliament to authorize a divorce and her deposition on grounds of adultery. He and his advisors did not count, however, on the enormous campaign that returned Caroline to England as a heroine, as a woman wronged by her rake of a husband, as living evidence of the regime's corruption. From the time she landed at Dover (5 June 1820) to her death (7 August 1821) London buzzed or roared repeatedly with demonstrations of support for her claims, countered only slightly by intermittent mobilizations on the king's behalf. In his entry for 6 July 1820, Clerk of the Council Charles Greville remarked: "it is certain hitherto that all ranks of men have been decidedly favourable to the queen, and disbelieve the charges against her. The military in London have shown alarming symptoms of dissatisfaction, so much so that it seems doubtful how far the Guards can be counted upon in case of any disturbance arising out of this subject" (Greville 1938: I, 100). That political entrepreneurs managed much of the queen's campaign does not gainsay the swell of popular support for her rights, or the glee with which ordinary people used the controversy as an occasion to voice other grievances against the crown.

At the time of George III's recovery from madness in 1789, his supporters had organized celebratory meetings, addresses, and processions all over the metropolis. When the king and queen had then appeared in public, crowds had cheered them enthusiastically; in theaters, audiences had joyously sung "God Save the King." By the king's death in 1820, he had been a popular figure for at least thirty years, despite—or perhaps even because of—his steady loss of power relative to Parliament (Colley 1992). His successor, George IV, long disliked as regent, inspired no such following. Still, the big difference between 1789 and 1820 did not lie in the new king's unpopularity. It lay in an emerging synthesis among established ceremonial, evasion of repression, opposition to the government, and organized campaigns to display public support for parliamentary reform. After the repression that followed Peterloo had stifled many reformers, Queen Caroline gave them a splendid opportunity to breathe freely again.

As the queen's "trial"—the 19 August opening of a parliamentary inquiry into the king's proposal to divorce and depose Caroline—approached, London reformers and radicals intensified their efforts. The radical shipwright John Gast organized and addressed a workers' meeting in support of the queen on 31 July, then had his address circulated widely for signatures. On 15 August no fewer than four distinct processions converged on the queen's residence, Brandenburgh House, to present addresses to Caroline: delegations from Middlesex, St. Leonard's Shoreditch, Hammersmith, and the artisans. The latter

> met a little before 12 o'clock, near St. Clement's church, and the crowd, which was very considerable, was there marshalled by a few persons who bore white wands, by way of distinction; they formed the crowd into companies of a convenient breadth to move through the streets without creating any inconvenient interruption. The Address itself, signed by 39,786 persons, was borne between two of the addressers, genteelly dressed in mourning, with rosettes of silk riband in the breasts of their coats; they were followed by about 100 others, walking two and two, attired in the same manner; about one hundred more followed in coloured clothes, some with their aprons on, others with silk coloured neckerchiefs, but the whole exceedingly clean. (LT 16 August 1820: 11)

Through all this the queen received daily advice from such reformers as Alderman Wood, had Francis Place organizing addresses to her and

William Cobbett writing her replies, and heard regularly from working-class radicals such as John Gast. Whatever her personal political proclivities, Caroline took a public position that aligned her with the standard critique of the government's corruption, incompetence, and injustice. Willy-nilly, she had joined the apparatus of a vast social movement.

The movement continued until after Caroline's death in August 1821, furthermore, since the cortege that took her body from Hammersmith (the location of Brandenburgh House) on the way to her native Brunswick occasioned a great demonstration, whose participants forced the hearse to pass through the City instead of bypassing it. A week later the funeral of two men killed by troops during that demonstration occasioned yet another march by thousands of workers—all this coordinated, and quarreled over, by activist reformers and radicals. The affair "had further shaken the prestige of monarchy and government, restored freedom of political agitation, brought trade societies into open political activity, and enabled [John] Gast to build up a radical trade organisation" (Prothero 1979: 153–154). It also confirmed the increased viability of social-movement politics in the face of a resistant state.

Contentious Actors

More so than in any other period under study, the concentration of our CG sample in 1819–20 and its confinement to southeastern England inadequately represents the trend of contention over the years from 1816 to 1827. That is true for several reasons: first because two adjacent years cannot establish a twelve-year trend; again because the years immediately preceding 1819 brought a great burst of conflict to the Southeast while the 1820s saw another decline; finally because the rest of Great Britain followed a rather different rhythm from the Southeast. To get a clear picture of British contention, we have to augment the detailed evidence from London and its vicinity with other sources describing the rest of Great Britain, especially the industrial North.

Still, the evidence from 1819 and 1820 contains important clues. As Table 6.3 indicates, the frequency of contentious gatherings in the Southeast greatly increased during the postwar years: from an average of 60 per covered year in the interval 1758–1811 to 265 per year in 1819 and 1820. The increase probably did not result merely from more intensive coverage, since it appeared in all our sources for the period. The numbers of CGs reported in each publication are shown in Table 6.4 (reports of many CGs appeared, of course, in more than one publication). Such mobilizations as those around parliamentary reform and Queen Caroline's rights generated unprecedented numbers of claim-making assemblies.

Meetings predominated in London and vicinity: if we include electoral assemblies, 65 percent of 1819's CGs, 51 percent in 1820, as compared with 27 percent in 1758–1781 and 49 percent in 1789–1811. After the many meetings of 1819 around such reformist issues as solidarity with the victims of Peterloo, the proportion of meetings declined in 1820 only because expressions of support for Queen Caroline also took the form of

Table 6.3. Occasions of contentious gatherings in Southeastern England, 1758–1820

Type of event	% of total for period				Total	N
	1758–1781	1789–1811	1819	1820		
Forced illumination of windows	4.3	0.5	0.0	2.9	1.9	23
Other attacks on persons or their property	46.5	12.1	3.1	1.5	16.4	190
Seizure of food or property	5.9	1.1	0.0	0.0	1.8	22
Resistance to governmental regulation or action	5.3	3.2	3.5	4.4	4.1	49
Meeting to communicate with national government	21.5	35.0	57.8	41.6	38.0	457
Electoral assembly	5.3	13.5	7.0	9.1	9.1	109
Strike, turnout, or gathering for wage demands	4.6	1.1	0.0	0.0	1.5	18
Other gathering	6.6	33.4	28.5	40.5	27.3	328
Total	100.0	99.9	99.9	100.0	100.1	1,203
Number of CGs	302	371	256	274	1,203	

delegations, processions, and cheering crowds, here classified as "other gatherings." The "other gatherings" of 1819 and 1820 also included an exceptional number of authorized local assemblies such as wardmotes dealing with municipal elections, parish administration, and other issues that bore only indirectly on national affairs. A full 144 of 1820's 274 CGs, nevertheless, concerned the king, the queen, or both at once. In the Southeast (although not in northern industrial districts) strikes, attacks on persons or property, and seizures of food or goods faded into nothingness.

The Napoleonic wars had indirectly promoted the rise of public meetings. Although toleration of religious gatherings, dispatch of parish business through authorized assemblies, and prying open of opportunities by special-purpose associations during the war years surely played their parts in the meeting's increasing prevalence, the main line of causality was something like the one shown in Figure 6.1. As Mark Harrison notes (1988), the parliamentary elections of 1812 brought a significant increase in public meetings, while the elections of 1819 secured the meeting as the centerpiece of political campaigns. Harrison does not note, however, the preceding segments of the causal sequence, from wars to taxes and military mobilization to parliamentary power to the increased salience of elections. Those segments explain why after the 1780s the proportion of all CGs that were meetings rose in close synchrony with the proportion in which Parliament was the object of claims.

Francis Place took the rise of meetings as evidence of the reform

Table 6.4. Number of CGs reported in periodicals, 1801–1820

Year	Annual Register	Gentleman's Magazine	London Chronicle	Times
1801	7	6	40	35
1807	4	5	40	93
1811	2	6	17	32
1819	3	14	87	234
1820	43	20	142	216

movement's civilizing influence. "Look even to Lancashire," he declared
in a letter to Thomas Hodgskin (12 September 1819):

> Within a few years a stranger walking through their towns was "touted,"
> i.e. hooted, and an "outcomling" was sometimes pelted with stones.
> "Lancashire brute" was the common and appropriate appellation. Until
> very lately it would have been dangerous to have assembled 500 of them
> on any occasion. Bakers and butchers would at the least have been
> plundered. Now 100,000 people may be collected together and no riot
> ensue, and why? Why, but for the fact before stated, that the people have
> an object, the pursuit of which gives them importance in their own eyes,
> elevates them in their own opinion, and thus it is that the very indi-
> viduals who would have been the leaders of the riot are the keepers of
> the peace. (Wallas 1898: 145–146)

His implied comparison between the "riots" of 1816 and the great assemblies of 1819 makes the point. But Place told only part of the story. The
fashioning and legalization of the public meeting—in which reform
agitators indeed played a significant part—itself made available a new
means of expression, a new vehicle of popular politics.

Note the practical importance of public meetings. They served not only
for their ostensible purpose of deliberation but also to justify assemblies
and discussions that authorities and enemies could otherwise easily forbid. A significant share of British repressive legislation and practice grew
precisely from negotiations between authorities and activists over the
proper limits of public meetings; the hue and cry over the yeomanry's
lethal attack on the crowd at Peterloo redoubled because the mass meeting's organizers had taken great pains to ensure that it would proceed in
a disciplined, legal manner. Increasingly meetings served not as decisionmaking devices but as demonstrations of a sort, as announcements that
considerable numbers of people were committing themselves publicly to
certain programs, causes, complaints, or demands.

The frequently prefabricated routine of electing a chair, hearing speeches,
adopting resolutions, and sending addresses or petitions to authorities
confirmed the demonstrative side of meetings. Banquets and their toasts
had long served similar purposes, and continued to assemble insiders at
the ends of great public gatherings (Epstein 1988). But festive dinners

took significantly greater effort, space, time, and money than public meetings involving the same numbers. Meetings offered partial, temporary approximations of the paraparliamentary conventions about which radicals often dreamed. If properly designed, they had the great advantage of remaining within the law, hence usually outside the reach of violent repression.

Like all large assemblies, to be sure, public meetings ran the risks of infiltration, subversion, repression, destructive division, or escalation to violent confrontation. A famous series of reform meetings in Spa Fields, London (15 November, 2 and 9 December 1816) illustrates those risks amply. London radicals including the Drs. Watson, Arthur Thistlewood, Thomas Preston, government spy-provocateur John Castle, and others hoped to use leading reformers as bait for a crowd they could then draw into insurrection. After Cobbett and a number of other leaders had refused, Henry Hunt stumbled part way into the trap. Before the first meeting, however, Hunt managed to substitute his own program of manhood suffrage, annual Parliaments, and ballots for the sweeping reorganizations of property his inciters were urging. At the 15 November meeting he called for more mass meetings representing the people's will, beginning with Parliament's next session at the end of January 1817; still the younger Watson was able to move and carry an adjournment of the meeting until 2 December, when the conspirators hoped to take charge.

On 2 December young Watson led part of the crowd that had assembled well before Hunt's arrival to assaults on gunshops and to a vain effort at recruiting soldiers at the Tower of London to their cause; unpaid sailors seized that moment of distraction to start their own looting. While the conspirators were stirring up minor confrontations elsewhere in the city, nevertheless, Hunt held the bulk of the audience at Spa Fields with a great speech on behalf of mass mobilization and parliamentary reform. At the Spa Fields meeting of 9 December Hunt addressed an even larger crowd, this time without competition from leaders of insurrection. The three Spa Fields meetings led directly to mass meetings elsewhere in Great Britain, to a first convention at the Crown and Anchor tavern on 22 January 1817, and to further assemblies at Spa Fields during that year; by this time a huge national series of meetings, marches, petitions, and demonstrations had begun.

Despite widespread repression over the next two years, the campaign hardly ceased. In Lancashire open-air meetings rapidly became standard political practice; in and around Manchester at least sixteen parliamentary reform meetings took place between 9 March and 1 September 1818 (Hall 1989). In Liverpool radicals "appropriated" residentially exclusive Clayton Square as a site for five reform meetings between February 1817 and the fall of 1819 (Harrison 1988: 162). The great mass meeting in Manchester's St. Peter's Fields on 16 August 1819, at which Hunt was again the featured speaker, belonged to the same series of mass demands for parliamentary reform; only the yeomanry's riding into the crowd with sabers drawn, seeking to arrest Hunt, turned it into something different and greater: Peterloo.

Antiradicals, for their part, did not merely promote governmental repression of radicals. They likewise adopted the mass meeting as a demonstration of support for their cause. Manchester loyalists held their first such meeting on 13 January 1817 (Glen 1984). Such demonstrations typically took the form of declarations of loyalty to the monarchy, hence to the settlement of 1689, thence to the religious establishment and the Orange cause. When Londoners attacked the Prince Regent's carriage on his return from Parliament (28 January 1817, the same day Admiral Cochrane delivered to Parliament the reform petition endorsed by the Crown and Anchor convention of 22 January), loyalist meetings multiplied as the House of Lords began an inquiry into revolutionary conspiracies and the House of Commons moved toward repressive measures against all sorts of societies, clubs, and Seditious Meetings.

Not all demonstrations of support for a cause took the form of orderly public assemblies. As elections to Parliament grew in importance, so did the frequency of contested elections and the participation of nonvoters in them. Partisans not only continued the eighteenth-century practices of accompanying favored candidates to the hustings, unhitching their horses to draw their carriages, jeering their opponents, and shouting as electors cast their votes, but also took to forceful intervention in the outcome. In June 1826 mayor Nicholas Grimshaw of Preston reported that:

> in consequence of the most serious outrages which had been committed by a Mob, armed with Bludgeons, at one of the Entrances of the Poll Booth for the Election now holding in that Borough, preventing the access of Voters to the Hustings. Captain Barrie, one of the Candidates had protested against the admission of any more Voters, until free access

was allowed to every voter; and that having in vain tried to force a free access by means of the Civil Power, except to such persons as the Mob chose to admit, he had been under the necessity of calling upon the Troop of Cavalry, stationed at Kirkham, to place itself at Broughton, four miles from Preston, on the road to Garstang, this morning by eight o'clock, to remain there until the close of the Election on Monday next. (HO 40/20, 22 June 1826)

Preston had one of Great Britain's broadest franchises. Cobbett had entered the Preston race against the Whig E. G. Stanley and the independent John Wood, with an agreement not to require Preston's Catholic voters to take the oath of supremacy. Then Robert Barrie (navy captain and resident commissioner in Kingston, Ontario) entered for the Tories, with the apparent intent of scaring off Cobbett's supporters by requiring the oath. The mayor and his election officials had at least implicitly conspired with Barrie and against Cobbett not only by insisting on the Anglican oath but also by physically blocking his electors from the polls (Spater 1982). The "bludgeons" Grimshaw mentioned were Cobbett's supporters' electoral staves cut into fours; until dragoons drove them away, they had used the bludgeons to keep supporters of Barrie and Stanley out of the channel that Grimshaw had assigned to Cobbett's electors, and that Cobbett himself, despairing of election, had opened to Wood's (Cobbett 1829). Both sides used force to influence the outcome.

That was not all. After a recession between 1789 and 1819, forced illuminations of windows revived with popular support for Queen Caroline. Chiefly because of Queen Caroline, furthermore, 111 of 1820's 274 CGs fell into the category "other gatherings." Residents of the Southeast not only cheered the queen repeatedly at her frequent public appearances but also took to organizing ostentatious processions to deliver addresses supporting either the king or (much more often) the queen. On 22 and 28 August 1820, for example, London crowds both cheered Queen Caroline and jeered the Duke of Wellington for his apparent siding with the king. In these events, the time-honored delegation and procession merged into the street demonstration. At year's end, furthermore, the standard meetings at which officers of London wards ended their terms and received thanks for their service became occasions for taking positions on the queen's rights as well as on parliamentary reform.

Nevertheless, older forms of direct action were fading. The Southeast's general decline in eighteenth-century forms of action and consolidation of the nineteenth-century repertoire show up in Table 6.5, which traces verbs in the CGs of 1819 and 1820. As compared with previous years, the verbs *chair, cheer, disperse,* and *resolve*—mostly associated with meetings and electoral assemblies—increased in frequency. On the decline over the long run were *attack, control, gather,* and *request,* all but the last of them typical actions in rough street politics. The campaign on behalf of Queen Caroline again reversed the long-term trend somewhat, as the verb categories *attack, control,* and *gather* rose to higher levels than they had occupied for twenty years, but not to their eighteenth-century prevalence.

The distribution of formations (Table 6.6) tells a similar story: a long-term movement toward formal assemblies and national actors complicated by the short-term effects of the Queen Caroline affair. Parliament, members of Parliament, and national officials reached new heights as objects of claims, but in 1820 so did royalty; both the prodigal queen-designate and the profligate king-elect received great attention from participants in contentious gatherings. (Chiefly because vestries across London passed resolutions in the spring of 1819 against a salary increase for Fire Act clergy, clergy likewise appeared more frequently than before as objects of claims.) Local assemblies of freeholders, residents, or vestries, who frequently initiated claims on national actors, likewise gained prominence. Local officials such as mayors and councilmen often figured because they served as middlemen, both receiving claims from their own constituencies and transmitting or initiating claims on higher authorities. Police, troops, judges, trade groups, unspecified crowds, and named individuals, in contrast, continued to decline in relative involvement.

Precisely because coordinated campaigns oriented to Parliament and the national government were gaining, issues of CGs became more volatile; meetings, processions, petition drives, and related forms of claim-making surged during a parliamentary debate or a governmental action, then subsided until the next governmental issue arose. As Table 6.7 shows, both direct attacks on malefactors and workers' claims concerning work declined over the long run in the Southeast. Issues of local government, in contrast, continued to rise, essentially because local assemblies called increasingly on Parliament to intervene in such matters as the powers of parish officials and the right to assemble, especially in the light of Peterloo

Table 6.5. Verbs in all actions of contentious gatherings, Southeastern England, 1758–1820

	% of total for period					
Verb	1758–1781	1789–1811	1819	1820	Total	N
Assemble	4.3	4.0	3.6	5.3	4.3	326
Attack	17.4	4.7	3.8	2.8	7.9	599
Chair	0.8	4.7	9.4	6.0	4.7	358
Cheer	1.2	4.2	3.7	8.9	4.3	323
Communicate	3.8	1.7	1.8	2.0	2.4	182
Control	15.0	8.0	4.0	4.1	8.5	639
Decry	1.3	1.6	1.6	1.7	1.5	115
Disperse	4.6	3.6	4.9	5.2	4.5	340
End	11.3	15.5	13.5	11.0	12.8	966
Fight	1.5	1.2	0.7	0.5	1.0	79
Gather	6.9	4.8	1.9	2.0	4.2	317
Meet	2.8	9.6	12.1	9.1	7.9	597
Move	9.7	6.2	3.2	5.6	6.5	494
Petition	1.0	1.0	0.5	0.2	0.7	54
Request	3.1	1.6	0.7	0.6	1.7	125
Resist	1.4	0.8	0.9	0.2	0.9	66
Resolve	1.6	13.7	23.4	19.1	13.2	996
Support	1.2	1.1	0.4	0.6	0.9	67
Other	11.1	12.0	9.7	15.2	12.0	907
Total	100.0	100.0	99.8	100.0	99.9	7,550
N	2,293	2,032	1,482	1,743	7,550	

(1819); the spreading practice of using the year-end meeting of a London ward to thank local officers who had taken appropriate positions on national issues such as parliamentary reform increased the prominence of local assemblies. Religion (in the worldly form of opposition to clerical salary increases) reared its head in 1819, only to dwindle in 1820. In 1820, meanwhile, the campaign of support for Queen Caroline brought CGs

Table 6.6. Formations participating in Southeastern contentious gatherings, 1758–1820

Type of formation	% of total for period					
	1758–1781	1789–1811	1819	1820	Total	N
Parliament, MP	4.5	15.5	16.4	17.3	16.8	341
National officials	3.0	2.2	3.4	4.3	3.9	79
Royalty	2.9	6.5	2.0	14.7	8.9	180
Gentlemen, nobles	2.6	4.5	3.6	3.6	3.6	72
Judges	4.5	2.5	1.6	0.8	1.2	24
Mayors	2.1	1.8	1.7	2.3	2.0	41
Other local officials	5.6	10.1	26.5	11.9	18.6	376
Clergy	0.2	0.7	5.2	1.0	2.9	59
Freeholders, electors	0.5	2.2	2.4	4.6	3.6	72
Other local assemblies	3.4	9.3	14.6	13.7	14.1	286
Trade	14.9	7.2	2.2	2.7	2.5	50
Other interest	2.8	7.1	5.3	4.0	4.6	93
Police	3.4	2.6	1.8	1.6	1.7	35
Troops	7.4	4.5	0.8	1.6	1.2	24
Unnamed crowd	11.3	4.0	2.6	2.8	2.7	55
Named individuals	9.9	3.2	2.0	2.7	2.4	49
Other	20.9	16.2	8.0	10.4	9.3	188
Total	99.8	100.1	100.1	100.0	100.0	2,024
N	1,223	1,189	929	1,095	2,024	

Note: Includes both actors and objects of claims.

Table 6.7. Major issues of contentious gatherings in Southeastern England, 1758–1820

| | % of total for period | | | | | |
Issue	1758–1781	1789–1811	1819	1820	Total	N
Attacks	22.1	6.7	3.9	4.0	9.4	113
Labor	7.6	0.3	0.0	0.0	2.0	24
Religion	6.9	2.2	22.3	1.1	7.4	89
Police	3.6	1.9	2.0	0.4	2.0	24
Election	5.6	10.5	5.9	4.4	6.9	83
National government	10.2	17.5	17.6	13.5	14.8	178
Royalty	5.3	15.4	2.0	52.6	18.4	222
Reform	1.3	2.2	3.5	1.8	2.2	26
Local government	6.9	10.0	19.1	16.4	12.6	152
Economy	3.3	7.8	5.5	1.1	4.7	56
Other	27.1	25.6	18.4	4.7	19.7	237
Total	99.9	100.1	100.2	100.0	100.1	1,204
N	303	371	256	274	1,204	

concerning royalty to a full majority of all the Southeast's contentious events.

Workers in Action

During the war years mass military service, the concentration of power in the national government, the expanding role of Parliament, and the proliferation of association-based popular politics on a country-wide scale had all drawn workers into increased involvement with national affairs. During the postwar period London's better-organized workers provided significant support for radical and reformist politics. During the Queen Caroline agitation, organized trades spoke up repeatedly on the proper conduct of the monarchy itself. The campaign on behalf of Queen Caroline, however, concentrated heavily in London, where she remained, made frequent public appearances, and died. Outside of the Southeast and across the wider span of years from 1816 to 1827, workers appeared with much greater frequency than in the CGs of London and its vicinity for 1819–1820. Away from London, machine-breaking, insurrection, and turbulent strikes figured importantly in the contention of 1816–1827. In the North, furthermore, workers also provided many activists for parliamentary reform.

We should distinguish between agricultural and industrial workers. Agricultural laborers mobilized mightily during the price-wage-unemployment squeeze of 1816. They marched, poached, burned haystacks and barns, sacked flour mills, attacked mole plows, smashed threshing machines, broke down enclosures, demanded poor relief, and seized grain. Except for lesser recurrences in East Anglia between 1822 and 1826, agricultural laborers then subsided, not to be heard from again until the "Swing" rebellion of 1830. Nor do they seem to have been much involved in the period's widespread demands for parliamentary reform.

Industrial workers remained much more active. During the first dozen postwar years the expanding textile regions of Lancashire, Cheshire, Nottinghamshire, and Yorkshire produced a spate of worker-based political mobilizations. The crucial proliferation occurred from 1816 to 1819; the repeal of the Combination Acts (1824) simply accelerated public efforts to create durable organization. Not only did friendly societies and similar local organizations multiply but also northern workers experimented continually with coordination on a larger scale: political unions, associations of Political Protestants, Hampden Clubs, systems of delegates, general unions grouping together many trades and localities. These organizations provided seedbeds for radical movements, conspiracies, and attempted insurrections. By the 1820s machine spinners formed the core of these organizing efforts, while handloom weavers (where they had survived) devoted a larger share of their energies to defensive attacks on machines and their owners. Like their agrarian counterparts, handloom weavers singled out machines they deemed to be reducing the demand for their work, thus condemning them to lower wages and less employment.

Significant clusters of attacks on powerlooms occurred in 1816, 1818, 1822, 1825, and 1826, with the industrial depressions of 1816 and 1826 the peaks of machine-breaking. In both those years great crowds of workers went from mill to mill methodically smashing the looms. By 1826, furthermore, magistrate Ralph Fletcher of Bolton was summarizing spy reports to the effect that clandestine workers' meetings explicitly linked the program of loom-smashing to general demands for abolition of the Corn Laws, reduction of taxes, and the end of "monarchical corruption" (HO 40/19, 6 May 1826). The government in Westminster thought the menace serious: "By the summer of 1826 almost 8,000 soldiers, one-quarter of the army in England, were stationed in the [Northern] district, mostly in Lancashire and Yorkshire" (Palmer 1988: 279).

Contrary to Duncan Bythell's characterization of weavers' actions in 1826 as a "blind display of hatred" against the powerloom (Bythell 1969: 199), they destroyed with startling discipline. On 27 April 1826 mill owner Daniel Hamer of Bury testified that

yesterday afternoon about four o'clock a multitude of persons to the number of Two Hundred came to the works of this Informant and his partner. That the principal part of these men were armed, a great portion of them with Sticks, others with Sledge Hammers, one person Informant saw had a musket, and the rest were armed with weapons of various descriptions. That Informant and his Father were near the works at this Time and seeing this Multitude approaching Informant and his Father went towards them. That when Informant and his Father came near to this Multitude, the Mob surrounded them. That the Mob said they were come to destroy the Power Looms at Informant's and his Father's Mills which they were determined to destroy before they left the place. The Mob asked Informant and his Father whereabouts in the Mill the Power Looms were. Informant and his Father refused to tell them. That the Mob then proceeded to break open the door of one of the Mills which they did by taking it off its hinges, that when the Mob had forced the door of the Mill Informant saw some of the Mob take Hammers out of their Pockets as they were going into the Mill. That Informant and his Father were standing at the Yard Gates of the Mill, about Forty or Fifty of the Mob went into the Mill. The Yard Gates are about Twenty yards from the Mill door. That the Mill the Mob went into was where the Power Looms are. That directly after the Mob had gone into the Mill Informant heard noises as if they were the blows of Hammers on the Machinery. Informant heard some of the Mob that were outside say "Let the windows alone, break nothing but the Power Looms." That the persons who went into the Mill stayed in about Ten Minutes. That when

> they came out of the Mill they said we have finished them. One of the Mob had got a Strap in his Hand belonging to the Machinery and some of the Mob observed "don't take any thing away with you we came here to break the Power Looms and we've broke them." That Informant heard no further observations made by the mob but on getting out of the Mill yard they set up a shout and went away. (HO 40/21; punctuation supplied)

The smashing of machines sprang from premeditation, organization, and a well-established theory of employment—or, rather, of *un*employment as a consequence of labor-saving machinery. The attacks occurred in a stir of meetings, delegations, and organizing efforts.

Meanwhile, miners and cotton spinners were pursuing parallel struggles with their employers by means of turnouts and related actions. In Tyneside, for example, keelmen (who hauled coal from shore to seagoing vessels in boats called keels, and who faced displacement by over-the-river spouts loading coal directly onto ships) raised great strikes in 1819 and 1822, but lost out when the government manned the keels with navy men who enjoyed military protection from the strikers (Flinn 1984; see also McCord 1967; Rowe 1968). In the Shropshire mines:

> On 2 February 1821, in the course of a strike over wage reductions in Shropshire, the yeomanry were sent in after engines had been put out of action and blacklegs threatened. Some two to three thousand miners assembled to resist them and answered the reading of the Riot Act with a shower of cinders. In the ensuing battle, subsequently known as 'Cinderloo,' the yeomanry finally retaliated by opening fire, killing one miner, and mortally wounding another. Many prisoners were taken, of whom one was subsequently convicted and hanged and several sentenced to nine months' hard labour. (Flinn 1984: 408–409)

Most disputes remained local and nonviolent. When employers themselves concerted on a large scale, however, they often united a great many workers against them.

In Oldham workers smashed machines during the summer of 1826, only to have an infantry detachment stationed in the town. With that protection, Oldham's larger employers declared in September that they were lowering wages to the levels prevailing in surrounding areas. Spinners immediately turned out, and employers soon began hiring strike-breakers. The struggle continued until the following spring. The spinners organized a "Committee of their Body which sat daily at Mr. Collitt's—a public house near the said Mills—organized their whole Body—and there regularly received advices, and issued their orders founded thereupon." Oldham's strikers paraded by the mills, picketed, broke windows of factories and millowners' houses, insulted and attacked strikebreakers, blocked piecers from entering, barricaded some of the blacklegs inside mills, finally broke into factories and dragged out their competitors. When some of the arrested ringleaders went free on bail, strikers paraded them through Oldham with a band, breaking the arresting constable's windows as they passed (HO 40/21, letter of manufacturers, 21 December 1826; see also Foster 1974).

The era's marches and insurrections, for all their spy-infiltrated failure, came from the same cloth. The Blanketeers' march from Manchester and vicinity (10 March 1817), the armed risings of Pentrich and Huddersfield (8–9 June 1817), Huddersfield again (31 March–1 April 1820), Glasgow (5–6 April 1820), and Grange Moor (11 April 1820) all depended on incomplete but extensive connections among radical workers throughout Great Britain. So, for that matter, did the extensive drilling and marching by paramilitary workers' forces in northern industrial regions during the mobilization of 1819. Even in the industrial North, however, large meetings addressing Parliament on behalf of parliamentary reform became commonplace. The trend toward formal assemblies and national actors prevailed over Great Britain as a whole.

Contending with Associations

Although Queen Caroline's claims gave reformers an unexpected opportunity to mobilize criticism of the government, the well-executed campaign on Caroline's behalf deviated from the long-term trend in one crucial way: it relied very little on publicly visible special-purpose associations. Among the dozens of crowds and assemblies of inhabitants in all of 1820's CGs concerning the queen, the only special-purpose associations that appeared as such were the General Pension Society, the Odd Fellows, and a set of benefit societies. At the margin of associations lay the delegations from constituted trades that attended Queen Caroline:

Merchant tailors	Lightermen and watermen
Shipwrights and caulkers	Letterpress printers
Operative coachmakers	Sawyers
Brass-founders	Drapers
Street-keepers	Grocers
Armourers	Cabinet-makers
Stay-makers	Furriers, skinners, and
Schoolmasters	leatherdressers
	Seamen

Meetings of constituted trades occupied a position resembling those of religious congregations, vestries, freeholders, and ward residents: they had all acquired protected rights of assembly to deliberate their common concerns, and enjoyed considerable latitude in defining those concerns. They thus differed from special-purpose associations, whose very rights to exist, meet, deliberate, and make claims frequently met challenges from authorities. Public meetings certainly figured in the Queen Caroline campaign, but chiefly as assemblies of localities or trades gathered to approve messages for Parliament or the queen rather than as convocations of special-purpose associations.

Elsewhere, however, specialized associations were coming into their own. The position of associations in British contention shifted notably between 1816 and 1827, with huge consequences for later struggles. From the 1760s to the 1780s elite political organizations such as the Wilkite Society of Supporters of the Bill of Rights, Christopher Wyvill's Yorkshire Association, and the Society for Abolition of the Slave Trade had greatly expanded their roles in claim-making at a national level. During the French Revolution's early years, organizations such as the Revolution Society and the Association for the Preservation of Liberty and Property against Republicans and Levellers (whether revolutionary, reformist, or loyalist in program) had incorporated significant numbers of workers and petty bourgeois into formal national-level political activity. Thus legal associations had significantly expanded their social bases.

During the war years an important share of the state's repression had aimed precisely at special-purpose political associations such as the London Corresponding Society and the United Englishmen. Parliament and the judiciary had collaborated in checking associations that undertook paraparliamentary programs: consulting, mobilizing, and assembling large numbers of people around issues over which Parliament held jurisdiction, then broadcasting the results of their deliberations. They had aimed especially at paraparliamentary associations opposing government policy.

The Seditious Societies Act of 1799, as the courts had come to apply it, permitted formally organized local groups to discuss public affairs for their own benefit and to prepare petitions for Parliament or the king, but not to create national organizations. Radical and reformist members of Parliament such as Sir Francis Burdett nevertheless repeatedly contrived to promote public claim-making that would reinforce the minority positions they represented within the Commons. Because of the threat of prosecution, organizers took care to create societies just within the law's perimeter or to act through previously existing authorized assemblies such as wardmotes, election rallies, and meetings of trades. Henry Hunt's mass platform relied chiefly on authorized assemblies whose petitions and resolutions would receive wide press coverage. After 1815, nevertheless, Major John Cartwright's Hampden Clubs linked reformers throughout Great Britain, friendly societies formed ostensibly to organize benefits for the members of a trade but less openly to provide them with a means of concerted action, Philanthropic or Union Societies united multiple trades on a local scale, reading and reform societies brought together a wider range of the local population, while the Society of Spencean Philanthropists and similar sectarian or quasi-revolutionary associations surfaced from their wartime underground. An associational basis for popular collective action was solidifying in Great Britain.

Associations, in turn, promoted the adoption of new means for making claims, notably innovations in the character of public meetings, publicity for claims, communications with Parliament, and coordination among multiple localities. Authorities and claimants, what is more, negotiated constantly (if often indirectly or covertly) over the permissible forms and actions of associations. The Hampden Clubs established their own bare legality, for example, by declaring that they were assembling to prepare petitions for Parliament. The government thus inadvertently promoted a crucial shift from petitioning the king through local magistrates or other dignitaries toward direct petitioning of Parliament. In a pattern that greatly generalized after 1820, Major Cartwright and Francis Burdett explicitly invited parliamentary petitions for reform that Sir Francis, an MP, could introduce as evidence of popular demands.

Political unions, in their turn, first took shape in calculated response to the Seditious Meetings Act of 1817, which forbade closed meetings planning explicit efforts to influence the government, but still tolerated public meetings to express more general support for parliamentary reform. The first so-named Political Union formed at Stockport, the first group of Political Protestants at Hull, both in 1818. On the loyalist side, the Society for the Suppression of Vice and the Constitutional Association were soon instigating prosecution of radicals. Radicals, moderates, and conservatives all relied increasingly on special-purpose associations.

The generality of associations gave a wide variety of people, some quite opposed to one another's politics, an interest in maintaining their rights. In 1825, urged by shipbuilders who saw their workers organizing energetically after the 1824 repeal of the Combination Acts, MP William Huskisson called for a bill to restrict workmen's associations. The proposed bill would, among other things, require that "no money could be subscribed to any such association without the consent of a magistrate, who would be the treasurer" (Prothero 1979: 169). Francis Place urged MP Joseph Hume to speak to the Attorney General, Copley, who would have to draft the bill.

> He did so, and put it to Mr. Attorney, how he could draw a bill on the plan proposed, so as not to make it the most obnoxious nonsense that ever had been proposed to Parliament? How, if money was not to be subscribed but by permission of a magistrate; and how, if none but a Justice of the Peace was ever to be a treasurer, school societies, Bible societies, charitable societies, and other useful associations, could exist? In fact, how any association for desirable purposes could be formed in which contributions were necessary, unless every such society first obtained an Act of Parliament? (Wallas 1898: 229)

Attorney General Copley declined to draft the bill. He saw clearly that otherwise he would wound a great many friendly interests while trying only to stab workers' organizations.

The most dramatic and crucial associational mobilization took place outside of Great Britain, in Ireland, but with enormous impact on British politics. Daniel O'Connell's founding of the Catholic Association expanded the role of mass-membership associations. Since the settlement of 1689 had excluded Catholics from Parliament and other public offices, the political "emancipation" of Catholics had remained a salient issue in

Ireland. Within Great Britain it had taken on renewed importance when the crown recruited Irish troops for its eighteenth-century wars and sought to exempt them from standard anti-Catholic oaths. In 1780 Lord George Gordon had led the Protestant Association against just such concessions to Catholics.

Thereafter, reformers had regularly used Catholic exclusion as evidence of the regime's impropriety and made Catholic emancipation part of their program, just as the exclusion of Jews and Protestant dissenters had intermittently become political issues for reformers; meanwhile, loyalists had obligingly defended the Anglican church as the regime's bedrock. As Britain had drawn overwhelmingly Catholic Ireland into a United Kingdom in 1801, George III himself had vetoed the proposal to integrate Catholics (Irish or otherwise) into the new realm's public life. Prime Minister Pitt, who had half-promised emancipation as an incentive to Union, thereupon resigned over the issue. Similarly, the Ministry of All the Talents resigned in 1807 over the king's blockage of minor concessions to Catholic officers in the British army.

The Catholic question brought multiple associations into play, even into existence. During the nineteenth century both reformers and religious activists knotted together Catholic emancipation and repeal of the Test and Corporation Acts, which excluded not only Catholics but all non-Anglicans from high public office. Religious associations—not only churches but also societies springing from them—had from the seventeenth century enjoyed an exceptional freedom to assemble and take positions with respect to public affairs. An elite Catholic Committee had formed in 1778 to work for Catholic relief and had lasted until 1792; successors included the Cisalpine Club and the Board of British Catholics (Hinde 1992). Protestant Dissenters, on their side, actually divided sharply among pro- and anti-Catholic positions. But such organizations as the General Body of Dissenting Ministers (a seventeenth-century survivor), the Dissenting Deputies of the Three Denominations (originating in 1732), the Protestant Society (founded in 1811), and the Unitarian Association (established in 1819) all supported the conjunction of Catholic emancipation and Repeal with varying degrees of publicity and enthusiasm (Davis 1966).

Reformers' attempts to push Catholic emancipation through Parliament during the reform agitation of 1816 to 1820 got nowhere. In 1821, with George IV in the process of succeeding his deceased father, a qualified Catholic emancipation bill passed the House of Commons but failed in the Lords. In August of that year George IV, newly crowned, actually visited Ireland in state, thus giving credence to the belief that he was sympathetic to Irish Catholics; before his marriage to Caroline he had, after all, secretly wed a Catholic woman. A new effort to pass an emancipation bill, even less successful than that of 1821, arose in 1822.

Even if the principal action of the early 1820s took place in Ireland, then, it had great resonance within Great Britain. It pervaded British elections of the 1820s. In East Retford (Nottinghamshire, a borough dissolved for corruption in 1828), Sir Henry Wright Wilson disturbed the serenity of 1826's election by entering late as an anti-Catholic candidate:

> Previously, however, to the arrival of Sir Henry, a prior candidate, who did not stay, Mr. W. A. Madocks had kindled considerable heat on this question; and a club was in existence, whose special object was to support Gentlemen inimical to the measure. A considerable party was consequently on foot before Sir H. W. Wilson appeared. Many, besides, under the name of "No Popery" were anxious to secure a third candidate. So that Sir Henry was at once surrounded with active partisans, and in possession of a popular voice: but his supporters were not voters, being chiefly persons altogether without a suffrage. (HO 40/20, 14 June 1826)

Despite the appointment of 200–300 special constables, Wilson's supporters assaulted candidate Robert Dundas, broke windows of the house where he fled for protection, stoned the Senior Bailiff (co-author of the letter just quoted) while he read the Riot Act, and dispersed only when a detachment of Life Guards rode down the crowd. After Wilson lost the election,

> Many insults were daily offered to persons supposed to be favorable to the two Gentlemen returned; especially, of a very gross kind, to Mr. H. Savile Foljambe, a Gentleman of consideration and a Banker residing here, who had been friendly to them. About a fortnight ago, twenty or thirty persons assembled before his House (great numbers looking on) and then raised loud shouts, drank toasts to the downfall of his Bank, and employed menacing, as well as insulting gestures so as to create such an apprehension in his mind as to make him think himself in danger if he

left his House. In the streets he was pursued with hootings, and otherwise made the object of shameful abuse. (HO 40/20, 10 July 1826)

In Nottinghamshire and elsewhere, anti-Catholicism drew vigorous popular support.

Within Catholic Ireland the question had enormous salience. The
Protestant Ascendancy monopolized Irish public office, the patronage that
accompanied it, and parliamentary representation, while the established
Protestant church drew tithes from Catholics and Protestants alike. In
1816, when Irish Catholics divided over the pope's willingness to concede
the British crown a limited veto of ecclesiastical appointments and policies
in return for admission of Catholics to office in the United Kingdom,
Daniel O'Connell had signaled his opposition to that compromise by an
unsuccessful proposal to create an oppositional Catholic Association. In
1823, after two failed attempts (in 1821 and 1822) to run pro-Catholic
bills through Parliament, he succeeded in forming such an association.
At first it consisted of just thirty-one members of the Irish Catholic elite.
But over the next year O'Connell engineered the association's alliance with
the Catholic clergy, its adoption of a program extending to general grievances of poor Irishmen, and its conversion into a mass-membership organization. In 1825, furthermore, it began organizing local Liberal Clubs
for the purpose of electing candidates who would work for Emancipation.

The idea of mass organization already hung heavy in the air. In 1818
the radical Dr. James Watson was trying to create a Universal Union Fund
of the Non-Represented People of the United Kingdom of Great Britain
and Ireland, with cells of ten clumped together into units of hundreds
and thousands, collecting dues of a penny per week (Prothero 1979).
During the Queen Caroline affair Henry Hunt had recommended the
creation of a radical mass-subscription organization with dues of a halfpenny or a penny per week, citing Methodists as a model (Belchem 1985).
The following year he actually attempted to form the Great Northern
Union as a permanent popular organization to agitate for reform. Hunt
tied it directly to a program of paying for the election of radical MPs, a
proposal whose opportunism upset the democratic purists among his followers. The Great Northern Union made a promising start, then collapsed.

O'Connell was the first to bring off the organizational feat on a national
scale, and the nation in question was Ireland. With dues (the famous

"Catholic Rent") as low as a penny per month, the Catholic Association rapidly became the most powerful political force in Ireland. Concentrating on a single issue, O'Connell accomplished in Ireland what advocates of a General Union had been unable to achieve in Great Britain. By early 1825 the association had acquired such mass and influence that the king demanded its dissolution. Parliament obligingly passed an Unlawful Societies Act banning the Catholic Association on significant and now-familiar grounds: that it was assuming the form and powers of an independent Parliament.

Another attempt to pass a Catholic relief bill (deliberately coupled, O'Connell assenting, with proposals raising the forty-shilling Irish franchise and establishing government-administered salaries for Catholic clergy) failed in 1825. Despite these defeats, O'Connell and the essential networks of the Catholic Association survived. The Irish elections of 1826, pivoting on the issue of Emancipation, produced an unprecedented rebellion of Catholic tenants against Protestant landlords. The Association reappeared in various guises along the very edge of the new repressive law, and Catholic priests played an ever larger part in its work. By the end of 1827 the so-called New Catholic Association (obvious successor to the Old) was preparing parish meetings throughout Ireland to demonstrate broad popular support for thoroughgoing Emancipation.

Two significant changes were intertwining. Catholic Emancipation, on the agenda of many reformers for half a century, was becoming a national political issue capable of mobilizing thousands of ordinary people, both for and against. At the same time a major move toward the modularity of contentious repertoires—toward the easy transferability of forms of action from one pair of actors, place, or issue to another—was occurring: a national mass-membership association openly demanding new legislation was muscling its way to an influential place in British politics. That organizational success soon provided a model and precedent for a wide variety of claim-making. A new mechanism—the mass-based, dues-fed, special-purpose association—entered the emerging apparatus of the national social movement.

Political Entrepreneurs, Radicals, and Reformers

All repertoires of contention leave places for political entrepreneurs and intermediaries, but the nature of those places depends on how firmly the repertoire is embedded in everyday routines of production, reproduction, and sociability. Although they generally knew the risks they were running, eighteenth-century Britons moved with relative ease from farm work to attacks on enclosures, from conversations in pubs to delegations seeking favors of landlords, from weaving to Rough Music for a weaver who worked below the established rate. In these cases local entrepreneurs and intermediaries played significant roles: local ringleaders on one side, local patrons and powerholders on the other. The relatively cosmopolitan, autonomous, and modular nineteenth-century forms of action, nevertheless, differed significantly. On the average, they relied less on patrons or intermediaries of any kind, located patrons or intermediaries much closer to national centers of power such as Parliament when they involved them, and depended more heavily on political entrepreneurs. Entrepreneurs knew how to organize meetings, create associations, connect existing organizations, mount demonstrations, get access to the press, consult with the police, write petitions, raise money, recruit participants for public events, and carry on the dozens of other requisites for social-movement action.

The work of political entrepreneurs appeared as both cause and effect of the shift in repertoires. The growing salience of Parliament as compared either with local targets of action or with the king and his ministers, for example, promoted the move to new forms of action such as the public meeting, but in so doing it also enhanced the leverage of entrepreneurs who could make connections with MPs, work out strategies to influence Parliament, and keep authorities from breaking up meetings. The same entrepreneurs experimented with new variants of claim-making, some of which succeeded and spread. During the years from 1816 to 1827, we have seen political entrepreneurs introducing mass-membership associations, mass meetings, and petition-procession-demonstrations as ways of doing public business.

Plenty of efforts failed, nevertheless. Among them was Cobbett's 1818 proposal to forge Bank of England notes, spread them through the country, and thus bring down the whole political system. Similarly, James Watson's program of organizing simultaneous (hence implicitly insurrectionary) mass meetings throughout the country in the aftermath of Peterloo proved impossible to realize. With respect to short-term objectives, the Queen Caroline agitation had at best a mixed result: helping block the queen's divorce and destitution, getting publicity for the analysis and program of reform, but never seating Caroline on the throne or changing the government. During 1819 T. J. Wooler's scheme of electing "legislatorial attorneys"—popularly selected counterparts to members of Parliament—for large towns lacking MPs attracted wide attention, but collapsed as authorities realized they needed no new authority to prosecute anyone who thus held a public election without royal warrant.

In these circumstances, political entrepreneurs succeeded or failed in three overlapping enterprises: attracting followers, organizing their action, and getting results with that action. So far as parliamentary and governmental outcomes are concerned, indeed, Britain's social-movement entrepreneurs gained no major victories between 1816 and 1827. They succeeded chiefly in keeping issues alive and activists connected.

It was not for lack of zeal that they accomplished no more. During the postwar years different segments of Britain's militant reformers and revolutionaries repeatedly marched, met, plotted, negotiated, created new organizations, braved prosecution, served time in jail, signed their names to risky programs and declarations, raised rebellions, and poured their energies into transformation of the political system. Not since the French Revolution's early years had such a heroic array of activists appeared in Britain. They ranged from insurrectionary ultraradicals such as Arthur Thistlewood, with their efforts to unite workers for direct attacks on the regime, to reformers such as Francis Place, who strove constantly to create peaceable but effective alliances among members of Parliament, farsighted gentlemen, and organized petty bourgeois.

Radicals and reformers agreed on what was wrong and what sort of change would be desirable in the long run more than they agreed on the proper means and time scale of action. They converged, nevertheless, in supporting organization of the masses as a basis for claim-making. At the radical end of the range, mass organization came to promise the means of a revolution in which an outraged people would take power into their own hands; an anti-Parliament would supplant the existing Parliament. At the reformist end, mass organization provided a means of pressure on Parliament and the government that would induce existing authorities to broaden suffrage, make Parliament more representative and responsive to popular will, chase rascals from government, and bring the reformers' sort of people in.

Radicals insisted on the short-run value of secret organization, direct action against authorities, and popular insurrection; they thereby became vulnerable to government-initiated infiltration and provocation, not to mention preemptive repression. Reformers called for legality, discipline, numbers, and incremental action over the long run; they thereby became vulnerable to delay, defection, and co-optation. The two groups saw each other's vulnerabilities more clearly than each other's strengths. They converged, nevertheless: if radicals were more willing than reformers to use illegal means and seek illegal ends, in the long perspective what differentiated them was chiefly the paths they saw as leading to rather similar outcomes: popular sovereignty, political democracy, diminished inequality, general prosperity.

Conclusions

During the first dozen postwar years Britain's predominant forms of collective action underwent a subtle but crucial change: the almost definitive installation of autonomous, modular, cosmopolitan nineteenth-century repertoires. Through the war years the repertoire of meetings, associations, demonstrations, and nationally oriented electoral campaigns had taken shape without crowding out the eighteenth-century repertoire. In the course of contention between 1816 and 1827, however, the parochial, particular, bifurcated eighteenth-century repertoire of contentious forms dwindled. The grain seizure, Rough Music, invasions of commons, pulling down of houses, and related forms of action receded markedly. In England and Scotland only scattered locations such as Otmoor (Oxfordshire) and the Scottish Highlands continued to experience attacks on enclosures beyond 1820 (Charlesworth 1983). In Wales concerted resistance to enclosures virtually ceased after a last burst in 1815–1820; thereafter destruction of tollgates, but little other direct action, characterized Welsh rural mobilizations into the 1840s. Although food prices figured prominently in the workers' struggles of 1816–1818, seizures of grain disappeared, direct action on the question merged with workers' attacks on mills, and struggles concerning food concentrated increasingly in industrial towns and cities.

Machine-breaking, it is true, occurred intermittently into the 1830s, especially where handloom weavers faced powerlooms or agricultural laborers confronted threshing machines. The 1826 depression brought a notable wave of machine-smashing in the industrial North. But even attacks on labor-displacing machinery diminished in relative prominence as public meetings, marches, and demonstrations gained ground. Cobbett's involvement in the North's industrial struggles, for example, consisted of running for Parliament from Preston in May 1826—a candidacy his opponents' ruthless street politics easily blocked.

On the occasion of that campaign, the informer George Bradley (who also signed his numerous reports George Bradbury and G___ B___) wrote from Walsall that Cobbett's supporters had invited him to Preston "to further the Ultimate ends of these Men whose work is to get a Voice in Parliament for the purpose of spreading principles subversive of the National faith, there principle object was it not for the Six Acts to call Meetings at all Places at one time where they can spread their principles under the specious pretext of Equal Representation in the House of Commons" (HO 40/20, 19 June 1826). Bradley/Bradbury reported that Cobbett's supporters hoped to regain the strength they had enjoyed between 1816 and 1819, and held to the prospect of armed insurrection on behalf of "Republican Government to be effected by force." (He suggested breaking up the movement by arresting and holding a number of leaders—including himself, to divert suspicion—whether or not the charges would stick.) Their program focused, nevertheless, on an effort to mobilize followers through public meetings and electoral campaigns. In a famous passage of his memoirs, Samuel Bamford praised Cobbett for moving readers from "riot" to campaigns for reform (Bamford 1967: II, 7). Cobbett, for his part, credited Bamford with converting him from advocacy of household suffrage to support of manhood suffrage.

Despite the persistence of machine-breaking, the nineteenth-century repertoire was consolidating rapidly in Great Britain. Not only the demonstration but also the special-purpose association, the public meeting, and the deliberate organization of a social movement were becoming dominant, widely available vehicles of contention as the direct attack on malefactors, the collective invasion of fields, the seizure of grain, and most of the other forms that had prevailed in the 1750s and 1760s faded away. Just as the ideology of a cross-industry general strike was forming, furthermore, the firm-by-firm strike was displacing the old turnout of all workers in a given industry and location. The novelties of picketing, boycotting, and attacking strikebreakers at mill entrances took shape in precisely that context of mill-by-mill action.

The autonomous, modular, cosmopolitan nineteenth-century repertoire was consolidating: street demonstrations, public meetings addressed
to national issues, and the devices of social movements all standardized
and became more prevalent. Despite radically restricted suffrage, the idea
and practice of popular sovereignty tacitly gained ground. We can reasonably speak of a *nationalization* and *parliamentarization* of contention.
Both Parliament and national officials became more prominent objects
of claim-making than they had been between the 1750s and the end of
the Napoleonic wars. As a consequence, the very timing of contention
came to depend more directly on the rhythm of major governmental
actions and of parliamentary debates. Although authorized local assemblies continued to play a major part in contentious claims, special-interest
associations and workers' organizations regained their prominence of the
early 1790s. Popular associations such as Hampden Clubs multiplied
despite repeated attempts to outlaw them. With Ireland formally integrated into the British polity, furthermore, the creation of the mass-subscription Catholic Association (likewise repeatedly banned and reborn)
offered a vivid model for political mobilization in Great Britain itself.

These processes continued over the long run; the repertoire shifts of
1816–1827 simply cumulated changes that had been proceeding for decades and had accelerated during the years of war with France. But
shorter-term changes in repression also promoted a rapid move toward
new repertoires after 1815. Relaxation of wartime controls over popular
claim-making allowed a surge of organization, communication, mobilization, and contention in 1815 and 1816, reversed temporarily in 1817–
1820, but became even more emphatic with the legal recasting of the early
1820s. Parliament removed death penalties its eighteenth-century predecessors had imposed on many forms of attack against bourgeois property.
It also revoked the Combination Acts of 1799, thus providing limited but
genuine authorization for workers' organizations, just so long as they were
not visibly devoted to restraint of trade. Starting in 1823 the ineffectual
repression of Daniel O'Connell's Catholic Association in Ireland provided
one more precedent and justification of popular association within Great
Britain. As a result, national associations, general federations of all trades,
political unions, and similar organizations gained new impetus. Repertoires
became modular, cosmopolitan, and autonomous almost across the board.

⁊ 7 ⁊

STRUGGLE AND REFORM,
1828–1834

DURING THE LAST DAYS of July 1830, a fragile worker-bourgeois coalition brought down the Bourbon monarchy of Charles X and seated Louis-Philippe d'Orléans on France's throne. After an election had gone against his government, the aging king Charles had not only shrunk the electorate and installed tight controls over the increasingly critical press but also dismissed the newly elected Chamber of Deputies and ordered new elections. An uprising in the streets of Paris then inspired insurrectionary seizures of power in many other French cities. Charles responded too slowly to keep his crown. Remembering reverberations of the French revolution that had begun four decades earlier, European rulers instantly fretted about encouragement the French example might give to radicals in their own domains. On 31 August Britain's Clerk of the Privy Council, C. C. F. Greville, confided to his diary:

On Sunday I met [Austrian ambassador] Esterhazy in Oxford Street with a face a yard long. He turned back with me, and told me there had been disturbances at Bruxelles, but that they had been put down by the gendarmerie. He was mightily alarmed, but said that his Government would recognize the French King directly, and in return for such general and prompt recognition as he was receiving he must restrain France from countenancing revolutions in other countries, and that, indeed, he had lost no time in declaring his intention to abstain from any meddling. In the evening Vaudreuil [first secretary of the French embassy] told me the same thing, and that he had received a despatch from M. de Molé [French foreign minister] desiring him to refuse passports to the Spaniards who wanted, on the strength of the French Revolution, to go and foment the discontents in Spain, and to all other foreigners who, being dissatisfied with their own Governments, could not obtain passports from their own Ministers. (Greville 1938: II, 39–40)

Greville recorded his fear that the Duke of Wellington, Britain's bluff, unreflective prime minister, might respond to the threat of revolutions on the continent by plunging his country into some violent, vindictive adventure. Hasty intervention, thought Greville, could precipitate another general European war.

Greville had grounds for concern. In October an insurrection in Brussels, then throughout the southern Low Countries, led to the declaration of Belgium's independence from the Kingdom of the Netherlands, which the victorious allies had stitched together and bestowed on the Prince of Orange in 1815. Over the next three years Dutch, French, and Prussian armies all invaded the territory, Britain sent a fleet to the Belgian coast, and the British repeatedly played arbiter. Under pressure from Britain and other great powers, Belgians elected as their king Leopold of Saxe-Coburg, pensioner of the British crown, widower of George IV's daughter Princess Charlotte, and counselor of queen-to-be Victoria. British presence did not, however, keep the French from trying to regain some of the Belgian territory they had lost in the peace settlement of 1815. In that enterprise Charles-Maurice Talleyrand-Périgord (onetime Bishop of Autun, Prince of Benevento by the blessing of Napoleon, wily politician and diplomat of Old Regime, Revolution, Empire, Hundred Days, Restoration, and another Revolution) served as *chef de jeu*. King Leopold shielded himself by remarrying, this time to the daughter of France's new king. Up to the international recognition of Belgium in 1839, the British government found itself dangerously involved in Belgian—hence in Dutch, Prussian, and French—affairs.

Despite his initial forebodings, Greville soon revised his estimate of France's revolutionary propensities. He learned with astonishment (as he recorded at the date of 9 September) that the new French regime had appointed the astute survivor Talleyrand as its ambassador to the United Kingdom. "He must be nearer eighty than seventy, and though his faculties are said to be as bright as ever (which I doubt), his infirmities are so great that it is inconceivable he should think of leaving his own house, and above all for another country, where public representation is unavoidable" (Greville 1938: II, 43). Among other afflictions, after all, Talleyrand had dragged a club foot since childhood.

The prince (who was in fact seventy-six years old) nonetheless betook himself to Great Britain. He received the homage of crowds in Dover on Friday 24 September and made a spectacular entry into London on 25 September:

> He appeared with tricolor ribbons, wearing a huge republican cockade on his hat and accompanied by three opera-style insurgents. The farce required a long speech: he called himself the representative of a popular government, thus symbolically establishing the July Monarchy in London. The street applauded his act; he won his plebiscite.
>
> The same evening [the Duke of] Wellington returned deliberately from the country and gave a state dinner to the prince, who appeared in a silk habit with gold-trimmed stockings, bemedalled, powdered, and wearing diamonds. So much for the tricolor ribbons! He had conquered the street; now it was time to conquer the salons. (Orieux 1970: 745)

Talleyrand did conquer London; he reigned there, at least in salons, until 1834.

Not long after his arrival Talleyrand installed his indispensable niece, the Duchess of Dino, as mistress of his own London salon. Both Talleyrand and the duchess often communicated with the new King Louis-Philippe through the king's sister Adelaide. On 2 November 1830 the duchess wrote Adelaide that she and Talleyrand had attended the king's opening of parliament that day, and when Talleyrand's carriage had appeared, "people started cries of LOUIS-PHILIPPE FOR EVER! NO CHARLES THE TENTH! That lasted from the House of Lords to Bond Street. There were also plenty of Long Live Prince Talleyrand! And when I came back with people wearing tricolor cockades people shouted A FRENCH LADY! They shouted and called out *vivas* all along the way (Talleyrand 1891: III, 459; the French original renders the uppercase words in English.) The duchess neglected to say that in the same procession people had cheered the English king but hooted his chief minister, the Duke of Wellington, and shouted against London's new police force. According to the *Morning Chronicle* of 3 November, "loud shouts were raised of 'Down with the New Police!' 'No martial law!' and the most hideous yells and execrations were directed against any members of the New Police who came in view."

The same day's *Times* reported that near Parliament two people waved tricolor flags, that ten or a dozen men wore tricolor cockades—direct allusions to the French revolution of July—and that people shouted both "No police" and "Vote by ballot." Later a gathering stoned police who had apprehended two pickpockets near St. James's. Elsewhere, roving bands broke windows and attacked a carriage wrongly rumored to be transporting Wellington. Police arrested at least 36 people. The following evening about 150 "mechanics and thieves" (as the *Times* of 5 November described them) paraded on Haymarket, shouting "Down with the police," "D__n the police."

Chastened by those experiences and warned of a likely attack on Wellington, the king and queen agreed to cancel their attendance at the City Dinner planned for Guildhall on 9 November, Lord Mayor's Day. "That decision," recalled Talleyrand in his memoirs, "caused great agitation in the metropolis. Menacing gatherings formed in the City, the stock market fell, and after a long discussion they postponed the dinner. But such an incident couldn't end there; it spurred discussion in Parliament, where Lord Brougham [newly elected as a reformist candidate from Yorkshire] had announced in the opening session that he would introduce a motion for parliamentary reform on 16 November" (Talleyrand 1891: III, 379–380). At the same session Wellington pledged his government's opposition to any such proposal.

On 8 November a meeting of the Radical Reform Association at the Rotunda (Blackfriars Road, Southwark) passed a resolution condemning the ministry for fearing to bring the king among his own people. As the session ended, meeting chair Henry Hunt went outside and spoke to a thousand or so followers who had gathered there. Thereafter members of Hunt's audience rushed over Blackfriars Bridge, "headed by a man bearing a tri-coloured flag" and shouting "No Wellington," "No Peel," and "Down with the Police." They cheered the statue of Charles I—the only British king to lose his head in a popular rebellion—at Charing Cross, then toured various public offices, Downing Street, and the Houses of Parliament before running into a cordon of New Police who dispersed them with truncheons (MC 9 November 1830).

That same day, government opponents stoned Wellington in Downing

Street as a crowd in Carlisle (Cumberland) burned effigies of Wellington and Home Secretary Peel. Meanwhile, through much of southeastern England groups of agricultural laborers with a sprinkling of artisans were assembling, marching, demanding wage increases, and attacking the properties of landlords, farmers, or parsons. The southeastern conflicts events came to be known as the Swing rebellion, for the mythical leader Captain Swing. Rebellion's wind was rising. Both in London and elsewhere, alarmed property holders wrote Peel advocating the formation of paramilitary volunteer forces to hold off the menace of revolution as well as public meetings to affirm support for king and government (HO 44/22). The government hastily filled the Tower of London's moats with water to forestall an attack on the citadel. It also ringed London with 7,000 troops and stationed 2,000 New Police in Westminster alone (Palmer 1988). Although the intensity of conflict abated at the Wellington ministry's resignation on 16 November, reformers, radicals, and defenders of the regime all maintained high levels of activity for the next year and a half.

Great Britain declined to emulate France in 1830 or later. No violent revolution occurred, no sustained urban insurrection, no effective promulgation of a revolutionary program, no sharp break in governmental continuity. Yet the conflicts and changes of 1828 to 1834 marked British politics for generations to come. They integrated merchants, master craftsmen, industrial capitalists, Protestant dissenters, and Catholics more fully into national political life than ever before. They undermined the Anglican religious establishment—and to some extent the coalition of landlords, parsons, and magistrates on which it rested—in both Ireland and Great Britain. They ensconced old radicals such as Cobbett and Hunt, who had served prison terms for their political agitation, in Parliament itself.

The conflicts and changes of 1828–1834 cemented in place a claim-making repertoire of meetings, marches, petition drives, electoral campaigns, social movements, associations, firm-by-firm strikes, and related forms of action—as compared to their predecessors, visibly cosmopolitan, autonomous, and modular. They produced an unprecedented mobilization of workers that carried over into Chartism and national trade union movements. They produced a definitive shift from virtual representation of localities and institutions toward the representation of propertied adult males; to that degree they democratized Great Britain. They drove Great

Britain as a whole (as distinguished from recurrently dissident Ireland) closer to a revolutionary situation than at any time since 1689.

Spurting Population, Expanding Economy, Consolidating State

The struggles did not issue from some momentary crisis of demography and economy. In contrast to the great shifts from the Napoleonic Wars to the postwar readjustment, social changes of the period from 1828 to 1834 generally accelerated or consolidated shifts that were already well defined by the early 1820s. In distant retrospect, to be sure, 1830 looks like a point of departure for widespread mechanization and capital concentration in British industry. Yet we have already witnessed the distress of handloom weavers as they faced the competition of powerlooms during the trade depression of 1826; their troubles did not begin in 1830. Although swings in industrial activity became more volatile after 1828, they had already affected the fates of thousands of workers in 1816 and 1817. In agriculture, despite the hastily enacted Corn Laws, imports resumed in 1815, with the consequence of a great depression from 1815 to the later 1830s. From war's end to the 1830s low-wage labor piled up, increasingly miserable, in southeastern agriculture and in regions of industrial handwork.

At least in England, the rate of population increase reached its all-time peak during the decade after 1816. Annual rates of increase (Wrigley and Schofield 1981: 209), ran as follows:

1801–1806: 1.35%	1821–1826: 1.55
1806–1811: 1.30	1826–1831: 1.37
1811–1816: 1.50	1831–1836: 1.21
1816–1821: 1.53	1836–1841: 1.20

As a result, record cohorts of youths began entering the market for wage-labor in the 1830s. The numbers of workers in agriculture continued to increase faster than the demand for their labor; indeed, their absolute number did not start to shrink until mid-century. At the same time, work continued to proletarianize, with higher and higher proportions of the labor force employed for wages on someone else's premises. In English agriculture landless laborers constituted roughly 49 percent of

Table 7.1. Government finance and real income in the United Kingdom, 1828–1834

Item	Annual total							Annual % change		
	1828	1829	1830	1831	1832	1833	1834	1789–1815	1816–1827	1828–1834
Revenue from customs	20.1	19.3	19.2	19.4	18.2	18.5	17.8	+5.5	+2.9	−2.0
Revenue from excise	20.0	22.2	21.0	20.0	17.5	17.9	17.7	+5.5	−3.2	−2.1
Revenue from stamps	7.1	7.4	7.4	7.3	7.2	7.2	7.1	+6.5	+0.4	+0.0
Revenue from land tax	5.1	5.2	5.3	5.4	5.2	5.2	5.2	+3.8	−5.8	+0.3
Debt service expenditure	29.4	29.3	29.1	29.2	28.3	28.3	28.5	+4.6	−0.9	−0.5
Civil government expenditure	6.2	5.0	5.4	4.9	5.0	4.7	4.3	+4.9	−0.2	−6.3
Expenditure on army/ordnance	9.8	9.5	9.3	8.6	8.7	8.9	7.9	+12.8	−13.1	−3.7
Expenditure on navy	6.4	5.7	5.9	5.3	5.7	4.9	4.4	+9.7	−9.0	−6.4
Total expenditure on military	16.2	15.2	15.2	13.9	14.4	13.8	12.3	+11.3	−11.7	−4.7
Farm laborer real income	22.6	23.2	23.8	24.3	24.9	25.5	26.0	+0.4	+0.1	+2.4
Middle worker real income	38.2	39.3	40.3	41.3	42.4	43.4	44.5	+0.4	+1.9	+2.6
Artisan real income	51.4	52.9	54.4	56.0	57.5	59.0	60.5	+0.4	+2.3	+2.8

Note: "Real income" is in 1851 pounds per year. Other figures are in millions of current pounds sterling.
Sources: Interpolations of real income from Lindert and Williamson 1983b; annual figures for governmental finances from Mitchell and Deane 1971.

all male workers in 1812, 76 percent in 1831, a peak 80 percent in 1851, before the hemorrhaging of proletarians from the countryside during the later nineteenth century (Tilly 1984).

Proletarians depended on current employment for income, on the current market for food, fuel, clothing, and lodging. Low-wage workers therefore became ever more vulnerable to swings in both prices and employment. As linear interpolations among scattered observations, the real income figures in Table 7.1 miss those year-to-year fluctuations. They do display, however, the widening gap between farm laborers and their industrial cousins, as well as the relatively prosperous times upon which artisans were entering. Nominal wages of common laborers—both agricultural and industrial—actually declined a little between 1827 and 1835; only a more rapid drop in food prices produced an estimated increase in their real income (Lindert and Williamson 1983b).

With nominal wages relatively immobile in the short run, fluctuations in prices for everyday necessities strongly affected the well-being of poor families, even when their wage-earners had jobs. Figure 7.1 traces a

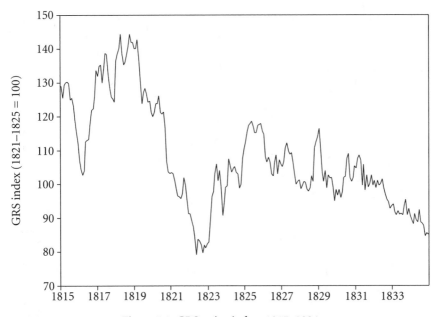

Figure 7.1. GRS price index, 1815–1834

well-known composite cost-of-living index (average prices 1821–1825 = 100) month by month from 1815 through 1834. The graph makes several things clear. First, over the period as a whole subsistence prices were dropping, with wide swings from year to year and season to season. Second, the price peaks immediately following the war towered over those of the 1820s and 1830s. Third, neither levels of contention as a whole nor sustained collective complaints about prices and wages corresponded closely to fluctuations in the cost of living; although one might attach importance to the high prices of 1819 and 1826, the falling prices of such contentious years as 1816, 1830, and 1832–1834 make any deterministic reasoning from cost of living to protest suspect.

Rapid increases in unemployment, in contrast, seem to have had a significant mobilizing effect, especially when they coincided with rising prices. With a lag for entry into the labor market, rapid population growth aggravated crises of unemployment. So, in the short run, did mechanization and the shift from long-term servants to day-laborers in agriculture or industry. Thus the industrial contraction of 1829–1830, although less severe from the perspective of total production than many previous trade depressions, produced a great surge of unemployment, and therefore widespread hardship. W. W. Rostow's famous Social Tension Chart, which gives equal weight to stylized estimates of unemployment and high wheat prices, reaches its summits of the entire period 1790–1850 in 1826 and 1829 (Rostow 1948).

Government, in any case, followed a different rhythm. After the state's vigorous expansion during the war years, the 1820s and 1830s brought a lull, a settling in, as the military contracted and even war-driven debt diminished. Table 7.1 provides some of the details: with the exception of a minor rise in the land tax, declines in all major categories of governmental receipts and expenditure between 1828 and 1834. To be more precise, gross government income and expenditure generally diminished from 1816 to 1832, then leveled off between 1832 and 1843 before starting to rise again in the later 1840s. The trend marks a stunning contrast with the war years. Once again we can represent the change in per capita annual tax burden in terms of daily wage equivalents, as shown in Table 7.2. By 1834 a notional average citizen was paying the equivalent of almost twice as many days' wages in taxes as his or her forebears of 1758, but only about two-thirds of the reckoning at war's end.

Despite the recent decline in taxation, Parliament's fiscal responsibilities during the war years had permanently augmented its power vis-à-vis both nation and crown. The frequent incompetence of George III (now interpreted as a recurrent consequence of porphyria) plus the political indolence of George IV and William IV probably accelerated the decline in royal power. Within Parliament, furthermore, the Commons had gained substantially at the expense of the Lords. In times of constitutional crisis, such as the struggle over Queen Caroline's rights in 1820, both crown and Lords remained crucial; they still played decisive parts in the decisions over Catholic Emancipation and reform. But, as those same crises revealed, ministers had become increasingly dependent on support of their parliamentary colleagues, and the House of Commons had become the focus of political decisions for all of the United Kingdom. Britain had arrived at a definitively different national politics from that of 1768, 1789, or 1801.

Between 1828 and 1834 successive governments engaged themselves heavily in reorganizing repression and facilitation. Unlike in the immediate postwar years, they were not so much adjusting the overall level of pressure on collective action as recasting repressive means, procedures, and penalties. The creation of the Metropolitan Police provides the most obvious example, but the substitution of transportation to the colonies for execution over a wide range of felonies likewise fits the pattern. So does political control: in contrast to such years as 1816 to 1819, despite huge, hostile mobilizations the government did not suspend *habeas corpus,* ban meetings or associations, clamp tight restrictions on the press, engage in essentially preventive arrests, or even prosecute extensively for

Table 7.2. Days' wages paid per capita in national taxes, 1785–1834

Year	Laborer	Spinner
1758	12	6
1789	14	8
1815	32	18
1827	23	12
1834	23	11

Sources: Interpolated and computed from Lindert and Williamson 1983b; Wrigley and Schofield 1981; and Mitchell and Deane 1971.

sedition. In the face of widespread industrial conflict, furthermore, Parliament made no effort to install equivalents of the Combination Acts it had repealed in 1824 and 1825. Although it seeded workers' organizations with spies, inhibited their public actions through policing and occasional prosecution, often intervened forcefully in strikes, and continued to harass the unstamped workers' press, the government generally recognized the legal right of workers' organizations to exist. Confronted with a massive rebellion of iron workers at Merthyr Tydfil (June 1831), the government chose to prosecute its captives not for the high treason urged by local magistrates but merely for riot.

Parliament had become both more powerful and more reluctant to undertake blatant repression of popular collective action. A proclamation condemning the paramilitary organization of Political Unions (1831), for example, entailed much less drastic action than its predecessors of 1816 or, especially, 1819. The Seditious Libel Act of 1830, while increasing the bonds required of newspaper publishers, eliminated banishment as the penalty for a second offense. The government extended the period available for review and appeal between a death sentence and its execution, consolidated a wide variety of laws and penalties concerning offenses against persons, abolished the routine provision of executed murderers' corpses to surgeons for dissection, and eliminated the hanging of executed criminals' bodies in chains. Some of the period's major legislation—notably the repeal of Test and Corporation Acts, Catholic Emancipation, and reform—actually facilitated collective action by integrating new categories of the population directly into national politics.

The trend toward facilitation and leniency suffered three major exceptions: reactions to the Swing rebellions, enactment of the Poor Law, and dealings with Ireland. In response to Swing, the government not only sent out troops in November 1830 but also passed measures reinforcing the recruitment of special constables, specifically condemning a wide range of actions taken by landless laborers, and assigning collective financial responsibility to hundreds for the destruction of threshing machines. By enhancing the powers of Poor Law Unions and shifting the balance away from parish cash relief of the poor toward incarceration, the Poor Law of 1834 further contained and demobilized the dependent poor. In Ireland major acts and proclamations included the Banning of Political Meetings (1828), the Suppression of Dangerous Societies (1829), the Irish County Franchise Act (raising the property qualification for parliamentary electors from 40s. to £10 in 1829, as part of the price for Catholic Emancipation), the Coercion Act (1832), the Local Disturbances Act (1833), the Peace Preservation Act (1834), and first steps toward the suppression of Orange Societies (1834). While the state certainly did not go limp, within Great Britain it moved away from the massive repression of popular collective action it had attempted, with decidedly mixed results, during the early postwar years.

Repertoires for the 1830s

The profile of public claim-making between 1828 and 1834 resembles a mountain range, with towering, spiked peaks in the nineteen months from November 1830 through May 1832—from the height of Swing to the passage of the Reform Act—between foothills before and after. The full catalog for 1828 through 1834 includes 6,884 CGs, an average of about 82 events per month, very unevenly distributed. Because events come so fast and furious, this chapter will resort to catalogs, graphs, and statistical summaries more extensively than earlier ones did. Figure 7.2, for example, identifies eighteen months in which our sources reported at least 100 CGs:

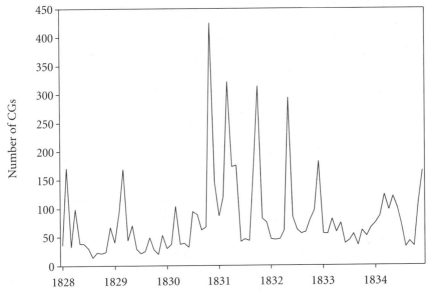

Figure 7.2. CGs per month, 1828–1834

February 1828 (171 CGs): public meetings (especially for petitions) on Test and Corporation repeal, election rallies and gatherings.

March 1829 (169): meetings, marches, demonstrations, attacks, and other actions concerning Catholic Emancipation.

March 1830 (104): resistance to New Police, meetings (especially petition meetings) opposing widow-burning in India, gatherings, attacks, and meetings complaining about distress, meetings against taxes.

November 1830 (425): Swing gatherings and attacks, resistance to New Police, meetings against slavery, meetings, marches, attacks, and other actions supporting parliamentary reform and/or opposing government officials.

December 1830 (147): antislavery meetings, reform meetings, wardmotes, demonstrations, attacks, and other actions, Swing attacks, turnouts, meetings against taxes.

February 1831 (120): turnouts, antislavery meetings (especially for petitions), meetings and other actions on reform, meetings against taxes.

March 1831 (322): turnouts, antislavery meetings, meetings, celebrations, window-breaking, and other actions on reform.

April 1831 (173): election rallies and meetings, antislavery meetings, meetings, demonstrations, window-breaking, and other actions concerning reform and/or opposing government officials.

May 1831 (175): election rallies, processions, and meetings, reform meetings and other actions.

September 1831 (168): reform meetings and other actions, coronation celebrations for William IV.

October 1831 (314): meetings on friendly societies bill, election gatherings, reform meetings, processions, demonstrations, attacks, and other actions, gatherings opposing government officials.

May 1832 (294): meetings on Irish education, meetings, petitions, celebrations, and other actions on parliamentary reform, workers' meetings and gatherings, gatherings in support of and opposition to government officials.

December 1832 (182): election rallies, gatherings, attacks, and meetings, London wardmotes defining political positions.

March 1834 (124): considerable variety of meetings (many of them for petitioning) concerning the Irish Coercion Bill, antislavery, Sabbath observance, taxes, and other issues.

May 1834 (121): meetings (often petition meetings) concerning separation of church and state, poor laws, church rates, tithes, and parliamentary reform.

June 1834 (101): election meetings and rallies, wide variety of meetings, especially for petitioning, notably about church rates, tithes, separation of church and state, gatherings in opposition to government officials.

November 1834 (107): meetings and other actions in opposition to the ministry, in favor of radical reform, including repeated burning of the anti-reform *London Times.*

December 1834 (166): electoral rallies and meetings, wardmotes taking political positions, meetings and other actions against the ministry and for reform.

In general, such surges occurred through the disproportionate multiplication of public meetings. Over the entire seven years, 75.4 percent of all CGs took the form of public meetings. Every one of the high-frequency months except Swing months November–December 1830 and reform-agitation month April 1831 featured a higher proportion of public meetings than that average. In March 1834 the share reached 117 of the 124 CGs, for 94.4 percent.

Months with many CGs also tended to be times of single-issue mobilization. In February 1828, for example, 145 of the 171 events concerned religious rights, while in October 1831 266 of the 314 CGs involved claim-making about parliamentary reform and another 16 concerned elections, which at that time likewise pivoted on reform. The chief exceptions were November–December 1830, when the Swing rebellion coincided with substantial mobilization for reform, and the more active months of 1834, when multi-issue politics began to thrive. Over the period as a whole, political entrepreneurs honed their social-movement skills, especially the technique of organizing multiple public meetings devoted to a single issue. The program-publicizing public meeting became by far the dominant technique of claim-making.

Figure 7.3 shows how much major issues surged, then subsided, as objects of contention. The lines for elections, reform-governmental change,

and religion also display the strong connection between popular contention and Parliament; we can almost read the rhythms of parliamentary
action in these regards directly from the curves. Contention concerning
the economy ran more autonomously, dominated as it was by the months
of Captain Swing, and filled as its lesser months were with locally oriented
turnouts, strikes, and other owner-worker conflicts. Even there the interplay of popular contention with parliamentary action made its mark; not
only did Parliament respond to Swing with a series of repressive measures,
but also the economic issues in question regularly included taxes, Corn
Laws, and other questions directly involving parliamentary policy. To
generalize, then, in the 1830s peaks of contention occurred chiefly as
political entrepreneurs organized numerous public meetings to broadcast
support for or opposition to particular programs requiring action of the
national government, especially Parliament.

Table 7.3 describes the ebb and flow of issues on an annual scale,
offering comparisons with previous years as well as between southeastern
England and the rest of Great Britain. Even at this level the surging of
issues comes across clearly: reform went from a mere 3 of 595 events in
1828 to a full 952 of 1831's 1,645 CGs, while religious questions motivated

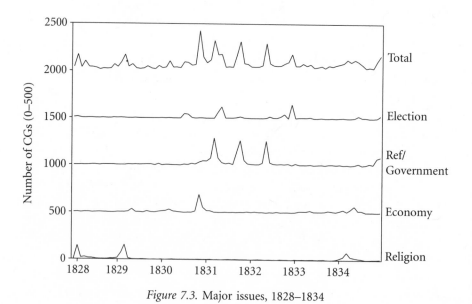

Figure 7.3. Major issues, 1828–1834

Table 7.3. Major issues of contentious gatherings in Great Britain, 1828–1834, and in the Southeast, 1758–1834

					% of total for period					
Issue	1828	1829	1830	1831	1832	1833	1834	1828–1834	S.E. 1828–1834	S.E. 1758–1820
Attacks	5.0	6.9	4.4	2.2	2.7	6.5	2.7	3.8	4.7	9.4
Labor	10.3	5.9	1.4	1.8	2.1	3.1	5.0	3.5	2.8	2.0
Religion	43.2	41.5	4.6	1.8	2.4	8.8	25.6	14.0	11.5	7.4
Police	0.8	3.1	6.5	1.8	2.3	5.0	2.6	3.1	5.3	2.0
Election	4.9	1.4	8.5	13.3	27.4	6.2	7.0	11.3	10.5	6.9
National government	6.9	12.0	6.0	5.2	8.8	11.4	19.5	9.5	9.6	14.8
Royalty	0.5	0.3	4.5	2.1	2.2	1.9	2.8	2.3	3.4	18.5
Reform	0.5	1.2	6.7	57.9	29.7	3.1	4.1	20.9	16.3	2.2
Local government	5.7	4.2	2.9	2.7	4.7	11.3	6.0	4.8	9.3	12.6
Economy	2.0	4.2	3.7	0.7	1.1	1.3	8.5	3.0	3.9	2.5
Machine breaking	0.0	0.0	10.3	0.2	0.1	0.0	0.0	1.9	0.7	0.0
Slavery	1.2	0.2	9.8	1.0	0.6	6.2	0.2	2.7	1.6	0.4
Taxes	1.3	2.2	6.3	2.3	1.2	13.9	4.1	4.1	5.8	2.2
Other	17.6	16.2	24.4	6.9	14.9	21.1	12.0	15.1	14.6	19.2
Total	100.0	100.0	100.0	100.0	100.0	100.0	100.0	100.0	100.0	100.0
N	595	641	1,164	1,645	1,111	674	1,054	6,884	3,068	1,203*

*Tabulations exclude 1758 mutiny originating in Portsmouth.

more than 40 percent of events in 1828 and 1829 only to subside to less than 2 percent in 1831.

Such categories, to be sure, overstate the distinctness of issues; as we have seen, in the later months of 1830 political entrepreneurs and ordinary claim-makers sometimes conjoined parliamentary reform, complaints about governmental performance, and resistance to the New Police, not to mention cheers for the recent French revolution. Furthermore, the passage of Test and Corporation repeal, Catholic Emancipation, and reform encouraged some of their beneficiaries to press for further religious innovations, notably the elimination of select vestries and the disestablishment of the Anglican Church. In the heat of reform mobilization (February 1831), indeed, John Cam Hobhouse, MP for Westminster, had introduced a bill calling for ratepayers' election of vestries by secret ballot, when the ballot itself was a crucial issue in the debate over reform. That is the point: increasingly the questions at issue in popular contention aimed at Parliament and national politics by means of sustained campaigns linking meetings, marches, demonstrations, petitions, pamphlets, and special-purpose associations. Issues intertwined. Social-movement politics flourished.

Table 7.3 also reveals how much reform and related issues engaged Great Britain outside of London: in the Southeast, 16.3 percent of the period's CGs concerned reform, while for Great Britain as a whole the proportion was even larger: 20.9 percent. Religious issues likewise mobilized a larger share of events outside the London region, with both Test and Corporation repeal and Catholic Emancipation drawing nationwide claims from associations, congregations, and local assemblies. Significantly more prevalent in the Southeast than elsewhere, according to our counts, were local government and police—the former very likely an illusion due to the focus of our sources on disputes in London wards, parishes, and councils, the latter resulting entirely from struggles over New Police.

With these exceptions, in the Southeast and elsewhere the profiles of dominant issues resembled each other. Judging from the range of events other historians (for example, Babington 1990; Belchem 1990; Bohstedt 1983; Charlesworth 1983; Colley 1992; Darvall 1934; Gilmour 1992; Hammond and Hammond 1917, 1920a, 1920b; Harrison 1988; Hole 1989; Logue 1979; Munger 1981a; Palmer 1988; Reed and Wells 1990; Rule 1986;

Stevenson 1992; Thomis and Grimmett 1982; Thompson 1963; Vogler 1991) have identified outside of London's hinterland during earlier years, convergence occurred during the postwar period; issues and actions became more similar in the London region and elsewhere. Within south-eastern England the mix of issues changed substantially: between 1828 and 1834 religion, police, elections, reform, the economy, and taxes all clearly gained relative to their prominence in 1758–1820, while claims on the national government, appeals to royalty, and attacks on persons or property all lost ground. Elsewhere in Great Britain, it seems, shifts in these directions were even more emphatic.

Events I have categorized as oriented to issues of "national government" featured open expressions of support or opposition for ministers or other high officials. As we have seen in the public hooting of Wellington and Peel, such expressions did not disappear in 1828. Indeed they tripled in absolute numbers, from roughly 14 per year between 1758 and 1820 to 42 per year in 1828–1834. Even the decline of claims on royalty was quite relative: about 17 CGs per year in the Southeast from 1758 to 1820, about 15 per year between 1828 and 1834. But claims concerning national policies multiplied far faster than those concerning nationally prominent persons. The whole pattern bespeaks an increasing focus of popular claim-making throughout Great Britain on the issues toward which Parliament was turning its attention, a parliamentarization of contention. The connection ran in both directions: Parliament's concerns stimulated popular contention as mass claim-making incited parliamentary action.

Table 7.4, which displays the occasions for CGs, amplifies the story. The catchall "other violent gatherings" includes the characteristic actions of Swing (except for machine-breaking) as well as two other sorts of events: violent strikes and meetings or demonstrations in which physical attacks of some kind occurred. The share of such events in the total declined substantially from earlier years: 11.7 percent of the Southeast's events in 1828–1834 as compared with 22.4 from 1758 to 1820. Although as a result of Swing other violent gatherings surged in 1830 with nearly one in five events, they occupied almost as large a share in 1829; during that year both violent strikes and boisterous gatherings around the issue of Catholic Emancipation made the difference. After 1830, however, all violent forms of claim-making dwindled.

Again, with religious and religio-political organizations sustaining much

Table 7.4. Occasions of contentious gatherings in Great Britain, 1828–1834, and in the Southeast, 1758–1834

									S.E.	S.E.
									1828–	1758–
Type of event	1828	1829	1830	1831	1832	1833	1834	1828–1834	1828–1834	1758–1820
									(%) of total for period	
Machine breaking	0.0	0.6	10.3	0.2	0.1	0.0	0.0	1.9	0.7	0.0
Smuggling	0.5	0.8	0.7	0.2	0.9	0.6	0.3	0.5	0.8	1.0
Food/market conflict	1.2	0.3	0.2	0.3	0.0	0.0	0.0	0.2	0.1	1.8
Other violent gatherings	12.1	18.7	19.1	10.5	12.2	10.4	8.0	12.7	11.7	22.4
Other unplanned gatherings	0.5	6.1	8.0	4.4	5.3	7.7	4.0	5.2	5.9	12.6
Authorized celebrations	0.5	1.1	0.7	0.8	0.4	0.4	2.6	0.9	1.2	1.1
Delegations	0.7	0.2	0.3	0.5	0.9	1.6	1.2	0.7	1.5	2.2
Demonstrations, parades	6.7	3.0	3.1	1.3	1.8	0.0	0.1	2.0	1.4	0.3
Strikes, turnouts	0.3	0.8	0.5	1.2	0.4	1.2	2.6	1.0	0.5	0.2
Associational meetings	48.1	23.2	12.1	7.1	7.4	8.8	6.5	13.1	14.7	6.8
Meetings of public assemblies	8.1	20.3	19.0	49.2	55.5	52.1	46.9	38.8	41.8	43.0
Other planned meetings	21.3	25.0	26.0	24.3	15.1	17.2	27.9	22.8	19.6	8.6
Total	100.0	100.0	100.0	100.0	100.0	100.0	100.0	100.0	100.0	100.0
Number of CGs	595	641	1,164	1,645	1,111	674	1,054	6,884	3,068	1,203

% of total for period

of the mobilization concerning Test and Corporation repeal and Catholic Emancipation, with friendly societies likewise voicing views on the bill Parliament fashioned to control them, associational meetings reached record heights in 1828 and 1829. During the reform campaign of 1830–1832, however, constituted public assemblies (for example, meetings of all inhabitants) and *ad hoc* public meetings (behind many of which associations actually lay) took up much more of the political burden; that predominance of constituted assemblies and open public meetings continued past the enactment of reform.

The distribution of actions (Table 7.5) confirms these alterations. The categories of verbs whose share increased by at least a third over 1758–1820 were *cheer, disperse, meet, petition,* and *support,* while *attack, control, gather,* and *move* waned—a clear shift from street confrontations to the politics of public meetings. Attacks and controlling actions again had their day in 1829–1831, years of Swing and widespread workers' confrontations, while petitioning and requesting gave way to assembling and resolving as the emphasis moved from the religious issues of 1828–1829 to reform and its aftermath. Increasingly people gathered chiefly to display their support for or opposition to a particular program rather than to take direct action that would forward or impede it.

As for formations making or receiving claims (Table 7.6), the roster of increases and decreases from 1758–1820 to 1828–1834 looks like this:

Increased share by 33% or more	*Decreased share by 33% or more*	
Parliament, MP	Royalty	Trade
National officials	Gentlemen, nobles	Troops
Police	Clergy	Crowd
Individual names	Freeholders, electors	

Although the substitution of police for troops, the waning of undifferentiated crowds in favor of explicitly named persons, and the declining prominence of trade disputes all deserve notice, the big news concerns the nationalization of participants, accompanied by a shift from royalty and nobility to Parliament itself. Among absent objects of claims in the Southeast, shares of major categories changed dramatically, as indicated in Table 7.7. We see a conjunction between the expansion of social-move-

Table 7.5. Verbs in all actions of contentious gatherings, Great Britain, 1828–1834, and Southeast, 1758–1834

	% of total for period									
Verb	1828	1829	1830	1831	1832	1833	1834	1828–1834	S.E. 1828–1834	S.E. 1758–1820
Assemble	2.4	3.4	6.0	4.4	6.4	6.1	7.8	5.3	4.8	4.3
Attack	3.8	6.9	7.9	7.2	7.4	5.7	4.4	6.6	4.9	7.9
Chair	0.3	0.5	1.7	4.4	3.6	5.0	5.0	3.2	4.7	4.7
Cheer	4.2	4.5	3.7	5.1	6.1	5.5	6.6	5.1	5.9	4.3
Communicate	1.8	2.4	2.3	2.1	2.4	1.8	1.5	2.1	2.0	2.4
Control	4.7	7.6	8.7	5.4	5.9	5.5	3.6	6.1	5.2	8.4
Decry	1.4	1.5	1.4	1.7	1.9	1.4	0.9	1.5	1.7	1.5
Disperse	5.8	5.7	4.5	5.1	6.6	5.8	5.9	5.5	6.4	4.5
End	16.1	13.1	13.3	12.2	11.2	14.1	16.7	13.3	11.9	12.8

Fight	1.0	0.7	0.8	0.4	0.8	1.3	0.8	0.7	0.7	1.0
Gather	1.2	1.6	4.4	2.6	3.1	2.9	3.1	2.9	2.5	4.2
Meet	15.4	11.1	6.8	9.9	8.8	11.9	11.9	10.1	10.9	7.9
Move	5.6	6.4	7.8	6.0	6.6	3.7	3.8	6.0	4.6	6.5
Petition	11.3	7.4	5.6	5.4	3.6	3.8	6.9	5.8	4.0	0.7
Request	2.7	2.5	4.9	1.2	1.0	1.1	0.8	2.0	1.9	1.7
Resist	1.1	1.4	1.6	0.6	0.5	0.8	0.6	0.9	0.9	0.9
Resolve	4.2	4.2	2.9	9.9	10.3	12.5	10.2	8.0	11.6	13.2
Support	2.1	2.5	1.5	0.8	0.5	0.6	0.7	1.1	1.2	0.9
Other	14.9	16.9	14.1	15.6	13.4	10.5	9.0	13.8	14.2	12.0
Total	100.0	100.0	100.0	100.0	100.0	100.0	100.0	100.0	100.0	100.0
N	2,726	3,600	7,047	10,127	6,375	3,288	4,600	37,763	16,499	7,541

Table 7.6. Formations participating in contentious gatherings in Great Britain, 1828–1834, and in the Southeast, 1758–1834

| | | | | | | | | | 1828– | S.E. 1828– | S.E. 1758– |
Formation	1828	1829	1830	1831	1832	1833	1834	1834	1834	1820
					% of total for period					
Parliament, MP	20.8	15.8	13.2	23.3	27.6	26.5	25.9	21.8	21.0	13.1
National officials	4.5	3.3	2.3	5.7	5.8	3.6	5.3	4.5	5.0	3.2
Royalty	0.6	0.8	2.1	7.7	3.7	1.7	5.3	3.9	4.2	6.6
Gentlemen, nobles	2.5	3.0	1.6	1.9	1.7	2.0	2.6	2.1	2.1	3.5
Judges	2.2	2.9	4.9	1.8	2.5	2.0	2.0	2.7	2.0	2.5
Mayors	1.6	1.6	1.0	2.4	1.7	1.5	1.6	1.7	1.6	2.0
Other local officials	5.4	5.5	4.2	6.8	6.7	11.5	8.5	6.7	11.0	12.7
Clergy	0.4	1.5	1.4	0.9	0.7	0.6	0.4	0.9	0.9	1.6

Freeholders, electors	0.9	2.3	1.7	1.0	1.1	1.5	1.0	1.3	1.5	2.3
Other local assemblies	5.2	5.8	6.6	16.7	13.5	12.8	11.7	11.3	10.3	9.9
Trade	5.4	9.4	6.2	3.7	2.9	6.7	5.3	5.2	4.3	7.2
Other interest	10.3	5.6	3.8	3.8	5.9	4.5	6.2	5.2	4.8	4.8
Police	2.6	4.1	2.9	2.3	3.4	4.1	2.8	3.0	3.8	2.4
Troops	1.4	2.1	2.1	1.6	1.4	1.1	0.6	1.5	1.0	3.8
Unnamed crowd	1.5	2.8	8.7	2.6	2.9	2.1	1.1	3.5	2.9	5.4
Named individuals	8.8	10.1	14.3	6.8	4.4	3.4	2.6	7.5	6.6	4.7
Other	25.7	23.3	23.0	11.1	14.2	14.4	17.1	17.2	16.2	14.3
Total	100.0	100.0	100.0	100.0	100.0	100.0	100.0	100.0	100.0	100.0
N	1,780	2,249	4,291	5,855	3,697	1,978	2,898	22,748	10,207	4,436

Note: Includes both actors and objects of claims.

Table 7.7. Absent objects of claims, Southeastern England, 1758–1834

Category	1758–1795	1801–1820	1828–1830	1831–1834
Parliament/MP	34.6	37.2	50.3	58.3
Royalty	22.8	19.9	7.1	14.9
National officials	6.8	9.7	11.3	12.2
Local officials	8.0	11.1	4.1	6.4
Other	17.8	22.1	27.2	8.2
Total	100.0	100.0	100.0	100.0

Note: The decline of royalty reversed temporarily in 1831 and 1832 because of King William's crucial role in the threat to pack a House of Lords that remained hostile to the Reform Bill.

ment tactics and the aiming of public displays at national authorities, especially Parliament. Note the differences in average CGs between months in which Parliament was and was not in session indicated by Table 7.8: while all sorts of contentious events were at least slightly more frequent in months of parliamentary session from the 1750s to the 1830s, the concentration of claim-making in sessions increased signally after 1820, especially for public meetings of named associations.

The Political Crisis of 1828–1834

Over the long run the increasing centrality of Parliament resulted especially from the government's mobilization for the Napoleonic wars, whose enormous demands for money, men, supplies, and controls over economic life made parliamentary decisions ever more crucial to the state's operation. The struggles of 1828 to 1834 reinforced Parliament's position; repeatedly the government responded to challenges not by deploying its existing powers of repression, persuasion, or reward but by turning to the House of Commons for new legislation. Since challengers usually had sympathizers, interpreters, allies, or even direct representatives among MPs—Sir Francis Burdett, for example, had been concerting his parliamentary action with reformers outside Parliament since 1796—the turn to Parliament engaged the government ever more directly in negotiation with challengers.

Challengers, moreover, allied or merged with one another in the effort to influence parliamentary decisions; a web of activism united Test and Corporation, Catholic Emancipation, reform and, to some extent, Swing and antislavery. The web extended all the way to Ireland, where repeal of the Union with Great Britain had gained widespread popular appeal, and alliances with British radicals were multiplying through such organizers as Feargus O'Connor (Epstein 1982). Political entrepreneurs became more crucial than ever before, as the formation of coalitions, the hammering out of programs, the sounding out of authorities, and the preparation of publicly visible actions preoccupied claim-makers. The classic governmental strategy for dealing with major social movements began to crystallize: monitor and channel the statement of claims, bargain selectively with the minimum coalition of challengers that seems likely to contain the movement yet produce tolerable demands, split and shield that coalition from its rivals, make necessary concessions, co-opt the challengers'

Table 7.8. Mean CGs per month for parliament in session/not in session, 1758–1834

Type of CGs and period	Parliament in session	Parliament not in session	Correlation
All CGs			
1758–1820	8.36	6.34	+.09
1828–1834	40.32	30.03	+.21
Violent gatherings			
1758–1820	1.79	1.62	−.03
1828–1834	5.38	3.90	+.06
Associational meetings			
1758–1820	0.63	0.30	+.15
1828–1834	6.96	2.71	+.37
Public assemblies			
1758–1820	3.51	3.10	+.08
1828–1834	16.11	13.81	+.09
Other meetings			
1758–1820	0.80	0.38	+.16
1828–1834	7.53	6.58	+.06

Correlation: Pearsonian correlation coefficient between number of events in category during a month and number of days of parliamentary session that month.

leaders, repress the more extreme claimants, and promote demobilization of the rest.

The classic strategy produces paradoxical results, since in its early phases it actually encourages mobilization and claim-making by three different groups of contenders: those whose interests any concessions to the challengers would attack; rivals whose demands the government chooses to ignore or repress; bystanders whose leaders sense the possibility that the government will be newly receptive to their demands. Where the initial challenge is momentous and the government engagement in selection and concession visible, the result is a cascade of claim-making, increasingly fierce struggle, a series of settlements, and then subsidence. In retrospect we often call this sort of sequence a cycle of protest or a political crisis. More visibly and coherently than in the contentious surges of 1790–1795 and 1815–1820, such a crisis played itself out in the United Kingdom between 1828 and 1834. It moved from questions of religious qualifications for office to questions of policing and, overwhelmingly, of parliamentary reform, to the accompaniment of industrial and agrarian struggles.

The crisis opened with questions of religious qualifications for office. Since the settlement of 1689 the Test and Corporation (T&C) Acts (passed *seriatim* in 1661, 1673, and 1678, then confirmed in the Glorious Revolution) had restricted major British public offices, including membership in Parliament, to members of the Anglican church. In fact, Protestant Dissenters frequently held office through *ad hoc* parliamentary dispensation, but the exclusive legal principle stood. Catholics, Jews, declared deists, and avowed atheists remained outside the fold. With the incorporation of Ireland into Parliament and the United Kingdom in 1801, exclusion of Catholics produced even more blatant inequality. Thenceforth, the political rights of religious groups became a more pressing national issue, one linked to parliamentary reform by the principles and practices of exclusion from national politics. In its various guises, Daniel O'Connell's mass-membership Catholic Association became Ireland's principal vehicle of agitation for Emancipation, a substantial force in Great Britain as well.

In 1828 Parliament repealed the Test and Corporation Acts amid considerable popular clamor; while still excluding known non-Christians, repeal made non-Anglican Protestants permanently eligible for most public offices. That same year, however, Parliament once again rejected

Table 7.9. Parlimentary petitions regarding religious issues, 1828

| | Test and Corporation repeal | | Catholic emancipation | | |
	For	Against	For	Against	Divided
Petitions	1,206	28	732	333	0
CGs	183	0	16	21	4

Catholic Emancipation. As measured by petitions recorded in *Votes and Proceedings of Parliament* or CGs in our catalog, T&C agitation overshadowed Catholic Emancipation as an issue that year (see Table 7.9). Once it occurred, T&C repeal split Dissenters: some moved away from their implicit alliance with Catholics to the government's anti-Catholic side, but others stuck with Catholic Emancipation as an issue of political rights and religious liberty. Toward the end of 1828 opponents of Emancipation mobilized through a campaign emulating both the successful drive for T&C repeal and the Catholic movement itself; meetings and petitions to Parliament multiplied.

Kent led the way with an anti-Catholic meeting of 20,000 people or more at Penenden Heath (24 October 1828) and the creation of the first anti-Catholic Brunswick Constitutional Club outside of London. (The London original had formed in July as a Protestant Club of peers and MPs at the instigation of the king's brother, the Duke of Cumberland, but at Lord Eldon's urging soon changed its name and started co-opting new members.) Thereafter Brunswick Clubs, often drawing on the existing membership of Pitt and Orange clubs, became major vehicles of anti-Catholic campaigning in both Great Britain and Ireland. During 1829 the distribution of petitions and CGs with respect to Catholic Emancipation inside Great Britain ran as follows:

	For	*Against*	*Divided*
Petitions	1,001	2,169	0
CGs	99	141	2

By these indications, the balance of mobilization within Great Britain ran strongly *against* Emancipation.

Ireland, however, produced quite the opposite preponderance: Brunswick Clubs made very little headway while the Catholic Association expanded its campaign on behalf of Catholic rights. During the year, in the face of vast movements pro and con in Ireland and Great Britain, Wellington and Peel finally (and quite reluctantly) engineered its passage. They attempted to limit political damage by dissolving O'Connell's Catholic Association, increasing the property requirements for suffrage in Ireland, and restricting activities of any future political associations on the island. Mobilization on behalf of religious rights subsided immediately. But the precedent stood: government had made major concessions in response to a deliberately organized, associationally based social movement. Almost immediately, reformers seized the precedent.

Embattled Bobbies

The question of New Police intersected that of reform and echoed that of Irish political mobilization. On the model of the constabulary he had organized in Ireland as Chief Secretary there between 1812 and 1818, in September 1829 Peel introduced to Westminster and a number of adjacent parishes the uniformed and disciplined Metropolitan Police that people came to call New Police, Peel's Bloody Gang, Blue Devils, Peelers, Lobsters, or, eventually, Bobbies; he placed the new force under direct control of his Home Office, abolished the old parish constabularies, yet levied increased taxes on parishes to pay for the new ones. The establishment of those police bothered not only the workers, radicals, and street criminals they were designed to control but also London ratepayers, parish officers, and magistrates whose previous authority over policing the New Police escaped; thus a variety of people saw the creation of the "gendarmes" (in Cobbett's epithet) as one more governmental tyranny. "Large mobs," recalled Francis Place, no admirer of mobs, "now assembled in the streets and assailed the police men, with all sorts of bad language, mud and stones, and on two or three occasions fighting with them" (BL ADD 27789). People fought the new force in Parliament, in public meetings, and in the streets.

The question of New Police occupied a curiously intermediate position: local because confined to the London metropolis, national because Peel stood behind the innovation and because it challenged the general decentralization of police powers in Great Britain. Many critics associated the metropolitan force with the tyranny of centralized, militarized European monarchies. A handbill dated 2 August 1830, two days after Louis-Philippe's revolutionary accession in France, put the issue this way:

REVOLUTION IN FRANCE
Citizens of England!
Take warning of the passing events in France.—Beware of a STANDING ARMY, and a MILITARY POLICE. If a New Police be requisite, let it emanate from the People, and be under their entire controul [sic]. Our Patriotic Sovereign wants not hirelings to support him—he desires publicity in all his actions, and relies with confidence on the justice of the People.—ENGLISHMEN! why should we pay for the support of a STANDING ARMY after Fifteen Years of profound Peace, when the burdens of the People are greater than they can bear? (HO 44/21)

The radical position associated uniformed, state-controlled police with wartime repression and arbitrary rule. It thereby linked the propertyholders' interest in cheap, non-intrusive government to the radical interest in free association and expression.

Contention concerning New Police took two main forms: local meetings to call for abolition of the police force and for remission of the taxes levied to support them, active resistance to the metropolitan constables as they exerted their new authority. The two forms were not as separate as they seem. For one similarity, both concentrated in the struggles over reform at the end of 1830. After a scattering of conflicts in 1829 and the first half of 1830, protests against the New Police bunched in the latter half of 1830: 8 CGs in September, 14 in October, 24 in November, then subsidence, only 14 more incidents through September 1833, and none thereafter. Of the 38 in October-November 1830, 14 were relatively staid public meetings, 5 nonviolent demonstrations or informal gatherings in which participants decried the (absent) police, and 19 violent encounters between police and civilians involving specific challenges to police jurisdiction. Police of some description took part in 65 of the 492 CGs that occurred somewhere in Great Britain during October or (especially) November; although crowds often resisted police when they took prisoners or broke up gatherings, only in the 19 CGs directly involving New Police did an open challenge to jurisdiction arise. To put it another way, during October and November 1830 every single time the New Police took part in a contentious gathering someone overtly resisted their authority. This concerted resistance to the new police force formed in the midst of mobilization for parliamentary reform.

For another similarity, themes carried over from one sort of struggle to another, with participants in meetings (depending on their political perspective) deploring the violence of police or of civilians, and participants in attacks echoing the condemnation of New Police as an unconstitutional innovation. On 9 November (the day after the Blackfriars Bridge march) occurred what Home Secretary Peel described in the Commons as "some unpleasant collisions between the police and the mob at Temple Bar, and other parts of the Strand" (MOP 10 November 1830). Those "collisions" grew out of the king's canceled visit to Guildhall, which had been scheduled for that day. In the afternoon of 9 November some 1,000–1,500 persons had gathered near Richard Carlile's shop in Fleet Street, heard a speech from William Wiblin, then rushed down Fleet Street, through Temple Bar, and along the Strand until they met detachments of New Police. On the way they shouted "Down with the police!" "No Peel!" and "No Wellington!" (MC and LT 10 November 1830). Police drove the demonstrators back in what may have been history's first organized baton charge by otherwise unarmed police (Miles 1988; available accounts also leave open the possibility that the police had already practiced their baton charge the previous evening, after the mass crossing of Blackfriars Bridge).

In the evening City Police (whom Peel, not wanting to jeopardize his 1829 bill by opposition from City of London politicians, had exempted from incorporation into the metropolitan force) protected Guildhall and the Lord Mayor's carriage from an "immense crowd" whose members forced passersby to doff their hats and shout "Huzzah." But toward 10 P.M. "perhaps three hundred men" from Spitalfields arrived at the City's edge, Temple Bar, armed with clubs; they found that the New Police had barred the gate from Westminster territory, which lay just outside. Francis Place reported that they had armed themselves by pulling down part of the Public Record Office, then under construction in Chancery Lane, and seizing its staves (BL ADD 27789).

City Police forced open the gate to assert their prerogative to control it, but also sought to disarm the Spitalfields workers. From inside the gate members of the crowd pelted the New Police with stones and wood. Later, a band of 200–300 men (no doubt essentially the same group) carried tricolor flags into Spitalfields, broke windows at a police station and elsewhere, then disappeared (AR 1830). This time we do not know the Spitalfields men's identities. But we do know that Spitalfields silkweavers had long supplied cudgel-bearers for Henry Hunt and radical reform. Once again the themes of police, popular liberties, political reform, and revolution intertwined.

Swing

Through the fall and winter of 1830 much of London's agricultural hinterland trembled to the marching of landless laborers, who wrote threatening letters, burned hayricks and farm buildings, ravaged threshing machines, drove out overseers of the poor, demanded wage rises, and visited workhouses, magistrates' homes, and rectories to call for higher poor relief or lower tithes. For a while authorities, noticing the coincidence between barn-burning and Cobbett's October lecture tour in Kent and Sussex, suspected Cobbett himself of being the great avenger Captain Swing, or a reasonable facsimile. Having failed to establish a direct connection, in July 1831 the government tried Cobbett for seditious libel on the grounds that his *Register* had inspired rural uprisings. He defended himself eloquently and secured discharge of the case in anticipation of a likely acquittal. Participants in the rebellion were not so lucky; eventually 252 of them received death sentences, and 19 of them actually died on the gallows, 16 of the 19 for arson.

At first glance, the so-called Swing rebellion looks like a fragment of another world: a futile, apolitical outburst of rural protest linked by shared misery and informal communication, a movement borrowing time-honored parochial forms of action for entirely local ends. Then the connections appear: concentration of events in London's market region, especially along main roads; disproportionate involvement of larger, open parishes with significant numbers of non-agricultural workers; a long precedent of parish wage-fixing in conjunction with local poor rates; prominence among Swing events of gatherings in which workers collectively demanded wage rises of local authorities, justifying their demands as founded on time-honored rights and sometimes making explicit references to current national politics (Armstrong 1988; Charlesworth 1978; Cirket 1978; Hobsbawm and Rudé 1968; Richards 1974; Singleton 1964). In Banbury (Oxfordshire) the gathering that went out to destroy Mr. Bolton's threshing machine in Neithorp on 29 November first burned two MPs in effigy for their vote against the motion for a select committee to investigate the Civil List, whose passage had brought down the Wellington government (MC 2 December 1830).

The connection to national politics also ran in another direction: although Wellington's tottering government sent out troops for the first time on 11 November, it was not until the Whig cabinet arrived on 17 November that the regime took coordinated action to repress the rebellion, beginning with Melbourne's proclamation of rewards for apprehension of participants on 23 November. Figure 7.4 presents five-day moving averages ending with the days shown for the number of CGs and for the number of events in the catalog prepared by E. J. Hobsbawm and George Rudé (1968). Both series show clearly the great acceleration of incidents after 8 November, the peak from 15 November to 1 December, the fading

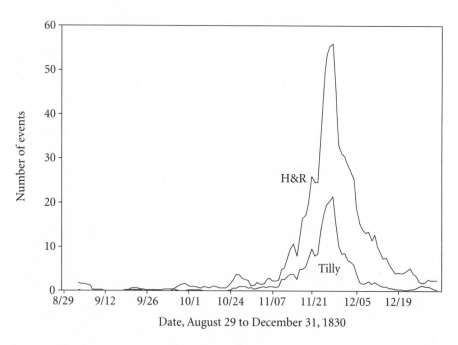

Figure 7.4. Swing events

away thereafter. The Swing action recalled the crises of 1816, 1818, and 1822—more exclusively rural, without their industrial machine-breaking, and greatly extended in time and space.

Swing's marches, solicitations, attacks, fires, and other forms of action were familiar in their era. They had surged to prominence during the agrarian struggles of the 1790s, and had reappeared intermittently from that point on, notably in 1816 and 1822. Consider the experience of John Marsh of Toppesfield, Essex, who rented out farm equipment and also operated his machines for farmers. On 16 January 1829, well before Swing, Marsh was running a threshing machine when "a party of labourers, in number thirty and upwards took away his machine by force, and conveyed it into the adjoining parish of Stambourne, where they broke it to pieces" (MC 28 January 1829). Toward the end of March, Marsh lost another machine when about twenty agricultural workers:

> proceeded to the place where the prosecutor's [that is, Marsh's] machine was at work and seized it; and a demand was made by the person who then had it in use, a Mr. John Hills, for its return, but that was refused unless it was promised that it should not be any more used in the parish. No such promise, however, was made, and the machine was accordingly removed. At this time, however, the prisoners were very quiet in their demeanour, and declared they would not, nor did they intend to injure the machine. Some time after the machine was found destroyed. (MC 4 August 1829)

The jury trying seven laborers for machine-breaking found them not guilty, apparently because the evidence did not link them directly to destruction of the thresher. Yet the jury was adjudicating a well-known form of retaliatory action. Threatening letters, the levying of contributions for beer, wage marches, and arson likewise had their precedents. Introduction of the Lucifer match in 1830 simply made it easier for a single person to set a big fire undetected. In East Anglia, for which John Archer has prepared a meticulous catalog of incendiarism, the years between 1815 and 1835 with more than twenty set fires included 1816, 1822, and each individual year from 1830 to 1835 (Archer 1990). After Swing, as overt resistance lost its efficacy, rural fires multiplied. "In no year before 1830, 1822 excepted," reports Archer, "did the number of fires attain the level and frequency of the post-1830 period" (ibid.: 73).

Within the swelling action of 1830, arson joined as only one of many connected forms of threat, coercion, and retaliation: 124 of the 924 events enumerated by Hobsbawm and Rudé for 1830. The main distinction of arson in the Swing events (exactly as its previous and subsequent history might suggest) was its greater relative frequency *outside* the peak of overt collective action during the last half of November. Figure 7.5 shows incendiary events as a much higher proportion of the total before 6 November and after 6 December. Except where the landed classes fell visibly on the defensive, anonymous threats and clandestine rick-burning served laborers as safer alternatives to public confrontations with farmers; arson and other covert action became more prominent when public contention became dangerous. During the rebellion's height, nevertheless, the two sometimes converged, as when gangs of workers went from breaking machines to firing farms or when laborers refused to help extinguish a set fire. During the later weeks of November, furthermore, rebellious assemblies of workers formed recurrently in villages to demand concessions from local landowners and authorities.

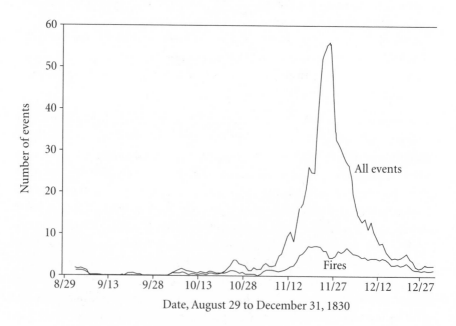

Figure 7.5. Fires, all events

Swing's cluster of marches and attacks began in Kent, chiefly in regions of mixed economy (neither market-gardening for London nor large wheat farms) near roads connecting to regional market towns. In Kent attacks on threshing machines took place almost exclusively in the Isle of Thanet or between Canterbury and Sandwich, two regions of intensive large-scale grain production for London. From "an evening paper" the *Times* of 27 October borrowed a Canterbury correspondent's characteristic account of events during the night of Saturday 23 October:

> It would seem that, about midnight on Saturday, a gang of men visited the farm of Mr. Quested, of Ash, whose fodder-stacks had been destroyed the previous night by the hand of an incendiary, and proceeded at once to break open his stable door, liberate the horses and turn them into the high road, to the number of 14 or 15. The men, however, were disturbed by two persons, who had been sent to watch the premises, and, it would appear, simultaneously, left the yard . . . Circumstances render it probable that the same party forthwith made their way towards Sandwich, where the revenge they meditated upon Mr. Quested was satiated in the complete destruction of a vast quantity of agricultural property belonging to a gentleman named [Robert] Castle . . . The barns, I am given to understand, were fired first, or rather discovered to be on fire; but scarcely had the discovery been made, than the stacks of corn, haulm, &c. of many hundred pounds' value, were in a complete blaze, and beyond human power to control.

The *Times* of 30 October added: "It is supposed that the bare fact of Mr. Castle's having a threshing machine on his premises was the cause of this visitation, as a better man or master, we understand, cannot exist."

By the beginning of November the laborers of many villages in Berkshire and, especially, Sussex were joining the action. Many attacks consisted of a band's movement from parish to parish, losing and recruiting participants as it went. During the latter half of November Berkshire and Hampshire became the principal centers of conflict, with laborers in Kent and Sussex continuing to struggle while their counterparts in Buckinghamshire, Dorset, and Wiltshire also took up the call. As the rebellions subsided in December, adjacent regions predominated. On the itineraries of our 285 Swing events we find 620 different locations, a little over two locations per CG. They were distributed as indicated in Table 7.10.

December's mopping up occurred outside the main regions of previous Swing activity. Except for sporadic arson, the chief forms of laborers' collective action then subsided rapidly. From 1831 through 1834 only five of the 4,484 CGs involved machine-breaking of any kind, and only two of them were agricultural: attacks on threshing machines at William Cross's farm near Dover (November 1831) and at Mr. Faircloth's farm in Croydon with Clapton (Cambridgeshire, September 1832). A venerable variety of vengeance was vanishing.

Radicals quickly seized upon the Swing events as material for their own propaganda. On 6 October the prolific propagandist Henry Hetherington issued a broadsheet titled "'Swing,' Eh?" concerning the rick-burning and machine-smashing of Kent. He used the recent Belgian revolution to suggest the possibility of revolution in Great Britain. Citing the *Brighton Gazette*, Hetherington attributed tight organization and radical intentions to the smashers and burners. "The Gentlemen and Farmers of Kent are in the greatest consternation," he reported:

> on account of the organized system of conflagration, from which so many of them have suffered. Every man who has ever employed an Irishman is in constant dread of a visit. The insurgents go about in bands

Table 7.10. Locations of Swing events, August–December 1830

County	August–October	November 1–15	November 16–30	December	Total
Berkshire	0	26	85	0	111
Buckinghamshire	0	0	22	7	29
Dorset	0	1	14	1	16
Hampshire	0	1	134	6	141
Kent	24	21	22	0	67
Sussex	0	51	31	3	85
Wiltshire	0	9	68	0	77
Other	0	1	68	25	94
Total	24	110	444	42	620

of one hundred and fifty, and coolly demand the keys of the barns to destroy the thrashing machines, and all idea of resistance is out of the question. Indeed, when gentlemen have applied to their servants to assist them in repelling the attack, they have meet [*sic*] with a flat refusal. The signals are given by sky-rocket and as many as fourteen stack-yards have been in flames at the same time. There has long been a sullen discontent among the peasantry of England; may the Aristocracy take warning in this. *The Sheffield Courant,* in noticing the Belgium affair, very properly remarks, "If we do not mistake the indications which appear in the political horizon, there are dangers nearer home, and on all sides, which our government may be too blind to see, but which, nevertheless, threaten Europe with terrible, sweeping, and extensive convulsions." (HO 40/25)

The broadsheet concluded oddly but ominously with the classic radical document "Nice Pickings," a list of the scandalous emoluments enjoyed by peers, bishops, and high officers of the realm. Nevertheless, the laborers of Kent, Berkshire, Hampshire, Sussex, and Wiltshire concentrated their claims almost exclusively on their own declining material situation, calling for short-term remedies to their own shrinking employments and incomes. In those regards they clung to eighteenth-century precedents. Meanwhile in London and elsewhere workers were joining with others in demands for long-term changes on a national scale.

Time for Reform

From 1830 to 1832 Great Britain experienced its greatest popular mobilization so far, a huge new campaign for parliamentary reform. The campaign drew on long-established networks of radicals and reformers. It drew heavily on the model, legal precedent, and organization left by the struggle over Catholic Emancipation. After defeat of the renewed bid for Emancipation in 1825, for example, a group close to Henry Hunt had formed the Friends of Civil and Religious Liberty. They aimed to link demands for parliamentary reform and religious inclusion. For several years they concentrated on private discussions and the distribution of tracts. Daniel O'Connell's election from Clare in 1828 opened the possibility that O'Connell would come to Westminster and claim his seat, thus daring the government to reject him. The prospect of a victorious alliance among reformers, Protestant Dissenters, Catholics, and Irish glimmered brighter than it had for years. The Friends began monthly meetings concentrating on Catholic Emancipation and the repeal of the Test and Corporation Acts while linking both to more general reforms.

The Friends of Civil and Religious Liberty subsided when O'Connell proved willing to compromise—or at least to postpone—reform as English radicals conceived of it in exchange for Emancipation. The settlement of 1829 that O'Connell helped negotiate actually restricted the Irish franchise, dissolved the Catholic Association, and gave Ireland's Lord Lieutenant extensive authority to ban any new popular associations. Nevertheless, the government's accession to demands forwarded by mass-membership associations tacitly recognized the right of British subjects to make other claims by means of similar associations. Thereafter, associational agitation multiplied.

In the aftermath of Emancipation's passage, indeed, Cobbett joined with Hunt and other activist members of the Friends to create the Friends of Radical Reform, soon to be known as the Radical Reform Association. In etymologically appropriate form, the word "radical" implied going to the root of the difficulty, as the Friends understood it: the need for manhood suffrage, the ballot, and annual election of Parliament. With the crucial qualification that most radicals joined the day's reformers in considering women and children to be politically unqualified dependents whose interests adult males could adequately represent, they were calling implicitly for popular sovereignty.

The new association again organized public meetings at the Mechanics' Institute until the mechanics, troubled by the dangerous pronouncements of Hunt, Cobbett, Robert Taylor, Richard Carlile, and Robert Owen on religion and politics, expelled them in April 1830 (MC 27 October 1830). The radicals soon began holding their public meetings at Southwark's Rotunda, which Carlile leased in May. It rapidly became London's principal platform for advocacy of thoroughgoing reform. "Rotundanist" or "Rotundist" became a local synonym for flaming radical.

London's agitation paralleled, and sometimes followed, mobilization elsewhere in the United Kingdom. In May 1829 Birmingham's ultra-Tory banker and currency reformer Thomas Attwood called explicitly for "Union—such as the Irish exhibited" as a means of organizing the middle and lower classes (Flick 1978: 18). Ultras argued that Parliament had passed Catholic Emancipation contrary to popular will, that broadening the franchise would therefore make it possible to reverse the wrong, or at least to prevent future outrages against the British heritage. Following this logic, in December of 1829 Attwood and other Birmingham Tories made an unlikely (some Tories thought unholy) coalition with local radicals. In January 1830 they announced the formation of a Birmingham Political Union (alias General Political Union of the Industrious Classes, for the Protection of Public Rights) dedicated to parliamentary reform. Political unions differed from other political associations precisely in their bundling together of diverse interests around the single issue of reform.

Without sharing Attwood's advocacy of paper money as the cure for most political ills or the Birmingham group's preference for household over manhood suffrage, Hunt, Cobbett, O'Connell (now an MP, back among the reformers, and already participating in the Birmingham Union), and others soon organized for London a Metropolitan Political Union as the next step toward a national organization. O'Connell's participation put that master-agitator's experience with Catholic Emancipation directly at their disposal. Hunt now saw the Radical Reform Association as a sort of steering committee for the mass-membership unions. The RRA and the MPU did not survive the year—cantankerous Cobbett, for one, broke with them almost immediately—but political unions soon became major vehicles of popular mobilization for reform throughout Great Britain.

As Hunt and his friends used the Radical Reform Association to spearhead their efforts in London, Britain's political entrepreneurs took advantage of greater governmental tolerance toward associational activity by forming hundreds of new associations to promote particular versions of reform. Political Unions, which proliferated throughout Great Britain in 1831 and 1832, offered the most successful model, although affiliates of the more radical and working-class National Union of the Working Classes gave them vigorous competition for a time. Once associations established constituencies, their activists often fanned out in two non-associational directions: holding meetings for the general public on issues of national concern, and placing such issues on the agendas of authorized assemblies such as wardmotes, ratepayers' meetings, and vestries. The latter tactic also served to nationalize local issues as in the campaign against select vestries—oligarchies in the realm of parish religious administration—between 1828 and 1834.

In the elections of July August 1830 impelled by George IV's death, parliamentary reform became a major campaign issue. With the mercurial Cobbett's support, Hunt stood unsuccessfully on a reform program in Preston, which already enjoyed an extremely broad franchise; he was finally to win a seat there in a December by-election. A number of MPs elected in the summer, including Henry Brougham, committed themselves to action on reform in the upcoming session. After the French revolution of late July, reformers began holding meetings in honor of the French and sending celebratory delegations to Paris. Wellington and Peel, however, announced their opposition to reform.

As 1830's fall parliamentary session approached, radicals and reformers began to knot together working-class mobilization, opposition to the police, condemnation of Wellington and Peel, advocacy of reform, menacing references to Swing, and invocation of the recent French revolution as a symbol of popular sovereignty—or at least as a threat of what might happen if the government blocked peaceful efforts at reform. A handbill signed "A True Englishman" commented on the scuffles of 8 November in these terms:

> Remember what the French and the Belgians have done! and what a pitiless, helpless, and cowardly people we seem. One hour of true liberty is worth ages of slavery! Consider, is it not more praiseworthy to meet a honorable death in defending your rights, than quietly die of starvation. Starvation stares you in the face, your wives, your families are starving, while your oppressors are rolling in luxury and wealth. Who began the riots on Tuesday? PEEL'S BLOOD-THIRSTY GANG. You are not Englishmen if suffer your heads to be wantonly broken by that Bloody Gang.
>
> Birmingham, Warwickshire, Kent, Essex, Sussex &c. are coming to assist us.
>
> Whatever you do, GET ARMS! BE FIRM; and the cause of Liberty will Triumph!!! (HO 44/22)

Some government agent or supporter may have designed this particular handbill to justify repression; spies and provocateurs abounded in 1830. But many authentic radical writings in the same vein circulated. When the increasingly reactionary poet-essayist Robert Southey came across a similar handbill later in November, "I deemed it my duty to lose no time in sending it to the Home Office" (Southey 1850: VI, 122).

For these reasons, both radicals and conservatives of the time often discussed the possibility of revolution. Once again they frequently referred to France as a model or a threat. After the French Revolution of 1830, even normally prudent Francis Place spoke the language of revolution—at least when it served his purpose. By then almost sixty years old, Place had been managing reformist and working-class politics for nearly forty years. Since his retirement from the tailoring business in 1817 he had worked close to full time at political entrepreneurship. From his leadership in the London Corresponding Society during the early 1790s to his daring advocacy of contraception (1820s) and engineering of the repeal of the Combination Acts' repeal (1824), he had long displayed an unusual combination of determination, resourcefulness, and political moderation. He had always, for example, rejected in principle the programs of mass insurrection that gained significant followings in the 1790s and again between Waterloo and Peterloo.

Place had little sympathy for street demonstrations, claiming: "that these mobs were composed of idle and miserable people who had no bond of union, no special and particular purpose, to induce them to hold together, nothing indeed to induce them to come together but a vague hope of plunder and that consequently as a body they were remarkably cowardly, that if attacked in a proper manner and treated as they deserved to be, there would soon be an end to all such mobs, and to all rioting" (BL ADD 27789). He accordingly advised Superintendent Thomas of the Metropolitan Police's C Division to have the force break up crowds with massed truncheons instead of attempting individual arrests; beginning with the street fights of 8 and 9 November 1830, the tactic caught on and spread with the London police model to the rest of the world (Palmer 1988).

In the spirit of Benthamite political economy, furthermore, Place maintained deep suspicion of national workers' unions. In October 1831 he was to reply to John Doherty's declaration that the people must seize reform by force with the remark that "it was absurd to expect such a combination among the working people as would enable them to defeat the army and others who would not quietly submit to be plundered. That the working people unaided by the middle class never had accomplished any national movement, and that it was insane in him to suppose that they could effect any change by force" (Wallas 1898: 266). Yet in 1830 Place waved the flag of revolution at Parliament in the manner of a roadworker who stops traffic to make way for heavy equipment: watch out, follow my signals, or you might get hurt!

Place mastered the art of writing quotable (hence publishable) letters for effect; we must always locate his correspondence in its strategic context. In 1830 he was trying to convince members of Parliament that timely concessions to reform would forestall widespread rebellion. At the start of November 1830 he wrote to his longtime collaborator MP Joseph Hume:

> There must be a radical change, not a sham reform but a radical change from the top to the bottom, and this you may if you please call a Revolution. The whole scheme of our Government is essentially corrupt, and no corrupt system ever yet reformed itself. Our System could not reform itself if it would. Take away the corruption and nothing remains. His Dukeship and his coadjutors know this as well as I do, but they think they can continue to cajole the people. Catholic Emancipation was to appease them. Repeal of taxes on Beer and on Leather was to satisfy them . . . But we are told: if all concession be refused the people will become outrageous, and no one can tell what may follow. Yes, I think any one can tell. There will be much grumbling and meeting and petitioning will follow. They will become more and more dissatisfied, and in time they will use force and after a while they will triumph. This is inevitable. (BL ADD 35148, LXXIX, 1 November 1830)

Writing to MP John Cam Hobhouse on 8 November (the very day of the radical march across Blackfriars Bridge), Place qualified his position. He cheered the king's cancellation of his "paltry contemptible procession to Guildhall" but urged that Hobhouse restrain his fellow reformers from forcing out the Tory government; better, Place thought, to let the Tories display their incompetence. He argued that "a present change of ministers would do more towards producing, or rather accelerating a revolution than all the other circumstances of the times taken together, and the time is not yet come when a radical change can be made either so effectually as to prevent other similar changes, or so beneficially as to answer the purposes of any class of reformers" (Rowe 1970: 9). Place did not, it seems, find the time ripe for revolution.

Home Secretary Peel nevertheless thought the threat sufficiently serious to justify repression. Steeped in his Irish experience, he had hoped, as radicals complained, that the New Police would help contain London's popular agitation (Palmer 1988). He consulted his law officers about prosecuting Cobbett, Hunt, or Carlile for their speeches at the Rotunda on 6, 8, and 9 November; the lawyers replied that juries would probably not find them seditious. By December, however, Solicitor General Gurney was remarking that on successive nights Cobbett, Hunt, Carlile, Taylor, John Gale Jones, and others "utter seditious inflammatory & blasphemous language of the most Shocking description before large Assemblages of persons who are attracted there by large printed Bills affix'd at the Doors & placarded about streets"; he then recommended prosecution (HO 48/28). During the following months the government did prosecute Cobbett and Carlile, failing to convict the former but sending the latter to prison.

Contentious gatherings of 1831 and 1832 conformed to the reform struggle's well-known timetable, with peaks of popular activity in March to May 1831 (Commons debate and passage of the Reform Bill, rejection by the House of Lords, general election), October 1831 (second rejection by the Lords, followed by violent demonstrations in Derby, Nottingham, Bristol, and elsewhere), and May 1832 (defeat of Whig government in Lords, failure to form Tory government, king's agreement to create new peers favorable to reform, return of Grey ministry, all to the background of frenzied political activity through much of Great Britain). Popular claim-making generally took the forms that had become standard during the previous decade: public meetings, demonstrations, petitions, creation of associations, conversion of elections into displays of popular support and opposition. Opponents and, especially, proponents of parliamentary reform plunged into social-movement activity.

This does not mean British claim-makers faded into gray decorum. At each juncture in the national struggle over reform, crowds somewhere in Britain not only marched, shouted, and displayed banners on behalf of their cause but also lit bonfires, burned effigies of anti-reformers, sacked their houses, and broke the windows of citizens who failed to illuminate at the call for celebration. As the reform campaign heated up in March and April 1831, for example, Scotland exploded with raucous demonstrations in Edinburgh, Avendale, Dalkeith, Dundee, Glasgow, and elsewhere.

In Bristol, when the anti-reform MP Charles Wetherell came to preside over jail delivery for the Spring Assizes of 1831, his opponents anticipated the greeting that would open three days of deadly violence when he returned at the end of October. On 9 April, as Wetherell arrived,

> An immense number of the populace met him at Totterdown, and saluted him with a general groan, which evidently startled him. He soon, however, recovered, and although the vociferations and groans became at times deafening, he affected to be unconscious of the scene. In the hall the tumult was renewed, accompanied by stamping of feet, when the Recorder [that is, Wetherell] said, if any person was taken into custody for disturbing the peace of the Court, he would instantly commit him. Another mode of annoyance was then resorted to, namely, the interruption of the reading of the Commission by violent coughing. At the conclusion loud cries of Boroughbridge were heard, and three cheers were given for reform. (MC 16 April 1831; although he served as Bristol's recorder, Wetherell represented Boroughbridge, Yorkshire, a rotten ["nomination"] borough where Sir Francis Burdett had held his first parliamentary seat, in Parliament)

When Wetherell reentered Bristol from Totterdown on 29 October, a waiting crowd stoned the constables sent to protect him, and violence escalated from there. Disguised as a postillion, Wetherell barely escaped the city's flaming Queen Square (Phillips 1992). But in April he already personified opposition to reform.

On 25 April, after London's Lord Mayor called for a general illumination and bell-ringing in honor of the king's dissolution of Parliament, setting the example by a brilliant lighting up of Mansion House, citizens rushed to display pro-reform lights and transparencies; in Blackheath, the owner of the Duke of Northumberland pub decked out his sign in mourning to signal his displeasure with the duke's opposition to reform. Throughout the London area crowds shattered the windows of unilluminated houses, including the Duke of Newcastle's mansion in Portman Square.

During the elections of spring 1831 nonvoters throughout Great Britain thronged the hustings and often intervened forcibly in the proceedings. In staunchly reformist Carmarthen, at the electoral assembly of 29 April 1831, "after the preliminary proceedings had been gone through and after John Jones Esquire the late member for the said Borough and John George

Phillips the Opposing Candidate had been put in nomination there appeared in the said Hall a very numerous assemblage of persons who acted in concert together as an Organized Mob and conducted themselves in a most tumultuous and riotous manner menacing and threatening all who might come forward as voters for the said John Jones" (HO 52/16, deposition of chief constable James Evans, 2 May 1831). For two days the nonvoting invaders were able to chase away anyone who tried to speak or vote for Jones, who had served in Parliament since 1815 and had represented the borough since 1821, but had brought popular thunder on himself by opposing the Reform Bill. They were unable, however, to prevent his eventual reelection.

So it went through the 670 CGs of March–May 1831: a whole country focused on parliamentary politics as never before (or at least not since 1689), a moving web of associations and political entrepreneurs, constant interplay between governmental politics and local affairs, the tempo of social movements. The 314 contentious events of October 1831 intensified and magnified the same sorts of actions—more marches, more bands and banners, more cheers for reformers and groans for anti-reformers, more immolated effigies, more window-breaking, more pitched battles with constables or troops, and meetings, meetings, meetings, overwhelmingly in favor of parliamentary reform. In the vast London demonstration of 12 October, according to the *Morning Chronicle* for the 13th, "about 300,000 inhabitants of the metropolis—chiefly tradespeople and industrious artisans, with the Parochial Officers at their head—walked in procession from their respective parishes to St. James's Palace."

The struggles of October brought political entrepreneurship to full flower. The newly formed National Political Union became an object of contention among factions led by Sir Francis Burdett (who favored concentrating on the Reform Bill), Francis Place (who advocated a broad alliance), and William Lovett (who held to the radical program), with Place maneuvering furiously to exclude Rotunda men from positions of prominence. It was a time of coffee-shop consultations, marches, and incessant public meetings. Even Place, whose preferred *modus operandi* kept him well behind the scenes, appeared by name in reports of a dozen public meetings from November 1831 to May 1832. Public displays of support for reform formed the roiled surface of a heaving sea.

The crisis of May 1832 therefore differed from its predecessors: not just more intense, but more controlled, more strongly oriented to pressure on the government, and especially the House of Lords, with programs to withhold taxes, to undertake a general strike, to have the Commons suspend government payments, to organize a run on the gold supply, to have the king name pro-reform peers. May's 294 CGs certainly included meetings aplenty—a full 260 of them—but they showed the marks of political entrepreneurship as never before. Despite persisting divisions among reformers (MP Henry Hunt, after all, was opposing the Reform Bill within Parliament and on the streets as a snare and delusion), the country came far closer than before to experiencing a single cleavage with credible force and genuine interests on both sides of the line.

The height of the crisis arrived with Wellington's unsuccessful attempt to form a government (12–18 May), which polarized the entire country and made some sort of revolution seem possible. Yet actual violence declined: verbs of attack characterized 4.6 percent of the action in the CGs of March-May 1831, 11.3 percent in October 1831, but only 1.6 percent in May 1832, while deaths in collective contention ran as indicated in Table 7.11. Merthyr Tydfil (June 1831), Bristol (October 1831), and three extraneous run-ins between smugglers and tax agents (February 1832) leave the dark spots on this calendar. From November through the Bill's passage in June, politically incited violence subsided dramatically. The coalition for reform—or rather against anti-reform—had achieved a remarkable focus and discipline.

Table 7.11. Deaths in contentious gatherings, January 1831 to June 1832

January 1831	0	October 1831	25
February 1831	0	November 1831	0
March 1831	0	December 1831	4
April 1831	0	January 1832	1
May 1831	1	February 1832	6
June 1831	17	March 1832	1
July 1831	1	April 1832	2
August 1831	2	May 1832	0
September 1831	2	June 1832	1

Fortunately, we do not have to determine the exact contribution of popular contention to the Reform Bill's passage, an exercise in hypotheticals that would require a much more extensive analysis of governmental decisionmaking and parliamentary politics than I have attempted here. The reform crisis suggests a number of important conclusions about popular contention in Britain: its strong, continuous, and increasing interaction with the high politics of parties and alliances; the consolidation of a cosmopolitan, autonomous, modular, cumulative, social-movement repertoire that had been falling into place piece by piece for several decades; the declining range and salience of the parochial, bifurcated, and particularized repertoires that had prevailed sixty or seventy years earlier; the importance of the struggle over Catholic Emancipation and its outcome in 1829 as a model, legal precedent, and source of organization for subsequent political mobilization; similar influence of the reform mobilization on post-reform politics, notably working-class attempts to acquire a share of national power; perpetuation of something we can reasonably call mass national politics with a popular voice.

Workers

When we close in on organized workers as such, however, we discover that the reform mobilization fails to exhaust, or even to describe, their history; action on issues of employment, production, and consumption followed a parallel but partly independent evolution. Between 1828 and 1834 British workers' claim-making ranged from Rough Music to rebellion to mass meetings and centrally organized strikes, with increasing emphasis on sustained action on a large scale. Our catalog from 1831 onward includes only two attacks on threshing machines and three episodes of industrial machine-breaking. Rough Music, donkeying, and similar forms of public humiliation likewise fell into decline. The period's only instances of donkeying, for example, took place in 1829—one in Norwich and three in the vicinity of Coventry. In all four cases the action blended into a workers' demonstration. The *Times* of 12 January clipped this report from the *Norwich Mercury:* "A large body of weavers paraded the streets on Monday, with three persons tied into a donkey-cart, with a label purporting them to have taken work under price. They were continually hooted, and all kind of filth thrown at them by the persons who accompanied the cart. We understand another person was taken out of his loom in his shirt-sleeves, and carried some distance." In Coventry and nearby outweaving villages such as Nuneaton and Bedworth, master ribbonmakers began introducing engine looms, displacing handloom weavers, and cutting their wages during the late 1820s. By May 1829 weavers were organizing major resistance.

During a ribbonweavers' turnout at Nuneaton, where a crowd of 500 or so had broken into a weaver's house to seize and donkey Coventry foreman John Taylor on 16 September 1829, even more action occurred the following Monday, 21 September:

a large body of Ribbon-weavers and other persons assembled in the Market-place at Nuneaton, and proceeded from thence to Nuneaton common, a place about half-a-mile distant from the town. Here they entered the house of a weaver, named Charles Lakin, and forcibly taking him from his abode, placed him on an ass, and conveyed him back, amidst the revilings of the mob, through Nuneaton to Attleborough, a hamlet close to the town. The offence for which this person was "donkeyed," as it was termed, was taking out work at a reduced price. At Attleborough, Lakin was released from his punishment, and another man, of the name of Longelow, mounted on the ass, and taken to Nuneaton, by a process similar to the foregoing; where he was set at liberty, in order that John Ellis, another obnoxious individual, might also be "donkeyed," but he could not be found; the mob then broke several windows in his house; from thence the rioters returned to Nuneaton-common, where they demolished upwards of 150 panes of glass in the factory of a person named Phillips, an extensive undertaker—that is, a kind of intermediate agent between the manufacturer and the journeymen. After this feat the mob dispersed. (MC 26 September 1829)

During the same turnout workers donkeyed two more of their fellows in nearby Bedworth during the next few days, then on Monday 28 September, "several hundred persons assembled on the road leading from Bedworth to Coventry, with a flag carried by two men, bearing the following inscription:—'Jackass them that work.' A donky [*sic*] was led by the side of these standard bearers, who carried the decree on their flag into effect both on men and women. Tickets for bread were distributed at different houses for the persons in distress" (LT 3 October 1829). Thus a classic humiliating ritual merged into a disciplined demonstration. From that point, industrial conflict continued to rage, but donkeying itself disappeared, at least through the end of 1834.

Our catalogs of CGs vastly underrepresent turnouts and strikes, for three reasons: our London-based sources gave less attention to events of all kinds outside the Southeast, while most turnouts and strikes took place outside; the same sources tended to neglect industrial conflicts unless they displayed exceptional features such as substantial violence; and our own rules included gatherings only if the reports explicitly described an assembly; in fact, few reports of turnouts or strikes did so. With these qualifications, the 73 CGs between 1828 and 1834 representing strikes or turnouts distribute approximately as other sources might lead us to expect: accelerating from late 1830 through the end of 1831 and again through most of 1834, concentrating in northern industrial districts, dividing roughly between craft-wide turnouts in areas of small-scale production and firm-by-firm shutdowns in areas and industries of concentrated capital. Treated as illegal or semilegal actions by local authorities and directed chiefly at localized clusters of masters, turnouts and strikes had none of the neat regularity and uniformity that public meetings and political demonstrations were taking on during the 1830s.

Larger strikes edged over into rebellion when challenged, as at Merthyr Tydfil during June 1831. In that Welsh town of iron mines and mills, a radical political union had spearheaded support for parliamentary reform in 1830, but the trade union federations that were proliferating elsewhere did not become visible until late in 1831, after the conflicts of June. During early phases of the electoral campaign in April–May 1831, hundreds of iron workers attended meetings, burned effigies, broke windows, and marched against enemies of reform. Three issues focused workers' local action at the same time: (1) wage reductions and layoffs at the Cyfarthfa mine and ironworks, (2) seizures of property for debt and assessment of damages against the window-breakers of April 1831 by the Merthyr Court of Requests, and (3) forestalling in the food market.

By 1 June workers were marching with reform banners, attacking the premises of high-priced shopkeepers and Court of Request officers, and taking back property the Court had confiscated. The following day:

The men who were standing out collected together in great numbers on Thursday, and being instigated by several men of bad character (some of whom have had their goods seized for debts contracted, and for which they were sued by the Court of Requests), they proceeded in large bodies to the house of Mr. Coffin, who is an officer of that Court, and demanded the books belonging to it, which being refused, they became very riotous and tumultuous, threatening to murder Mr. Coffin and others. It was at this period that the Magistrates got upon some chairs, but were very cruelly insulted by the mob, and were obliged to desist. They then broke into Coffin's house, smashed all his windows, and gutted the place of every article of furnitures, which they burnt in a heap in the middle of the street. (MC 11 June 1831)

On Friday 3 June a crowd surrounded a troop of 68 Highlanders, attacked the soldiers after failed negotiations, stoned them, and finally received their gunfire; eventually 16 people or more died of their wounds (Williams 1978). Squire and surgeon William Thomas reported that Lewis Lewis (alias Lewis the Huntsman) had climbed up a lamppost to say in Welsh, "We are met here to have our wages raised instead of which the Master's have brought the soldiers against us. Now, boys, if you are of the same mind as I am let us fall upon them and take their arms away" (deposition of 17 June 1831, HO 52/16, rough version, punctuation supplied); then the crowd began to press the troops, and the slaughter began. From Friday 3 June to Monday 6 June impromptu insurgents controlled Merthyr Tydfil. Only the deployment of hundreds of troops on Monday broke up a movement that had begun to connect miners and ironworkers throughout the region.

Eventually the magistrates charged 28 people, 2 of them women, tried 9 people before abandoning the prosecutions, condemned 5 to death, but actually hanged only 1, the legendary Richard Lewis, or Dic Penderyn; Lewis Lewis received a death sentence, then a commutation of his sentence to transportation (Williams 1978). Thenceforth political and workers' unions made the town a major center of Welsh militancy. By early August Anthony Hill was writing Melbourne from near Merthyr that "my workmen are still busily engaged in forming & maturing Union Lodges; and that the miners & colliers, most evidently do not settle to their work, as heretofore . . . they are only waiting some demonstration elsewhere and the removal of the Military, to exhibit their dissatisfaction & revenge, in fresh tumult" (HO 52/16, 3 August 1831).

During the summer and fall oath-taking workers' unions multiplied in Merthyr Tydfil and environs, mobilizing a great miners' strike firm by firm in September. Owners struck back by discharging union leaders and locking out their workers. By November 12 a correspondent was writing to the Monmouthshire newspaper *Merlin:* "This place is in a dreadful state. The moment the news arrived of the disturbance in Bristol, the Union Clubs all met—what happened I know not. All is quiet, but everyone is apprehensive. Thousands are out of employment and starving. The men know all that passes, and are evidently plotting. They talk of revolution" (Edwards 1926: 27). The unions were everywhere, and so was struggle.

From that point on, indeed, the very right to organize became a major issue for workers throughout Great Britain. More so than the 1820s, the 1830s saw repeated short-lived efforts to create general or national workers' federations combining economic and political programs: the National Union of the Working Classes, the National Association for the Protection of Labour, the General Trades Union, the Grand National Consolidated Trades Union all surged for a year or two, then subsided. Authorities watched these organizations and their subsidiaries closely for signs of insurrection and treasonous conspiracy, prosecuted their periodicals for failure to pay the stamp tax, but did not challenge their right to existence; given the simultaneous proliferation of bourgeois associations, such a challenge would have been difficult to sustain. Hence some of the surprise and indignation that greeted sentencing to transportation of the six agricultural laborers of Tolpuddle, Dorset, for violating the mutiny-inspired Unlawful Oaths Act of 1797 by swearing in members of their local mutual aid society—one of three prosecutions under the 1797 Act in 1834 (Orth 1991). Protests and demands for remission of the sentences came from great gatherings in Birmingham, Newcastle, Leeds, Huddersfield, Manchester, Oldham, Greenwich, and London, the most spectacular being the march of at least 25,000 workers, coordinated by the GNCTU, from Islington to St. James's to Southwark on 21 April.

The bourgeoisie did not remain silent. In adjacent columns of the *Times* for 3 May 1834 appeared the announcement of a Manchester meeting to discuss "the present critical situation in which trades' unions and associations are involved in consequence of the uncalled-for and severe interference of the Executive power" and a report from an inhabitants' meeting of Newbury and Speenhamland at which "Some members of the unions attended the meeting and were heard with attention, but their statements were not calculated to remove the impression that almost unanimously exists here against the improper formation of these clubs, or societies, or lodges, or any other cognomen by which they are known."

On 2 May inhabitants of St. Paul's, Covent Garden, met in the Vestry Room and passed a resolution reading: "The Meeting viewed with regret and alarm the combination of vast numbers of the working classes, who, influenced by interested and designing men, not only presumed, in the most arbitrary manner, to dictate to their employers, but, by acts of intimidation and violence, compelled the cooperation of many of their well-disposed fellow workmen, to the great inconvenience of trade, to the serious loss and injury to themselves and families, and to the disturbance of the public peace" (MC 3 May 1834). The final drive for parliamentary reform had depended on an uneasy coalition among masters, merchants, and workers, but had enfranchised many antagonists of workers' organizations while excluding most workers. In that regard it had sharpened the opposition of labor and capital in Great Britain.

During the years from 1828 to 1834 the expansion of capitalist property relations had profound but indirect effects on popular contention. True, in the period's strike waves and in the Swing rebellion we can see a relatively direct connection between capitalization and proletarianization, on one side, and demands for protection of workers, on the other. The underemployment of agricultural laborers and handloom weavers motivated a number of defensive actions on their parts. But the critical changes occurred in the organization of struggle: rising importance of special-purpose associations and federations as vehicles for workers' demands, expanded involvement of workers in national political campaigns, movement of workers toward the quest for explicitly political rights, politicization of conflicts between workers and employers over issues that had previously seemed alien to national politics. The junction of issues in Merthyr Tydfil's bitter strike illustrates perfectly the great politicization of economic relations that was taking place.

Glimmers of Revolution

Divisions ran deep in the Britain of 1830 to 1834, then, but did they approach revolutionary strength? In his great parliamentary speech of 2 March 1831 on behalf of reform, Macaulay said as much:

I support this plan, because I am sure that it is our best security against a revolution . . . We say, and we say justly, that it is not by mere numbers, but by property and intelligence, that the nation ought to be governed. Yet, saying this, we exclude from all share in the government great masses of property and intelligence, great numbers of those who are most interested in preserving tranquillity, and who know best how to preserve it. We do more. We drive over to the side of revolution those whom we shut out from power. (Macaulay 1900: I, 4–5)

Macaulay was not alone. Francis Place, we have seen, repeatedly conjured up revolutionary specters as he argued for orderly, moderate reform. Of May 1832 he later wrote, "The great peculiarity causing a difference between the Political Unions and the Unions of the working classes was, that the first desired the reform bill to prevent a revolution, the last desired its destruction as the means of producing a revolution" (BL ADD 27793). Place recollected that radicals then hoped or feared that Wellington would seize power by military means and provoke a rebellion. Critics of the government repeatedly flew the French tricolor and held out the French people as a revolutionary example. Amid all this talk of revolution, how close did Great Britain come?

A well-built revolution-detector would have two dials, one for revolutionary situations and the other for revolutionary outcomes. The gauge for revolutionary situations would measure how close a country came to dual or multiple sovereignty, in which at least two political blocs were exercising effective control over significant segments (territorial or administrative) of state power and each received compliance from some portion of the citizenry. The gauge for revolutionary outcomes, in contrast, would measure the extent to which state power actually changed hands, how fast, and how durably. In the French Revolution of 1830, for example, the situations dial of our imaginary machine would show high values from roughly 27 July (when barricades went up in working-class neighborhoods of Paris) to 4 August (when supporters of Louis-Philippe had displaced Bourbon authorities in the parallel insurrections of Toulouse, Bordeaux, Lille, Amiens, and Dijon); although struggles in the countryside continued through the fall and major new insurrections occurred in 1831 and 1832, full-fledged revolutionary situations opened up in Paris and elsewhere for about ten days. As for revolutionary outcomes, the gauge would show a significant change of regime effected quite rapidly, with a new royal line and a substantially renovated governmental staff in place throughout the country by late August, but only minor alterations in class power vis-à-vis the state. In neither regard would the July Revolution set off the high readings of the decade from 1789 to 1799, with its repeated deep divisions of public power, its prolonged civil wars, and its lurches from one ruling coalition to the next.

On such an instrument, how would British history register from the 1750s to the 1830s? On the situational dial, we might see vibrations in 1768–1769 (the Wilkes crisis), 1795–1797 (interlocking of subsistence struggles, radical activism, and mutinies), 1816–1820 (Peterloo, workers' attacks and rebellions, Queen Caroline) and 1830–1832 (from Swing to the Reform Bill), but none of the four readings would pass the critical level; if in 1832 withholding of taxes, a run on the banks, or armed insurrection had actually occurred under the control of radicals and reformers, that might have brought Britain into the dial's red zone. But none of these things happened. On the side of revolutionary outcomes, a long-run transfer of power from landed magnates toward commercial and industrial capitalists did occur, but with nothing like revolutionary speed. In 1830–1832 the expansion of the electorate, the weakening of patrimonial control over state office, and the soon-ruptured reform coalition of bourgeois and workers had revolutionary resonance, but no more than that. Both Catholic Emancipation and reform altered the operation of the British polity over the long run without constituting revolutionary breaks in the short run. Despite the talk of tricolors and anti-Parliaments, Great Britain remained well within the perimeter of non-revolution.

Readings change if we shift to the British Isles as a whole. For in Ireland from 1798 to 1803 the British state faced open insurrections backed by French intervention. Effective opposition to British rule reached revolutionary proportions in 1798, when large parts of the island fell under rebel control, and persisted intermittently until the crushing of Robert Emmet's attempted Dublin insurrection of 1803. Indeed, if we include Ireland, that breeding-ground of British repressive organization, British history from the fifteenth century to the present suddenly looks much more revolutionary. Within England, Wales, and Scotland, nevertheless, nothing like a full-fledged revolutionary situation, much less a revolutionary outcome, has appeared since the Scottish rising of 1745–1746.

Short of revolution, the successive popular mobilizations and parliamentary actions of 1828–1834 deeply altered British politics. The successful campaigns for repeal of Test and Corporation and for Catholic Emancipation weakened Anglican hegemony while loosening the tie between religious affiliation and relations with the government. Swing's repression practically eliminated machine-breaking and laborers' marches from the rural collective-action repertoire after rewarding them briefly. In Shrewsbury and elsewhere, reform mobilization and its outcome increased political partisanship and strengthened the connections between local and national political concerns (Phillips and Wetherell 1991). The arrival of bourgeois reformers in Parliament facilitated the elimination of select vestries, the passage of a Factory Act, the abolition of slavery, and the enactment of a New Poor Law.

More generally, popular politics nationalized as the role of Parliament became even more salient. Although workers continued to battle for the right to act in concert against their employers, for other purposes the public meeting, the demonstration, the petition drive, the formation of specialized associations, and related forms of social-movement politics became the standard means for pressing popular collective claims. Chartism, for all its division between proponents of physical force and political appeals, inherited the mighty accumulation of political experience, connections, and rights that occurred between 1828 and 1834. Mass popular politics had arrived on a national scale.

❦ 8 ❧

FROM DONKEYING TO DEMONSTRATING

HISTORY IS A FOREST of a million trees. Wild beasts run through it, vines hide its branches, strange birds sing in its upper reaches, and wildflowers burst out in its clearings. It is coherent, interdependent, lawful . . . and complicated! We can explain its particular features, discover recurrent causal mechanisms in its evolution, and provide overall accounts of its changes. But woe to the ecologist or historian who seeks to catalog, reconstruct, vivisect, and explain every niche, every creature, every change of a particular forest; madness lies that way. British history from the 1750s to the 1830s offers about as thick a grove as any other three-quarters of a century in any single country, and therefore defies reduction to simple explanations. Yet it deserves careful exploration: the British thicket matters both because of what happened within it and because of its influence on other parts of the great historical woodland. Within Great Britain, durable mass national politics came into being, perhaps for the first time anywhere in the world, as capital-concentrated industrialization proceeded, proletarianization accelerated, and a warmaking state expanded its powers. Outside, pursuit of a world-spanning series of wars, construction of a great empire, penetration of distant markets with cheap manufactured goods, and export of British political models altered the lives of whole peoples in Europe, North America, and elsewhere.

On the trail of popular claim-making, we have tramped in this book through the forest of British politics from the 1750s to the 1830s. Such an itinerary does not take us very close to the springs of British foreign policy, the swamps of dynastic intrigue, or the brambles of ministerial bargaining. But it does reveal features and connections that other paths ignore: the profound, if indirect, influence of mobilization for war on the texture of popular politics, the deep alteration of contentious repertoires, the strong influence of entrepreneurship and precedent in that alteration, and much more. Previous chapters have repeatedly called attention to those features and connections without providing a general map of them or reviewing that map's adequacy. Mapping will occupy this final chapter.

Remember the destination we chose at the outset. We have been asking about changes in British popular contention—ordinary people's collective making of claims that bear on other people's interests—between the 1750s and the 1830s. What happened? How, when, and where? Why did it happen? What difference did it make? What implications does the experience have for British history in general? For European history? For our general understanding of political processes? Such queries motivate this chapter's three separate trips through the British forest: one to recast the historical narrative, another to consider implications of that recast narrative for the foundations of contention, and a third to examine implications of the same experience for the growth of mass national politics and of democracy in general.

As a reminder of what we must explain, Table 8.1 offers a numerical summary of changes in the proportions of different sorts of CG from 1758 to 1834. This way of presenting the evidence has significant limits: the categories overlap, as in the small number of routine meetings forcibly broken up by opponents, which appear here not as meetings but as violent gatherings. The absence of breakdowns by location, group, and issue hides the uneven selectivity by which changes occurred in different niches of the British polity. The forms themselves were evolving, so that elements of what would become the demonstration—a performance absent as such in the 1760s but fairly well delineated by the 1830s—show up in elections, holiday celebrations, and turnouts of the 1760s. The catalog greatly underestimates the frequency of turnouts and strikes, thereby understating workers' overall involvement in claim-making. All these features make the summary quite schematic.

Despite its limitations, the statistical evidence establishes a substantial decline in the proportion of violent gatherings such as attacks on poorhouses, affrays of hunters with game wardens, and donkeying of renegade workers from roughly 1789 onward—from 75 percent or so of all events in the early years to the order of 15 percent during the 1830s. Other

Table 8.1. Occasions of contentious gatherings, 1758–1834 (% distribution by year)

Year	Violent gathering	Other unplanned gathering	Election meeting	Authorized assembly	Association meeting	Other public meeting	Other*	Total	Number
1758	85.7	0.0	0.0	14.3	0.0	0.0	0.0	100.0	14
1759	75.0	0.0	0.0	8.3	8.3	0.0	8.3	99.9	12
1768	69.4	21.6	0.9	1.8	0.9	1.8	3.6	100.0	111
1769	28.4	19.4	11.9	32.8	3.0	1.5	3.0	100.0	67
1780	74.3	2.9	0.0	20.0	0.0	1.4	1.4	100.0	70
1781	48.3	6.9	3.4	37.9	3.4	0.0	0.0	99.9	29
1789	15.4	19.2	3.8	51.9	5.8	1.9	1.9	99.9	52
1795	15.7	13.9	0.9	55.6	6.5	4.6	2.8	100.0	108
1801	25.5	36.4	0.0	16.4	10.9	9.1	1.8	100.1	55
1807	13.0	8.3	30.6	22.2	9.3	12.0	4.6	100.0	108

									N
1811	16.7	10.4	2.1	31.3	18.8	18.8	2.1	100.2	48
1819	8.2	6.3	3.9	66.4	6.6	8.2	0.4	100.0	256
1820	8.0	15.3	4.4	40.1	8.8	13.9	9.5	100.0	274
1828	12.6	1.2	2.2	7.6	48.2	19.8	8.4	100.0	595
1829	19.8	6.4	0.8	20.1	22.9	24.6	5.3	99.9	641
1830	30.0	8.2	5.3	18.2	12.1	21.6	4.6	100.0	1,164
1831	11.0	4.7	9.9	46.9	6.4	17.3	3.8	100.0	1,645
1832	13.2	5.3	22.6	39.4	7.0	9.0	3.4	99.9	1,111
1833	11.0	7.7	5.7	47.6	8.8	16.0	3.3	100.1	674
1834	8.3	4.0	5.9	42.0	6.4	26.9	6.5	100.0	1,054
Total	16.4	6.6	8.2	34.9	11.9	17.3	4.6	99.9	8,088
N	1,327	532	663	2,826	966	1,399	375	8,088	

*Celebration, delegation, parade, demonstration, strike, turnout.

unplanned gatherings (market conflicts, nonviolent responses to the arrivals of dignitaries, heroes, or blackguards, and so on) fluctuated more than violent incidents, with a weak, irregular diminution after 1801. Collective acts of retaliation, resistance, and direct physical control lost much of the prominence they had assumed in the 1750s and 1760s.

Nonviolent, indirect, annunciatory, and preplanned interactions waxed much more than violent events waned. Authorized assemblies such as wardmotes, elections, religious ceremonies, vestry meetings, and scheduled gatherings of ratepayers became mainstays of claim-making by 1769, and occupied even larger shares of all events from 1789 onward; they reached a maximum two-thirds of all CGs in 1819. Meetings of named associations (for example, Society of Supporters of the Bill of Rights, Hampden Clubs, Catholic Association) grew more important over time, although except for the Catholic Emancipation campaign of 1828–1829 they never surpassed the proportions of local assemblies. Other public meetings (often organized by associations, but open to the general public) grew much more prominent after 1800, and by the 1830s played a large part in claim-making. Meanwhile, elections fluctuated trendlessly as a function of parliamentary history and royal successions. The crude figures indicate a decisive shift from spur-of-the-moment provocation and violent retribution toward planned gatherings aimed at declaring collective positions with regard to public issues.

What, then, must we explain? Focusing on occasions of public collective claim-making, we find large alterations in the means by which people—especially ordinary people—stated demands, complaints, and expressions of support. Before 1789, to begin with, we discover repeated occasions on which ordinary people participated in one or more of the following interactions with other people:

> *Claim-making within authorized public assemblies* (for example, Lord Mayor's Day): taking of positions by means of cheers, jeers, attacks, and displays of symbols; attacks on supporters of electoral candidates; parading and chairing of candidates; taking sides at public executions; attacks or professions of support for pilloried prisoners; salutation or deprecation of public figures (for example, royalty) at theaters; collective response to lines and characters in plays or other entertainments; breaking up of theaters at unsatisfactory performances.

Celebrations and other popularly initiated gatherings: collective cheering, jeering, or stoning of public figures or their conveyances; popularly initiated public celebrations of major events (for example, Wilkes's elections), with cheering, drinking, display of partisan symbols, fireworks, and so on, sometimes with forced participation of reluctant persons; forced illuminations, including attacks on windows of householders who fail to illuminate; faction fights (for example, Irish vs. English, rival groups of military).

Attacks on popularly designated offenses and offenders: Rough Music; ridicule and/or destruction of symbols, effigies, and/or property of public figures and moral offenders; verbal and physical attacks on malefactors seen in public places; pulling down and/or sacking of dangerous or offensive houses, including workhouses and brothels; smashing of shops and bars whose proprietors are accused of unfair dealing or of violating public morality; collective seizures of food, often coupled with sacking the merchant's premises and/or public sale of the food below current market price; blockage or diversion of food shipments; destruction of tollgates; collective invasions of enclosed land, often including destruction of fences or hedges.

Workers' sanctions over members of their trades: turnouts by workers in multiple shops of a local trade; workers' marches to public authorities in trade disputes; donkeying, or otherwise humiliating, workers who violated collective agreements; destroying goods (for example, silk in looms and/or the looms themselves) of workers or masters who violate collective agreements.

Attacks on coercive authorities: liberation of prisoners; resistance to police intervention in gatherings and entertainments; resistance to press gangs; fights between hunters and gamekeepers; battles between smugglers and royal officers; forcible opposition to evictions; military mutinies.

From their initiators' viewpoints, most of these interactions stressed resistance or revenge. Still, many of them had dual versions, expressing either denigration or approval; thus spectators at an execution could voice condemnation of either victim or executioner, while enforcers of illumination could turn quickly from celebrating in the streets to breaking unlighted windows. A number of them borrowed or parodied forms of action sometimes employed or commanded by authorities: illumination, hanging in effigy, toasts, cheers, attendance at the pillory, setting of prices, even the pulling down of condemned buildings. No one population, however, ever used more than a fraction of these contentious means, and their precise routines varied from place to place. Actual repertoires therefore differed among populations even more than the list suggests.

When it came to nobility, gentry, bourgeoisie, and some privileged groups—notably religious congregations and trades having chartered relations with public authorities—a few other performances occurred: public meetings, banquets, processions, delegations, and preparation of petitions. For all their later importance, those performances remained rare before 1789. The ruling classes, after all, constituted at maximum only one person in fifty; like most well-connected oligarchies, they enjoyed multiple means of exercising power outside of public claim-making. For the rest of the population, we can reasonably call characteristic eighteenth-century performances *parochial, particular,* and *bifurcated*—mostly local in scope, adopting forms and symbols peculiar to the relationship between claimants and the objects of their claims, either acting directly on a local relationship or asking privileged intermediaries to convey claims to more distant authorities.

Although (as we should expect) their issues and relative frequencies varied significantly from one period to another, the array of contentious forms available from the 1750s to the 1780s greatly resembled those which had prevailed during the seventeenth and early eighteenth centuries. Between James I's accession in 1603 and Charles II's flight in 1642, K. J. Lindley (1983) catalogs raucous public celebrations, attacks on popularly designated miscreants, pulling down of brothels and playhouses, and attempted rescues of prisoners—all familiar forms of claim-making during the later eighteenth century. During the Civil War, it is true, military engagements, mutinies, and collective resistance to military depredations multiplied in manners quite distinct from anything that happened within Great Britain from 1758 to 1789; that burst of activity should warn us against any strictly linear model of change, *a fortiori* against the illusion that no alterations in contention occurred before the eighteenth century. Otherwise, the destruction of enclosures, attacks on houses of public enemies, expulsions of tax collectors, and other popular interactions of the Civil War period fit easily into the eighteenth-century catalog (Underdown 1985; Morrill and Walter 1985).

Although he sometimes disguises them with the misleading labels "demonstration" and "riot", Tim Harris discovers a similar array of performances in London during the later seventeenth century. In his rich account, bonfires, burning of effigies, pulling down of brothels, and attacks on troops figure repeatedly. He shows us the importance of political clubs for the elite, as of trade groups for ordinary workers, and emphasizes the crucial place of authorized assemblies. "The typical tactic for tory crowds," he reports, "was to organize bonfires at which loyal healths were drunk, effigies of leading whigs and/or Jack Presbyter burnt, along with associated symbols such as a mock bill of exclusion or solemn league and covenant. Royal birthdays were obvious occasions for such demonstrations" (Harris 1987: 168). With different symbols and occasions, as we have seen, many similar events occurred from the 1750s to the 1790s. The chief mutation of repertoires from the reign of Charles II to the later eighteenth century seems to have been the disappearance of the quasi-military march, where "Rioters typically modelled themselves on the trained bands, dividing themselves into regiments, each with its captain and lieutenant, and each marching behind colours borne by an ensign" (ibid.: 25). In London of the 1750s and later, the only trace of this format appears in bannered processions of sailors, coalheavers, weavers, or other trades to demand redress of their masters. Although Harris is documenting a period of intense politicization, he describes an essentially parochial, particular, and bifurcated repertoire of contention.

Similarly, in 1715's London Nicholas Rogers discovers shouts against the new Hanoverian regime at the Lord Mayor's banquet, attacks on an anti-Tory preacher, cheers at the release from the pillory of a man being punished for speaking against George I, Tory-Whig street battles at a Whig mug-house, bonfires, effigies, parades, window-smashing, and the sacking of a Presbyterian meeting house—the quintessence of what I have called the eighteenth-century repertoire (Rogers 1989). The issues and actors differed considerably—1715 was not 1768 or 1780—but the array of claim-making performances on which people drew in 1715 had much in common with that of a half-century later. Around Bristol in the 1750s, Rogers chronicles the following events:

colliers' attacks on turnpike gates;
a march in which "'a mob of many hundred colliers and other
    country people headed by a captain and colours' entered Bristol

by Lawford's Gate and proceeded to the Council House to protest to the Corporation about the high price of grain and to urge that all exportation of wheat should be stopped," then boarded a ship and started to unload the grain;

a later attempt to rescue from jail one of the persons arrested on that occasion;

a consequent confrontation with soldiers from Gloucester and constables; and

a raucous election. (Rogers 1989: 291–299, quotation from 292)

Again we encounter interactions readily recognizable in the later eighteenth-century repertoire.

With some variation from place to place, group to group, issue to issue, and performance to performance, these forms of interaction flourished until the eighteenth century's end, then began an uneven decline. Although few of them absolutely vanished, most of them had become rare events by the 1830s. The turnout, it is true, survived in artisanal trades well into the nineteenth century. For a time in the 1830s installation of the New Poor Law revived attacks on poorhouses and overseers of the poor. In some regions rural arson persisted into the 1840s. The revival of tollgate attacks in the Rebecca riots of 1839 to 1843 (so named for their mythical avenging heroine, whose male disciples often donned women's clothing for the work of destruction) and of machine-breaking during the Plug Plot conflicts of 1842 (so named for Staffordshire colliers' pulling of boiler plugs at their pitheads) stood out as unusual and retrograde events for their time—but they did occur.

Contention over food, drink, and shoddy goods or service continued into the twentieth century, but by the 1830s it had virtually stopped occasioning collective seizures, forced sales, or smashing of the premises; if relatively classic blockage and price-fixing recurred in Cornwall and coastal Scotland during 1847, even in persistent Devon the so-called "food riots" of 1867, which essentially closed the genre's history, mixed street marches with attacks on high-priced bakers' shops rather than seizures and sales (Charlesworth 1983; Storch 1982b). World War I's occasional organized attacks on high-priced merchants only distantly reflected their eighteenth-century predecessors (Coles 1978).

Workers' confrontations with capitalists and authorities likewise swelled many times after 1834, but then rarely involved physical attacks on goods, buildings, machines, or masters. British strikes have intermittently produced violence up to our own time but, as Roger Geary (1985) has chronicled, twentieth-century strike violence has flowed chiefly from confrontations between massed strikers and strikebreakers or between picketers and police. Although the great majority of British demonstrations have long occurred without physical destruction, a minority continue to stimulate violence when counter-demonstrators intervene or when police seek to contain unruly demonstrators. Victorian elections and their public drinking generated many a street brawl (Richter 1971). In short, conflict did not subside definitively between 1750 and 1840, but its most frequent eighteenth-century forms dwindled. They dwindled despite the fact that from a strictly technical viewpoint most eighteenth-century performances remained feasible for years beyond their demise.

By the 1830s a distinctly different set of claim-making performances prevailed: petition marches, demonstrations, firm-by-firm strikes, election rallies, and a wide variety of public meetings, many of them coordinated by special-purpose associations and/or political entrepreneurs. On average, we can reasonably call these performances *cosmopolitan, autonomous,* and *modular:* cosmopolitan because both the scope of action and the objects of claims commonly spanned multiple localities; autonomous because the organizers of such performances frequently scheduled and located them in advance at their own initiative rather than taking advantage of authorized assemblies or routine confluences of people; modular because people employed very similar performances across a wide range of issues, groups, localities, and objects of claims.

Such performances often coalesced into the new sort of campaign we call a social movement, a great promoter of modularity through its organizers' orchestration of like performances in widely dispersed settings. As a correlate of modularity, far fewer distinct performances comprised the nineteenth-century repertoire. In the widespread adoption of formal public meetings as vehicles for claim-making, to take the most obvious case, uniformity triumphed on a national scale. Innovation continued, perhaps even intensified in the heat of strategic interaction, but it took place within and at the boundaries of a few available performances: new sorts of meeting, variants on the firm-by-firm strike, different demands in demonstrations, and so on. Even aside from abandoned eighteenth-century forms of contention, many technically feasible and possibly efficacious performances—for example, mass consumer boycotts and deliberate obstruction of communication channels—simply did not occur.

The repertoire's narrowing had another significant implication: that disparities in modes of public claim-making between ordinary people and members of the ruling classes declined, that contention democratized. Democratization happened to some extent as a result of the broadening of means that were already available to the rich and powerful, but not to others, during the eighteenth century; the club, the public meeting, the organized petition, the procession generalized from the privileged to the underprivileged. But it also occurred via the creation of new performances such as the demonstration and new campaigns such as the social movement, in both of which members of several social classes often collaborated, however temporarily.

In the formation of a cosmopolitan, modular, autonomous repertoire of contention, we can distinguish *grosso modo* among three phases:

a period of *invention* from the 1760s to the 1780s, when Great
    Britain saw its first secular popular associations, its first mass
    petition marches, its first demonstrative uses of public meetings,
    its first firm-by-firm strikes, and so on through a fertile cluster of
    innovations;

a period of *consolidation* chiefly during the French Wars, when the
    standard performances of public meetings, demonstrations,
    popular electoral campaigns, and social movements took shape in
    implicit, if grudging, coordination with authorities; and

a period of *expansion* from 1815 onward in which these standard
    performances—especially different variants of the public
    meeting—became the overwhelmingly dominant settings for
    claim-making and the forms that had prevailed before 1800
    entered definitive decline.

Let us take care not to force all the different times of contention into just these three boxes. Peaks and troughs of contention occurred before 1758 as they did after then, and the quality of action varied from one to the other; bursts of claim-making in 1640, 1689, 1715, 1768, and 1819 differed in character, not just in quantity, from the claim-making of calmer years. Within campaigns and even within events, tactical times followed partly independent logics, depending on strategic interaction among allies and enemies; even the highly segmented Swing rebellion displayed intense communication, small-scale coordination, and nearly simultaneous responses to actions of the national government. The triad invention/consolidation/expansion simply schematizes decade-to-decade changes between the 1750s and the 1830s.

This periodization follows a retrospective rationale; it looks back from 1834 at the origins of a new repertoire rather than forward from 1758 at the transformation of contention as a whole. Performances in the parochial, particular, bifurcated eighteenth-century repertoire actually flourished through the period of the later repertoire's invention, altered somewhat but by no means disappeared during the period of consolidation, then declined significantly during the later repertoire's expansion. Thus seizures of food multiplied in such high-priced years as 1766, 1771–1773, 1794–1796, and 1799–1801, but during the last two of these crises marches and mass confrontations with authorities became much more common. After that, the diminishing and increasingly peripheral food struggles of 1810–1813, 1816–1818, 1847, and 1867 marked the performance's decline; the rapid price rises of 1825–1826 and 1828–1829 elicited strong responses from workers, but not seizures of food. Again, forced illuminations occurred widely during the times of Wilkes and Gordon, became a rarer yet still standard way of displaying support for government or a cause during the war years, recurred in 1820 (Queen Caroline) and 1831–1832 (reform), but over all dwindled rapidly after 1815.

Like those of the eighteenth-century repertoire, the newer performances varied somewhat in timetable, with the claim-making public meeting already well established at a time when the turnout still retained its dominance in zones of artisanal production. Attacks on labor-displacing machines and landless laborers' threatening marches from farm to farm actually rose to an all-time height between 1810 and 1830 before fading rapidly away. Resistance to uniformed, bureaucratized police welled up with the establishment of London's force in 1829, and continued through much of the nineteenth century as similar reorganizations of policing occurred elsewhere in Great Britain (Storch 1975, 1976). Yet on the whole dominant modes of contention changed in tandem and in surges, facilitating one another but also responding simultaneously to shifts in the national structure of political opportunity.

Recall other changes that accompanied the installation of cosmopolitan, autonomous, modular forms of claim-making. The frequency of physical violence in contention greatly declined. In control over contentious gatherings, uniformed police displaced troops, militias, and yeomanry. Special-purpose associations came to play a much larger role in organizing and leading the public presentation of demands. Because campaigns occurred on a large scale and in similar forms across much of the country, innovations such as new symbols, demands, slogans, or tactics spread much more rapidly and widely than they had during the eighteenth century.

Relations of contention to national politics also changed. Waves of action oriented to a single issue—notably a pending action of parliament or government—rolled in with increasing frequency. Parliament and its members became far more central to the action, especially as objects of claims. While workers continued to struggle with their own local employers, even they connected their troubles with national politics much more explicitly and frequently than had their eighteenth-century predecessors. The transformation of repertoires moved Great Britain toward mass national politics.

Although preceding chapters have made them familiar, another close look at the great mutations of repertoires reveals several puzzling features. They involved a shift from a good deal of direct action—punishment or rectification here and now, immediate contact with objects of reprobation or admiration, physical seizure or damage of persons and property—to overwhelmingly indirect and cumulative action designed to demonstrate that many separate groups supported or opposed a particular program. They involved greatly increased reliance on connections among dispersed populations through printed matter, associations, and political brokers. They involved substantially augmented requirements for anticipation, preparation, coordination, publicity, and timing. They involved a radical narrowing of the standard forms of claim-making. They involved expanded opportunity for authorities and police to forecast, infiltrate, negotiate with, and channel claim-making actions.

The predominant nineteenth-century repertoire included, furthermore, a very limited set of forms among all those which were, in their time, technically feasible. While one might have thought that a "modernization" of collective interaction would pass through greater differentiation, in important regards the opposite happened: even more so than the earlier listing suggests, eighteenth-century forms varied as a function of locality, issue, and relations between claimants and the objects of their claims, so much so that E. P. Thompson once wondered aloud whether Rough Music constituted a unitary phenomenon or simply a convenient name for a wide variety of loosely related shaming performances (Thompson 1981). Their nineteenth-century successors acquired much greater uniformity across localities, issues, populations, and subject-object relations. Narrowed from their occasional seventeenth-century employment to humiliate political reprobates, the various eighteenth-century forms of donkeying almost always related members of a local trade with another member of the same trade whom they considered to have violated their collective agreements. Nineteenth-century meetings, in contrast, centered on local groups' statement of their positions with respect to issues currently under parliamentary consideration, but extended widely across the spectra of issues, groups, relations, and localities.

Ordinary British people, in short, abandoned contentious methods that had produced results fairly often, at least on a local scale, for a more costly, more restricted set of methods in which a single action rarely produced decisive effects, and whose cumulative outcome remained at best contingent. All in all, claim-making Britons seem to have traded simple, sturdy, reliable hammers and hoes for great wheezing steam engines consuming vast quantities of fuel, requiring constant cleaning, and destined to spend much of their time under repair.

To Retell the Story

Let us therefore recognize what tales these changes do *not* tell. They do not tell a story of modernization, of displacing archaic, ineffectual means of interaction by more dynamic, efficient, powerful means; on the contrary, prevailing eighteenth-century forms often worked better than their successors, since on-the-spot actors often expelled an offending worker, broke down a tollgate, made food available at a lower price, and so on, while with the nineteenth-century forms no single interaction ever had the prospect of realizing its claims then and there. They do not tell a story of disorder, of impulsive acting out in response to excessively rapid or painful social change, since they feature extensive organization, debate, and premeditation. They do not tell a story of "social control" in which ordinary people gave up their hopes of justice in the face of repression, visible or invisible. Far from it: they display growing demands for one version or another of popular sovereignty, as well as modest governmental concessions to those demands in the form of expanded rights to associate and assemble, reductions in religious restrictions on officeholding, and steps toward parliamentary reform.

Relating the shifts of repertoires as a story of "protest," on the other hand, ignores the frequency with which nineteenth-century sorts of claim-making promoted not reactive rage but innovations such as Catholic Emancipation and parliamentary reform. Reducing them to expressions of changing "mentalities," "public opinion," or "popular attitudes" forgets both the differential access that various groups had to these forms of expression and the organizational effort that drawing people into them frequently entailed. Compressing these changes into "class formation" neglects the broadening cross-class availability of the nineteenth-century forms. But to treat them as one more example of British common sense, of pragmatism, of statesmanlike accommodation, of collaboration among classes, is to deny what the evidence reveals: the struggle and danger they entailed at such moments as Peterloo, the fierce tactical disagreements among radicals and reformers, the fearful determination with which Britain's rulers fought against most of these innovations from the watershed of John Wilkes to the heyday of Henry Hunt.

The history of British contention from the 1750s to the 1830s resembles an evolutionary cusp, where members of disparate populations encounter one another in a time of rapid environmental change, try multiple strategies for survival, alter their collective boundaries, relations, and characteristics in manners that none of them could have intended, and in the process remake the very environment in which they live. No one class, faction, instinct, or historical law willed the profound mutations of popular politics that occurred in Great Britain from the 1750s to the 1830s, or even caused them unwittingly. After the fact, we can discern causal order in the complexity, but at the time no one could know how it would all turn out. Contingent history means that the same causes in slightly different combinations could produce significantly different outcomes. In retelling the story, then, let us attempt a difficult but essential dual enterprise: to avoid comparing what happened with some ideal course of events we or some people of the time might have preferred, yet also to consider what else could have happened in the circumstances of the day.

The evolution of struggles over food illustrates the problem and its solution. In 1766, early in the period we have been examining, Parliament allowed the 5s. per quarter bounty on exported wheat (suspended in February 1766 after a round of grain seizures) to resume when an economic slump (hence income loss among wage workers who relied on the market for their food) and crop failure coincided in southern England. Throughout the South, especially in industrial sections of the West Country, people gathered to attack mills and warehouses, blocked grain shipments, intervened in markets, and drove down prices through intimidation (Charlesworth 1983; Charlesworth and Randall 1987; Hayter 1978; Shelton 1973; Williams 1984). While workers often blamed the national government and local officials for their handling of the crisis, they confined their action almost exclusively to regaining control over food and its price.

The acute crisis of 1794–1796 concatenated not only harvest failure and industrial recession but also substantial requisitions of food for the military. It produced what may have been the greatest proliferation of grain seizures England ever experienced. This time blockages, seizures, and direct interventions into market pricing occurred in abundance (Bohstedt 1983; Booth 1977; Charlesworth 1983; Wells 1988). But so did public meetings, demonstrations, and takeovers of markets by military units, especially the militia; in the Southeast, 9 of our 13 food-connected CGs from 1795 took the shape of meetings demanding or offering help for the hungry. A clear politicization of struggles over food was occurring.

By the 1810s the political recasting of food-oriented conflicts had gone even farther. The struggles of 1810–1813, which concentrated heavily in the industrial sections of the North, articulated closely with machine-breaking, strikes, and working-class political demands. The interactions of 1816–1818, which followed the setting of a high import threshold in the Corn Law amendment of 1815, clustered especially in East Anglia. There agricultural laborers broke agricultural machinery, sought to fix wages and prices, besieged magistrates, and marched into towns demanding redress (Armstrong 1988; Charlesworth 1983). On 18 May 1816, for example, people began assembling in the market place of Brandon (Suffolk) at about 9 A.M. An hour or so later fifty-odd armed men

marched into the square carrying white and red flags. Willett, the butcher, who was amongst the crowd, told [William] Peverett [an agricultural laborer] that the parish would let them have flour at 2s. 6d. if they would disperse, and asked for a deputation to go along with him to meet the magistrates. Helen Dyer, a married woman, had earlier told Willett that, although she could not read, she had a paper containing the crowd's demands, which she wanted shown to the magistrates. On it was written *"Bread or Blood in Brandon this day."* (Peacock 1965: 79; italics in original)

At the deputation's demand, Magistrate Burch sent away the dragoons another magistrate had requisitioned, and agreed to a meeting with the principal inhabitants. The meeting agreed on a 2s. daily allowance for the poor and the sale of flour at 2s. 6d. a stone. Nevertheless, some minor stoning and window-breaking occurred that evening, and the following day a group destroyed the house and shop of Willett the butcher (ibid.: 80–81). Although the confrontation at Brandon had few of a London reform meeting's lineaments, it belonged to a different genre from the grain seizures of 1766. Outright seizures of food, as distinguished from demands that authorities control prices and assure supplies, had still figured prominently in 1794–1796 and 1800–1801. They appeared only peripherally in the conflicts of the 1810s, and almost vanished thereafter.

The word "politicization" blurs the history of subsistence struggles. From the beginning, they took place in a known political context, local or national. From 1766 to the 1830s government action—bounties on exports, diversion of local supplies to military forces, Corn Laws, failures to enforce prohibitions on profiteering—aggravated every subsistence crisis, and provided some of the justification for popular retaliation against millers, bakers, farmers, merchants, and local authorities. Thus the history of grain seizures and related actions resulted from the intersection of commodity market fluctuations, governmental interventions, and changing employment patterns. Yet with time the workers who retaliated against accused hoarders and profiteers, blocked grain shipments, seized food, and demanded publicly enforced fair prices also moved increasingly toward the creation of trade unions and the linking of industrial justice to parliamentary reform (Charlesworth 1993). More and more the issues of food supplies and prices fell subsidiary to the programs of unions and movements for reform.

That outcome was not inevitable. From the late sixteenth to the early nineteenth century, the national government had frequently responded

to widespread grain seizures by strong intervention in commodity markets, just as local authorities had often tried to mitigate the effects of
crises through price controls, restrictions on shipments, subsidized sales,
and direct financial aid to poor households. If Parliament in its turn had
leaned more heavily toward market restrictions, protection of workers'
rights, and regulation of manufacturing, the course of food-related struggles would have run differently: no doubt the seizure of food would have
accompanied price and supply crises much longer, and the integration of
subsistence questions into the new repertoire would have taken more
time. Thus an alternative alimentary history, closely related in its causes
to the one that actually unfolded, remained possible in eighteenth- and
nineteenth-century Britain. In its sphere, it would have produced a different history of contention.

To Meet in Public

Performances within the new repertoire likewise illustrate the possibility
of alternative histories. Consider the public meeting, that workhorse of
nineteenth-century contention. More than 5,800 of our 8,000-odd CGs
took the form of scheduled assemblies in which people made collective
claims, most often in the form of resolutions and petitions; their number
and proportion increased from decade to decade. At our starting-point
of the 1750s, the only groups regularly using public meetings to do their
business were members of the ruling classes with their clubs and banquets, religious congregations, some privileged trades, agencies of government such as county magistracies or common councils, and duly constituted assemblies of freeholders, electors, vestrymen, or similar public
bodies. The first visible expansion of the public meeting occurred toward
1780, as both the Protestant Association and various reform committees
began to use such gatherings not only to deliberate but to advertise their
political preferences.

For years thereafter the government—caught between the well-established precedent of elite assembly and its own opposition to the creation
of any body that would compete with the priority of Parliament as the
voice of national will—remained warily repressive about opinion-pro-
claiming public meetings. The government began to monitor meetings,
sending spies and examining reports of their proceedings for evidence of
sedition or political presumption. Yet the Anti-Slavery Society, the Revo-

lution Society, the London Corresponding Society, and most other re-form-oriented associations increasingly used well-advertised meetings not just to deliberate but to broadcast their programs, complaints, and demands. Organized workers continued to operate under the threat of prosecution for conspiracy, but their unions and mutual-aid societies likewise turned to meeting regularly and debating public issues. The very intensification of surveillance and repression sharpened the distinction between illegal and legal meetings, thereby ironically reducing the government's own capacity to eliminate threatening meetings that remained within legal bounds.

In London and elsewhere coffeehouses and taverns came to be the favored sites of organized political debate and position-taking. Meanwhile, turnouts, elections, and public holidays provided precedents, models and, to some extent, occasions for open-air gatherings that exceeded the capacities of public buildings. Before the massive repression of the later 1790s, public meetings began to take their places as elements in coordinated campaigns to mobilize publicity and support for well-defined political programs.

During the 1790s as well began a decisive shift toward Parliament as the object of collective claims; both local powerholders and (especially) the monarch became less salient as targets of publicly concerted demands. The connections between parliamentary and popular consideration of issues, notably in the form of controversial bills, tightened greatly. With the relaxation of wartime controls after 1815, association-driven reform meetings multiplied, then the scope of issues taken up via meetings broadened enormously. Either to call a local meeting for discussion of a single issue or to place that issue on the agenda of an already-scheduled meeting became the most common ways to publicize popular support for a program; resolutions, petitions, and newspaper reports translated the proceedings into visible segments of the public record, parallel to the speeches made by members of Parliament.

What else could have happened? Imagine three alternative scenarios: Containment, Revolution, and Invention. In Containment, we see Great Britain approaching the mid-nineteenth century with essentially the same contentious repertoire that had prevailed in the 1750s: claim-making within authorized public assemblies, celebrations and other popularly initiated gatherings, attacks on popularly designated offenses and offenders, workers' sanctions over members of their trades, and attacks on coercive authorities. To suppose Containment, we must also postulate continuous repression sufficient to keep workers from broadening their trade meetings into adjacent political activity, to limit church services, elections, and parish assemblies in similar ways, and to prevent effective cross-class alliances against the regime. With those suppositions, we might also construct a nineteenth-century world in which such eighteenth-century procedures as Rough Music and donkeying moved actively into the political arena—as indeed they did in France between the Restoration of 1815 and the Revolution of 1848. Such a world would promote a popular politics that was even more class-segregated than was the actual politics of nineteenth-century Great Britain.

What about Revolution? We need not import France's blood and thunder; we need only imagine that popular programs of mass platform and anti-Parliament prevailed, most likely during the divisions of the 1790s, perhaps with French assistance. In that case, we find at least a more thoroughgoing version of the 1832 Reform Act, with mobilized workers acquiring a significantly more direct voice in national politics, and considerably earlier. Such a scenario could bypass the expansion of the public meeting if the revolutionary process created a system of popular sovereignty via local, regional, and national legislative bodies retaining the exclusive right to deliberate public affairs. Previous insistence on a parliamentary monopoly of public deliberation could easily have promoted such an exclusive system. As the experience of many a revolution indicates, such legislative bodies often restrict and infiltrate paraparliamentary political activity instead of promoting it.

Invention? The varieties of British public meeting took their shapes and acquired their legal protection from the interlocking histories of parish assemblies, religious congregations, chartered trades, and parliamentary elections. Out of those histories, however, one could also construct a more differentiated, almost corporatist set of institutions, with separate means and channels of representation for localities, religious groups, trades, and forms of property, each of them connected hierarchically with national centers of power through patron-client chains. Contention within such a system would take one of two forms: great struggles and coalitions among corporate sectors on a regional or national scale, maneuvering for preference within different levels of each corporation. Again, Europe provides many examples of politics in this genre.

Or we might bind our Inventions more closely to what actually happened: instead of the public meeting, an expansion and regularization of petitioning that would have restricted the right of petition to authorized bodies, but turned it into a sort of continuous plebiscite, vote, or public-opinion survey directed toward Parliament and the government. During the great campaigns for Abolition, Catholic Emancipation, and parliamentary reform, after all, petitions did flow in by the thousands. Under these circumstances, we would expect even greater exclusion from public politics than actually occurred of unchartered population segments such as agricultural laborers and handloom weavers.

Is such speculation idle? No, even short of assigning probabilities to these alternative scenarios, their construction serves two important purposes. First, it helps identify what difference the public meeting and other political practices associated with it made: they facilitated publicly visible cross-class alliances, articulated with a press that could report events publicizing political programs, provided an alternative to patronage, sent messages directly to Parliament without encroaching too obviously on Parliament's prerogatives, and so on. Second, to ask why the alternatives did not materialize is also to ask what caused the changes that did occur; every valid explanation implies selection among possibilities. In this case, even the simple sketches of alternatives I have just offered identify likely factors in the great shift of repertoires: expanding powers of Parliament, vesting of increasingly burdensome local and regional government in partly autonomous assemblies, proletarianization that weakened the political patronage of landlords and master craftsmen, and increasing reliance on Catholic and Dissenting populations for military manpower. They also make more plausible the three-stage scheme of invention, consolidation, and expansion I proposed earlier, with the Seven Years War and the American wars as backdrops to invention, the French wars as backdrop to consolidation, and the postwar adjustment doubling with an acceleration of capital-concentrated industrialization as backdrops to expansion.

Catholics in Politics

The three periods of intense struggle over Catholic rights that intersect our catalog—1780, 1807, and 1828–1829—summarize the same general trends in contention as dramatically as successive frames in a comic strip. In 1780 action centered on Lord George Gordon, his Protestant Association, and London's anti-Catholic crowds, all of them resisting the concessions being made to Catholics in order to assure military recruitment and service of Irish Catholics. With the more or less simultaneous mobilization of the Yorkshire Association and its counterparts, it marked the first large creation of paraparliamentary organization since the Civil War. Much of the action spurred by Gordon consisted of smashing and burning, but it coincided with widespread popular and elite support for continued exclusion of Catholics from the British polity. It exposed the state's vulnerability to popular violence, since authorities dithered and bickered about jurisdiction for several days before intervening decisively to stop attacks on Catholic targets.

By 1807 reformers were frequently demanding relaxation of anti-Catholic penal laws. The entry of Ireland into the Union (1801), with Pitt's half-promise to extend Catholic political rights, had made the issue all the more salient. In 1807, nevertheless, war and military recruitment still figured as a stimulus to contention, since over George III's resistance parliamentary Whigs were trying to legalize the service of Catholic officers through the rank of colonel in England as the government had done for service within Ireland. This time the action consisted of delegations, decorous ruling-class meetings, and extensive (if finally unsuccessful) maneuvering behind the scenes. Another crisis passed with little popular mobilization in Great Britain.

By 1828 Catholic Emancipation had become the rallying issue of an unprecedented social movement in Ireland and was rapidly becoming the focus of both movement and counter-movement in Great Britain. Daniel O'Connell and his Catholic Association on one side, the Earl of Winchilsea and his Brunswick Clubs on the other, with an array of reformers and political pragmatists scattered across the intervening space, organized the campaign of meetings, petitions, marches, pamphlets, and coalition-making that marked nineteenth-century national social movements and counter-movements. This time popular pressure contributed to the passage of long-resisted legislation. From 1780 to 1829, then, popular interaction on Catholic rights always maintained some connection with parliamentary maneuvering, but the connection tightened; between those years Catholic-Protestant contention made the transition from popular vengeance on stigmatized individuals to mass movements oriented toward displays of support for rival parliamentary programs on a national scale.

What else could have happened? Do not forget that Ireland rose repeatedly in open insurrection from 1798 to 1803, that Irish resistance to British rule and French aid to that resistance promoted the integration of Ireland into the United Kingdom, which in turn made starker and more problematic the disparity between Catholic and Protestant political rights. Do not forget either that in the same period Britain was perfectly capable of imposing military control on dissident minorities in its colonies. Those two strands of causality make plausible alternative scenarios involving armed confrontation between Britain and Ireland, faction-making of the kind that occurred with Wilkes and the American Revolution, even stronger fusion of Irish, Catholic, and reform issues as the basis of division within British politics, and consequent deviation from the social-movement path to Catholic Emancipation as a managed parliamentary question.

Other possibilities existed as well: a much earlier extension of Catholic rights under a more indulgent king, political success for the Protestant Association of 1780, or so great a Brunswick mobilization in 1829 that ministers, king, and Parliament would not have dared to compromise with O'Connell and the Catholic Association. In reckoning the alternatives, we begin to sense the importance to what actually happened of the junction between Catholic Emancipation and Irish dissidence, the consequent advantages to reformers of taking up the Catholic issue despite widespread popular anti-Catholicism in Great Britain, as well as the dangers that fusion of Reform and Emancipation presented to Britain's rulers. To retell the story is to recount possibilities, only some of them realized, and to reason about the causes that selected those outcomes which occurred over others.

Toward Explanation

As these examples make clear, particular issues and forms of interaction had their own histories, their own politics. Yet many of the histories had family resemblances that fitted them into a more general history of popular contention. Viewed broadly, the differences between eighteenth- and nineteenth-century repertoires conformed to the contrasting principles schematized in Table 8.2. We find autonomous means of interaction displacing the frequent borrowing of authorities' forms in satire or ear-

Table 8.2. Contrasting principles of eighteenth- and nineteenth-century repertoires

Eighteenth century	Nineteenth century
1. People's frequent employment of the authorities' normal means of action, either as caricature or as a deliberate, if temporary, assumption of the authorities' prerogatives in the name of the local community.	1. Use of relatively autonomous means of action, of a kind rarely or never employed by authorities.
2. Convergence on the residences of wrongdoers and the sites of wrongdoing, as opposed to seats and symbols of public power.	2. Preference for previously planned action in visible public places.
3. Extensive use of authorized public celebrations and assemblies for the presentation of grievances and demands.	3. Deliberate organization of assemblies for the articulation of claims.
4. Common appearance of the participants as members or representatives of constituted corporate groups and communities rather than of special interests.	4. Participation as members or representatives of special interests, constituted public bodies, and named associations.
5. A tendency to act directly against local enemies but to appeal to powerful patrons for redress of wrongs beyond the reach of the local community and, especially, for representation vis-à-vis outside authorities.	5. Direct challenges to rivals or authorities, especially national authorities and their representatives.
6. Repeated adoption of rich, irreverent symbolism in the form of effigies, dumb show, and ritual objects to state grievances and demands.	6. Display of programs, slogans, and symbols of common membership such as flags, colors, and lettered banners.
7. Shaping of action to particular circumstances and localities.	7. Preference for forms of action easily transferred from one circumstance or locality to another.
8. Summary: *parochial, particular, and bifurcated.*	8. Summary: *cosmopolitan, modular, and autonomous.*

nest, assembly in symbolically charged public places displacing the descent on a dishonored house or dishonorable person, and so on through a decisive series of mutations. In now familiar terms, *parochial, particular, bifurcated* forms of claim-making gave way to *cosmopolitan, modular, autonomous* forms.

Notice what the shifts (parochial cosmopolitan), (particular modular), and (bifurcated autonomous) imply. They portray a decisive shift away from short-term effectiveness toward long-term cumulation of efforts. They describe a declining covariation among group, relation, issue, and action in favor of all-purpose means of claim-making. They entail, on the average, significantly sharper breaks of collective contention from the locales and routines of everyday social relations. They rest on elaborated communication and coordination among distant populations and groups. They suggest an accretion of political memory, shared symbols, common programs, tactical knowledge, and organization for collective interaction on a larger than local scale.

The substantial shifts of repertoire involve decisive movement toward social-movement logic: toward sustained, ostentatious challenges to authorities in the name of disadvantaged or threatened populations, toward displays of support for well-articulated programs and demands, toward the cumulative acting out of worthiness, unity, numbers, and commitment on behalf of the cause. They therefore assign increased importance to organizers, brokers, and political entrepreneurs. Finally, they imply increased orientation of national officials and Parliament to publicly organized interests, both local and national.

More generally, the massive changes in contention embody *parliamentarization* and *nationalization* of claim-making. With increasing frequency people, including ordinary people acting collectively, made claims on Parliament, individual members of Parliament, and national officials. Local powerholders and the crown became less salient objects of claims. The timing of claim-making came to depend more closely on the rhythms of parliamentary discussion and governmental action. While authorized local assemblies such as wardmotes and vestry meetings continued to provide the setting for many claims on national authorities, workers' organizations, special-interest associations, and public meetings open to all inhabitants (or at least to all "respectable" inhabitants) took on increasing importance as vehicles for claim-making. In the 1820s and 1830s, despite repeated governmental efforts to squash the Catholic Association, mass-subscription organizations on a national scale acquired both legal standing and political influence.

Such a bundle of changes contains some unexpected items. The abandonment of effective direct action for uncertain and costly indirect action remains bemusing. The two repertoires coexisted longer than any simple representation of changing political opportunities can account for. On conventional ideas of transition from community to association and local to national, one might have expected special-interest associations to displace authorized local assemblies much more than they did; it looks as though the legal protection and precedent provided by the deeply rooted rights of qualified residents to public deliberation gave strong advantages to any association that could ally with, infiltrate, or persuade such an assembly to take a public position. In a similar way, election campaigns gained importance as occasions for expressions of political preference among electors and the disfranchised alike.

That does not end the surprises. Far from obscuring local events, in some respects the nationalization of contention actually increased the resonance of exemplary local conflicts such as the agricultural machine-breaking of 1830 and the 1834 prosecution of Tolpuddle laborers for swearing commitment to their friendly society. Finally, Ireland looms up repeatedly in British contention, as a source of contentious issues, as a site of contention overflowing into Great Britain, as a proving-ground for governmental dealing with mobilization and contention, as a stimulus to political reorganization. On beginning this inquiry, I expected none of these findings, and found no reason in available histories to expect any of them. After the fact, nevertheless, it is not hard to rationalize them as consequences of the very historical processes by which British repertoires altered.

Four processes converged in the shift to cosmopolitan, autonomous, modular repertoires, in the nationalization and parliamentarization of contention. First, war-driven expansion, strengthening, and centralization of the British state gave increasing political advantage to groups that could convey their demands directly to Parliament, whose fiscal and regulative powers augmented from decade to decade. Access to local patrons and exploiters therefore proved decreasingly feasible and efficacious. Struggles over living costs, for example, shifted from less and less effective seizures of grain and local wage-setting to lobbying of Parliament over Poor Laws and Corn Laws. In the process Parliament—critical to every decision concerning governmental revenue, expenditure, and personnel—occupied ever more space in political decisions. Parliament's increasing prominence, in its turn, augmented the importance of parliamentary elections as determinants of public policy, occasions of policy debates, and opportunities for advocates of causes to publicize and promote their programs.

Second, capitalization, commercialization, and proletarianization of economic life undermined old networks of patronage, weakened local craft organization as a basis of collective interaction, sharpened the division between wage-earners and employers, gave workers increasing incentives and opportunities to band together on a regional or national scale, and promoted an alliance (however contingent and temporary) among workers and capitalists in favor of democratic openings in national politics. At the same time, employers' efforts to rationalize production in the face of sharpening competition generated workers' resistance to wage cuts, losses of control over working conditions, and elimination of jobs. Donkeying and cutting, for instance, diminished in efficacy as local groups of masters lost their inclination and capacity to bargain out community-wide wage schedules with their journeymen. Similarly, proletarianizing agricultural workers lost what little collective capacity they had previously enjoyed to maintain their livelihoods in the face of cost-cutting landlords and farmers. Again, struggles over food shifted from community seizures of local supplies to concerted agitation for action by authorities. Meanwhile, major strikes and workers' movements became increasingly entangled with politics on a national scale.

Third, population growth, migration, urbanization, and the creation of larger producing organizations transformed local social ties, giving political advantages to actors that could create, manipulate, alter, or infiltrate flexible, efficient assemblies and associations. Assemblies, associations, and political entrepreneurs provided the means of connecting and coordinating the actions of many dispersed clusters of people simultaneously. Not only the idea but also the feasibility and effectiveness of a union federation or a national network of political clubs generalized.

Fourth, within limits set by these first three processes and in constant interaction with authorities, contention accumulated its own history of shared beliefs, memories, models, precedents, and social ties, which underlay the use for claim-making of public assemblies, marches, petitions, delegations, and special-purpose associations. The recurrent effort to organize general unions and stage general strikes in the 1830s rested in part on the venerable program of the mass platform and on shared memories of simultaneous meetings and insurrections between 1815 and 1820. The right to assemble peaceably in the name of an association, as exercised in the 1820s and 1830s, drew on confrontations, attempted prosecutions, and organized political campaigns extending back to John Wilkes and his supporters.

The first three clusters of changes constrained the fourth, but did not determine it. Growth of the state, capitalization, and demographic change incrementally undermined the conditions for effectiveness of eighteenth-century forms of claim-making and created conditions under which the nineteenth-century forms became relatively effective. Yet people's adaptation to changed conditions of effectiveness was neither rapid, direct, nor fully conscious. Because the structural changes proceeded unevenly in different sectors and regions, at any given time the successes and failures of other contending groups sent mixed messages about the consequences of different interactions; thus between 1815 and 1820 landless laborers were smashing agricultural machinery while many of their industrial cousins were attending meetings in support of parliamentary reform. Prior histories of groups and localities affected their shared understandings of what was possible, desirable, proper, and efficacious, as the long-established parliamentary protection of Spitalfields weavers inclined them toward appeals for government intervention and direct involvement in national politics more than most weavers elsewhere. Governmental repression and facilitation channeled contention to some degree, as when the rescinding of the Combination Acts and partial legalization of friendly societies encouraged the formation of publicly authorized workers' associations as vehicles of collective interaction, both legal and illegal. These interweaving elements constituted a giant exercise in collective learning.

Neither the learning nor its consequences ran all in one direction. Other parties to claim-making—authorities, repressive forces, allies, rivals, enemies, bystanders, possible beneficiaries—learned from their own observations and adaptations. Note, for example, how the anti-Catholic Brunswick Clubs of 1828–1829 adapted forms of organization and agitation pioneered by the Catholic Association, as well as how the New

Police rapidly became skilled at containing demonstrators. Contention, furthermore, changed national politics. It did so in at least four ways: (1) by requiring rulers to negotiate, at least indirectly, over such issues as political rights of religious minorities and treatment of the poor; (2) by stimulating repressive efforts such as the organization of the New Police, which had their own durable effects on governmental organization as they reshaped local collective action; (3) by transforming durable connections among different groups of participants in collective interaction, notably when alliances formed between segments of the ruling classes and activists from the ranks of ordinary people, as in the Queen Caroline affair; and (4) (more rarely) by generating struggles and realignments among powerholders such as those which swirled around John Wilkes, Catholic Emancipation, and parliamentary reform. Now and then popular collective interaction contributed to a fifth outcome: a direct, genuine recasting of national power structure; expanded suffrage for merchants and manufacturers provided by the Reform Act of 1832 gave them political weights they had not previously wielded. Changes in forms of contention not only constrained further contention but also affected routine politics in each of these regards.

As a barber's mirror sometimes brings into view gray hair, bald spots, and cranial bumps their owner does not ordinarily see, the evidence in this book reflects changes in contention at an unusual angle. Existing histories of popular contention have given workers' struggles and changes in production much greater prominence than they have received in my analysis. Part of that de-emphasis results from the sources on which I have relied; London-based periodicals underreport British strikes and day-to-day confrontations between workers and local powerholders while overreporting interactions between national authorities and claimants of all sorts. They also provide less direct evidence concerning transformations of production than concerning reorganizations of state power. Finally, restriction of the CG catalog before 1828 to Kent, Middlesex, Surrey, and Sussex cants the viewfinder away from such major centers of economic change and worker activity as Lancashire and Yorkshire. Even without this selectivity, evidence drawn disproportionately from public claim-making would understate the importance of economic change, which influences contention more incrementally and indirectly—but no less profoundly—than does alteration of the state.

Still, the book's angle of vision provides new insight into the mutations of popular contention in Great Britain, even with respect to workers and economic change. For we have frequently seen workers making claims in other guises: as members of the local citizenry, as parishioners, as users of local markets, as participants in political associations, as representatives of various creeds, and many more. Instead of arguing that in all these conditions they remained "really" or "essentially" workers, we should recognize that economic and political change interact with contention to determine what identities are actually available for public claim-making. Repertoires of contention and politically available identities change in tandem with each other. Their changes then alter the relative political advantages of different social relations and actors. Between the 1750s and the 1830s, workers by no means withdrew from politics, contentious or otherwise. On the contrary, their political activity expanded, but they became involved politically in many more guises than as workers alone.

Social Movements and Demonstrations

We can see the interplay between routine and publicly contentious politics in the British invention of social movements and demonstrations. A social movement consists of the deliberate, ostentatious mounting of a sustained challenge to powerholders in the name of a disadvantaged population living under the jurisdiction or influence of those powerholders. It entails the mobilization of large numbers of people around a set of claims by means of meetings, processions, demonstrations, petitions, slogans, symbols, committees, publicly proclaimed strategies, and related means. If its authors aim at national authorities, we can call the movement national as well. A social movement gains strength from observers', authorities', and opponents' perceptions that the movement's supporters constitute a numerous, committed, unified, worthy mass that is prepared to risk breaking with routine politics in pursuit of its program. (Worthiness results from uprightness, subjection to injustice or, better, some combination of the two; oppressed, upright people have a perennial claim on outside support.) Badges, slogans, rituals, disciplined marches, mass meetings, militant pronouncements, and access to the mass media enhance that image—although they run the risk of ridicule and self-exposure if participants actually appear to be few, uncertain, corrupt, or divided among themselves. A social-movement strategy has its greatest effect in the presence of binding elections, of visible opportunities for insurrection, or both. In fact, social movements have generally waxed and waned with the rise and fall of electoral politics.

Social movements work with inherent contradictions, one with respect to support, the other with respect to outcomes. On the side of *support,* social-movement leaders gain from maximizing the multiple of four factors: numbers, commitment, worthiness, and unity; if any of them falls to zero, the movement misfires. Unity itself works ambivalently, since in some circumstances, notably where supporters seek to advance a particular religious, ethnic, or sexual identity, social movements gain from an appearance of homogeneity in origin and life, while in others, notably where supporters claim that their issue engages all citizens, the sharing of a grievance across heterogeneous populations actually gives that grievance force. The drive for numbers proceeds either by mobilizing the less committed or by forming coalitions with like-minded groups. Either strategy almost necessarily diminishes both the average level of commitment (as gauged, for example, by readiness to endure hardship and injury for the cause) and the unity of population or program.

On the side of *outcomes,* successful claim-making becomes more probable, on the whole, in the presence of moderate demands, sustained negotiation, and cooperation with authorities or other powerful actors. But such successes lead to co-optation of leaders, breakaways by zealots, and integration into routine politics, which in turn commonly reduce the movement's appeal to its potential beneficiaries. Organizers at all levels spend much of their energy concealing, balancing, and mitigating these contradictions.

We must distinguish social-movement *organizations* like the Catholic Association from the social movement—the series of challenges—as such. Although social-movement leaders always strive to portray their supporters as unified and committed, a single organization rarely sustains or contains a whole social movement. The effort to augment numbers and breadth usually engages political entrepreneurs in negotiating coalitions with existing organizations, creating new ones where gaps exist, and knitting organizations together through networks of activists. Hence the frequency of such names as "front," "coalition," or "union" for the supporters of a particular challenge. Shifting, conglomerate sets of people participate in social movements. So it certainly happened in Great Britain.

Since both sustained, deliberate national challenges and associations committed to such challenges evolved in fits and starts, it is arbitrary to set a precise date for the first appearance of each in British—or any other—national history. Squinting, one can certainly see something of the social movement and the social-movement organization in John Wilkes's Society of Supporters of the Bill of Rights or Lord George Gordon's Protestant Association. The antislavery agitation of the 1780s and thereafter, which nestled within the protective wall of established churches, likewise anticipated tactics of later social movements. Yet any plausible criterion indicates that during the 1760s the social movement was a rare or nonexistent way of doing political business, while during the 1830s many different interests seized on its use. As indexed by catalogs of contentious gatherings, it first appeared intermittently during the years of the French Revolution (for example in the reform campaigns of the London Corresponding Society). The national social movement, furthermore, entered British repertoires of contention as a widely available form only after 1815. Much as a distinguished line of mechanics conceived, introduced, and perfected the power loom, British political entrepreneurs such as John Wilkes, Lord George Gordon, Christopher Wyvill, William Wilberforce, Francis Burdett, Francis Place, William Cobbett, Henry Hunt, Richard Carlile, and John Gast collectively and incrementally *invented* the national social movement as a routine way of making claims.

Social movements took shape as established forms of interaction in a para-electoral, paraparliamentary setting, and retained marks of that setting. As their inventors half-understood, social-movement interactions and social constructions countered the objections that ruling classes and authorities commonly made to inconvenient demands from relatively powerless people: that they were a handful of malcontents, that the bulk of the people in their category disagreed with them, that they had adequate legal means of redress, that their actions threatened public order, that unscrupulous powerseekers were manipulating them, that they were asking for impossible or destructive concessions. Such objections to popular claims became more likely when people were not acting on local objects, especially renegades among their own numbers, but making demands on national powerholders. The public rebuttal of such negative judgments became more crucial and effective to the extent that the judgments came from national officials, that numerous governmental opponents existed who might ally themselves with challengers on the

enemy-of-my-enemy principle, and that members of the audience themselves had an investment in the right to challenge and be heard.

Unlike sacking an official's house or hanging a minister in effigy,
social-movement tactics answered the charges eloquently:

> We are many;
> we (or the objects of our solicitude) are worthy and unjustly
> disadvantaged;
> we agree among ourselves and with the objects of our solicitude;
> we are committed, disciplined, and legal.

Like the arrival of many partisan and vociferous non-voters at contested
parliamentary elections, the deployment of disciplined numbers challenged the claim of the ruling classes that they adequately represented
the nation. It also conveyed an implicit threat of retaliation against
violators of the popular will. The display of unity, commitment, discipline,
and legality reinforced the challenge by declaring the dissidents a force
to be reckoned with, a force at the disposal of its collective will, a force
that would remain within legal channels so long as authorities were
prepared to bargain, but could well turn to creation of antiparliamentary
means, direct action against individual malefactors, or even open insurrection. Hence the tenacity with which authorities sought to check particular social movements and the means of their action.

As it took shape in the 1820s, the British social movement included
several recurrent elements: the creation of associations visibly devoted to
the promotion of a particular program; the holding of public meetings
to publicize the program and dramatize the extent of public support for
it; the production of addresses, pamphlets, and other texts on behalf of
the program; a search for publicity in newspapers and other periodicals,
including periodicals organized deliberately for the purpose by movement
supporters; the submission of petitions to public authorities, and especially to Parliament, often in collusion with parliamentary supporters who
used the petitions as occasions for debate on the subject; the organization
of marches, processions, ceremonies, dinners, and demonstrations. Not
every movement employed all these forms. But in the cases of Queen
Caroline and parliamentary reform we can see all of them in play at one
time or another.

Although Major Cartwright's Hampden Clubs and their successors the
political unions of 1817 onward also served as examples, Daniel O'Con-

nell's Catholic Association played a major part in integrating special-purpose associations into the British social movement on a national scale. When London's reformers used social-movement tactics in their campaign for Queen Caroline, they made relatively little public use of specialized associations, relying instead on previously authorized assemblies of various kinds. The Catholic Association and its reincarnations flaunted their mass base, their national scale, their strategic coordination, and their commitment to a circumscribed set of demands. Even after legal dissolution their connection with a successful national campaign made them a compelling model for the mounting of very different claims, including claims for parliamentary reform.

The individual performance we now call a demonstration entered Britain's repertoires of contention in essentially the same way as the sort of campaign we now call a social movement, indeed as social movements' indispensable device. A demonstration entails gathering deliberately in a visible, symbolically important place, displaying signs of shared commitment to some claim on authorities, then dispersing (see Favre 1990; Lindenberger 1993; Sommier 1993). Demonstrations have many variants: with or without marches through the streets, with or without speeches, with or without the trappings of parades such as uniforms, costumes, banners, signs, musicians, songs, and chanted slogans. Like miniature social movements, demonstrations broadcast a multiple of numbers, unity, worthiness, and commitment to a cause, with signs of intense commitment or great worthiness compensating to some degree for small numbers. Again we can find antecedents of the demonstration among the eighteenth century's CGs. During the food crises of 1795–1796 and 1801–1802, local people sometimes paraded symbols of their distress such as a loaf on a stick through the streets instead of making direct attacks on millers or bakers. Such a parade directed the challenge to local authorities more than to the merchants and manufacturers of food. Mass marches in honor of the French Revolution likewise sometimes qualified as quasi- or demi-demonstrations. The cheering, jeering, and chairing of candidates in parliamentary elections likewise contained some elements of the demonstration. Still, the demonstration came to be a standard way of making public claims in Great Britain only after 1815.

In Lancashire workers began to organize demonstrations recurrently in 1816. They never ceased. On 27 May, for example, magistrate Ralph Fletcher reported that Bolton's demonstrators had exhibited a shuttle covered with mourning crepe (HO 42/151). In September a large crowd proceeded through the streets of Bolton dragging a wagon that carried effigies of a starving soldier and an old woman begging for bread, then dumped the wagon in the river. This time Fletcher interpreted the action as meant "to ridicule the charitable endeavors of the well disposed to relieve by their contributions the necessities of the poor and also by showing the unprofitable nature of a soldier's life to dissuade others from entering into the army—and again by drowning the effigy to manifest their hatred of the profession" (Munger 1977: 173–174, citing HO 41/153). In earlier decades Britons had devastated effigies of Lord Bute, Tom Paine, and many other public figures in focused acts of revenge, but by combining image, action, and massed numbers the people of Bolton were dramatizing their theory that the government's warmaking had ruined the people as they broadcast their demand for public redress of that wrong.

During the great 1818 Manchester area cotton textile strikes, mule spinners "organized striking factory workers into mass processions and solemnly marched three and four abreast through the streets of Manchester, a tactic which the dyers also had employed"; in a clear demonstration of numbers, commitment, unity, and worthiness, they dramatized the strikers' discipline and sobriety (Hall 1989: 452). Elsewhere in Lancashire bands, flags, and coffins containing simulated weavers' skeletons became regular accouterments of orderly marches through the streets. Although this performance recalled seventeenth-century quasi-military marches in some respects, by 1818 it had lost its air of mutiny; it was standardizing and narrowing into a generally peaceful instrument of social movements. Despite the implicit or explicit threat of disruptive action that accompanied many demonstrations, marchers often wore their best clothes, sported uniform ribbons, proceeded in ranks under the banners of their trades, and displayed collective self-control. Thus ordinary people were adopting the demonstration as a standard way of making claims. During the 1820s and 1830s demonstrations and social movements proliferated in British politics.

National and International Politics

Over the long run of 1758 to 1834 changes in state, capital, demography, and contention's accumulated history interwove to promote a shift toward collective interaction that was large in scale and national in scope. In addition, they enhanced the strategic advantage and maneuvering room of formally constituted associations, especially those with national constituencies, as bases for collective interaction. They made parliamentary elections more critical to national issues, encouraged contested elections, drew nonvoters more intensely into electoral campaigns, gave political organizers greater scope for strategic interaction, and encouraged the formation of "paraparliamentary" politics in such guises as national social movements, large-scale petition drives, and calls for a mass platform. Such activities in turn expanded the utilization of local assemblies such as vestries and wardmotes in national struggles over power and policy. These processes sharpened the conflict between two different conceptions and organizations of national politics: one vesting fundamental power in a compact between regime and Parliament, the other treating both of them as instruments of a sovereign people.

To the extent that popular politics nationalized, relations between the British government and the rest of the world became salient in domestic contention. When war had reached into local life in the guise of militia recruitment, press gangs, rising taxes, or diversion of food stocks to the military, it had long stimulated local struggles. American policy figured importantly in the conflicts around John Wilkes in the 1760s. But ostensibly foreign affairs gained new salience in popular struggles with the expansion of empire, the Napoleonic Wars, the creation of a United Kingdom with Ireland, the intensification of economic interchanges and population flows between Ireland and Great Britain, the formation of nationwide networks of collective interaction, and the general shift of contention toward Parliament and national officials. Widow-burning in India, slavery in the colonies, and policy toward France or Belgium generated meetings, petitions, resolutions, letters to newspapers, and impassioned pamphlets.

Most of all, Irish affairs interacted closely with British domestic politics. Irish Catholics made the question of Catholic Emancipation urgent in Great Britain, and Irish mobilization over the question tipped the balance toward the compromise of 1829. That ratification of agitation by a mass-subscription association, in its turn, opened the way to greatly expanded agitation by political unions, workers' organizations, and other associations in the British campaign for parliamentary reform. A government that had conceded so much to a mass organization of Irish priests, peasants, and landless laborers could hardly deny their English, Welsh, and Scottish counterparts rights to organize. Thus Ireland gained its revenge for unwilling service as laboratory for British techniques of repression.

Let me caution one last time against interpreting the transformation of repertoires as unmitigated advance—the irresistible rise of the working class, political modernization, democratization, or something of the sort. Two aspects of the story forbid any such interpretation. First, the history rested not on clairvoyant progress but on fogbound struggle. Although themes such as mass platform and the rights of freeborn Englishmen did give some continuity and direction to claim-making, most alterations of contentious repertoires resulted from tactical maneuvering in which few people reflected on long-term changes in means of action, and no one anticipated the long-term consequences. Wilkes and his followers fought deliberately against his exclusion from Parliament, against general warrants, and for the right to criticize government policy, but they did not deliberately set out to establish the petition march or the election celebration as ways of exerting political pressure. Nevertheless, their maneuvering had that effect.

Second, the move from eighteenth-century to nineteenth-century forms of interaction cost actual and potential claim-makers plenty. British citizens gave up a wide range of interactions that were fairly easy to implement on a local scale, that applied rewards and punishments directly to their objects, that often produced results visible to their participants and the local community. They gave up attacks on enclosures, destruction of tollgates, Rough Music, and other effective performances for means of expression offering few short-term results on a local scale while requiring extensive preparation and coordination. Those means of expression, furthermore, strongly limited who could act on what occasion or interest. Public meetings, petition drives, firm-by-firm strikes, and social-movement tactics as a whole left landless agricultural laborers—a population still growing and increasingly miserable until the middle of the nineteenth century—without effective means of bidding for the wages and employment they knew they needed; the suppression of machine-breaking, the policing of marches, and the containment of arson deprived them of leverage that had sometimes served them well.

More generally, the old repertoire's decline spelled a loss of collective power for workers in localized crafts, clients in patron-client chains, and people whose welfare depended on small-scale community moral pressure. The new repertoire gave disproportionate advantages to people who worked in larger firms, belonged to specialized associations, enjoyed local property rights, and connected with political organizers. That organizational life in general was moving in their direction, that the shift in organizational life promoted the change of repertoires, does not gainsay the losses sustained by those ordinary people whose lives were not moving in that direction, or were moving more slowly than those of their fellow citizens.

The British repertoire of contention changed deeply because the entire structure of political opportunity changed. The repertoire change itself altered political opportunities for different segments of the population. That interaction produced what the ruling classes saw as incessant danger, but what we in comfortable retrospect see as rudiments of mass national politics and elements of parliamentary democracy.

Foundations of Popular Contention

British experience from the 1750s to the 1830s offers valuable lessons for students of popular contention elsewhere. As promised, in this book I have highlighted explanations of popular contention in terms of struggle: various combinations of shared understanding and collective contest rather than social stress and unreasoned impulse. I have, however, made more concessions to imposed consciousness and top-down political mobilization than the purest accounts of struggle allow; the evidence shows, in fact, that the distance between everyday experience and collective interaction increased with the formation of new social-movement repertoires. Cutting the silk from a renegade worker's loom or seizing high-priced food for public distribution satisfied locally shared standards of justice much more immediately than cheers in a meeting hall for a speaker who denounced governmental corruption and called for parliamentary reform.

Analyses in previous chapters have made a case for a strong version of the repertoire metaphor, for the following ideas:

1. that the current array of known, practiced means for collective contention significantly limits the interactions people use in making claims;
2. that not merely their availability as knowledge and skill but their embedding in established identities and concrete social relations—with fellow workers, with local authorities, with police, with families, and

more—lends priority to the existing repertoire over hypothetically superior alternatives;

3. that the array changes incrementally as a result of shared experience in contention;

4. that participants in collective contention are constantly innovating in small ways as part of strategic interaction, but chiefly at the edges of existing performances;

5. that a few of those innovations stick—especially as a consequence of being associated with visible, significant gains for at least one party; but

6. that the course and outcomes of contention also depend on (a) the changing organization and social positions of various potential contenders and (b) fluctuations and long-term alterations in political opportunity structure, as defined by the organization of power, patterns of repression or facilitation, and presence of various potential allies or enemies.

Repertoires changed as a consequence of collective learning within strong structural limits.

Who learned? Of course, particular individuals acquired memories, understandings, and skills in the course of watching or participating in contention. But repertoires and their characteristic performances belonged to social relations among collective identities in something like the same way that distinctive dialects inhere not in individuals' voices but in conversations among connected sets of persons. Any set of persons at risk to make joint claims constitutes a potential identity. Identities take on actuality in performance: both routine social interaction and claim-making itself. Some identities emerge chiefly from routine social interaction in work, neighborhood, school, religious practice, kinship, or friendship, while others emerge chiefly from collective interaction. Thus in the 1820s the identity "Catholic" pervaded a wide range of social relations, then became the basis of sustained challenges to the British government, while "member of the Stockport Political Union" or "supporter of Queen Caroline" designated identities shared chiefly in the public political arena.

Both broad and narrow identities showed up as formations in our catalog of contentious gatherings, but narrowly political identities became more prominent with time. Increasingly, groups of people identified themselves publicly as supporters of ———, opponents of ———, members of————, each defining a position with respect to actions by constituted authorities. Conversely, ties weakened between contentious identities and identities embedded in everyday social life, such as neighbor or parent. In a loose sense, each actualized identity had its own repertoire of claim-making performances. More accurately, however, repertoires belonged to pairs or larger compounds of identities. The routines of web-cutting and donkeying belonged chiefly to sets of workers within the same local trade, although constables and local authorities occasionally became involved in them as well. Particular kinds of public meetings linked self-defined interests to Parliament or the king, but also to pub-owners, rivals, enemies, mayors, and police. Sets of linked identities learned from collective contention.

What did they learn? Imagine a matrix of outcomes by interactions, say all possible outcomes of contention on the horizontal axis, all possible procedures for making contentious claims on the vertical (see Figure 8.1). People attach varying degrees of intrinsic desirability and undesirability—intrinsic costs and benefits, if you will—to the possible performances arrayed on the vertical axis. To the possible outcomes on the horizontal, they attach both (a) relative desirabilities and (b) relative probabilities as

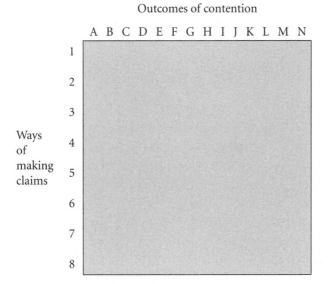

Figure 8.1. Interactions and outcomes in contention

a function of the performances they adopt. Within the cells of the matrix (for example 8B = a rise in wages as the result of a turnout, 3L = abolition of slavery as the result of a petition) resides causal reasoning (however implicit or invalid) about the relationship between performance and outcome; that causal reasoning obviously includes estimates of likely reactions by allies, enemies, and objects of claims. Causal reasoning permits movement in either direction: from proposed performances to likely outcomes, from desired outcomes to appropriate performances.

In this conceptualization, potential sets of collaborative actors share matrices, one per opportunity for action. The matrices alter continuously as a function of changing opportunities, changing capabilities, observations of other people's struggles, and, especially, the potential actors' own experience in making claims. Jointly, people learn and act on the changing matrices. Over and over we have witnessed the rich, irregular, unarticulated analogs of those matrices in the pulling down of poorhouses, seizures of grain, attacks on press gangs, cheers for Queen Caroline, campaigns to repeal the Test and Corporation Acts, and a panorama of other interactions.

The scheme simplifies radically, assuming perfect agreement among all participants in joint claim-making, ignoring the significance of leaders and entrepreneurs in identification of new possibilities or in realigning estimates on the vertical and horizontal axes, neglecting the way such evaluations shift in the course of contentious interaction itself, collapsing relations with third parties such as allies, enemies, police, patrons, and reluctant families of potential activists into computations of actors alone. It also sums up values over whole performances, when participants surely vary in their evaluation of different elements of performances; after all, a workers' march from Guildhall to Parliament could include shouting slogans, meeting famous leaders, confronting MPs, breaking windows, battling policemen, and much more, each item having its own particular attraction or repulsion. Nevertheless, the simplification makes three essential points: that collective contention depended on powerful shared understandings; that for any particular population, situation, and relation to others, previous history had made only a limited number of joint means of claim-making available, leaving many technically feasible and possibly fruitful means unavailable; that understandings concerning those means altered continuously as a result of collective learning.

Collective learning altered people's shared orientations to past, present, and future. For the past, different sets of potential actors accumulated and recreated common memories of grievances, interactions, and outcomes. For the present, the same people fashioned definitions of current problems, threats, and opportunities. For the future, near and far, they constructed stories of possibilities and probabilities in the same regards as well as of their parts in the different available scenarios. Thus mutable shared understandings linked past with future, and thereby constrained present claim-making. I have neither rolled out this conceptual machinery each time it was whirring in the background nor provided systematic evidence for each of its connections. Yet it has informed the analysis from beginning to end.

As British experience illustrates repeatedly, innovation in repertoires occurs chiefly at the edges of existing performances, as someone stretches known routines past familiar limits. When observers or objects of claims show surprise and indignation at a contentious performance, we have reason to suspect that innovation is occurring. Remember Benjamin Franklin's shock at Wilkesite use of electoral celebrations to force cries of "Wilkes and Liberty" from reluctant travelers, the government's forceful reaction to Lord George Gordon's arrival at Parliament with a mass petition and 14,000 followers, and the 1834 *Morning Chronicle*'s hostility to workers' use of their fellows' funerals to voice disapproval of the Tolpuddle Martyrs' conviction and transportation. In each of these instances and many more, a performance's novelty led authorities and unsympathetic observers to demand restriction or banning of unruly actions that later became commonplace.

Some innovations, nevertheless, aim not so much at making a new dent in authorities' defenses as at rousing supporters of the cause and broadcasting their message; the ingenious deployment of the number 45 during Wilkes's campaigns illustrates this sort of innovation. In either case, most innovations disappear after brief trials. Surviving forms of interaction generally take their strength from association with visible successes for one participant in claim-making or another: the conversion of petition-bearing delegations into mass marches, the multiplication of political unions, the containment of demonstrators by New Police.

Innovations in the policing of contention also illustrate a subtler, longer-term process of containment: the channeling and narrowing of contention by interaction between claimants and authorities. Throughout the three-quarters of a century we have been scrutinizing, authorities and their repressive agents responded selectively to the different performances challengers had their disposal, generally rewarding or at least tolerating those which communicated peaceable subordination and battling those which either presumed some form of popular sovereignty or threatened damage to persons and property of the ruling classes. This implicit strategy left avenging interactions among workers and neighbors largely unpunished unless they spilled over into property-holders' precincts, but favored humble appeals to patrons while bringing troops out against invaders of enclosed fields, smashers of capitalists' machines, and meetings devoted to the mass platform. The repressive strategy worked, more or less; although it involved ratifying challengers' rights to make some sorts of claims, it also rendered more costly to their participants those actions which threatened the existing structure of power and property, while helping narrow even generally acceptable performances to their less threatening elements. Just as the firm-by-firm strike shed its acts of vengeance and intimidation, the demonstration lost much of its short-run danger in the course of becoming better established.

Since all parties were acting strategically, however, channeling and narrowing had another side. Challengers repeatedly took advantage of entering wedges, either adapting occasions and performances whose utilization authorities could hardly block, or seizing precedents provided by powerholders' accommodations to other challengers. In the first category fall the recurrent use of authorized occasions for public gathering such as markets, holidays, executions, and elections to show support for popular heroes, opposition to popular villains, or commitment to controversial programs; the Queen Caroline campaign, undertaken in a time of renewed repression, amply illustrates this strategy. In the second we find the organization of antislavery campaigns within existing churches, laborers' demands that farmers smash their own threshing machines during the Swing rebellion, and direct use of the Catholic Association's successes to justify agitation by means of reform-oriented political unions. Indeed, political unions had initially taken shape during 1818 as petitioning organizations that could evade restrictions of 1817's Seditious Meetings Act; the right to petition provided an entering wedge even when the state had filled other gaps in the polity's wall. In these detailed ways, strategic interaction among challengers, allies, rivals, enemies, and authorities altered both repertoires of contention and political opportunity structures.

Strategic interaction generated change from within contentious repertoires. From outside, change in the social environment of contenders and contention also produced important alterations in the forms of claim-making. In the particular circumstances of eighteenth- and nineteenth-century Britain, much of the stimulus to change in political opportunity structure and in the organization of various contenders, not to mention the immediate incentives to make contentious claims, arose from economic capitalization and war-driven expansion of the state. Capitalism and state growth are not, however, universals; in other circumstances we will find population movements, the disintegration of empires, religious revival, or environmental degradation at work on political opportunity structure and contenders' organization, then through them on patterns of contention. The universals in my formulation, if any there be, concern the transformation of repertoires, hence of contention itself, as a function of alterations in political opportunity structure, contenders' organized identities, and the cumulative history of collective struggles.

Mass National Politics and Democracy

We can of course argue about whether the Protestant Reformation, the English Revolution, the Fronde, the Dutch Patriot movement, the French Revolution, or other great European mobilizations before 1800 constituted leaps into mass national politics. Whatever we say on that score, the British experience between the 1750s and the 1830s will stand as a major example of durable transition from relatively parochial to substantially national popular political life. During the nineteenth century, frequent references in local struggles to national parties, policies, and powers; connections between parliamentary maneuvering and local mobilization; confirmation of MPs as advocates and counselors for regional constituencies; enlarged participation in contested elections, and much more, testify to expanded participation of ordinary people in the exercise of power on a national scale. Although nothing like popular sovereignty had arisen in land- and capital-dominated nineteenth-century Great Britain, even landlords and capitalists had to consider the relations between their own interests and the claims organized workers, Irish Catholics, or unenfranchised opponents of slavery were making on the state.

To put it differently, Great Britain had created citizenship, a greatly expanded set of mutual rights and obligations linking the state to a whole category of people defined chiefly by long-term legal residence within the state's territory. New rights and obligations concerned military service, taxation, voting, assembly, association, religious practice, access to the judicial system, legal penalties, economic welfare, working conditions, and other significant zones of human activity. Even after 1832, to be sure, such rights and obligations remained starkly unequal, different for men and women, adults and children, propertied and propertyless, masters and servants, titled and untitled, Protestant and Catholic, Anglican and Dissenting, British and Irish, employed and unemployed. Still, Britain had moved from an eighteenth-century situation of relatively indirect rule, in which magistrates, parsons, landlords, and local councils had done most of the governmental deciding and administering with considerable autonomy, to one of much more direct rule, in which Parliament and national officials exercised extensive central control over the enforcement of these rights and obligations.

Changes in judicial activity illustrate the movement toward direct rule unexpectedly well: reduction of the once-enormous autonomous powers of Justices of the Peace, abandonment of exemplary execution, flogging, or stocking of a few offenders as a frightening spectacle for those who got away or who might contemplate offending the next time, substitution of more general prosecution, imprisonment, and transportation to the colonies, displacement of local constables by nationally regulated police forces that engaged both in routine patrolling and crowd control. All these bespeak a national state reaching into local niches with unprecedented assiduity. Thus told, the story sounds like an unalloyed tale of oppression, Leviathan realized. But the transformation also gave British citizens more extensive access to protective policing, courts that acted in partial independence of local tyrannies or rivalries, and due process for minor offenses. It produced rights as well as obligations and subjugations.

The same sort of explanation that applies to the transition from eighteenth- to nineteenth-century repertoires appears to account for the broadening of citizenship and nationalization of popular politics: the cumulative bargaining out of new relations between subjects and national authorities within the changing threats and opportunities created by the state's expansion and the economy's capitalization. Indeed the two processes overlapped, since in such processes as the partial incorporation of Irish Catholics into the British polity and the incomplete reform of Parliament we see popular contention and other forms of bargaining intersect.

This does not mean that always and everywhere the development of mass national politics and extensive citizenship depends on the coincidence of capitalism and state expansion, although elsewhere in Europe similar coincidences did produce similar developments during the nineteenth and twentieth centuries. Other trajectories to broad citizenship and mass national politics surely pass through colonization and decolonization, state socialism, and revolution, as Barrington Moore declared long ago (Moore 1966). It means that in trajectories like the British one the outcome bears stigmata of its capitalist and statist origins, right down to property-based differentials in citizenship. It also means that the crucial precipitants of mass national politics and broadened citizenship include any and all generators of strong demands by state authorities on their subjects coupled with effective resistance and bargaining by those subjects, especially when state demands bypass established patrons and intermediaries to reach directly into households and communities.

What of democracy? Mass national politics and broadened citizenship do not in themselves constitute or guarantee democracy; they have coexisted with many tyrannies and formed the program of many a populist dictatorship. We can call a polity democratic to the degree that it features (1) broad citizenship, (2) equal citizenship, (3) binding consultation of citizens with respect to state policies and personnel, (4) protection of citizens from arbitrary action of state agents. No perfectly democratic polity has ever existed, at least on a large scale, but we can array historical polities by their approximation of the four criteria. For convenience, we can think of each of the four features as running from 0 (none) to 1 (complete), so that 1100 describes a fascist tyranny with broad, equal citizenship but no binding consultation or protection, while 1011 describes a near-democracy featuring very unequal citizenship rights. All real cases, of course, take intermediate values on the four scores. In this perspective, mass national politics and broad citizenship stand as necessary but not sufficient conditions for democracy; in addition, democracy requires relative equality of citizenship, binding consultation, and protection.

Notice what this conception does *not* do. It does not make general equality of means or opportunity a criterion of democracy; equality refers only to claims on and from the state in a person's capacity as citizen. As much as it invites a search for institutions guaranteeing democratic outcomes, it does not stipulate any particular political institutions as defining features of democracy. It ignores the unequal treatment of non-citizens, disregarding any disabilities they suffer with respect to binding consultation and protection from arbitrary state action. It certainly does not require intelligent communication, patriotism, legitimacy, happiness, or prosperity. It leaves theoretically and empirically open the relationship of democracy to general economic equality, care for non-citizens, social justice, communication, and innumerable other features that people sometimes consider inseparable from democracy.

The proposed conception of democracy *does* declare that a polity is undemocratic to the degree that citizens' political rights and obligations vary by gender, race, religion, national origin, wealth, or any other general set of categories, that it is likewise undemocratic to the extent that large numbers of people subject to the state's jurisdiction lack access to citizenship. It makes binding consultation and protection from arbitrary state action, furthermore, matters of degree—recognizing, for example, that in large democratic states the sheer existence of parliaments limits consultation and state agents sometimes commit injustices. Even breadth and equality, after all, have their limits; when Paul Peterson (1992: 151) proposes "that all citizens, even our youngest, should cast votes or have their votes cast for them by their parents or guardians," he must concede that the infants his proposal would enfranchise generally lack the reasoned political self-interest his argument requires; hence the extra votes his scheme entrusts to parents and guardians. The definition, in short, simply allows us to designate polities as democratic *insofar as* they embody broad, equal citizenship which gives its beneficiaries binding consultation and protection from arbitrary state action.

As in the case of citizenship, more than one process can yield these outcomes, although all relevant processes seem to include substantial demilitarization of the general population and subordination of the military to civilian control. European experience suggests strong hypotheses concerning the social bases of democracy's components:

1. *Protection from arbitrary state action* depends on (a) subordination of the military to civilian control, and (b) class coalitions in which old powerholders ally with relatively powerless but large segments of the population (for example bourgeois and workers), thus extending old privileges and protections.

2. *Binding consultation* depends on (a) subordination of the military to civilian control, (b) extensive domestic taxation (as opposed, for example, to state revenues drawn directly from exports), and (c) representation with respect to the assessment and collection of taxes.
3. *Equal citizenship* depends on (a) broad class coalitions including powerholders, and (b) creation and expansion of electoral systems.
4. *Broad citizenship* depends on (a) extensive domestic taxation, (b) broad class coalitions, and (c) direct recruitment of large military services from the domestic population.

We might reasonably hypothesize that the relative strength of these factors prior to democratization also affects the kind of democracy that emerges, for example that systems growing up chiefly through subordination of the military via defeat in war, military occupation, or some other cause will emphasize protection and breadth more than equality or binding consultation, while domestic taxation alone will promote binding consultation and breadth of citizenship while leaving equality and protection more uncertain. As Hanspeter Kriesi has pointed out, democracy operates quite differently in Switzerland and the Netherlands as a result of the contrast between Switzerland's federal coalescence and the transformation of the Dutch state under French conquest in the 1790s; the Dutch creation of a centralized bureaucracy and a subordinated military promoted a greater emphasis on breadth and equality of citizenship, which in turn led to the incorporation of the population's competing segments by means of "pillarization" in parallel organizations rather than the creation of multiple local niches for different kinds of politics. The Swiss system operates quite differently, tolerating considerable inequality among geographically segregated niches (Kriesi 1990).

In Great Britain the process of state expansion had enormous importance for citizenship. Remember that by "citizenship" we still mean rights and mutual obligations binding state agents and a category of persons defined exclusively by their legal attachment to the same state. Between 1750 and 1815 such rights and obligations multiplied as a result of the state's pursuit of war. War had its most visible effects in the realms of taxation and military service. Total taxes collected, as we have seen, rose from about £17 million in 1790 to almost £80 million in 1815, a 371 percent increase during a period when the cost of living was rising about

45 percent; war-driven taxes reached an extraordinary height: about 35 percent of Britain's total commodity output (Mathias and O'Brien 1976; O'Brien 1988, 1989).

Military service, including civil defense, likewise expanded enormously in scope. As Linda Colley sums up: "In Great Britain, as in other major European powers, it was training in arms under the auspices of the state that was the most common collective working-class experience in the late eighteenth and nineteenth centuries, not labour in a factory, or membership of a radical political organization or an illegal trade union" (Colley 1992: 312). Through the increasingly visible presence of the tax collector, the recruiting sergeant, the militia commander, the press gang, and the Member of Parliament, ordinary British people acquired much more extensive direct contact with the state than they had experienced since the revolutionary period of 1640–1660. This time it lasted.

From multiplied encounters with agents of the state, Britons acquired a growing sense of Britishness, which did not keep many of them from attacking press gangs, evading tax collectors, or joining radical movements; on the contrary, the nationalization of daily life and consciousness nationalized British struggles and resistance to authorities as well. In the process, direct obligations between subjects and state gained enough scope and intensity to merit the name citizenship. As a revolution and a vast military mobilization were creating French citizens across the Channel, reaction to them were creating British citizens in England, Scotland, and Wales.

What of democracy? As of 1750 we can plausibly describe Great Britain as a 0001, a paternalistic polity involving narrow, unequal citizenship and only partial binding consultation of those aristocrats and gentry who enjoyed something like citizens' privileges, but substantial protections from arbitrary state action for them. The narrowness of citizenship did not reside so much in the small parliamentary electorate—although the roughly 300,000 voters in a total population of 7.5 million certainly constituted a compact oligarchy—as in the mediation of most Britons' relations with the state through local and regional notables such as the Justices of the Peace, who enjoyed great autonomy in their exercise of state-authorized positions.

By 1835 Great Britain had moved closer to 1001 or even 1011, as a broader but arguably more unequal citizenry enjoyed extensive rights to assemble, associate, and communicate their grievances directly to the state, although the exclusion of the population's vast majority from the suffrage made binding consultation questionable. The Reform Act of 1832 had not greatly expanded the electorate, despite shifting the basis of representation from chartered privilege to population and wealth. But contention of the previous seventy-five years had significantly enlarged citizenship by establishing numerous channels, including mass associations, election campaigns, and public assemblies, through which even non-voters exercised strong collective claims to be heard directly by agents of the state. The working-class Chartist program of 1838–1848 demanded an extension of democracy by means of equalization: universal suffrage, secret ballot, annual elections, salaried Members of Parliament, no property qualification for MPs, and equal electoral districts, a call for 1111 (with the unstated presumption that British subjects already enjoyed a measure of protection from arbitrary state action). The movement collapsed in 1848, but its program gradually passed into law through the acts of 1867–1868, 1885, 1918, and auxiliary legislation. Through struggle from inside and outside the polity, the breadth and equality of citizenship increased as popular consultation—chiefly in the form of periodic elections—became more binding and protections extended as well.

Military mobilizations continued to inflate the state and extend the range of citizenship during the twentieth century (Cronin 1991). By the enactment of female suffrage in 1918, Great Britain edged into the category of 1111 (in a more differentiated scale, perhaps .75, .80, .60, .75), by no means a "full" democracy, but nonetheless unusually democratic among the states of its time (Cronin 1983). Thereafter, the chief alterations in citizenship consisted of openings to residents of former colonies and extensions of the state services or payments to which citizens had a right. If we included Ireland or British overseas colonies in the evaluation of democracy, to be sure, Britain's democracy scores would all plummet. Still that makes the point: Even in the days of the British Empire and the United Kingdom of Great Britain and Ireland (roughly 1800–1945), the polity commanding Wales, Scotland, and England remained somewhat distinct from the rest, and within its own confines significantly more democratic than they.

In a telling simplification, T. H. Marshall described the whole process of democratization as a movement from civic to political to social rights (Marshall 1950). Marshall's formulation misleads us in two important ways: by substituting a neat succession for a tangled intertwining of civic, political, and social rights, and by erasing many curtailments of rights, for example the massive repression of 1795–1799 and the defeat of Chartism in the 1840s. Nevertheless, Marshall's scheme correctly calls attention to the alternation among relative emphases on the breadth of citizenship, its equality, its protections against arbitrary state action, and control of citizens over state personnel and policy. British history of the last two centuries illustrates the truism that changes in the character of the state and of citizenship entail alterations in the extent and character of democracy.

Once we recognize the importance of military activity to the British state's transformation, British history takes on a delightful irony. In the world as a whole, autonomous militaries generally inhibit democracy, even when they seize power in the name of democratic programs. They regularly inhibit democracy by diminishing the protections of citizens against arbitrary state action, and often do so by blocking the definitiveness of popular consultation—annulling or falsifying elections, bypassing or intimidating Parliaments, evading public surveillance of their activities. Yet in Britain the state's military expansion indirectly fostered democratization. It did so through the struggle and bargaining it generated, which fortified citizenship and subordinated military activity to parliamentary control.

The process began in the sixteenth century with Tudor checking of great lords' private armies and fortified castles. It ended, for practical purposes, in the nineteenth century with the elimination of press gangs. An aristocratically led military continued to draw a major share of the state budget, retained great freedom of action in Ireland and the colonies, and enjoyed great prestige at home, yet as such never wielded autonomous power in domestic politics after 1660. Reliance of the British military on Parliament for finance and supply—still an acute issue in the struggles that led up to the revolution of 1640—eventually subordinated the army and navy to civilian, parliamentary control. In retrospect, we see the crucial importance of that subordination to the later creation of British democracy.

Parallel processes produced military subordination, and thereby promoted democracy, elsewhere in Europe. Where they had less force, as in Iberia and the Balkans, autonomous militaries posed barriers against democracy into the twentieth century. In Iberia the weakening of the monarchy through Napoleon's conquest and the subsequent resurgence of military leaders in the peninsula's reconquest facilitated military intervention throughout the nineteenth century, while in the Balkans both the casting off of Ottoman control and the promotion of local military resistance to the Ottomans by neighboring powers such as the Russian empire similarly fortified the long-term involvement of militaries in politics. *Per contra,* Iberian and Balkan experiences underline the crucial importance of military subordination to democracy.

Great Britain's experience with popular contention, mass national politics, citizenship, and democracy did not, then, blaze the trail for all other European countries; it marked only one path through the forest. Still it was an important path, an example others could not ignore, a crucial case of intersection among capitalist growth, state expansion, and engagement of ordinary people in national politics. For us, it also serves as a profound source of evidence and reflection on the meaning of popular struggle.

Sources and Methods

In order to discipline both narrative and analysis, I have centered this research on a catalog of *contentious gatherings* (CGs). A contentious gathering is an occasion on which a number of people (here, a minimum of ten) outside of the government gathered in a publicly accessible place and made claims on at least one person outside their own number, claims which if realized would affect the interests of their object. (Such claims include expressions of support.) Following this definition, my collaborators and I cataloged every contentious gathering in Middlesex, Surrey, Kent, or Sussex mentioned in any of four publications (*Gentleman's Magazine*, the *Annual Register*, the *London Chronicle*, and, from 1789 onward, the *Times* of London) in 1758, 1759, 1768, 1769, 1780, 1781, 1789, 1795, 1801, 1807, 1811, 1819, or 1820, for a total of 1,204 events. We also inventoried every contentious gathering in Great Britain—England, Wales, or Scotland—mentioned in any of seven publications (*Gentleman's Magazine*, the *Annual Register*, the *Morning Chronicle*, the *Times*, *Mirror of Parliament*, *Hansard's Parliamentary Debates*, *Votes and Proceedings of Parliament*) and occurring during the seven years from 1828 to 1834, for a total of 6,884 events. (We actually read the periodicals through June 1835 in order to catch retrospective evidence of events in earlier years.) We prepared a machine-readable description of each event, including the key words the periodicals used to characterize it. Although my collaborators and I often consulted archival material and the work of other historians when analyzing particular events, the machine-readable records contain only the information drawn from the periodicals. This large catalog constitutes the core of my evidence on changes and variations in collective-action repertoires.

Although I have done the analyses reported in this book on my own, successive groups of researchers at the University of Michigan and the New School for Social Research, working under my direction, took about twelve years to prepare the machine-readable catalog of CGs that constitutes the book's principal source of evidence. We separated identification of sources from enumeration and description of qualifying events: on a first careful pass through the periodicals we tagged every article that mentioned an action (for example the calling of a meeting or the continuation of a strike) that might be part of a CG, on a second pass we copied the articles, and then we sorted the mentions by time and place before screening the events for their conformity to our basic definitions. For context and correction, we placed the events not meeting our criteria in a separate file, from which (among other things) we drew the catalog of "routine assemblies" mentioned below.

Each time a bundle of reports drawn from our basic periodicals qualified an event as a CG, my collaborators and I prepared a machine-readable record containing the following parts:

1. A general description of the *event,* one per CG, for a total of 8,088 records.
2. A description of each *formation*—each person or set of persons acting in a distinguishable manner—within each CG (27,184 records).
3. A description of each *action*—any participating formations's movement or change with respect to the claims being made, including new utterances, cheers, or displays of sentiments—within each CG (50,875 records); when two or more formations changed action simultaneously, as in the outbreak of a fight, we transcribed their doings as separate actions within the same action-phase.
4. An identification of each *source* (including sources supplementary to our standard periodicals) we consulted in preparing the event for coding (21,030 records).
5. An identification of each *location* in which any part of the CG took place (11,054 records).
6. An enumeration of additional *names* the sources gave any formation (28,995 records).
7. An enumeration of *individuals* mentioned as members of any formation (26,318 records).
8. Supplementary information on the geographical or numerical *size* of any formation (18,413 records).

9. The detailed *texts* from which we drew summary descriptions of actions (76,189 records).

10. *Comments* on any aspect of the CG or its description (5,450 records).

Except for straightforward items such as day of the week or county names, these records do not contain codes in the usual sense of the term; on the whole, we transcribed words from the texts or (when that was not feasible) paraphrases of those words. Instead of coding names given to formations into broad categories, for example, we transcribed the actual words used in our sources. Thus the transcription of each action includes the actor's name, a verb characterizing the action, and (where there was one) the action's object.

We minimized inferences and syntheses concerning events and their contexts, with the idea that it was better to leave the machine-readable record as a reduced but relatively faithful transcription of the texts, and to encourage users of the records to make their inferences or syntheses systematic and self-conscious. We divided the record into reported actions before, during, and after the CG itself—that is, before any two participating formations began interacting on that occasion, and after the last two stopped interacting.

Thus the attempt of pressed sailors to escape from their ship in Portsmouth (January 1758) described in Chapter 1 involved five formations: escaping sailors, marines who shot at them, the subset of the sailors whom the marines wounded, a ship's lieutenant who ordered them to fire, and the Lords of the Admiralty to whom the mutinous sailors appealed unsuccessfully; we omitted workmen on the dock and officers who undoubtedly accompanied the arrested soldiers back to Portsmouth because our sources did not report any interaction (not even cheers or imprecations) between them and clearly designated participants in the contention. According to our report, the event took place in two different locations: at the jetty in Portsmouth, and at the Admiralty in Westminster. (It is debatable whether we should have added locations for the sailors' march from Portsmouth to London as well as their return in irons to Portsmouth; we omitted intermediate locations because our sources did not mention them explicitly.) We recorded nine actions, of which one took place after the CG ended:

Seventy men gather on board the Namur.
The men force their way onto the dock.

The lieutenant orders marines to fire.

Marines fire.

They wound one or two sailors.

The men set out for London.

Fifteen of them attempt to gain audience at the Admiralty.

Lords of the Admiralty order them put in irons.

The gathering ends.

The sailors are court-martialed and sentenced.

Obviously the accounts would have allowed us to record more intermediate steps; the nine we actually set down represent the major changes in location and in claim-making. In our central action record the sequence of actions appears in a kind of pidgin English (all verbs, for example, remaining in the present tense), while the supplementary record contains extensive extracts from the text.

Although some names repeat from CG to CG, the records contain about 12,000 different formation names, about 2,500 distinct verbs, and so on through the various items they describe. My own analyses of the records generally grouped those thousands of individual designations into from four to sixty categories, depending on the purpose at hand. How many distinctions I made within and among such categories varied with the character of the analysis. The great virtue of this apparently obsessive recording of detail is, precisely, to permit the regrouping of elements as questions change or refine.

In addition to the machine-readable descriptions of CGs, our files include a variety of other evidence, machine-readable and otherwise:

1. Machine-readable descriptions of 1,982 "routine assemblies"—gatherings in the Southeast (Kent, Middlesex, Surrey, or Sussex) during 1758, 1759, 1768, 1769, 1780, 1781, 1789, 1795, 1801, 1807, 1811, 1819, or 1820 in which no one made claims that would have qualified the event as contentious.

2. Machine-readable descriptions of 818 locations (parishes, towns, wards, and other sites) in Kent, Surrey, Sussex, or Middlesex.

3. Machine-readable transcriptions of total population, urban population, proportion of land cultivated, and 35 other characteristics for all counties of Great Britain, chiefly as of 1831.

4. A separate file of machine-readable descriptions of 285 CGs forming part of the "Swing" rebellion of 1830.
5. Machine-readable transcriptions of 1,039 events from the "Swing" rebellion catalogued in the appendix to Eric Hobsbawm and George Rudé, *Captain Swing.*
6. Another separate file of 1,680 CGs belonging to the reform mobilization of 1830–1832.
7. Machine-readable transcriptions of all entries in Kent's London street directories of trades and businesses for 1759, 1768, 1801, and 1828, plus 5 percent of all entries for 1781, 1795, and 1811.
8. Machine-readable descriptions of 9,889 CGs from 1758 through 1834 we identified in readings of John Belchem, *'Orator' Hunt;* John Bohstedt, *Riots and Community Politics;* James Bradley, *Popular Politics and the American Revolution in England;* John Brewer, *Party Ideology and Popular Politics at the Accession of George III;* Michael Carter, *Peasants and Poachers;* Frank Darvall, *Popular Disturbances and Public Order in Regency England;* Carlos Flick, *The Birmingham Political Union and the Movements for Reform in Britain;* John Foster, *Class Struggle and the Industrial Revolution;* Albert Goodwin, *The Friends of Liberty;* J. L. and Barbara Hammond, *The Town Labourer, The Skilled Labourer,* and *The Village Labourer;* Mark Harrison, *Crowds and History;* Anthony Hayter, *The Army and the Crowd in Mid-Georgian England;* R. G. Kirby, *The Voice of the People;* Kenneth Logue, *Popular Disturbances in Scotland;* A. J. Peacock, *Bread or Blood;* Iorwerth Prothero, *Artisans and Politics in Early Nineteenth Century London;* Bernard Reaney, *The Class Struggle in Nineteenth Century Oxfordshire;* D. J. Rowe, *London Radicalism, 1830–1843;* George Rudé, *Wilkes and Liberty;* Walter Shelton, *English Hunger and Industrial Disorders;* John Stevenson, *Popular Disturbances in England;* and E. P. Thompson, *The Making of the English Working Class.*
9. Standing files containing the dossiers (and often more detail) for machine-readable files 1 through 8, plus the main files of CGs.
10. Additional descriptive material on major events and sequences of events.
11. Microfilms or photocopies of about 20,000 pages of manuscripts in British archives (especially the Public Record Office, London) from 1740 to 1860, drawn especially from administrative and political correspondence concerning control of collective action.

I have deposited documented versions of files 1 through 7 in the Inter-University Consortium for Political and Social Research, Ann Arbor, Michigan, for distribution to other scholars.

Comparisons

My group has compared its descriptions and enumerations of CGs with other historical publications, with other periodicals, and with archival material. In addition to such spot comparisons as the one with Roger Wells reported in Chapter 2 and those with Hobsbawm-Rudé and Bohstedt reported below, we staged a number of confrontations with periodicals, notably parallel readings of our own sources, the *Lancaster Gazette, Cobbett's Political Register,* and *The Scotsman* for 1828 and 1829. We searched for all reported gatherings in all sources, singled out those whose descriptions clearly qualified them as CGs (for example explicitly described the making of claims on others), then asked: (1) What sorts of events does one source report, but not the other? (2) What differences among sources appear in descriptions of the same events—especially differences bearing on our ability to decide whether they qualify as CGs?

From 1828, for example, of 33 events reported in the *Lancaster Gazette* that qualified as CGs 23 also appeared in our files, but in 2 of the 23 (both public meetings, one in support of a strike, the other in support of catholic claims) our sources provided insufficient information to qualify the events as CGs; the 10 events our sources failed to mention occurred in Manchester (2), Leeds, Wigan, Westmoreland, Halton, Bury, Rochdale, Lancaster, and Darrington, and included 5 violent gatherings, 3 public meetings (on slavery, tithes, and parish issues), an election gathering, and a gathering in support of government officials. In compensation, however, our sources reported a full 90 qualifying CGs for Lancashire in 1828—including 59 left unreported in the *Lancaster Gazette*—and scores more for adjacent counties. Local and specialized periodicals sometimes reported more events within their own purviews than our national periodicals, but not always, and rarely with significantly more detail.

When we turned to comparisons with Home Office correspondence, the weight shifted decisively: periodicals yielded far more events than the collected correspondence concerning a given region and period. For 1828, for example, we searched HO 43/36, 51/31, 52/05, 62/1, 64/11, and 64/16, finding only 3 events from our own collection, each of them described less fully than in our periodicals. Other comparisons concerned North-umberland from January through June 1831 (HO 52/14) plus Berkshire, Devonshire, and Lancashire 1828–1834 (relevant county collections of HO 52). In general, such comparisons indicate that our sources (1) significantly overrepresent London and its immediate hinterland, (2) greatly underrepresent distant locations, especially outside of major cities, (3) underrepresent industrial conflicts, (4) identify far larger numbers of CGs than comparable series of Home Office correspondence, and (5) on average—but by no means always—offer more general accounts of the events in question.

Let us look more closely at two comparisons with other historians' work. For all years of 1790–1810, John Bohstedt has assembled a catalog of "riots" from all of England and Wales. (Despite my strenuous efforts to dissuade him, Bohstedt adopted the authorities' terms "riot" and "mob.") In a riot, by his definition, fifty or more people assembled and tried to damage or seize property, attack someone, or coerce someone to act and/or to desist from action (Bohstedt 1983: 4). Bohstedt identified every event meeting his criteria in HO 42, *The Observer*, the *Morning Chronicle*, the *Annual Register*, and (when one or both of the other newspapers was missing) the *Times* or the *London Chronicle*. Altogether his search yielded 617 such events.

Bohstedt's coverage, like mine, was surely more complete for pitched battles than for industrial conflicts or everyday struggles over food; Roger Wells writes scathingly of the lacunae in Bohstedt's coverage of "food riots," as he would no doubt of mine (Wells 1988: 91–92). Bohstedt's procedure closely resembled mine, except in the following ways:

1. Bohstedt's enumeration covered all twenty-one years, while mine covered only five.
2. Bohstedt took information from all of England and Wales, while for this period I took it only for Kent, Middlesex, Surrey, and Sussex.
3. Bohstedt restricted his attention to "riots" as just defined; my CGs included every event that Bohstedt would consider a riot, but many more nonviolent gatherings as well. Bohstedt counts an average of 32 riots per year for England and Wales, while my sample for the period includes an average of 8 violent events (out of 64 CGs of all kinds) per year for the Southeast.
4. Bohstedt's catalog drew from HO 42 as well as the periodicals; although

I read selectively in the relevant archives, including HO 42, for supplementary information on particular events and on repression, my
catalog itself drew only from periodicals.

We should not, therefore, expect the two bodies of evidence to resemble
each other closely. Bohstedt, furthermore, concentrates his rich analysis
on differences among localities and types of events rather than changes
over time. Nevertheless, it is worth asking whether Bohstedt discovered
the same characteristics and trends at a national scale as my collection
displays for the Southeast.

Bohstedt partitions the issues in his "riots" as indicated in Table A.1.
Although our categories are not entirely compatible, the distribution
suggests a considerably larger representation of military struggles—recruiting, mutinies, and military-civilian brawls—than appear among the
Southeast's CGs for 1789, 1795, 1801, 1807, and 1811. My sample, meanwhile, contains a significantly higher proportion of manifestly political
and ideological issues; Catholic claims, elections, royalty, national government, and local government together account for 54.5 percent of all CGs
in the sample years. The difference probably results chiefly from a fact
already noted: contention involving the military was, almost by definition,

Table A.1. Issues in Bohstedt's "riots," 1790–1810

Issue	London	Provinces	Total
Food	4.1%	48.0%	39.2%
Labor	4.9	7.8	7.2
Military	25.2	20.7	21.6
Political/ideological	13.8	9.6	10.2
Brawls	16.3	2.8	5.5
Miscellaneous	35.0	9.3	14.4
Unknown	0.8	2.0	1.8
Total	100.1	99.9	99.9
Number of events	123	494	617

Source: Bohstedt 1983: 14.

more likely to generate violence (hence to qualify for Bohstedt's collection), while meetings and demonstrations concerning political issues frequently took place quite peacefully.

Bohstedt suggests that the "older tradition of bargaining through riot"—in grain seizures, invasions of enclosed fields, mutinies, wage disputes, and similar events—"reached its climax in these two decades" (Bohstedt 1983: 209). He denies that technological change, innovations in military recruitment, or advance of the market in themselves frequently generated riots in defense of older privileges and social arrangements. He sees the effects of those big transformations as real but far more indirect: proto-industrialization and nationalization of the food market eventually "knocked the props from under a locally enforceable 'moral economy'" (ibid.: 216). Bohstedt argues, furthermore, that contrary to a common belief among working-class historians the big changes in outlook did not move the populace from loyalism to radicalism: "The war years did not witness a simple spiritual progress of 'the people' from 'natural' but 'backward' loyalism to 'enlightened' radicalism; what was genuinely new during that time was an unprecedented widening of the organized political public on both sides. Rather than conversion, the significant transition was mobilization, the emergence of perceptions and organizations having regional and national, not merely local, horizons" (ibid.: 219). In other words, the character of larger-scale collective violence changed little, but its political context altered; a nationalization of contention occurred.

In that regard, Bohstedt's evidence and mine coincide. The CGs of 1789–1815 show clear signs of nationalization. Bohstedt is surely right, furthermore, to insist that major economic changes affected popular contention chiefly through their long-term impact on interests and organization rather than through their generation of the immediate stimuli to conflict. A final point of approximate agreement: in the Southeast, violent events changed character and context between 1789 and 1811 much less than did nonviolent events, or than did the relative predominance of different sorts of events.

There, however, we begin to see differences between Bohstedt's findings and mine. According to my evidence from the Southeast, the character of popular contention changed dramatically during the war years. The differences probably result from Bohstedt's concentration on collective violence—"riots"—on a large scale. The occasions of violence changed less between 1790 and 1810 than the occasions for nonviolent contention. But the nonviolent share of all events increased dramatically. In the Southeast, and most likely in Great Britain as a whole, the growth of associations, public meetings, and related means of claim-making coupled closely with the nationalization of popular programs and complaints. It became significantly more common for ordinary people to address their demands and statements of preference to and through Parliament. The transmission ran in both directions: people who had demands or grievances more frequently addressed them directly to an MP or to Parliament as a whole, Parliament's consideration of a bill more frequently incited popular mobilization and the collective statement of preferences.

We also have a chance to compare the enumeration of CGs for the "Swing" rebellion of 1830 with an authoritative catalog, that of Hobsbawm and Rudé (1968). Neither set is complete; if, for example, we take all mentions of arson in Kent between 14 June 1830 and 31 January 1831, we find 42 incidents in both the Hobsbawm-Rudé catalog and the initial file of reports my group assembled before its *triage* for CGs, 11 in Hobsbawm-Rudé alone and 33 in Tilly alone. Roger Wells (Reed and Wells 1990: 165–166) has characteristically scored Hobsbawm and Rudé for missing incidents in Sussex and elsewhere. By our criteria, in any case, most of these incidents do not qualify as contentious gatherings.

Taking only events mentioned in our sources with strong indications of a gathering of 10 or more people, our enumeration includes 285 CGs from 29 August through 31 December 1830. Over the same period, Hobsbawm and Rudé cataloged 924 events: just over three times as many. Their much larger number of events stems from three differences between the compilations: (1) Hobsbawm and Rudé's enumeration of events in a wider range of sources, including archival material; (2) their adoption of a much more generous criterion, which included threats, arson, and machine-breaking where the authors and numbers of participants were unknown; (3) the fact that we consolidated actions in adjacent parishes or on adjacent days into a single event if we had evidence of substantial overlap in the persons involved. Nevertheless, if we take events having precise starting dates in both collections, the correlation between the numbers of events per day in the two enumerations is .95; day after day there appear roughly one CG for every three or four events in the Hobsbawm-Rudé collection. Given the differences in sources and criteria, the correspondence is striking.

Table A.2. Day of week for Swing events in Tilly and Hobsbawm-Rudé catalogs

Day	Tilly	Hobsbawm-Rudé
Sunday	20	82
Monday	65	212
Tuesday	60	138
Wednesday	40	132
Thursday	30	105
Friday	34	121
Saturday	22	89
Total	271	324

The starting points of Swing events distributed quite unevenly across the week, as indicated in Table A.2. Where we can date them securely, about 45 percent of Swing events began on Monday or Tuesday, after the weekend's parleys, on days of frequent leisure for both agricultural and industrial workers. The two independent compilations agree very closely on that distribution as well.

Previous Reports of the Research

Over the many years this study required, my group issued a number of technical papers and provisional research reports. Here is a list of the more widely circulated of those papers (CRSO = Center for Research on Social Organization, University of Michigan; CSSC = Center for Studies of Social Change, New School for Social Research):

Brown, Brian (1981): "Industrial Capitalism, Conflict, and Working-Class Contention in Lancashire 1842," in Louise A. Tilly and Charles Tilly, eds., *Class Conflict and Collective Action.* Beverly Hills: Sage.

Correa, Maria Emilia (1985): "The Legal Context of Collective Action: A Chronology of Events in Great Britain, 1700–1834," CSSC Working Paper 21.

Espaillat, Carmen, and Vina A. Lanzona (1993): "Repression and Facilitation in Great Britain, Ireland, and the United Kingdom, 1750–1835," CSSC Working Paper 160.

Horn, Nancy, and Charles Tilly (1986): "Catalogs of Contention in Britain, 1758–1834," CSSC Working Paper 32.

Kim, Hyun (1986): "The Parliamentary History of Great Britain: A Chronology of the Debates and Proceedings of Both Houses of Parliament (for twenty selected years: 1758–59, 1768–69, 1780–81, 1785, 1801, 1807, 1811, 1819–20)," CSSC Working Paper 25. (1987): "Social Change and Collective Action in Norfolk, 1820–1840," CSSC Working Paper 47.

Lal, Radhika (1987): "Social Change and Contention in Berkshire, 1820–1840," CSSC Working Paper 45.

Munger, Frank (1974): "A Comparison of the Dissatisfactions and Collective Action Models of Protest: The Case of the Working Classes of Lancashire, England: 1793–1830," CRSO Working Paper 105; presented to the annual meeting of the American Sociological Association. (1977): "Popular Protest and Its Suppression in Early Nineteenth-Century Lancashire, England: A Study in Theories of Protest and Repression," Ph.D. diss. in sociology, University of Michigan. (1979): "Measuring Repression of Popular Protest by English Justices of the Peace in the Industrial Revolution," *Historical Methods* 12: 76–83. (1981a): "Contentious Gatherings in Lancashire, England, 1750–1830," in Louise A. Tilly and Charles Tilly, eds., *Class Conflict and Collective Action.* Beverly Hills: Sage. (1981b): "Suppression of Popular Gatherings in England, 1800–1830," *American Journal of Legal History* 25: 111–140.

Murphy, Fred (1987): "Social Change and Contention in the County of Devon, 1800–1840," CSSC Working Paper 53.

Pearlman, Michael (1977a): "Great Britain, 1828–1834: Historiography and Selected Bibliography," CRSO Working Paper 159. (1977b): "Some Political Issues in Nineteenth-Century Britain, Part One: The Government and Workers' Associations, the Rural Rebellions of 1830, Parish Government, Catholic Emancipation," CRSO Working Paper 160. (1977c): "Some Political Issues in Nineteenth-Century Britain, Part Two: The Rights of Collective Association and Assembly; Parliamentary Reform; Industrial Conflict," CRSO Working Paper 165.

Poland, Diane (1987): "Social Change and Contention in Edinburgh, 1820–1840," CSSC Working Paper 55.

Schweitzer, R. A. (1979): "A Study of Contentious Gatherings in Early Nineteenth-Century Great Britain," *Historical Methods* 12: 1–4. (1980): "British Catholic Emancipation, Prototype of Reform?" CRSO Working Paper 220.

Schweitzer, R. A., and Steven C. Simmons (1981): "Interactive, Direct-Entry Approaches to Contentious Gathering Event Files," *Social Science History* 5: 317–342.

Schweitzer, R. A., Charles Tilly, and John Boyd (1980): "The Texture of Contention in Britain, 1828–1829," CRSO Working Paper 211.

Seth, Anuradha (1987): "Social Change and Contention in Lancashire, 1820–1840," CSSC Working Paper 39.

Skinner, Rebecca, and Carlos de la Torre (1988): "Social Change and Contention in Warwick, 1800–1840," CSSC Working Paper 70.

Stanley, Erica A. (1983): "The GBS Topographical Survey of London," CRSO Working Paper 308. (1984): "Kent's Directories of London, 1759–1828: A Guide to the Machine-Readable Transcription," CRSO Working Paper 309.

Steinberg, Marc W. (1983): "Class Consciousness, Interests, and Their Articulation among the English Working Class, 1828–1831," CRSO Working Paper 292. (1989): "Worthy of Hire: Discourse, Ideology, and Collective Action among English Working-Class Trade Groups, 1800–1830," Ph.D. diss. in sociology, University of Michigan. 2 vols.

Tilly, Charles (1977): "Collective Action in England and America, 1765–1775," in Don E. Fehrenbacher and Richard Maxwell Brown, eds., *Tradition, Conflict and Modernization: Perspectives on the American Revolution*. New York: Academic Press. (1978): *From Mobilization to Revolution*. Reading, Mass.: Addison-Wesley. (1979): "Repertoires of Contention in America and Britain, 1750–1830," in Mayer N. Zald and John D. McCarthy, eds., *The Dynamics of Social Movements*. Cambridge, Mass.: Winthrop. (1980): "How (and, to Some Extent, Why) to Study British Contention," CRSO Working Paper 212. (1981): "The Web of Contention in Eighteenth-Century Cities," in Louise A. Tilly and Charles Tilly, eds., *Class Conflict and Collective Action*. Beverly Hills: Sage. (1982a): "Britain Creates the Social Movement," in James Cronin and Jonathan Schneer, eds., *Social Conflict and the Political Order in Modern Britain*. London: Croom Helm. (1982b): "British Conflicts, 1828–1831," CRSO Working Paper 255. (1982c): "Proletarianization and Rural Collective Action in East Anglia and Elsewhere, 1500–1900," *Peasant Studies* 10: 5–34. (1983): "Speaking Your Mind without Elections, Surveys, or Social Movements," *Public Opinion Quarterly* 47: 461–478. (1985a): "De Londres (1768) à Paris (1788)," in Jean Nicolas, ed., *Mouvements populaires et conscience sociale, XVIe-XIXe siècles*. Paris: Maloine. (1986a): "European Violence and Collective Action since 1700," *Social Research* 53: 159–184. (1986b): "Structural Change and Contention in Great Britain, 1758–1834," CSSC Working Paper 36. (1987a): "The Analysis of Popular Collective Action," *European Journal of Operational Research* 30: 223–229. (1987b): "GBS + GCL = ?" *Connections* 10: 94–105. (1987c): "Twenty Years of British Contention," CSSC Working Paper 52. (1989): "Collective Violence in European Perspective," in Ted Robert Gurr, ed., *Violence in America*, vol. 2. Newbury Park: Sage. (1991a): "From Mutiny to Mass Mobilization in Great Britain, 1758–1834," CSSC Working Paper 109. (1991b): "Revolution, War, and Other Struggles in Great Britain, 1789–1815," CSSC Working Paper 127. (1992): "How to Detect, Describe, and Explain Repertoires of Contention," CSSC Working Paper 150. (1993b): "Contentious Repertoires in Great Britain, 1758–1834," *Social Science History* 17: 253–280. (1993c): "Social Movements as Historically Specific Clusters of Political Performances," CSSC Working Paper 162.

Tilly, Charles, and R. A. Schweitzer (1982): "How London and Its Conflicts Changed Shape, 1758–1834," *Historical Methods* 5: 67–77.

Table A.3. Formations participating directly in contentious gatherings, 1758–1834

| | Southeastern England | | | | | | |
| | % of annual total | | | | | | |
Type of formation	1758	1759	1768	1769	1780	1781	1789
Parliament, MP	0.0	0.0	0.2	3.9	7.5	1.1	2.8
National officials	0.0	0.0	1.5	2.0	2.9	5.3	0.9
Royalty	0.0	4.4	1.0	2.0	0.4	2.1	6.5
Gentlemen, nobles	0.0	2.2	2.7	5.4	2.1	1.1	6.5
Judges	0.0	0.0	2.5	1.5	2.1	2.1	0.0
Mayor	5.9	0.0	1.7	4.4	0.8	0.0	2.8
Other local officials	2.9	2.2	0.7	11.2	5.0	11.6	6.5
Clergy	2.9	0.0	0.0	0.0	0.8	0.0	0.0
Freeholders/electors	2.9	0.0	0.7	0.5	0.4	0.0	6.5
Other local assemblies	0.0	6.7	4.4	6.8	1.7	3.2	5.6
Members of trade	14.7	0.0	26.8	18.0	2.9	8.4	15.7
Other interest	2.9	2.2	3.2	0.5	2.9	4.2	9.3
Police	2.9	4.4	3.2	3.9	4.1	6.3	2.8
Troops	8.8	17.8	6.4	3.9	9.5	15.8	0.9
Unnamed crowd	14.7	13.3	11.6	6.3	25.7	4.2	4.6
Named individual	11.8	15.6	9.4	9.3	13.7	4.2	4.6
Other	29.4	31.1	23.9	20.5	17.4	30.5	24.1
Total	99.8	99.9	99.9	100.1	99.9	100.1	100.1
N	34	45	406	205	241	95	108

Table A.3 (continued)

Type of formation	Southeastern England						
	% of annual total						
	1795	1801	1807	1811	1819	1820	1828
Parliament, MP	4.3	0.0	12.4	10.1	7.7	14.1	4.4
National officials	1.1	1.4	0.4	0.8	1.7	1.4	3.3
Royalty	2.9	4.1	2.5	3.4	0.6	6.7	0.3
Gentlemen, nobles	3.2	4.8	4.5	14.3	3.7	4.7	3.1
Judges	2.2	2.8	1.2	0.0	0.6	0.7	1.1
Mayor	1.4	2.8	2.1	2.5	1.4	2.7	2.0
Other local officials	14.1	4.8	13.6	9.2	30.2	13.2	10.1
Clergy	0.0	3.4	0.4	0.0	0.9	0.6	0.3
Freeholders/electors	2.9	4.1	0.8	2.5	3.4	6.2	0.5
Other local assemblies	13.4	9.0	13.2	12.6	21.0	18.7	8.6
Members of trade	10.1	9.7	4.5	5.9	2.5	3.7	7.0
Other interest	7.2	6.9	12.4	8.4	6.9	4.2	12.7
Police	2.9	2.8	4.1	4.2	2.5	2.2	4.1
Troops	10.5	5.5	1.2	4.2	0.9	2.1	1.5
Unnamed crowd	7.2	6.2	3.3	5.0	3.7	3.9	2.6
Named individual	3.2	6.9	3.3	0.8	2.5	3.7	13.4
Other	13.4	24.8	19.8	16.0	9.7	11.1	25.1
Total	100.0	100.0	99.7	99.9	99.9	99.9	100.1
N	277	145	242	119	648	804	614

Table A.3 (continued)

Type of formation	Southeastern England % of annual total							
	1829	1830	1831	1832	1833	1834	Total	N
Parliament, MP	5.3	4.2	9.3	15.6	10.6	10.2	8.4	878
National officials	1.8	1.5	2.3	2.9	1.7	2.7	2.0	213
Royalty	0.4	1.9	1.4	1.0	0.8	1.5	1.8	185
Gentlemen, nobles	4.6	2.2	3.0	1.9	2.0	2.7	3.2	332
Judges	1.0	1.4	0.5	1.0	0.4	0.7	1.0	105
Mayor	1.4	0.9	2.9	1.7	2.5	1.1	1.9	200
Other local officials	11.9	7.2	14.5	12.1	17.5	17.5	13.1	1,372
Clergy	1.7	1.6	0.5	0.6	0.4	0.7	0.8	81
Freeholders/electors	3.7	2.7	1.8	1.7	2.7	1.4	2.4	251
Other local assemblies	8.1	7.7	25.6	13.7	15.9	15.6	14.0	1,471
Members of trade	5.5	8.5	3.7	3.1	5.5	6.2	6.5	681
Other interest	5.7	5.8	5.1	7.3	7.7	8.8	6.6	696
Police	4.4	5.4	4.4	5.3	6.4	6.1	4.5	474
Troops	1.3	2.6	0.7	1.7	1.0	0.6	2.4	248
Unnamed crowd	2.6	8.2	3.6	4.3	3.1	2.6	5.1	536
Named individual	13.4	10.4	9.9	4.5	4.9	4.3	7.4	776
Other	27.2	27.8	10.7	21.6	16.9	17.4	18.9	1,985
Total	100.0	100.0	99.9	100.0	100.0	100.1	100.0	10,484
N	703	1,289	1,459	1,144	905	1,001	10,484	

Table A.3 (continued)

Type of formation	Other Great Britain								
	% of annual total								
	1828	1829	1830	1831	1832	1833	1834	Total	N
Parliament, MP	1.2	2.3	3.9	8.6	9.5	9.3	8.4	6.5	546
National officials	3.0	0.3	1.5	1.8	2.0	3.4	6.9	2.3	197
Royalty	0.4	0.3	0.5	0.1	0.6	1.0	0.5	0.4	35
Gentlemen, nobles	2.5	2.7	1.8	2.3	2.3	3.6	4.2	2.5	212
Judges	1.1	1.9	2.0	2.0	2.0	1.8	1.4	1.8	155
Mayor	1.9	2.2	1.1	2.8	2.7	0.4	2.2	2.0	172
Other local officials	2.1	2.6	2.6	4.6	5.8	5.1	3.4	3.9	324
Clergy	0.9	1.8	1.4	0.6	0.5	0.8	0.4	0.9	77
Freeholders/electors	1.9	2.4	1.5	1.3	1.5	1.2	1.6	1.6	131
Other local assemblies	6.2	7.5	9.3	27.1	24.5	21.7	19.4	18.0	1,508
Members of trade	6.7	14.3	6.6	6.6	4.4	12.6	6.1	7.4	620
Other interest	14.3	6.6	4.0	6.0	8.1	2.8	8.1	6.6	551
Police	2.6	6.2	2.4	2.8	4.5	4.1	1.4	3.3	275
Troops	2.3	3.8	2.5	3.3	2.3	2.2	1.1	2.6	221
Unnamed crowd	1.8	5.0	14.2	4.3	4.3	2.6	0.7	5.9	495
Named individual	9.0	10.8	21.0	8.9	6.9	3.2	1.3	10.3	861
Other	42.3	29.4	23.7	17.0	18.2	24.5	32.8	24.0	2,013
Total	100.2	100.1	100.0	100.1	100.1	100.3	99.9	100.0	8,393
N	568	929	1,861	2,209	1,382	507	937	8,393	

Note: Excludes spectators, bystanders, and absent objects of claims, as well as one 1758 CG originating in Portsmouth and passing through London.

Table A.4. Most common subject-verb-object combinations, 1758–1834 (combinations appearing in at least 0.5% of all actions having objects during the period)

1758–1801 (2021 actions)

Interest-Delib[erate]-Parl[iament]	Workers-Attack-Workers	Workers-Attack-Trade
Workers-Attack-Repressive	Workers-Control-Workers	Workers-Control-Other
Trade-Delib-Parl	Crowd-Claim-Other	Crowd-Attack-Trade
Crowd-Attack-Crowd	Crowd-Attack-Repressive	Crowd-Attack-Locals
Crowd-Attack-Officials	Crowd-Attack-Electors	Crowd-Attack-Government
Crowd-Attack-Other	Crowd-Control-Crowd	Crowd-Control-Repressive
Crowd-Control-Officials	Crowd-Control-Other	Crowd-Cheer-Royalty
Crowd-Enter-Other	Repressive-Attack-Crowd	Repressive-Control-Crowd
Repressive-Control-Pariahs	Repressive-Control-Other	Repressive-Enter-Crowd
Repressive-Other-Crowd	Locals-Cheer-Officials	Locals-Delib-Locals
Locals-Delib-Inhabitants	Officials-Control-Repressive	Officials-Control-Other
Officials-Delib-Locals	Officials-Delib-Inhabitants	Electors-Claim-Royalty
Electors-Delib-Parl	Inhabitants-Delib-Officials	Inhabitants-Delib-Parl
Inhabitants-Delib-Royalty	Other-Attack-Crowd	Other-Control-Other

1807–1820 (2365 actions)

Interest-Cheer-Government	Interest-Delib-Parl	Trade-Delib-Parl
Crowd-Attack-Crowd	Crowd-Attack-Repressive	Crowd-Attack-Locals
Crowd-Attack-Government	Crowd-Attack-Other	Crowd-Control-Crowd
Crowd-Control-Other	Crowd-Cheer-Government	Crowd-Cheer-Parl
Crowd-Cheer-Royalty	Crowd-Communicate-Parl	Crowd-Communicate-Royalty
Repressive-Control-Crowd	Locals-Cheer-Parl	Locals-Delib-Locals
Locals-Delib-Officials	Locals-Delib-Parl	Locals-Delib-Inhabitants
Locals-Delib-Royalty	Officials-Delib-Inhabitants	Electors-Claim-Royalty
Electors-Cheer-Parl	Electors-Delib-Parl	Government-Delib-Government
Parl-Delib-Locals	Parl-Delib-Inhabitants	Inhabitants-Claim-Locals
Inhabitants-Claim-Parl	Inhabitants-Claim-Royalty	Inhabitants-Cheer-Locals
Inhabitants-Cheer-Officials	Inhabitants-Cheer-Parl	Inhabitants-Cheer-Royalty
Inhabitants-Delib-Locals	Inhabitants-Delib-Officials	Inhabitants-Delib-Royalty
Inhabitants-Delib-Other		

1828–1831 (13,333 actions)

Interest-Claim-Parl	Church-Claim-Parl	Workers-Attack-Other
Crowd-Claim-Other	Crowd-Attack-Constables	Crowd-Attack-Repressive
Crowd-Attack-Locals	Crowd-Attack-Other	Crowd-Control-Crowd

Table A.4 *(continued)*

Crowd-Control-Other	Crowd-Enter-Other	Constables-Control-Crowd
Repressive-Attack-Crowd	Repressive-Control-Crowd	Locals-Claim-Parl
Locals-Cheer-Parl	Locals-Cheer-Other	Locals-Delib-Inhabitants
Officials-Control-Crowd	Electors-Claim-Parl	Electors-Cheer-Parl
Electors-Delib-Parl	Inhabitants-Claim-Locals	Inhabitants-Claim-Royalty
Inhabitants-Cheer-Government	Inhabitants-Cheer-Parl	Inhabitants-Cheer-Other
Inhabitants-Delib-Locals	Inhabitants-Delib-Officials	Inhabitants-Delib-Parl
Inhabitants-Delib-Royalty	Other-Control-Crowd	Other-Delib-Inhabitants

1832–1834 (7520 actions)

Interest-Claim-Parl	Interest-Cheer-Parl	Interest-Delib-Parl
Church-Claim-Parl	Crowd-Attack-Constables	Crowd-Attack-Repressive
Crowd-Attack-Locals	Crowd-Attack-Other	Crowd-Control-Other
Repressive-Control-Crowd	Repressive-Control-Other	Locals-Attack-Locals
Locals-Delib-Locals	Locals-Delib-Electors	Locals-Delib-Parl
Locals-Delib-Inhabitants	Officials-Delib-Inhabitants	Electors-Claim-Parl
Electors-Cheer-Government	Electors-Cheer-Parl	Electors-Communicate-Parl
Electors-Delib-Parl	Government-Cheer-Parl	Parl-Delib-Inhabitants

Pariahs-Attack-Constables	Inhabitants-Claim-Locals	Inhabitants-Claim-Parl
Inhabitants-Claim-Royalty	Inhabitants-Cheer-Locals	Inhabitants-Cheer-Government
Inhabitants-Cheer-Parl	Inhabitants-Communicate-Parl	Inhabitants-Delib-Locals
Inhabitants-Delib-Officials	Inhabitants-Delib-Government	Inhabitants-Delib-Parl
Inhabitants-Delib-Royalty	Other-Attack-Repressive	

Total 1758–1834 (25,239 actions)

Interest-Claim-Parl	Interest-Delib-Parl	Church-Claim-Parl
Crowd-Claim-Other	Crowd-Attack-Locals	Crowd-Attack-Government
Crowd-Attack-Other	Crowd-Control-Crowd	Crowd-Control-Repressive
Crowd-Control-Other	Crowd-Enter-Other	Repressive-Control-Crowd
Locals-Claim-Parl	Locals-Cheer-Parl	Locals-Delib-Locals
Locals-Delib-Parl	Locals-Delib-Inhabitants	Officials-Control-Crowd
Officials-Delib-Inhabitants	Electors-Claim-Parl	Electors-Cheer-Parl
Electors-Communicate-Parl	Electors-Delib-Parl	Parl-Delib-Inhabitants
Inhabitants-Claim-Officials	Inhabitants-Claim-Parl	Inhabitants-Claim-Royalty
Inhabitants-Cheer-Officials	Inhabitants-Cheer-Parl	Inhabitants-Delib-Locals
Inhabitants-Delib-Officials	Inhabitants-Delib-Government	Inhabitants-Delib-Parl
Inhabitants-Delib-Royalty		

Table A.5. Verb categories, subcategories, and sample items (Ns for verbs having objects; total = 25,239)

Claim (N = 4,331)
Delegate (5): depute
Petition (2,223): petition
Request (1,327): appeal, apply, ask, ask leave, ask support, beg, beseech, call, call for . . .
Address (776): address

Attack (N = 3,906)
Attack (3,006): abuse, alarm, annoy, assault, attack, batter, beat, beat in, beat off . . .
Decry (710): accuse, assail, boo, censure, challenge, complain, condemn, decline, decry . . .
Fight (190): affray, arm, battle, combat, conflict, contend, contest, engage, fight . . .

Control (N = 3,768)
Control (3,060): abduct, acquit, apprehend, arouse, arrange, arrest, assign, calm, capture . . .
Donkey (5): donkey
Oppose (242): oppose
Resist (461): defy, deny, mutiny, object, protest, question, rebuke, rebut . . .

Cheer (N = 3,713)
Cheer (2,140): cheer
Support (460): admire, aid, applaud, approve, assent, assist, avow, bear, carry . . .
Thank (1,113): thank

Communicate (N = 1,552)
Communicate (783): advertise, advise, affirm, announce, chant, clamour, comment . . .
Hear Petition (40): hear petition
Negotiate (232): accede, accept, admit, agitate, agree, allow, answer, assert, bicker . . .
Receive (497): receive

Deliberate (N = 5,697)
Chair (1,546): chair
Deliberate (182): address, adopt, amend, answer, appoint, argue, bring to, bring before . . .
Meet (162): meet
Resolve (3,807): frame, resolve

Enter (N = 1,122)
Disperse (232): disperse
Enter (30): enter
March (38): file off, march, parade, process
Move (784): abandon, abate, accompany, accost, advance, appear, approach, arrive, ascend . . .
Proceed (38): embark, press in, proceed

Table A.5 (continued)

Other (N = 1,005)

Adjourn (18): adjourn
Assemble (89): assemble, compose
Attempt (161): attempt
Block (264): barricade, bind, block, close, close in, close out, contain, disrupt, enclose, exclude . . .
Bracket (51): bar, continue, desist, encounter, finish, persevere, stop
Celebrate (9): celebrate, dance, entertain, illuminate, play, rally, rejoice, strike up
Demonstrate (28): demonstrate
Dine (9): breakfast, consume, dine, drink, eat
End (17): end
Gather (11): convene, frequent, gather, reassemble, throng
Give (113): give
Hunt (3): hunt, poach
Observe (87): ignore, look at, look for, notice, observe, perceive, recognize . . .
Other (145): acquiesce, act, appease, assure, attempt, augment, avoid, belabour . . .
Smuggle (1): smuggle
Turn out (26): turn out
Vote (118): elect, outvote, poll, re-elect, vote

Table A.6. Formation categories, subcategories, and sample items (first subject and object formations named in actions having both subjects and objects; total = 50,478)

Church (N = 874)
Catholics (78): Catholics, London-Area Catholics, Romish-School Owner
Church (157): Society of Friends
Protestants (639): Protestant Dissenters, Protestant Ministers, Quakers, Wesleyans

Constables (N = 1,672)
Constables (664): beadles and constables, constable, constable and officers . . .
Gamekeepers (223): keepers
Militia (71): Derbyshire Militia, Islington Volunteers, Militia, Oxford Militia . . .
New Police (118): New Police
Sheriff (596): High Sheriff, London Sheriffs, Sheriff, Sheriff's Officer . . .

Crowd (N = 6,781)
Crowd (959): assemblage, assembly, audience, band, crowd, rabble
Mob (3,867): gang, Gordon rioters, mob, principal rioter, ringleader . . .
Numbers (133): multitude, numerous party, several
Persons (1,366): boys, children, Chinese, company, concourse of persons . . .
Someone (456): somebody, someone

Electors (N = 2,700)
Deputation (261): delegation, deputation, representatives
Electors (1,296): electors
Freeholders (1,143): borough proprietors, freeholders, freemen, house owner . . .

Government (N = 2,318)
Gentlemen (491): gentlemen, ladies and gentlemen, nobility and gentry . . .
Government (130): Assize Court, civil power, constituted authorities, court . . .
Ministers (981): King's Ministers, Majesty's Privy Council, Ministers, Present Ministry
Nobles (716): nobility, nobles

Inhabitants (N = 7,264)
Inhabitants (7,264): inhabitants [with localities], house occupants, neighbors, populace

Interest (N = 1,406)
Farmers (231): farmers, farmers and graziers, yeoman
Firm (102): bank directors, Court of Directors, Court of Proprietors, East India Company . . .
Friendly Society (91): Benefit Societies, Benevolent Institution
Interest (213): advocates of free speech, bank owners, bank volunteers, canal proponents . . .
Procession (63): procession
Society (706): African and Asiatic Society, Agricultural Association, Christian Knowledge
   Society . . .

Table A.6 (continued)

Locals (N = 5,378)

Churchwardens (732): churchwardens
Clergy (398): Archbishop of Canterbury, Bishop of ___, Church Ministers, clergy . . .
Committee (144): chairman, committee
Local Officials (1,496): beadles, borough gaoler, collector, deputy, vestry . . .
Mayor (867): Lord Mayor, Mayor, Mayor and Aldermen, Mayor and Corporation . . .
Opponents (86): members of Opposition, Opposition, Queen's detractors . . .
Parishioners (221): parish, parishioners
Party (537): party [with qualifier]
Select Vestry (97): select vestry
Supporters (663): advisers, friends [of ___], supporters, sympathizers . . .
Wardmote (134): wardmote

Officials (N = 2,198)

Aldermen (714): aldermen
Common Council (231): Common Council, Common Hall, Common Serjeant, Councilmen
  . . .
Judge (872): judge, justice
Official (381): Admiralty, Ambassador, Attorney General, Chief Officers, Commissioner . . .

Other (N = 4,989)

Individual name (4,199): individual name when identified as separate formation
Other (790): associates of prisoner, Mr. Banister and singers, boroughmongers . . .

Pariahs (N = 1,152)

Hunters (312): hunters, poachers
Irish (192): Irish, Irishmen
Poor (134): beggar, charity children, lower order of people, paupers, poor, vagrants
Prisoners (261): defendants, hostages, prisoners
Wrongdoers (253): assailants, child-molester, criminals, deserter, encroachers, enemy . . .

Parliament (N = 6,724)

House of Commons (420): Commons, House of Commons
House of Lords (324): House of Lords, Lords
MP [Member of Parliament] (2804): MP or name
Parliament (3176): legislature, Parliament

Repressive (N = 2,217)

Police (1,117): body of officers, city marshal, Bridewell keeper, marshal . . .
Troops (1,100): sergeant, captain, cavalry, Coldstream Guards, colonel . . .

Table A.6 (continued)

Royalty (N = 1,419)

Royalty (1,419): King, King and Government, Majesties, Prince Regent, Queen . . .

Trade (N = 1,616)

Masters (216): chief mate, employers, master, Master _____, shipowners . . .
Trade (1,400): actor, American sailors, army clothier, baker, baker's man . . .

Workers (N = 1,770)

Blacklegs (250): blacklegs
Labourers (496): labourers
Weavers (406): engine-loom weavers, journeymen weavers, single-hand weavers . . .
Workers (843): artificers, artisans, brass-founders, bridgeman, brother draymen . . .

Major Acts by the British Government Directly Affecting Popular Association and Collective Action, 1750–1834

This chronology excludes many acts in and with respect to Ireland. It also excludes frequent alterations to the laws of vagrancy and trespass. See Espaillat and Lanzona 1993 for a much more complete listing.

1750: Parliament expanded the capital provisions of the Mutiny Act of 1715, which covered the use of troops to control civilian populations, to "every act of direct disobedience, whether active or passive"; other significant extensions occurred in 1766, 1784, and 1797.

1757: The Militia Act established widespread domestic military service for national defense and crowd control; significant revisions occurred in 1758, 1761, 1802, and 1803.

1774: Among a number of experiments and innovations around this time, the Westminster Watching Act codified police practice in Westminster and adjacent areas.

1776: A new Militia Act empowered the king to call out the militia for a limited period in cases of rebellion if Parliament was not sitting, while the Criminal Law Act authorized the punishment by hard labor of offenders who were liable to transportation to the colonies.

1780: In response to the Gordon Riots, the government eased the conditions for military or police intervention in riot, regularized the Bow Street Patrol, and created a single Home Secretary with responsibility for domestic order.

1787: The Vagrants and Criminals Act allowed Justices to send vagrants to jail as an alternative to houses of correction, authorized corporal punishment, and expanded the category of "idle and disorderly" to men who allowed their families to become chargeable to poor rates by neglecting their work or squandering their wages, as well as soldiers and sailors found wandering and begging.

1792: Middlesex Justice Act established police offices and salaried justices in the London area; a Proclamation against Seditious Writings and Assemblies enjoined magistrates to more vigorous action against subversives; on the facilitative side, Fox's Libel Act gave juries the responsibility for deciding whether words constituted libel, seditious or otherwise.

1793: Greville's Aliens Act strengthened political control of foreigners; the Act for Encouragement of Friendly Societies (revised significantly in 1795, 1809, and 1819) authorized their existence but also subjected them to official registration.

1794: Suspension of *habeas corpus;* illegalization of the United Irishmen.

1795: The Treasonable Practices Act and the Seditious Meetings Act greatly restricted the rights of speech, press, and assembly, while the Manning the Navy Act (reinforced in 1798) facilitated the pressing of vagrants and paupers.

1797: Act against Unlawful Oaths (strengthened in 1812) prohibited swearing into secret societies.

1798: The Act for the Defence of the Realm authorized the calling out of civilian posses against threats to public order.

1799, 1800: The Combination Laws and the Unlawful Societies Act forbade combinations in restraint of trade as well as societies established for "seditious and treasonable purposes"; United Irishmen specifically proscribed.

1801: *Habeas corpus* suspended in Scotland.

1803: At the renewal of hostilities with France, another Act for the Defence of the Realm.

1811–1812: Multiple judicial and parliamentary actions against machine-breaking.

1816: Habeas Corpus Amendment Act generalized the right, including application to victims of press gangs; the Pillory Abolition Act replaced the pillory with imprisonment and/or fines, while the Malicious Damage Act (Scotland) increased penalties for attacks on property, including machines.

1817: Coercion Acts and Seditious Meetings Act temporarily suspended *habeas corpus* (restored in 1818), extended the 1798 provisions against seditious meetings, renewed penalties for inducing soldiers and sailors to violate their duty, and increased protection for the king; the government prosecuted many writers and printers.

1819: The Six Acts provided for speedy trial in cases of misdemeanor, increased penalties for seditious libel, imposed the newspaper stamp duty on periodicals containing news, forbade training of persons in the use of arms, and empowered magistrates to search for and seize arms; the Poor Relief Act authorized select vestries and paid assistant overseers for tighter control over paupers.

1820: The Malicious Trespass Act permitted summary punishment of persons willfully or maliciously damaging or trespassing public or private property, while the Unlawful Drilling Act outlawed armed processions.

1823: Repeal of numerous statutes (including the Black Act) imposing the death sentence for property crimes.

1824: Repeal of the Combination Acts (with amendments in 1825); the Act for the Punishment of Idle and Disorderly Persons, Rogues and Vagabonds made the 1822 controls permanent.

1825: Repeal of death sentence for assaulting or obstructing a revenue officer.

1827: The Remedies Against the Hundred Act consolidated the law concerning citizen involvement in the suppression of affrays, riots, and felonies, while Peel's Acts revamped the criminal code and reduced the number of capital offenses.

1829: The Metropolitan Police Act (modified in 1833) established the uniformed London police, while the Friendly Societies Act eased restrictions on workers' mutual-aid organizations but imposed strict registration and a ban on politics.

1830: The Lighting and Watching Act enabled municipalities to set up police and lighting authorities without separate parliamentary acts, while the Seditious Libel Act both eliminated banishment for libel and increased the bonds required of newspaper publishers.

1831: The Special Constables and Tumultuous Risings Acts strengthened policing of events like those of the Swing rebellion, while a proclamation against political unions forbade their organization along military lines.

1832: The Punishment of Death Act and the Forgery Act reduced the range of the death penalty, while the Threshing Machine Act made inhabitants of a hundred (a local judicial unit) collectively responsible for damage.

1833: The Consolidating Act and a new Lighting and Watching Act tightened up the police legislation of 1829 and 1830 as the Factory Act restricted the work of women and children, and the Abolition of Slavery Act covered all British colonies.

1834: The Transportation Act and the Hanging in Chains Act again reduced the applicability of the death penalty and eliminated the hanging of criminals' bodies in chains, as the New Poor Law Amendment Act instituted major changes in local poor relief, on the whole favoring incarceration, reduction of benefits, and diminished eligibility.

References

A list of earlier reports from this research appears in Appendix 1; I have not repeated those items here. In some cases I have cited both an edited volume and an individual article from that volume on the grounds that the volume as a whole provides information or ideas generally relevant to this book.

Abelove, Henry, et al. (1983): *Visions of History: Interviews with E. P. Thompson, Eric Hobsbawm, Sheila Rowbotham, Linda Gordon, Natalie Zemon Davis, William Appleman Williams, Staughton Lynd, David Montgomery, Herbert Gutman, Vincent Harding, John Womack, C. L. R. James, and Moshe Lewin.* New York: Pantheon.

Alapuro, Risto (1988): *State and Revolution in Finland.* Berkeley: University of California Press.

Alberoni, Francesco (1968): *Statu nascenti.* Bologna: Il Mulino.

Allen, Robert C. (1982): "The Efficiency and Distributional Consequences of Eighteenth-Century Enclosures," *Economic Journal* 92: 937–953.

Amey, Geoffrey (1979): *City Under Fire: The Bristol Riots and Aftermath.* Guildford: Lutterworth Press.

Aminzade, Ronald (1981): *Class, Politics, and Early Industrial Capitalism: A Study of Mid-Nineteenth-Century Toulouse.* Albany: State University of New York Press.

Anderson, James, ed. (1986): *The Rise of the Modern State.* Brighton, Sussex: Wheatsheaf.

Andreucci, Franco, and Alessandra Pescarolo (1989): *Gli spazi del potere. Aree, regioni, Stati: Le coordinate territoriali della storia contemporanea.* Florence: Istituto Ernesto Ragionieri.

Apfel, William, and Peter Dunkley (1985): "English Rural Society and the New Poor Law: Bedfordshire, 1834–47," *Social History* 10: 37–68.

Archer, John E. (1990): *By a Flash and a Scare: Incendiarism, Animal Maiming, and Poaching in East Anglia 1815–1870.* Oxford: Clarendon Press.

Arnold, Rollo (1974): "The 'Revolt of the Field' in Kent, 1872–1879," *Past and Present* 64: 71–95.

Armstrong, Alan (1988): *Farmworkers: A Social and Economic History, 1770–1980.* London: Batsford.

Arnstein, Walter L. (1973): "The Survival of the Victorian Aristocracy," in Frederic Cople Jaher, ed., *The Rich, the Well Born, and the Powerful.* Urbana: University of Illinois Press.

Ashcraft, Richard (1993): "Liberal Political Theory and Working-Class Radicalism in Nineteenth-Century England," *Political Theory* 21: 249–272.

Aspinall, Arthur (1949): *Politics and the Press, c1780–1850.* London: Home and VanThal.

Aya, Rod (1990): *Rethinking Revolutions and Collective Violence: Studies on Concept, Theory, and Method.* Amsterdam: Het Spinhuis.

Ayer, A. J. (1989): *Thomas Paine.* London: Faber and Faber. First published in 1988.

Babington, Anthony (1990): *Military Intervention in Britain: From the Gordon Riots to the Gibraltar Incident.* London: Routledge and Kegan Paul.

Baer, Marc (1992): *Theatre and Disorder in Late Georgian London.* Oxford: Clarendon Press.

Bailyn, Bernard (1986): *Voyagers to the West: A Passage in the Peopling of America on the Eve of the Revolution.* New York: Knopf.

Balbus, Isaac (1973): *The Dialectics of Legal Repression: Black Rebels before the American Criminal Courts.* New York: Russell Sage Foundation.

Bamford, Samuel (1967): W. H. Chaloner, ed., *The Autobiography of Samuel Bamford.* 2 vols. London: Frank Cass.

Barnett, Corelli (1974): *Britain and Her Army, 1509–1970: A Military, Political and Social Survey.* Harmondsworth: Penguin. First published in 1970.

Barry, Jonathan (1993): "Identité urbaine et classes moyennes dans l'Angleterre moderne," *Annales; Economies, Sociétés, Civilisations* 48: 853–884.

Bates, Robert H. (1988): "Lessons from History, or the Perfidy of English Exceptionalism and the Significance of Historical France," *World Politics* 40: 499–516.

Battestin, Martin C., and Ruthe R. Battestin (1989): *Henry Fielding. A Life.* London: Routledge.

Baugh, Daniel A. (1975): "The Cost of Poor Relief in South-East England, 1790–1834," *Economic History Review,* 2d ser., 28: 50–68.

Baxter, J. L., and F. K. Donnelly (1974): "The Revolutionary 'Underground' in the West Riding: Myth or Reality?" *Past and Present* 64: 124–132.

Baylen, Joseph O., and Norbert J. Gossman (1979): *Biographical Dictionary of Modern British Radicals.* Vol. 1: 1770–1830. Hassocks, Sussex: Harvester.

Beattie, John (1974): "The Pattern of Crime in England, 1660–1800," *Past and Present* 62: 47–95. (1986): *Crime and the Courts in England, 1660–1800.* Princeton: Princeton University Press.

Beckett, J. V. (1984): "The Pattern of Landownership in England and Wales, 1660–1880," *Economic History Review,* 2d ser., 37: 1–22. (1986): *The Aristocracy in England, 1660–1914.* Oxford: Blackwell.

Beer, Samuel H. (1957): "The Representation of Interests in British Government: Historical Background," *American Political Science Review* 51: 613–650.

Behagg, Clive (1979): "Custom, Class and Change: The Trade Societies of Birmingham," *Social History* 4: 455–480.

Belchem, John (1978): "Henry Hunt and the Evolution of the Mass Platform," *English Historical Review* 93: 739–778. (1981): "Republicanism, Popular Constitutionalism and the Radical Platform in Early Nineteenth-Century England," *Social History* 6: 1–32. (1985a): "'Orator' Hunt, 1773–1835," *History Today* 35: 21–27. (1985b): *"Orator" Hunt: Henry Hunt and Working-Class Radicalism*. Oxford: Clarendon Press. (1988): "Radical Language and Ideology in Early Nineteenth-Century England: The Challenge of the Platform," *Albion* 20: 247–259. (1990): *Industrialization and the Working Class: The English Experience, 1750–1900*. Aldershot: Scolar Press. (1992): Ed., *Popular Politics, Riot and Labour: Essays in Liverpool History 1790–1940*. Liverpool: Liverpool University Press.

Beloff, Max (1938): *Public Order and Popular Disturbances, 1660–1714*. London: Humphrey Milford/Oxford University Press.

Bendix, Reinhard (1964): *Nation-Building and Citizenship*. New York: Wiley. (1967): "Tradition and Modernity Considered," *Comparative Studies in Society and History* 9: 292–346.

Berg, Maxine (1985): *The Age of Manufactures: Industry, Innovation and Work in Britain, 1700–1820*. Oxford: Blackwell.

Bermeo, Nancy (1989–90): "Review Article: Rethinking Regime Change," *Comparative Politics* 22: 359–377.

Berting, Jan, and Wim Blockmans, eds. (1987): *Beyond Progress and Development: Macro-Political and Macro-Societal Change*. Aldershot: Avebury.

Best, G. F. A. (1958): "The Protestant Constitution and Its Supporters, 1800–1829," *Transactions of the Royal Historical Society* 5th ser., 8: 105–127. (1967): "Popular Protestantism in Victorian Britain," in Robert Robson, ed., *Ideas and Institutions of Victorian Britain*. London: G. Bell and Sons.

Best, Geoffrey (1982): *War and Society in Revolutionary Europe, 1770–1870*. London: Fontana.

Binder, Leonard, et al. (1971): *Crises and Sequences in Political Development*. Princeton: Princeton University Press.

Binney, J. E. D. (1958): *British Public Finance and Administration, 1774–92*. Oxford: Clarendon Press.

Birnbaum, Pierre (1982): *La logique de l'Etat*. Paris: Fayard. (1988): *States and Collective Action: The European Experience*. Cambridge: Cambridge University Press.

Black, Eugene (1963): *The Association: British Extraparliamentary Political Organization, 1769–1793*. Cambridge, Mass.: Harvard University Press. (1969): *British Politics in the Nineteenth Century*. London: Macmillan.

Black, Jeremy (1988): "Britain's Foreign Alliances in the Eighteenth Century," *Albion* 20: 573–602.

Black, Robert A., and Claire G. Gilmore (1990): "Crowding Out during Britain's Industrial Revolution," *Journal of Economic History* 50: 109–132.

Blickle, Peter (1988): *Unruhen in der ständischen Gesellschaft, 1300–1800.* Munich: Oldenbourg. Enzyklopädie Deutscher Geschichte, vol. 1.

Bohstedt, John (1983): *Riots and Community Politics in England and Wales, 1790–1810.* Cambridge, Mass.: Harvard University Press. (1988): "Gender, Household and Community Politics: Women in English Riots, 1790–1810," *Past and Present* 120: 88–122. (1990): "The Myth of the Feminine Food Riot: Women as Proto-Citizens in English Community Politics, 1790–1810," in Harriet B. Applewhite and Darline G. Levy, eds., *Women and Politics in the Age of the Democratic Revolution.* Ann Arbor: University of Michigan Press. (1992): "The Moral Economy and the Discipline of Historical Context," *Journal of Social History* 26: 265–284.

Bonnell, Victoria (1983): *Roots of Revolution: Workers' Politics and Organizations in St. Petersburg and Moscow, 1900–1914.* Berkeley: University of California Press.

Bonwick, Colin (1977): *English Radicals and the American Revolution.* Chapel Hill: University of North Carolina Press.

Booth, Alan (1977): "Food Riots in the North-West of England 1790–1801," *Past and Present* 77: 84–107. (1983): "Popular Loyalism and Public Violence in the North-West of England, 1790–1800," *Social History* 8: 295–314.

Bordo, Michael D., and Eugene N. White (1991): "A Tale of Two Currencies: British and French Finance during the Napoleonic Wars," *Journal of Economic History* 51: 303–316.

Botz, Gerhard (1976): *Gewalt in der Politik. Attentate, Zusammenstösse, Putschversuche, Unruhen in Österreich 1918 bis 1934.* Munich: Wilhelm Fink.

Boyer, George R. (1990): *An Economic History of the English Poor Law, 1750–1850.* Cambridge: Cambridge University Press.

Braddick, Michael (1991): "State Formation and Social Change in Early Modern England: A Problem Stated and Approaches Suggested," *Social History* 16: 1–18.

Bradley, James E. (1986): *Popular Politics and the American Revolution in England: Petitions, the Crown, and Public Opinion.* Macon: Mercer University Press.

Brewer, John (1976): *Party Ideology and Popular Politics at the Accession of George III.* Cambridge: Cambridge University Press. (1979–80): "Theater and Counter-Theater in Georgian Politics: The Mock Elections at Garrat," *Radical History Review* 22: 7–40. (1980): "The Wilkites and the Law, 1763–74: A Study of Radical Notions of Governance," in John Brewer and John Styles, eds., *An Ungovernable People: The English and Their Law in the Seventeenth and Eighteenth Centuries.* New Brunswick, N.J.: Rutgers University Press. (1989): *The Sinews of Power: War, Money and the English State, 1688–1783.* New York: Knopf.

Briggs, Asa (1950–52): "The Background of the Parliamentary Reform Movement in Three English Cities (1830–32)," *Cambridge Historical Journal* 10: 293–317. (1956): "Middle-Class Consciousness in English Politics, 1780–1846," *Past and Present* 60: 65–74. (1976): "Peasant Movements and Agrarian Problems in England and Wales from the End of the XVIIth Century up to Our Time," *Cahiers*

Internationaux d'Histoire Economique et Sociale 6: 308–332. (1979): "The Language of 'Mass' and 'Masses' in Nineteenth-Century England," in David E. Martin and David Rubinstein, eds., *Ideology and the Labour Movement: Essays Presented to John Saville*. London: Croom Helm.

Bright, Charles, and Susan Harding (1984): eds., *Statemaking and Social Movements*. Ann Arbor: University of Michigan Press.

British Museum (1870–1954): *Catalog of Prints and Drawings in the British Museum. Division 1: Political and Personal Satires*. 11 vols. London: British Museum.

Brock, Michael (1974): *The Great Reform Act*. New York: Humanities Press.

Broeker, Galen (1970): *Rural Disorder and Police Reform in Ireland, 1812–36*. London: Routledge and Kegan Paul.

Brogden, Mike (1987): "The Emergence of the Police: The Colonial Dimension," *British Journal of Criminology* 27: 4–14.

Brown, Richard Maxwell, and Don E. Fehrenbacher, eds. (1977): *Tradition, Conflict, and Modernization: Perspectives on the American Revolution*. New York: Academic Press.

Brundage, Anthony (1978): *The Making of the New Poor Law, 1832–1839*. London: Hutchinson.

Bryson, Anne (1992): "Riotous Liverpool, 1815–1860," in John Belchem, ed., *Popular Politics, Riot and Labour: Essays in Liverpool History, 1790–1940*. Liverpool: Liverpool University Press.

Bulst, Neithard, and Jean-Philippe Genet, eds. (1988): *La ville, la bourgeoisie et la genèse de l'Etat moderne (XIIe-XVIIIe siècles):* Paris: Editions du Centre National de la Recherche Scientifique.

Bumsted, J. M. (1982): *The People's Clearance: Highland Emigration to British North America, 1770–1815*. Edinburgh: Edinburgh University Press.

Burke, Edmund (1910): *Reflections on the French Revolution and Other Essays*. London: J. M. Dent. *Reflections* first published in 1790. (1963): *Edmund Burke: Selected Writings and Speeches*, ed. Peter J. Stanlis. Garden City, N.Y.: Doubleday Anchor. "Thoughts on the Cause of the Present Discontents" first published in 1770.

Burke, Edmund III, ed. (1988): *Global Crises and Social Movements: Artisans, Peasants, Populists, and the World Economy*. Boulder, Colo.: Westview.

Burstein, Paul (1981): "The Sociology of Democratic Politics and Government," *Annual Review of Sociology* 7: 291–319. (1988): "Political Sociology," in Edgar Borgatta and Karen Cook, eds., *The Future of Sociology*. Newbury Park, Calif.: Sage.

Burton, Michael G. (1984): "Elites and Collective Protest," *Sociological Quarterly* 25: 45–66.

Butterfield, Herbert (1968): *George III, Lord North, and the People, 1779–80*. New York: Russell and Russell. First published in 1949.

Bythell, Duncan (1969): *The Handloom Weavers: A Study in the English Cotton Industry during the Industrial Revolution*. Cambridge: Cambridge University Press.

Cahill, Gilbert A. (1957): "Irish Catholicism and English Toryism," *Review of Politics* 19: 62–77.

Calder-Marshall, Arthur (1971): "The Spa Fields Riots, 1816," *History Today* 21: 407–415.

Calhoun, Craig (1982): *The Question of Class Struggle: Social Foundations of Popular Radicalism during the Industrial Revolution*. Chicago: University of Chicago Press (1991): "The Problem of Identity in Collective Action," in Joan Huber, ed., *Macro-Micro Linkages in Sociology*. Newbury Park, Calif.: Sage..

Cameron, David R. (1974): "Toward a Theory of Political Mobilization," *Journal of Politics* 36: 138–171.

Cameron, Rondo (1990): "La révolution industrielle manquée," *Social Science History* 14: 559–566.

Cannon, John (1973): *Parliamentary Reform, 1640–1832*. Cambridge: Cambridge University Press.

Caple, Jeremy (1990): *The Bristol Riots of 1831 and Social Reform in Britain*. Lewiston, N.Y.: Edwin Mellen Press.

Carter, Michael J. (1980): *Peasants and Poachers: A Study in Rural Disorder in Norfolk*. Woodbridge, Suffolk: Boydell.

Chambers, J. D. (n.d.): *The Vale of Trent, 1670–1800*. London: Cambridge University Press; *Economic History Review*, supplements, 3.

Charlesworth, Andrew (1978): *Social Protest in a Rural Society: The Spatial Diffusion of the Captain Swing Disturbances of 1830–1831*. Liverpool: Department of Geography, University of Liverpool. Historical Geography Research Series, no. 1. (1980): "The Development of the English Rural Proletariat and Social Protest, 1700–1850: A Comment," *Journal of Peasant Studies* 8: 101–111. (1983): Ed., *An Atlas of Rural Protest in Britain, 1548–1900*. London: Croom Helm. (1991): "An Agenda for Historical Studies of Rural Protest in Britain, 1750–1850," *Rural History* 2: 231–240. (1993): "From the Moral Economy of Devon to the Political Economy of Manchester, 1790–1812," *Social History* 18: 205–218. (1994): "The Spatial Diffusion of Riots: Popular Disturbances in England and Wales, 1750–1850," *Rural History* 5: 1–22.

Charlesworth, Andrew, and Adrian J. Randall (1987): "Morals, Markets and the English Crowd in 1766," *Past and Present* 114: 200–213.

Chartres, John A. (1973): "The Marketing of Agricultural Produce in Metropolitan Western England in the Late Seventeenth and Eighteenth Centuries," in Michael Havinden, ed., *Husbandry and Marketing in the South-West, 1500–1800*. Exeter: Department of Economic History, University of Exeter.

Chase, Malcolm (1988): *"The People's Farm": English Radical Agrarianism, 1775–1840*. Oxford: Clarendon Press.

Checkland, S. G., and E. O. A. Checkland, eds. (1974): *The Poor Law Report of 1834*. Harmondsworth: Penguin.

Chester, Norman (1981): *The English Administrative System, 1780–1870*. Oxford: Clarendon Press.

Chevenix Trench, Charles (1967): *The Poacher and the Squire: A History of Poaching and Game Preservation in England*. London: Longmans.

Christie, Ian R. (1977): "British Politics and the American Revolution," *Albion* 9: 205–226. (1984): *Stress and Stability in Late Eighteenth-Century Britain: Reflections on the British Avoidance of Revolution*. Oxford: Clarendon Press.

Cirket, A. F. (1978): "The 1830 Riots in Bedfordshire: Background and Events," *Publications of the Bedfordshire Historical Record Society* 57: 75–112.

Claeys, Gregory (1994): "The Origins of the Rights of Labor: Republicanism, Commerce, and the Construction of Modern Social Theory in Britain, 1796–1805," *Journal of Modern History* 66: 249–290.

Clark, Anna (1990): "Queen Caroline and the Sexual Politics of Popular Culture in London, 1820," *Representations* 31: 47–68.

Clark, Gregory (1993): "Agriculture and the Industrial Revolution, 1700–1850," in Joel Mokyr, ed., *The British Industrial Revolution*. Boulder, Colo.: Westview.

Clark, J. C. D. (1985): *English Society, 1688–1832*. Cambridge: Cambridge University Press. (1986): *Revolution and Rebellion: State and Society in England in the Seventeenth and Eighteenth Centuries*. Cambridge: Cambridge University Press. (1989): "English History's Forgotten Context: Scotland, Ireland, Wales," *Historical Journal* 32: 211–228. (1990): "Revolution in the English Atlantic Empire, 1660–1800," in E. E. Rice, ed., *Revolution and Counter-Revolution*. Oxford: Basil Blackwell. (1991): "Sovereignty: The British Experience," *Times Literary Supplement*, 29 November: 15–16. (1994a): *The Language of Liberty, 1660–1832: Political Discourse and Social Dynamics in the Anglo-American World*. Cambridge: Cambridge University Press. (1994b): "Success Stories," *Times Literary Supplement*, 11 March: 11–12.

Clark, Samuel D., and J. S. Donnelly, eds. (1983): *Irish Peasants: Violence and Political Unrest, 1780–1914*. Madison: University of Wisconsin Press.

Clarke, John (1977): *The Price of Progress: Cobbett's England, 1780–1835*. London: Granada.

Clarke, John, Chas Critcher, and Richard Johnson, eds. (1979): *Working Class Culture: Studies in History and Theory*. London: Hutchinson.

Clay, Christopher (1968): "Marriage, Inheritance, and the Rise of Large Estates in England, 1660–1815," *Economic History Review*, 2d ser., 21: 503–518.

Cobbett, William (1829): *The Poor Man's Friend, or Essays on the Rights and Duties of the Poor*. London: the author. Rpt. Fairfield, N.J.: Augustus M. Kelley, 1977. (1967): *Rural Rides*, ed. George Woodcock. Harmondsworth: Penguin. First published in 1830.

Cockburn, Henry (1971): *Memorials of His Time*. Edinburgh: James Thin. First published in 1856.

Cockburn, J. S. (1991): "Patterns of Violence in English Society: Homicide in Kent, 1560–1985," *Past and Present* 130: 70–106.

Cohen, Jean (1985): "Strategy or Identity: New Theoretical Paradigms and Contemporary Social Movements," *Social Research* 52: 663–716.

Cohen, Jean L., and Andrew Arato (1992): *Civil Society and Political Theory*. Cambridge, Mass.: MIT Press.

Cohen, Stanley, and Andrew Scull, eds. (1983): *Social Control and the State: Historical and Comparative Essays*. Oxford: Martin Robertson.

Cohen, Emmeline W. (1965): *The Growth of the British Civil Service, 1780–1939*. London: Frank Cass. First published in 1941.

Cole, G. D. H. (1930): *The Life of Robert Owen*. London: Macmillan.

Cole, G. D. H., and Raymond Postgate (1961): *The British People, 1746–1946*. London: Methuen. First published in 1946.

Coleman, D. C. (1987): *History and the Economic Past: An Account of the Rise and Decline of Economic History in Britain*. Oxford: Clarendon Press.

Coles, Anthony James (1978): "The Moral Economy of the Crowd: Some Twentieth-Century Food Riots," *Journal of British Studies* 18: 157–176.

Colley, Linda (1980): "Eighteenth-Century English Radicalism before Wilkes," *Transactions of the Royal Historical Society* 31: 1–19. (1984): "The Apotheosis of George III: Loyalty, Royalty and the British Nation, 1760–1820," *Past and Present* 102: 94–129. (1986a): "Whose Nation? Class and National Consciousness in Britain, 1750–1830," *Past and Present* 113: 97–117. (1986b): "The Politics of Eighteenth-Century British History," *Journal of British Studies* 25: 359–379. (1992): *Britons: Forging the Nation, 1707–1837*. New Haven: Yale University Press.

Colquhoun, Patrick (1800): *A Treatise on the Police of the Metropolis*. 6th ed. London: Joseph Mawman. (1806): *A Treatise on Indigence*. London: J. Hatchard. (1815): *A Treatise on the Wealth, Power, and Resources of the British Empire*. London: Joseph Mawman.

Cooper, J. P. (1967): "The Social Distribution of Land and Men in England, 1436–1700," *Economic History Review*, 2d ser., 20: 419–440. (1978): "In Search of Agrarian Capitalism," *Past and Present* 80: 20–65.

Corfield, P. J. (1982): *The Impact of English Towns, 1700–1800*. Oxford: Oxford University Press.

Corrigan, Philip (1980): *Capitalism, State Formation and Marxist Theory: Historical Investigations*. London: Quartet Books.

Corrigan, Philip, and Derek Sayer (1985): *The Great Arch: English State Formation as Cultural Revolution*. Oxford: Basil Blackwell.

Couser, Walter H., Jr., et al., eds. (1986): *Resistance, Politics, and the American Struggle for Independence, 1765–1775*. Boulder, Colo.: Lynne Rienner.

Cowherd, Raymond G. (1956): *The Politics of English Dissent: The Religious Aspects of Liberal and Humanitarian Reform Movements from 1815 to 1848*. New York: New York University Press.

Crafts, N. F. R. (1985): *British Economic Growth during the Industrial Revolution*. Oxford: Clarendon Press. (1989): "Real Wages, Inequality and Economic Growth in Britain, 1750–1850: A Review of Recent Research," in Peter Scholliers, ed., *Real Wages in 19th and 20th Century Europe: Historical and Comparative Perspectives*. New York: Berg.

Crafts, N. F. R. and C. K. Harley (1992): "Output Growth and the British Industrial

Revolution: A Restatement of the Crafts-Harley View," *Economic History Review* 45: 703–770.

Cronin, James E. (1983): "Politics, Class Structure, and the Enduring Weakness of British Social Democracy," *Journal of Social History* 16: 123–142. (1988): "The British State and the Structure of Political Opportunity," *Journal of British Studies* 27: 199–231. (1991): *The Politics of State Expansion: War, State and Society in Twentieth-Century Britain.* London: Routledge. (1993): "Neither Exceptional nor Peculiar: Towards the Comparative Study of Labor in Advanced Society," *International Review of Social History* 38, pt. 1: 59–75.

Cronin, James E., and Jonathan Schneer, eds. (1982): *Social Conflict and the Political Order in Modern Britain.* London: Croom Helm.

Crouzet, François (1958): *L'Économie britannique et le blocus continental (1806–1813):* 2 vols. Paris: Presses Universitaires de France.

Cunningham, Hugh (1981): "The Language of Patriotism," *History Workshop Journal* 12: 8–33.

Dann, Otto, and John Dinwiddy, eds. (1988): *Nationalism in the Age of the French Revolution.* London: Hambledon.

Darvall, T. O. (1934): *Popular Disturbances and Public Order in Regency England.* Oxford: Oxford University Press.

Davis, David Brion (1987): "Capitalism, Abolitionism, and Hegemony," in Barbara Solow and Stanley Engerman, eds., *British Capitalism and Caribbean Slavery: The Legacy of Eric Williams.* Cambridge: Cambridge University Press.

Davis, Richard W. (1966): "The Strategy of 'Dissent' in the Repeal Campaign, 1820–1828," *Journal of Modern History* 38: 374–406. (1971): *Dissent in Politics, 1780–1830: The Political Life of William Smith, MP.* London: Epworth Press.

Deane, Phyllis, and W. A. Cole, eds. (1971): *British Economic Growth, 1688–1959.* 2d ed. Cambridge: University of Cambridge, Department of Applied Economics Monographs, 8.

Dekker, Rudolf (1982): *Holland in beroering. Oproeren in de 17de en 18de eeuw.* Baarn: Amboeken.

DeNardo, James (1985): *Power in Numbers.* Princeton: Princeton University Press.

Deutsch, Karl (1966): *Nationalism and Social Communication.* 2d ed. Cambridge, Mass.: MIT Press.

Di Palma, Giuseppe (1990): *To Craft Democracies: An Essay on Democratic Transitions.* Berkeley: University of California Press.

Dickinson, Harry T. (1976): "The Eighteenth-Century Debate on the Sovereignty of Parliament," *Transactions of the Royal Historical Society* 26: 189–210. (1989): "Counter-revolution in Britain in the 1790s," *Tijdschrift voor Geschiedenis* 102: 354–367. (1990): "Popular Loyalism in Britain in the 1790s," in Eckhart Hellmuth, ed., *The Transformation of Political Culture: England and Germany in the Late Eighteenth Century.* London: German Historical Institute and Oxford University Press.

Dickson, P. G. M. (1967): *The Financial Revolution in England: A Study in the Development of Public Credit, 1688–1756.* London: Macmillan.

Digby, Anne (1975): "The Labour Market and the Continuity of Social Policy after 1834: The Case of the Eastern Counties," *Economic History Review,* 2d ser., 28: 69–83. (1978): *Pauper Palaces.* London: Routledge and Kegan Paul.

Dinwiddy, J. R. (1971): *Christopher Wyvill and Reform, 1790–1820.* Borthwick Papers, 39. York: St. Anthony's Press. (1973): "'The Patriotic Linen-Draper': Robert Waithman and the Revival of Radicalism in the City of London, 1795–1818," *Bulletin of the Institute of Historical Research* 46: 72–94. (1974): "The 'Black Lamp' in Yorkshire 1801–1802," *Past and Present* 64: 113–123. (1979): "Luddism and Politics in the Northern Counties," *Social History* 4: 33–63. (1980): "Sir Francis Burdett and Burdettite Radicalism," *History* 65: 17–31. (1990): "Conceptions of Revolution in the English Radicalism of the 1790s," in Eckhart Hellmuth, ed., *The Transformation of Political Culture: England and Germany in the Late Eighteenth Century.* London: German Historical Institute and Oxford University Press.

Ditchfield, G. M. (1978): "Dissent and Toleration: Lord Stanhope's Bill of 1789," *Journal of Ecclesiastical History* 29: 51–73.

Dobson, C. R. (1980): *Masters and Journeymen. A Prehistory of Industrial Relations 1717–1800.* London: Croom Helm.

Dodgshon, R. A., and R. A. Butlin, eds. (1978): *An Historical Geography of England and Wales.* London: Academic Press.

Donnelly, F. K. (1976): "Ideology and Early English Working-Class History: Edward Thompson and His Critics," *Social History* 2: 219–238. (1988): "Levellerism in Eighteenth- and Early Nineteenth-Century Britain," *Albion* 20: 261–169.

Donnelly, F. K., and J. L. Baxter (1975): "Sheffield and the English Revolutionary Tradition, 1791–1820," *International Review of Social History* 20: 398–423.

Dozier, Robert R. (1983): *For King, Constitution, and Country.* Lexington: University of Kentucky Press.

Drescher, Seymour (1980): "Two Variants of Anti-Slavery: Religious Organization and Social Mobilization in Britain and France, 1780–1870," in Christine Bolt and Seymour Drescher, eds., *Anti-Slavery, Religion, and Reform.* Folkestone: Dawson-Archon. (1982): "Public Opinion and the Destruction of British Colonial Slavery," in James Walvin, ed., *Slavery and British Society, 1776–1846.* Baton Rouge: Louisiana State University Press. (1986): *Capitalism and Antislavery: British Mobilization in Comparative Perspective.* London: Macmillan. (1990): "People and Parliament: The Rhetoric of the British Slave Trade," *Journal of Interdisciplinary History* 20: 564–580. (1991): "British Way, French Way: Opinion Building and Revolution in the Second French Slave Emancipation," *American Historical Review* 96: 709–734. (1994): "Whose Abolition? Popular Pressure and the Ending of the British Slave Trade," *Past and Present* 143: 136–166.

Duffy, Michael (1987): *Soldiers, Sugar, and Seapower: The British Expeditions to the West Indies and the War against Revolutionary France.* Oxford: Clarendon Press.

Dunbabin, J. P. D. (1974): *Rural Discontent in Nineteenth-Century Britain.* New York: Holmes and Meier.

Dunkley, Peter (1981): "Whigs and Paupers: The Reform of the English Poor Laws, 1830–1834," *Journal of British Studies* 20: 124–149. (1982): *The Crisis of the Old Poor Law in England, 1795–1834: An Interpretive Essay.* New York: Garland.

Dyck, Ian (1993): "William Cobbett and the Rural Radical Platform," *Social History* 18: 185–204.

Eden, Sir Frederick Morton (1929): *The State of the Poor.* New York: Dutton. First published in 1797.

Edsall, Nicholas (1971): *The Anti-Poor Law Movement, 1834–44.* Manchester: Manchester University Press.

Edwards, Ness (1926): *The History of the South Wales Miners.* London: Labour Publishing Company.

Egret, Jean (1962): *La Pré-Révolution française, 1787–1788.* Paris: Presses Universitaires de France.

Eisenberg, Christiane (1989): "The Comparative View in Labour History: Old and New Interpretations of the English and German Labour Movements before 1914," *International Review of Social History* 34: 403–432.

Eley, Geoff (1981): "Re-Thinking the Political: Social History and Political Culture in 18th and 19th Century Britain," *Archiv für Sozialgeschichte* 21: 427–449. (1992): "Nations, Publics, and Political Cultures: Placing Habermas in the Nineteenth Century," in Craig Calhoun, ed., *Habermas and the Public Sphere.* Cambridge, Mass.: MIT Press.

Ellis, Aytoun (1956): *The Penny Universities: A History of the Coffee-Houses.* London: Secker and Warburg.

Emsley, Clive (1975): "Political Disaffection and the British Army in 1792," *Bulletin of the Institute of Historical Research* 48: 230–245. (1978): "The London 'Insurrection' of December 1792: Fact, Fiction, or Fantasy?" *Journal of British Studies* 17: 66–86. (1979): *British Society and the French Wars, 1793–1815.* Totowa, N.J.: Rowman and Littlefield. (1983a): *Policing and Its Context, 1750–1870.* London: Macmillan. (1983b): "The Military and Popular Disorder in England, 1790–1801," *Journal of the Society for Army Historical Research* 61: 10–21, 96–112. (1989): "The Impact of the French Revolution on British Politics and Society," in Ceri Crossley and Ian Small, eds., *The French Revolution and British Culture.* Oxford: Oxford University Press. (1991): *The English Police: A Political and Social History.* Hemel Hempstead: Harvester Wheatsheaf.

Engels, Frederick (1969): *The Condition of the Working Class in England.* London: Granada. First published (in German) in 1845.

Ennis, James G. (1987): "Fields of Action: Structure in Movements' Tactical Repertoires," *Sociological Forum* 2: 520–533.

Epstein, James (1982): *The Lion of Freedom: Feargus O'Connor and the Chartist Movement, 1832–1842.* London: Croom Helm. (1988): "Radical Dining, Toasting and Symbolic Expression in Early Nineteenth-Century Lancashire: Rituals of

Solidarity," *Albion* 20: 271–191. (1989): "Understanding the Cap of Liberty: Symbolic Practice and Social Conflict in Early Nineteenth-Century England," *Past and Present* 122: 75–118. (1990): "The Constitutional Idiom: Radical Reasoning, Rhetoric and Action in Early Nineteenth Century England," *Journal of Social History* 23: 553–574.

Epstein, James, and Dorothy Thompson, eds. (1982): *The Chartist Experience.* London: Macmillan.

Evans, Eric J. (1976): *The Contentious Tithe: The Tithe Problem and English Agriculture, 1750–1850.* London: Routledge and Kegan Paul. (1994): "National Consciousness? The Ambivalence of English Identity in the Eighteenth Century," in Claus Bjørn, Alexander Grant, and Keith J. Stringer, eds., *Nations, Nationalism and Patriotism in the European Past.* Copenhagen: Academic Press.

Evans, Eric J. (1983): *The Forging of the Modern State: Early Industrial Britain, 1783–1870.* London: Longman.

Evans, Peter, et al., eds. (1985): *Bringing the State Back In.* New York: Cambridge University Press.

Favre, Pierre, ed. (1990): *La Manifestation.* Paris: Presses de la Fondation Nationale des Sciences Politiques.

Feinstein, Charles (1988): "The Rise and Fall of the Williamson Curve," *Journal of Economic History* 48: 699–729.

Ferguson, Henry (1960): "The Birmingham Political Union and the Government, 1831–32," *Victorian Studies* 3: 261–276.

Fernandez, Roberto, and Doug McAdam (1988): "Social Networks and Social Movements: Multiorganizational Fields and Recruitment to Mississippi Freedom Summer," *Sociological Forum* 3: 357–382.

Fitzmaurice, Lord (1912): *Life of William, Earl of Shelburne.* 2 vols. 2d ed. London: Macmillan.

Fitzpatrick, David (1985): "Review Essay: Unrest in Rural Ireland," *Irish Economic and Social History* 12: 98–105.

Fletcher, Anthony (1968): *Tudor Rebellions.* London: Longmans.

Fletcher, Anthony, and John Stevenson, eds. (1985): *Order and Disorder in Early Modern England.* Cambridge: Cambridge University Press.

Flick, Carlos (1978): *The Birmingham Political Union and the Movements for Reform in Britain, 1830–1839.* Hamden, Conn.: Archon Books.

Flinn, Michael, et al. (1977): *Scottish Population History from the 17th Century to the 1930s.* Cambridge: Cambridge University Press. (1984): *The History of the British Coal Industry,* vol. 2, *1700–1830: The Industrial Revolution.* Oxford: Clarendon.

Floud, Roderick, and Donald McCloskey, eds. (1981): *The Economic History of Britain since 1700,* vol. 1, *1700–1860.* Cambridge: Cambridge University Press.

Floud, Roderick, and Kenneth W. Wachter (1982): "Poverty and Physical Stature: Evidence on the Standard of Living of London Boys, 1770–1870," *Social Science History* 6: 422–452.

Fogel, Robert W. (1994): "Economic Growth, Population Theory, and Physiology:

The Bearing of Long-Term Processes on the Making of Economic Policy." Working Paper 4638. Cambridge, Mass.: National Bureau of Economic Research.

Fores, Michael (1981): "The Myth of a British Industrial Revolution," *History* 66: 181–198.

Foster, John (1974): *Class Struggle and the Industrial Revolution: Early Industrial Capitalism in Three Towns.* London: Weidenfeld and Nicolson.

Fox, N. E. (1978): "The Spread of the Threshing Machine in Central Southern England," *Agricultural History Review* 26: 26–28.

Franklin, Benjamin (1972): *The Papers of Benjamin Franklin,* vol. 14, *January 1 through December 31, 1768,* ed. William B. Willcox. New Haven: Yale University Press.

Franzosi, Roberto (1987): "The Press as a Source of Socio-Historical Data: Issues in the Methodology of Data Collection from Newspapers," *Historical Methods* 20: 5–16.

Fraser, Peter (1961): "Public Petitioning and Parliament before 1832," *History* 46: 195–211. (1970): "The Agitation for Parliamentary Reform," in J. T. Ward, ed., *Popular Movements, c. 1830–1850.* London: Macmillan.

French, David (1990): *The British Way in Warfare, 1688–2000.* London: Unwin Hyman.

Friedeburg, Robert von (1991): "Dörfliche Gesellschaft und die Integration sozialen Protests durch Liberale und Konservative im 19. Jahrhundert. Desiderate und Perspektiven der Forschung im deutsch-englischen Vergleich," *Geschichte und Gesellschaft* 17: 279–310.

Fryer, W. B. (1965): *Republic or Restoration in France? 1794–7: The Politics of French Royalism, with Particular Reference to the Activities of A. B. J. d'André.* Manchester: Manchester University Press.

Gadian, D. S. (1978): "Class Consciousness in Oldham and Other Northwest Industrial Towns, 1830–1850," *Historical Journal* 21: 161–172. (1986): "Class Formation and Class Action in North-West Industrial Towns, 1830–50," in R. J. Morris, ed., *Class, Power and Social Structure in British Nineteenth-Century Towns.* Leicester: Leicester University Press.

Gailus, Manfred, and Heinrich Volkmann (1994): *Der Kampf um das tägliche Brot. Nahrungsmangel, Versorgungspolitik und Protest 1770–1990.* Opladen: Westdeutscher Verlag.

Gamson, William A. (1987): "Introduction," in Mayer N. Zald and John D. McCarthy, eds., *Social Movements in an Organizational Society.* New Brunswick, N.J.: Transaction.

Gamson, William A., Bruce Fireman, and Steven Rytina (1982): *Encounters with Unjust Authority.* Homewood, Ill.: Dorsey.

Gash, Norman (1971): *Politics in the Age of Peel: A Study in the Technique of Parliamentary Representation, 1830–1850.* New York: Norton. First published in 1953. (1978): "After Waterloo: British Society and the Legacy of the Napoleonic Wars," *Transactions of the Royal Historical Society,* 5th ser., 28: 145–157. (1979): *Aristocracy and People: Britain, 1815–1865.* Cambridge, Mass.: Harvard University Press.

Gatrell, V. A. C. (1982): "Incorporation and the Pursuit of Liberal Hegemony in Manchester, 1790–1839," in Derek Fraser, ed., *Municipal Reform and the Industrial City.* Leicester: Leicester University Press.

Gayer, Arthur D., W. W. Rostow, and Anna Jacobson Schwartz (1975): *The Growth and Fluctuation of the British Economy, 1790–1850.* New York: Barnes and Noble. New ed. 2 vols. First published in 1953.

Geary, Roger (1985): *Policing Industrial Disputes: 1893 to 1985.* Cambridge: Cambridge University Press.

Genet, Jean-Philippe, and Michel Le Mené, eds. (1987): *Genèse de l'État moderne: Prélèvement et redistribution.* Paris: Editions du Centre National de la Recherche Scientifique.

Gilbert, Alan D. (1976): *Religion and Society in Industrial England.* London: Longman.

Gilje, Paul A. (1987): *The Road to Mobocracy: Popular Disorder in New York City, 1763–1834.* Chapel Hill: University of North Carolina Press.

Gillis, John (1974): *Youth and History: Tradition and Change in European Age Relations.* New York: Academic.

Gilmour, Ian (1992): *Riot, Risings and Revolution: Governance and Violence in Eighteenth-Century England.* London: Hutchinson.

Ginter, Donald E. (1966): "The Loyalist Association Movement of 1792–93 and British Public Opinion," *Historical Journal* 9: 179–190.

Giugni, Marco G., and Hanspeter Kriesi (1990): "Nouveaux mouvements sociaux dans les années '80: Evolution et perspectives," *Annuaire suisse de science politique* 30: 79–100.

Glen, Robert (1984): *Urban Workers in the Early Industrial Revolution.* London: St. Martin.

Godechot, Jacques (1965): *La prise de la Bastille.* Paris: Gallimard.

Golby, J. M., and A. W. Purdue (1984): *The Civilisation of the Crowd: Popular Culture in England 1750–1900.* London: Batsford.

Goldie, Mark (1987): "Levelling the Levellers," *Times Literary Supplement,* 23 January: 88.

Goldstone, Jack A. (1986): "The Demographic Revolution in England: a Re-examination," *Population Studies* 49: 5–33. (1991): *Revolution and Rebellion in the Early Modern World.* Berkeley: University of California Press.

Goodwin, Albert (1979): *The Friends of Liberty: The English Democratic Movement in the Age of the French Revolution.* Cambridge, Mass.: Harvard University Press.

Gosden, P. H. J. H. (1961): *The Friendly Societies in England 1815–1875.* Manchester: Manchester University Press.

Gossez, Rémi (1953): "La résistance à l'impôt: Les quarante-cinq centimes," *Bibliothèque de la Révolution de 1848* 15: 89–132.

Grace, Frank (1980): "Food Riots in Suffolk in the Eighteenth Century," *Suffolk Review* 5: 32–46.

Gray, Daniel Savage (1975): "'Prisoners, Wanderers, and Deserters': Recruiting for the King's German Legion, 1803–1815," *Journal of the Society for Army Historical Research* 53: 148–158.

Greengrass, Mark, ed. (1991): *Conquest and Coalescence: The Shaping of the State in Early Modern Europe.* London: Edward Arnold.

Greer, Allan (1990): "From Folklore to Revolution: Charivaris and the Lower Canadian Rebellion of 1837," *Social History* 15: 25–43.

Grego, Joseph (1892): *A History of Parliamentary Elections and Electioneering from the Stuarts to Queen Victoria.* London: Chatto and Windus.

Greville, C. C. F. (1938): *The Greville Memoirs, 1814–1860,* ed. Lytton Strachey and Roger Fulford. 3 vols. London: Macmillan.

Grew, Raymond, ed. (1978): *Crises of Political Development in Europe and the United States.* Princeton: Princeton University Press.

Gurr, Ted Robert (1976): *Rogues, Rebels and Reformers: A Political History of Urban Crime and Conflict.* Beverly Hills: Sage. (1980): Ed., *Handbook of Political Conflict.* New York: Free Press. (1986): "Persisting Patterns of Repression and Rebellion: Foundations for a General Theory of Political Coercion" in Margaret P. Karns, ed., *Persistent Patterns and Emerging Structures in a Waning Century.* New York: Praeger Special Studies for the International Studies Association. (1989): Ed., *Violence in America.* 2 vols. Newbury Park, Calif.: Sage.

Gurr, Ted Robert, Keith Jaggers, and Will H. Moore (1990): "The Transformation of the Western State: The Growth of Democracy, Autocracy, and State Power since 1800," *Studies in Comparative International Development* 25: 73–108.

Hagen, William W. (1988): "Capitalism and the Countryside in Early Modern Europe: Interpretations, Models, Debates," *Agricultural History* 62: 13–47.

Haimson, Leopold, and Charles Tilly, eds. (1989): *Strikes, Wars, and Revolutions in an International Perspective: Strike Waves in the Late Nineteenth and Early Twentieth Centuries.* Cambridge: Cambridge University Press.

Hair, P. E. H. (1971): "Deaths from Violence in Britain: A Tentative Secular Survey," *Population Studies* 25: 5–24.

Halebsky, Sandor (1976): Mass Society and Political Conflict: Toward a Reconstruction of Theory. Cambridge: Cambridge University Press.

Hall, John A., and G. John Ikenberry: (1989): *The State.* Minneapolis: University of Minnesota Press.

Hall, Robert G. (1989): "Tyranny, Work and Politics: The 1818 Strike Wave in the English Cotton District," *International Review of Social History* 34: 433–470.

Hamburger, Joseph (1963): *James Mill and the Art of Revolution.* New Haven: Yale University Press.

Hamilton, Earl J. (1950): "Origin and Growth of the National Debt in France and England," in *Studi in onore di Gino Luzzatto.* Milano: Giuffré.

Hammond, J. L., and Barbara Hammond (1917): *The Town Labourer, 1760–1832.* London: Longmans. (1920a): *The Skilled Labourer, 1760–1832.* London: Longmans. (1920b): *The Village Labourer, 1760–1832.* London: Longmans.

Hampson, E. M. (1934): *The Treatment of Poverty in Cambridgeshire, 1597–1834.* Cambridge: Cambridge University Press.

Hanagan, Michael P. (1980): *The Logic of Solidarity: Artisans and Industrial Workers in Three French Towns, 1871–1914.* Urbana: University of Illinois Press. (1989): *Nascent Proletarians: Class Formation in Post-Revolutionary France.* Oxford: Basil Blackwell.

Hanagan, Michael, and Charles Stephenson, eds. (1986): *Proletarians and Protest: The Roots of Class Formation in an Industrializing World.* New York: Greenwood.

Hanagan, Michael, and Charles Tilly, eds. (1989): "Solidary Logics," *Theory and Society* 17 (special issue):

Hardin, Russell (1983): *Collective Action.* Baltimore: Johns Hopkins University Press.

Harley, C. Knick (1982): "British Industrialization before 1841: Evidence of Slower Growth during the Industrial Revolution," *Journal of Economic History* 42: 267–290. (1993): "Reassessing the Industrial Revolution: A Macro View," in Joel Mokyr, ed., *The British Industrial Revolution.* Boulder, Colo.: Westview.

Harris, Tim (1987): *London Crowds in the Reign of Charles II.* Cambridge: Cambridge University Press.

Harrison, Mark (1988): *Crowds and History: Mass Phenomena in English Towns, 1790–1835.* Cambridge: Cambridge University Press.

't Hart, Marjolein (1991): "'The Devil or the Dutch': Holland's Impact on the Financial Revolution in England, 1643–1694," *Parliaments, Estates and Representation* 11: 39–52.

Hartwell, R. M. (1969): "Economic Change in England and Europe, 1789–1830," in C. W. Crawley, ed., *The New Cambridge Modern History,* vol. 10, *War and Peace in an Age of Upheaval, 1793–1830.* Cambridge: Cambridge University Press. (1990): "Was There an Industrial Revolution?" *Social Science History* 14: 567–576.

d'Haussez, Baron (1833): *La Grande Bretagne en mil huit cent trente trois.* 2 vols. Paris: Urbain Canel.

Hay, Douglas (1982): "War, Dearth and Theft in the Eighteenth Century: The Record of the English Courts," *Past and Present* 95: 117–160.

Hay, Douglas, et al. (1975): *Albion's Fatal Tree: Crime and Society in Eighteenth-Century England.* New York: Pantheon.

Hay, Douglas, and Francis Snyder (1989): "Using the Criminal Law, 1750–1850: Policing, Private Prosecution, and the State," in Douglas Hay and Francis Snyder, eds., *Policing and Prosecution in Britain, 1750–1850.* Oxford: Clarendon Press.

Hayter, Anthony (1978): *The Army and the Crowd in Mid-Georgian England.* Totowa, N.J.: Rowman and Littlefield.

Hearn, Francis (1978): *Domination, Legitimation, and Resistance: The Incorporation of the Nineteenth-Century English Working Class.* Westport, Conn.: Greenwood.

Hechter, Michael (1975): *Internal Colonialism: The Celtic Fringe in British National Development, 1583–1966.* Berkeley: University of California Press. (1987): *Principles of Group Solidarity.* Berkeley: University of California Press.

Held, David (1987): *Models of Democracy.* Stanford: Stanford University Press.

Hellmuth, Eckhart (1990): "Towards a Comparative Study of Political Culture: The Cases of Late Eighteenth-Century England and Germany," in Eckhart Hellmuth, ed.,

The Transformation of Political Culture: England and Germany in the Late Eighteenth Century. London: German Historical Institute and Oxford University Press.

Henriques, U. R. Q. (1968): "The Jewish Emancipation Controversy in Nineteenth-Century Britain," *Past and Present* 40: 126–146.

Hibbert, Christopher (1958): *King Mob: The Story of Lord George Gordon and the London Riots of 1780.* Cleveland: World.

Hill, B. W. (1985): *British Parliamentary Parties, 1742–1832: From the Fall of Walpole to the First Reform Act.* London: George Allen and Unwin.

Hinde, Wendy (1992): *Catholic Emancipation: A Shake to Men's Minds.* Oxford: Blackwell.

Hirsch, Eric L. (1990): "Sacrifice for the Cause: Group Processes, Recruitment, and Commitment in a Student Social Movement," *American Sociological Review* 55: 243–254.

Hirschman, Albert O. (1991): *The Rhetoric of Reaction: Perversity, Futility, Jeopardy.* Cambridge, Mass.: Harvard University Press. (1993): "The Rhetoric of Reaction—Two Years Later," *Government and Opposition* 28: 291–314.

Hobsbawm, E. J. (1957): "Methodism and the Threat of Revolution in Britain," *History Today* 7: 115–124. (1959): *Primitive Rebels.* Manchester: Manchester University Press. (1964): *Labouring Men.* London: Weidenfeld. (1968): *Industry and Empire: An Economic History of Britain since 1750.* London: Weidenfeld and Nicolson. (1971): "Class Consciousness in History," in Istvan Meszaros, ed., *Aspects of History and Class Consciousness.* London: Routledge and Kegan Paul. (1973): *Revolutionaries.* London: Weidenfeld and Nicolson. (1986): "Revolution," in Roy Porter and Mikulas Teich, eds., *Revolution in History.* Cambridge: Cambridge University Press.

Hobsbawm, E. J., and George Rudé (1968): *Captain Swing.* New York: Pantheon.

Hochstadt, Steve (1982): "Social History and Politics: A Materialist View," *Social History* 7: 75–83.

Hoerder, Dirk (1977): *Crowd Action in a Revolutionary Society: Massachusetts, 1765–1780.* New York: Academic Press.

Hohenberg, Paul M., and Lynn Hollen Lees (1985): *The Making of Urban Europe, 1000–1950.* Cambridge, Mass.: Harvard University Press.

Hole, Robert (1989): *Pulpits, Politics and Public Order in England, 1760–1832.* Cambridge: Cambridge University Press.

Hollis, Patricia, ed. (1974): *Pressure from Without in Early Victorian England.* London: Edward Arnold. (1979): *The Pauper Press: A Study in Working-Class Radicalism of the 1830s.* Oxford: Oxford University Press. (1973): *Class and Conflict in Nineteenth-Century England, 1815–1850.* London: Routledge and Kegan Paul. (1980): "Anti-Slavery and British Working-Class Radicalism in the Years of Reform," in Christine Bolt and Seymour Drescher, eds., *Anti-Slavery, Religion and Reform.* Folkestone: Dawson/Archon.

Holmes, Geoffrey, and Daniel Szechi (1993): *The Age of Oligarchy: Pre-industrial Britain, 1722–1783.* London: Longman.

Holton, Robert J. (1978): "The Crowd in History: Some Problems of Theory and Method," *Social History* 3: 219–234.

Hone, J. A. (1982): *For the Cause of Truth: Radicalism in London, 1796–1821.* Oxford: Oxford University Press.

Honeyman, Katrina (1982): *Origins of Enterprise: Business Leadership in the Industrial Revolution.* Manchester: Manchester University Press.

Hoppit, Julian (1986): "Financial Crises in Eighteenth-Century England," *Economic History Review,* 2d ser., 39: 39–58.

Horn, Pamela (1979): "The Mutiny of the Oxfordshire Militia in 1795," *Cake and Cockhorse* 7: 232–241. (1980): *The Rural World, 1780–1850: Social Change in the English Countryside.* New York: St. Martin's.

Hoskins, W. G. (1935): *Industry, Trade and People in Exeter, 1688–1800.* Manchester: Manchester University Press.

Hudson, Pat (1986): *The Genesis of Industrial Capital: A Study of the West Riding Wool Textile Industry, c. 1750–1850.* Cambridge: Cambridge University Press. (1990): Ed., *Regions and Industries: A Perspective on the Industrial Revolution in Britain.* Cambridge: Cambridge University Press.

Hueckel, Glenn (1973): "War and the British Economy, 1793–1815: A General Equilibrium Analysis," *Explorations in Economic History* 10: 365–396. (1976): "Relative Prices and Supply Response in English Agriculture during the Napoleonic Wars," *Economic History Review,* 2d ser., 29: 401–414. (1981): "Agriculture during Industrialization," in R. C. Floud and D. N. McCloskey, eds., *The Economic History of Britain since 1700,* vol. 1. Cambridge: Cambridge University Press.

Humphries, Jane (1990): "Enclosures, Common Rights, and Women: The Proletarianization of Families in the Late Eighteenth and Early Nineteenth Centuries," *Journal of Economic History* 50: 17–42.

Hunt, E. H. (1981): *British Labour History, 1815–1914.* London: Weidenfeld and Nicolson.

Hunt, Lynn (1984): *Politics, Culture, and Class in the French Revolution.* Berkeley: University of California Press.

Huntington, Samuel P. (1968): *Political Order in Changing Societies.* New Haven: Yale University Press.

Huntington, Samuel P., and Jorge I. Domínguez (1975): "Political Development," in Fred I. Greenstein and Nelson W. Polsby, eds., *Handbook of Political Science,* vol. 3, *Macropolitical Theory.* Reading, Mass.: Addison-Wesley.

Husung, Hans-Gerhard (1983): *Protest und Repression im Vormärz: Norddeutschland zwischen Restauration und Revolution.* Göttingen: Vandenhoeck and Ruprecht.

Innes, Joanna (1987): "Jonathan Clark, Social History and England's 'Ancien Regime',' *Past and Present* 115: 165–200. (1990): "Parliament and the Shaping of Eighteenth-Century English Social Policy," *Transactions of the Royal Historical Society* 40: 63–93. (1991): "Representative Histories: Recent Studies of Popular Politics and Political Culture in Eighteenth- and Early Nineteenth-Century England," *Journal of Historical Sociology* 4: 182–211. (1994): "The Domestic Face of the

Military-Fiscal State," in Lawrence Stone, ed., *An Imperial State at War: Britain from 1689 to 1815*. London: Routledge.

Jaggard, Edwin (1983): "Cornwall Politics, 1826–1832: Another Face of Reform?" *Journal of British Studies* 22: 80–97.

Jenkins, J. Craig (1983): "Resource Mobilization Theory and the Study of Social Movements," *Annual Review of Sociology* 9: 527–553. (1985): *The Politics of Insurgency: The Farm Worker Movement in the 1960s*. New York: Columbia University Press.

Jessop, Bob (1972): *Social Order, Reform and Revolution: A Power Exchange and Institutionalization Perspective*. London: Macmillan.

Jewson, C. B. (1975): *The Jacobin City: A Portrait of Norwich in Its Reaction to the French Revolution, 1788–1802*. Glasgow: Blackie and Son.

John, A. H. (1955): "War and the English Economy, 1700–1763," *Economic History Review*, 2d ser., 7: 329–344. (1976): "English Agricultural Improvement and Grain Exports, 1660–1765," in D. C. Coleman and A. H. John, eds., *Trade, Government and Economy in Pre-Industrial England*. London: Weidenfeld and Nicolson.

Jones, David (1973): *Before Rebecca: Popular Protests in Wales, 1793–1835*. London: Allen Lane. (1979): "The Poacher: A Study in Victorian Crime and Protest," *Historical Journal* 22: 825–860. (1982): *Crime, Protest, Community and Police in Nineteenth-Century Britain*. London: Routledge and Kegan Paul. (1983): "The New Police, Crime and People in England and Wales, 1829–1888," *Transactions of the Royal Historical Society*, 5th ser., 33: 151–168. (1989): *Rebecca's Children: A Study of Rural Society, Crime, and Protest*. Oxford: Clarendon Press.

Jones, Philip D. (1980): "The Bristol Bridge Riot and Its Antecedents: Eighteenth-Century Perception of the Crowd," *Journal of British Studies* 19: 74–92.

Joyce, Patrick, ed. (1987): *The Historical Meanings of Work*. Cambridge: Cambridge University Press. (1991): *Visions of the People: Industrial England and the Question of Class, 1848–1914*. Cambridge: Cambridge University Press.

Karl, Terry Lynn (1990): "Dilemmas of Democratization in Latin America," *Comparative Politics* 23: 1–21.

Katznelson, Ira, and Aristide Zolberg (1986): *Working-Class Formation: Nineteenth-Century Patterns in Western Europe and the United States*. Princeton: Princeton University Press.

Kennedy, William (1964): *English Taxation, 1640–1799: An Essay on Policy and Opinion*. New York: Augustus Kelley. First published in 1913.

Kerbo, Harold R. (1982): "Movements of 'Crisis' and Movements of 'Affluence': A Critique of Deprivation and Resource Mobilization Theories," *Journal of Conflict Resolution* 26: 645–663.

Kerr, Barbara (1962): "The Dorset Agricultural Labourers, 1750–1850," *Proceedings of the Dorset Natural History and Archaeology Society* 84: 158–177.

Kimmel, Michael S. (1990): *Revolution: A Sociological Interpretation*. Philadelphia: Temple University Press.

King, Peter (1989): "Gleaners, Farmers and the Failure of Legal Sanctions in England, 1750–1850," *Past and Present* 125: 116–150.

Kirby, R. G., and A. E. Musson (1975): *The Voice of the People: John Doherty, 1798–1854.* Manchester: Manchester University Press.

Kirk, Neville (1985): *The Growth of Working Class Reformism in Mid-Victorian England.* Urbana: University of Illinois Press. (1987): "In Defence of Class: A Critique of Recent Revisionist Writing upon the Nineteenth-Century English Working Class," *International Review of Social History* 32: 2–47.

Kitschelt, Herbert (1993): "Social Movements, Political Parties, and Democratic Theory," *Annals of the American Academy of Political and Social Science* 528: 13–29.

Klandermans, Bert (1984): "Mobilization and Participation: Social-Psychological Expansions of Resource Mobilization Theory," *American Sociological Review* 49: 583–600. (1989): Ed., *Organizing for Change: Social Movement Organizations in Europe and the United States.* International Social Movement Research, 2. Greenwich, Conn.: JAI Press.

Klandermans, Bert, Hanspeter Kriesi, and Sidney Tarrow, eds. (1988): *From Structure to Action: Comparing Social Movement Research across Cultures.* International Social Movement Research, 1. Greenwich, Conn.: JAI Press.

Klausen, Kurt Klaudi (1988): *Konflikter, Kollektive Aktioner og Protestbevaegelser i Danmark.* Copenhagen: Samfunds Fagsnyt.

Knoke, David (1990): *Organizing for Collective Action: The Political Economies of Associations.* New York: Aldine de Gruyter.

Knott, John (1986): *Popular Opposition to the 1834 Poor Law.* New York: St. Martin's.

Koditschek, Theodore (1989): "The Dynamics of Class Formation in Nineteenth-Century Bradford," in A. L. Beier, David Cannadine, and James M. Rosenheim, eds., *The First Modern Society.* Cambridge: Cambridge University Press. (1990): *Class Formation and Urban-Industrial Society: Bradford, 1750–1850.* Cambridge: Cambridge University Press.

Komlos, John (1990): "Nutrition, Population Growth, and the Industrial Revolution in England," *Social Science History* 14: 69–92.

Kornhauser, William (1959): *The Politics of Mass Society.* New York: Free Press.

Korpi, Walter (1974): "Conflict and the Balance of Power," *Acta Sociologica* 17: 99–114.

Kramnick, Isaac (1990): *Republicanism and Bourgeois Radicalism: Political Ideology in Late Eighteenth-Century England and America.* Ithaca: Cornell University Press.

Kriesi, Hanspeter (1990): "Federalism and Pillarization: The Netherlands and Switzerland Compared," *Acta Politica* 25: 433–450.

Kriesi, Hanspeter, et al. (1981): *Politische Aktivierung in der Schweiz, 1945–1978.* Diessenhoffen: Ruegger.

Kumar, Krishnan (1983): "Class and Political Action in Nineteenth-Century England. Theoretical and Comparative Perspectives," *Archives Européennes de Sociologie* 24: 3–43.

Kussmaul, Ann (1981): *Servants in Husbandry in Early Modern England.* Cambridge:

Cambridge University Press. (1990): *A General View of the Rural Economy of England, 1538–1840.* Cambridge: Cambridge University Press.

Langbein, John H. (1983): "*Albion's* Fatal Flaws," *Past and Present* 98: 96–120.

Langford, Paul (1980): "Old Whigs, Old Tories and the American Revolution," *Journal of Imperial and Commonwealth History* 8: 106–130. (1988): "Property and 'Virtual Representation' in Eighteenth-Century England," *Historical Journal* 31: 83–116. (1989): *A Polite and Commercial People: England, 1727–1783.* Oxford: Clarendon Press. (1990): "The English Clergy and the American Revolution," in Eckhart Hellmuth, ed., *The Transformation of Political Culture: England and Germany in the Late Eighteenth Century.* London: German Historical Institute and Oxford University Press. (1991): *Public Life and the Propertied Englishman, 1689–1798.* Oxford: Clarendon Press.

Laqueur, Thomas (1976): *Religion and Respectability: Sunday Schools and Working Class Culture, 1780–1850.* New Haven: Yale University Press. (1982): "The Queen Caroline Affair: Politics as Art in the Reign of George IV," *Journal of Modern History* 54: 417–466. (1983): "Bodies, Death, and Pauper Funerals," *Representations* 1: 109–131. (1989): "Crowds, Carnival and the State in English Executions, 1604–1868," in A. L. Beier, David Cannadine, and James M. Rosenheim, eds., *The First Modern Society:.* Cambridge: Cambridge University Press.

Lawrence, Jon, and Miles Taylor (1993): "The Poverty of Protest: Gareth Stedman Jones and the Politics of Language—A Reply," *Social History* 18: 1–16.

Lawton, Richard (1977): "Regional Population Trends in England and Wales, 1750–1971," in John Hobcraft and Philip Rees, eds., *Regional Demographic Development.* London: Croom Helm.

Lazonick, William (1990): *Competitive Advantage on the Shop Floor.* Cambridge, Mass.: Harvard University Press.

Lee, C. H. (1986): *The British Economy since 1700: A Macroeconomic Perspective.* Cambridge: Cambridge University Press.

Lehmann, William C. (1960): *John Millar of Glasgow, 1735–1801: His Life and Thought and His Contributions to Sociological Analysis.* Cambridge: Cambridge University Press.

Lerner, Daniel (1956): *The Passing of Traditional Society: Modernizing the Middle East.* New York: Free Press. (1967): "Comparative Analysis of Processes of Modernization," in Horace Miner, ed., *The City in Modern Africa.* New York: Praeger.

Leslie-Melville, R. (1934): *The Life and Work of Sir John Fielding.* London: Lincoln Williams.

Levack, Brian P. (1987): *The Formation of the British State: England, Scotland, and the Union, 1603–1707.* Oxford: Clarendon Press.

Levi, Margaret (1983): "The Predatory Theory of Rule," in Michael Hechter, ed., *The Microfoundations of Macrosociology.* Philadelphia: Temple University Press. (1988): *Of Rule and Revenue.* Berkeley: University of California Press.

Levine, David (1984): "Production, Reproduction, and the Proletarian Family in England, 1500–1851," in David Levine, ed., *Proletarianization and Family History.*

Orlando, Fla.: Academic Press. (1987): *Reproducing Families.* Cambridge: Cambridge University Press.

Lewis, George Cornewall (1970): *Remarks on the Use and Abuse of Some Political Terms,* ed. Charles Frederick Mullett. Columbia: University of Missouri Press. First published in 1832.

Lillywhite, Bryant (1963): *London Coffee Houses: A Reference Book of Coffee Houses of the Seventeenth, Eighteenth, and Nineteenth Centuries.* London: George Allen and Unwin.

Lindenberger, Thomas (1993): "Politique de rue et action de classe à Berlin avant la Première Guerre mondiale," *Genèses* 12: 47–68.

Lindert, Peter H. (1980): "English Occupations, 1670–1811," *Journal of Economic History* 40: 685–712. (1983): "English Living Standards, Population Growth, and Wrigley-Schofield," *Explorations in Economic History* 20: 131–155. (1986): "Unequal English Wealth since 1670," *Journal of Political Economy* 94: 1127–1162.

Lindert, Peter H., and Jeffrey G. Williamson (1982): "Revising England's Social Tables, 1688–1812," *Explorations in Economic History* 19: 385–408. (1983a): "Reinterpreting Britain's Social Tables, 1688–1913," *Explorations in Economic History* 20: 94–109. (1983b): "English Workers' Living Standards during the Industrial Revolution: A New Look," *Economic History Review,* 2d ser., 36: 1–25.

Lindley, D. J. (1983): "Riot Prevention and Control in Early Stuart London," *Transactions of the Royal Historical Society,* 5th ser., 33: 109–126.

Linebaugh, Peter (1992): *The London Hanged: Crime and Civil Society in the Eighteenth Century.* Cambridge: Cambridge University Press.

Lis, Catharina (1986): *Social Change and the Labouring Poor: Antwerp, 1770–1860.* New Haven: Yale University Press.

Lofland, John (1981): "Collective Behavior: The Elementary Forms," in Morris Rosenberg and Ralph Turner, eds., *Social Psychology: Sociological Perspectives.* New York: Basic Books.

Logue, Kenneth J. (1979): *Popular Disturbances in Scotland, 1780–1815.* Edinburgh: John Donald.

Lottes, Gunther (1979): *Politische Aufklärung und plebejisches Publikum. Zur Theorie und Praxis des englischen Radikalismus im späten 18. Jahrhundert.* Munich: Oldenbourg.

Macaulay, Thomas Babington (1900): *Miscellanies: Complete Writings of Lord Macaulay,* vols. 17–20. Boston: Houghton Mifflin.

MacDermot, Brian, ed. (1992): *The Irish Catholic Petition of 1905: The Diary of Denys Scully.* Dublin: Irish Academic Press.

Macdonagh, Oliver (1977): *Early Victorian Government, 1830–1870.* New York: Holmes and Meier.

Macfarlane, Alan (1986): "Socio-economic Revolution in England and the Origin of the Modern World," in Roy Porter and Mikulas Teich, eds., *Revolution in History.* Cambridge: Cambridge University Press.

Machin, G. I. T. (1963): "The No-Popery Movement in Britain in 1828–9," *Historical*

Journal 6: 193–211. (1964): *The Catholic Question in English Politics, 1820 to 1830.* Oxford: Clarendon Press. (1979): "Resistance to Repeal of the Test and Corporation Acts, 1828," *Historical Journal* 22: 115–139.

Macpherson, C. B. (1962): *The Political Theory of Possessive Individualism.* Oxford: Clarendon Press.

Main, J. M. (1965–67): "Radical Westminster, 1807–1820," *Historical Studies* 12: 186–204.

Malcolmson, Robert W. (1984): "Workers' Combinations in Eighteenth-Century England," in Margaret Jacob and James Jacob, eds., *The Origins of Anglo-American Radicalism.* London: George Allen and Unwin.

Mann, Michael (1986): *The Sources of Social Power, I: A History of Power from the Beginning to A.D. 1760.* Cambridge: Cambridge University Press. (1988): *States, War and Capitalism.* Oxford: Blackwell. (1990): ed., *The Rise and Decline of the Nation State.* Oxford: Blackwell. (1993): *The Sources of Social Power, II: The Rise of Classes and Nation-States, 1760–1914.* Cambridge: Cambridge University Press.

Manning, Roger B. (1988): *Village Revolts: Social Protest and Popular Disturbances in England, 1509–1640.* Oxford: Clarendon Press.

Markoff, John (1985): "The Social Geography of Rural Revolt at the Beginning of the French Revolution," *American Sociological Review* 50: 761–781. (1986): "Contexts and Forms of Rural Revolt: France in 1789," *Journal of Conflict Resolution* 30: 253–289.

Marshall, Dorothy (1968): *Dr. Johnson's London.* New York: Wiley.

Marshall, T. H. (1950): *Citizenship and Social Class.* Cambridge: Cambridge University Press.

Marston, Sallie A. (1989): "Public Rituals and Community Power: St. Patrick's Day Parades in Lowell, Massachusetts, 1841–1874," *Political Geography Quarterly* 8: 255–269.

Martin, J. M. (1967): "The Parliamentary Enclosure Movement and Rural Society in Warwickshire," *Agricultural History Review* 15: 19–39. (1979): "The Small Landowner and Parliamentary Enclosure in Warwickshire," *Economic History Review* 32: 328–343.

Martin, Roger H. (1978): "Evangelical Dissenters and Wesleyan-Style Itinerant Ministries at the End of the Eighteenth Century," *Methodist History* 16: 169–184.

Marvel, Howard P. (1977): "Factory Regulation: A Reinterpretation of Early English Experience," *Journal of Law and Economics* 20: 379–402.

Marwell, Gerald (1981): "Altruism and the Problem of Collective Action" in V. Derlega and J. Grzelk, eds., *Cooperation and Helping Behavior.* New York: Academic Press.

Marwell, Gerald, and Pamela Oliver (1993): *The Critical Mass in Collective Action: A Micro-Social Theory.* Cambridge: Cambridge University Press.

Marx, Karl (1973): "Review of Guizot's Book on the English Revolution," in Karl Marx, *Surveys from Exile,* ed. David Fernbach. London: Allen Lane. Written in 1850.

Mather, F. C. (1959): *Public Order in the Age of the Chartists.* Manchester: Manchester University Press.

Mathias, Peter (1979): *The Transformation of England: Essays in the Economic and*

Social History of England in the Eighteenth Century. New York: Columbia University Press. (1983): *The First Industrial Nation: An Economic History of Britain, 1700–1914.* 2d ed. London: Methuen.

Mathias, Peter, and Patrick O'Brien (1976): "Taxation in Britain and France, 1715–1810: A Comparison of the Social and Economic Incidence of Taxes Collected for the Central Governments," *Journal of European Economic History* 5: 601–650. (1978): "The Incidence of Taxes and the Burden of Proof," *Journal of European Economic History* 7: 211–213.

Mayer, Arno (1981): *The Persistence of the Old Regime.* New York: Pantheon.

Mayer, Margit (1990): "Social Movement Research and Social Movement Practice: The U.S. Pattern," in Dieter Rucht, ed., *Research on Social Movements: The State of the Art in Western Europe and the USA.* Frankfurt and Boulder: Campus/Westview.

Mayfield, David, and Susan Thorne (1992): "Social History and Its Discontents: Gareth Stedman Jones and the Politics of Language," *Social History* 17: 165–188.

McAdam, Doug (1982): *Political Process and the Development of Black Insurgency, 1930–1970.* Chicago: University of Chicago Press. (1988): *Freedom Summer.* New York: Oxford University Press.

McAdam, Doug, John D. McCarthy, and Mayer N. Zald (1988): "Social Movements," in Neil J. Smelser, ed., *Handbook of Sociology.* Newbury Park: Sage.

McCalman, Iain D. (1987): "Ultra-radicalism and Convivial Debating-Clubs in London, 1795–1838," *English Historical Review* 102: 309–333. (1988): *Radical Underworld: Prophets, Revolutionaries and Pornographers in London, 1795–1840.* Cambridge: Cambridge University Press.

McCarthy, John D., David W. Britt, and Mark Wolfson (1991): "The Institutional Channeling of Social Movements by the State in the United States," *Research in Social Movements, Conflicts and Change* 13: 45–76.

McCloskey, Donald N. (1978): "A Mismeasurement of the Incidence of Taxation in Britain and France, 1715–1810," *Journal of European Economic History* 7: 209–210.

McCord, Norman (1967): "Tyneside Discontents and Peterloo," *Northern History* 2: 91–111. (1972): "Some Aspects of North-East England in the Nineteenth Century," *Northern History* 7: 73–88.

McCord, Norman, and David E. Brewster (1968): "Some Labour Troubles of the 1790s in North East England," *International Review of Social History* 13: 366–383.

McKendrick, Neil, John Brewer, and J. H. Plumb (1985): *The Birth of a Consumer Society: The Commercialization of Eighteenth-Century England.* Bloomington: Indiana University Press. First published in 1982.

McPhail, Clark (1991): *The Myth of the Madding Crowd.* New York: Aldine De Gruyter.

McPhail, Clark, and Ronald T. Wohlstein (1983): "Individual and Collective Behaviors within Gatherings, Demonstrations, and Riots," *Annual Review of Sociology* 9: 579–600. (1986): "Collective Locomotion," *American Sociological Review* 51: 447–481.

Melucci, Alberto (1985): "The Symbolic Challenge of Contemporary Movements," *Social Research* 52: 789–816. (1989): *Nomads of the Present: Social Movements and Individual Need in Contemporary Society.* Philadelphia: Temple University Press.

Mercier, Louis-Sébastien (1982): *Parallèle de Paris et de Londres.* Paris: Didier.

Metcalfe, Andrew (1988): *For Freedom and Dignity: Historical Agency and Class Structures in the Coalfields of NSW.* Sydney: Allen and Unwin Australia.

Meyer, David S. (1993): "Protest Cycles and Political Process: American Peace Movements in the Nuclear Age," *Political Research Quarterly* 47: 451–479.

Meyer, David S., and Douglas R. Imig (1993): "Political Opportunity and the Rise and Decline of Interest Group Sectors," *Social Science Journal* 30: 253–270.

Mikkelsen, Flemming (1986): ed., *Protest og Opror.* Aarhus: Modtryk.

Miles, Dudley (1988): *Francis Place, 1771–1854: The Life of a Remarkable Radical.* New York: St. Martin's.

Miller, David W. (1983): "Who Was Captain Rock? A Study of Agrarian Unrest in Pre-Famine Ireland," manuscript, Carnegie-Mellon University.

Miller, N. C. (1968): "John Cartwright and Radical Parliamentary Reform, 1808–1819," *English Historical Review* 83: 705–728.

Miller, Wilbur R. (1977): *Cops and Bobbies: Police Authority in New York and London, 1830–1870.* Chicago: University of Chicago Press.

Milton-Smith, John (1972): "Earl Gray's Cabinet and the Objects of Parliamentary Reform," *Historical Journal* 15: 55–74.

Mingay, G. E. (1989): ed., *The Agrarian History of England and Wales, VI: 1750–1850.* Cambridge: Cambridge University Press.

Mitchell, Austin (1967): *The Whigs in Opposition, 1815–1830.* Oxford: Clarendon Press.

Mitchell, B. R., and Phyllis Deane (1971): *Abstract of British Historical Statistics.* Cambridge: Cambridge University Press.

Mitchell, Harvey (1965): *The Underground War against Revolutionary France: The Missions of William Wickham, 1794–1800.* Oxford: Clarendon Press. (1991): "Edmund Burke's Language of Politics and His Audience," *Studies on Voltaire and the Eighteenth Century* 287: 335–360.

Mokyr, Joel (1987): "Has the Industrial Revolution Been Crowded Out? Some Reflections on Crafts and Williamson," *Explorations in Economic History* 24: 293–319. (1993): "The New Economic History and the Industrial Revolution" in Joel Mokyr, ed., *The British Industrial Revolution: An Economic Perspective.* Boulder: Westview.

Mommsen, Wolfgang, and Gerhard Hirschfeld (1982): *Social Protest, Violence and Terror in Nineteenth- and Twentieth-Century Europe.* New York: St. Martins, 1982.

Money, John (1971a): "Taverns, Coffee Houses and Clubs: Local Politics and Popular Articulacy in the Birmingham Area in the Age of the American Revolution," *Historical Journal* 14: 15–47. (1971b): "Birmingham and the West Midlands, 1760–1793: Politics and Regional Identity in the English Provinces in the Later Eighteenth Century," *Midland History* 1: 1–19. (1977): *Experience and Identity: Birmingham and the West Midlands, 1760–1800.* Manchester: Manchester University Press. (1990): "Freemasonry and the Fabric of Loyalism in Hanoverian England," in Eckhart Hellmuth, ed., *The Transformation of Political Culture: England and Germany in the Late Eighteenth Century.* London: German Historical Institute and Oxford University Press.

Moore, Barrington, Jr. (1966): *Social Origins of Dictatorship and Democracy.* Boston: Beacon. (1979): *Injustice: The Social Bases of Obedience and Revolt.* White Plains, N.Y.: M. E. Sharpe.

Moore, D. C. (1961): "The Other Face of Reform," *Victorian Studies* 5: 7–34. (1966): "Concession or Cure: The Sociological Premises of the First Reform Act," *Historical Journal* 9: 39–59.

Moorhouse, H. F. (1973): "The Political Incorporation of the British Working Class: An Interpretation," *Sociology* 7: 341–359.

Morawska, Ewa, and Willfried Spohn (1994): "'Cultural Pluralism' in Historical Sociology: Recent Theoretical Directions," in Diana Crane, ed., *The Sociology of Culture: Emerging Theoretical Perspectives.* Oxford: Blackwell.

Morgan, Edmund S. (1988): *Inventing the People: The Rise of Popular Sovereignty in England and America.* New York: Norton.

Morineau, Michel (1980): "Budgets de l'Etat et gestion des finances royales en France au dix-huitième siècle," *Revue Historique* 264: 289–336.

Morrill, J. S., and J. D. Walter (1985): "Order and Disorder in the English Revolution," in Anthony Fletcher and John Stevenson, eds., *Order and Disorder in Early Modern England.* Cambridge: Cambridge University Press.

Morris, Aldon, and Cedric Herring (1987): "Theory and Research in Social Movements: A Critical Review," *Annual Review of Political Science* 2: 137–195.

Morris, Aldon D., and Carol McClurg Mueller (1992): eds., *Frontiers in Social Movement Theory.* New Haven: Yale University Press.

Morris, R. J. (1976): *Cholera, 1832: Social Response to an Epidemic.* New York: Holmes and Meier. (1979): *Class and Class Consciousness in the Industrial Revolution, 1789–1850.* London: Macmillan. (1983): "Voluntary Societies and British Urban Elites, 1780–1850: An Analysis," *Historical Journal* 26: 95–118. (1986): "Introduction: Class, Power and Social Structure in British Nineteenth-Century Towns," in R. J. Morris, ed., *Class, Power and Social Structure in British Nineteenth-Century Towns.* Leicester: Leicester University Press. (1990): "Clubs, Societies, and Associations," in F. M. L. Thompson, ed., *The Cambridge Social History of Britain, 1750–1950,* vol. 3: *Social Agencies and Institutions.* Cambridge: Cambridge University Press.

Moss, B. H. (1993): "Republican Socialism and the Making of the Working Class in Britain, France, and the United States: A Critique of Thompsonian Culturalism," *Comparative Studies in Society and History* 35: 390–413.

Muller, Edward N. (1985): "Income Inequality, Regime Repressiveness, and Political Violence," *American Sociological Review* 50: 47–61.

Munsche, P. B. (1981a): "The Gamekeeper and English Rural Society, 1660–1830,"

Journal of British Studies 20: 82–105. (1981b): *Gentlemen and Poachers: The English Game Laws, 1671–1831.* Cambridge: Cambridge University Press.

Murray, Norman (1978): *The Scottish Hand Loom Weavers, 1790–1850: A Social History.* Edinburgh: John Donald.

Muskett, Paul (1980): "A Picturesque Little Rebellion? The Suffolk Workhouses of 1765," *Bulletin of the Society for the Study of Labour History* 41: 28–31.

Musson, A. E. (1963): *British Trade Unions, 1800–1875.* London: Macmillan. (1978): *The Growth of British Industry.* New York: Holmes and Meier.

Nardin, Terry (1972): "Conflicting Conceptions of Political Violence," in Cornelius P. Cotter, ed., *Political Science Annual.* Indianapolis: Bobbs-Merrill.

Nelson, Joan M. (1987): "Political Participation," in Myron Weiner and Samuel P. Huntington, eds., *Understanding Political Development.* Boston: Little, Brown.

Nettement, Alfred (1866): *Histoire de la Restauration.* Paris: Jacques Lecoffre. 8 vols.

Newby, Howard (1979): *The Deferential Worker: A Study of Farm Workers in East Anglia.* Madison: University of Wisconsin Press.

Nicolas, Jean (1985): ed., *Mouvements populaires et conscience sociale, XVIe-XIXe siècles.* Paris: Maloine.

Nicholas, Stephen J., and Jacqueline M. Nicholas (1992): "Male Literacy, 'Deskilling,' and the Industrial Revolution," *Journal of Interdisciplinary History* 23: 1–18.

Norman, E. R. (1976): *Church and Society in England, 1770–1970.* Oxford: Clarendon Press.

North, Douglass, and Robert Paul Thomas (1973): *The Rise of the Western World: A New Economic History.* Cambridge: Cambridge University Press.

Nusteling, Hubert P. H. (1993): "English Population Statistics for the First Half of the Nineteenth Century: A New Answer to Old Questions," *Annales de Démographie Historique* 1993: 171–189.

Nuttall, Geoffrey F. (1971): "Assembly and Association in Dissent, 1689–1831," in G. J. Cuming and Derek Baker, eds., *Councils and Assemblies: Papers Read at the Eighth Summer Meeting and the Ninth Winter Meeting of the Ecclesiastical History Society.* Cambridge: Cambridge University Press.

Nye, John Vincent (1992): "Guerre, commerce, guerre commerciale: L'Économie politique des échanges franco-anglais réexaminée," *Annales: Économies, Sociétés, Civilisations* 47: 613–631.

Oberschall, Anthony (1973): *Social Conflict and Social Movements.* Englewood Cliffs, N.J.: Prentice-Hall. (1978): "Theories of Social Conflict," *Annual Review of Sociology* 4: 291–316. (1993): *Social Movements.* New Brunswick, N.J.: Transaction.

O'Brien, Conor Cruise (1992): *The Great Melody: A Thematic Biography and Commented Anthology of Edmund Burke.* Chicago: University of Chicago Press.

O'Brien, Patrick K. (1988): "The Political Economy of British Taxation, 1660–1815," *Economic History Review* 41: 1–32. (1989): "The Impact of the Revolutionary and Napoleonic Wars, 1793–1815, on the Long-run Growth of the British Economy," *Review* 12: 335–395. (1991a): "The Foundations of European Industrialization: From the Perspective of the World," *Journal of Historical Sociology* 4: 288–316. (1991b): "Power with Profit: The State and the Economy, 1688–1815," inaugural lecture, University of London.

O'Donnell, Guillermo, and Philippe C. Schmitter (1986): *Transitions from Authoritarian Rule: Tentative Conclusions about Uncertain Democracies.* Baltimore: Johns Hopkins University Press.

O'Ferrall, Fergus (1985): *Catholic Emancipation: Daniel O'Connell and the Birth of Irish Democracy, 1820–30.* Dublin: Gill and Macmillan.

O'Gorman, Frank (1982): *The Emergence of the British Two-Party System, 1760–1832.* London: Arnold. (1984): "Electoral Deference in 'Unreformed' England: 1760–1832," *Journal of Modern History* 56: 391–429. (1989): *Voters, Patrons, and Parties: The Unreformed Electoral System of Hanoverian England, 1734–1832.* Oxford: Clarendon Press. (1992): "Campaign Rituals and Ceremonies: The Social Meaning of Elections in England 1780–1860," *Past and Present* 135: 79–115.

Oliver, Pamela (1984): "'If You Don't Do It, Nobody Else Will': Active and Token Contributions to Local Collective Action," *American Sociological Review* 49: 601–610.

Olson, Mancur (1965): *The Logic of Collective Action.* Cambridge, Mass.: Harvard University Press. (1978): *The Rise and Decline of Nations.* New Haven: Yale University Press.

Olzak, Susan (1989): "Analysis of Events in the Study of Collective Action," *Annual Review of Sociology* 15: 119–141. (1992): *The Dynamics of Ethnic Competition and Conflict.* Stanford: Stanford University Press.

Orieux, Jean (1970): *Talleyrand ou le sphinx incompris.* Paris: Flammarion.

Ormrud, David (1985): *English Grain Exports and the Structure of Agrarian Capitalism, 1700–1760.* Hull: Hull University Press.

Orth, John V. (1991): *Combination and Conspiracy: A Legal History of Trade Unionism, 1721–1906.* Oxford: Clarendon Press.

Orum, Anthony (1988): "Political Sociology," in Neil J. Smelser, ed., *Handbook of Sociology.* Newbury Park: Sage.

Outhwaite, R. B. (1991): *Dearth, Public Policy and Social Disturbance in England, 1550–1800.* London: Macmillan.

Paine, Thomas (1984): *Rights of Man.* Harmondsworth: Penguin. First published in 1984.

Palmer, Stanley H. (1988): *Police and Protest in England and Ireland, 1780–1850.* Cambridge: Cambridge University Press.

Parssinen, T. M. (1972): "The Revolutionary Party in London, 1816–20," *Bulletin of the Institute of Historical Research* 14: 266–282. (1973): "Association, Convention and Anti-Parliament in British Radical Politics, 1771–1848," *English Historical Review* 88: 504–533.

Parssinen, T. M., and I. J. Prothero (1977): "The London Tailors' Strike of 1834 and the Collapse of the Grand National Consolidated Trades Union: A Police Spy's Report," *International Review of Social History* 22: 64–107.

Pawson, Eric (1977): *Transport and Economy: The Turnpike Roads of Eighteenth-Century Britain*. London: Academic Press.

Payne, Harry C. (1975): "Elite versus Popular Mentality in the Eighteenth Century," *Historical Reflections* 2: 183–208.

Peacock, A. J. (1965): *Bread or Blood: The Agrarian Riots in East Anglia, 1816*. London: Gollancz. (1971): "The Revolt of the Field in East Anglia," in L. M. Munby, ed., *The Luddites and Other Essays*. London: Katanka. (1974): "Village Radicalism in East Anglia, 1800–50," in J. P. D. Dunbabin (with A. J. Peacock), *Rural Discontent in Nineteenth-Century Britain*. New York: Holmes and Meier.

Peattie, Lisa, and Martin Rein (1983): *Women's Claims: A Study in Political Economy*. Oxford: Oxford University Press.

Peirce, David, Peter N. Grabosky, and Ted Robert Gurr (1977): "London: The Politics of Crime and Conflict, 1800 to the 1970s," in Ted Robert Gurr et al., *The Politics of Crime and Conflict: A Comparative History of Four Cities*. Beverly Hills: Sage.

Perkin, Harold (1969): *The Origins of Modern English Society, 1780–1880*. London: Routledge and Kegan Paul.

Perrot, Michelle (1974): *Les ouvriers en grève*. Paris: Mouton. 2 vols.

Peterson, Paul E. (1992): "An Immodest Proposal," *Daedalus* 121, no. 4: 151–174.

Philips, David (1980): "'A New Engine of Power and Authority': The Institutionalization of Law-Enforcement in England, 1780–1830," in V. A. C. Gatrell, Bruce Lenman, and Geoffrey Parker, eds., *Crime and the Law: The Social History of Crime in Western Europe since 1500*. London: Europa. (1989): "Good Men to Associate and Bad Men to Conspire: Associations for the Prosecution of Felons in England, 1760–1860," in Douglas Hay and Francis Snyder, eds., *Policing and Prosecution in Britain, 1750–1850*. Oxford: Clarendon Press.

Phillips, John A. (1982): *Electoral Behavior in Unreformed England: Plumpers, Splitters, and Straights*. Princeton: Princeton University Press. (1990): "Municipal Politics in Later Eighteenth-Century Maidstone: Electoral Polarization in the Reign of George III," in Eckhart Hellmuth, ed., *The Transformation of Political Culture: England and Germany in the Late Eighteenth Century*. London: German Historical Institute and Oxford University Press. (1992): *The Great Reform Bill in the Boroughs: English Electoral Behaviour, 1818–1841*. Oxford: Clarendon Press.

Phillips, John A., and Charles Wetherell (1991): "The Great Reform Bill of 1832 and the Rise of Partisanship," *Journal of Modern History* 63: 621–646.

Philp, Mark (1991): ed., *The French Revolution and British Popular Politics*. Cambridge: Cambridge University Press.

Place, Francis (1972): *The Autobiography of Francis Place (1771–1854)*, ed. Mary Thale. Cambridge: Cambridge University Press.

Poggi, Gianfranco (1990): *The State: Its Nature, Development and Prospects*. Stanford: Stanford University Press.

Pollard, Sidney, and David W. Crossley (1968): *The Wealth of Britain, 1085–1966*. London: B. T. Batsford.

Porta, Donatella della, and Gianfranco Pasquino (1983): eds., *Terrorismo e violenza politica*. Bologna: Il Mulino.

Porta, Donatella della, and Sidney Tarrow (1986): "Unwanted Children: Political Violence and the Cycle of Protest in Italy, 1966–1973," *European Journal of Political Research* 14: 607–632.

Powell, G. Bingham (1973): "Incremental Democratization: The British Reform Act of 1832" in Gabriel A. Almond, Scott C. Flanagan, and Robert J. Mundt, eds., *Crisis, Choice and Change: Historical Studies of Political Development*. Boston: Little, Brown.

Prest, John (1977): *Politics in the Age of Cobden*. London: Macmillan.

Price, Richard N. (1975): "The Other Face of Respectability: Violence in the Manchester Brickmaking Trade, 1859–1870," *Past and Present* 66: 110–132. (1986): *Labour in British Society: An Interpretive History*. London: Croom Helm. (1991): "The Future of British Labour History," *International Review of Social History* 36: 249–260.

Prothero, Iorwerth (1979): *Artisans and Politics in Early Nineteenth-Century London: John Gast and His Times*. Folkestone: Dawson.

Quadagno, Jill (1982): *Aging in Early Industrial Society: Work, Family and Social Policy in Nineteenth-Century England*. New York: Academic Press. (1992): "Social Movements and State Transformation: Labor Unions and Racial Conflict in the War on Poverty," *American Sociological Review* 57: 616–634.

Radzinowicz, Leon (1968): *A History of English Criminal Law and Its Administration from 1750*, vol. 4: *Grappling for Control*. London: Stevens and Sons.

Randall, Adrian J. (1982): "The Shearmen and the Wiltshire Outrages of 1802: Trade Unionism and Industrial Violence," *Social History* 7: 283–304. (1986): "The Philosophy of Luddism: The Case of the West of England Woolen Workers, ca. 1790–1809," *Technology and Culture* 27: 1–17. (1989): "Work, Culture and Resistance to Machinery in the West of England Woollen Industry," in Pat Hudson, ed., *Regions and Industries: A Perspective on the Industrial Revolution in Britain*. Cambridge: Cambridge University Press. (1990): "New Languages or Old? Labour, Capital, and Discourse in the Industrial Revolution," *Social History* 15: 195–216. (1991): *Before the Luddites: Custom, Community and Machinery in the English Woollen Industry, 1776–1809*. Cambridge: Cambridge University Press.

Rasler, Karen (1986): "War, Accommodation, and Violence in the United States, 1890–1970," *American Political Science Review* 80: 921–945.

Ratcliffe, B. M., and W. H. Chaloner (1977): eds., *A French Sociologist Looks at Britain: Gustave d'Eichthal and British Society in 1828*. Manchester: Manchester University Press.

Read, Donald (1958): *Peterloo: The 'Massacre' and Its Background*. Manchester: Manchester University Press.

Reaney, Bernard (1970): *The Class Struggle in 19th Century Oxfordshire: The Social and Communal Background to the Otmoor Disturbances of 1830 to 1835*. History Workshop Pamphlets, 3. Oxford: History Workshop.

Reay, Barry (1990): *The Last Rising of the Agricultural Labourers: Rural Life and Protest in Nineteenth-Century England.* Oxford: Clarendon Press.

Reed, Mick, and Roger Wells (1990): eds., *Class, Conflict and Protest in the English Countryside, 1700–1880.* London: Frank Cass.

Reid, Douglas A. (1976): "The Decline of Saint Monday, 1766–1876," *Past and Present* 71: 76–101.

Rice, E. E. (1990): ed., *Revolution and Counter-Revolution.* Oxford: Blackwell.

Richards, Eric (1974): "Captain Swing in the West Midlands," *International Review of Social History* 19: 86–99.

Richardson, Ruth (1987): *Death, Dissection and the Destitute.* London: Routledge and Kegan Paul.

Richter, Donald (1971): "The Role of Mob Riot in Victorian Elections, 1865–1885," *Victorian Studies* 14–15: 19–28.

Rimlinger, Gaston V. (1960): "The Legitimation of Protest: A Comparative Study in Labor History," *Comparative Studies in Society and History* 2: 329–343.

Robinson, Dwight E. (1987): "Secret of British Power in the Age of Sail: Admiralty Records of the Coasting Fleet," *American Neptune* 48: 5–21.

Rogers, Nicholas (1973): "Aristocratic Clientage, Trade and Independency: Popular Politics in Pre-Radical Westminster," *Past and Present* 61: 70–106. (1978): "Popular Protest in Early Hanoverian London," *Past and Present* 79: 70–100. (1984): "The Urban Opposition to Whig Oligarchy, 1720–60," in Margaret Jacob and James Jacob, eds., *The Origins of Anglo-American Radicalism.* London: George Allen and Unwin. (1989): *Whigs and Cities: Popular Politics in the Age of Walpole and Pitt.* Oxford: Clarendon Press. (1990): "Crowd and People in the Gordon Riots," in Eckhart Hellmuth, ed., *The Transformation of Political Culture: England and Germany in the Late Eighteenth Century.* London: German Historical Institute and Oxford University Press.

Rose, Arthur G. (1963–64): "Early Cotton Riots in Lancashire, 1769–1779," *Transactions of the Lancashire and Cheshire Antiquarian Society* 73–74: 60–100.

Rose, R. B. (1959): "Eighteenth-Century Price-Riots, the French Revolution and the Jacobin Maximum," *International Review of Social History* 4: 432–445. (1960): "The Priestley Riots of 1791," *Past and Present* 18: 68–88. (1961): "Eighteenth-Century Price Riots and Public Policy in England," *International Review of Social History* 6: 277–292. (1965): "The Origins of Working-Class Radicalism in Birmingham," *Labour History* 9: 6–14.

Rose, Richard (1964): *Politics in England.* Boston: Little, Brown.

Rose, Sonya O. (1992): *Limited Livelihoods: Gender and Class in Nineteenth-Century England.* Berkeley: University of California Press.

Rosenfeld, Rachel A., and Kathryn B. Ward (1991): "The Contemporary U.S. Women's Movement: An Empirical Example of Competition Theory," *Sociological Forum* 6: 471–500.

Rostow, W. W. (1948): *The British Economy of the Nineteenth Century.* Oxford: Clarendon Press.

Rowe, D. J. (1967): "The London Working Men's Association and the 'People's Charter,'" *Past and Present* 36: 73–86. (1968): "The Strikes of the Tyneside Keelmen in 1809 and 1819," *International Review of Social History* 13: 58–75. (1970): ed., *London Radicalism, 1830–1843: A Selection from the Papers of Francis Place*. Chatham, Kent: W. and J. Mackay. Published for London Record Society. (1977): "London Radicalism in the Era of the Great Reform Bill," in John Stevenson, ed., *London in the Age of Reform*. Oxford: Blackwell.

Roy, William (1984): "Class Conflict and Social Change in Historical Perspective," *Annual Review of Sociology* 10: 483–506.

Royle, Edward, and James Walvin (1982): *English Radicals and Reformers, 1760–1848*. Lexington: University Press of Kentucky.

Rubinstein, W. D. (1987): *Elites and the Wealthy in Modern British History: Essays in Social and Economic History*. Brighton: Harvester.

Rudé, George (1962): *Wilkes and Liberty*. Oxford: Clarendon Press. (1964): *The Crowd in History*. New York: Wiley. (1967): "English Rural and Urban Disturbances on the Eve of the First Reform Bill, 1830–1831," *Past and Present* 37: 87–102. (1969a): "Why Was There No Revolution in England in 1830 or 1848?" in Manfred Kossok, ed., *Studien über die Revolution*, pp. 231–244. Berlin: Akademie Verlag. (1969b): "The 'Pre-Industrial' Crowd," *Flinders Journal of History and Politics* 1: 4–18. (1971a): *Hanoverian London, 1714–1808*. London: Secker and Warburg. (1971b): *Paris and London in the Eighteenth Century: Studies in Popular Protest*. New York: Viking. (1973): "Protest and Punishment in Nineteenth-Century Britain," *Albion* 5: 1–23. (1978): *Protest and Punishment: The Story of the Social and Political Protesters Transported to Australia, 1788–1868*. Oxford: Clarendon Press. (1979–80): "L'Idéologie de la contestation populaire à l'époque pré-industrielle," *Europa* 3: 7–17.

Rueschemeyer, Dietrich, Evelyne Huber Stephens, and John D. Stephens (1992): *Capitalist Development and Democracy*. Chicago: University of Chicago Press.

Rule, James (1988): *Theories of Civil Violence*. Berkeley: University of California Press.

Rule, John (1979): "Social Crime in the Rural South in the Eighteenth and Early Nineteenth Centuries," *Southern History* 1: 135–153. (1981): *The Experience of Labour in Eighteenth-Century Industry*. London: Croom Helm. (1986): *The Labouring Classes in Early Industrial England, 1750–1850*. London: Longman.

Sabel, Charles F. (1982): *Work and Politics: The Division of Labor in Industry*. Cambridge: Cambridge University Press.

Salaman, Redcliffe N. (1985): *The History and Social Influence of the Potato*. Cambridge: Cambridge University Press. Revised impression. First published in 1949.

Salert, Barbara, and John Sprague (1980): *The Dynamics of Riots*. Ann Arbor: Inter-University Consortium for Political and Social Research.

Samuel, Raphael (1981): ed., *People's History and Socialist Theory*. London: Routledge and Kegan Paul.

Schieder, Theodor (1973): ed., *Revolution und Gesellschaft: Theorie und Praxis der Systemveränderung*. Freiburg im Breisgau: Herder.

Schumaker, Paul D. (1978): "The Scope of Political Conflict and the Effectiveness of Constraints in Contemporary Urban Protest," *Sociological Quarterly* 19: 168–184.

Schutz, Barry M., and Robert O. Slater (1990): eds., *Revolution and Political Change in the Third World*. Boulder: Lynne Rienner.

Schwarz, L. D. (1972): "Occupations and Incomes in Late Eighteenth-Century East London," *East London Papers* 14: 87–100. (1979): "Income Distribution and Social Structure in London in the Late Eighteenth Century," *Economic History Review*, 2d ser., 32: 250–259. (1982): "Social Class and Social Geography: The Middle Classes in London at the End of the Eighteenth Century," *Social History* 7: 167–185. (1992): *London in the Age of Industrialisation: Entrepreneurs, Labour Force and Living Conditions, 1700–1850*. Cambridge: Cambridge University Press.

Scott, James C. (1985): *Weapons of the Weak: Everyday Forms of Peasant Resistance*. New Haven: Yale University Press. (1990): *Domination and the Arts of Resistance*. New Haven: Yale University Press.

Scott, Joan Wallach (1987): "On Language, Gender, and Working-Class History," *International Labor and Working-Class History* 31: 1–13. (1988): *Gender and the Politics of History*. New York: Columbia University Press.

Searby, Peter (1977): "Paternalism, Disturbance and Parliamentary Reform: Society and Politics in Coventry, 1819–1832," *International Review of Social History* 22: 198–225.

Seed, John (1985): "Gentlemen Dissenters: The Social and Political Meanings of Rational Dissent in the 1770s and 1780s," *Historical Journal* 28: 299–325. (1993): "Capital and Class Formation in Early Industrial England," *Social History* 18: 17–30.

Seligman, Adam (1992): *The Idea of Civil Society*. New York: Free Press.

Sen, Amartya (1981): *Poverty and Famines: An Essay on Entitlement and Deprivations*. Oxford: Clarendon Press.

Sewell, William H., Jr. (1980): *Work and Revolution: The Language of Labor from the Old Regime to 1848*. New York: Cambridge University Press. (1990a): "Rethinking Labor History: Toward a Post-Materialist Rhetoric," paper presented to the annual meeting of the Society for French Historical Studies, Baltimore. (1990b): "Collective Violence and Collective Loyalties in France: Why the French Revolution Made a Difference," *Politics and Society* 18: 527–552.

Sharp, Buchanan (1980): *In Contempt of All Authority: Rural Artisans and Riot in the West of England, 1586–1660*. Berkeley: University of California Press.

Shelton, Walter J. (1973): *English Hunger and Industrial Disorders: A Study of Social Conflict during the First Decade of George III's Reign*. London: Macmillan.

Sheppard, Francis (1958): *Local Government in St. Marylebone, 1688–1835: A Study of the Vestry and the Turnpike Trust*. London: Athlone Press. (1971): *London, 1808–1870: The Infernal Wen*. London: Secker and Warburg.

Silberman, Bernard S. (1993): *Cages of Reason: The Rise of the Rational State in France, Japan, the United States, and Great Britain*. Chicago: University of Chicago Press.

Singleton, F. (1964): "Captain Swing in East Anglia," *Bulletin of the Society for the Study of Labour History* 9: 13–15.

Skocpol, Theda (1979): *States and Social Revolutions: A Comparative Analysis of France, Russia, and China.* Cambridge: Cambridge University Press.

Smelser, Neil J. (1959): *Social Change in the Industrial Revolution.* Chicago: University of Chicago Press.

Smith, Dennis (1982): *Conflict and Compromise: Class Formation in English Society, 1830–1914. A Comparative Study of Birmingham and Sheffield.* London: Routledge.

Smith, W. A. (1965): "Anglo-Colonial Society and the Mob, 1740–1775," Ph.D. dissertation, Claremont Graduate School and University Center.

Snell, K. D. M. (1985): *Annals of the Labouring Poor: Social Change and Agrarian England, 1660–1900.* Cambridge: Cambridge University Press.

Snow, David A., et al. (1986): "Frame Alignment and Mobilization," *American Sociological Review* 51: 464–481.

Soffer, R. N. (1965): "Attitudes and Allegiances in the Unskilled North, 1830–1850," *International Review of Social History* 10: 429–454.

Somers, Margaret R. (1992): "Narrativity, Narrative Identity, and Social Action: Rethinking English Working-Class Formation," *Social Science History* 16: 591–630. (1993): "Citizenship and the Place of the Public Sphere: Law, Community, and Political Culture in the Transition to Democracy," *American Sociological Review* 58: 587–620.

Sommier, Isabelle (1993): "La CGT: Du service d'ordre au service d'accueil," *Genèses* 12: 69–88.

Southey, Charles Cuthbert (1850): *The Life and Correspondence of the Late Robert Southey.* London: Longman, Brown, Green and Longmans. 6 vols.

Southey, Robert (1832): *Essays, Moral and Political.* London: John Murray. 2 vols.

Spater, George (1982): *William Cobbett: The Poor Man's Friend.* Cambridge: Cambridge University Press. 2 vols.

Spohn, Willfried (1990): "Toward a Historical Sociology of Working-Class Formation," *Critical Sociology* 17: 75–90.

Spring, David (1980): "An Outsider's View: Alexis de Tocqueville on Aristocratic Society and Politics in 19th-Century England," *Albion* 12: 122–131.

Stedman Jones, Gareth (1983): *Languages of Class: Studies in English Working Class History, 1832–1982.* Cambridge: Cambridge University Press.

Steinberg, Marc W. (1991a): "Talkin' Class: Discourse, Ideology and Their Roles in Class Conflict," in Scott McNall, Rhonda Levine, and Rick Fantasia, eds., *Bringing Class Back In.* Boulder: Westview. (1991b): "The Re-Making of the English Working Class?" *Theory and Society* 20: 173–198.

Stephens, John D. (1989): "Democratic Transition and Breakdown in Western Europe, 1870–1939: A Test of the Moore Thesis," *American Journal of Sociology* 94: 1019–1077.

Stevens, John (1977): *England's Last Revolution: Pentrich, 1817.* Hartington, Derbyshire: Moorland.

Stevenson, John (1974): "Food Riots in England, 1792–1818," in John Stevenson and Roland Quinault, eds., *Popular Protest and Public Order: Six Studies in British*

History, 1790–1920. London: George Allen and Unwin. (1977a): ed., *London in the Age of Reform.* Oxford: Blackwell. (1977b): "Social Control and the Prevention of Riots in England, 1789–1829," in A. P. Donajgrodzki, ed., *Social Control in Nineteenth-Century Britain.* London: Croom Helm. (1979): *Popular Disturbances in England, 1700–1870.* London: Longman. (1992): *Popular Disturbances in England, 1700–1832.* 2d ed. London: Longman.

Stohl, Michael (1976): *War and Domestic Political Violence: The American Capacity for Repression and Reaction.* Beverly Hills: Sage.

Stone, Lawrence (1947): "State Control in Sixteenth-Century England," *Economic History Review* 17: 103–120. (1974): "The Size and Composition of the Oxford Student Body, 1580–1909," in Lawrence Stone, ed., *The University in Society,* vol. 1: *Oxford and Cambridge from the 14th to the Early 19th Century.* Princeton: Princeton University Press. (1983): "Interpersonal Violence in English Society, 1300–1980," *Past and Present* 101: 22–33. (1994): ed., *An Imperial State at War: Britain from 1689 to 1815.* London: Routledge.

Stone, Lawrence, and Jeanne C. Fawtier Stone (1984): *An Open Elite? England, 1540–1880.* Oxford: Clarendon Press.

Storch, Robert D. (1975): "The Plague of the Blue Locusts: Police Reform and Popular Resistance in Northern England, 1840–57," *International Review of Social History* 20: 61–90. (1976): "The Policeman as Domestic Missionary: Urban Discipline and Popular Culture in Northern England, 1850–1880" *Journal of Social History* 9: 481–509. (1982a): "'Please to Remember the Fifth of November': Conflict, Solidarity and Public Order in Southern England, 1815–1900," in Robert D. Storch, ed., *Popular Culture and Custom in Nineteenth-Century England.* London: Croom Helm. (1982b): "Popular Festivity and Consumer Protest: Food Price Disturbances in the Southwest and Oxfordshire in 1867," *Albion* 14: 209–234.

Talleyrand-Périgord, Charles-Maurice de (1891): *Mémoires du prince de Talleyrand,* ed. duc de Broglie. Paris: Calmann-Lévy. 5 vols.

Tarrow, Sidney (1988): "National Politics and Collective Action: Recent Theory and Research in Western Europe and the United States," *Annual Review of Sociology:* 421–440. (1989a): *Struggle, Politics, and Reform: Collective Action, Social Movements, and Cycles of Protest.* Western Societies Program, Occasional Paper no. 21. Ithaca: Center for International Studies, Cornell University. (1989b): *Democracy and Disorder: Social Conflict, Political Protest and Democracy in Italy, 1966–1973.* New York: Oxford University Press. (1993): "Modular Collective Action and the Rise of the Social Movement: Why the French Revolution Was Not Enough," *Politics and Society* 21: 69–90. (1994): *Power in Movement.* Cambridge: Cambridge University Press.

Taylor, John G. (1979): *From Mobilization to Modes of Production: A Critique of the Sociologies of Development and Underdevelopment.* Atlantic Highlands, N.J.: Humanities Press.

Taylor, Michael (1975): "The Theory of Collective Choice," in Fred I. Greenstein and

Nelson Polsby, eds., *Handbook of Political Science*, vol. 3. Reading, Mass.: Addison-Wesley.

Te Brake, Wayne (1989): *Regents and Rebels: The Revolutionary World of the 18th-Century Dutch City.* Oxford: Blackwell. (1990): "How Much in How Little? Dutch Revolution in Comparative Perspective," *Tijdschrift voor Sociale Geschiedenis* 16: 349–363.

Teitelbaum, Michael (1984): *The British Fertility Decline: Demographic Transition in the Crucible of the Industrial Revolution.* Princeton: Princeton University Press.

Temperley, Howard (1981): "The Ideology of Antislavery," in David Eltis and James Walvin, eds., *The Abolition of the Atlantic Slave Trade: Origins and Effects in Europe, Africa, and the Americas.* Madison: University of Wisconsin Press.

Thale, Mary (1989): "London Debating Societies in the 1790s," *Historical Journal* 32: 57–86.

Thane, Pat (1990): "Government and Society in England and Wales, 1750–1914," in F. M. L. Thompson, ed., *The Cambridge Social History of Britain, 1750–1950*, vol. 3: *Social Agencies and Institutions.* Cambridge: Cambridge University Press.

Thirsk, Joan, and Jean Imray (1958): eds., *Suffolk Farming in the Nineteenth Century.* Ipswich: Suffolk Records Office.

Thomas, Michael (1975): "The Rioting Crowd in Derbyshire in the 18th Century," *Derbyshire Archaeological Journal* 95: 37–47.

Thomas, P. D. G. (1975): *British Politics and the Stamp Act Crisis: The First Phase of the American Revolution, 1763–1767.* Oxford: Clarendon Press.

Thomas, W. E. S. (1962): "Francis Place and Working-Class History," *Historical Journal* 1: 61–79.

Thomas, William (1970): "Whigs and Radicals in Westminster: The Election of 1819," *Guildhall Miscellany* 3: 174–217.

Thomas, Keith (1978): "The United Kingdom" in Raymond Grew, ed., *Crises of Political Development in Europe and the United States.* Princeton: Princeton University Press.

Thomis, Malcolm I., and Jennifer Grimmett (1982): *Women in Protest, 1800–1850.* New York: St. Martin's.

Thomis, Malcolm I., and Peter Holt (1977): *Threats of Revolution in Britain, 1789–1848.* London: Macmillan.

Thompson, E. P. (1963): *The Making of the English Working Class.* London: Gollancz. (1968): "English Trade Unionism and Other Labour Movements before 1790," *Bulletin of the Society for the Study of Labour History* 17: 19–24. (1971): "The Moral Economy of the English Crowd in the Eighteenth Century," *Past and Present* 50: 76–136. (1972): "Rough Music: Le Charivari anglais," *Annales: Economies, Sociétés, Civilisations* 27: 285–312. (1975): *Whigs and Hunters: The Origin of the Black Act.* New York: Pantheon. (1976): "Modes de domination et révolutions en Angleterre," *Actes de la Recherche en Sciences Sociales* 2: 133–151. (1978): "Eighteenth-Century English Society: Class Struggle without Class?" *Social History* 3: 133–165. (1981): "'Rough Music' et charivari: Quelques réflexions complémentaires," in Jacques Le Goff and Jean-Claude Schmitt, eds., *Le*

Charivari. Paris: Ecole des Hautes Etudes en Sciences Sociales. (1991): *Customs in Common*. London: Merlin Press. (1994): "Hunting the Jacobin Fox," *Past and Present* 142: 94–140.

Thompson, F. M. L. (1990) ed., *The Cambridge Social History of Britain*. Cambridge: Cambridge University Press. 3 vols.

Thurston, Gavin (1967): *The Clerkenwell Riot: The Killing of Constable Culley*. London: George Allen and Unwin.

Tilly, Charles (1984): "Demographic Origins of the European Proletariat," in David Levine, ed., *Proletarianization and Family History*. New York: Academic Press. (1985): *Big Structures, Large Processes, Huge Comparisons*. New York: Russell Sage Foundation. (1986): *The Contentious French*. Cambridge, Mass.: Harvard University Press. (1988): "Misreading, Then Re-Reading, Nineteenth-Century Social Change," in Barry Wellman and S. D. Berkowitz, eds., *Social Structures: A Network Approach*. Cambridge: Cambridge University Press. (1990): *Coercion, Capital, and European States, A.D. 990–1990*. Oxford: Blackwell. (1993): *European Revolutions, 1492–1992*. Oxford: Blackwell.

Tilly, Charles, Louise Tilly, and Richard Tilly (1975): *The Rebellious Century, 1830–1930*. Cambridge, Mass.: Harvard University Press.

Tilly, Richard (1980): *Kapital, Staat und sozialer Protest in der deutschen Industrialisierung*. Göttingen: Vandenhoeck and Ruprecht.

Tocqueville, Alexis de (1958): *Voyages en Angleterre, Irlande, Suisse et Algérie*, ed. J. P. Mayer. Paris: Gallimard. Oeuvres, papiers et correspondances d'Alexis de Tocqueville, 5.

Torsvik, Per (1981): ed., *Mobilization, Center-Periphery Structures and Nation-Building*. Bergen: Universitetsforlaget.

Touraine, Alain (1981): *The Voice and the Eye: An Analysis of Social Movements*. Cambridge: Cambridge University Press. (1985): "An Introduction to the Study of Social Movements," *Social Research* 52: 749–788.

Traugott, Mark (1978): "Reconceiving Social Movements," *Social Problems* 26: 38–49. (1985): *Armies of the Poor: Determinants of Working-Class Participation in the Parisian Insurrection of June 1848*. Princeton: Princeton University Press.

Tunzelmann, G. N. von (1978): *Steam Power and British Industrialization to 1860*. Oxford: Clarendon Press.

Turberville, A. S., and F. Beckwith (1943): "Leeds and Parliamentary Reform, 1820–1832," *Thoresby Miscellany* 12, pt. 1: 1–88.

Turner, Bryan S. (1990): "Outline of a Theory of Citizenship," *Sociology* 24: 189–218.

Turner, Michael, and Dennis Mills (1986): eds., *Land and Property: The English Land Tax, 1692–1832*. New York: St. Martin's.

Tyrrell, Ian (1986): *The Absent Marx: Class Analysis and Liberal History in Twentieth-Century America*. Westport, Conn.: Greenwood.

Underdown, David (1985): *Revel, Riot, and Rebellion: Popular Politics and Culture in England, 1603–1660*. Oxford: Clarendon Press.

Useem, Michael (1975): *Protest Movements in America*. Indianapolis: Bobbs-Merrill.

Valverde, Marianna (1988): "'Giving the Female a Domestic Turn': The Social, Legal and Moral Regulation of Women's Work in British Cotton Mills, 1820–1850," *Journal of Social History* 21: 619–634.

Vernon, James (1993): *Politics and the People: A Study in English Popular Culture c. 1815–1867.* Cambridge: Cambridge University Press.

Vester, Michael (1970): *Die Entstehung des Proletariats als Lernprozess: Die Entstehung antikapitalistischer Theorie und Praxis in England, 1792–1848.* Frankfurt am Main: Europaïsche Verlaganstalt.

Vincent, David (1977): ed., *Testaments of Radicalism: Memoirs of Working Class Politicians, 1790–1885.* London: Europa Publications.

Vogler, Richard (1991): *Reading the Riot Act: The Magistracy, the Police and the Army in Civil Disorder.* Milton Keynes: Open University Press.

Vries, Jan de (1984): *European Urbanization, 1500–1800.* Cambridge, Mass.: Harvard University Press.

Wahrman, Dror (1992): "Virtual Representation: Parliamentary Reporting and Languages of Class in the 1790s," *Past and Present* 136: 83–113.

Wallas, Graham (1898): *The Life of Francis Place, 1771–1854.* London: Longmans.

Walsh, Edward J. (1988): *Democracy in the Shadows: Citizen Mobilization in the Wake of the Accident at Three Mile Island.* New York: Greenwood.

Walsh, Richard (1959): *Charleston's Sons of Liberty.* Columbia: University of South Carolina Press.

Walter, John (1989): "The Social Economy of Dearth in Early Modern England," in John Walter and Roger Schofield, eds., *Famine, Disease, and the Social Order in Early Modern Society.* Cambridge: Cambridge University Press.

Walter, John, and Keith Wrightson (1976): "Dearth and the Social Order in Early Modern England," *Past and Present* 71: 22–42.

Walvin, James (1980): "The Rise of British Popular Sentiment for Abolition, 1787–1832," in Christine Bolt and Seymour Drescher, eds., *Anti-Slavery, Religion, and Reform: Essays in Memory of Roger Anstey.* Folkestone: Dawson/Archon. (1981): "The Public Campaign in England against Slavery, 1787–1834," in David Eltis and James Walvin, eds., *The Abolition of the Atlantic Slave Trade: Origins and Effects in Europe, Africa and the Americas.* Madison: University of Wisconsin Press. (1984): *English Urban Life, 1776–1851.* London: Hutchinson.

Ward, Bernard (1912): *The Eve of Catholic Emancipation, 1803–1829.* London: Longmans.

Ward, J. T. (1962): *The Factory Movement, 1830–1850.* London: Macmillan. (1970): ed., *Popular Movements, c. 1830–1850.* London: Macmillan.

Wasson, Ellis Archer (1985): "The Great Whigs and Parliamentary Reform, 1809–1830," *Journal of British Studies* 24: 434–464.

Waterman, Harvey (1981): "Reasons and Reason: Collective Political Activity in Comparative and Historical Perspective," *World Politics* 23: 554–589.

Watson, J. Steven (1960): *The Reign of George III, 1760–1815.* Oxford History of England, vol. 12. Oxford: Clarendon Press.

Webb, Sidney, and Beatrice Webb (1920): *The History of Trade Unionism.* London:

Longmans. (1963): *English Poor Law History,* pt. 1: *The Old Poor Law.* Hamden, Conn.: Archon. *English Local Government,* vol. 7. First published in 1927.

Weiner, Myron, and Samuel P. Huntington (1987): eds., *Understanding Political Development.* Boston: Little, Brown.

Weir, David R. (1984a): "Rather Never Than Late: Celibacy and Age at Marriage in English Cohort Fertility, 1541–1871," *Journal of Family History* 9: 340–354. (1984b): "Life under Pressure: France and England, 1670–1870," *Journal of Economic History* 44: 27–47. (1989): "Markets and Mortality in France," in John Walter and Roger Schofield, eds., *Famine, Disease, and the Social Order in Early Modern Society.* Cambridge: Cambridge University Press.

Weisbrod, Bernd (1990): "Der englische 'Sonderweg' in der neueren Geschichte," *Geschichte und Gesellschaft* 16: 233–252.

Weisser, Henry (1975): *British Working-Class Movements and Europe, 1815–1848.* Manchester: Manchester University Press.

Wellenreuther, Hermann (1979): *Repräsentation und Grossgrundbesitz in England, 1730–1770.* Stuttgart: Klett-Cotta.

Weller, Robert P., and Scott E. Guggenheim (1982): eds., *Power and Protest in the Countryside: Studies of Rural Unrest in Asia, Europe, and Latin America.* Durham, N.C.: Duke University Policy Studies.

Wells, Roger A. E. (1977): *Dearth and Distress in Yorkshire, 1793–1802.* Borthwick Papers, no. 52. York: Borthwick Institute of Historical Research, University of York. (1978): "Counting Riots in Eighteenth-Century England," *Bulletin of the Society for the Study of Labour History* 37: 68–72. (1979): "The Development of the English Rural Proletariat and Social Protest, 1700–1850," *Journal of Peasant Studies* 6: 116–139. (1980): "Social Conflict and Protest in the English Countryside in the Early Nineteenth Century: A Rejoinder," *Journal of Peasant Studies* 9: 514–530. (1983): *Insurrection: The British Experience, 1795–1803.* Gloucester: Alan Sutton. (1988): *Wretched Faces: Famine in Wartime England, 1793–1801.* Gloucester: Alan Sutton. (1990): "Social Protest, Class, Conflict and Consciousness, in the English Countryside, 1700–1880," in Mick Reed and Roger Wells, eds., *Class, Conflict and Protest in the English Countryside, 1700–1880.* London: Frank Cass.

Western, J. R. (1956): "The Volunteer Movement as an Anti-Revolutionary Force," *English Historical Review* 71: 603–614. (1965): *The English Militia in the Eighteenth Century: The Story of a Political Issue, 1660–1802.* London: Routledge and Kegan Paul.

White, Louise (1976): "Rational Theories of Participation," *Journal of Conflict Resolution* 20: 255–278.

Wiener, Joel (1983): *Radicalism and Freethought in Nineteenth-Century Britain: The Life of Richard Carlile.* Westport, Conn.: Greenwood.

Williams, Basil, and C. H. Stuart (1962): *The Whig Supremacy, 1714–1760.* 2d. ed. Oxford: Clarendon Press.

Williams, Dale Edward (1984): "Morals, Markets and the English Crowd in 1766," *Past and Present* 104: 56–73.

Williams, Gwyn W. (1968): *Artisans and Sans-Culottes: Popular Movements in France and Britain during the French Revolution.* London: Arnold. (1978): *The Merthyr Rising.* London: Croom Helm.

Williams, Raymond (1983): *Cobbett.* Oxford: Oxford University Press.

Williamson, Jeffrey G. (1982): "Was the Industrial Revolution Worth It? Disamenities and Death in 19th-Century British Towns," *Explorations in Economic History* 19: 221–245. (1985a): *Did British Capitalism Breed Inequality?* Boston: Allen and Unwin. (1985b): "The Historical Content of the Classical Labor Surplus Model," *Population and Development Review* 11: 171–191.

Willis, Richard E. (1976): "'An Handful of Violent People': the Nature of the Foxite Opposition, 1794–1801," *Albion* 8: 236–254.

Wilson, John (1977): "Social Protest and Social Control," *Social Problems* 24: 469–481.

Wilson, Kenneth L., and Anthony Orum (1976): "Mobilizing People for Collective Political Action," *Journal of Political and Military Sociology* 4: 187–202.

Wood, Ellen Maiksins (1991): *The Pristine Culture of Capitalism: A Historical Essay on Old Regimes and Modern States.* London: Verso.

Wood, James L., and Maurice Jackson (1982): *Social Movements: Development, Participation, and Dynamics.* Belmont, Calif.: Wadsworth.

Wood, Gordon S. (1992): *The Radicalism of the American Revolution.* New York: Knopf.

Woodcock, George (1989): "The Meaning of Revolution in Britain, 1770–1800," in Ceri Crossley and Ian Small, eds., *The French Revolution and British Culture.* Oxford: Oxford University Press.

Worrall, David (1992): *Radical Culture. Discourse, Resistance and Surveillance, 1790–1820.* Detroit: Wayne State University Press.

Wright, D. G. (1988): *Popular Radicalism: The Working-Class Experience, 1780–1880.* London: Longman.

Wrightson, Keith, and David Levine (1979): *Poverty and Piety in an English Village: Terling, 1525–1700.* New York: Academic Press. (1991): *The Making of an Industrial Society: Whickham, 1560–1765.* Oxford: Clarendon Press.

Wrigley, E. A. (1986): "Men on the Land and Men in the Countryside: Employment in Agriculture in Early-Nineteenth-Century England," in Lloyd Bonfield, Richard M. Smith, and Keith Wrightson, eds., *The World We Have Gained: Histories of Population and Social Structure.* Oxford: Basil Blackwell. (1987): *People, Cities and Wealth.* Oxford: Blackwell. (1988): *Continuity, Chance and Change: The Character of the Industrial Revolution in England.* Cambridge: Cambridge University Press. (1994): "Society and the Economy in the Eighteenth Century," in Lawrence Stone, ed., *An Imperial State at War: Britain from 1689 to 1815.* London: Routledge.

Wrigley, E. A., and R. S. Schofield (1981): *The Population History of England, 1541–1871: A Reconstruction.* Cambridge, Mass.: Harvard University Press. (1983): "English Population History from Family Reconstitution: Summary Results, 1600–1799," *Population Studies* 37: 157–184.

Yeo, Eileen (1971): "Robert Owen and Radical Culture," in Sidney Pollard and John Salt, eds., *Robert Owen: Prophet of the Poor.* London: Macmillan.

Young, Alfred (1976): ed., *The American Revolution.* DeKalb: Northern Illinois University Press.

Zagorin, Perez (1982): *Rebels and Rulers, 1500–1660.* 2 vols. Cambridge: Cambridge University Press.

Zald, Mayer N., and John D. McCarthy (1979): eds., *The Dynamics of Social Movements.* Cambridge: Winthrop. (1987): eds., *Social Movements in an Organizational Society.* New Brunswick, N.J.: Transaction.

Zimmerman, Ekkart (1983): *Political Violence, Crises and Revolutions.* Cambridge: Schenkman.

Index